D0084049

Praise for *Health Economics*:

"A very thorough introduction to health economics combining the important theoretical literature from economics, including neighboring fields, with an account of the actual systems which allocate medical care in its various dimensions."

Kenneth J. Arrow, Joan Kenney Professor of Economics,
Professor of Operations Research, Emeritus, and Stanford Health
Policy Fellow, USA, and Nobel Prize-winning economist

"With a readable, breezy style and a deft touch at explaining sophisticated concepts, *Health Economics* approaches health and health care from a uniquely modern and engaging economic perspective. This book should have very broad appeal. It will reward even the most well-informed readers who seek to understand the challenges facing the US health care system, as well as anyone who would like to learn about applied economics or policy analysis."

Alan Garber, Provost of Harvard University, Mallinckrodt Professor
of Health Care Policy, Harvard Medical School and Professor
of Economics, Harvard Kennedy School, USA

"This comprehensive and up-to-the-minute book offers an engaging introduction to the complex subject of health economics, covering every aspect of the market from compensation for doctors and nurses, to technological change, to the Affordable Care Act. I look forward to using this book in the classroom."

Janet M. Currie, Henry Putnam Professor of Economics and Public Affairs,
Director of the Center for Health and Well-Being, Princeton University, USA

"This is an exceptionally rich and comprehensive undergraduate textbook in Health Economics. It covers the traditional building blocks of health economics, but also extends to behavioral health economics, public health economics and addresses pertinent policy questions that different countries with different health care models face. This book is a must for health economics courses throughout the world and a definite recommend as secondary reading for courses on the economics of the welfare state."

Maarten Lindeboom, Professor of Economics, VU University, the Netherlands

"A welcome new textbook that includes highly accessible treatment of the most important topics in modern health economics. This will be a student favorite."

William Dow, Henry J. Kaiser Professor of Health Economics,
University of California, Berkeley, USA

"An exceptionally well-written textbook, broad in coverage, refreshingly non-technical, but nevertheless scholarly and thorough. Innovative chapters like economic epidemiology and thoughtful insights on demographic change as well as a review of new developments on public health economics and behavioral economics are most valuable; well-discussed phenomena like moral hazard and adverse selection are presented in a highly accessible manner."

Konrad Obermann, Mannheim Institute of Public Health,
Heidelberg University, Germany

JAY **BHATTACHARYA**

TIMOTHY **HYDE**

PETER **TU**

HEALTH ECONOMICS

© Jay Bhattacharya, Timothy Hyde, Peter Tu 2014

All rights reserved. No reproduction, copy or transmission of this publication may be made without written permission.

No portion of this publication may be reproduced, copied or transmitted save with written permission or in accordance with the provisions of the Copyright, Designs and Patents Act 1988, or under the terms of any licence permitting limited copying issued by the Copyright Licensing Agency, Saffron House, 6–10 Kirby Street, London EC1N 8TS.

Any person who does any unauthorized act in relation to this publication may be liable to criminal prosecution and civil claims for damages.

The authors have asserted their rights to be identified as the authors of this work in accordance with the Copyright, Designs and Patents Act 1988.

First published 2014 by
PALGRAVE MACMILLAN

Palgrave Macmillan in the UK is an imprint of Macmillan Publishers Limited, registered in England, company number 785998, 4 Crinan Street, London, N1 9XW.

Palgrave Macmillan in the US is a division of St Martin's Press LLC, 175 Fifth Avenue, New York, NY 10010.

Palgrave Macmillan is the global academic imprint of the above companies and has companies and representatives throughout the world.

Palgrave® and Macmillan® are registered trademarks in the United States, the United Kingdom, Europe and other countries.

ISBN 978–1–137–02996–6

This book is printed on paper suitable for recycling and made from fully managed and sustained forest sources. Logging, pulping and manufacturing processes are expected to conform to the environmental regulations of the country of origin.

A catalogue record for this book is available from the British Library.

A catalog record for this book is available from the Library of Congress.

Printed and bound in Lebanon

To my teachers and students. – JB
To our families and friends. – TH, PT

BRIEF CONTENTS

About the authors   xvii
Preface   xviii
Suggested pathways through the book   xxii
Authors' acknowledgments   xxiv
Publisher's acknowledgments   xxvi

1 Why health economics?   1

I DEMAND FOR HEALTH AND HEALTH CARE

2 Demand for health care   8
3 Demand for health: the Grossman model   28
4 Socioeconomic disparities in health   51

II SUPPLY OF HEALTH CARE

5 The labor market for physicians   78
6 The hospital industry   100

III INFORMATION ECONOMICS

7   Demand for insurance   126
8   Adverse selection: Akerlof's market for lemons   141
9   Adverse selection: the Rothschild–Stiglitz model   162
10 Adverse selection in real markets   184
11 Moral hazard   203

IV ECONOMICS OF HEALTH INNOVATION

12 Pharmaceuticals and the economics of innovation   230
13 Technology and the price of health care   255
14 Health technology assessment   278

V HEALTH POLICY

15 The health policy conundrum   306
16 The Beveridge model: nationalized health care   328
17 The Bismarck model: social health insurance   354

18   The American model   372
19   Population aging and the future of health policy   402

VI   PUBLIC HEALTH ECONOMICS

20   The economics of health externalities   428
21   Economic epidemiology   449
22   Obesity   472

VII   BEHAVIORAL HEALTH ECONOMICS

23   Prospect theory   496
24   Time inconsistency and health   525

Bibliography   549
List of figures   574
List of tables   577
Index   579

CONTENTS

About the authors   xvii
Preface   xviii
Suggested pathways through the book   xxii
Authors' acknowledgments   xxiv
Publisher's acknowledgments   xxvi

1   **Why health economics?**   1
    1.1   The health care economy is massive   1
    1.2   Health is uncertain and contagious   2
    1.3   Health economics is public finance   3
    1.4   Welfare economics   4
    1.5   A special note for non-American readers   4

I   **DEMAND FOR HEALTH AND HEALTH CARE**

2   **Demand for health care**   8
    2.1   Experiments on the demand for health care   9
    2.2   Is demand for health care downward-sloping?   12
    2.3   Measuring price sensitivity with elasticities   19
    2.4   Does the price of health care affect health?   21
    2.5   Conclusion   23
    2.6   Exercises   24

3   **Demand for health: the Grossman model**   28
    3.1   A day in the life of the Grossman model   28
    3.2   An optimal day   33
    3.3   Extending Grossman from cradle to grave   39
    3.4   Comparative statics   42
    3.5   Unifying the Grossman model   45
    3.6   Conclusion   47
    3.7   Exercises   47

4   **Socioeconomic disparities in health**   51
    4.1   The pervasiveness of health inequality   52
    4.2   The Grossman model and health disparities   57
    4.3   The efficient producer hypothesis   58
    4.4   The thrifty phenotype hypothesis   59
    4.5   The direct income hypothesis   62

4.6	The allostatic load hypothesis	63
4.7	The productive time hypothesis	66
4.8	Time preference: the Fuchs hypothesis	68
4.9	Conclusion	70
4.10	Exercises	71

II   SUPPLY OF HEALTH CARE

5	**The labor market for physicians**	**78**
5.1	The training of physicians	79
5.2	Physician wages	83
5.3	Barriers to entry	88
5.4	Physician agency	90
5.5	Racial discrimination by physicians	94
5.6	Conclusion	96
5.7	Exercises	96

6	**The hospital industry**	**100**
6.1	The rise and decline of the modern hospital	100
6.2	The relationship between hospitals and physicians	103
6.3	The relationship between hospitals and other hospitals	107
6.4	Nonprofits and hospital production	112
6.5	The relationship between hospitals and payers	115
6.6	Conclusion	119
6.7	Exercises	119

III   INFORMATION ECONOMICS

7	**Demand for insurance**	**126**
7.1	Declining marginal utility of income	126
7.2	Uncertainty	127
7.3	Risk aversion	128
7.4	Uncertainty and insurance	131
7.5	Comparing insurance contracts	135
7.6	Conclusion	137
7.7	Exercises	138

8	**Adverse selection: Akerlof's market for lemons**	**141**
8.1	The intuition behind the market for lemons	142
8.2	A formal statement of the Akerlof model	143
8.3	The adverse selection death spiral	150
8.4	When can the market for lemons work?	152
8.5	Conclusion	155
8.6	Exercises	156

9	**Adverse selection: the Rothschild–Stiglitz model**	**162**
9.1	The I_H–I_S space	162
9.2	Indifference curves in I_H–I_S space	163
9.3	The full-insurance line	165

9.4	The zero-profit line	165
9.5	The feasible contract wedge	167
9.6	Finding an equilibrium	168
9.7	Heterogeneous risk types	170
9.8	Indifference curves for the robust and the frail	171
9.9	Information asymmetry and the pooling equilibrium	172
9.10	Finding a separating equilibrium (sometimes)	174
9.11	Can markets solve adverse selection?	177
9.12	Conclusion	179
9.13	Exercises	180

10   Adverse selection in real markets   184

10.1	Predictions of asymmetric information models	185
10.2	Adverse selection in health insurance	187
10.3	Adverse selection in other markets	190
10.4	What prevents adverse selection?	195
10.5	Conclusion	197
10.6	Exercises	198

11   Moral hazard   203

11.1	What is moral hazard?	204
11.2	A graphical representation of moral hazard	206
11.3	How to limit moral hazard	209
11.4	Evidence of moral hazard in health insurance	213
11.5	The tradeoff between moral hazard and risk reduction	217
11.6	The upside of moral hazard?	221
11.7	Conclusion	223
11.8	Exercises	223

IV   ECONOMICS OF HEALTH INNOVATION

12   Pharmaceuticals and the economics of innovation   230

12.1	The life cycle of a drug	231
12.2	The uncertainty and costs of drug development	232
12.3	Patents	233
12.4	Induced innovation	240
12.5	Regulation of the pharmaceutical industry	244
12.6	Conclusion	249
12.7	Exercises	250

13   Technology and the price of health care   255

13.1	Technology and the rise in medical expenditures	257
13.2	New technology and medical inflation	262
13.3	Technology overuse: the Dartmouth Atlas	265
13.4	Theories to explain the Dartmouth findings	266
13.5	Conclusion	274
13.6	Exercises	275

14	**Health technology assessment**	**278**
14.1	Cost-effectiveness analysis	279
14.2	Evaluating multiple treatments: the cost-effectiveness frontier	282
14.3	Measuring costs	285
14.4	Measuring effectiveness	287
14.5	Cost–benefit analysis: picking the optimal treatment	292
14.6	Valuing life	296
14.7	Conclusion	300
14.8	Exercises	301

(V) HEALTH POLICY

15	**The health policy conundrum**	**306**
15.1	Arrow's impossibility theorem	306
15.2	The health policy trilemma	307
15.3	How should health insurance markets work?	309
15.4	How should moral hazard be controlled?	313
15.5	How should health care provision be regulated?	317
15.6	Comparing national health policies	321
15.7	Conclusion	325
15.8	Exercises	326
16	**The Beveridge model: nationalized health care**	**328**
16.1	A brief tour of the Beveridge world	329
16.2	Rationing health care without prices	331
16.3	Queuing	331
16.4	Health technology assessment	339
16.5	Competition in Beveridge systems	342
16.6	Injecting competition	345
16.7	Conclusion	351
16.8	Exercises	352
17	**The Bismarck model: social health insurance**	**354**
17.1	A brief tour of the Bismarck world	355
17.2	Health insurance markets in the Bismarck model	359
17.3	Containing costs with price controls	364
17.4	Conclusion	368
17.5	Exercises	370
18	**The American model**	**372**
18.1	Employer-sponsored health insurance	373
18.2	The managed care alternative	380
18.3	Medicare: universal coverage for the elderly and the severely disabled	384
18.4	Medicaid: subsidized coverage for the poor	389
18.5	Uninsurance	393
18.6	2010 health reform	394
18.7	Conclusion	397
18.8	Exercises	397

19 Population aging and the future of health policy   **402**

19.1   Why is the world aging?   403
19.2   Health care system sustainability   407
19.3   Forecasting the future of health expenditures   410
19.4   Policy responses to population aging   416
19.5   Conclusion   420
19.6   Exercises   420

VI PUBLIC HEALTH ECONOMICS

20   The economics of health externalities   **428**

20.1   Externalities in health   429
20.2   Pigouvian subsidies and taxes   434
20.3   The Coase theorem   437
20.4   The economics of organ transplantation   440
20.5   Conclusion   444
20.6   Exercises   445

21   Economic epidemiology   **449**

21.1   The demand for self-protection   449
21.2   The SIR model of infectious disease   454
21.3   Disease control   458
21.4   Applications of economic epidemiology   463
21.5   Conclusion   467
21.6   Exercises   467

22   Obesity   **472**

22.1   The widespread rise in obesity   473
22.2   What explains increasing obesity?   476
22.3   The costs of obesity   480
22.4   Is obesity a public health crisis?   482
22.5   Obesity contagion in social networks   486
22.6   Other justifications for public health intervention   488
22.7   Conclusion   490
22.8   Exercises   491

VII BEHAVIORAL HEALTH ECONOMICS

23   Prospect theory   **496**

23.1   Modeling decisions under uncertainty   497
23.2   Misjudging probabilities   500
23.3   Framing   505
23.4   Loss aversion   507
23.5   A formal introduction to prospect theory   511
23.6   Implications for health economics   517
23.7   Conclusion   519
23.8   Exercises   520

24   Time inconsistency and health   **525**

24.1   The beta-delta discounting model   526

24.2   Time-consistent preferences   527

24.3   Time-inconsistent preferences: myopia and hot brains   529

24.4   Demand for commitment mechanisms   534

24.5   Behavioral welfare economics   538

24.6   Conclusion   542

24.7   Exercises   543

Bibliography   549

List of figures   574

List of tables   577

Index   579

ABOUT THE AUTHORS

Jay Bhattacharya is an associate professor of medicine at Stanford University, a research associate at the National Bureau of Economic Research, and a senior fellow at the Stanford Institute for Economic Policy Research. His research focuses on the constraints that vulnerable populations face in making decisions that affect their health status. He is particularly interested in the effects, both intended and unintended, of government policies and programs designed to benefit vulnerable populations. He has published studies on the economic constraints facing the elderly, adolescents, patients with HIV/AIDS, and the obese.

He worked for three years as an economist at the RAND Corporation in Santa Monica, California, where he also taught health economics as a visiting assistant professor at the University of California, Los Angeles. He has a BA in economics, an MD and a PhD from Stanford University. His preferences are shockingly time-consistent, so he has no demand whatsoever for commitment devices.

Timothy Hyde is a doctoral student at Yale University studying health economics and the economics of information. His past research projects include a game-theoretic model of workplace discrimination and an exploration of the effects of loosening licensure requirements for doctors in the US. As far as his health insurer knows, he enjoys a daily morning jog and has never so much as heard of In-N-Out Burger.

Peter Tu is a doctoral student in economics at Harvard University. His past research includes an auction theory-based analysis of market power in the viatical settlement market. At the moment his favorite economics topic is moral hazard. Health insurers (and anyone looking to take him out to dinner) have been forewarned!

PREFACE

I have been teaching health economics now for nearly 15 years, first at the RAND Corporation and at the University of California-Los Angeles, and for over a decade at Stanford University. Health economics is a fantastic way to introduce students to the power of economic thinking to make sense of complicated real-world problems. The importance and ubiquity of health economics in policy debates makes it easy to motivate students from many diverse disciplinary backgrounds to learn economic principles. My students have included undergraduates, doctors, medical students, health policy students, and graduate students in economics and other disciplines. My fellow health economists around the world together reach an even wider variety of students.

Over the years, a major frustration in teaching my course has been the lack of a textbook suitable for all of these audiences. I have tried many of the top available books, but they either lack economic sophistication or engage in a health policy discussion that is out of date or too vague to be useful to students. Every year, I feel the need to supplement these texts with many primary readings from the health economics literature, which is great for doctoral students studying to become health economists, but perhaps not so good for the other audiences. After years of complaining to my students that there is no appropriate textbook available, I found the ideal opportunity to write one when two of my students approached me with the desire to help produce one. Their energy and intelligence carried us through many rough spots in the process of researching and writing this book.

My goal was to write a textbook that provides teachers with a roadmap for designing full lectures without needing to remind themselves about the relevant literature or to study up on the latest research. The book is designed to be a ready companion to professors who want to foster lively and rigorous discussion of the current developments and debates in modern health economics.

Our major focus during the writing process was maintaining a tight link between theory and policy. Too often in health economics and other disciplines, questions of policy or empirical evidence are divorced from theoretical models that help us make sense of them. We believe the only reason the theoretical models are interesting in the first place is that they provide a framework for thinking about empirical studies and policy. Meanwhile, discussions of policy unmoored from theoretical predictions are unfocused and often misleading. This textbook reflects a belief that for a complete education, neither theory nor policy can stand alone, and we draw many explicit connections between the models of health economics discussed in the first half of the book and the policy dilemmas presented in the second half.

Working on this book has provided me an opportunity to learn many things about health economics that I thought I knew, but found I really did not. It has also served as an occasion to reflect with gratitude on the many great people – students and teachers – from whom I have learned over the years. I hope that professors and students alike find this book useful in starting many stimulating and well-informed conversations about health economics and health policy.

— Jay

When we sat in Jay's class as students, learning health economics for the first time, we quickly developed an interest in the subject. But we were even more interested in Jay's endless personal anecdotes, his self-deprecating humor about his (fictional) video game addiction, and continual allusions to *The Simpsons* – especially Springfield's discount health care provider, Dr Nick. During the lecture on Akerlof's Market for Lemons, we heard about Cal Worthington, a legendary used-car salesman from southern California whose outlandish commercials blanketed the airwaves in the 1980s. The next week, in the context of a lesson on time-inconsistent preferences, raconteur Jay told us about his nightly decision during grad school: should he take the direct route home and face the temptation of a midnight snack at McDonald's, or take the long route home instead?

All Jay's varied diversions had one thing in common: they helped connect a health economics concept with an amusing story or memorable quote in the mind of the students. While it might have seemed to some students that Jay was constantly distracted from the material at hand, they learned and remembered much more than they realized by the course's end.

So our major task during the writing process was keeping the book lively and enjoyable, trying to capture some of Jay's exuberant teaching style in print. We know firsthand that most textbooks are not very much fun to read, mostly because they must cover great expanses of technical, complex material. We did our best to buck this trend without sacrificing any economics. We firmly believe that health economics can be interesting and relevant for every last student, as it was for us, and we think adding some enjoyment to the learning process helps achieve that goal. Recognizing that students are the ones that spend the most time using textbooks, we aimed to make the text as user-relevant and user-friendly as possible.

Naturally, the book includes coverage of core topics such as insurance markets and health policy debates around the world. But we have also included other topical material that can be found every day in the popular press: socioeconomic disparities in health, the obesity epidemic, and behavioral health economics, to name just a few. As students, we enjoyed these topics during Jay's class, and we hope their inclusion will help the book appeal to a broad cross-section of students and underscore the relevance of health economics for all audiences.

We both learned a phenomenal amount in helping put this textbook together. Thanks to Jay's guidance and mentorship, we have matured in our economic thinking and have begun to think about many topics, both within health economics and beyond, in a new light. We are immeasurably grateful to Jay for offering us this apprenticeship, and we are excited to share with our readers all that we have learned.

— Tim and Peter

How to teach with this book

Pathways through the book

We hope that health economics professors, veterans and first-time teachers alike can quickly create new syllabi for their classes using this book. Alas, there may not be time to cover all the material in this book in one term or semester – in Jay's ten-week course at Stanford, he usually only covers material equivalent to 17 of the 24 chapters. In the following pages we propose several different pathways through the book, which professors might find useful in structuring their syllabi. These pathways have been designed with a 13-week course in mind, and are customized to courses with a particular focus (for example, public health or health policy). They highlight chapters to focus on and other chapters that might be less pertinent. We have endeavored to make the book as modular as possible; professors can skip some chapters and move on to the rest of the book without trouble.

Level of mathematics

It should be noted that some of the chapters are more mathematically advanced than others, especially those that present models of adverse selection and behavioral economics. The intended audience for this book is a class of advanced undergraduates, but we feel it also has something to offer to introductory economics students, doctors, public health students, and economics doctoral students. We are confident that professors can fruitfully use this book with mathematically inexperienced audiences as effectively as they can with mathematically sophisticated students. The instructor's guide available on the companion site provides many helpful suggestions for tailoring this book for students of many different backgrounds.

Reading guide online

The companion website also includes a reading guide, providing an overview of several articles in the literature that are relevant to the content in each chapter. Advanced students will benefit from gaining some first-hand exposure to the research process that provided the basis for our textbook, and the reading guide can help professors and students determine which articles to read for additional insights that the book has not been able to include for reasons of space.

Online resources

A number of online resources are available to lecturers and students using this book. Students have free access to:

- Answers to the Comprehension questions at the end of every chapter in the book.
- A reading guide with suggestions about how to approach the journal articles and academic papers that students may be assigned to read.

Lecturers have access to a password-protected section of the website, including:

- PowerPoint lecture slides for each chapter that can be edited for individual use.

- An additional PowerPoint slide deck covering material on the 2010 US health reform in greater detail than the text provides.
- An Instructor Manual providing guideline answers to the analytical problems and essay questions in the book.

These resources can be found at: **www.palgrave.com/economics/bht**.

SUGGESTED PATHWAYS THROUGH THE BOOK OVER A 13–WEEK COURSE

WEEK OF COURSE			SUGGESTED CHAPTERS
	Broad interest (full book)	Broad interest, less math-intensive	Public health/medicine focus
1	1, 2	1, 2	1, 2
2	3, 4	3	3
3	5, 6	4, 5	4
4	7, 8	6, 7	5
5	9, 10	10	6, 7
6	11, 12	11	10, 11
7	13, 14	12, 13	13
8	15	14	14
9	16, 17*	15	15
10	18*	16, 17*	18*
11	19, 20	18*	20, 21
12	21, 22	19, 20	22
13	23, 24	21, 22	23, 24
Chapters to emphasize		3, 10, 11, 14	4, 5, 13, 14, 22
Chapters not covered		8, 9, 23, 24	8, 9, 16, 17, 19
Advice for teachers		Skip the most math-intensive chapters (adverse selection theory and behavioral economics), and leave extra time for the semi-technical chapters that remain: Grossman model, moral hazard, and health technology assessment.	Skip adverse selection theory chapters and some health policy chapters, and emphasize the following public health issues: health disparities, physician labor markets health technology, health technology assessment, and obesity.

* Reorder or substitute to emphasize the locally relevant policy chapter.

(by subject focus)

Health policy focus	Industrial organization focus	Economic theory focus
1, 2	1, 2	1, 2
3, 4	3, 4	3
5, 6	5	5, 6
7, 8	6	7, 8
9, 10	7, 8	9
11, 12	9, 10	11
13, 14	11, 13	12, 13
15	12	15
16	14	18*
17	15	20
18	18*	21, 22
19	19, 20	23
20, 22	21, 22	24
16, 17, 19	5, 6, 12, 14	3, 9, 11, 20, 23, 24
21, 23, 24	16, 17, 23, 24	4, 10, 14, 16, 17, 19
Skip economic epidemiology and behavioral economics, and leave plenty of time for each of the five health policy chapters.	Skip behavioral economics and some policy chapters, and leave extra time for chapters on physicians, hospitals, pharmaceuticals, and health technology assessment.	Skip empirically minded chapters and some policy chapters, and leave extra time for the Grossman model, the RS model, moral hazard, welfare economics, and behavioral economics.

AUTHORS' ACKNOWLEDGMENTS

Writing a textbook is an enormous undertaking. It is something that no three people can do themselves, and there are innumerable others who helped usher this book into being. What follows is a woefully incomplete list of those who contributed.

First, thanks to all the folks at Palgrave Macmillan, **Jaime Marshall**, **Helen Bugler**, and **Aléta Bezuidenhout**, who helped mold our book from the earliest stages. Thanks also to **Nikini Jayatunga**, whose tireless work securing permissions for our use of figures and images sped up our production schedule by months if not years.

Thanks are also due to the legion of reviewers who read our sometimes incoherent rough drafts, provided needed constructive criticism, or good old-fashioned encouragement when we needed it. These include **Marty Gaynor**, **Karen Eggleston**, **Eran Bendavid**, **Sarah Markowitz**, **Neeraj Sood**, **Doug Owens**, **Jeremy Goldhaber-Fiebert**, **Bill Vogt**, **Mikko Packalen**, **Grant Miller**, **Helen Levy**, **Raphael Godefroy**, **John Cawley**, **Karen Eggleston**, **Mike Grossman**, **Geoffrey Joyce**, **Tom Deleire**, **Tom Philipson**, **Han Hong**, **Ernie Berndt**, **Kanaka Shetty**, **Darius Lakdawalla**, **Dana Goldman**, **Vincenzo Atella**, **Aki Yoshikawa**, **Martin Connor**, **Daniella Perlroth**, **Oddvar Kaarboe**, **Kate Bundorf**, **Amy Finkelstein**, **Alan Garber**, and **Tom MaCurdy**.

Thanks also to **John Taylor** and **Victor Fuchs** for their valuable insights into the world of textbook publishing, to **Sid Le**, **Kara Raphael**, **Scott Roberts**, **Micol Marchetti-Bowick**, **Rebecca McKibbin**, **Paula Obler**, **Kyna Fong**, **Jodie Ha**, **Patricia Foo** and **Misha Dworsky** for their helpful comments and contributions, and to the innocent students in the Econ 126 class of 2011, who endured the test-teaching of the first of our chapters. Thanks are due to all the students who have taken Econ 126 over the years – the lessons learned by both teacher and students in those classes have gone into the writing of this textbook.

Last but not least, thanks to **Stephan Seiler**, **Mark Stabile**, and **Jonas Schreyogg**, who taught us so much about the national health care systems of Britain, Canada, and Germany (respectively).

We also owe a great debt of gratitude to **Allen Cox**, who enthusiastically embraced the challenge of creating comic illustrations for technical economic concepts. The cartoons he created are absolutely sensational, and we are confident that most students will consider these the highlight of the book.

Thanks to **Nancy Lonhart**, **Melissa Miller**, **Christine Geibel**, **Samantha Chu**, **Jeanette Cowan**, and **Chelsea Bell**, who kept PCOR running with ruthless efficiency. Without them, Jay's calendar would be a tangle of missed deadlines and overdue responsibilities, and Tim and Peter would still be roaming the halls of PCOR, looking for an office.

Jay would be remiss (and in a world of trouble) if he forgot to thank his family for putting up with all of the late nights working on the book. To Cathy he owes more than he ever repays, and to his children Jodie, Matthew, and Benji he is grateful for giving him many reasons to come home from work. Jay also thanks his mom and God, for obvious reasons. Tim would like to thank his family and friends who supported him when he told them about his professor's harebrained scheme to write a textbook. Peter tips his hat to his family, his friends, and his mentors, all of whom he cannot thank enough.

Finally, a special word of thanks for **Lena Schoemaker** and **Neesha Joseph**, without whom this book would be in a perpetual state of near-completeness. Their work editing the first draft, correcting innumerable typos, brainstorming many of the exercises, and broadening the international scope of many chapters was simply indispensable.

The authors are also grateful to the following people who acted as external reviewers and made many useful and insightful suggestions which have resulted in a better book.

Kurt Brekke, Norwegian School of Economics, Norway
Anthony Culyer, University of York, UK
Derek DeLia, Rutgers University, US
William H. Dow, University of California, Berkeley, US
Tracy Falba, Duke University, US
Karen Grépin, New York University, US
Mireia Jofre-Bonet, City University London, UK
Oddvar Kaarbøe, University of Bergen, Norway
Amanda Kowalski, Yale University, US
Marten Lindeboom, VU University, Amsterdam, the Netherlands
Zoe McLaren, University of Michigan, US
Konrad Obermann, Heidelberg University, Germany
Victoria Phillips, Emory University, US
Dylan Roby, University of California, Los Angeles, US
Victoria Serra-Sastre, City University London, UK
Nils-Olov Stålhammar, University of Gothenburg, Sweden
Sophie Whyte, Sheffield University, UK

PUBLISHER'S ACKNOWLEDGMENTS

The authors and publishers are grateful to the following for permission to reproduce copyright material.

The American Economic Association and the named authors for our Table 2.14 'Various measures of predicted annual use of medical services by income group' from Manning, W. G., Newhouse, J. P., Duan, N., Keeler, E.B., Leibowitz, A. (1987) 'Health Insurance and the Demand for Medical Care: Evidence from a Randomized Experiment', *The American Economic Review*, Vol. 77, No. 3 pp. 251–277; our Figure 4.5 'Health inequalities by condition' from Case, A., Lubotsky, D., and Paxson, C. (2002), 'Economic Status and Health in Childhood: The Origins of the Gradient', *American Economic Review*, 92(5):1308–1334; our Figure 4.6 'Health inequalities among Canadian children' from Currie, J. and Stabile, M. (2003), 'Socioeconomic Status and Child Health: Why Is the Relationship Stronger for Older Children?', *American Economic Review*, 93(5):1813–1823; our Figure 4.11 'HDL cholesterol levels in baboons and British civil servants by social status' from Smith, J. P. (1999), 'Healthy Bodies and Thick Wallets: the dual relation between health and economic status', *The Journal of Economic Perspectives*, 13(2):145–166; our Figure 10.4 'Premium cost per dollar unit of life insurance coverage' from Cawley, J. and Philipson, T. (1999), 'An Empirical Examination of Information Barriers to Trade in Insurance', *American Economic Review*, 89(4): 827–846; our Figure 24.2 'Imputed annual discount rates from several time discounting studies' from Frederick, S., Loewenstein, G., and O'Donoghue, T. (2002), 'Time discounting and time preference: A critical review', *Journal of Economic Literature*, 40(2):351–401.

The Dartmouth Institute for our Figure 13.8 'Relationship between health care use and supply of hospital beds' from Dartmouth Atlas Project (2008), *Tracking the Care of Patients with Severe Chronic Illness, Technical report.*

De Gruyter for our Figure 13.9 'Trends in HIV survival and expenditures in the U.S. (a) HIV survival curves, 1980–2000, (b) HIV expenditures, 1986–2004' from Philipson, T. J. and Jena, A. B. (2006), 'Who benefits from new medical technologies? Estimates of consumer and producer surpluses for HIV/AIDS drugs', *Forum for Health Economics & Policy*. The original is available from the De Gruyter website.

The Econometric Society for our Table 23.1 'Survey questions and responses illustrating the certainty effect', our Table 23.2 'Survey questions with prospective gains and prospective losses', our Table 23.4 'An example of cancellation and coding during the editing stage', our Table 23.5 'Problem 1 and Problem 2 illustrating the certainty effect' from Kahneman, D. and Tversky, A. (1979), 'Prospect Theory: An Analysis of Decision under Risk', *Econometrica*, 47(2):263–291.

Elsevier for our Figure 4.2 'Male survival curves by educational attainment' and our Figure 15.4 'Health expenditures and average life expectancy of females, at age 65 by country' from Bhattacharya, J. and Lakdawalla, D. (2006), 'Does Medicare benefit the poor?', *Journal of Public Economics*, 90(1-2):277–292; our Table 4.3 'Adult characteristics according to timing of prenatal exposure to the Dutch famine' from Roseboom, T. J., van der Meulen, J. H., Ravelli, A., Osmond, C., Barker, D. J., and Bleker, O. P. (2001), 'Effects of prenatal exposure to the Dutch famine on adult disease in later life: an overview', *Molecular and Cellular Endocrinology*, 185:93–98; our Table 5.1 'Estimated IRR for various professional careers versus a typical college degree-requiring job in the United States, 1970–80' from Burstein, P. L. and Cromwell, J. (1985), 'Relative incomes and rates of return for U.S. physicians', *Journal of health economics*, 4(1):63–78; our Figure 12.1 'Cumulative success rate of drugs entering the three clinical FDA approval phases' from DiMasi, J. A., Hansen, R. W., and Grabowski, H. G. (2003), 'The price of innovation: new estimates of drug development costs', *Journal of Health Economics*, 22(2):151–85; our Figure 21.1 'Epidemiological and economic cost of diseases with varying severity' from Philipson, T. J. (2000), 'Economic Epidemiology and Infectious Diseases' in Newhouse, J., editor, *Handbook of Health Economics*; our Figure 22.4 'Food prices have fallen steadily since World War II' from Lakdawalla, D. and Philipson, T. (2009), 'The Growth of Obesity and Technological Change', *Economics Human Biology*, 7(3):283–293; and our Figure 23.4 'Different evaluations of utility due to different reference points' from Winter, L. and Parker, B. (2007) 'Current Health and Preferences for Life-Prolonging Treatments: An Application of Prospect Theory to End-of-Life Decision Making', *Social Science & Medicine*, 65(8):1695–707.

The Kaiser Family Foundation for our Figure 18.3 'Distribution of U.S. private health insurance customers by plan type' from *Employer Health Benefits 2012 Annual Survey*, (#8345) The Henry J. Kaiser Family Foundation & HRET, September 2012.

Management Science for our Table 12.2 'Distribution of returns for drugs introduced in the U.S. between 1970 and 1979' from 'A New Look at the Returns and Risks to Pharmaceutical R&D', Grabowski, H. and Vernon, J., *Management Science*, Vol. 36, 7, 1990.

The National Academy of Sciences for our Table 4.4 'Hazard rate of coronary heart disease, stroke, and total cardiovascular disease, compared to average birth rate cohort' from Goldman, D. P. and Smith, J. P. (2002), 'Can Patient Self-Management Help Explain the SES Health Gradient?', *Proceedings of the National Academy of Sciences*, 99(16):10929–10934.

OECD for permission to use data from OECD Health Data 2012 in our Figure 13.1 'Health care expenditures as a proportion of U.S. GDP, 1960-present'; in our Table 13.1 'Technology adoption by nation per million people', in our Table 17.1 'Health care technology utilization in select countries following different health policy models in 2010', in our Table 17.2 'Health care spending as a percentage of GDP in select countries following different health policy models in 2010' and from OECD Health Data 2003 in our Figure 22.3 'Rising obesity rates in seventeen Organization for seventeen Economic Cooperation and Development (OECD) countries'.

Oxford University Press for our Table 2.1 'Evidence for outpatient care: (b) Oregon Medicaid Experiment', our Table 2.2 'Evidence for inpatient care: (b) Oregon Medicaid Experiment', our Table 2.3 'Evidence for emergency care: (b) Oregon Medicaid Experiment', our Table 2.11 'Effect of lottery win on health in the Oregon Medicaid Experiment', our Table 11.2 'Preventative care test frequency in the Oregon Medicaid Experiment', our Table 11.4 'Health care utilization in the past six months, Oregon Medicaid Experiment' from Amy Finkelstein et al. (2012) 'The Oregon Health Insurance Experiment: Evidence from the First Year', *Quarterly Journal of Economics*, 127(3): 1057–1106, Supplementary Data; our Figure 2.3 'Emergency and non-emergency visits by age' from Card, D., Dobkin, C., and Maestas, N. (2009). 'Does Medicare Save Lives?', *Quarterly Journal of Economics*, 124(2):597–636; our Figure 4.3 'Mortality rate among British ducal families and commoners' from Harris, B. (2004), 'Public Health, Nutrition, and the Decline of Mortality: The McKeown Thesis Revisited', *Social History of Medicine*, 17(3):379–407; our Figure 4.7 'Health inequalities by race' from Cutler, D., Lleras-Muney, A. and Vogl, T., (2011) 'Socioeconomic Status and Health: Dimensions and Mechanisms' in *The Oxford Handbook of Health Economics*, Glied, S. & Smith, P. (eds.) pp. 124–163; our Table 12.1 'Sample of drug categories with age range of principal users', adapted from Acemoglu, D. and Linn, J. (2004), 'Market Size in Innovation: Theory and Evidence from the Pharmaceutical Industry', *Quarterly Journal of Economics*, 119(3):1049–1090; our Figure 12.5 'Distribution of newly-approved drugs by approximate target age demographic' from Acemoglu, D. and Linn, J. (2004), 'Market Size in Innovation: Theory and Evidence from the Pharmaceutical Industry', *Quarterly Journal of Economics*, 119(3):1049–1090; and our Table 13.2 'Life expectancy of AMI patients in the U.S. Medicare system and average costs of AMI treatment over time' from Cutler, D., McClellan, M. B., Newhouse, J., and Remler, D. (1998), 'Are medical prices declining? Evidence from heart attack treatments', *Quarterly Journal of Economics*, 113(4):991–1024.

RAND for permission to use data in our Table 2.1 'Evidence for outpatient care: (a) RAND HIE Study', our Table 2.8 'Antibiotic use in the RAND HIE', our Figure 2.4 'Data on outpatient and dental care', our Table 11.3 'Evidence from the RAND HIE' from Keeler E., Buchanan, J. L., Rolph, J. E., Hanley, J. M., and Reboussin, D. M. (1988). *The Demand for Episodes of Medical Treatment in the Health Insurance Experiment*; in our Tables 2.2, Table 2.3 'Evidence for inpatient care: (a) RAND HIE Study', 2.5 'Percentage with preventative pediatric care in three years, by age and care type', 2.6 'Per-capita mental health expenditures, by plan type', 2.7 'Dental care utilization by income level', 2.9 'Evidence on mortality rates', 2.10 'Health indicators by insurance plan in the RAND HIE', 2.15 'Percentage with preventative care in three years from the RAND HIE study', 11.1 'Evidence of ex ante moral hazard from the RAND HIE' from Newhouse, J. P. (1993), *Free for All? Evidence from the RAND Health Insurance Experiment*; in our Figure 19.6 'Future Elderly Model: Effect of an Anti-Aging Drug' from Goldman, D., Shekelle, P., Bhattacharya, J., Hurd, M., Joyce, G., Lakdawalla, D., Matsui, D., Newberry, S., Panis, C., and Shang, B. (2004), Health status and medical treatment of the future elderly: Final Report. Technical report, RAND Technical Report TR-169-CMS and for permission for our Table 2.4, adapted from 'Mean health care expenditures in the CHRIE, in yuan' from Cretin, S., Williams, A., and Sine, J. (2006), *China Rural Health Insurance Experiment, Technical report.*

The Statistics Bureau, Ministry of Internal Affairs and Communications, Japan for our Figure 19.2 'Japanese Population Aging' from Statistics Bureau, (2012), *Statistical Handbook of Japan 2012, Technical report.*

The United Nations for our Figure 19.1 'European Population Aging' from United Nations (2011), *World Population Prospects: The 2010 Revision, Technical report*, Department of Economic and Social Affairs.

The University of Chicago Press for our Figure 12.6 'Predicted and actual number of new chemical entities (NCEs) before and after the 1962 Kefauver-Harris Amendment' from Peltzman, S. (1973), 'An Evaluation of Consumer Protection Legislation: The 1962 Drug Amendments', *Journal of Political Economy*, 81(5):1049; our Figure 22.2 'Estimated average body mass index of American males in various age cohorts, 1863–1991' from Costa, D. and Steckel, R. H. (1997), 'Long-Term Trends in Health, Welfare, and Economic Growth in the United States', in Steckel, R. H. and Floud, R., editors, *Health and Welfare during Industrialization*; our Table 23.6 'Selling and buying price for Duke lottery winners and sellers' from Carmon and Ariely (2000), 'Focusing on the Forgone: How Value Can Appear So Different to Buyers and Sellers', *Journal of Consumer Research*, 27:3, 360–370.

The University of Wisconsin Press for our Figure 21.7 'Differential measles vaccination rates by prevalence for babies born in 1989' from Philipson, T. (1996), 'Private Vaccination and Public Health: An Empirical Examination for U.S. Measles', *The Journal of Human Resources*, 31(3):611–630.

The Wall Street Journal for our Figure 6.3 'Prices for common procedures from California chargemasters in 2004' from Lagnado, L. (2004), 'Medical Markup: California Hospitals Open Books, Showing Huge Price Differences'.

Wiley for our Figure 21.6 'Estimated prevalence and hazard rate of HIV in San Francisco' from Geoffard, P. and Philipson, T. (1996), 'Rational Epidemics and their Public Control', *International Economic Review*, pp. 603–624.

The World Health Organisation for our Table 21.2 'Yearly costs of smallpox and the smallpox eradication campaign', adapted from Fenner, F., Henderson, D. A., Arita, I., and Ladnyi, I. D. (1988), *Smallpox and its Eradication.*

The publishers are also grateful to the following suppliers of images in the book:

Bananastock, Brand X Pictures, Center for Disease Control and Prevention – Public Health Image Library, Corbis, Fotolia, Gary Becker, Getty, Image Source, Imperial College Healthcare NHS Trust, Intuitive Surgical, iStockphoto.com, Kenneth Arrow, PhotoDisc, Photostock, Superstock.

1   WHY HEALTH ECONOMICS?

Almost everyone in the world has a good reason to care about health economics. The following quiz can determine whether or not health economics is important to you:

- Do you have finite resources to draw upon in case you get sick?
- Are you incapable of predicting the future with perfect accuracy?
- Do you live in a country that levies taxes on its citizens?

If you answered "yes" to any of these questions, health economics is important to your well-being, and understanding it can make you healthier and happier. (Or perhaps you will be happier once you get *less* healthy. We will discuss that possibility in Chapter 3.)

Health economics is not just an alphabet soup of esoteric acronyms like HMO and QALY. Nor is it an endless droning debate about arcane minutiae pertaining to the national budget. Instead, it is a lively field where we study real-life health decisions: why people lie to insurance companies about their health, why people smoke even when they know exactly how bad it is for them, and why health insurance might make you fat. Understanding health economics not only helps you make better decisions about your health, it is also inherently intriguing and compelling, even fun.

Understanding health economics is vital. Our argument rests on three facts: the health care economy is massive and expensive; health is a major source of uncertainty and risk; and governments around the world are deeply involved in financing health care systems.

1.1   The health care economy is massive

The gross domestic product (GDP) of the US in 2008 was just about $14 trillion. This means that $14 trillion worth of economic activity took place in the US that year. People spent money on a mind-bogglingly vast array of goods and services: meals at restaurants, baseball tickets, gasoline, new houses and cars, raw materials and machinery for factories, salaries for soldiers and schoolteachers, and retirement benefits (to name just a few).

Perhaps even more mind-boggling is the fact that one out of every six dollars spent in the US that year was spent on health care, to pay for things like checkups at the doctor's office, bariatric surgeries, anti-cholesterol medicines, and new investments in medical research. This statistic is all the more shocking when we compare today's mammoth health care sector to that of fifty years ago. In 1960, barely one out of every *twenty* dollars spent in the US went toward health care.

The trend has been similar in countries around the world, although no one spends quite as much on health care as Americans. In the past hundred years, the health care sector has grown massively across the developed world. Part of the story of this expansion in health care has to do with the wealth of scientific discoveries and technological improvements that have occurred in the last century, as we will see in Chapter 13. Today, billions are

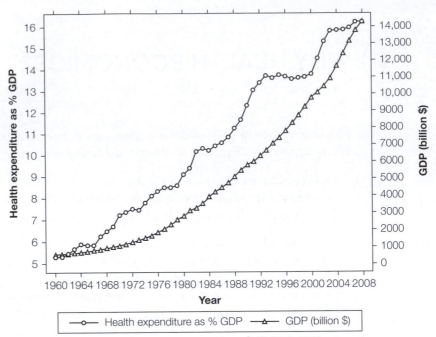

Figure 1.1. *Health care expenditure as a proportion of US GDP, 1960–present.*

Source: Data from the US Center for Medicare and Medicaid Services, Office of the Actuary.

spent on insulin, antibiotics, chemotherapy, open heart surgery, and blood transfusions – but none of these things even existed in 1900.

The size of the health care sector also means that millions of people make a living working in the health care sector. In Chapters 5, 6, and 12 we will explore the role of doctors, hospitals, and drug companies in the health care economy, and learn about some unusual features of the markets for their services.

What do we get for all of this money we spend on health care? And are we spending too much or too little? Health care can certainly extend lifespans and improve quality of life, but then Americans, for all of their expenditures, are not the longest-living or healthiest people on the globe. These complicated questions are examined in much more depth in Chapter 14.

1.2   Health is uncertain and contagious

So the health care sector is quite large, but why are the economics of health any *different* from the economics at work in other, smaller markets, like the market for televisions or the market for bananas? Basic economic theory concludes that any competitive market, in the absence of externalities and asymmetric information, will produce an efficient outcome where there is no way to make anyone better off without making someone else worse off. Why should we assume that the market for health care is operating inefficiently or in need of any government intervention? For many years, economists did not treat health economics differently at all. But a seminal paper published in 1963 by Stanford professor Kenneth Arrow established health economics as its own field of study.

Arrow argued that health is different from other goods, and a source of "special economic problems," for one major reason: *uncertainty*. Most people know roughly how many

Kenneth Arrow, founding father of health economics. Arrow won a Nobel Prize in 1972. Credit: With permission of Kenneth Arrow.

televisions or bananas they are likely to buy in the next week, but demand for health care is highly uncertain. An unforeseen broken leg or heart attack can suddenly create demand for expensive health care services. Because most people are averse to risk, health-related uncertainty is unpleasant and, as we will see in Chapter 7, this uncertainty motivates individuals to demand health insurance.

The ubiquity of insurance in health care distinguishes it from other markets. Insurance markets are peculiar because they feature information asymmetries between buyers and sellers. Simply put, health insurance customers tend to know more about their health risks than insurance companies do. This would not be a problem if sickly insurance customers volunteered information about their health. But this is not in their self-interest because health insurers would charge them more for coverage. Instead, sickly customers have a strong incentive to masquerade as healthy customers. In a sense, most of the problems in health economics stem from the fact that people have every incentive to lie about their health. In Chapters 8 through 11, we will discuss the twin problems that arise in markets with information asymmetry: *adverse selection* and *moral hazard*.

Additionally, health care markets are rife with externalities because health status is a uniquely contagious quantity. It probably does not matter very much to you if your neighbor decides to purchase a television or eat a banana. But it certainly does matter if your co-workers decide to skip their flu shots or come to the office with tuberculosis. The fact that other people's health decisions affect you – and that your health decisions affect others – can undermine the efficient functioning of markets. In Chapters 20 through 22, we discuss health externalities and the economics of public health.

1.3   Health economics is public finance

Headquarters of the world's largest health insurance company? The US Capitol Building in Washington, DC. Credit: Image Source.

So health care is expensive, and health is a source of uncertainty and externalities. But what if you are healthy, face little risk of falling ill, and have generous insurance coverage to pay for treatment if you do? Even then, health economics should still be of interest to you because governments are deeply involved in the health care economy. Each year, the size of your tax bill depends greatly on the decisions of politicians and bureaucrats about how to manage your nation's health care system.

The prominent role of governments in health care goes as far back as the 1880s, when German Chancellor Otto von Bismarck established a national health care system to gain political advantage over the Socialist Party. After World War II, more governments became extensively involved in health care markets as many countries introduced new government-financed insurance programs. Notable examples include national, single-payer health insurance systems like the National Health Service (NHS), in the UK and Medicare and Medicaid in the US.

By 2008, when one out of every six dollars spent in America was spent on health care, one out of every two of those dollars was spent by the government. And this is in a country with a health system that is relatively private. In countries like the UK, Sweden, and Canada, the government is responsible for the vast majority of health care expenditures. In Chapter 15, we introduce the range of health policy options that countries use to steward their health care systems.

The pressure on governments to finance the costs of health care will grow in the coming decades. As we will see in Chapter 19, increasing life expectancies and aging populations throughout the developed world will place enormous stress on public health insurance systems which are responsible for paying for health care. In addition, governments will have to cope with ongoing questions about whether or not to pay for expensive new medical technologies.

Together, these trends imply that health care will be an ever-growing item on government balance sheets. The critical role that governments play in health care means that all taxpayers – even healthy and rich ones – have a stake in ongoing political debates about uninsurance, cost-effectiveness, and the regulation of health care markets.

1.4   Welfare economics

Given the major role of government in health care, and the high stakes of the debate for taxpayers and patients, disagreement in health policy debates is inevitable. In practice, debates about health policy are among the most emotional and vociferous in all of politics. Sometimes these disagreements turn on *normative* issues, which are different ideas of how the world should be. Some people feel that adequate health care is a human right, while others feel that no government should be allowed to force anyone to purchase health insurance. These are philosophical questions that no amount of economic analysis can resolve.

But all too often these debates concern *positive* issues, which are different ideas of how the world actually is. One role of health economics is to decrease the level of unnecessary disagreement about health policy by determining positive facts. Do strict patent protections for newly developed drugs increase innovation? How much will it cost Medicare to pay for a new expensive type of laproscopic surgery? Does a tax on fatty foods save money and make people healthier? How much would consumers save if individuals without medical degrees were allowed to offer health care services just like doctors? Unlike normative questions, these questions are amenable to careful economic reasoning.

In order to answer these questions, though, we need a coherent way of thinking that allows us to measure the costs and benefits of any policy proposal. Throughout this book we use the principles of *welfare economics*, an approach that will be familiar to most economics students. The central contention of welfare economics is that people know what is best for them. Their preferences – as revealed by their choices under constraints – are the best guide for determining good policy.

But welfare economics, as useful as it is for analyzing health economics, is not universally accepted. We end the book with Chapters 23 and 24, which cover prospect theory and time inconsistency, respectively. These chapters cover *behavioral economics*, a growing field that challenges the fundamental assumptions of the welfare economics framework and calls into question much of what we think we know about health economics.

1.5   A special note for non-American readers

If you live and receive health care in a country other than the US, a few of the topics we discuss in this book that make sense to American students will seem, well, foreign. In many countries, including Canada and the UK, patients almost never pay directly out of their own pockets when they receive basic health care, except for peripheral services like dentistry and prescription drugs. But in the US, patients sometimes pay out of pocket for routine health care like flu shots and visits to the doctor.

Another major difference is that, in almost all developed countries, uninsurance is extremely rare or even nonexistent. Insurance is either provided for free by the government, or provided by a mix of public and private insurers. But in America, some people are not eligible for government insurance and cannot afford (or do not want) to buy private insurance.

Paying out of pocket for health care and going without insurance may be unfamiliar at first, but these concepts will come up over and over again in this book. This is because we focus largely on private markets for health insurance and for health care. This may seem a strange choice given that, as we have just pointed out, so much of the world's health care is not delivered this way. But learning how health insurance and hospitals work in private markets is key for understanding two major health economics concepts: adverse selection and moral hazard. It is also crucial to understanding what motivates other countries to operate their systems in other ways.

Because the US currently provides the best examples of private health insurance markets and private markets for hospitals and doctors, much of the evidence we study will come from American data. Then, in Chapters 15 through 18, we will turn to a discussion of international health policy. By that point, we will have spent enough time understanding private markets to think intelligently about the vast array of policies in place in different countries. Understanding the economics of private health markets provides a deep insight into the functioning and tradeoffs implicit in public health provision.

I   DEMAND FOR HEALTH AND HEALTH CARE

2   Demand for health care   8

3   Demand for health: the
    Grossman model   28

4   Socioeconomic disparities
    in health   51

② DEMAND FOR HEALTH CARE

Before we left for college, our parents counseled us always to follow the doctor's advice and never to skimp on health care. If the doctor says get a flu shot, get one. If the doctor says get ten flu shots, get all ten – even if they cost $100 each.[1] While our parents' counsel was loving advice, it implies that health care is so valuable that it is worth ignoring any and all economic tradeoffs. In the words of introductory economics, our parents are encouraging us to be *price-inelastic* or *price-insensitive* when it comes to health care.

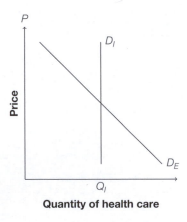

Figure 2.1. *A price-inelastic demand curve, D_I, and price-elastic one, D_E. This chapter discusses which curve more accurately resembles the demand for health care.*

Are people actually price-insensitive when it comes to health care? Or does demand for health care respond to price, even for health care that may be a matter of life and death?

Figure 2.1 shows two possible demand curves. D_I reflects our parents' advice: the individual with this demand curve is insensitive to price. He wants a certain level of care Q_I and is willing to pay any price to get it. D_E, on the other hand, represents the demand of an individual sensitive to price. She takes price into account when deciding how much care to seek. A non-vertical curve like D_E is said to be *downward-sloping*.

Figure 2.1 may seem simple, but it lies at the center of health economics. Much of the policy debate about how best to organize the provision of health care is grounded in two questions:

- Is the demand curve for health care downward-sloping? Put another way, are people sensitive to the price of health care?
- If the answer to the above question is "yes," people who face different prices or have different willingness to pay get different amounts of care. Do they end up with different health outcomes as a result?

If the answer to the first question is "no," and the demand curve for health care resembles D_I, then the economics of health and medical care is of little interest. The incentives of patients seeking care are inconsequential; instead, there exists a medically optimal level

---

1 One of the authors, despite being both a professional economist and a medical doctor, gives this questionable advice to his children.

of health (Q_l). Achieving that optimum is a medical problem to be solved by doctors and medical researchers. It is not an economic problem to be solved by utility-maximizing consumers. In this world, health economics is an accounting exercise involving the comparison of different medical treatments and the measurement of different medical outcomes. Health economists studying incentives and markets have little to add.

But the evidence we outline in this chapter overwhelmingly suggests that the answer to the first question above is "yes" – consumers are price-sensitive when it comes to medical care. People with different budget constraints, different life expectancies, different qualities of life evaluate the tradeoff between medical care and other goods differently. One person may decide to skip a knee replacement surgery to pay for his child's tuition. Another person may decide to get laser eye surgery rather than a fancy Christmas gift for his spouse. Determining the right amount of care is not merely a medical matter, but is the outcome of economic tradeoffs that balance the marginal cost of care against the marginal benefit of that care. In other words, demand for health care is downward-sloping.

In many countries, this is rarely an issue because all citizens are entitled to subsidized health insurance or are eligible for free care from the government. But in some countries, notably the US, people must routinely decide how much to pay for care. In those contexts, evidence suggests that people who face different prices or have different abilities to pay for health care receive unequal amounts of health care. But even in countries where patients pay nothing for care at the point of service, whether health care demand is downward-sloping has important consequences for the design of good health care policy, as we will see throughout the book.

Are people who can better afford health care healthier because they receive more and better care? If so, what should a society do, if anything, in response to this possible inequity? These questions underlie the ferocious political debate about health care in every country and motivate much of our study in this textbook.

2.1   Experiments on the demand for health care

Imagine a consultant working on his first case. He is tasked with helping a surgeon predict what will happen to her customer base if she raises prices. To do so, the consultant sets out to plot a demand curve for the surgeon's services.

One method he might use to plot this demand curve is to take a survey of the surgeon's patients and ask them if they would have chosen a different surgeon if the price had been higher or lower. One major problem with this approach is that it ignores the population of people who are not currently patients of the surgeon. A change in price for the surgeon's services may have a different effect on that population. Since the surgeon's patients are likely to be more devoted to her than patients who do not know her, they may be less sensitive to price changes than the people not surveyed.

Alternatively, the consultant could commission a survey of the entire local population. He asks respondents whether they visit surgeons like his client and how much they pay. The main advantage of this approach is that different groups of people – covered by different insurance plans – face different prices for surgical visits. This allows the consultant to construct a demand curve, since he observes different levels of demand at different effective prices. Unlike the first survey, respondents are not asked to conduct any hypothetical thought experiments.

But this survey design is also problematic because the prices that respondents face are not randomly assigned. People choose their insurance plans based on what is advantageous to them. For instance, a respondent who knows he is likely to require surgery will search for an insurance carrier that comprehensively covers surgical services. As a result, people with generous insurance – and therefore facing lower out-of-pocket costs – are exactly the people who are most likely to demand surgery in the first place.

This non-random selection distorts the estimated demand curve because the groups facing each price level differ in important ways. In this case, the people who choose generous insurance are sicker than the typical population, and consequently have higher demand for services. Conversely, people who choose less generous insurance are healthier and have lower demand. Figure 2.2 shows what the measured demand curve D_M might look like if the true demand curve is actually D_T. Under these conditions, the consultant underestimates the demand at the high price P_H and overestimates the demand at the low price P_L.

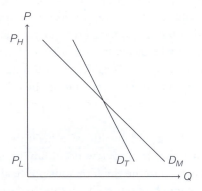

Figure 2.2. *True demand, D_T, and measured demand, D_M, in a non-randomized study. A non-randomized study such as a broad survey will tend to overestimate health care demand at low prices (and underestimate demand at high prices) because the people who face low prices are the same ones who purchased generous insurance coverage and tend to need more services.*

To calculate a true demand curve, we need to find how the *same* population reacts to different prices. Ideally, we would track the same population in two parallel universes where they face different price levels, but of course this thought experiment cannot be performed in real life. The next best alternative is a **randomized experiment** that assigns treatments randomly to different groups of study participants. Randomization generates experimental groups that are statistically similar. Done correctly, this becomes the best approximation for the parallel universes with actually identical groups. Distortions like the one in Figure 2.2 disappear if there are no meaningful differences between the groups except for the random assignment.

Definition	2.1

Randomized experiment: a study that assigns treatments randomly to different groups of study participants. A **randomized controlled experiment** includes a control group which is randomly chosen and receives either no treatment, a placebo treatment, or the usual treatment they would have received if not enrolled in the trial. Such studies provide the most persuasive evidence on questions of causality in the social sciences and medicine.

Two randomized health insurance experiments

For this chapter, we rely primarily on two influential randomized experiments of health care demand: the **RAND Health Insurance Experiment (HIE)** and the **Oregon Medicaid Experiment**. The RAND study, conducted between 1974 and 1982, was particularly

groundbreaking because it was the first large-scale randomized study in which insurance status was randomly assigned, and it is still the only such study ever conducted in the US. Before RAND, there were many non-randomized studies but little consensus about the effects of price on the demand for health care. Since the RAND HIE was published, there has been little dispute that the demand curve for health care is not vertical but in fact downward-sloping.

For the HIE, the RAND researchers randomly assigned two thousand families from six American cities to one of several different health insurance plans for several years. These plans varied on the generosity of coverage; in particular, the plans had different **copayment rates**.

The copayment rate for an insurance plan is the fraction of the medical bill for which the patient is responsible. Thus, people assigned to

Parallel universes would be the ideal setting for estimating demand curves, but researchers lack the grant money to build such a testing environment. They rely on randomized experiments instead. Credit: © rolffimages – Fotolia.com.

different plans had to pay different prices for the same services. There were four different plans: one plan with completely free care (0% copayment rate), and three other **cost-sharing plans** with 25%, 50%, and 95% copayments.[2] Because the plans studied in the RAND HIE differed in only this respect, they are ideal for estimating the effect of price on health care decisions.

Definition	2.2

Copayment rate: the fraction of the medical bill for which the patient is responsible. A **cost-sharing plan** is one with a positive copayment rate, so that costs are shared between the insured and the insurer.

One problem with the RAND HIE is that the health economy has changed in fundamental ways since the 1980s. Consequently, the results found in the RAND HIE may not apply to the demand for health care today. A recent study, the Oregon Medicaid Experiment, provides an interesting update to the RAND results. In general, like the RAND HIE, the Oregon Medicaid Experiment finds downward-sloping demand for health care (Finkelstein et al. 2011).

Unlike the RAND HIE, the Oregon Medicaid Experiment did not assign participants to different insurance plans. Instead, it compared two groups of low-income adult Oregonians: (a) people who won a 2008 lottery to receive the opportunity to apply for public

---

2 In addition to plans that varied on the copayment rate, there were also other plans including a health maintenance organization (HMO) plan and an individual deductible plan. Interested readers should check out *Free for All?* by Joseph Newhouse (1993) for an in-depth look at the experiment and many details that we lack the space to cover here.

health insurance coverage through Medicaid, and (b) lottery entrants who did not win and were not given a chance to apply for Medicaid. In effect, this lottery randomly assigned insurance coverage to a subset of the winners. Hence, the lottery winners tended to face lower out-of-pocket prices for care.

The approaches of the RAND HIE and the Oregon Medicaid Experiment each have their advantages and disadvantages. The Oregon Medicaid Experiment exclusively focuses on a low-income population, unlike the RAND HIE, which studied a nationally representative population. Furthermore, the RAND HIE used a direct randomization of health insurance coverage, while the Oregon Medicaid Experiment relied on a randomization scheme that was only indirectly related to insurance coverage (Medicaid enrollment was not automatic for lottery winners; they were only 25 percentage points more likely to be covered in the year following the lottery than the lottery losers were). Lastly, the Oregon Medicaid Experiment included an uninsured group that was in part randomly assigned, while the RAND HIE did not include any participants who were totally without insurance.

2.2   Is demand for health care downward-sloping?

If we wish to estimate a demand curve for health care, there are two basic questions to answer before we can even start: How do we define quantity, Q? And how do we define price, P? This may be simple in some cases: in the market for bubblegum, quantity is naturally defined as the number of sticks purchased and price as the cost of a stick.

Matters are more complicated when it comes to health care. A quick visit to the doctor's office is not equivalent to an overnight stay at the hospital. Counting both as one unit of health care is not appropriate, nor is it clear if an overnight stay should count as five doctor's visits or one hundred. Researchers handle this difficulty by measuring separate demand curves for different kinds of care.

Measuring price in health care is also not straightforward. Most health care is paid for by third parties such as private health insurers or the government. Unlike bubblegum buyers, patients pay a *premium*, or an upfront cost, to join an insurance plan, and in exchange they pay lower out-of-pocket prices for each medical service they receive. When calculating demand, the appropriate measure of price is the marginal cost that patients pay when consuming a fixed amount of care. Researchers treat the copayment rate as a measure of price because it is proportional to the marginal cost faced by patients.

The remainder of this section summarizes the experimental evidence on downward-sloping demand for different types of health care.

Outpatient care

If you have ever visited the doctor's office, hospital, or emergency room and gone home the same day, you were the recipient of **outpatient care**. Depending on the severity of your condition, you may not care that your insurance company requires you to pay $20 for the visit. If you have a broken leg, you still want a cast set even if you have to pay the fee. On the other hand, if you just have a runny nose, you might choose chicken soup and *Simpsons* reruns instead of a visit to the doctor.

Definition | **2.3**

Outpatient care: any interaction with a doctor or other medical care professional that does not involve an overnight stay. Typically, more severe cases will require overnight stays for patient monitoring and recovery, so outpatient cases tend to be less complex.

Outpatient care is also sometimes called **ambulatory care**.

In the health insurance experiments, participants faced different prices for outpatient care. What effect did this have on demand for outpatient services? Both the RAND HIE and the Oregon Medicaid Experiment report the effects of price changes on the demand for outpatient care. The effects are large and show that demand curves for these services are downward-sloping.

Table 2.1. *Evidence for outpatient care: (a) RAND HIE Study. (b) Oregon Medicaid Experiment.*

(a)

Plan	Avg # of annual episodes by condition		
	Total	Acute	Chronic
Free	2.99	2.29	0.70
25%	2.32	1.78	0.54
50%	2.11	1.60	0.51
95%	1.90	1.44	0.46

(b)

	% with visit	No. of visits
Lottery winners	63.6	2.22
Lottery losers	57.4	1.91

Sources: (a) Keeler et al. (1988). With permission from RAND. (b) Amy Finkelstein et al. (2012) The Oregon Health Insurance Experiment: evidence from the first year, *Quarterly Journal of Economics*, 127(3): 1057–1106, Supplementary Data. With permission from Oxford University Press.

Table 2.1(a) shows evidence from the RAND HIE that, as patient cost-sharing increases, the number of episodes of outpatient care decreases sharply. People assigned to the 95% group, for example, had 36% fewer episodes of outpatient care than those in the free plan.

While this result is striking, even more surprising is that patients with *chronic* conditions and *acute* conditions had similar downward-sloping demand. Chronic conditions, such as diabetes and high blood pressure, are health problems that persist over long periods of time and require sustained treatment. Non-chronic or acute conditions are those with sudden onset such as a cold or a broken leg. People assigned to the 95% group had 34% fewer episodes of chronic outpatient care than those in the free plan, and 37% fewer episodes of acute outpatient care.

The Oregon Medicaid Experiment also provides evidence for downward-sloping demand in outpatient care. Table 2.1(b) shows that lottery winners who are more likely to be Medicaid enrollees were 24 percentage points more likely to have an outpatient visit over a six-month period, and had 36% more visits on average, when compared with lottery losers who were unlikely to be on Medicaid.

Inpatient and emergency room care

Imagine that you see your doctor and she tells you that your condition is sufficiently serious that you must stay overnight in the hospital for monitoring. The doctor is admitting you to the hospital for **inpatient care**.

Definition	2.4

Inpatient care: any interaction with a doctor or other medical care professional that involves an overnight stay at a hospital.

Given the severity of your condition, it seems unlikely in this case that you would be too worried about the 20% copayment that the insurance company will charge for the visit, even though the visit will ultimately be very expensive. In fact, even a 50% copayment rate would not deter you from heeding the doctor's orders and staying overnight. What this thought experiment suggests is that demand for inpatient care may not be as sensitive to price as outpatient care is. Does the evidence from these health insurance experiments line up with this intuition?

The evidence on this question is mixed. The data on inpatient care from the Oregon Medicaid Experiment corroborates our intuition in part. Table 2.2(b) shows that though lottery winners had more inpatient visits than lottery losers over a six-month period, the difference was not statistically significant. The evidence does not allow us to conclude that this population is price-sensitive with respect to its demand for inpatient care.

By contrast, the RAND HIE study does find downward-sloping demand for inpatient care. Members of the 95% copayment group were 24% less likely to have inpatient care than members of the free plan in an average year (see Table 2.2(a)). However, the drop in service use at higher prices was smaller than the corresponding drop for outpatient care. Like the Oregon Medicaid Experiment, the RAND HIE finds demand for inpatient care is not as sensitive to price as outpatient care is.

Table 2.2. *Evidence for inpatient care: (a) RAND HIE Study. (b) Oregon Medicaid Experiment.*

(a)

Plan	Avg # of Annual Visits
Free	0.133
25%	0.109
50%	0.099
95%	0.098

(b)

	% with visit	No. of visits
Lottery winners	7.4	0.103
Lottery losers	7.2	0.097

No significant difference at the $p = 10\%$ level.

* Indicates significantly different from the free plan at the $p = 5\%$ level.
** Indicates significantly different from the free plan at the $p = 1\%$ level.

Sources: (a) Keeler et al. (1988). With permission from RAND. (b) Amy Finkelstein et al. (2012) The Oregon Health Insurance Experiment: evidence from the first year, *Quarterly Journal of Economics*, 127(3): 1057–1106, Supplementary Data. With permission from Oxford University Press.

Intuitively, we would expect that the more severe a condition is, the less price-sensitive patients will be with respect to its treatment. This explains why study participants seemed to be more price-sensitive for outpatient care than inpatient care. By this logic, demand for emergency room (ER) care by deathly ill patients should be completely price-insensitive: regardless of costs, people will seek ER care in cases of life and death.

Nonetheless, there is evidence that demand for emergency care slopes downward. While the Oregon Medicaid Experiment finds no statistically significant difference in the rates of ER visits (Table 2.3(b)), participants in the RAND HIE were sensitive to price.

Table 2.3. *Evidence for emergency care: (a) RAND HIE Study. (b) Oregon Medicaid Experiment.*

(a)

Plan	Probability of ER use
Free	22%
25%	19%*
50%	20%
95%	15%**

(b)

	% with visit	No. of visits
Lottery winners	26.7	0.48
Lottery losers	26.1	0.47

No significant difference at the $p = 10\%$ level.

* Indicates significantly different from the free plan at the $p = 5\%$ level.
** Indicates significantly different from the free plan at the $p = 1\%$ level.

Sources: (a) Newhouse (1993). With permission from RAND. (b) Amy Finkelstein et al. (2012) The Oregon Health Insurance Experiment: evidence from the first year, *Quarterly Journal of Economics,* 127(3): 1057–1106, Supplementary Data. With permission from Oxford University Press.

Table 2.3(a) shows that people in the cost-sharing groups were less likely to visit the ER than people on the free plan.

This result is at least a bit surprising; if all ER visits are truly for dire emergencies, this means that demand for life-saving care is downward-sloping. But not every ER visit is actually a matter of life or death. Many patients visit the ER for less urgent matters because they do not have a regular primary care doctor, have nowhere else to go, or have overestimated the severity of their condition (Garcia et al. 2010). When patients face high prices, it is these nonurgent ER visits that are most likely deterred.

Other evidence on outpatient, inpatient, and emergency care

Other studies also provide convincing evidence that demand for inpatient and emergency care slopes downward. The China Rural Health Insurance Experiment (CRHIE), conducted by RAND researchers and largely modeled on the RAND HIE, finds similar patterns. Like the RAND experiment, the CRHIE randomly assigned participants to insurance plans with different copayment rates. The participants were drawn from 26 villages in rural China, and their health expenditures were tracked over a two-year period from 1988 to 1989 (Cretin et al. 2006).

CRHIE participants with more generous insurance plans incurred more medical costs than participants with less generous plans, just as in the RAND HIE and the Oregon Medicaid Experiment (Table 2.4). As with the American experiments, the difference is more pronounced for outpatient expenditures: those in the most generous plan incurred more than twice as much outpatient cost per person compared with the people in the least

Table 2.4. *Mean health care expenditures in the CRHIE, in yuan.*

Copayment rate	Outpatient care	Inpatient care
20%	13.49	4.51
30%	12.04	1.18
40%	10.72	3.88
50%	9.52	3.61
60%	8.42	3.36
70%	7.43	3.14
80%	6.54	2.95

Source: Based on Table 8 in Cretin et al. (2006). With permission from RAND.

generous plan, but only about 53% more inpatient costs. Just like RAND HIE participants and Oregon Medicaid lottery entrants, health care consumers in rural China show signs of price-sensitivity, especially when it comes to outpatient care.

Data from non-experimental studies provides more corroborating evidence for both downward-sloping demand and different rates of price-sensitivity for different kinds of care. One non-experimental strategy researchers have used is to study people who suddenly change insurance status from uninsured to insured. If demand is indeed downward-sloping, we would expect to see an increase in the use of medical services when an individual becomes insured. But if urgent care is less price-sensitive, then we would expect to see less of a jump in those services when individuals gain insurance coverage.

Most US citizens become eligible to enroll in Medicare when they turn 65, including many people who were uninsured before that age. Card et al. (2009) use this fact in an analysis of California hospital admissions data to measure the effect of insurance coverage on demand. The number of planned hospital admissions per patient jumps by 15% from age 64 to age 65 when Medicare coverage begins. Even if this jump reflects "pent-up demand" – a phenomenon where individuals who know they will soon have insurance access delay costly procedures – it is evidence that people are sensitive to price when it comes to planned hospital admissions. By contrast, unplanned hospitalizations that begin in the ER increase by only 2.5% at that age (Figure 2.3). Again, when life is at stake, the price of care seems to matter a lot less, or not at all.

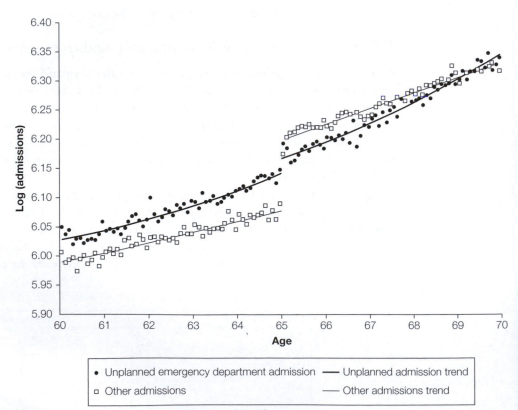

Figure 2.3. *Emergency and non-emergency visits by age.*

Source: Figure 2 in D. Card, C. Dobkin and N. Maestas (2009). Does Medicare save lives?, *Quarterly Journal of Economics*, 124(2): 597–636, by permission of Oxford University Press.

A related approach takes advantage of a change in policy extending insurance to a well-defined group in the population. For instance, in 2000, the French government made a free complementary insurance plan available to the poorest 10% of French residents. In an analysis of this policy, Grignon and Perronnin (2008) find that people in this group who previously lacked complementary coverage increased their use of medical care services.

Pediatric care

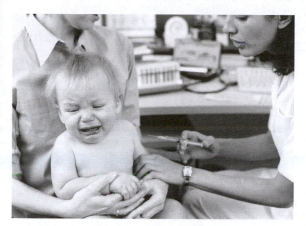

This child probably wishes his parents were more price-sensitive.
Credit: Bananastock.

We have seen plenty of evidence that demand slopes downward for all different sorts of care. People trade off their health against other goals in almost every conceivable situation. But consider now pediatric care, that is, care for infants and children which is typically paid for by parents. Despite all the evidence we have seen for downward-sloping demand, it is hard to imagine that parents would skimp on care for their children because of price.

And yet evidence from the RAND HIE shows parents are price-sensitive even with respect to health care for their children. Families on the free plan were significantly more likely to have sought immunizations and other preventative care for infants, toddlers, and young children (ages 0–6) than families with positive copayment rates (Table 2.5). This is evidence that even the demand curve for pediatric care slopes downward, although this pattern does not seem to extend to older children and adolescents (ages 7–16).

Table 2.5. *Percentage with preventative pediatric care over three years, by age and care type.*

	0–6 years		7–16 years	
	Immunization	Any preventative	Immunization	Any preventative
Free	58.9	82.5	21.2	64.8
Copayment	48.7*	73.7*	21.7	59.6

* Statistically significant discrepancy from free plan.

Source: Newhouse (1993). With permission from RAND.

Other types of care

The RAND HIE and Oregon Medicaid Experiment also gathered use and spending data for **mental health care**, **dental care**, and **prescription drug use**. In each case, both studies find strong evidence of downward-sloping demand.

Table 2.6 displays evidence that per-capita expenditures on ambulatory mental health care depend on plan type. Participants on the free plan used more than twice as much mental health care in dollar terms as the participants with the 95% copayments.

The demand for dental care is even more price-sensitive than the demand for outpatient medical care. Nearly 58% of low-income participants on the free plan visited the dentist annually, compared with only 40% of the low-income participants on the 95% plan, and incurred about 47% more total dental expenditures (Table 2.7). Similar patterns hold for

Table 2.6. *Per-capita mental health expenditures, by plan type.*

Plan	Mean expense ($)	Percentage of free plan
Free	42.2	–
25%	28.4	67%
50%	13.1	33%
95%	18.1	43%

Source: Newhouse (1993). With permission from RAND.

Table 2.7. *Dental care utilization by income level.*

	Low-income group[†]		High-income group[†]	
	Percentage with any use	Average expenditures ($)	Percentage with any use	Average expenditures ($)
Free	57.8	317	74.7	339
95%	39.8*	216*	61.3*	234*

* Statistically significant discrepancy from free plan.
† The low-income group comprises the third of households with the lowest incomes. The high-income group comprises the third of households with the highest incomes.

Source: Newhouse (1993). With permission from RAND.

high-income participants, indicating that families on tight budgets are not the only ones sensitive to price when taking care of their teeth.

Prescription drugs are no exception to the general rule of downward-sloping demand. Both the RAND HIE and the Oregon study find evidence that patients facing lower prices use more prescription drugs. The case of antibiotic drugs is particularly interesting. When patients have an illness caused by a bacterial condition, it is medically appropriate to prescribe antibiotics. But when a patient suffers from a viral infection, antibiotics are powerless against the patient's condition and even potentially harmful because antibiotic use can breed resistant bacterial strains.

Despite the futility of antibiotics for treating viruses, patients with colds (which are caused by viruses) often pressure their doctors to prescribe antibiotics anyway, not realizing the uselessness of such treatment. Doctors know better, but in busy practices they are prone to relent and prescribe antibiotics anyway. The RAND HIE provides evidence of this fact: patients with viral infections commonly received antibiotic prescriptions (Table 2.8).

Raising the price of antibiotics has both a bad effect and a good effect. Among patients with bacterial illnesses, those in the free plan received more antibiotic prescriptions than those in the cost-sharing plans. Thus, it is possible that some sick patients in the cost-sharing plans went without antibiotics, when such prescriptions would have been useful. Among patients suffering viral infections, cost-sharing also reduced the use of antibiotics.

Table 2.8. *Antibiotic use in the RAND HIE.*

	No. of antibiotics per person	
Plan	Bacterial conditions	Viral conditions
Free	0.47	0.17
Copay	0.24**	0.08**

** Statistically significant discrepancy from the free plan.
Source: Keeler et al. (1988). With permission from RAND.

In this case, the lower price of antibiotics for people on the free plan offered no health benefits, while potentially abetting the evolution of resistant bacterial strains.

2.3   Measuring price sensitivity with elasticities

Evidence from the randomized experiments establishes that the demand for inpatient and outpatient care slopes downward, but we have not directly examined the demand curve implied by this evidence. Figure 2.4 plots data on the use of outpatient care and dental care from Keeler et al. (1988) in the form of a traditional demand curve.

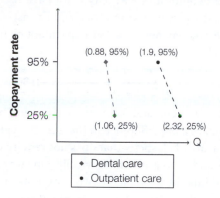

Figure 2.4. *Data on outpatient and dental care.*

Source: Keeler et al. (1988). With permission from RAND.

One simple measure of price sensitivity for each type of care is the slope of the line plotted between the two points of measured demand. The problem is that the units of the quantity demanded are not comparable. A dental visit is not the same as an outpatient visit. Hence, the fact that one slope is greater than the other is not meaningful for comparing price sensitivities between the two goods. Instead, we need a measure of price sensitivity that is not affected by the units in which either price or quantity are measured. The **elasticity of demand** provides just such a measure.

Definition	2.5

Elasticity of demand: the ratio that represents how a fixed percentage change in the price of a good leads to a change in the quantity demanded, measured as a percentage change from the original quantity.

Let Q_1 be the original quantity demanded at the price P_1 and let Q_2 be the new quantity demanded after the price changes from P_1 to P_2. The **elasticity** ϵ between these two points is defined as

$$\epsilon = \frac{(Q_2 - Q_1)/Q_1}{(P_2 - P_1)/P_1} \qquad (2.1)$$

For instance, suppose an individual starts with an insurance plan with a 25% copayment rate and switches to a plan with a 95% copayment rate. This represents a 280% increase in the price of care for the individual: $^{(95-25)}/_{25} \times 100\% = 280\%$. Figure 2.4 shows how her quantity of outpatient care demanded changes with the switch in insurance: it decreases from 2.32 episodes per year to 1.9, an 18% decline. The elasticity of demand for this individual is

$$\epsilon = \frac{(Q_2 - Q_1)/Q_1}{(P_2 - P_1)/P_1} = \frac{(1.9 - 2.32)/2.32}{(95\% - 25\%)/25\%} = \frac{-0.18}{2.8} = -0.06$$

A similar calculation shows that the elasticity of demand for dental care is also -0.06, even though the slope of the demand curve for dental care looks steeper; comparing slopes can be deceptive. Elasticity is useful for comparing demand curves for various goods, or the demand curve for the same good in different places or settings, because it is *unitless*. We can use elasticities to compare downward-sloping demand for different types of health care or for the same type of care in different studies. While it was already evident that the demand curves for these goods are downward-sloping, these calculations affirm that demand for these goods is relatively inelastic ($-1 < \epsilon < 0$).

One problem with the definition of elasticity ϵ we have used so far is it treats price changes from P_1 to P_2 and P_2 to P_1 asymmetrically. For instance, if the individual had instead switched from a 95% copayment to a 25% copayment plan, her elasticity of demand for outpatient care would be

$$\epsilon = \frac{(Q_2 - Q_1)/Q_1}{(P_2 - P_1)/P_1} = \frac{(2.32 - 1.9)/1.9}{(25\% - 95\%)/95\%} = \frac{0.22}{-0.74} = -0.30$$

Analogously, her elasticity of demand for dental care would be -0.28. The choice of a starting point for price makes a big difference in the ultimate calculation of elasticity.

We would prefer a measure of elasticity that does not require us to pick a starting point and treats price increases and decreases symmetrically. One way around this problem is to measure elasticity at the midpoint between the two endpoints of the demand curve, rather than at the endpoints themselves. This alternate formulation is called the **arc elasticity**.

Definition | 2.6

Let (Q_1, P_1) and (Q_2, P_2) be two points on a single demand curve. The **arc elasticity** ϵ_{arc} between these two points is defined as

$$\epsilon_{arc} = \frac{\Delta Q/(Q_1 + Q_2)}{\Delta P/(P_1 + P_2)} \tag{2.2}$$

where $\Delta Q = Q_2 - Q_1$ and $\Delta P = P_2 - P_1$.

When we apply formula (2.2) to the data from Figure 2.4, we find that the arc elasticity of demand for outpatient care is -0.17 and for dental is -0.16.

Figure 2.5 shows the arc elasticity of demand for various health care goods implied by the RAND HIE, alongside estimated elasticities for several other common goods. Demand for medical care goods tends to be inelastic ($-1 < \epsilon_{arc} < 0$). Meanwhile, the demand for goods such as restaurant meals and fresh tomatoes is more elastic ($\epsilon < -1$).

Evidence from the RAND HIE and the Oregon Medicaid Experiment suggests that demand for medical care is quite inelastic. But an arc elasticity calculation is an average measure, so it may not fully capture the range of behavior of all health care consumers. For instance, it is possible that those who spend the most on health care are less sensitive to the price of additional care. Kowalski (2009) analyzes non-experimental data from a large US employer and finds that the 5% of the population that spent the most on medical care are far less price-sensitive than the general population, while typical members of the population are fairly *elastic* in their demand.

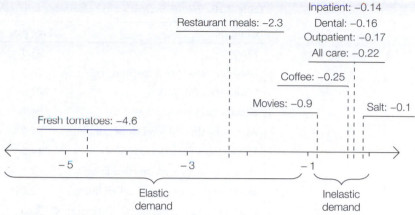

Figure 2.5. *Elasticities of various goods.*

Source: Developed from Newhouse (1993) and Gwartney et al. (2008).

2.4   Does the price of health care affect health?

The previous section showcased the overwhelming evidence that demand for health care is downward-sloping. Though more exigent needs such as inpatient care and ER care seem less sensitive to price, it is clear that people do sometimes skimp on health care, despite parents' advice. The next important question is: How much impact, if any, does the price of health care have on *health* itself?

The simplest way to compare the health of different groups is with mortality rates. The Oregon Medicaid Experiment tracked participant survival rates, and did not find a significant difference between the survival of Medicaid lottery winners and lottery losers in the first year after the lottery (Table 2.9(b)). By contrast, a different study of the Medicaid program in the US does find that insurance coverage reduces mortality. Meyer and Wherry (2012) analyze the expansion of health insurance to a population of poor children in the US. They find that providing Medicaid to black children increased their probability of survival to their late teens by between 13% and 18% relative to similar black children who were not eligible for the Medicaid expansion because they were born before an arbitrary age cutoff date.

Like the Oregon Medicaid Experiment, the RAND HIE also failed to find a mortality difference between treatment groups. The risk of dying for all participants is nearly

Table 2.9. *Evidence on mortality rates: (a) RAND HIE Study. (b) Oregon Medicaid Experiment.*

(a) Relative mortality rate				(b) Absolute two-year mortality rate	
	All participants	High-risk participants[a]			All participants
Free	0.99	1.90		Lottery winners	0.8%
Copay	1	2.10[*]		Lottery losers	0.8%

[a] Participants were classified as high risk based on their blood pressure, cholesterol levels, and smoking habits at the beginning of the study.

[*] Indicates significantly different from the free plan at the $p = 5\%$ level.

Sources: (a) Newhouse (1993). With permission from RAND. (b) Amy Finkelstein et al. (2012) The Oregon Health Insurance Experiment: evidence from the first year, *Quarterly Journal of Economics*, 127(3): 1057–1106, Supplementary Data. With permission from Oxford University Press.

Table 2.10. *Health indicators by insurance plan in the RAND HIE.*

Condition	Free plan	Copay plan
FEV_1^a	95.0	94.8
Diastolic blood pressure (mm Hg)	78.0	78.8*
Cholesterol (mg/dl)	203	202
Glucose (mg/dl)	94.7	94.2
Abnormal thyroid level (% of sample)	2.4	1.7
Hemoglobin (g/100 ml)	14.5	14.5
Functional far vision (Snellen lines)	2.4	2.5*
Functional near vision (Snellen lines)	2.35	2.44*
Chronic joint symptoms (% of sample)	30.0	31.6

[a] FEV is forced expiratory volume in 1 second.
* Indicates significantly different from the free plan at the $p = 5\%$ level.
Source: Newhouse (1993). With permission from RAND.

identical under the free plan and under the copayment plans: those in the free plan were 99% as likely to die during the experiment as those in the cost-sharing plans (Table 2.9(a)).

But free insurance did seem to have an impact on the mortality rates among the most vulnerable participants in the RAND HIE. At the beginning of the study, participants were categorized into risk categories based on their blood pressure, cholesterol level, and smoking habits. The high-risk people on the free plan were 10% less likely to die than high-risk participants on the cost-sharing plans.

Mortality is an extreme outcome. So the fact that people in different plans did not differ in their mortality rates does not mean that more affordable care does not yield any health benefits. In addition to mortality, the RAND HIE tracked various health indicators such as cholesterol levels and blood pressure. Table 2.10 shows some of the differences in health indicators between members of the free plan and members of cost-sharing plans measured in the RAND HIE. Out of 23 health comparisons, the only statistically significant differences between the plans were in blood pressure, myopia, and presbyopia.[3] With the exception of blood pressure, there were no medically important differences as a result of more generous insurance coverage. Even this difference in blood pressure was concentrated among the low-income and high-risk study participants (Newhouse 1993).

As in the RAND HIE, investigators in the Oregon Medicaid Experiment measured the effect of insurance coverage on health status. One key measure evaluated was self-reported health. By this measure, Medicaid lottery winners were healthier than lottery losers twelve months after the lottery. Lottery winners reported better overall health, more healthy days, and lower rates of depression than lottery losers did (Table 2.11). This survey evidence suggests that the lottery winners benefited as a result of the lower price of health care they faced, even though Table 2.9(b) shows there were no mortality differences.

The Oregon investigators found that lottery winners with diabetes had lower blood sugar levels, and that lottery winners with depression were more likely to be receiving

A Snellen chart for testing vision. According to the RAND HIE, members on the free plan could read an average of 0.1 lines farther down the chart than members on the cost-sharing plan. Credit: Getty.

---

3 Both myopia and presbyopia are vision-related problems. Myopia is near-sightedness, and presbyopia is far-sightedness.

Table 2.11. *Effect of lottery win on health in the first year of the Oregon Medicaid Experiment.*

	Lottery winners	Lottery losers
Survived one year after lottery	99.2%	99.2%
Self-reported health good	58.7%	54.8%**
Self-reported health fair or better	88.9%	86.0%**
Health about the same or better over last six months	74.7%	71.4%**
No. of days physical health good	22.2	21.9*
No. of days mental health good	19.3	18.7**
Did not screen positive for depression in last two weeks	69.4%	67.1%**

* Difference between lottery winners statistically significant at the $p = 5\%$ level.
** Difference between lottery winners statistically significant at the $p = 1\%$ level.

Source: Amy Finkelstein et al. (2012) The Oregon Health Insurance Experiment: evidence from the first year, *Quarterly Journal of Economics*, 127(3): 1057–1106, Supplementary Data. With permission from Oxford University Press.

treatment. However, as in the RAND study, Oregon investigators found little statistically significant evidence of health differences for many health outcomes between lottery winners and lottery losers in the first two years of the experiment (Baicker et al., 2013). Rates of hypertension and high cholesterol, for instance, were statistically quite similar. Together, the studies imply that more affordable care does not measurably improve health for most of the population, but can improve health for at-risk groups.

Findings from several non-experimental studies largely support this conclusion. Studies of vulnerable sub populations, including Wisconsin car accident victims, low-income pregnant mothers on Medicaid, elderly Seattle-area veterans, and dying HIV patients, all find that more affordable health care improves health (Levy and Meltzer 2004; Doyle 2005; Currie and Gruber 1996; Fihn and Wicher 1988; Goldman et al. 2001). On the other hand, evidence on broader populations of self-employed workers finds no mortality differences as a result of insurance coverage, just like the RAND HIE did (Perry and Rosen 2004).

2.5   Conclusion

It seems clear that demand for health care is in fact downward-sloping. Evidence shows unequivocally that people take price into account when deciding how much medical care to seek, even for serious conditions. In short, economic tradeoffs matter even in the world of health. This means that economic analysis is relevant in the world of health care.

Downward-sloping demand implies a fundamental tradeoff for the design of any health care system. If health care is free at the point of service (as it is in many countries), people will demand a lot of care, even care that is not particularly useful for improving their health. For instance, in the RAND HIE, members of the free plan had the same health status outcomes and mortality rates on average as the people on the cost-sharing plans.

On the other hand, if health care is not free, some patients will respond by seeking less care. High prices for health care may have deadly consequences for the most vulnerable segments of the population such as the poor and the chronically ill. Ultimately, this tradeoff between economic efficiency and social equity forms the core of the health policy debate.

2.6   Exercises

Comprehension questions

Indicate whether the statement is true or false, and justify your answer. Be sure to cite evidence from the chapter and state any additional assumptions you may need.

1 Unlike with most types of goods, deriving a demand curve for health care is quite simple because people rarely skimp on health care.
2 The RAND study was especially useful for measuring price elasticities because it randomly assigned insurance plans to participants (as opposed to letting them choose).
3 The Oregon Medicaid Experiment is not truly "randomized" because lottery winners did not all end up with insurance, and some lottery losers did end up with insurance.
4 The RAND HIE found that people assigned to the free health plan had the same rate of hospitalization as people assigned to the cost-sharing plans.
5 In the RAND HIE, the arc elasticity of demand for inpatient care was larger (in absolute value) than the arc elasticity of demand for outpatient care.
6 Unlike the usual measure of elasticity, an arc elasticity can be calculated from just one price–quantity data point.
7 Both the RAND and Oregon studies find that demand for health care is approximately unit elastic, that is, $\epsilon \approx -1$.
8 In the RAND HIE, being assigned more generous insurance did not generally improve participants' health outcomes, except among certain subgroups.
9 To date, no major health insurance experiment has studied the impact of *un*insurance, just different levels of insurance.
10 Results from the Oregon Medicaid Experiment suggest that having health insurance has a positive impact on health status.

Analytical problems

11 Suppose you are collecting data from a country like Japan where the government sets the price of health care. Each prefecture in Japan has a different set of prices (for example, Tokyo has higher prices than rural Hokkaido). Data for 1999 is displayed in Table 2.12.

Table 2.12. *Outpatient utilization in Tokyo and Hokkaido, 1999.*

Region	Outpatient visits	Price/visit
Tokyo	1.25/month	20¥
Hokkaido	1.5/month	10¥

a What is the arc price elasticity of demand for health care consumers in Japan (using only this data)?
b Suppose that incomes are generally much higher in Tokyo than Hokkaido. Is your answer to the last question an overestimate or underestimate of price elasticity? Justify your answer. [*Hint*: It may be helpful to plot the data points from Table 2.12 and consider likely demand curves for Tokyo and Hokkaido.]

c   Using your estimated elasticity, what would the demand for health care be if the price in Tokyo were raised to 30¥ per visit? What would the demand in Hokkaido be if the price were lowered to 5¥ per visit?

You continue your observations of the Japanese health care system into the year 2000. For inscrutable reasons having to do with internal Japanese politics, the government changed the price in both Tokyo and Hokkaido that year, and you observe the demand recorded in Table 2.13.

Table 2.13. *Outpatient utilization in Tokyo and Hokkaido, 2000.*

Region	Outpatient visits	Price/visit
Tokyo	1.0/month	30¥
Hokkaido	1.2/month	15¥

d   Calculate the price elasticity of demand for health care in Japan using only data from the year 2000.

e   Use data from both years to calculate the elasticity of demand for health care for Tokyo and Hokkaido separately.

f   Using your estimated elasticities, what would the demand for health care in each prefecture be if the price were raised to 60¥ per visit next year (for both prefectures)?

g   Combine the Tokyo and Hokkaido estimates from Exercise 11(e) to get a single estimate of the price elasticity of health care demand for all of Japan. Assume that Tokyo is five times as populous as all of Hokkaido.

12 **Preventative care** refers to care taken to prevent future diseases rather than to treat current ones. Compared with ER care, preventative care is rarely urgent, and benefits can be difficult to measure: if you had the flu vaccine this year but did not catch the flu, it is impossible to tell if it was the shot or assiduous hand-washing that preserved you.

a   Given this description of preventative care, would you expect preventative care to be more or less price-sensitive compared with inpatient care? Why?

b   Table 2.14 shows evidence on preventative care from the RAND HIE. Summarize the data in the table and note any interesting patterns. Was your prediction correct?

Table 2.14. *Percentage with preventative care in the three years from the RAND HIE Study.*

	Males 17–44	Males 45–64	Females 17–44		Females 45–64	
	Any care	Any care	Any care	Pap test	Any care	Pap test
Free	27.2%	39.1%	83.7%	72.2%	76.9%	65.0%
Copay	23.1%	27.4%	76.9%**	65.8%	65.3%**	52.8%**

** indicates statistically significant difference from the free plan at the $p = 1\%$ level.

Source: Newhouse (1993). With permission from RAND.

13   In this exercise, assume that the term "admission" in Table 2.15 refers to inpatient care, while "any use" refers to inpatient and outpatient care.

Table 2.15 contains a lot of information. Without looking at any specific values, summarize what type of data the table contains. Give an example of a broad question about income levels and demand for health care that the table might have the potential to answer.

Table 2.15. *Various measures of predicted annual use of medical services by income group.*

	Income			Significance tests t on contrast of:	
Plan	Lowest third mean	Middle third mean	Highest third mean	Middle vs. lowest thirds[a]	Highest vs. lowest thirds[a]
Likelihood of any use (percent)					
Free	82.8	87.4	90.1	4.91	5.90
Family pay					
25 percent	71.8	80.1	84.8	5.45	6.28
50 percent	64.7	76.2	82.3	4.35	4.86
95 percent	61.7	68.9	73.8	3.96	4.64
Likelihood of one or more admissions (percent)					
Free	10.63	10.14	10.35	−0.91	−0.35
Family pay					
25 percent	10.03	8.44	7.97	−2.95	−2.75
50 percent	9.08	8.06	7.77	−1.78	−1.66
95 percent	8.77	7.38	7.07	−2.79	−2.46
Expenses (1984 $)					
Free	788	736	809	−1.78	0.53
Family pay					
25 percent	680	588	623	−3.17	−1.47
50 percent	610	550	590	−1.89	−0.49
95 percent	581	494	527	−3.09	−1.41

Note: Excludes dental and outpatient psychotherapy. Predictions for enrollment population carried forward for all years of the study.
[a] The t-statistics are corrected for intertemporal and intrafamily correlation. The statistics test the null hypothesis that the mean of the middle (highest) third equals the mean of the lowest third; for example, the 4.91 figure implies we can reject at the 0.001 level the hypothesis that in the free plan the likelihood of any use for the lowest and middle thirds of the income distribution are equal.

Source: Manning et al. (1987). Reprinted with permission from the American Economic Association.

Essay questions

14   Here is a selection from an abstract of a recent study entitled "The effect of health insurance coverage on the use of medical services" by Michael Anderson, Carlos Dobkin, and Tal Gross (2010). NBER Working paper No. 15823.

Substantial uncertainty exists regarding the causal effect of health insurance on the utilization of care. Most studies cannot determine whether the large differences in healthcare utilization between the insured and the uninsured are due to insurance status or to other unobserved differences between the two groups. In this paper, we exploit a sharp change in insurance coverage rates that results from young adults "aging out" of their parents insurance plans to estimate the effect of insurance coverage on the utilization of emergency department (ED) and inpatient services. [*In the US, children are eligible for insurance coverage through their parents' insurance only up to their 23rd birthday, at which point they lose eligibility.*] Using the National Health Interview Survey (NHIS) and a census of emergency department records and hospital discharge records from seven states, we find that aging out results in an abrupt 5 to 8 percentage point reduction in the probability of having health insurance. We find that not having insurance leads to a 40 percent reduction in ED visits and a 61 percent reduction in inpatient hospital admissions.

a What two groups are being compared in this study?
b Identify at least one important methodological difference between the design of this study and the RAND HIE. Give a hypothetical reason why this difference would bias the results.
c Are the findings of this study generally consistent with the findings from the Oregon Medicaid Experiment?

Students can find answers to the comprehension questions and lecturers can access an Instructor Manual with guideline answers to the analytical problems and essay questions at **www.palgrave.com/economics/bht**.

3 DEMAND FOR HEALTH: THE GROSSMAN MODEL

Is health something that happens to you, or something that you choose? Clearly, it is a little of both. A heart attack is an unpredictable event that can happen at any time, even to the young and fit. Getting hit by a bus is also bad for your health, and may be outside your control as well. But there are many actions you can take that reduce the likelihood of heart attacks or bus accidents. Cutting back on Big Macs, for instance, might reduce your heart attack risk, while cloistering yourself in your home virtually eliminates the prospect of a bus collision.

The situation is even more complicated when we consider that a single, seemingly beneficial action can have a wide variety of costs and consequences. For instance, you can take up jogging to keep in shape and avoid heart attacks, but this may increase your exposure to buses. And even if you manage to steer clear of buses, taking time out of your day to jog will reduce the time available for other healthy activities like body-building or pilates. As always, every use of time has an opportunity cost and every decision implies a tradeoff.

Furthermore, health is not the only important thing in life. You probably value many other things, not all of which will extend your lifespan. Maybe, like the authors, you enjoy the occasional jig-saw puzzle or video game. These pursuits, while admirable, reduce the time available for activities that improve health. Maybe you also enjoy snacking on chocolate-chip cookies, which is not very time-consuming but may make you gain weight.

When Sid Meier's Civilization *was first released in 1991, one of the authors spent sixteen straight hours crushing the Mongols. These were hours he could have spent jogging instead.*
Credit: Edward Mallia – iStockphoto.com.

Finally, your health decisions need to be considered in the context of your entire lifespan. Health is a form of capital – it is a valuable asset that pays dividends throughout your life but depreciates as you age. So managing your health over your lifetime is an economic problem that is similar, in some ways, to managing a stock portfolio.

We need a framework that captures all of the complex tradeoffs involved in health management. It should model health as a consumption good, an input into the enjoyment of other goods, and a capital good all at the same time. The Grossman model, developed by Michael Grossman in 1972, provides such a framework by treating health as something that people decide in part for themselves, rather than something that happens to them. The model provides a powerful set of explanations for a variety of health phenomena, including the link between socioeconomic status and health (Grossman 1972).

3.1   A day in the life of the Grossman model

The Grossman model ties together the health decisions that people make on a day-to-day basis in a framework that encompasses their entire lifespan. We start with the single-period utility function because the function for lifetime utility is built upon that.

Single-period utility

The Grossman model starts with a simplification: in any given period, an individual's utility is based on her health and the other non-health goods she consumes. So the first role health plays in the model is as a *consumption good*. Like the number of chocolate-chip cookies eaten or hours of video games played, one's health contributes directly to utility. An individual's utility for the period t is given by

$$U_t = U(H_t, Z_t) \tag{3.1}$$

where:

- H_t is the level of health, and
- Z_t is a composite good that represents everything else – video games, opera tickets, paintballing, company of friends – that a well-adjusted utility function includes. We refer to Z as the **home good**.

Note that health *care* does not appear explicitly in this utility function, so in this model the number of vaccines received affects utility only through health H (rather than affecting it directly).

While H and Z are distinct contributors to the utility function, there may be occasions when choices made by the individual simultaneously change H and Z. These choices may pose interesting tradeoffs for the individual. For instance, eating a double-double cheeseburger may contribute positively to Z but also clog the individual's arteries and cause a reduction in H. On the other hand, exercising may increase both the home good Z and health H.

Time constraints within a single period

In addition to the possible tradeoffs between H and Z, there are other constraints that limit the individual's ability to gain utility. Perhaps the most important of these is the time constraint – there are only 24 hours in the day. This leads us to the next important piece of the Grossman model: our individual divides her time between exactly four different activities. She can spend her time working, playing, improving her health, or lying in bed sick. In any given period t, the individual has Θ units of time at her disposal, and faces the following time constraint:

$$\Theta = T^W + T^Z + T^H + T^S \tag{3.2}$$

where:

- T^W is time spent working,
- T^Z is time spent playing,
- T^H is time spent improving health, and
- T^S is time spent sick.

In this formula, we suppress the t subscripts on each term to keep the notation simple, but please remember that there is a new stock of Θ units of time to spend in each period, and hence a new constraint. We will include t subscripts when needed for clarity.

Each of these activities plays a different role in the Grossman model and contributes to the individual's utility in a different way. Each hour spent working (T^W) produces income, which can then be used to buy medical care (which contributes to H) or jigsaw puzzles (which contributes to the home good Z). But it is not enough for the individual to simply own a pile of jigsaw puzzles that she never solves. To produce Z, she must actually open the box and piece the puzzle together; that is, she must spend time at play (T^Z). Similarly, she might buy a yoga mat or treadmill with her earned income, but she must spend time using them (T^H) in order to actually produce H.

The time spent sick, T^S, is a different kind of activity. It does not contribute to H or Z, and hence does not increase utility. It *does* impose an opportunity cost, because each hour spent sick is an hour not spent at the gym, or at work, or at the opera. Time spent sick is therefore lost time, and there are only Θ hours in a day. Why would she choose to spend any time sick? She may not have a choice. In the Grossman model, T^S is entirely determined by H and is not a voluntary activity.

Consider *The Simpson's* character Homer, who works at the Springfield Nuclear Power Plant. On Monday, he goes to work (T^W), earning enough income to purchase the latest Troy McClure DVD and a box of day-old donuts. On Tuesday, he decides to skip work, forgoing income in order to spend quality time in front of the television with his donuts and new DVD (T^Z). His activities on Tuesday increase the home good Z, because Homer derives enjoyment from Troy McClure's acting and the taste of jelly donuts. Unfortunately, his day is sedentary – devoid entirely of exercise (T^H) or any physical movement whatsoever. As a result, his health H deteriorates rapidly.

By Wednesday morning, Homer is feeling very sick, so he visits his doctor Dr Nick, taking an hour out of his morning to do so (T^H). Dr Nick writes him a note excusing him from work for another day – his advice for Homer is to take placebo medication. The visit and the medication, which cost $50, improve Homer's H somewhat, but it cannot salvage his Wednesday.

Donuts, a major source of Z *(and negative* H*) for Homer Simpson.* Credit: © ksena32 – Fotolia.com.

Homer is so miserable he cannot even drag himself out of bed to watch Troy McClure for a fifteenth time or eat any of the remaining stale donuts (T^S). For Homer, this is just wasted time. In just three days, Homer has illustrated most of the dynamics of the Grossman model.

Table 3.1 lists examples of activities that fit into each category, and summarizes the purpose and impact of each on the individual's utility.

Production of H and Z

We focus next on the process of producing H and Z. In the usual economic model of consumer behavior, all inputs into utility are purchased directly on the market. In this case, however, neither H nor Z can be purchased in a store. Instead, the individual must combine market commodities that she purchases with personal time to produce her two inputs into utility. In other words, for both health H and the home good Z, there are two distinct categories of inputs: market goods and personal time.

Table 3.1. *Activities in the Grossman model.*

Activity	Example	Purpose
Working (T^W)	Working at a power plant; playing professional sports; teaching health economics	Earn income to purchase items that will enhance H and Z
Playing (T^Z)	Doing a jigsaw puzzle; going to the opera; logging onto Facebook	Enhance Z
Improving health (T^H)	Jogging; undergoing surgery; beauty rest	Enhance H
Being sick (T^S)	Spending the day home in bed, doing nothing	None; T^S is always wasted time

We have already assigned variables to the personal time inputs that create H and Z: T^H and T^Z respectively. We want to refer to the market goods with shorthand notation as well. Let M be the market inputs for health (for example, health care or exercise equipment), and let J be the market inputs for the home good Z (for example, jigsaw puzzles or video games).

Despite the similarities between H and Z, there is at least one important difference. While Z is a *flow* that is created and consumed each period, H is a *stock* that accumulates or deteriorates from period to period. Decisions made about the individual's health ten years ago affect her today, just as her decisions today will affect her ten years from now. In a sense, the level of H reflects the complete history of past inputs and decisions pertaining to health. By contrast, enjoyment from today's home good is forgotten by tomorrow and does not contribute to tomorrow's Z.

In any given period t, before the individual has allocated any time or money, Z_t starts out at 0. H_t starts out at H_{t-1}, but is modified by the health decisions and purchases the individual makes during period t. The individual treats H_{t-1} as a given during period t, since she cannot go back into the past and change her history of health decisions, which determined H_{t-1}.

Hence, H_t and Z_t are determined by the following production functions:

$$H_t = H(H_{t-1}, T_t^H, M_t)$$
$$Z_t = Z(T_t^Z, J_t) \tag{3.3}$$

where:

- M_t represents market inputs like vaccines and treadmills into health H during period t, and
- J_t represents market inputs like video games and opera tickets into the home good Z.

The market budget constraint

In addition to the time constraint, the individual faces a more traditional budget constraint – she cannot spend more than she earns. Suppose that when the individual works, she earns a wage of w dollars per unit of time. Recall that her total time working in period t is T_t^W, so her total income Y_t for the period t is

$$Y_t = w \cdot T_t^W$$

The Grossman model does not specify how wages w are determined, but presumably the individual's education and other factors determine the wage she faces.

In any given period, the individual can spend her income on two items: market inputs into health (M_t) and the home good (J_t). Let p_M and p_J represent the prices of these two goods. She thus faces the following budget constraint:

$$p_M \cdot M_t + p_J \cdot J_t \leq w \cdot T_t^W = Y_t \tag{3.4}$$

To simplify matters, we assume that the individual cannot save leftover income to spend in future periods. With this additional assumption, the budget inequality becomes an equality:

$$p_M \cdot M_t + p_J \cdot J_t = w \cdot T_t^W = Y_t$$

The time and budget constraints are not independent. They are linked through the individual's decisions about time spent working (T^W). For instance, if the individual is so sick that she has no time to work, she will not be able to earn income to purchase any M or J, the inputs into the production of H and Z.

Sick time and productive time

We turn next to the relationship between health levels H and sick time T^S. The link is intuitive: the healthier the individual is, the less time she spends sick in a given period and the more productive time T^P she has available. Productive time is simply the complement of T^S and is the sum of time spent on the other three useful activities of working, playing, and improving health:

$$T^P \equiv \Theta - T^S = T^W + T^Z + T^H \tag{3.5}$$

In the Grossman model, there are diminishing marginal returns to productive time from health. If a person is already healthy enough to have very little sick time, then additional improvements in health yield little additional productive time. Conversely, if a person is very unhealthy, even small improvements in health can yield substantial decreases in sick time. This is the second role of health in the Grossman model. In addition to its role as a consumption good, health is an *input to the production* of productive time. Figure 3.1 is the illness-avoidance function. It plots the relationship between T^S and H in the Grossman model. T^S falls as health H improves, but the effect of better health on T^S also shrinks as health improves.

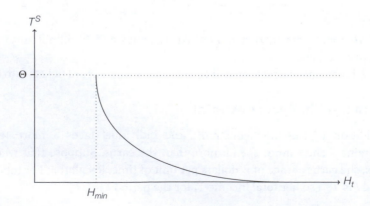

Figure 3.1. *Illness-avoidance function. As health (H) increases, sick time (T^S) falls. At H$_{min}$, there is no productive time for any other activities left since health is so low.*

A careful examination of this figure shows that there is a point, labeled H_{min} on the H-axis, such that the individual's T^S equals Θ. This means she is sick for the entire period, with no time left to work, play, or even seek medical care. In this way, the model provides an economic definition of death. The individual has no productive time left, and cannot generate any more health. She remains at H_{min} for all remaining periods and is effectively dead.

Let us go back to the case where the individual is still alive, with $H > H_{min}$. The only way to reduce sick time T^S is to improve health. So any market inputs or personal time dedicated to improving health create extra productive time. This new-found productive time can be reinvested in health-improving activities (T^H), but it can also be put to use as time spent working (T^W) or playing (T^Z). Ultimately, the purpose of reducing sick time is to have more productive time for producing more H and Z.

We have already discussed *two* important roles of health H in any given period. First, it enters directly into utility, as can be seen in equation (3.1). The individual cares about health for its own sake because it feels good to be healthy. Second, it expands the total amount of productive time available to the individual, allowing her to spend more time on things she actually cares about and less time sick in bed. In other words, you need to be healthy to have fun.

There is a third role that health plays in improving utility, but this additional role is not realized within a single period. Because health is a form of *stock*, high levels of health in one period lead to high levels of health in subsequent periods (see equation (3.3)). This third role is sometimes called the investment aspect of health. We will discuss this further in Section 3.3.

Three roles of health in the Grossman model

1 Health is a *consumption good*. It contributes directly to the individual's utility function each period. Being healthy is valuable in and of itself.
2 Health is an *input into production*. It generates productive time T^P which is useful for producing more H and Z.
3 Health is a form of *capital*. Unlike the home good, it endures from period to period. It can accumulate (or depreciate) over time, so improvements in health today can lead to better health tomorrow.

3.2   An optimal day

In the previous section, we discussed some of the key assumptions underlying the behavior of an individual in the Grossman model during a single period. There are many moving parts to the model. The subject of this section is how those parts move together, and how they jointly determine the optimal values of H and Z each period. In the previous section, we maintained a focus on the decisions an individual makes during a single period. Of course, decisions about health in this period have consequences in future periods, because H is a stock. As we will see in the next section, the individual makes decisions with this aspect of health in mind. The optimal levels of H and Z in any given period depend on decisions that are right for a *lifetime*, not just for a single period.

In this section, however, we first suppose that the individual is optimizing utility over just one period in order to demonstrate the major tradeoffs within the model. While this is a simplification, it is one that builds intuition for what follows. In subsequent sections, we relax this simplification and consider optimization over the whole lifespan.

The production possibility frontier for H and Z

A production possibility set traces out all of the possible combinations of H and Z that are attainable given an individual's budget and time constraints. The edge or frontier of this set is called the *production possibility frontier* (PPF) and should be familiar to students of economics. It is helpful to think about what the PPF looks like in the Grossman model, as the constraints facing the individual are not the same as those consumers face in a typical decision model.

In a standard model of consumer decision-making, if a consumer decides to devote all his resources to one good, he can attain a maximal level of that good. For instance, in a model of how consumers split their money between apples and bananas, every apple that the consumer buys results in less money left over to buy bananas. This results in a PPF that resembles Figure 3.2(a). An individual who devotes all resources to H will have no resources left to buy Z. Conversely, an individual who devotes all his resources to Z will have no H. The problem with this typical PPF in the context of the Grossman model is that, as we have seen, an individual with low H will have few resources to produce any Z at all. In the figure, points such as the one labeled "P" are not attainable and therefore should not be within the boundary of the PPF.

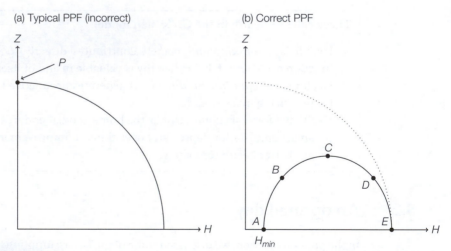

(a) Typical PPF (incorrect)   (b) Correct PPF

Figure 3.2. *Production possibility frontier (PPF) in the Grossman model. The incorrect PPF (a) describes health and the home good as substitutes. The maximum level of the home good is attained when health is 0. The problem with this PPF is that an individual with low* H *will have few resources to produce any* Z. *Points such as the one labeled "P" are not attainable and therefore are not within the boundary of the true PPF (b).*

Figure 3.2(b) presents the correct PPF that is consistent with the budget and time constraints of the Grossman model. It is easiest to see why this frontier is shaped the way it is by examining five extreme points labeled in the figure.

- At point A, the individual is at H_{min}, and hence has no productive time available to work, play, or improve health. As a consequence, he cannot afford any of the home good Z.

- At point *B*, the individual is healthier, and has some time available for productive activities. Since his health is still low, he is on the steep portion of the illness-avoidance function (Figure 3.1). Even small improvements in health yield large increases in productive time. We could call this the *free-lunch zone*: an hour spent increasing health yields more than an hour reduction in sick time. The individual can increase *Z* without giving up *H*.
- At point *C*, the free lunch is over. One extra hour spent on health yields exactly one extra hour of productive time T^p. The individual is still not as healthy as he could be, because he is not spending all his time jogging or all of his money on medical care. At point *C*, the individual enjoys the maximum amount of *Z* possible. If he tries to increase *Z* by shifting resources from health to the home good, the increase in sick time will outweigh the gain in the resources available for *Z* production. If he tries to increase *Z* by increasing *H* in an attempt to gain more productive time, he will again fail. Increases in health will not produce enough extra productive time to offset the time he must dedicate to improving *H*.
- Point *D* is in the *tradeoff zone*, which consists of all the points between *C* and *E*. Because the individual is on the flat part of the illness-avoidance function (Figure 3.1), increases in *H* yield only small decreases in sick time. In order to finance any increase in *H*, he must shift resources away from *Z*.
- At point *E*, the individual spends all of his time and money on health, totally ignoring the home good. As a result, *Z* is 0 and *H* is at its maximum attainable value.

Picking the optimal *H* and *Z* within a period

How does the individual choose the optimal mix of *H* and *Z*? Just as in any consumer demand model, the individual picks *H* and *Z* to maximize his utility subject to the constraints he faces. Suppose the individual picks a point, such as *A* or *B* in the free-lunch zone of Figure 3.3 (that is, any point on the PPF between *A* and *C*). In that zone, he can simultaneously increase both *H* and *Z* simply by shifting resources around. Because of this and the fact that *H* and *Z* are positive inputs into his utility function, he never finds it optimal to remain in the free-lunch zone.

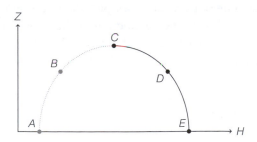

Figure 3.3. *Points A and B are in the free-lunch zone of this individual's PPF curve, since C is strictly better than both. The individual would never choose a point left of C.*

This may be counter-intuitive; why would it be non-optimal to have a free lunch? The answer is that allocations in the free-lunch zone do not take advantage of all opportunities and leave free *H* and *Z* on the table. For this reason, we gray out the zone in Figure 3.4 to indicate that no one who values *H* and *Z* would ever choose allocations there.

We know that the optimal allocation will be in the tradeoff zone on the PPF; that is, any point between *C* and *E*. The exact allocation he picks depends on his tastes for health and the home good. His utility function (equation (3.1)) describes his preferences over *H*

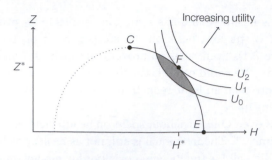

Figure 3.4. *Single-period indifference curves.*

and Z. Recall that in this section we have adopted the simplification that utility is maximized over one period. In the full version of the Grossman model, individuals consider tradeoffs across periods as well. We consider this in Section 3.3.

Recall that an indifference curve maps out the set of allocations that yield the same given level of utility. In Figure 3.4, we plot three example indifference curves. U_2 represents the highest level of utility of these three. The individual would love to be at U_2, but none of the points on that curve are feasible because the indifference curve does not intersect the PPF.

By contrast, the individual can obtain utility level U_0 by picking an allocation inside the PPF that is on the U_0 indifference curve. This is not optimal though, because any point in the shaded region between U_0 and the PPF would increase his utility. All of these points lie inside the PPF, so they are all feasible.

The allocation represented by F is optimal because it generates the highest utility level possible. Unlike with U_0, there is no room between U_1 and the PPF to improve the allocation. And unlike with U_2, U_1 is actually attainable because it intersects the PPF. In fact, at F, U_1 and the PPF are tangent. H^* and Z^* denote the optimal levels of health and the home good.

For this typically shaped utility function, the individual picks a level of H^* that is less than the maximum. He is willing to give up some health in order to gain utility from other goods. Rather than spend all his time jogging and all his money on checkups, he buys video games and jigsaw puzzles to play with

"There is nothing worse than fussiness about one's health, in excess of normal physical training" – *Plato, The Republic. Plato avoided point* E *in Figure 3.4, preferring to concentrate on* Z *(in his case, the search for truth).*
Credit: Zu_09 – iStockphoto.com.

in his leisure time. At the same time, he does not pick the maximum level of Z because he also values better health. This is a key prediction of the Grossman model – that in maximizing their utility, people make tradeoffs that lead to less than maximal health.

This is true for the typical utility function, but the model also allows for exotic preferences. For instance, consider someone who cares only about her health and nothing else. That individual will have indifference curves that are vertical lines, because a change in Z does not affect her utility. Figure 3.5 shows that the optimal allocation for this individual falls at point E, with health at its maximum and Z at 0.

Another possibility is an individual who only cares about Z. This individual will have horizontal indifference curves, since H does not enter his utility function. Figure 3.5 shows that the optimal allocation for this individual will fall at point C, with Z at its maximum. The striking outcome here is that even though H does not enter the individual's utility function, his optimal level of H is still positive. Recall that there are two possible motives for choosing H in the single-period model: because it directly enters the utility function and because it increases productive time. In this case, the individual picks a positive level of H solely because of the latter motive.

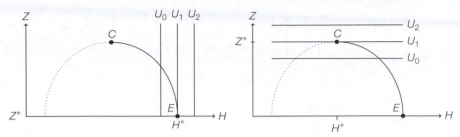

Figure 3.5. *Exotic indifference curves.*

The labor–leisure–health improvement tradeoff

The individual has to navigate a complicated set of tradeoffs in deciding how to spend his time. In this subsection, we take a closer look at these tradeoffs and how the individual's utility function and constraints interact. In a sense, we already looked at this tradeoff when we considered the tradeoff between H and Z. In order to allocate resources between H and Z, the individual first allocates his time across the four activities: work (T^W), play (T^Z), health improvement (T^H), and illness (T^S).

This is a complicated decision process in any given period, but the problem is simplified by the fact that the individual's prior health, over which he has no current control, plays a key role in determining current health. Current decisions about health will affect his future health, but that is little help to him in the current period.

The total productive time he has available, T^P, is thus determined by his health. Figure 3.6 shows this relationship. This figure is derived directly from Figure 3.1, where we plotted T^S against H. Remember that $T^S + T^P = \Theta$, so that both figures are plotting the same relationship between health and productivity. Total productive time, not surprisingly, is increasing in health, but there are diminishing marginal returns.

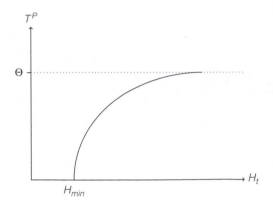

Figure 3.6. *At low levels of health, small improvements reap large increases in productive time,* T^P, *and large drops in sick time,* T^S. *But the same amount of health improvement at high levels of health returns a much smaller gain in* T^P. *Thus, marginal returns to health are diminishing.*

So we can simplify the individual's choice. He now has T^P available to him to allocate among three activities: work, play, and health improvement. This is still a complicated choice, but easier than the choice he previously faced.

Figure 3.7 shows the set of possible allocations for his productive time, plotted in three-dimensional space. At point A, the individual is a workaholic: he devotes all of his productive time to work and none to play or health improvement. Similarly, points B and C represent the extreme healthaholic and playaholic, respectively.

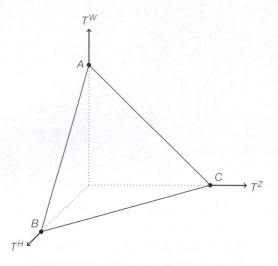

Figure 3.7. *After suffering time sick, the individual allocates productive time* $T^P = \Omega - T^S$ *between labor* T^W, *play* T^Z, *and health improvement* T^H. *The decision is shown here as a three-dimensional tradeoff. Later, we hold* T^H *fixed and study the decision in two dimensions.*

Visually, it is easier to think about decisions in two dimensions. So let us suppose the individual has already made a final decision about time spent on health improvement T^H. We are doing this to make the tradeoffs easier to see, but the reader should always remember that T^H, T^W, T^Z, and all the other decision variables are chosen simultaneously in the Grossman model.

If we assume that the individual has already decided T^H, then the individual has only two ways to spend his remaining time: labor T^W and leisure T^Z. Figure 3.8 shows this tradeoff, along with indifference curves that illustrate his preferences between work and play. He must balance his desire to play, which helps produce Z, with the necessity to work, which allows him to buy inputs into H and Z. The shape of the indifference curve U_0 in this figure is therefore indirectly derived from his utility function for H and Z. This indifference curve is the "same" indifference curve we saw in Figure 3.4, projected onto a different set of axes.

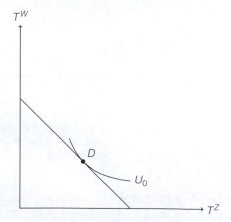

Figure 3.8. *Once sick time* T^S *and health-improvement time* T^H *are set, the individual allocates the remaining time between work* T^W *and play* T^Z. *D is the optimal allocation of time, where the indifference curve* U_0 *is tangent to the time constraint.*

The individual chooses the optimal levels of work and play using a familiar mechanism. He picks T^W and T^Z at the point where his indifference curve is tangent to the constraint he faces. In Figure 3.8, this is shown at point D. This individual in question is neither a workaholic nor a playaholic because he allocates some time to each activity.

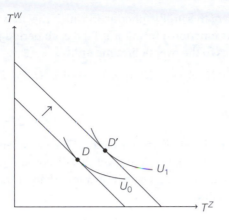

Figure 3.9. *When health improves, more productive time is available. The individual can spend more time both at work and at play. Graphically, the individual's time constraint shifts outward, and allows him to reach D′, a new optimum with more* T^W, T^Z, *and utility than* D.

This analysis helps us see more clearly the value of health improvement. Imagine that the individual had spent previous periods jogging and quitting smoking instead of his usual slothful routine of video games and jelly donuts. He would have entered this period in better health, and consequently, would have suffered lower T^S and had more productive time at his disposal. Figure 3.9 shows the payoff of this prior health investment. The constraint shifts outward, allowing more time for both labor and leisure.

Improved health from previous periods and reducing T^S is not the only way to gain more time for labor and leisure. Alternatively, the individual could sacrifice some time spent on health improvement T^H in this period in order to free up time for work and play. Of course, this will have repercussions in future periods on his health and other outcomes.

3.3   Extending Grossman from cradle to grave

So far, our examination of the Grossman model focused on the life of an individual in a single period. This allowed for an introduction to the basic mechanics of the model, and demonstrated the important tradeoffs (between health and other goods, between useless sick time and costly health investment, between labor and leisure). But as we also hinted, health is a stock; decisions made in the past impact today, and decisions today have implications in future periods. In this section, we examine the full multi-period version of the Grossman model and study how the individual navigates the tradeoffs between health, work, and play over an entire lifespan.

The multi-period utility function

We are finally ready to present the full range of our individual's preferences. He values health and home goods in every single period of his life:

$$U = U(H_0, Z_0, H_1, Z_1, \ldots, H_{\Omega-1}, Z_{\Omega-1}, H_\Omega, Z_\Omega)$$

where:

- H_t is the level of health in period $t = 0 \ldots \Omega$,
- Z_t is the amount of the home good in period t, and
- Ω is the length of the lifespan in periods.

As we shall see later, Ω is actually chosen by the individual.

We consider a version of this utility function in which the individual separates decisions in each period. With this functional form for utility, each period produces a *flow* of utility $U(H_t, Z_t)$ that contributes to the overall lifetime utility:

$$U = U(H_0, Z_0) + \delta U(H_1, Z_1) + \delta^2 U(H_2, Z_2) + \cdots + \delta^{\Omega} U(H_{\Omega}, Z_{\Omega})$$

$$= \sum_{t=0}^{\Omega} \delta^t U(H_t, Z_t) \tag{3.6}$$

where $\delta \in (0, 1)$ is the individual's discount factor. Since δ is between 0 and 1, when δ is raised to a power it becomes smaller. We need this discount factor to represent the fact that the individual values the current utility flow more than he values the same amount of utility flow in any future period.

Health as an investment good

Now that we have introduced the multi-period utility function, we are ready to discuss the third role of health (recall that the first two roles of health were as a consumption good and as an input in the production of healthy time). Health is a form of human capital akin to knowledge or education. All capital goods have a few things in common. They store value from investments in previous periods, but they also depreciate in value over time.

Health is no exception. The human body, like a car or pizza oven, may last for a long time but suffers the typical wear and tear that comes even with careful use. Let γ be the rate of depreciation; this measures how fast health H dissipates from period to period.

We are now ready to revise the production function for health (see equation (3.3)) so that it reflects the depreciation of health over time:

$$H_t = H\left((1 - \gamma)H_{t-1}, T_t^H, M_t\right) \tag{3.7}$$

As we will see, depreciation of health plays a critical role in determining the optimal level of health investment.

Return to health capital

Health is a capital good, which is another way of saying it is an investment with its own rate of return. However, health has a particular feature – at low levels of health, small investments have enormous returns to productive time.

Let us consider a thought experiment: What happens to an individual's lifetime utility when her health in any one period is magically increased by a small amount? This increase in health has repercussions on her health and utility level in each period for the rest of her lifespan. The total increase in lifetime utility, which is the "return" to this increase in health, depends on her starting level of H. The marginal lifetime returns to health are high at low levels of health and low at high levels of health because of the diminishing marginal returns to health (recall Figure 3.6).

Figure 3.10 shows how the marginal lifetime returns to health change with the initial level of H. This curve is called the **marginal efficiency of capital** (*MEC*) because it indicates how efficient each unit of health capital is in increasing lifetime utility. Recall that these returns are measured over the lifespan and include all benefits of health. Ironically, the highest returns to health are available when the individual is dying, $H \approx H_{min}$. Even then, an investment to health does not have infinite returns. The *cost* of making that investment may be so high that even high returns do not justify investing.

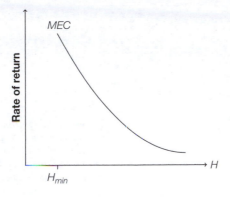

Figure 3.10. *The marginal efficiency of health capital curve (MEC) captures all lifetime return from a marginal investment in health at any given level of health stock. That the MEC curve is downward-sloping reflects the diminishing marginal returns to health.*

What are the costs of investing in H? First, there is the opportunity cost; the individual forgoes putting her resources in other market investment options. Let us suppose these alternative market investments pay an interest rate r. For ease of discussion, we earlier assumed the individual cannot save income from period to period, but here we relax that assumption to make clear that there is an opportunity cost to using health as a savings vehicle.

Depreciation due to aging γ acts as a second type of cost of investing in H. Suppose the individual invests in health. In order to guarantee the same rate of return as the market investment opportunity, health must pay a return of at least $r + \gamma$. If the return were any less, then depreciation lowers the effective return to health below r, making the market opportunity more attractive. Thus, the market rate of return to the alternative investment plus depreciation $(r + \gamma)$ is the effective price of health capital.

Most students of economics are used to thinking about opportunity costs, but it may be confusing to think of depreciation as a *cost* of capital as well. In what sense does health get more expensive when γ rises? Think about the fact that, in order to have the same amount

Actually, the Grossman model is named after economist Michael Grossman, who developed it as part of his PhD dissertation.

Credit: Allen Cox.

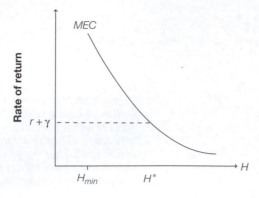

Figure 3.11. *Optimal investment in health depends both on the opportunity cost of forgone market investment opportunities* r *and the individual's depreciation of health* γ. *High* r *and* γ *lower the individual's optimal level of health.*

of health later, you need to buy more now if the depreciation rate is high. The depreciation rate acts like a kind of continual tax on any health the individual produces.

The *MEC* curve determines the optimal amount of health H^* for the individual. On a traditional demand curve for a given good, the quantity associated with a particular price is the optimal demand for the good at that price. Similarly, the *MEC* curve shows the optimal health level associated with the market price of health investment, $r + \gamma$. At this price level, the individual optimally chooses H^*. And at H^*, the marginal cost of health investment ($r + \gamma$) balances the marginal benefit of health investment.

3.4   Comparative statics

The measure of a model is its ability to represent complex realities and make predictions. The Grossman model is best known for providing economic explanations for two well-known empirical health phenomena: better health among the educated, and declining health among the aging. We use comparative statics to study the health of the college graduate versus that of the high-school dropout, and the health of the twentysomething versus that of the senior citizen. This side-by-side analysis allows us to better understand the power of the Grossman model.

Education and the efficiency of producing health

There is much evidence of a relationship between health and socioeconomic status (SES). People who are better educated or wealthier tend also to enjoy longer life expectancies and fewer health problems. This correlation is known as the **SES health gradient** and will be studied further in the next chapter.

There are several different explanations for the gradient advanced by sociologists, doctors, and economists. The Grossman model posits one: the gradient arises because the well-educated are more efficient producers of health. For any given hour dedicated to T^H or dollar devoted to purchasing health-related goods M, a college graduate reaps more health improvement than a high-school dropout. This difference may take the form of a better understanding of a doctor's instructions or more sophistication about purchasing medicine. In the language of the Grossman model, the more-educated person gains more health stock for each unit of health investment.

Graphically, this increased efficiency manifests as an upward shift of the marginal efficiency of health capital curve *MEC*. Because better-educated people are more efficient health producers, they receive higher returns from health investment at any H. In Exercise 13, the student will have the opportunity to further explore the effect of changes in wage on health.

Figure 3.12 displays the MEC curve of two different individuals, one a college graduate (MEC_C) and the other a high-school dropout (MEC_H). The two have different education backgrounds but are otherwise exactly the same: they share the same preferences for labor and leisure, the same taste for Z and H, and the same depreciation rate γ and return for market investments r. Hence, if not for their education differences, the Grossman model would predict their lives would be identical.

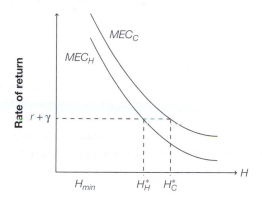

Figure 3.12. *Empirical evidence consistently finds that the more-educated enjoy better health than the less-educated. One hypothesis for explaining this difference is that the college-educated are more efficient producers of health. This is graphically depicted as a higher* MEC *curve for the college graduate (*MEC_C*) compared with the high-school dropout (*MEC_H*).*

But their education differences matter a lot. In Figure 3.12, the college graduate's higher MEC_C means that her optimal level of health H_C^* is higher than the high-school dropout's H_H^*, even though both face the same cost of capital $r + \gamma$. Because the college graduate is more efficient in producing health, it makes sense for her to invest more in her health. The high-school dropout, on the other hand, does not produce health as efficiently, so investments in health offer lower returns. It makes more sense for him to focus on Z.

This disparity in education and resulting differential in health has major implications. Not only will the college-educated person be healthier throughout her life, as empirical evidence suggests, but, as we see later in this section, she also enjoys a lengthier lifespan.

Aging and endogenous death

A second important payoff of the Grossman model is that it provides an economic explanation for why health optimally deteriorates with age. We might ask why not make investments so that H stays high forever? The Grossman model predicts that it is too costly to stay forever young.

There is a basic biological reality of aging: whatever health assets a person has (strong bones, unclogged arteries, plentiful neurons) not only tend to diminish over time, but tend to diminish at a *faster rate* as he ages. In economic terms, the depreciation rate γ does not stay constant over a lifetime. As the individual ages, his γ also increases.

Now consider what happens when the individual's γ begins to rise as he ages. The cost to capital ($r + \gamma$) rises, and he would have to invest more and more resources to maintain the same level of health over time. As the cost of health rises, the aging individual will be

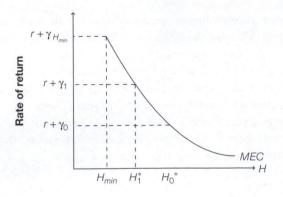

Figure 3.13. *As the individual ages, his depreciation of health increases from γ_0 to γ_1 and finally, to $\gamma_{H_{min}}$. Such a high depreciation level means any investments in health decay immediately, so the individual may not want to invest in health at all. This is the Grossman model's treatment of death.*

less willing to spend his productive time and money on H and will start devoting a greater proportion of his dwindling resources to Z.

Figure 3.13 shows that, as the cost of capital $r + \gamma$ rises with age (since γ is always increasing), the optimal health H^* will decline. As γ continues its inexorable climb, eventually H^* falls to H_{min}.

At H_{min}, all available time is lost to T^S. The individual has no time to spend on labor, leisure, or health improvement, and therefore cannot produce any H or Z ever again. The reasonable question at this juncture is why any rational actor might choose to set $H = H_{min}$ for any period. How could death possibly be utility-maximizing?

Consider the alternative: Under what circumstances would it be optimal to live forever? Imagine, contrary to biological realities, depreciation of health stays at a γ of 5% from age 0 onward. It is possible to show that, in the Grossman model, a constant depreciation rate results in an equilibrium level of health H_e^* that never changes. In each period, 5% of H drains away, but the individual invests exactly enough resources to replenish his supply of H right back up to H_e^*. After this equilibrium is reached, every future period is identical. The individual lives out an infinite lifespan at H_e^*. This is a pretty outlandish result, even for an economics model. Unfortunately, we would need a fountain of youth for this happy result.

The key insight is that increasing depreciation γ makes it less and less attractive to invest scarce resources in health. To see why the high depreciation rate makes health investments less appealing, consider what would happen if a student knew that he would forget 99% of whatever he studied before a big exam. How would that affect his willingness to hit the books? This "why bother?" attitude dissuades aging individuals from investing in health in the Grossman model.

Fans of the critically acclaimed 2006 film *Little Miss Sunshine* may recall the free-wheeling, foul-mouthed Grandpa character with a destructive heroin habit. At one point in the movie he makes a comment that exemplifies the logic of the Grossman model. After his family discovers his heroin addiction, he counsels his grandson against the habit:

GRANDPA: Don't you get ideas. When you're young, you're crazy to do that s***.

FRANK: What about you?

GRANDPA: Me?! I'm old! You get to be my age - you're crazy *not* to do it.

Neither the Grossman model nor the authors of this textbook endorse recreational drug use among the elderly.[1] Nevertheless, the Grandpa's life choices indicate an understanding of health as a depreciating capital commodity. It seems that, rather than making costly investments (e.g. abstaining from heroin) to maintain a health stock that is dissipating rapidly anyway, he opts to shift his resources to producing more Z (e.g. a heroin-induced high) even at the expense of his health.

3.5   Unifying the Grossman model

At this point, we have introduced four different graphs, each of which illustrates a different tradeoff or constraint in the Grossman model.

- The **production possibilities frontier** (PPF) in Figure 3.4 demonstrates the tradeoff between health production and home good production.
- The **health production** schedule in Figure 3.6 relates health to availability of productive time T^P for work, play, and health improvement.
- The **labor–leisure** graph in Figure 3.7 illustrates the tradeoffs in allocating finite time between work and play.
- The **marginal efficiency of capital** (MEC) curve in Figure 3.11 plots the marginal lifetime utility returns against initial levels of health.

The aim of this section is to tie together these four diagrams. The preferences they illustrate are intimately related in a single, multi-dimensional utility function that underlies all four graphs. The indifference curves in the PPF diagram and the work–play tradeoff diagram may seem unrelated, but they actually reflect the same underlying tastes for H and Z. The tradeoffs and constraints that people face are also multi-dimensional.

Figure 3.14 combines these four graphs and aligns the axes so as to illuminate the connections between the components of each figure. All the diagrams in this figure are snapshots of an optimization problem taking place in high-dimensional space. Each graph in Figure 3.14 is a projection of an aspect of this problem onto a two-dimensional plane. Simultaneously solving for the optimum in each diagram results in the bundle of H_t, Z_t, T_t^H, T_t^Z, T_t^W, T_t^S, M_t, J_t that maximizes the individual's lifetime utility.

To better see how the diagrams interrelate, Figure 3.14 shows the effect of an increase in age discussed in Section 3.4. It depicts the decisions of the same individual at two different stages of his life: the "young" period, denoted by subscript Y, and the "old" period, denoted by subscript O.

Recall that the direct result of the aging process is an increase in depreciation rate γ, which is represented in part (a). As a result of the higher depreciation, the optimal level of H decreases as the aging individual shifts investments away from health. Accordingly, the optimal level of health of the individual in the old period H_O^* is less than H_Y^*.

This lower level of health inevitably results in lower productive time, as the individual suffers more sick time in the old period as shown in part (b). The decline in productive time in turn limits the available time for work and play as shown in part (c). Having less productive time also reduces the time and money available to the individual for

---

1   Indeed, the Grandpa reaches H_{min} before the final scene.

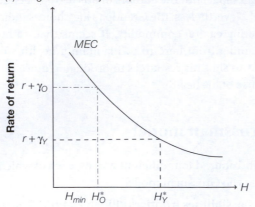

(a) Marginal efficiency of capital

(b) Health production curve

(c) Labor–leisure graph

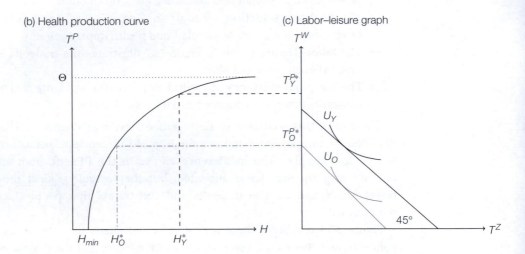

(d) Production possibility frontier

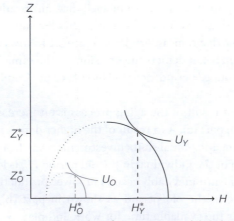

Figure 3.14. *The combined Grossman model shifting with age.*

production of H and Z. This shrinks inward the individual's PPF and results in a lower level of overall utility (shown in part (d)).

3.6   Conclusion

The Grossman model begins with the premise that health is a *choice*, at least when considered over a long period of time. People may start with different endowments, and in any given period may not have a large degree of control, but over time small decisions add up to large changes in health. This idea, combined with declining marginal productivity of health investments and binding time constraints, leads to powerful predictions about health and aging, health and socioeconomic status, and labor–leisure tradeoffs, among others. Our task in future chapters is to examine whether the empirical evidence is consistent with these predictions.

3.7   Exercises

Comprehension questions

Indicate whether the statement is true or false, and justify your answer. Be sure to cite evidence from the chapter and state any additional assumptions you may need. Review the basic assumptions of the Grossman model before answering these questions.

1 In real life, investments in health can generate long-lasting benefits, but the Grossman model neglects this aspect of health.
2 In the framework of the Grossman model, an individual's level of health is completely controlled by her actions. Thus, in any given period, an individual is unconstrained in her choice of health status.
3 In the Grossman model, the marginal efficiency of investment in health care declines as health improves.
4 Aging shifts the marginal efficiency of investment in health curve inward.
5 An hour spent exercising always pays for itself by decreasing the time spent sick by more than an hour.
6 Assume the PPF is as pictured in Figure 3.3. People might choose point E as their optimum even if they value the home good Z.
7 In the Grossman model, optimal health status declines with age.
8 The fact that older people spend more on health care is evidence against the Grossman model, which predicts that spending will decline as δ increases.
9 People who drop out of high school are able to produce more health than college graduates because they have more free time to invest in health production.
10 According to the Grossman model, people choose an optimal time to die (barring any unforeseen accidents).

Analytical problems

11 The Grossman model envisions consumers deciding between investments in health H and investments in home goods Z. Figure 3.15 depicts a typical consumer's production possibility frontier for health and home goods.

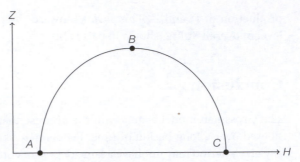

Figure 3.15. *The PPF in the Grossman model.*

   a Succinctly describe why the graph is shaped the way it is between points *A* and *B*.

   b Succinctly describe why the graph is shaped the way it is between points *B* and *C*.

   c Would any consumer with typical preferences ever pick a point on the graph between *A* and *B*? Explain succinctly (using Figure 3.15) why or why not.

12 Suppose a new miracle pill is discovered that increases both the marginal health effects of health investment (at any given level of health investment) and the maximum level of attainable health from H_{max} to a higher H_{max}.

   a Draw the old PPF before the discovery of the miracle pill.

   b On this same graph, draw a new PPF that corresponds to the description of the miracle pill.

   c How will the miracle pill affect H^*?

   d How will the miracle pill affect the rate of jogging?

13 **Differences in wage levels.** Suppose individual *A* received a much better education than individual *B*, and consequently earns twice as much per hour of labor.

   a If both individuals work 40 hours a week, who will have greater H^*? Why?

   b If both individuals work enough hours so as to earn exactly $50,000 per year, who will have greater H^*? Why?

   c Draw a set of axes labeled T^W and T^Z that resemble Figure 3.8. Draw a line labeled *A* that shows individual *A*'s time constraint during a given period (say, one month), and draw another time constraint for individual *B*. Explain why and how they differ due to choices in previous periods.

   d On this same set of axes, draw representative indifference curves for both individual *A* and individual *B*, including ones that lie tangent to their respective time constraints. Based on the way you drew your curves, does individual *A* earn less than twice as much or more than twice as much as individual *B*?

   e Explain briefly why your answer to Exercise 13(a) may change if you found out that individual *A* had to spend ten times as many hours on homework during her schooling years as individual *B* did.

   f Explain why it is optimal for individual *B* to invest less in health when she is already less healthy than *A*. Why does she not invest more to "catch up"?

14 True or false? According to the Grossman model, if a new drug were discovered that eliminated the steady deterioration of health that accompanies aging – but does not eliminate sudden events like heart attacks or being hit by a bus – then the demand for jelly donuts, french fries, and physical activity in the presence of buses would decline. Justify your answer.

15 How does aging change the shape or size of the PPF in the Grossman model from period to period? Draw a graph to demonstrate the effect of aging, and include a short paragraph of text justifying the changing shape or size of the PPF.

16 **Nutritional economics.** Suppose we are considering a hungry individual in the Grossman model deciding what to have for dinner. His options are listed in Table 3.2. Each dish has an effect on the level of the home good Z and health H.

Table 3.2. *Meal options in the Grossman model.*

Meal	Home good (Z)	Health (H)
Steak and eggs	+7	−2
Kale salad with broccoli	−2	+5
Entire box of cookies	+10	−20

a Suppose the diner's single-period utility function is as follows:

$$U = 3Z + H$$

If the diner is trying to maximize his single-period utility, and he can only select one item from Table 3.2, which meal would he choose?

b A miracle pill is discovered that halves the negative health impact of cookies. How does this impact the diner's choice?

c What effect does the miracle pill have on the diner's health H? Interpret this result. Does this mean the diner would be better off without the miracle pill?

d If the diner is instead trying to maximize his lifetime utility and not just his single-period utility, how might your answer to Exercise 16(a) change? Is he likely to value Z or H more in the lifetime context than the single-period context? Explain your answer, and be sure to invoke the concept of a capital good.

Essay questions

17 One curious finding from the RAND Health Insurance Experiment was that the rate of treated bone fractures per capita was higher in the group of families that had been assigned to the free insurance plan, compared with those in the high copayment plans. Concisely describe how the Grossman model might explain the fact that people facing higher prices for health care would break bones less often. Be sure to discuss the concept of marginal efficiency of health investment.

18 **Munchausen's syndrome.** Munchausen's syndrome is a psychiatric disease first recognized by doctors in the 1950s. Sufferers will feign unusual medical symptoms and seek out the most complicated treatments and procedures, typically out of a desire to gain the sympathy and attention of family, friends, and medical professionals. In some sense, we could say that health care enters into the utility function of the afflicted. As much as most people viscerally dislike sitting in a doctor's waiting room or undergoing surgery at a hospital, people with Munchausen's often cannot get enough.

Imagine an individual in the Grossman model who suddenly develops Munchausen's syndrome. How would this affect her optimal level of H^*? Explain your answer, and make sure your explanation discusses the three roles of health in the model.

19 A recent paper entitled "Inheritances, health, and death" by Beomsoo Kim and Christopher Ruhm (NBER Working Paper No. 15364, 2009) reports the following:

> We examine how wealth shocks, in the form of inheritances, affect the mortality rates, health status and health behaviors of older adults, using data from eight waves of the Health and Retirement Survey (HRS). Our main finding is that bequests do not have substantial effects on health, although some improvements in quality-of-life are possible. This absence occurs despite increases in out-of-pocket (OOP) spending on health care and in the utilization of medical services, especially discretionary and non-lifesaving types such as dental care. Nor can we find a convincing indication of changes in lifestyles that offset the benefits of increased medical care. Inheritances are associated with higher alcohol consumption, but with no change in smoking or exercise and a possible decrease in obesity.

Interpret these findings using the Grossman model as a framework. In particular, comment on how exogenous income shocks change decisions about health status in the Grossman model. Is the evidence in this report consistent or inconsistent with your interpretation of the predictions of the Grossman model? Does this report support or contradict the theory that one's wealth level determines health status?

Students can find answers to the comprehension questions and lecturers can access an Instructor Manual with guideline answers to the analytical problems and essay questions at **www.palgrave.com/economics/bht**.

4 SOCIOECONOMIC DISPARITIES IN HEALTH

How long will you live? The answer to that question has a lot to do with your standing in society – financial, social, and otherwise. Understanding and explaining the links between socioeconomic status (SES) and health has attracted the efforts of economists, sociologists, epidemiologists, public health researchers, and biologists alike. Few other areas of health economics have garnered as much attention in recent years.

All this scholarly attention to socioeconomic health disparities is merited because they are incredibly pervasive. Health disparities appear in every country on Earth, and in different historical settings as well. We show evidence of health disparities across education, race, employment grade, income, and birth weight. We will even present evidence that health disparities exist in non-human societies.

While the widespread existence of health disparities may be an obvious point, the reasons behind these disparities are a rich source of scholarly investigation and controversy. Researchers have proposed many theories to explain the link between SES and health. Some theories emphasize the effect of SES on health; others emphasize the opposite pathway from health to SES; and yet others emphasize alternate variables that explain the connection between SES and health. Figure 4.1 shows the different causal pathways that might underlie these findings.

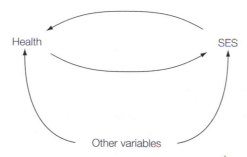

Figure 4.1. *Causal relationship between health, socioeconomic status, and other variables.*

While many theories of health disparities exist, this chapter highlights six prominent theories implicating various factors: adherence to medical advice, early life events, income levels, the stress of being poor, work capacity, and impatience. In Chapter 5, we discuss one other prominent theory: discrimination by doctors. While Figure 4.1 provides one useful way to organize these theories, it is helpful to also consider them through the lens of an economic model. The Grossman model discussed in Chapter 3 provides just such a structure, and we will use it as an organizing principle throughout this chapter.

As with much of health economics, understanding how the evidence relates to economic theory has implications for health policy. For instance, if health disparities arise *in utero* (that is, before people are even born), the optimal policy response will be very different than if health disparities only arise later in life.

4.1   The pervasiveness of health inequality

Health inequality exists in every society. The prevalence of health disparities across different strata is not a phenomenon unique to a particular country, nor is it unique to our time or even to our species. Here, we document the evidence for health disparities in a variety of settings.

Perhaps the most basic measure of health status for a population is survival or life expectancy. Imagine a large population of people, all the same age. As they get older, some of the people in this group will start to die off, while others live on. We can depict the plight of this population with a *survival curve*, a graph that tracks the fraction of the group still alive at each age.

Figure 4.2 shows two such survival curves for American males. One curve (solid line) is calculated for college graduates, while the other curve (dotted line) is calculated for high-school dropouts. The figure shows that 18-year-olds who will eventually graduate from college are likely to survive longer than 18-year-old high-school dropouts. Imagine a high-school class with 100 college-bound young men and 100 other young men who will drop out before graduation. These curves suggest that about 85 of the college graduates would live to attend their fiftieth reunion, but only 60 of the high-school dropouts would survive to that time. Strikingly, the college graduates are 25 percentage points more likely to survive to age 68.

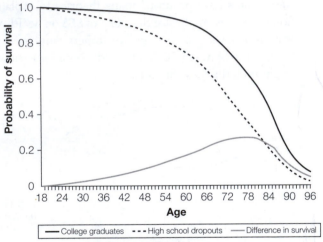

Figure 4.2. *Male survival curves by educational attainment.*

Source: Figure 1 from Bhattacharya and Lakdawalla (2006). Reprinted with permission from Elsevier.

Historical health disparities

Such mortality disparities have existed at least since the beginning of the industrial age and probably much longer. Demographer T. H. Hollingsworth (1965) tracked the life expectancy at birth among members of British ducal families between 1750 and 1900 (Figure 4.3). At the beginning of this period, British nobility had the same average life expectancy as the rest of the British population. By 1900, the children of British dukes could expect to live nearly twenty years longer than their commoner counterparts. Antonovsky (1967) cites similar studies with diverse data sources ranging from 1820s France to civil-war-era Rhode Island, all of which find life expectancy or mortality disparities between the rich and the poor.

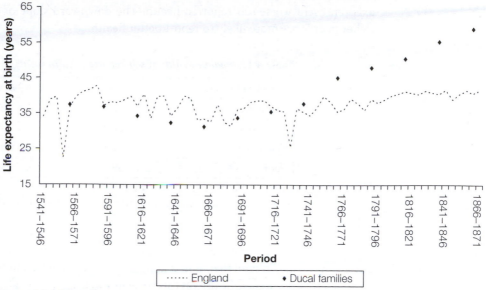

Figure 4.3. *Mortality rate among British ducal families and commoners.*

Source: Reproduced from B. Harris (2004). Public health, nutrition, and the decline of mortality: the McKeown thesis revisited, *Social History of Medicine*, 17(3): 379–407, by permission of Oxford University Press. Original data from T. H. Hollingsworth (1965) and Wrigley et al. (1997).

Disparities across income levels

Mortality or life expectancy is an extreme measure of health; two people living out the same lifespan could enjoy very different levels of health. In fact, health disparities emerge almost no matter how health is measured. For instance, another commonly used measure of health is *self-reported health status*, usually delineated on a scale ranging from 1 (poor health) to 5 (excellent health).

High-income individuals routinely self-report better health status on this scale than low-income individuals. Figure 4.4 shows nationally representative evidence on this point from the United States. Family income is plotted against average self-reported health, and each line represents a different age group. In the graph, higher numbers on the vertical

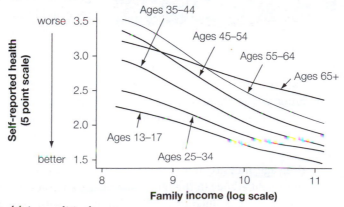

Figure 4.4. *Health inequalities by age.*

Source; From Figure 1 in Case et al. (2002). With permission of the American Economic Association.

axis represent worse self-reported health. The downward slope of each line means that richer people are more likely to report better health.

Table 4.1. *Median wealth by self-reported health status.*

1984 health status	1984 wealth	1994 wealth
Excellent	68.3	127.9
Very good	66.3	90.9
Good	51.8	64.9
Poor	39.2	34.7

Wealth is reported in thousands of 1996 dollars.

Source: Based on Table 1 in Smith (1999). With permission of the American Economic Association.

Self-reported health on a five-point scale may seem a crude measure of health status, but it is more meaningful than it first appears. In a national US study of individuals, study participants ranked their health on this scale in 1984. They were also asked detailed questions about their wealth. Table 4.1 corroborates the result from Figure 4.4: those with better self-reported health tend to be wealthier. Ten years later, the individuals who reported poor health in 1984 had seen a drop in household wealth, while those who reported excellent health in 1984 saw their wealth nearly double. Apparently, self-reported health status is a powerful predictor of future wealth.

Young man suffering from a hay fever attack – a small price to pay for being wealthy. Credit: © lichtmeister – Fotolia.com.

Health disparities across income levels exist for more objective measures of health as well. Several different patterns occur, including cases where the poor have worse outcomes, where the rich have worse outcomes, where the disparities emerge only with age, and where no disparities exist at all.

For instance, in the US, children from wealthy families are less likely to suffer from congenital heart defects (see Figure 4.5; in this figure, as well as in Figure 4.4, higher values represent *worse* health). This pattern is consistent with the gradient we have seen so far in mortality and self-reported health. Furthermore, this evidence from newborns indicates that disparities in health may emerge even before birth.

Unlike congenital heart defects, the prevalence of hay fever displays a distinctly different pattern. There is no measured difference between rich and poor among infants, but among older children, the rich are more likely to have been diagnosed with hay fever. One explanation is that children from richer families are more likely to see a doctor and thus more likely to be diagnosed than children from poorer families.

Finally, bronchitis prevalence does not seem to vary consistently with income. As children age, they are more likely to be diagnosed with myopia or have other vision problems, but no difference in the rate of diagnoses emerges between poor and rich. At young ages, the prevalence–income relationship is flat, with poor and rich children equally likely to be diagnosed. In pre-pubescence and adolescence (as with hay fever), richer children are

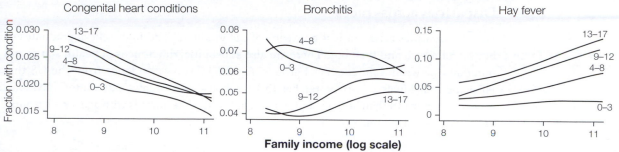

Figure 4.5. *Health inequalities by condition.*

Source: Figure 2 in Case et al. (2002). With permission of the American Economic Association.

more likely to be diagnosed with bronchitis. But hay fever and bronchitis are exceptions to the usual rule that poorer children are more likely to be sick than richer children.

Disparities in countries with universal health insurance

While this evidence of health disparities from the US is overwhelming, we might wonder whether different countries with different health systems have fewer or less obvious socioeconomic disparities. A country like Canada, for instance, has universal health insurance, which may reduce health outcome differences between rich and poor. But the evidence shows health disparities persisting in Canada as well as other countries with different health care systems. Infants born to poor families in Canada are nearly twice as likely to have poor self-reported health than those born to rich families. This gap in self-reported health widens dramatically after age ten (see Figure 4.6).

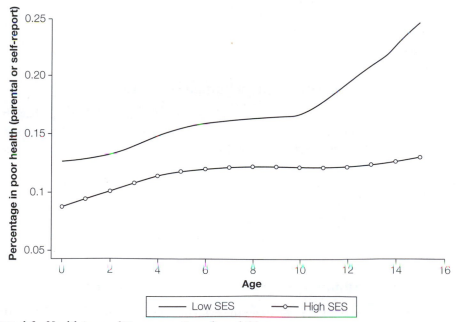

Figure 4.6. *Health inequalities among Canadian children.*

Source: Currie and Stabile (2003). With permission of the American Economic Association.

Disparities across races

Health disparities arise not just between college graduates and high-school graduates or between the rich and the poor. There are also substantial differences in health status and outcomes between different racial groups. Figure 4.7 shows evidence from the US that Hispanic individuals report better health than black individuals, and white individuals report better health than both groups. Health naturally deteriorates with age for all groups, but racial disparities remain.

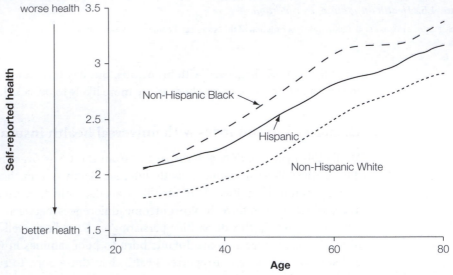

Figure 4.7. *Health inequalities by race.*

Notes: The curves reflect local linear regression estimates. The regressions are weighted using the survey weights provided by the NHIS.

Source: From *The Oxford Handbook of Health Economics*, edited by Sherry Glied and Peter C. Smith (2011), Ch. 7, Socioeconomic status and health: dimensions and mechanisms, by David M. Cutler, Adriana Lleras-Muney, and Tom Vogl, pp. 124–163, Figure 7.5b from p. 134. Reprinted by permission of Oxford University Press.

Disparities in non-human societies

Finally, health disparities between different social groups have been found even in non-human societies. Biologist Robert Sapolsky has spent decades studying social interactions and hierarchies among baboon troops in East Africa. He consistently found that dominant baboons at the top of their social hierarchies are in better health than subordinate baboons. For instance, Sapolsky and Mott (1987) show that dominant baboons have higher levels of high-density lipoprotein (HDL) – the "good cholesterol" – which in humans is correlated with lower rates of heart disease. Sapolsky has argued that this disparity arises because dominant baboons suffer lower stress: they relax by pounding the heads of subordinate baboons.

Summary of evidence for health disparities

Table 4.2 summarizes the evidence we have discussed for health disparities in various contexts. We argue that health disparities are not an accidental or atypical outcome but are a pervasive feature of human (and non-human) societies. It is tempting to try to explain

Table 4.2. *Summary of evidence for health disparities in different populations.*

Factor	Measure of health	Disparity	Evidence
Education	Life expectancy	Better-educated live longer	Male survival curves (Fig. 4.2)
Wealth	Self-reported health	Wealthier report better health	NHIS data from US (Fig. 4.4), Canadian kids (Fig. 4.6)
	Prevalence of congenital heart disease and other conditions	Wealthier less likely to have disease	NHIS data (Fig. 4.5)
Race	Self-reported health	Whites report better health than Hispanics, blacks	NHIS data from US (Fig. 4.7)
Social standing	Life expectancy	Dominant class lives longer	Ducal study in England (Fig. 4.3)
	HDL levels	Dominant class has better HDL levels	Sapolsky study of baboons

each instance of this phenomenon with its own theory. For example, one theory for racial disparities in health is racial discrimination by doctors and nurses. There may be some truth to this theory, but even so it could not possibly explain the evidence for health disparities in industrial-age England or baboon troops in the Serengeti. We search for broader theories that work in multiple settings.

In the next sections, we discuss the most prominent theories that have been advanced to explain health disparities and the evidence supporting each. These theories are not mutually exclusive, and it seems likely that no single theory will ever explain all of the many health disparities.

4.2   The Grossman model and health disparities

The Grossman model discussed in Chapter 3 provides an excellent organizing framework for thinking about health disparities. It encapsulates a family of hypotheses that have been advanced to explain health differences across socioeconomic groups.

Recall from our discussion of the Grossman model that the marginal efficiency of capital (*MEC*) curve plays a critical role in determining optimal health. The *MEC* curve indicates how much lifetime utility each additional unit of health capital creates. If two individuals have different *MEC* curves, as in Figure 4.8, they

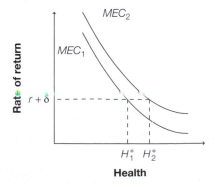

Figure 4.8. *Two* MEC *curves.*

will choose different optimal levels of health even if they are identical in every other way. Each of the hypotheses we discuss in this section implies different *MEC* curves for different socioeconomic groups, and hence different optimal health levels.

How would different *MEC* curves arise for different groups? The Grossman model has many moving parts and parameters, such as health productivity, resource constraints, health depreciation rate, total productive time, and rate of time discounting. Differences in any of these parameters can result in different *MEC* curves and different optimal health decisions. Although not always framed this way by researchers, each of the theories we discuss below can be interpreted in terms of the Grossman model.

4.3   The efficient producer hypothesis

The fact that education and health are correlated does not necessarily imply a causal connection between them. Lleras-Muney (2005) searches for a causal effect of education by statistically exploiting changes in compulsory education laws in the US during the early twentieth century. She finds that an additional year of schooling caused as much as a 1.7-year increase in life expectancy for those born in 1925.

So Lleras-Muney (2005) finds that education improves health, but the mechanism is not clear. The **efficient producer hypothesis** postulates that better-educated individuals are more efficient producers of health than less well-educated individuals. Recall that the Grossman model predicts that people who are more efficient health producers will have higher levels of optimal health. If this hypothesis is accurate, then we expect a health disparity across people with different educational levels, such as the mortality–education gradient found by Lleras-Muney.

Definition	4.1

Efficient producer hypothesis: health disparities exist because better-educated individuals are more efficient producers of health than less well-educated individuals.

There are many reasons why education might lead to more efficient health production. For instance, there may be lessons learned in school that allow students to take better care of themselves. Alternatively, schooling may teach students to be more patient and more willing to make investments that pay off over a long period of time, like health.

A third possible mechanism is that better-educated consumers are more likely to adhere to treatment regimens that require diligence, and better able to navigate complex treatment plans. Consumers who are better readers may also be more able to follow directions that come with prescription drugs. Those more comfortable with math skills may have an easier time figuring out the right dose of insulin, or following through with a diet that requires careful tracking of calories.

Goldman and Smith (2002) focus on the possibility that differences in patient self-management can explain the relationship between health and education. They study people with two diseases, HIV and Type I diabetes, that require intensive patient participation in treatment. HIV patients undergoing anti-retroviral therapies must be vigilant about taking multiple drugs each day without fail; even a few missed doses can lead to a higher level of virus within the body. Diabetics, similarly, must calibrate doses of insulin carefully several times a day in order to control blood sugar levels and reduce the risk of complications.

If there is any validity to the efficient producer hypothesis, then highly educated patients should be better able to adhere to these complex treatment regimens. In fact, this is exactly what the data says. In the study, better-educated HIV patients had better self-reported adherence, defined as having taken all medications on schedule in each of the last seven days. Education, in this case, seems to correlate strongly with the sorts of skills that permit HIV patients to keep track of which drugs they are supposed to take, the appropriate doses, and when they need to take them. This adherence differential explains entirely the health disparity between well-educated and poorly educated HIV patients. Highly educated HIV patients are thus more efficient producers of health.

For diabetic patients, Goldman and Smith found that a randomized intervention promoting intensive adherence to insulin therapy had different effects on people with different educational levels. The less schooling people had, the more effective the intensive treatment was on future adherence as compared with those with more schooling. In the study, patients randomly assigned to the intensive support treatment were given more help to stay on their prescribed therapy. This is exactly as predicted by the efficient producer hypothesis since people with more education presumably do not need this extra support to adhere to their prescribed insulin therapy. See Exercise 12 for more on their results.

4.4   The thrifty phenotype hypothesis

Adherence to medical advice is not the only way that people can differ in their health productivity. There may be genetic reasons why some individuals are less efficient at producing health, even with the same resources. Strictly speaking, this theory is a form of the efficient producer hypothesis, but we devote a separate section to it because of the prominent and distinct role this theory has played in the scholarly debate.

The **thrifty phenotype hypothesis** posits that health outcomes throughout life are determined in part by deprivation that occurs in early childhood or even in the womb. Children from poorer families may suffer more deprivation during gestation and infancy, which may explain observed health disparities.

The thrifty phenotype hypothesis suggests that the link between early deprivation and negative adult health outcomes is a result of gene activation. Children born during times of resource deprivation are more likely to activate certain "thrifty" genes that optimize for sparse conditions, for example ones that instruct cells to hoard fat within the body. These children are well-adapted for famine conditions, but may suffer relatively poor health if they end up living in environments with abundant resources. Their thrifty genes, so helpful for deprivation during infancy, may predispose them to obesity, diabetes, and other undesirable health outcomes in adulthood.

Definition | 4.2

Thrifty phenotype hypothesis: resource deprivation *in utero* and during early childhood can lead to activation of "thrifty" genes optimized for sparse conditions. Individuals with such genes activated are poorly adapted for abundant conditions and may develop diabetes, obesity, and other disorders. Health disparities arise because poorer individuals are more likely to face this sort of deprivation early in life.

Researchers also refer to this hypothesis as the **Barker hypothesis**.

The British National Cohort Study of children born in March 1946 provides evidence that adverse health events in early life, plausibly the result of poverty, are linked to poor adult health outcomes. Individuals with low birth weight, slow fetal growth, or respiratory illnesses as infants were more likely to suffer from hypertension, chronic obstructive pulmonary disease, and schizophrenia as adults (Wadsworth and Kuh 1997). This is one of several national longitudinal studies, which track the health of survey participants over time, that show similar trends. For instance, Coneus and Spiess (2012) show similar findings in Germany.

But this study does not definitively establish a causal link between early-life deprivation and poor health outcomes. The children who suffered health problems in early life in the British study could have been different from the other children in several other ways, and perhaps some of those differences drove the adult health outcomes. The best way to establish causality is a scientific experiment like the RAND HIE, but in this case that would involve randomly assigning children to prenatal deprivation. That would allow us to compare a group of children with early-life deprivation (the treatment group) to a substantially similar group of children who enjoyed abundant resources early in life (the control group), but such an experiment would be extremely unethical.

Instead, researchers look to evidence from **natural experiments**, environmental shocks that create a treatment group and a control group naturally. In the last year of World War II, for example, parts of Holland suffered a devastating famine as the result of a German blockade. While tragic, this shock created two groups of Dutch babies: those in gestation during the famine, and those conceived immediately afterwards. The groups were demographically similar, except for the fact that the first group experienced massive nutritional deprivation *in utero*, while the latter group did not experience the same extreme level of deprivation.

The major problem with non-experimental studies is *selection bias*, the bias introduced when treatment is chosen and that people who select into treatment differ in important ways from people in the control group. The virtue of a good natural experiment is that it limits selection bias.

Definition	4.3

Natural experiment: a study that uses an environmental shock that creates a treatment group and a control group naturally. This is useful for identifying causal effects because it eliminates selection bias.

Examples of potential natural experiments include:

- a famine that affects one cohort of babies and not another;
- an earthquake that affects only one half of a country;
- a spike in immigration that affects one region and not another;
- a government policy implemented in one state but not a similar neighboring state;
- an unusually large snowfall one winter but not the next.

Evidence developed by Roseboom et al. (2001) shows that individuals gestating during the famine suffered worse health in adulthood than those not conceived until the famine was over (Table 4.3). The babies exposed to starvation *in utero* grew up to experience higher rates of diabetes, lower levels of HDL (good cholesterol), higher incidence of obstructive airway disease, and worse overall health, although not all these results are statistically significant. According to the thrifty phenotype theory, this is because these individuals' genes were optimized for starvation conditions, and not as well adapted for postwar abundance as their younger counterparts' genes.

Table 4.3. *Adult characteristics according to timing of prenatal exposure to the Dutch famine.*

Cohort	Late gestation during famine	Early gestation during famine	Conceived after famine
Type 2 diabetes	21%	16%	15%
HDL cholesterol (mmol/l)	1.32	1.26*	1.32
Obstructive airway disease	15.0%	23.0%	17.3%
General health poor	6.4	10.3*	5.3

* Indicates statistically significant difference from the unexposed cohort.

Source: Table 1 from Roseboom et al. (2001). Copyright (2001), with permission from Elsevier.

The Dutch famine is not the only famine to be studied as a natural experiment. Between 1958 and 1961, China implemented a set of reform policies known as the Great Leap Forward. The reforms included the collectivization of farms and the reassignment of farmers from agriculture to heavy industry. These in combination with other policies led to a massive famine that killed tens of millions throughout China. Chen and Zhou (2007) compare those *in utero* during the famine against those conceived after the famine. They find that those who lived through the famine *in utero* and survived to adulthood were about three centimeters shorter than those conceived afterwards. These survivors also worked shorter hours and earned less income than their slightly younger counterparts. This latter evidence is also consistent with efficient producer hypothesis.

Economist Douglas Almond and his colleagues have studied three other natural experiments in search of the link between early-life deprivation and adult outcomes: the 1918 influenza epidemic (Almond 2006); the 1986 Chernobyl disaster (Almond et al. 2009); and Ramadan, the Muslim holy month of fasting (Almond and Mazumder 2007). In each case, researchers compared individuals affected by the events *in utero* with others who were conceived immediately thereafter, or others who lived in nearby unaffected areas in the case of the Chernobyl incident. In each case, the evidence supports the hypothesis that shocks in early life have adverse impacts on outcomes in later life.

These findings have spurred interest in policy changes that improve fetal health. For example, Currie and Walker (2011) study the introduction of the electronic toll collection system E-ZPass in New Jersey around 1999. The E-ZPass system streamlined payments at toll plazas, eliminating long lines of idling cars and sharply reducing air pollution in the surrounding environment. The authors study babies born to women living within two kilometers of a toll plaza, and found the risk of birth prematurity fell by 10.8% and the likelihood of low birth weight dropped by 11.8% after the introduction of E-ZPass. The thrifty phenotype hypothesis suggests that these babies will enjoy better health outcomes throughout life thanks to less pollution exposure *in utero*.

4.5   The direct income hypothesis

In some sense, the evidence that the rich are in better health is utterly unsurprising. Richer people are better off on many dimensions: by virtue of their wealth, they can afford to send their children to better schools, drive fancier cars, or dine at nicer restaurants. Similarly, they can afford better doctors, gym memberships, and live in healthier neighborhoods with more outdoor parks and less pollution. From this viewpoint, there is nothing mysterious to explain about health disparities.

Definition | 4.4

Direct income hypothesis: health disparities arise because the rich have more resources available to invest in health.

The key to better health, according to Lindahl (2005).
Credit: © philhol – Fotolia.com.

Again, the Grossman model provides a way to think about this argument. Consider two individuals who are identical in every way except that individual R earns a high wage, and individual P earns a low wage.

As Figure 4.9 illustrates, the rich individual R has an expanded production possibility frontier (PPF) because of the extra financial resources at her disposal. Her optimal levels of health H and home good Z are both higher than the optimal levels of her poorer counterpart. Staying healthy is more important to the richer individual because her time is more valuable. Because the returns to health are greater, her MEC curve will be shifted up relative to the MEC curve of the poorer individual.

Differences in wage are not the only way that financial resources can create health disparities. People with more wealth, whatever the source, have more resources available for health production. So the Grossman model would predict better health even for lottery winners, even though their productivity and wages do not change overnight as a result of their great luck. Lindahl (2005) shows that this is indeed the case: a

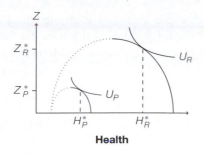

Figure 4.9. *The rich individual* R *earns higher wages than the poor individual* P *and therefore has more money at her disposal to purchase medical goods and home goods. Consequently, her PPF curve is shifted outward and her optimal level of health is higher.*

lottery win that increased income by just 10% decreased the five-year mortality rate from 6% to 4% in a sample of Swedish lottery participants.

4.6   The allostatic load hypothesis

The allostatic load hypothesis of health disparities emphasizes stress as the main mechanism linking socioeconomic status and health. The stress response in humans is vitally important to survival. In the face of threats, the body releases a hormone called adrenaline produced by the adrenal glands located just above the kidneys. This is known as the "fight or flight" response. In response to the adrenaline rush, the body shunts blood to the muscles and lungs, and away from the kidneys and stomach, in an attempt to prioritize the body parts most useful for fighting or fleeing (Sapolsky 1995).

This response can save the life of someone face to face with a saber-tooth tiger. But if the stress response is prolonged or repeated, it becomes unhealthy. The body adapts to frequent stress response by producing hormones like glucocorticoids. In the short run, glucocorticoids shut down the immune system and increase metabolism. But repeated or prolonged exposure to glucocorticoids triggers a biochemical cascade that can lead to memory loss, strokes, and neuron death; it accelerates the aging of the brain. This is one reason why students often get sick after taking final exams: the "fight or flight" response carries them through studying and test-taking but the weakened immune system eventually leads to infection.

In the Grossman model, the aging process is captured in the rate of depreciation of health capital δ. A person under prolonged or repeated stress has a higher δ than a person who lives a more relaxed life, even at the same biological age. Figure 4.10 shows the consequences of high stress: optimal health will be lower because health investment is less worthwhile. This holds even though the efficiency of health production is the same (that is, even though both individuals face the same *MEC* curve).

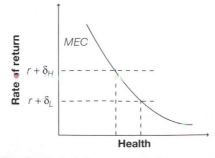

Figure 4.10. *An individual with prolonged or repeated stress faces a higher rate of health depreciation* δ_H *and chooses a lower optimal health level as a result.*

In modern life, the stress response is more frequently triggered by threats that look nothing like a saber-tooth tiger, such as final exams, overbearing bosses, and mortgage payments. Such repeated stress creates a cumulative physiological burden known as **allostatic load**. The allostatic load theory predicts that people on the lower end of the socioeconomic status suffer more stress and face worse health outcomes as a result.

Definition | 4.5

Allostatic load: cumulative physiologic toll exacted on the body over time by efforts to adapt to life experiences.

Source: Seeman et al. (1997).

Marmot et al. (1978) and Marmot et al. (1991) track the health status of British civil servants from the beginning of their career to test the allostatic load hypothesis. These are known as the Whitehall studies, named for the London street where many British government employees work.

The British civil servants are a particularly interesting group for study, since though there are distinct employment grades, people who apply and become civil servants are relatively homogeneous in backgrounds and workplace environments. In addition, all British civil servants are enrolled in the National Health Service and have similar access to health care. Given this homogeneity, sharp gradients in health disparity between high-grade and low-grade employees would be surprising.

The Whitehall studies find that morbidity and mortality rates are highest among the lowest-grade civil servants, and conversely, lowest among the highest-grade civil servants. The mortality rate for the lowest-level workers was over three times higher than for the highest-grade administrators. There were also sharp socioeconomic gradients in the rates of heart disease, diabetes, and asthma. Behavioral and physical differences like smoking, obesity, high blood pressure, and high cholesterol explain only part of the disparity.

Marmot et al. (1991) find that lower-grade civil servants report lower job satisfaction, lower job control, and more stressful life events. They argue that these civil servants suffer higher allostatic load than their higher-grade colleagues. Consistent with the allostatic load hypothesis, higher job stress correlates strongly with poorer health outcomes. Another strong conclusion from the Whitehall studies is that equalizing access to care does not eliminate health disparities. This echoes the conclusions drawn from the RAND HIE (see Chapter 2).

Nelson's Column in Trafalgar Square, near Whitehall in central London. Despite an exalted socioeconomic status, Admiral Horatio Nelson died at a young age. Credit: *Jonathan Ling – iStockphoto.com.*

Smith (1999) makes an explicit comparison between the British civil servants in the Whitehall studies and the baboon troops studied by Sapolsky and Mott (1987). Both high-grade British civil servants and dominant baboons have higher levels of high-density lipoprotein (HDL) cholesterol. Higher levels of HDL cholesterol are correlated with lower rates of heart disease, at least in humans. Figure 4.11 shows HDL cholesterol rates for both British civil servants and baboons. This is suggestive evidence that being on the low end of a social hierarchy produces high allostatic load and adverse physiological outcomes.

The income inequality hypothesis

Perhaps it is not absolute income that determines health outcomes but instead the *distribution of income* within a society. Societies with more unequal income distributions,

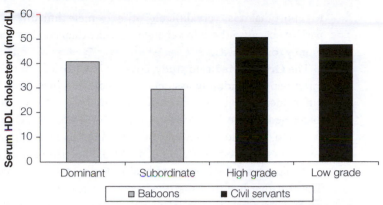

Figure 4.11. *HDL cholesterol levels in baboons and British civil servants by social status.*

Source: Figure 1 from Smith (1999). Reprinted with permission from the American Economic Association.

according to **income inequality hypothesis**, will have worse health. Under this theory, more equal societies are also less stressful ones, and therefore, according to the allostatic load hypothesis, are generally more healthy (Wilkinson and Pickett 2006).

Definition	4.6

Income inequality hypothesis: health disparities are caused by income inequality, which in and of itself is a source of allostatic load for the poor.

The income inequality hypothesis, if true, has important policy implications. If in fact higher levels of inequality have a negative impact on health outcomes, then policymakers should aim at reducing inequality within a community, not just elevating average health. The hypothesis also means that health status in a society may decline even as average income rises if that increase is confined just to the richest groups.

There is a vast empirical literature attempting to document the correlation between society-wide inequality and average health status (Wilkinson and Pickett 2006). All of these studies rely on aggregate data at the international level, the state level, or the country level, and are vulnerable to omitted variable bias. There is much disagreement in the literature about whether the correlation between societal inequality and health is causal (Deaton 2003).

Access to care hypothesis

One advantage of high income is the ability to afford more generous health insurance and more lavish health care. Conversely, people with lower income tend to have less generous insurance and face higher prices for care. This reasoning leads to another possible explanation for health disparities: differences in access to health care.

Bindman et al. (1995) find that low self-reported access to care is strongly predictive of higher rates of hospitalization for chronic conditions: asthma, hypertension, congestive heart failure, and chronic obstructive pulmonary disease. These hospitalizations are largely preventable and are considered indicators of poor overall health and inadequate outpatient care. As expected, it is the uninsured or Medicaid-insured who are more likely to report that it is "very difficult" or "extremely difficult" to get medical care when needed, perhaps because these lower-income individuals do not have the time to seek care or the money to pay for it.

The Oregon Medicaid study, covered in Chapter 2, found similar evidence when examining people randomly assigned to Medicaid coverage. Though mortality rates did not differ due to insurance coverage, diabetic patients with Medicaid were more likely to be diagnosed and to be taking appropriate medication. One possible mechanism is better access to care: those on Medicaid were more likely to report having a regular place of care and a personal doctor (Baiker et al. 2013; Finkelstein et al. 2011).

While a plausible source of health disparities, access cannot explain the whole story. The fact that health disparities persist even in societies with universal health insurance coverage suggests that equalizing access to care does not eliminate health disparities. Two studies we have already discussed – the study of Canadian youth (Currie and Stabile 2003) and the Whitehall studies (Marmot et al. 1978, 1991) – illustrate this point. In the Canadian study, health inequalities between the rich and the poor expanded during adolescence, despite universal access to health care in Canada (Figure 4.6). In the Whitehall study, there were sharp health disparities across different job grades, even though the study participants comprised a relatively homogeneous population – British civil servants – with universal access to health care through the National Health Service.

4.7   The productive time hypothesis

So far our discussion of health disparities has focused on the causal pathway leading from socioeconomic status to health. While there is much compelling evidence for this pathway, there is also evidence of the reverse pathway: changes in health can affect subsequent socioeconomic status as well. Indeed, the Grossman model predicts that worsening health diminishes productive time and hence the ability to produce income. We call this the **productive time hypothesis**.

Definition	4.7

Productive time hypothesis: SES differences are caused by disparities in health. Worsening health diminishes productive time and hence the ability to produce income.

Table 4.1 from Smith (1999) shows one indirect piece of evidence that is consistent with the productive time hypothesis. Survey respondents reporting poor health in 1984 lost wealth over the next decade, while those who reported excellent health in 1984 saw their assets nearly double over the same time period.

Smith (1999) also reports more direct evidence from the Health and Retirement Study (HRS). People newly diagnosed in 1992 with severe chronic diseases such as cancer or heart disease had lost on average $17,000 in wealth by 1994, representing about 7% of household income. This loss cannot be explained by higher medical bills alone: over the same period, average out-of-pocket medical expenses totalled only about $2,300.

The respondents who were newly diagnosed with severe chronic conditions in 1992 also tended to work less or leave work completely; 21% left the workforce between 1992 and

1994 in the wake of their diagnosis. Even those who remained employed worked about four fewer hours per week on average. In total, this reduction in working time resulted in a decrease in earnings of about $2,600. This labor force exit is exactly as the productive time hypothesis predicts, although the decrease in earnings is not enough to explain the total decrease in wealth either.

It seems clear from the HRS data that health shocks late in life can alter socioeconomic status. There is also good evidence that health shocks early in life – even before birth – play a fundamental role in determining education levels, poverty, and other economic outcomes.

For instance, Barreca (2010) studies the effect of malaria exposure *in utero* in the US between 1900 and 1936. Babies born in states and years in which temperatures were ideal for *Anopheles* mosquito breeding were substantially more likely to end up in poverty by 1960 than babies born in other states and times. They also tended to end their schooling earlier in life. This evidence is consistent with the productive time hypothesis – the babies exposed to malaria were presumably sicker during childhood and had less time and energy to invest in their own human capital development.

Similarly, Oreopoulos et al. (2008) and Black et al. (2007) study twins and siblings to measure the effect of poor health in infancy on later-life outcomes. The benefit of studying twins and siblings is that they share a common background and typically grow up in similar environments. This research strategy helps isolate the effect of birth weight and other measures of newborn health. Both studies find lower mortality rates for healthier babies, along with higher educational attainment and higher earnings in adulthood. In addition, they find that low birth weight children suffer higher mortality rates relative to their twins or siblings; this is causal evidence in favor of the thrifty phenotype hypothesis.

The Grossman model predicts that the productive time hypothesis is more relevant to people with poor health. Figure 4.12 shows the diminishing marginal returns to health in terms of productive time. Health changes have a larger effect on total productive time for relatively unhealthy individuals like those at point *A* in the figure. Healthier individuals like those at point *B* are in the flat portion of the curve; for them, changes in health have only minor effects on total productive time.

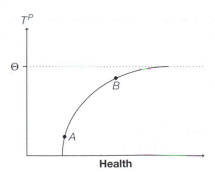

Figure 4.12. *The production function of productive time* T^P.

One consequence of this reasoning is that we should find strong evidence for the productive time hypothesis in poorer countries where the average level of health is lower. Thomas et al. (2004) conducted a randomized experiment in Indonesia in which half the subjects received a weekly iron supplement of 120 mg for a year. The other half took a placebo pill over the same time period.

Male and female subjects who received the iron treatment were much less likely to be anemic. The men who received the treatment were also more likely to work. And among self-employed males, earnings were likely to be much higher. In general, the men receiving iron supplements were more productive than the placebo group. The evidence from this randomized study is consistent with the idea that the productive time hypothesis applies strongly in poorer countries. If this result can be generalized beyond iron supplements and anemia, then small investments in health improvement in poor countries may yield large economic returns.

The iron supplement study is a good example of the productive time hypothesis because of the medical consequences of anemia. Anemia is a condition defined as a shortage of hemoglobin or red blood cells, which carry oxygen throughout the body. Iron deficiency is a common cause of anemia. Because anemia can lead to lethargy and the inability to concentrate, anemic individuals typically have much lower capacity for work. In Grossman parlance, anemic individuals have lower H and greater T^S.

4.8   Time preference: the Fuchs hypothesis

Fuchs (1982) suggests that the observed correlation between socioeconomic status and health is actually caused by an unobserved third variable: patience. People who are patient show high tolerance for delayed gratification. And people who are willing to delay gratification invest more in both education and health status. In other words, patience may explain the correlation between health and education.

Definition | 4.8

Fuchs hypothesis: both health and SES disparities are simultaneously caused by innate differences in the willingness to delay gratification. Individuals with a lower rate of time discounting (who are therefore more patient) invest more in both health and education.

The Grossman model provides a good framework for studying this argument. An individual's lifetime utility is

$$U = U(H_0, Z_0) + \delta U(H_1, Z_1) + \delta^2 U(H_2, Z_2) + \cdots + \delta^\Omega U(H_\Omega, Z_\Omega)$$

$$= \sum_{t=0}^{\Omega} \delta^t U(H_t, Z_t) \tag{4.1}$$

where $\delta \in [0, 1]$ is the individual's time discount factor (not to be confused with γ, her depreciation rate). When an individual's δ is low, near 0, she is impatient. Utility from future periods is discounted heavily, and even high levels of utility in the far future do not appeal greatly to the individual. When an individual's δ is near 1, by contrast, she is patient; the prospect of high utility in the future is appealing and she will be more reluctant to trade future utility away for utility in the present.

Now consider two individuals, Bart and Lisa, who are identical in every way except that Bart is impatient (with low δ) and Lisa is patient (with high δ). Who has a higher optimal level of health H^*?

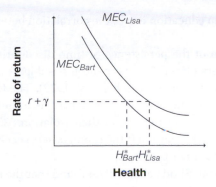

Figure 4.13. *Lisa gains more lifetime utility from a small increase in health than the impatient Bart because patient Lisa values utility in future periods highly. Consequently, her* MEC *curve is shifted upward and her optimal level of health is higher.*

Consider the impact of time discounting on the *MEC* curve. Lisa, who values utility in future periods more, benefits more from each unit of health investment than Bart does because the benefits of health are realized mostly in future periods. Consequently, Lisa's *MEC* curve lies above Bart's *MEC* curve, and her optimal level of health is higher (see Figure 4.13).

This link between patience and investment should be intuitive. To invest in health (or any type of capital), an individual spends resources now in order to gain in the future. For someone who discounts future utility heavily, this is an unattractive option: Why spend time and money to build up health (H) for future periods when it could be spent on gaining utility from other goods (Z) today?

An identical argument can be made with regard to education, which is a different kind of human capital that also requires investment. Students must forgo income, sleeping in, and entertainment in exchange for learning, which pays off only in the future. People who discount the future heavily are less willing to make this tradeoff.

This time-discounting theory predicts that people who do not discount the future very heavily will be well educated and healthy, while people who *do* discount the future heavily will be poorly educated, unhealthy, and the happier for it. Then, even if there is no causal connection between education levels and health, we would still expect to see the strong correlation between education and health that we do observe.

More evidence that suggests that time discounting is an innate quantity rather than a learned quantity comes from research on smoking patterns. Suppose the lessons learned in college cause people to avoid smoking. Then a 17-year-old in twelfth grade would have the same propensity to smoke as any other 17-year-old in twelfth grade, even if one were an aspiring astrophysicist destined for college and the other were planning to enter the workforce right after high-school graduation. Only once the aspiring astrophysicist actually gains an educational advantage will she be less likely to smoke than her high-school peer.

Alternatively, suppose that the Fuchs hypothesis is true. Then the aspiring astrophysicist invests more in education because she innately has more patience than her high-school peers. Under this hypothesis, we would expect the 17-year-old aspiring astrophysicist to *already* be less likely to smoke, even in the twelfth grade. It is not the lessons of college that cause her not to smoke, but instead her innate patience.

Using data on smoking patterns and education history from the Stanford Heart Disease Prevention Program, Farrell and Fuchs (1982) test the Fuchs hypothesis. They find that, even at age 17, students who go on to college have a lower rate of smoking. Hence, future education disparities predict current disparities in smoking rates. This result suggests that time discounting rather than education drives the correlation between education and health.

In a charming demonstration of the persistence of time-discounting attitudes, a different set of Stanford researchers placed four-year-old test subjects in a room alone in front of a plate with a single marshmallow (Mischel et al. 1972). The four-year-olds were told that if they could resist eating the marshmallow for a few minutes, they would be rewarded with several marshmallows at the end of their isolation. While some kids ate the marshmallow as soon as the investigator left the room, others successfully resisted the temptation and were rewarded for their patience.

Following up on this experiment, Shoda et al. (1990) found that the kids who were able to delay gratification as four-year-olds, scored much better on math and language tests as 18-year-olds. The ability to delay gratification is persistent and explains why the kids who waited for the extra marshmallows were also more successful academically, since academic success also requires delayed gratification.

Cutler and Lleras-Muney (2010) find in national survey data from the US and the UK that higher-educated people are less likely to take unnecessary risks like not wearing seat belts and more likely to take preventative health measures like cancer screenings. This result, in itself, is consistent with the Fuchs hypothesis. However, Cutler and Lleras-Muney (2010) find that including proxy variables for time preference *increases* the strength of the relationship between education and risk-taking, contrary to the Fuchs hypothesis. This finding would suggest that heterogeneity in time-discounting rates is not a primary driver of health disparities.

4.9   Conclusion

Each of the theories outlined above works within the logic of the Grossman model, but each one explains the connection between health and socioeconomic status in its own way. The first four theories we discussed – the *efficient producer hypothesis*, the *thrifty phenotype hypothesis*, the *direct income effect* and the *allostatic load hypothesis* – all describe ways in which more wealth or better education lead to improved health. The *productive time hypothesis* reverses that causal argument; it posits that improved health leads to better SES. Finally, the *Fuchs hypothesis* argues that a third variable, time discounting or "patience", determines both health and wealth.

Each theory has supporting evidence, and it could well be the case that they all help explain socioeconomic health disparities. Figure 4.14 summarizes the causal structure of the Grossman family of theories.

This is an active and contentious area of research, and it seems likely that future work in health economics will clarify issues that at this point remain murky. But a few things have been well established:

- better-educated people are more efficient producers of health, even with the same resources;
- health events early in life have important consequences throughout the lifespan;
- stress plays an important role in producing health disparities;
- equalizing access to care does not eliminate health disparities;
- there is a bi-directional relationship between health and socioeconomic status.

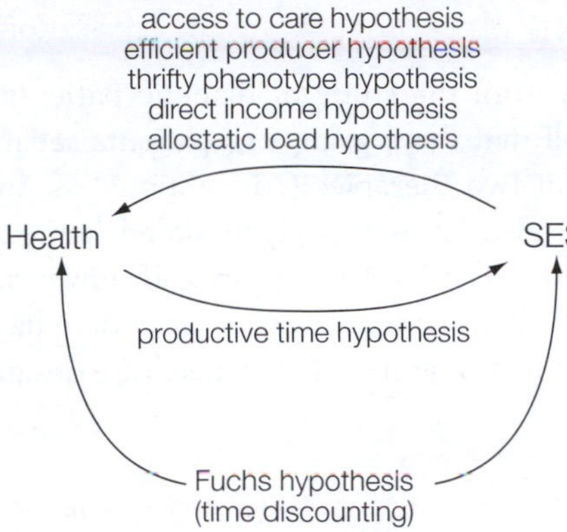

access to care hypothesis
efficient producer hypothesis
thrifty phenotype hypothesis
direct income hypothesis
allostatic load hypothesis

Health   SES

productive time hypothesis

Fuchs hypothesis
(time discounting)

Figure 4.14. *Causal relationship between health, socioeconomic status, and other variables.*

Policies aimed at reducing health disparities must cope with these facts. Because health disparities have a multifaceted set of causes, policymakers must be mindful of unintended consequences when addressing the root causes of health disparities.

4.10   Exercises

Comprehension questions

Indicate whether the statement is true or false, and justify your answer. Be sure to cite evidence from the chapter and state any additional assumptions you may need.

1   In the US, well-educated males can expect to live longer than poorly educated males.
2   Unlike in the US, there are no socioeconomic status gradients in health in countries that provide universal health care coverage to all citizens. That is, in such countries, poorer and richer citizens have (on average) the same health.
3   Health status earlier in life is a good predictor of wealth later in life.
4   According to Smith (1999), nearly all of the differences in health outcomes between rich and poor in America can be attributed to differences in access to medical care.
5   The thrifty phenotype hypothesis states that early-life events after birth have a strong influence on health status even in adulthood.
6   People who have a newly diagnosed chronic disease, such as diabetes, often suffer large declines in their wealth over time. This decline in wealth is entirely explained by decreased hours of work.
7   In the Whitehall study, access to health care was a key variable determining the relative health outcomes of high- and low-grade British civil servants.
8   One leading theory about why the poor are in worse health than the rich is that the rich enjoy a greater allostatic load.
9   In a study of babies born during the Dutch famine toward the end of World War II, those exposed to the famine *in utero* were more likely than those not as exposed to be obese as adults.
10   In Canada, unlike in the US, the gap between rich children and poor children in health status does not widen as children age.
11   There is a consensus among health economists that socioeconomic status has a major impact on health, but health does not have a significant effect on SES.

Analytical problems

12 Table 4.4 shows results from the study of diabetic patients discussed in Goldman
and Smith (2002). Recall that three groups of patients separated by education level
were treated with one of two therapies (conventional vs. intensive). Their average
hemoglobin A1c levels (also known as glycosylated hemoglobin) before and after
the experiment are reported. Note that, as in golf, lower scores are better on the
hemoglobin A1c test, which measures how well the patient has kept blood glucose levels in control. Most treatment regimens for diabetes are designed to keep hemoglobin
A1c levels low.

Table 4.4. *Improvement in hemoglobin measurement for diabetics by treatment regime
and age.*

Group	Glycosylated hemoglobin		
	Postgraduate degree	College grad/ some college	HS degree/some secondary
Conventional therapy only ($n = 495$)			
Baseline	8.42	8.76	8.96
End-to-study	8.88	9.08	9.59
Difference	0.46	0.32	0.63
Intensive treatment only ($n = 490$)			
Baseline	8.04	8.86	8.93
End-of-study	7.18	7.30	7.43
Difference	−0.85	−1.56	−1.51
Treatment effect*	−1.31	−1.88[†]	−2.14[‡]

* Treatment effect is the improvement in glycemic control among the intensive treatment group relative to
conventional therapy. Average follow-up period was 72 months. Significance levels are for a test of equivalence
with the postgraduate category and control for duration in study, gender, marital status, and age. Intensive
treatment was more efficacious for the less educated.
[†] $P < 0.10$.
[‡] $P < 0.05$.

Source: Goldman and Smith (2002). Copyright (2002) National Academy of Sciences, USA. Reproduced with
permission.

As the figure indicates, average hemoglobin A1c levels deteriorated for patients in the
control group, but improved for patients in the treatment group.

a   In all three groups of conventional-therapy patients, glucose levels got worse.
Which of the conventional therapy groups had the biggest deterioration in average
glycosylated hemoglobin levels?

b   Which intensive-treatment group had the biggest improvement in average glycosylated hemoglobin levels?

c   For which group of patients did the intensive-treatment intervention seem to have
the biggest effect compared with the conventional therapy? The smallest effect?

d   Explain how this evidence is consistent with the efficient producer hypothesis.

13 Table 4.5 shows data from Rich-Edwards et al. (2005) on the prevalence of various
afflictions among female nurses who were born at different weights.

Table 4.5. *Hazard rate of coronary heart disease, stroke, and total cardiovascular disease, compared with average birth rate cohort.*

Cohort	Average birth weight	Low birth weight	Very low birth weight	Extremely low birth weight
Birth weight (kg)	3.2–3.9	2.5–3.2	2.3–2.5	< 2.3
Coronary heart disease	100%	130%*	148%*	131%
Stroke	100%	116%	105%	123%
All cardiovascular disease	100%	123%*	129%*	127%

* Indicates statistically significant difference from the average birth weight cohort.
Hazard ratios are adjusted for age and body mass index (BMI).

Source: Data from Table 1 in Rich-Edwards et al. (2005).

a   Is it a coincidence that all nurses born at average birth weight suffer from coronary heart disease, stroke, and all cardiovascular disease at the exact same rate?

b   Summarize the data in the figure in one or two concise sentences.

c   Discuss the data in light of what you know about the thrifty phenotype hypothesis.

14 **Simpson's paradox.** Recently, the king of the mythical nation of Pcoria was diagnosed with cancer. He noticed that many other nobles in his court had also been diagnosed with cancer recently. He dispatched his two best health economists to study cancer rates in Pcoria's two towns. Their results are recorded in Table 4.6. Before you begin, recall that Pcoria's two towns are very different. Eastville is a poor area, home to numerous factories that produce prodigious amounts of pollution. Weston is the home of the king's court and is filled with pristine parks and hiking trails.

Table 4.6. *Information from the cancer rate study commissioned by the King of Pcoria.*

	Eastville		Weston	
	Population	Cancer rate	Population	Cancer rate
Nobles	100	50%	900	10%
Peasants	1,000	40%	500	8%

a   The king's economists conclude that there is a health disparity between nobles and peasants when it comes to cancer rates. Succinctly state the health disparity.

b   Calculate the nationwide cancer rate for nobles and the nationwide cancer rate for peasants. What do you find?

c   This effect is called *Simpson's paradox* or the amalgamation paradox. Explain how the distribution of nobles and peasants and the geography of Pcoria contribute to the paradoxical result. Which health disparity hypothesis from the chapter does this exemplify?

d   Consider Table 4.7, which substitutes variable names for the cancer rate data. Simpson's paradox occurs when the cancer rate is higher for nobles in each town but higher for peasants nationwide. Express these three conditions in terms of the variable names in the table.

e   Use your answer from Exercise d to prove that Simpson's paradox cannot occur if the populations of nobles and peasants are the same in both towns (that is, $a = c$ and $b = d$).

Table 4.7. *Generalized version of Table 4.6.*

	Eastville		Weston	
	Population	Cancer rate	Population	Cancer rate
Nobles	a	w	c	y
Peasants	b	x	d	z

f   Do you think Simpson's paradox might invalidate some of the evidence for health disparities cited in this chapter? Why or why not?

Essay questions

15   The following is an excerpt from the abstract of a recent journal article entitled "The effects of maternal fasting during Ramadan on birth and adult outcomes" by Almond and Mazumder (2007). Ramadan is the traditional month of daytime fasting by Muslims.

> We use the Islamic holy month of Ramadan as a natural experiment for evaluating the short and long-term effects of fasting during pregnancy. Using Michigan natality data we show that *in utero* exposure to Ramadan among Arab births results in lower birthweight and reduced gestation length. Preconception exposure to Ramadan is also associated with fewer male births. Using Census data in Uganda we also find that Muslims who were born nine months after Ramadan are 22 percent ($p = 0.02$) more likely to be disabled as adults. Effects are found for vision, hearing, and especially for mental (or learning) disabilities.

   a   Describe how one or more theories discussed in this chapter might explain the findings by Almond and Mazumder.

   b   Suppose that a scientific study determines that fasting during Ramadan actually has no causal effect on fetal health. What other factor could explain the Michigan results? Do you think your explanation is likely?

16   Below is the abstract of a recent National Bureau of Economic Research working paper entitled "Positive and negative mental health consequences of early childhood television watching" by Waldman et al. (2012):

> An extensive literature in medicine investigates the health consequences of early childhood television watching. However, this literature does not address the issue of reverse causation, i.e., does early childhood television watching cause specific health outcomes or do children more likely to have these health outcomes watch more television? This paper uses a natural experiment to investigate the health consequences of early childhood television watching and so is not subject to questions concerning reverse causation. Specifically, we use repeated cross-sectional data from 1972 through 1992 on county-level mental retardation rates, county-level autism rates, and county-level children's cable-television subscription rates to investigate how early childhood television watching affects the prevalence of mental retardation and autism. We find a strong negative correlation between average county-level cable subscription rates when a birth cohort is below three and subsequent mental retardation diagnosis rates, but a strong positive correlation between the same cable

subscription rates and subsequent autism diagnosis rates. Our results thus suggest that early childhood television watching has important positive and negative health consequences.

a   Assuming the findings of this paper are correct, connect their results to one or more of the hypotheses discussed in this chapter.

b   The researchers assume that higher rainfall in a county will lead to higher cable subscription rates (because people in those counties are more likely to stay inside and watch TV). In other words, they treat rainfall amounts as a random influence on cable subscription rates. Explain why a natural experiment is important to identify a causal effect. In this case, what selection biases are the researchers concerned about?

c   Assume that this natural experiment is invalid and that cable subscription rates are instead totally determined by income (that is, rich families are more likely to buy cable, and the local weather plays no role). Interpret their evidence in light of this possibility.

Students can find answers to the comprehension questions and lecturers can access an Instructor Manual with guideline answers to the analytical problems and essay questions at **www.palgrave.com/economics/bht**.

II SUPPLY OF HEALTH CARE

5   The labor market for
    physicians   78
6   The hospital industry   100

5 THE LABOR MARKET FOR PHYSICIANS

A 59-year-old woman on her walk to work unexpectedly falls to the sidewalk and is unable to get up. A passerby calls for an ambulance and she is rushed to the hospital. An emergency-room doctor examines her and finds her conscious but groggy. Her speech is slurred, and she is unable to move her right arm or leg. The doctor concludes that she has almost certainly suffered a stroke.

Now the doctor must make a vital decision on her behalf. Broadly speaking, there are two distinct types of strokes: clotting and bleeding. One possibility is that a blood clot in the patient has lodged in the wrong place. This is called an ischemic stroke. Another possibility is that an artery in her brain, for whatever reason, has ruptured and she is bleeding internally. This is called a hemorrhagic stroke. Both cut off blood supply to the brain.

The diagnostic problem that the doctor faces is that these two possibilities require dramatically different treatments. If it is a clot that has caused the stroke, the correct course of treatment is to give her a drug that dissolves the clot. If the treatment is applied in time, the damage from the stroke may be minimal and reversible. Unfortunately, if the cause is a ruptured blood vessel, this course of treatment is counterproductive and may even kill her.

The doctor must decide what to do quickly with incomplete information. The patient entrusts the doctor with her life – she is in no position to help decide, and even if she were healthy she has no experience distinguishing between an ischemic and hemorrhagic stroke.

From the patient's point of view, it would be best if the doctor focuses only on the medicine and leaves out of his decision-making all matters extraneous to her health and well-being. The patient hopes the doctor does not consider his own financial well-being and that he leaves aside any prejudices he might have. Most of all, the patient hopes that her doctor knows what he is doing. In her groggy state, she cannot tell how capable her doctor is, so she has to trust that regulatory agencies have barred unqualified physicians from practicing. But such regulations may come with the cost of more expensive health care and shortages in doctor supply.

The economic literature on the physician labor market emphasizes tradeoffs that are implicit throughout this story. How should doctors be trained to minimize harm to patients? How should the patient be compensated for mistakes that doctors make, and what consequences will that have for how doctors practice? If doctors are allowed to set the required standard for what it means to be a high-quality doctor (and who else would know enough to do so?), does this mean they will earn monopoly rents? Our goal in this chapter is to make clear the tradeoffs inherent in regulating the market for physicians.

5.1   The training of physicians

There is a consensus among nations that, before they can practice, physicians must receive an education in both basic sciences and clinical training. And in all countries, this training requires several years to complete. But nations differ in how long the training takes, and how physicians must demonstrate their competency.

Medical school

In most European countries, aspiring physicians enter medical school directly out of high school. Conversely, almost all medical schools in the US and Canada require a bachelor's degree for admittance, so students there must first attend an undergraduate institution. They can pursue a major or concentration in any field they choose, but to apply for medical school they also must complete a pre-medical curriculum of biology, physics, chemistry, mathematics, and English.

Entry into medical school is a selective and competitive process. Only about one in two people who apply to US medical school each year are accepted to any schools, though this rate fluctuates and has been as low as one in three in years past. Entry into the most selective schools is even more difficult. For instance, the University of California, San Francisco, received 6,767 applications in 2011 for only 149 slots. In the UK too, the admissions process is quite selective. In 2004, there were over twice as many applicants as spaces at the UK medical schools (Powis et al. 2007).

Given the difference in the ages in which students enter medical school, the length of medical school predictably differs across countries as well. In the US, it typically lasts four years; in the UK, five years; and in France, students need up to six or seven years to fully complete their studies. In all cases, the first portion of medical school focuses mostly on classroom work: students study topics like anatomy, physiology, pharmacology, pathology, and biochemistry.

During the second half of medical school, focus shifts from classroom work to clinical and patient management skills. Students serve as junior members on teams taking care of patients in teaching hospitals and go through monthly rotations on different teams in specialty areas such as internal medicine, surgery, pediatrics, and gynecology. These rotations help students learn about the different branches of medicine and prepare students to select a specialty.

Though the subject matter is similar across medical schools, the tuition cost shouldered by students varies tremendously across countries. Four years of medical training in the US can cost around $140,000 at public schools and $225,000 at private ones (Morrison 2005). Meanwhile, both the German and French governments heavily subsidize medical school so that students pay only €200 to €500 a year (Segouin et al. 2007; Chenot 2009). The cost of medical schools has an impact on who attends medical school and the makeup of the labor market of physicians. We discuss this effect in Section 5.2.

Residency

Medical school is only the beginning of the process of learning to be a doctor. Graduates fresh out of medical school are not qualified to take care of patients on their own; they have spent years in the classroom learning anatomy and pharmacology, but relatively little time caring for patients. One of the main jobs of doctors is helping patients make life-and-death decisions with incomplete information and often under great time pressure. No classroom experience by itself can equip someone to perform such tasks.

Becoming a doctor thus requires an extensive, hands-on apprenticeship, called a residency in the US. In the final year of medical school, students pick a specialty within medicine – such as surgery, pediatrics, or internal medicine – and then apply to residency programs that train physicians in that specialty. Residency is an intense and arduous time for young physicians. Work weeks typically extend up to 80 hours and sometimes more, and a single shift can last 36 hours or longer. Most of the learning in residency takes place under the supervision of veteran doctors called attending physicians who help trainees perform surgeries, make clinical decisions, and manage patients.

Upon completion of their first year of residency, called an internship, doctors can earn their license to practice medicine, which also gives them the right to prescribe drugs. Though legally permitted to practice at this point, few doctors leave residency after their internship, because insurers are reluctant to reimburse incompletely trained doctors for their services.

After residency, which typically takes at least three years and can take much longer depending on the specialty, some doctors continue their medical training in a subspecialty (Figure 5.1). For example, in order to practice as a cardiologist, a doctor must complete a three-year internal medicine residency and then a cardiology fellowship, which may take an additional five years.

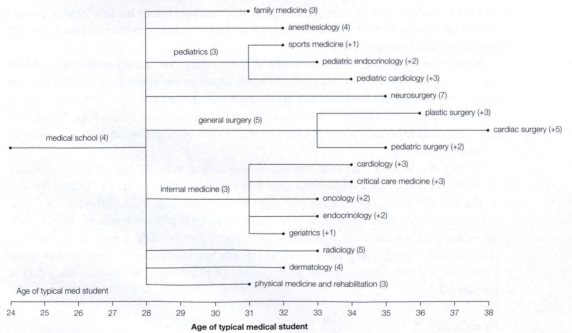

Figure 5.1. *Time requirements in years for various residency and fellowship programs in the US.*

Source: Data from GME Directory 2010–2011.

Resident inexperience and the July effect

On-the-job training is an inherent part of the residency system. The unofficial motto that guides much of medical training is "See one, do one, teach one." Although this process is largely unobserved by patients, even the greenest residents routinely participate in medical procedures and surgeries, including highly complex ones. As Atul Gawande underscores in *Complications* (2002), any surgeon who has mastered a procedure originally had to perform that same procedure for the very first time – likely on a patient who had no awareness of what was happening.

Such on-the-job experience is clearly indispensable to training competent and experienced doctors, but it is inevitable that inexperienced residents will make some mistakes.

American medical professionals have long spoken of a "July effect," a reference to the month of the year when experienced residents finish their terms and fresh medical school graduates take their place (Young et al. 2011). Because experience levels decline abruptly in American teaching hospitals in July, some fear that the quality of medical care available at these hospitals plummets during the first few weeks of the new term. In the UK, where residency programs transition later in the summer, the same phenomenon is called the "August killing season."

Empirically, there is substantial evidence that the July effect is real. For instance, US counties with teaching hospitals experience a 10% spike in fatal medication errors in July, while counties without teaching hospitals do not (Phillips and Barker 2010). Some studies fail to find a significant effect on mortality (Huckman and Barro 2005; Bakaeen et al. 2009), but a comprehensive review of the literature suggests otherwise. In a review of 39 recent studies of resident changeover, Young et al. (2011) find substantial evidence that patient mortality increased and hospital efficiency suffered in the periods immediately following a changeover.

If the July effect is real, Americans should be very careful handling fireworks on Independence Day (July 4). Credit: © *Carlos Santa Maria – Fotolia.com.*

Physician work-hours

Physicians are among the longest-working professionals; a doctor's work-"day" can last more than 24 hours. There are patients to treat, operations to conduct, and innumerable forms to complete. Even a single surgery can last longer than a typical 9-to-5 work-day: a surgeon performing a pancreaticoduodenectomy, for example, may be in the operating room for ten straight hours.[1]

So it is unsurprising that physicians frequently clock more than 60 work-hours in a week (Dorsey et al. 2003). The time spent in the hospital may be even greater for residents. Historically, a resident on call overnight once every three nights would routinely work up to 30 hours consecutively and 96 hours or more in a single week (Steinbrook 2002).

---

1 A pancreaticoduodenectomy, commonly known as a Whipple procedure, is performed to remove part of the pancreas and part of the small intestine.

The fatigue of working long hours may impair a physician's cognitive abilities, which in turn may have adverse effects on patient health. Taffinder et al. (1998) and Eastridge et al. (2003) compare the performance of well-rested surgeons and sleep-deprived ones on a virtual-reality laparoscopic surgery simulator. Taffinder et al. find that surgeons with no sleep needed 14% more time and committed 20% more errors than surgeons who operated on the simulator after a full night of sleep. Likewise, Eastridge et al. find a significant difference in the number of errors.

A converse hypothesis argues that longer work-hours for physicians and residents actually has benefits for patient health in the long run. If doctors work continuously for long periods, a hospitalized patient may remain with the same doctor for her entire stay. This not only improves the patient experience, but more importantly, requires fewer hand-offs between different physicians, thereby minimizing the chance that crucial information is mishandled (Arora et al. 2005).

In 2003, the Accreditation Council for Graduate Medical Education (ACGME) implemented limits on the number of hours that residents in the US are permitted to work. Doctors-in-training were not to work in excess of 24 consecutive hours and no more than 80 hours in a single week.[2]

The ACGME ruling created a natural experiment to estimate the impact on patient outcomes of limiting resident work-hours, as only teaching hospitals with residency programs were affected by the new limits. If health outcomes changed in teaching hospitals but not in non-teaching ones, researchers could identify the difference as the result of the new ACGME limits. However, studies found little to no difference in mortality outcomes in the two years following the reform (Volpp et al. 2007; Prasad et al. 2009). Shetty and Bhattacharya (2007) do find a small decrease in mortality risk for medical patients, but no significant change for surgical patients. These results suggest that constrained resident hours may improve outcomes for patients in teaching hospitals, but the effects are not large. However, the studies consider only patient deaths – they do not track possible changes in the number of non-fatal errors.

One explanation for the lack of a measurable effect is that the ACGME's policy may not have been completely effective at limiting work-hours. One survey found that 83.6% of survey respondents violated the regulation at least once during the year after policy implementation (Landrigan et al. 2006).

Landrigan et al. (2004) conducted a randomized experiment at the Brigham and Woman's intensive care unit (ICU) at Harvard to study the effect of work-hour limitations on physician errors. The experiment randomly assigned two teams, one to a traditional schedule and one to a shorter work week. They closely monitored each team to ensure that neither deviated from its assigned schedule. Those in the traditional schedule averaged 77 to 81 hours a week and up to 34 consecutive hours. The alternative schedule limited shifts to a maximum of 16 hours and averaged 60 to 63 work-hours a week. A physician observer accompanied each intern to chronicle (and intercept) medical errors.

---

2 One of the authors, who was in medical school before these limits were established, once toiled 112 hours in an obstetrics ward in a single week. He was exhausted by the end but three new mothers were grateful for his efforts – or at least the efforts of the more experienced doctors who were there to correct his mistakes.

They found that interns on the traditional schedule committed 35.9% more serious medical errors than the interns on the limited schedule. That difference included 20.8% more medication errors and 5.6 times as many diagnostic errors. Patient outcomes, however, did not differ significantly between the two groups, because senior physicians intercepted most serious errors.

This highlights a policy tradeoff. Residency is designed to be a safe place for new doctors to gain experience and make errors without harming patients. An unintended consequence of work-hour limits may be that residents get less supervised practice before the end of their residency. Though no study has examined this tradeoff explicitly, it may be the case that work-hour restrictions reduce errors by residents at the expense of increasing errors by recent graduates of residency programs.

Other nations have also grappled with the tradeoffs in imposing restrictions on resident work-hours (Woodrow et al. 2006). In Canada, resident unions have negotiated for and won work-hour legislation in each province. While the exact ceiling varies from province to province, they roughly match the 80-hour limit in the US (Romanchuk 2004).

Physicians in Europe, meanwhile, are subject to the European Union's Working Time Directive (WTD), which establishes a maximum 48-hour work week. This edict, aimed at ensuring quality of life for European workers, has raised worries about shortages in health services and reduced opportunity of training for doctors (Sheldon 2004; Maxwell et al. 2010). However, an independent review commissioned by England's National Health Service in 2010 argues that even under the WTD proper training can be delivered as long as effective supervision is given (Temple 2010).

5.2   Physician wages

The content and length of physician training is similar across nations. But physician wages vary tremendously across countries. In the US, physician salaries are high compared with salaries in other professions. But becoming a physician requires years of expensive training, both in medical school and during residency. As Adam Smith (1776) observed in *Wealth of Nations*, "wages vary with the cost of learning the business." In order to see if this fact fully explains the high salaries of working physicians, we must consider income over the entire lifespan.

Returns to medical training

Consider a student who is thinking of becoming a doctor but is also considering another career, such as professional surfing. If he decides to become a surfer, he can start earning money right away. On the other hand, becoming a licensed physician requires four years of medical school as well as additional years of residency training. In the US, four years of medical school can cost between $140,000 and $225,000, though in most European countries it is free or heavily subsidized. Then physicians go through a period of low-paying residency before becoming fully licensed to practice. Only at this late date does the physician begin earning a high salary. Figure 5.2 portrays the two income paths for professional surfers and licensed physicians in the US and in western Europe.

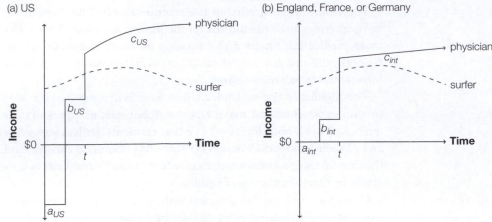

Figure 5.2. *The surfer earns a moderate income over his entire career. (a) In the US, an aspiring physician earns negative income while in medical school (interval a_{US}) and then relatively low income during residency (interval b_{US}). After that though, he makes a very high income (interval c_{US}). (b) In countries where medical school is entirely or heavily subsidized, physicians-in-training sacrifice less income early on (interval a_{int}) but also tend to earn less after graduation.*

As long as the college graduate enjoys ripping waves about as much as he enjoys seeing patients – that is, so long as the only relevant difference between the professions is the income stream – he should pick the career that maximizes the **net present value** (NPV) of his income. In this context, NPV captures how valuable a lifetime stream of income is to an individual today. It depends on the total amount of income, the individual's discount rate, and the degree of backloading in the income stream. Recall that the discount factor δ is a number between 0 and 1 that indicates how much a person values utility in future periods and in essence how much patience that person has. A higher δ indicates that the person values future utility nearly as much as present utility, implying greater patience.

Definition   5.1

Net present value (NPV): the discounted sum of all future earnings from $t = 0$ onward. The discount factor δ is between 0 and 1 and is a measure of how much less the individual values future income than present income:

$$\text{NPV} = \sum_{t=0}^{T} \delta^t I(t) \tag{5.1}$$

The discount *factor* δ can be expressed also as a function of a discount *rate* r:

$$\delta = \frac{1}{1+r} \tag{5.2}$$

Expressed in this way, high values of r indicate impatience. It is convenient to express δ this way, because the discount rate r presents a direct comparison with market interest rates. Suppose someone has a discount factor of $\delta = 0.9$. Then applying equation (5.2) yields $r = 0.11$. This person would rather spend his money than save it unless the bank offers an interest rate greater than 11%.

The returns to a surfing career are frontloaded and the returns to a career in medicine are backloaded, so the more impatient college graduate will pursue surfing while the patient one pursues medicine.

College graduates with high values of discount rate r, and therefore low discount factors δ, are impatient and value the quick returns of a surfing career more than the delayed returns from a career in medicine. Graduates with low values of r are patient and are more likely to pursue medical careers. Thus, as discount rate r moves from 0 to 1, the person is more and more impatient, and therefore more likely to go into surfing. This also means that somewhere between 0 and 1, there is a specific discount rate r^* such that the person is indifferent between surfing and medicine. At r^*, the person values the financial returns from both careers equally. This r^* is known as the **internal rate of return** (IRR) of going into medicine versus surfing.

"I actually just couldn't stand the sight of blood."
Credit: © AZP Worldwide – Fotolia.com.

Definition 5.2

Internal rate of return (IRR): the discount rate r^* of an investment that would imply a net present value of 0 for that investment versus the best alternative. If $I_p(t)$ is the income in period t from the investment, and $I_s(t)$ is the income in period t from the alternative, then the internal rate of return r^* satisfies the following equation:

$$\sum_{t=0}^{T} \frac{I_p(t)}{(1+r^*)^t} - \sum_{t=0}^{T} \frac{I_s(t)}{(1+r^*)^t} = 0 \tag{5.3}$$

If the internal rate of return is *higher* than an individual's discount rate, he should make the investment – the future returns are worth the wait. If the internal rate of return is *lower* than an individual's discount rate, he should not make the investment – the future returns are not worth the wait (see Figure 5.3).

There is a long history of economists interested in calculating the IRR of a career in medicine. Nobel laureate Milton Friedman wrote his dissertation in the 1930s on measuring the IRR of becoming a physician versus a lawyer in the US (Friedman and Kuznets 1945). Burstein and Cromwell (1985) find that internal rates of return for entry into medicine or dentistry in the US were over 10% in the 1970s, even when accounting for differences in work-hours (Table 5.1). Other recent estimates using data from the 1990s indicate that the IRR has only grown over time (Weeks and Wallace 2002).

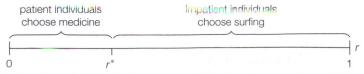

Figure 5.3. *Career choice depends on discount rate. If the internal rate of return r^* increases, more people will be inclined to become physicians.*

Table 5.1. *Estimated IRR for various professional careers versus a typical college-degree-requiring job in the US, 1970–1980.*

Year	All physicians	General practitioners	Dentists	Lawyers*
1970	11.8%	12.1%	16.1%	7.0%
1971	11.6%	13.2%	—	6.6%
1972	10.7%	12.2%	14.4%	5.7%
1973	10.8%	12.5%	—	6.7%
1974	12.0%	14.5%	14.9%	7.1%
1975	11.6%	12.3%	—	7.1%
1976	10.5%	12.4%	15.8%	7.1%
1977	10.2%	13.3%	—	6.8%
1978	11.0%	13.0%	16.3%	6.8%
1979	11.6%	14.5%	—	7.2%
1980	12.1%	14.2%	—	7.2%

Internal rates of return were calculated in reference to the earnings of the population of college graduates, and adjusted for differences in work-hours.
*The internal rates of return reported for lawyers are *not* adjusted for differences in work-hours.
Source: Burstein and Cromwell (1985). With permission from Elsevier.

In fact, in the US the internal rates of return for a professional career are substantially higher than the market interest rate. By itself, this means that these professional careers are good investments. This presents an economic puzzle: How can the rates of return for entering these careers remain so high? Presumably people would be attracted to these high returns, so more and more people would decide to go to medical school. A glut of new doctors would compete salaries down to a point where the IRR of becoming a physician is no longer higher than the market interest rate.

The fact that the IRR has instead remained high suggests that there are obstacles to entry into medicine. First, it may be the case that few people have an aptitude for medical practice, so many people attracted to medicine would not be able to find jobs as physicians even with medical training. Alternatively, the supply of physicians may be constrained by the number of slots in medical schools and restrictions in the immigration of physicians. We discuss these possible obstacles further in Section 5.3.

Returns to specialization

Almost all doctors are well paid, but doctors within certain specialty fields – like surgery, cardiology, and radiology – command even higher salaries (Table 5.2). Entering these specialties requires newly minted physicians to complete longer residency periods. So doctors graduating from medical school and selecting an area of specialty face a dilemma similar to that of the college graduate discussed earlier: Are they willing to defer income in the short term (that is, complete a longer residency) in order to enjoy higher income later?

It turns out that pursuing a highly paid specialty field is almost always worthwhile, even considering the longer low-paid residency. Nicholson (2002) estimates that the internal

Table 5.2. *Survey data on average hourly wage and work-hours in various medical specialties in the US, 2004–2005.*

Specialty	Mean hourly wage	Mean work-hours/week
Neurologic surgery	$132	58
Immunology	$112	49
Orthopedic surgery	$108	61
Dermatology	$103	45
Gastroenterology	$93	57
General surgery	$86	61
Obstetrics and gynecology	$83	57
Psychiatry	$72	45
Geriatric medicine	$57	53
Internal medicine and pediatrics	$50	57

Source: Data from Leigh et al. (2010).

rates of return for physicians entering into radiology, orthopedic surgery, general surgery, obstetrics/gynecology, and anesthesiology in 1998 exceeded 25%. He finds that entering these specialties would still be advantageous even if their residency positions did not pay *at all*.

Can the huge returns to high-paying medical specialties possibly be a competitive labor market outcome? It is actually possible for high salary differentials to persist in competitive equilibrium if . . .

- . . . *specialists work more.* If specialists work consistently more than non-specialists, then their extra wages are compensation for longer hours and the burden of working late nights or early mornings.
- . . . *specialists train longer.* If specialists have to spend many more years in residency than non-specialists, then higher wages are necessary to induce them to take those extra years to train.
- . . . *specialists retire earlier.* If specialists tend to retire earlier, either because their longer schedules wear them out or because their physical dexterity (a key attribute for surgeons) diminishes rapidly with age, then annual salary differentials are not the best way to compare specialists and non-specialists. The NPV or IRR comparisons are more appropriate, because they account for lifetime income.
- . . . *specialists are more highly skilled.* If specialists have rare abilities that make them particularly well suited to their demanding jobs, then they should enjoy a wage premium even in a competitive labor market.

Bhattacharya (2005) examines data on young physicians and uses an IRR calculation to find that differences in work-hours, training requirements, career length, and ability (as measured by test scores) can only explain half of the salary premiums for medical specialists. Surprisingly, differences in ability at the end of medical school do not explain any of the differences in returns between high-income and low-income specialties. Since these four explanations do not account for all of the difference between specialist and non-specialist salaries, presumably the remaining differences must be due to barriers to entry to becoming a specialist.

5.3   Barriers to entry

Early in American history, the marketplace for physician services was largely unregulated and doctors were in plentiful supply. Kessel (1958) depicts a nineteenth-century medical marketplace that was unfettered and competitive:

> With very few exceptions, anyone who wanted to practice [medicine] was free to hang a shingle outside and declare himself available. Medical schools were easy to start, were easy to get into, and provided ... a varied menu of medical training that covered the complete quality spectrum.

In the present day, the market for physicians is much more tightly regulated, with various restrictions on entering medical school and practicing medicine. The bulk of evidence suggests that these barriers to entry allow physicians to earn **monopoly rents**, extra wages above the competitive level that accrue to producers in a market where supply is artificially constrained. This section details those barriers and discusses the costs and benefits of policies that restrict physician supply.

Definition	5.3

Monopoly rents: extra wages above the competitive level that accrue to producers in a market where supply is artificially constrained.

The rise of the AMA

The conditions described by Kessel (1958) did not persist. In the nineteenth century, a movement to regulate medical practice began to take shape. Early attempts included an 1827 meeting of doctors in Northampton, Massachusetts, to agree upon certain basic standards for medical education and an 1835 effort by the faculty at the Medical College of Georgia to create an organization to oversee medical practice. In 1847, the American Medical Association (AMA) was founded and immediately took up the cause of ensuring that all practicing doctors had a "suitable preliminary education" and a uniform set of "elevated requirements" for the MD degree.

At first, the AMA focused its resources on an extensive licensure campaign. It persuaded states to require anyone who wanted to practice as a physician to obtain a license to do so. States mandated that physicians complete an examination or a certain amount of training to become licensed. While successful in convincing many states to license the practice of medicine, the AMA was not without detractors. Kessel recounts a speech by a Massachusetts state legislator who acknowledged the virtue of medical cures but compared doctors and medical professionals to "a powerful trade union [demanding] legislation against the competition of the 'scabs.'"

The AMA turned its focus to closing low-quality medical schools in the early twentieth century. The release of an influential 1910 report by Abraham Flexner – which corroborated a 1906 AMA finding that nearly half of the 160 medical schools then in existence were of unacceptably low quality – was a turning point in American medical history. The Flexner report convinced state legislatures and medical examining boards to appoint the AMA as certifier of all MD-granting institutions. The number of medical schools and medical students began declining precipitously thereafter, and the number of medical students did not return to its 1910 level for over thirty years. Only in the twenty-first century has the number of US medical schools rebounded to the 1910 level.

Present-day barriers in the US physician labor market

In the decades since the Flexner report, the AMA, together with the American Association of Medical Colleges (AAMC), has consolidated control over the training process for US physicians. Together they run the Liaison Committee on Medical Education (LCME), which manages the pipeline of new physicians into the US labor market. These organizations decide which medical schools deserve accreditation, impose strict caps on medical school class sizes, and limit residency program enrollment. The caps on medical school class size are strict enough that less than half of all applicants were admitted to US medical schools in each year from 2006 to 2010 (Vassev and Geraci 2010). There may be a pool of qualified individuals who would like to become doctors but do not have the opportunity to even begin the training process.

For physicians to practice on their own, they must obtain a license. In the US, states grant licenses to physicians who have successfully completed medical school, the first year of residency, and a national licensing examination. This is a significant constraint because physicians who attempt to practice without a license can be thrown in jail.

International medical graduates (IMGs) from overseas medical schools face additional barriers to entering the American physician labor market (Educational Commission for Foreign Medical Graduates 2012). Those without the legal ability to work in the US must vie for a limited number of H1-B visas for highly skilled immigrants. They must pass the same licensing tests required of American medical graduates and complete a US residency (even if they have been practicing successfully overseas for years). Non-native English speakers must also pass a clinical skills assessment testing their ability to interact with English-speaking patients. Meeting these requirements is an onerous process and a logistical challenge. While most tests are available online, the clinical skills assessment is only offered in five US cities and requires a fee of $1,350 as of 2012 (applicants are responsible for their own travel expenses). Over 40% of IMGs who apply for licenses to practice medicine in America ultimately do not succeed.

Some have called for nurses and physician assistants to play a larger role in providing health care in order to alleviate physician shortages or bring down prices, especially in rural areas where doctors are particularly scarce (Pohl et al. 2011). But the growing number of nurses who provide services traditionally performed by physicians also face barriers. Most states allow nurse practitioners to provide certain kinds of care such as managing diabetic patients, suturing minor wounds, or prescribing physical therapy. There are limits, though: nurses are not allowed to prescribe medication and physician assistants cannot conduct major surgeries.

Insurers, including Medicare and Medicaid, have policies that make it harder for nurses to compete. Medicare and other insurers routinely pay nurses less than licensed physicians for providing the same service, and many states require nurses to be supervised or associated with a physician in order to get payment. These policies prevent nurses from opening their own practices to compete directly with doctors, and put them at a competitive disadvantage.

Practitioners of alternative medicine, like chiropractors, homeopaths, and acupuncturists, also face barriers to providing services that compete with traditional, allopathic physician services (Anderson et al. 2000). All fifty states require chiropractors to be licensed, and many states also require acupuncturists to be licensed, further constraining the supply of health care providers.

The implicit tradeoff of barriers to entry

Barriers to entry in the labor market for physicians result in monopoly rents. Friedman and Kuznets (1945), Leffler (1978), Svorny (1987), and Anderson et al. (2000) all find evidence that various barriers to entry increase US physician salaries. Outside the US, the same story holds. Immigrant licensure policies create rents for physicians in Israel (Kugler and Sauer 2005) and a lottery for medical school admission in the Netherlands generates large rents for physicians there (Ketel 2011).

These rents, which are estimated to approach 25% of total physician compensation in some cases, are costly because they raise prices for anyone who seeks to purchase physician labor. In theory, a perfectly competitive labor market would dissipate these rents as more and more health care providers flood into the market, lowering prices for all consumers.

But training and licensure requirements for physicians have existed since ancient times (Leffler 1978). Why do they endure? Policies restricting entry into the physician labor market are defended by the AMA and others on the grounds that these policies assure high physician quality. The barriers are designed to ensure that anyone who completes medical school and becomes licensed to practice medicine is a qualified doctor. Unlike in the days before the AMA, dangerously unqualified people cannot offer medical services to unwitting patients.

In the typical market, consumers are given the prerogative to make determinations about supplier quality and make purchases accordingly. Consumers who demand high quality, pay for it with higher prices, while others may opt for lower-quality alternatives if the price is right. The market for physicians may be atypical though, because physicians offer a suite of complex services. If it is costly for consumers to distinguish good physicians from bad on their own, it may be worthwhile for consumers to defer to regulatory bodies like the AMA to decide which physicians should be allowed to practice.

Is it worth paying more for physician services (in the form of monopoly rents) if it means that consumers do not have to spend time or money investigating which physicians are qualified? This is the tradeoff a society weighs when it considers a licensure regime for physicians. If the search costs to consumers in an unregulated market exceed monopoly rents in a regulated market, then barriers to entry may improve welfare after all.

5.4   Physician agency

By stepping into a doctor's office, the patient is anointing the physician as an agent for his health. One major role of physicians is to advise patients about their health in settings where patients have very little technical knowledge about medicine. Physicians thus have a professional responsibility to serve as good stewards for their patients since it is difficult for patients to assess whether the doctor is doing the right thing. The patient hopes that the doctor will conduct himself "only for the good of [the] patients, keeping . . . far from all intentional ill-doing," in keeping with the Hippocratic Oath. Doctors who follow this dictum are good agents for their patients' health.

Physicians face incentives that may cause them to deviate from perfect agency. For financial, legal, or personal reasons, the physician might overprescribe procedures, underprescribe treatment, or not treat certain patients altogether. The next sections discuss why physicians may deviate from perfect agency in theory and practice. Chapter 15 explores these themes in the context of health policy.

Physician-induced demand

One of the primary things patients pay doctors for is information. Doctors are trained to interpret subtle signs and make treatment recommendations on that basis. Unless the patient is savvy about matters of health – what certain diagnoses mean and what the proper treatment should be – he is likely to be swayed by the doctor's recommendations. In a sense, the uninformed patient is at the mercy of his doctor.

This information asymmetry between doctor and patient creates an opening for doctors to prescribe more services than patients want or need. Doctors may not serve as perfect agents for their patients. Patients want good advice and treatment that maintains or restores their health. Doctors want this, but they may also design treatment with an eye toward other goals such as their own financial well-being. If so, a doctor may induce a patient to demand more than the patient would want if he were better informed. This phenomenon is called **physician-induced demand** (PID).

Definition | **5.4**

Physician-induced demand (PID): extra demand for medical goods and services induced by the advice of a physician who takes into account goals other than the patient's objectives, such as the physician's own financial gain (McGuire 2000).

Financial gain might motivate physicians to induce demand, but there are also costs to inducement (otherwise, doctors would induce without restraint or remorse). Evans (1974) posits that physicians suffer psychic costs such as guilt as a result of misleading patients away from their self-interest. Ethical norms and a particularly strong sense of professionalism among doctors tend to discourage inducement. Stano (1987a) draws an analogy between inducements and advertising. Like advertising, inducement increases demand but also consumes resources. So even the profit-maximizing doctor does not seek infinite inducement.

Another impediment to inducement is competition. When physicians have market power, they have strong incentives to induce, because they earn economic profits on each patient treated. In a competitive market, profits are zero, so there is nothing to gain from inducement to offset the psychic costs (Stano 1987b).

The empirical evidence suggests that physicians do indeed change their practices in response to financial incentives. Hickson et al. (1987) randomly assigned a group of pediatric residents to be either paid by a fixed salary or paid according to the number of services rendered. If these physicians were good agents for patient health, then we would expect the treatment patterns of the two groups to be statistically indistinguishable, because payment structure has nothing to do with patient health outcomes. But the evidence shows that fee-for-service physicians not only scheduled more visits per patient than salaried physicians did, they also scheduled more visits than were recommended by the American Academy of Pediatrics.

A separate observational study found that orthopedists and neurologists who owned their own MRI machines ordered more MRI tests than did physicians who had to refer patients to outside firms for MRI scans. Under the PID theory, the financial gain from billing for more diagnostic tests lured doctors into inducing more demand for MRI scans (Baker 2010). Mitchell (2008) tells a similar story about physician ownership of specialty treatment clinics. Physicians who recently became owners of back and spine clinics were more likely to recommend surgery than they were before owning their own clinics. Yip (1998) finds that thoracic surgeons compensated for a round of cuts to Medicare fees in 1990 by performing more surgeries.

The PID phenomenon poses a challenge for insurers who manage physician incentives through reimbursement policies. Setting high reimbursements could lead doctors to overprescribe certain procedures. But lowering reimbursements might cause physicians to switch patients to other, more lucrative services. The quandary of PID motivated Medicare actuaries in the late 1980s to lower surgical fees by an additional 6.5% to account for the anticipated volume inducements by physicians. The lack of evidence that volume actually increased for surgeries in subsequent years could suggest either that any effect of PID is small or that physicians opted to induce demand for more lucrative services whose fees had not been reduced (McGuire 2000).

Defensive medicine

PID occurs when physicians overprescribe treatment for personal financial gain, but there are other reasons why doctors might deviate from optimal medical practice. One theory proposes that doctors order superfluous tests or procedures to reduce the risk of medical malpractice lawsuits. This may manifest in extra diagnostic tests, low-value treatments, and even unnecessary invasive procedures. Doctors may also reject or refer away high-risk patients (or litigious ones) to reduce malpractice risk. This is known as **defensive medicine**.

Definition	5.5

Defensive medicine: deviations from optimal medical practice in order to reduce the risk of conflict with patients, especially in the form of malpractice lawsuits.

Fear of malpractice suits is not unfounded: medical errors do occur and invite liability lawsuits. Jena et al. (2011) find that between 1991 and 2005, 7.4% of all US physicians covered by a large liability insurer faced at least one malpractice claim in any given year. From these annual percentages, they extrapolate that 75% of physicians in low-risk specialties and 99% in high-risk specialties will have suffered at least one malpractice claim by the end of their careers. The average payout on successful claims was $274,887, though

78% of claims did not result in payouts. Even unsuccessful malpractice claims can still be injurious to physicians, as they still have the power to damage reputations and can require time and resources to defeat.

Physicians widely admit to practicing defensive medicine in this liability environment. Among high-risk practitioners in Pennsylvania, 93% of doctors surveyed reported practicing defensive medicine, 59% conducted more diagnostic tests than they thought were medically necessary, and 39% avoided caring for high-risk patients in order to reduce their exposure to liability (Studdert et al. 2005). Doctors practice defensive medicine in Europe too, even though malpractice litigation risk is lower there than in the US. Surveys of Dutch family physicians found that 17% of referrals and 27% of tests were ordered for defensive reasons, largely due to a desire to avoid personal conflicts with patients (Veldhuis 1994).

Survey data is self-reported, so the percentages might understate the degree of defensive medicine if physicians are not consciously defensive, or they might be inflated if physicians misidentify optimal medical behavior as defensive. Other researchers have relied on changing legal climates as natural experiments to measure the extent of defensive medicine. Throughout the 1980s, many states instituted caps on the damages patients could recover through malpractice suits as part of a broader movement towards tort reform. Some states adopted these reforms in the early days of the movement, while others adopted them later or not at all.

Several researchers have used this wave of tort reforms in the 1980s to study defensive medicine. Kessler and McClellan (1996) find that lower liability pressure as a result of the reforms led to a 5–9% decline in medical expenditures for patients with serious heart diseases. The lower expenditures did not produce significant effects on health outcomes. Helland and Showalter (2006), studying the same reforms, estimate that a 10% decrease in expected liability costs leads doctors to increase their work-hours by 2.85%. Apparently, capping liability did reduce the incentives of doctors to practice defensive medicine and even led some doctors to increase their caseload.

Mello et al. (2010) estimate that the financial costs as a result of the medical liability system in the US reached $55.6 billion annually in 2008 dollars or 2.4% of US health care spending. Their estimate includes the costs of actual payouts from malpractice claims, attorney fees, and higher medical costs due to defensive medicine, but omits social costs like the damage to reputation from liability suits, which are more difficult to quantify.

Another way that doctors respond to liability risk is through the purchase of liability insurance. Liability insurance, like health insurance, smooths consumption by charging a premium to doctors and reimbursing those doctors who face malpractice claims.[3] If liability insurance were full and could completely insure physicians from all the costs of malpractice claims, then there would be little incentive for doctors to practice defensive medicine.

Full liability insurance might induce another perverse incentive though. Rather than being overly cautious about care, fully insured doctors might be less diligent in protecting against errors, because the risk of malpractice now is shouldered entirely by their insurer. If so, full liability insurance might lead to more medical errors, more malpractice claims, and more malpractice payments. This is why liability insurers are reluctant to offer full malpractice insurance packages.[4]

---

3 See Chapter 7 for a more complete discussion.
4 See Chapter 11 for more about this tradeoff.

5.5   Racial discrimination by physicians

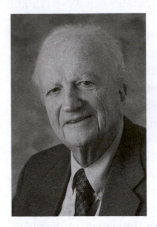

The difficulty patients face in assessing physician behavior opens the door for another pernicious consequence of physician agency – racial discrimination. If physicians harbor racial animus or act on unfounded stereotypes, minority patients may lose trust in their doctors' advice or receive worse care. Researchers have uncovered differential treatment rates by race in heart attack care, organ transplantation, and many other areas of medicine (Werner et al. 2005; Liu et al. 2011). Some have even proposed that racial discrimination by physicians is responsible for the health disparity between different racial groups noted in Chapter 4. However, racial differences in treatment may be an optimal response driven by biological or behavior differences, at least in some cases.

Types of discrimination

1992 Nobel laureate Gary Becker pioneered the application of economic principles to topics in sociology, including the study of racial discrimination. He is famous for what is known as the Rotten Kid Theorem. Credit: *Gary Becker.*

Discrimination by physicians might take a few different forms. Maybe some doctors prefer not to interact closely with black patients and cannot diagnose them or advise them effectively. Maybe they are less willing to exert themselves and do everything within their power to help black patients. These are theories of *taste-based discrimination*. Alternatively, doctors might treat black patients differently because of biological differences between races or because the doctors believe black patients are less likely to follow up with medications or other doctor's orders and are not good candidates for treatment in the first place. This is an example of *statistical discrimination*. The important distinction from a welfare point of view is between *efficient* discrimination and *inefficient* discrimination.

Definition	5.6

Discrimination: Racial discrimination in medicine, defined as differential treatment rates for different racial groups, can be the result of several forces including racial animus (taste-based discrimination) and stereotyping based on biological differences (statistical discrimination). Discrimination can be medically efficient or inefficient.

Taste-based discrimination: preferential medical treatment for certain groups of patients due to the tastes of the physician, whether conscious or subconscious.

Statistical discrimination: differential medical treatment for certain groups of patients based on stereotypes of their biological or behavioral tendencies.

Efficient discrimination: differential treatment by race that improves patient outcomes on average.

Inefficient discrimination: differential treatment by race that harms patients on average.

Evaluating treatment disparities

One of many realms in which racial differentials have been noted is treatment decisions for acute myocardial infarction (AMI). Shulman et al. (1999) conducted a study of physician practice patterns to measure this differential. In this study, they invented fictional patient histories involving angina pectoris, chest pain that may be an indicator of an impending AMI. The researchers then wrote an interview script for professional actors, some black and some white, to recite while being filmed sitting in a consultation room wearing a hospital gown. They created pairs of videos with identical transcripts, hand motions, and background props. In each pair of video clips, the only difference was the race of the "patient."

These patient history videos were shown to a sample of doctors, who were asked to make treatment recommendations for the hypothetical patients. The physicians, who were overwhelmingly white males, were significantly less likely to recommend black patients with chest pain for cardiac catheterization. This disparity arose despite the fact that the researchers designed the patient histories and interview transcripts to be identical across patients of different races.

This disparity in treatment is certainly evidence of discrimination – but what kind? The question remains whether the discrimination is taste-based or statistical and whether it leads to optimal or suboptimal outcomes for blacks and whites. Generally speaking, taste-based discrimination is inefficient because some factor other than a patient's welfare is affecting treatment decisions. Statistical discrimination, though, may be efficient if there is evidence that it makes medical sense to treat racial groups differently in some situations.

For example, medical research shows that optimal treatment for hypertension (high blood pressure) in black patients is different from the optimal treatment for whites. Gupta et al. (2010) argue that diuretics and ACE inhibitors should be used as first-line treatment for black hypertensive patients, while beta blockers and calcium channel blockers are the preferred treatment for white patients. In the case of hypertension, statistical discrimination actually saves lives.

Testing for inefficient discrimination

Chandra and Staiger (2010) attempt to determine whether the discriminatory prescriptions noted by Shulman et al. (1999) and others are efficient or inefficient using a subtle test. They analyze the medical records of black and white Medicare patients admitted to US emergency rooms suffering from AMI. They compare the rates at which black and white patients undergo procedures involving reperfusion (catheterization or open heart surgery). They find that black patients are slightly less likely to receive reperfusion than white patients, even after controlling other relevant risk factors. The differential reperfusion rates imply discrimination just like the Shulman et al. (1999) audit study.

Suppose this discrimination is the result of tastes, and also suppose that some patients can be expected to benefit more from reperfusion than others. Perhaps white doctors are willing to put in every effort to save white patients, and so recommend reperfusion even for white patients for whom it may only be marginally useful. Meanwhile, they only recommend reperfusion for black patients who will definitely benefit from it, and do not bother to treat marginal black patients who may not significantly benefit from reperfusion.

Under this hypothesis, the average benefit for black patients receiving reperfusion would be *higher* than white patients receiving reperfusion. Intuitively, this makes sense because, under this assumption, borderline white patients with bad prognoses are being included in the reperfusion group, while borderline black patients are not.

Surprisingly, the researchers find that reperfusion benefits black patients *less* than it benefits white patients; thirty-day survival rates among black patients are improved with reperfusion, but the improvement is larger for white patients. This evidence is inconsistent with the hypothesis of discrimination against blacks and even suggests the reverse: physicians are either overtreating black patients or undertreating white patients. This finding makes clear a weakness of the audit study approach, because it shows that differential rates of treatment do not necessarily imply harmful discrimination.

5.6   Conclusion

Periodically we hear reports of shortages of certain types of doctors: primary care physicians, family medicine doctors, and – increasingly, with our aging population – geriatric care specialists (see Chapter 19). In free markets, the concept of a supply shortage has little economic meaning in the long run. If people are clamoring for more supply (that is, if demand is sufficient), new suppliers will enter the marketplace.

As we have seen, the labor market for physicians does not quite work this way. Physician supply does not respond quickly to demand changes because there are so many impediments to new suppliers entering in any given specialty. The training process for new doctors is long and arduous, and residency is so specialized that doctors cannot switch readily from specialty to specialty when the market demands it. Finally, significant barriers to entry play a role in diminishing the number of doctors available.

These training requirements and other barriers limit the supply of doctors, but they also benefit patients like the 59-year-old stroke victim who opened this chapter. She can be confident that her doctors have been trained to provide good care.

But doctors, as central as they are to the health care system, are not the only players who contribute to her health. Physicians coexist with hospitals, insurance companies, and pharmaceutical developers that also play their own role in health care provision. In the next chapter we examine the economics of the hospital industry and its recent evolution.

5.7   Exercises

Comprehension questions

Indicate whether the statement is true or false, and justify your answer. Be sure to cite evidence from the chapter and state any additional assumptions you may need.

1 Physicians in the US are licensed to practice medicine immediately after they complete medical school.
2 The internal rate of return is defined as the interest rate that makes the net present value of an investment stream exactly equal to zero.
3 Consider two investment streams w and z which pay out some amount, $w(t)$ and $z(t)$, in each period t. (The amount may be negative in some periods.) If the interest rate is exactly equal to the internal rate of return of $w(t)$, the net present value of choosing w over z is zero.
4 The number of US medical schools decreased drastically between 1900 and 1950.
5 The full economic cost of medical school includes mainly tuition, room, and board for the school.

6 Compared with doctors who are paid on a fee-for-service basis by health insurers, doctors who are paid on a capitated (per-patient) basis have incentives to provide too much care.

7 In part, physicians' salaries are higher than secretaries' salaries because it takes more years to train to become a physician than it does to become a secretary.

8 The fact that practicing surgeons who have finished residency earn more than practicing pediatricians implies that the rate of return of choosing surgery exceeds the rate of return of choosing pediatrics for a medical school graduate.

9 Once length of residency and hours of work are taken into account, the internal rate of return of choosing a specialized branch of medicine over a more generalized branch is roughly equal to the real rate of interest in the economy.

10 If physicians are earning monopoly rents, then there must be more barriers to entry in the labor market for physicians than is socially optimal.

Analytical problems

11 **Fun with IRR.** Suppose you have just graduated from college and are deciding on a career. Your four career options, along with your salary in each of the four earning periods, are displayed in Table 5.3. Assume that any career will only last four periods before retirement.

Table 5.3. *Career options and salary information for Exercises 11 and 12.*

Occupation	Salary			
	Period 0	Period 1	Period 2	Period 3
Ophthalmologist	−5	1	10	12
Accountant	2	3	4	5
Starving artist	1	1	1	1
Sports superstar	15	0	0	0

a Assume your discount factor $\delta = 0.95$. Interpret this assumption.

b Find the value of the interest rate r that corresponds to your discount factor.

c Assuming $\delta = 0.95$, calculate the net present value (NPV) of becoming an ophthalmologist and of becoming an accountant. Which career do you prefer?

d Will the internal rate of return (IRR) for becoming an ophthalmologist as opposed to an accountant be greater or less than your answer to Exercise 11(b)?

e Now assume $\delta = 0.6$. Calculate both the corresponding interest rate and the net present value (NPV) of becoming an ophthalmologist and of becoming an accountant. Now which job do you prefer?

f Find the IRR for becoming an ophthalmologist as opposed to an accountant. That is, find a value of r^* that equates these two NPVs. [*Hint*: you will probably want to use a graphing calculator or an online equation solver to find r^*.]

12 **More fun with IRR.** Refer to Table 5.3 about the payouts available at different jobs.

a Find the IRR for becoming an ophthalmologist as opposed to a professional sports star. Compare your result with the IRR from the previous exercise and interpret this difference in terms of the concept of patience.

    b Find the IRR for becoming an accountant as opposed to an ophthalmologist. How can you interpret a negative IRR?

    c The IRR for becoming an accountant as opposed to a starving artist is infinite. Explain why this makes sense.

    d Does the NPV of salaries in the various professions tell you everything you need to know about picking a career? What does this calculation leave out?

13 In each of the following situations, indicate whether the physician's discriminatory action is taste-based or statistical.

    a An American physician detests interacting with French people, so she always gives French patients quicker examinations than she gives Americans.

    b A physician believes that Hispanic patients are less likely to follow through with an expensive therapeutic regimen that leads to major side effects, so he never prescribes it for them.

    c A surgeon has heard that it is very difficult for black patients to find bio-compatible matches on the kidney donor waitlist. As a result, he is more aggressive in trying to save a black patient's kidneys than a white patient's kidneys.

    d A hospitalist believes that the nurses at her hospital routinely discriminate against Asian patients due to subconscious racism. She always spends a little more time ensuring that her Asian patients are receiving the right medication.

Essay questions

14 A recent study by Prof. Jessica Reyes at Amherst College finds that female gynecologists (doctors who specialize in women's reproductive health) charge a standard fee for a basic patient visit that is $4.81 (on average) higher than male gynecologists charge. Furthermore, she finds that waiting lists to see female gynecologists are 1.14 weeks longer than waiting lists to see male gynecologists.

    a Give two possible explanations for Prof. Reyes' findings. One explanation should focus on the demand side of the market for gynecologists; the other should focus on the supply side.

    b Are the longer waiting times and higher fees for female gynecologists evidence that the market for gynecological services is not competitive? Give two answers to this question – one assuming that your demand-side explanation from Exercise 14(a) is correct, and one assuming that your supply-side explanation is correct.

    c Has Prof. Reyes uncovered evidence that there is discrimination in the residency training market for gynecologists? If so, is this discrimination against male gynecologists or female gynecologists? Again give two answers to this question – one assuming that your demand-side explanation from Exercise 14(a) is correct, and one assuming that your supply-side explanation is correct.

15 Below is an excerpt from the abstract of a 2002 journal article entitled "Does regulation affect economic outcomes? The case of dentistry" by Morris Kleiner and Robert Kudrle:

> Theory suggests that more restrictive licensing may raise prices and at the same time raise demand by reducing uncertainty about the quality of the services. This article uses unique data on the dental health of incoming Air Force personnel to analyze empirically the effects of varying licensing stringency

among the states. It finds that tougher licensing does not improve outcomes.

a   Explain the basic tradeoff a state makes when it tightens regulations on licenses for physicians, dentists, or any other professionals. What are the costs and benefits?

b   Kleiner and Kudrle find that cadets hailing from states with tougher licensing regimes for dentists do not have healthier teeth on average. Argue that the tougher licensing regimes might be efficient, even if those states also have higher prices for dental services.

c   Assume also that states choose strict or lenient licensure regimes at random (this is probably not the case), and that states with strict licensure have higher prices but no better dental health. Argue that the tough licensing regimes are inefficient.

d   Why could you not conduct a similar study about licensing regimes for physicians using the same data on US Air Force cadets?

Students can find answers to the comprehension questions and lecturers can access an Instructor Manual with guideline answers to the analytical problems and essay questions at **www.palgrave.com/economics/bht**.

THE HOSPITAL INDUSTRY

Today the mention of a hospital invokes the image of a pristine fortress with clean, white rooms and futuristic technology. It is bustling with nurses, physicians, surgeons, other specialists, and administrators taking care of patients and moving from task to task with clockwork efficiency. A hospital is a place where the sick seek state-of-the-art treatments for whatever ails them.

But today's hospitals would have astonished a visitor from the mid-1800s. In that era, hospitals were generally viewed as squalid places where only the most indigent, desperate members of society sought care. The density of patients packed into unkempt wards coupled with a primitive understanding of germ theory led to higher mortality rates after surgery in hospitals than in homes. Unsurprisingly, members of the upper and middle classes did their best to avoid the hospital, and since most doctors made home visits or held private practices, avoiding the hospital was never all that difficult for those who could afford it (Starr 1982).

Several innovations arrived in the late 1800s to fundamentally transform hospitals. The introduction of anesthesia turned surgery from brutal and risky to life-saving and humane. Aseptic techniques motivated by a better understanding of germs ensured that surgeries proceeded only in sterile environments. The invention of X-ray technology in the 1890s further enabled doctors to diagnose and treat disease and injury.

The dramatic increase in the power of surgery also demanded dramatically more resources – surgeons needed sterile rooms in which to operate, the support staff to conduct these operations, and beds to monitor patient recovery. By the early 1900s, hospitals were becoming the places for medical care, and the earlier stigma associated with hospitals was starting to fade.

With higher costs, hospitals also began developing controversial ways of funding themselves. In the early 1900s, most hospitals were affiliated with religious institutions, and most refrained from charging fees to poorer patients who stayed in densely packed wards rather than private rooms. Some hospitals operated by soliciting donations from altruistic patrons, others by charging richer patients for staying in private rooms. Modern hospital financing looks very different. Insurance systems are responsible for almost all payments. Increasingly, hospitals are adopting for-profit models and eschewing the traditional nonprofit model of religious charity.

6.1 The rise and decline of the modern hospital

The Hill-Burton Act and the rise of the hospital

Scientific progress, such as the discovery of penicillin and other advances, transformed the hospital from simply a place to die into a vital input into improving the health of a population. By the middle of the twentieth century, there was growing concern that there was an insufficient number of hospitals in the US to adequately care for everyone, especially in rural areas. Furthermore, the rising costs of care put hospitals increasingly out of reach of the poor, even in cases of medical emergencies.

In 1946, the US Congress passed the Hill-Burton Act which was designed to address both of these problems. The Act provided substantial monies for the building of hospitals around the country with a preference toward underserved rural areas. Furthermore, the Act mandated that any hospital accepting Hill-Burton money would be required to provide free or low-cost care for the poor and indigent. Federal funding and the rise in demand together inspired a spree of hospital building around the country which continued more or less unabated until 1974 (Figure 6.1). The number of hospitals increased by 16% and the total number of hospital beds by 12% during this period.

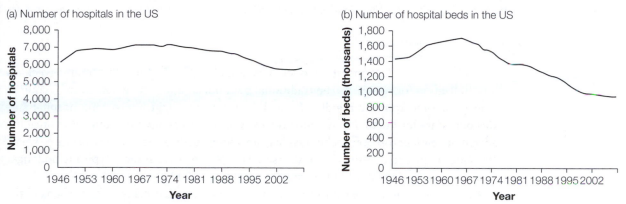

Figure 6.1. *Recent trends in US hospitals. (a) Number of hospitals in the US. (b) Number of hospital beds in the US.*

Source: Data from American Hospital Association (2010).

The transition to outpatient care

In 1974, the number of hospitals peaked and has been declining ever since. In fact, the probability of being hospitalized in any given year has dropped sharply since then as well. Even as the number of hospitals and hospital beds was growing in the mid-1900s, the average length of a hospital stay has steadily declined since 1946 (Figure 6.2). In American hospitals, average lengths of stay are the shortest in the developed world. Hospitals are still important providers of inpatient care for the severely ill and they continue to generate enormous expenditures. However, hospitals no longer play the predominant role in providing medical care. Instead, a large portion of medical care now takes place outside the hospital, in outpatient clinics.

There are at least two important reasons for the decline of inpatient care, one technological and one economic.

Many of the scientific advances in medical care over the past decades have made it possible to perform services that previously required overnight hospital care in outpatient settings; hospitals are therefore less necessary than they once were. One good example of technological change is the development of laparoscopic surgery. In laparoscopic surgery, surgeons rely on a small camera, rather than a gaping incision, to see into the patient's body. It came into widespread use during the 1980s and 1990s and has greatly shortened the recovery time for many surgeries.

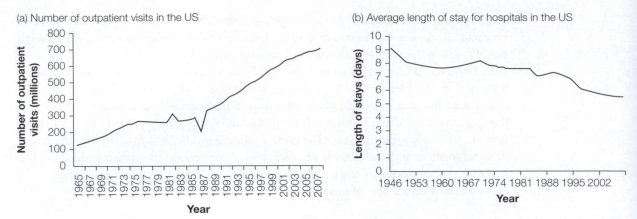

Figure 6.2. *Recent trends in US hospitals. (a) Number of outpatient visits in the US. (b) Average length of stay for hospitals in the US.*

Source: Data from American Hospital Association (2010).

Cholecystectomy, an operation to remove the gallbladder, historically required weeks of hospitalization for recovery. The traditional method, an open cholecystectomy, required a deep incision from the middle of the abdomen to the right hip. A long hospital stay was necessary for doctors to monitor recovery and to treat any infections. But since the advent of new laparoscopic techniques, a gallbladder can be removed with just three small, strategically-placed incisions in most cases. This less invasive surgery typically no longer requires an overnight stay in the hospital (Ahmad et al. 2008).

A second reason for the transition to outpatient care is that insurers have changed the way they compensate hospitals. These changes have made hospital stays, especially long ones, less lucrative for hospitals, particularly in the US. In 1984, the US Medicare program, which provides universal health insurance coverage for the elderly, introduced a prospective payment system for hospital reimbursement known as the diagnosis-related groups (DRG) payment system (Cutler 1995). Prior to this change, hospitals were paid on a fee-for-service (FFS) basis for each day that a patient stayed in the hospital and for each service performed. Since fees were set above marginal cost, hospitals had financial incentives to provide even marginally necessary services and extend hospital stays. Before the DRG system, Medicare faced all the financial risks associated with ongoing hospital stays.

Under the DRG system, hospitals receive a fixed fee that depends on the patient's diagnosis at the time of hospital admission and on nothing else. In particular, hospitals do not receive extra payment if the patient stays in the hospital for a long time or receives costly services. Unlike with the FFS system, the hospital bears the majority of the financial risk associated with long hospital stays. Perhaps unsurprisingly, the introduction of the DRG system preceded a sharp drop in the average hospital length of stay in the US (see Figure 6.2). In subsequent years, many European health systems with private hospitals have moved towards a DRG system.

In contrast with the US, Japanese hospitals are still paid on an FFS basis (though recent reforms have introduced a partial and voluntary system of prospective payment). Though Japan's average length of stay has declined over the past decades, presumably because of advances in medical technology, it is still substantially higher than the average length of stay in the US. Under Japan's fee-for-service payment system, hospitals have little incentive to avoid lengthy hospital stays (see Chapter 17).

Despite all the technological advancements of the last century, hospitals remain dangerous places. They are still places where sick people are housed in close quarters and can spread diseases to one another. Hospitals are also breeding grounds for drug-resistant bacteria that threaten the health of the elderly and the immuno-compromised. Given these considerations, the recent trend away from inpatient care to outpatient care is welcome.

6.2   The relationship between hospitals and physicians

Today, the modern hospital combines the great expertise of medical professionals with expensive technologies. Running a large hospital is a coordination challenge that requires extensive manpower for tasks such as managing the operating room, conducting blood tests and X-rays, and dispensing drugs.

People tend to think of "good hospitals" as ones with excellent physicians who are well trained and have decades of experience in their various medical specialties. But while the physician may be the face of the hospital in the patient's mind, it is a vast support staff of nurses, orderlies, clerical workers, and executives who keep the hospital running. We will see that hospitals are organizations that can learn from experience just as physicians do. A good hospital is not necessarily the one with the best doctors, but the one whose doctors and support staff work together best.

The internal organization of hospitals

Harris (1977) argues that hospitals should be thought of as two separate economic entities: the physician staff and the administrative staff. The physician staff treats patients and demands medical goods and services like syringes, MRI tests, operating rooms, and nursing care. The administrative staff consists of nurses, executives, and other hospital employees who work to supply these inputs demanded by physicians. The physician staff and administrative staff face different incentives but are together responsible for the decisions made by hospitals, such as the adoption of new technologies.

Unlike the administrative staff, physicians are often not direct employees of the hospital. In the US, physicians may run their own private practices but refer their sickest patients to hospitals. Then as part of their relationship with the hospital, the physicians can use its resources to continue treating their patients. The patient or his insurance continues to pay the physician and pays the hospital separately for its facilities. The administrative staff does not interfere with the doctor's treatment of patients. Given the power that doctors often wield in hospital settings, hospitals have long been known as the "physicians' workbench."

The fact that doctors are not employees of the hospitals tends to undermine their incentive to control hospital costs. Instead, doctors plead with hospital administrators to adopt every technological innovation to treat their patients, even if they are expensive or useless. The hospital administrators control the budget but typically lack the medical knowledge to judge the relative value of different innovations for patient health. This bargaining process between doctors and administrators can result in wasteful spending to install cost-ineffective technology. This allocation of decision power has been cited as a possible explanation for why hospital costs have grown so much in past decades.

In practice, there are three different models of the relationship between physicians and hospitals. The first is the "physician's workbench" relationship, described by the Harris model, in which hospitals provide a place for physicians to do their work, but do not directly employ them. The Harris model describes most American hospitals reasonably well.

The standard example of learning comes from a pin factory described in Adam Smith's Wealth of Nations *(1776). Specialization of labor within the factory enabled workers to become better at a very specific task – like straightening a wire or sharpening the point of a pin – through repeated practice. Credit: © Georgios Kollidas – Fotolia.com.*

The second type of relationship between physicians and hospitals involves physicians as direct employees of a hospital or hospital system. In the UK, for instance, most physicians are employees of the National Health System, which runs most of the nation's hospitals. This type of arrangement is becoming more popular in the US as well, even at private hospitals.

The final type of relationship involves physician ownership of hospitals, which is traditionally justified as a way to avoid the commercialization of medicine (Rodwin and Okamoto 2000). In Japan, for example, it is a common for a physician or a small group of physicians to own small hospitals and clinics.

These alternate types of relationships avoid the conflict of interest between physicians and administrators. But because doctors must also be mindful of costs, there is the potential that doctors will fail to serve as ideal agents for their patients. For instance, sometimes doctors may choose to save the hospital money rather than exploring every possible avenue of treatment.

The volume–outcome relationship and learning by doing

Within hospitals, economists have long noticed a positive correlation between the number of cases and the outcome of those cases. For example, surgeons and hospitals who perform the same procedure over and over again seem to have better post-operative results and fewer complications. This relationship between volume and outcome is called the **volume–outcome relationship**.

Definition	6.1

Volume–outcome relationship: the observed positive correlation between the number of procedures performed (volume) and patient outcomes.

One hypothesis for the volume–outcome relationship is *learning by doing*, the process whereby people get better at doing tasks they perform repeatedly. To what extent can the volume–outcome relationship be attributed to learning by doing? It certainly seems plausible for surgical teams who complete a complex procedure nearly every day to outperform teams at hospitals who complete the same procedure only a few times a year.

On the other hand, the volume–outcome relationship may be the result of selective referral patterns: doctors may prefer to direct their patients to the most highly skilled surgeons. Even if there is no learning by doing, this selective referral hypothesis would explain the volume–outcome relationship. The best surgeons, who tend to have the best patient outcomes, receive the most referrals, and as a result, a positive relationship emerges between volume and outcomes. Under this alternate hypothesis, the direction of causation is reversed from learning by doing: variation in outcome causes variation in volume and not the other way around. Both the learning-by-doing hypothesis and the selective-referral hypothesis seem plausible, and evidence has been found in support of both (Luft et al. 1987).

Recent studies have highlighted the fact that the strength of the volume–outcome relationship in hospitals varies dramatically across different procedure types. Birkmeyer

Table 6.1. *Surgical mortality rates for various Medicare procedures, by hospital volume.*

Procedure	Hospital volume		
	Lowest 20%	Middle 20%	Highest 20%
Coronary-artery bypass grafting[a]	6.1	5.3*	4.8*
Aortic-valve replacement[b]	9.9	9.1*	7.6*
Carotid endarterectomy[c]	2.0	1.8*	1.7*
Pancreatic resection[d]	17.6	11.6*	3.8*
Nepherectomy[e]	3.6	2.7*	2.6*

[a] Coronary-artery bypass grafting (CABG) involves replacing one or more clogged coronary arteries, which provide blood to the heart muscle, with a vein typically taken from the thigh.
[b] The aortic valve mediates blood flow between the heart's left ventricle and the aorta, which is the biggest artery in the body. It can be replaced with a mechanical valve or an aortic valve from a pig or a cow.
[c] Carotid endarterectomy involves the removal of atherosclerotic plaque from the carotid artery in the human neck. The surgery requires partially blocking blood flow to the brain, so it must be completed quickly.
[d] The removal of part of the pancreas is a complex surgical procedure that typically takes several hours to complete. Cancer is a common reason why pancreatic resections are performed.
[e] Nepherectomy is the removal of the kidney: *-ectomy* means removal, and *nepher-* means kidney.
* Indicates statistically significant difference from hospitals with the lowest 20% of volumes.

Source: Data from Birkmeyer et al. (2002).

et al. (2002) use Medicare data from the 1990s and find evidence of volume–outcome relationships for all 14 procedures they study. A selection of their results is shown in Table 6.1. Even in the sample, substantial variation exists: the correlation is stronger for pancreatic resection than it is for carotid endarterectomy. Meta-analyses of volume–outcome studies similarly find wide variation by procedure type (Halm et al. 2002).

Hospital experience versus physician experience

It is clear that *hospital* volume is correlated with outcomes. It is also true that *physician* volume is correlated with outcomes. Which one is more closely related? A recent study compares the volume–outcome relationship for individual physicians with the volume–outcome relationship for hospitals. McGrath et al. (2000) study the outcomes of Medicare patients undergoing percutaneous coronary intervention (PCI) to unclog their coronary arteries, tracking both 30-day mortality and the rate of follow-up coronary artery bypass graft (CABG) surgery. If a patient needs CABG surgery soon after a PCI, it is an indication the PCI failed to keep the coronary artery unclogged, so the need for CABG can be seen as evidence of an ineffective PCI.

In both cases, patients experience significantly worse outcomes when served by low-volume providers compared with high-volume providers. But as is apparent in the data, the volume–outcome relationship for hospitals is greater in magnitude. For instance, an increase in hospital PCI volume from 75 to 200 annually results in a decline in 30-day mortality from about 4% to 3%, while a similar increase in physician PCI volume is not associated with any decrease. In the case of PCI, the experience of the hospital seems to be more important than the experience of the attending surgeon.

The finding that hospital experience matters so much might be surprising, but it makes sense as surgeries are complicated exercises that require the coordination of several hospital employees, not just the leading physician. A typical procedure involves not only the surgeons, anesthesiologists, and nurses present in the operating room, but also pharmacists and operating assistants who gather the tools and information for the doctors.

And after the surgery, a separate post-operative team might be managing the patient's recovery.

Errors may occur before, during, and after a surgery. For instance, before a cataract surgery on a patient's left eye, the surgeon might mistakenly mark the patient's right eye for operation. During the actual surgery, the anesthesiologist might overdose the patient. And after the surgery, the team caring for the patient might not have been told about the patient's diabetes, resulting in a medication error. De Vries et al. (2010) estimate that more than half of all surgical errors actually occur outside the operating room.

A key to preventing these errors is often to implement systems at the hospital level that require multiple people to double-check each step of the patient's care. De Vries et al. find that hospitals perform significantly better when employing a checklist system designed to promote communication between the different hospital employees involved in any surgery. Given the coordination across the hospital that is necessary to care for a patient, it is not surprising that organizations appear to gain from learning by doing as much as or more than individual doctors do.

The rise of the hospitalists

Despite the well-documented benefits of learning by doing, few doctors in the US specialized exclusively in hospital care before the mid-1990s. Such specialists, known as **hospitalists**, had existed in Canada and the UK before this time, but almost all hospitalized patients in the US were cared for by their primary care doctor, rather than an in-house physician specializing in hospital care (Wachter and Goldman 1996).

Since the mid-1990s, the hospitalist model has experienced tremendous growth in the US. These hospitalists perform the same types of procedures as primary care doctors, but only treat patients who have been hospitalized. Several reasons have been proposed for this change, including cost pressures on physicians and hospitals, increased time burdens on primary care physicians, and the declining role of inpatient care within the medical system (Wachter and Goldman 2002). The evidence on learning by doing in medicine may also be motivating this shift. There is much potential for learning by doing by hospitalists, who typically spend six months or more of the year in hospital settings. Their experience may make them more efficient at treating hospitalized patients than non-hospitalists who only treat inpatients sporadically.

A meta-analysis of 33 studies published between 1998 and 2008 shows that hospitalists usually outperform their non-hospitalist counterparts, such as community doctors and general internists, in terms of reducing patient length of stay and lowering total medical expenditures at hospitals (Peterson 2009). A few studies also show better mortality outcomes for patients treated by hospitalists. Most of these studies feature randomized assignment of patients to hospitalists and non-hospitalists, so they provide strong causal evidence of the benefits of treatment by specialists.

Another hypothesized benefit to having hospitalists care for inpatients is that hospitalists tend to be more rapid and efficient adopters of new technologies. One possible mechanism is that hospitalists have greater incentive to stay abreast of advancements in the care of inpatients, because that is their focus. This willingness to try new technologies can benefit other patients in the same hospital. Because hospitalists are around the hospital continuously, they are more likely to develop social networks along which knowledge can diffuse (Meltzer 2009).

Health economist and physician David Meltzer relates the story of the adoption of low-molecular-weight heparin (LMWH), a drug used to treat stroke patients, at the University of Chicago Medical Center. A single hospitalist learned about the drug and was the first to use it on a patient at the center. Other doctors, including non-hospitalists and trainees who were on the team caring for that patient, observed this and subsequently rotated onto new teams in the months that followed. They, in turn, introduced LMWH to their new colleagues, further spreading knowledge of the drug throughout the hospital.

6.3   The relationship between hospitals and other hospitals

Like suppliers in other industries, hospitals compete with one another for customers – in this case, patients. But several characteristics about the market for health care make hospital competition dissimilar from competition in other industries.

First, in some countries, access to health care is seen as a basic right, and hospitals are forbidden from denying anyone care. Second, building and staffing a new hospital requires high initial investment costs and often some form of government approval. These high barriers to entry can impede competitors from entering the market. Lastly, the ubiquity of insurance in this market distorts the typical economics of supply and demand. As a result of these quirks in the hospital market, the standard analysis of competition must be amended.

Differentiated product oligopoly

Many economic theories start with the assumption that markets are perfectly competitive. While no market is truly *perfectly* competitive, the market for hospitals strays further away from this ideal than most. For one, entry is not easy. New hospitals have to invest substantial funds in erecting buildings, installing technologies, and hiring physicians and administrators. Governments also regulate the entry of health care providers. In most US states, firms are required to obtain a Certificate of Need approval from the state government before building a new hospital or expanding an existing one. These barriers restrict entry into the hospital market, so there are often only a few hospitals competing for patients in a given geographic area. Economists typically model these markets as *oligopolies* (Gaynor and Town 2013).

Additionally, hospitals are not perfect substitutes for one another. Each hospital may appear superficially similar – they all have operating rooms and radiology labs – but in fact they differ on both the set of services they offer and the quality of each service.

The type of care a heart attack victim receives in the emergency room may depend on whether the hospital is equipped with a catheterization lab (McClellan et al. 1994). Even two hospitals with catheterization labs may provide different quality of care depending on which hospital's staff and doctors are more experienced.

And even if the standard of medical care is exactly equal across hospitals, patients may have some loyalty to their own physician or a surgeon they worked with in the past. Patients also live different distances away from different hospitals. Especially in an emergency, travel time can differentiate the services of each hospital.

Because of the barriers to entry and the differences between suppliers, economists model the hospital market as a **differentiated product oligopoly**.

Definition	6.2

Differentiated product oligopoly: a model of competition in which there are few firms as a result of barriers that restrict entry, and in which the products supplied by the firms are not perfect substitutes for each other.

Suppose that the marginal cost of performing a hip replacement surgery is $10,000. This includes the cost of all the resources necessary for the operation: alcohol swabs, a surgeon's time, medical imaging equipment, and everything else. Further suppose an avaricious hospital tries to make more money by charging $11,000 for each hip replacement surgery it conducts. In a perfectly competitive market, this move would be economically suicidal: a new hospital would enter the market, charge $10,500 for the same procedure, and attract every last customer from the first hospital. Other firms would enter until the price stabilizes at $10,000.

But this story relies on two critical assumptions: easy entry of new firms and the identicalness of goods. As we have discussed, neither assumption holds in a differentiated product oligopoly. As a result, a hospital in an oligopoly might get away with charging $11,000 without losing all its customers. Some customers may stay because they feel a loyalty to their longtime hospital, believe that the hip replacement offered by this hospital is superior, or are unwilling to travel to more distant hospitals for a discount. Furthermore, it may be infeasible for an enterprising firm to build a new hospital to undercut the expensive one.

Because oligopolistic firms are not simply price-takers, but can instead price above marginal cost and earn positive economic profits, they are said to have *market power*. Firms that have market power face downward-sloping demand – unlike firms in perfectly competitive markets, a firm with market power can raise prices without losing all its customers. Market power is undesirable for society because it leads to high prices for consumers, less productive output, and lower social welfare.

Oligopolistic firms wield some market power, but their power is limited because, unlike monopolists, they do face some competition. Suppose the same hospital decided to charge $1,000,000 for each hip replacement surgery in an attempt to leverage its market power. Now many or all of its patients would probably leave, even if they live far from other hospitals or feel an intense loyalty to their doctors.

Because there are few firms in oligopoly markets, it might become possible for all firms to cooperate, agree to maintain high prices together, and split up the available profits. This practice, called *collusion*, is forbidden by governments because it exacerbates the social welfare loss from oligopoly. But it still might happen illegally if firms can communicate in secret or tacitly signal their intentions to each other through prices. Strategic behavior by oligopolists can also be non-cooperative. For example, incumbent firms may temporarily lower prices below marginal cost to bankrupt competitors and extend their market power. Strategic pricing behavior cannot happen in perfectly competitive markets, since prices are constrained to equal marginal cost.

Oligopoly markets fall somewhere between perfectly competitive markets and monopolies. Oligopolies cause the same problems that monopolies do (high prices and low output), but due to the presence of limited competition, these problems are not as severe with oligopolies as they are with monopolies.

To determine whether hospital markets are oligopolies as theory suggests, economists use a measure of market concentration called the **Herfindahl–Hirschman Index** (HHI), which ranges between 0 and 1. A low HHI indicates that a market is fairly competitive, with customers spread out evenly across many firms. A high HHI means that a small group of firms dominates the market, and may indicate an oligopolistic market.

Definition | **6.3**

Herfindahl–Hirschman Index: a measure of market concentration. It is the sum of the squared market shares of all of the firms in a market:

$$HHI = \sum_i s_i^2$$

where s_i is the market share of firm i. The highest possible HHI is 1, indicating that one firm controls the entire market. Theoretically, the lowest possible HHI is 0, indicating an infinite number of firms with infinitely small market shares.

The US Department of Justice and the Federal Trade Commission, which share responsibility for regulating competition in markets, label a market as "concentrated" if its HHI is greater than 0.18, and "highly concentrated" if its HHI is greater than 0.25. By this measure, hospital markets in the US are not very competitive: the HHI for the hospital market in the average American metroposition area was 0.33 in 2006 (Gaynor and Town 2013).

This evidence suggests that hospitals do indeed have some market power and there may be too little competition in hospital markets. If so, policies aimed at increasing competition will lead to lower prices and better outcomes for patients. But hospital markets have another unusual property: incomplete price competition. Unlike nearly all other markets, markets with this property do not necessarily benefit from more competition.

Price competition

In most markets, suppliers attempt to attract customers by offering lower prices than their competitors. In perfectly competitive markets, and even to some extent in oligopolistic markets, consumers punish firms that charge high prices by taking their business elsewhere. If a drug store decides to start charging $100 for a generic painkiller, customers would quickly abandon that store and buy their painkillers elsewhere. Price competition keeps markets efficient by forcing firms to offer their clients good value or face the risk of bankruptcy. But when price competition is limited, this check on inefficiently high prices may disappear.

Insurance, which is ubiquitous in health care markets generally and hospital markets specifically, can interfere with price competition and may eliminate it completely. For example, patients in the US covered by Medicare pay only a fixed amount per hospital visit, and medical costs in the UK are completely covered by the National Health Service (NHS). Thus, insured patients have diminished incentive to search for the lowest-cost providers. If most of the burden of higher medical prices is shouldered by the insurer, then patients may be indifferent between expensive and inexpensive hospitals. This distortion of incentives for insured patients is known as *moral hazard*, a phenomenon that appears again and again in health care markets (see Chapter 11).

Moreover, search costs are often high and price information can be hard to come by. In emergencies such as a heart attack, the patient is rushed to the nearest emergency room, without concern for price. And in most medical situations, the full price of treatment is usually uncertain, depending on a yet-unknown diagnosis and various complications that arise during treatment.

In many health care systems, medical prices are actually set by the government. For example, Medicare and Medicaid in the US determine at the beginning of each year how much it will pay for each group of treatments for a subset of the American population. Similarly the UK's NHS determines the payment for hospital care. In these cases, hospitals cannot lower prices to attract more patients. But more generally, even when payers are not unilaterally setting hospital prices, the presence of insurance always undermines price competition.

Price competition is not totally absent in hospital markets though. For instance, any patient who must cover some of the costs of her own care – usually in the form of a copayment – still has some incentive to avoid pricey hospitals. And insurers themselves also foster price competition by directing patients to less expensive hospitals. For instance, managed care organizations (MCOs) in the US operate by restricting enrollees to a list of approved health care providers. MCOs often exclude expensive hospitals from their lists to maintain lower costs.

Quality competition

What happens when hospitals are no longer forced to compete on price? They tend to raise prices and compete with each other on quality instead. Quality is a broad concept that encompasses many aspects of a hospital visit, including the comfort of hospital beds, the availability of advanced technologies, and even the effort or vigilance of the staff. If a hospital can get away with charging high prices, it can attract patients with lavish, high-quality care and then charge them or their insurers a fortune for their stay.

The higher quality also serves to convince physicians to refer their patients to those hospitals. Hospitals offering the highest quality attract the most patients, while hospitals with the least lose patients, money, and may even have to shut down. When there are many hospitals competing for the same set of customers, a never-ending race for the best medical technology can develop. This is known as the **medical arms race hypothesis** (Dranove and Satterthwaite 2000).

Definition | **6.4**

Medical arms race hypothesis: hospitals compete on quality by adopting the best medical technologies available to appeal to physicians and their patients. This competition results in a race for each hospital to have the best medical technologies available and may cause overconsumption of medical technology.

If the medical arms race hypothesis is true, then competition among hospitals can be bad for society. The more hospitals compete with each other, the more frenzied the arms race becomes. Each hospital purchases expensive machinery, and redundancy occurs as multiple hospitals invest in the same fixed costs. Moreover, if physician-induced demand is present, then access to medical resources makes the use of such resources more frequent, even if that use is extraneous. So the excess technologies may also increase consumption, and health care expenditures will rise without corresponding improvements in health outcomes.

Empirical investigations into the medical arms race hypothesis have returned mixed findings. Most studies use positive correlations between competition in an area and the costs per admission as proxy evidence for a medical arms race. A hospital competing with many other hospitals in the area would invest more in medical resources and also generate higher expenditures per patient. Indeed, Robinson and Luft (1985) find that US hospitals in more competitive markets have higher expenditures. These hospitals also tend to have higher ratios of employees to patients, more angioplasty and coronary bypass facilities, and more mammography, heart surgery, and catheterization services (Robinson 1988; Robinson and Luft 1987; Luft et al. 1987).

Yet, the extent of the medical arms race might have shifted over time as a result of changes in the competitive landscape. For example, the increased popularity of MCOs during the 1980s in the US might have tamped down the medical arms race. Because MCOs vertically integrate the payer and provider of health care, they are sensitive to both hospital costs and patient bills. This sensitivity may limit any medical arms race if hospitals are more reluctant to invest in expensive technologies. Zwanziger and Melnick (1988) studied California hospitals between 1983 and 1985 and found that the positive correlation between competition and costs found in 1983 disappeared by 1985. Connor et al. (1997) similarly found that the correlation for hospitals nationwide greatly subsided by 1994 (see Chapter 18 for more on MCOs).

If the US medical arms race has cooled, then more hospital competition may not increase social loss. Nonetheless, Devers et al. (2003), after interviewing hospital executives in 1996 and again in 2001, have found that hospitals may be reviving their non-price competition strategies. The authors attribute this change to the waning popularity of MCOs and the rise of outpatient clinics that also compete with hospitals for patients (Berenson et al. 2006). If so, a medical arms race may be brewing again.

Only rarely does the medical arms race devolve into open medical warfare.

Credit: Allen Cox.

However, Dranove and Satterthwaite (1992) argue that even those studies that find positive correlations between competition and per-patient hospital expenditures may not actually be evidence of a medical arms race. They propose an alternative explanation for the correlation. More hospitals within a region can arise as a response to greater demand there, and that higher demand alone can produce a positive correlation. Meanwhile hospitals in smaller markets face less demand and therefore less return to installing MRI machines, angioplasty facilities, and other technology investments. As a result, these hospitals are unlikely to adopt the new technologies as quickly.

Thus, a positive competition–cost correlation could be the result of differing regional demand and not a medical arms race. Dranove and Satterthwaite test their hypothesis by applying an empirical strategy that controls for traits of different regional markets, and they find little support for the medical arms race hypothesis, even before 1983.

Hospital competition and patient outcomes

Thus, the standard prediction that more competition will improve welfare in the face of oligopolistic pricing may not hold in this market. Under certain conditions, increased hospital competition may actually lower consumer welfare by worsening patient outcomes. The exact effect of competition can depend greatly on many variables in the market environment (Gaynor and Town 2013).

Kessler and McClellan (2000) study the impact of hospital competition on all non-rural Medicare patients in the US treated for acute myocardial infarctions (AMI). They compared patient outcomes and medical costs for treatment in regions with more competition and regions with less. At least since 1991, more competitive regions seem to yield better results, including both lower costs and lower patient mortality. This suggests that more competition improves welfare for AMI patients.

Gowrisankaran and Town (2003) also study AMI patients on Medicare but focus on a specific geographical area in California: Los Angeles County. Unlike Kessler and McClellan, they find worse mortality rates in the more competitive parts of the county. This difference may have arisen because the first study used nationwide data, whereas Gowrisankaran and Town examined only one small region. Together, the studies suggest that the relationship between hospital competition and patient outcomes is not clear.

Even in markets with private insurance, the effect of competition on patient outcomes is unclear. Escarce et al. (2006) track mortality for six conditions: AMI, hip fracture, stroke, gastrointestinal hemorrhage, congestive heart failure, and diabetes. They find that higher competition led to better mortality outcomes for five of the conditions in California and for all six conditions in New York. In contrast, mortality did not vary with the level of competition for any of the six conditions at hospitals in Wisconsin.

In the UK, most hospitals are government-run. Nonetheless, various government reforms have tried to inject some elements of competition into the market. For example, some reforms in the 1990s permitted competitive bidding by hospitals for government contracts. Others in the 2000s permitted patients to choose which hospitals they visited for surgery and granted more autonomy to hospital administrators.

Two studies focus on NHS reforms in the 2000s that permitted greater patient choice in hospitals and more autonomy in hospital administration, even while health care prices remained centrally decided by the government (Gaynor et al. 2010; Cooper et al. 2011). Both find that mortality rates from AMI were lower in markets in more hospital competition. However, Propper et al. (2008) studying the 1990s reforms find that competition reduced waiting times, but also raised patient mortality rates.

Learning by doing may also explain why greater competition among hospitals may hurt patient outcomes. When many hospitals compete in a local area for a fixed number of patients, the number of patients treated at each hospital is low, so opportunities for learning-by-doing are also few. Meanwhile, a monopolistic hospital may charge high prices, which lowers patient welfare, but may gain invaluable experience through access to a large number of patients, which benefits the local community and more than compensates for the high prices (Lakdawalla and Philipson 1998; Gaynor and Town 2013).

The ambiguous relationship between competition and patient outcomes has motivated all nations to regulate the hospital industry. Certain governments have even taken the step of nationalizing their hospital industries and eliminating private competition altogether. We discuss more specifically the merits and drawbacks of different policy choices in Chapter 15.

6.4   Nonprofits and hospital production

Another motivation for public involvement in the provision of health care is equity. The notion that everyone should have access to basic health care underlies laws in the US that forbid any hospital from denying emergency care to anyone for any reason, including inability to pay. In the UK, nearly all hospitals are government-run and publicly financed. Medical care at these hospitals is completely free to all citizens. In the US, public hospitals do charge their insured customers, but they offer free services to the indigent and usually provide the less lucrative services that private hospitals sometimes avoid (Horwitz 2005).

However, there is only a small percentage of public hospitals in the US, and these are typically run by state and local governments. In 2009, about 20% of American hospitals were publicly run. This may be one reason for the major presence of nonprofit firms in America's hospital industry. In the US, 75% of private hospitals were nonprofit in 2009 (American Hospital Association 2010).

In this section, we discuss the costs and benefits of nonprofit organization, as well as four prominent theories that seek to explain why nonprofits exist at all. The first three theories posit that altruistic preferences, government failure, and distrust of for-profits explain the existence of nonprofit firms. The final theory argues that nonprofits and for-profits are not all that dissimilar and that nonprofit status is an accounting technique motivated by a desire to evade corporate income taxes.

The costs and benefits of nonprofit organization

Unlike for-profit hospitals, nonprofit ones are exempt from certain taxes and are typically better able to attract donations because the government considers those contributions tax-deductible. However, in exchange for these benefits, nonprofits are forbidden from selling stock to raise capital or formally distributing profits to owners. Table 6.2 summarizes these costs and benefits, and Table 6.3 lists the four theories for the existence of nonprofits that we discuss next.

Table 6.2. *The costs and benefits of nonprofit status under US law.*

Benefits of nonprofit status	*Costs* of nonprofit status
• Exempt from corporate income taxes	• Forbidden from selling stock to raise capital
• Donors receive tax deduction for donations	• Cannot formally distribute profits to owners
	• Restricted to certain charitable activities

The government-failure theory

The government-failure theory of nonprofits predicts that nonprofit firms arise when the political process fails to provide as much of a charitable good or service as some members of the community would like to see. Some people gain utility if they know that homeless people in their city are receiving free medical care or if the local performing arts are thriving, even if they do not receive any direct benefits. In this case, the government responds to this altruistic sentiment by providing some subsidies for medical care and support for theater companies. Those people most interested in charitable services, though, may not consider these government efforts sufficient (Weisbrod 1975).

Mother Teresa was a Catholic nun who established orphanages in India and became world-famous for her ministry to the poor. She was outspoken in her belief that governments and other institutions fail to care for the poor.   Credit: © zatletic – Fotolia.com.

Some might donate their time and effort individually to make up the shortfall in charitable services provision, but many people might lack the requisite time or skills to contribute. Under this theory, a nonprofit firm is a vehicle to organize the labor and capital of the people who demand more charity. As long as donors are willing to support altruistic causes above and beyond what the government provides, nonprofit firms will exist to satisfy this demand.

The altruistic-motive theory

Alternatively, nonprofits may arise as a reflection of the goals of altruistic owners (Newhouse 1970; Rose-Ackerman 1996). Consider a hospital run by a board of trustees. The board wants the hospital to succeed financially, but may also be concerned with the quantity and quality of medical services provided, especially to individuals who cannot afford them at market rates. They are willing to accept reduced profits in exchange for more output or higher-quality output. If a firm cares about something other than profit, it is not behaving like the typical profit-maximizing firm that economists study.

A firm that is not interested solely in maximizing profit may organize as a nonprofit because of the costs and benefits outlined in Table 6.2. Nonprofit legal status can help the firm increase output by reducing tax liability and attracting donations. These extra funds can allow nonprofit hospitals to build a new wing, add extra beds, or install the latest medical technologies.

Asymmetric information and a failure of trust

Theoretically, nonprofit firms are not necessary to remedy shortfalls in government offerings or fulfill the goals of altruistic owners. For-profit firms could perform these functions as well; they could seek charitable donations and offer increased output while still making a profit. But Arrow (1963) argues that for-profit firms fail as charitable enterprises because of asymmetric information combined with a lack of trust. Donors may believe that for-profit firms are capable of high-quality charity work but do not trust these firms to use their donations exclusively for charity. It is difficult for donors to verify how exactly donations are put to use, and the firms have no reliable way to prove they are spending funds the way they claim. This lack of trust provides an opening for nonprofits to exist, because donors tend to trust the motivations of nonprofits more.

If this theory is correct, nonprofit firms should advertise their status whenever they interact with customers, because it is an advantage in attracting donations. However, David (2008) finds that few nonprofit firms in the hospital and nursing home sectors specifically call attention to their nonprofit status on their websites or in yellow page listings. This finding should be interpreted in light of the fact that donations make up only a small fraction of the operating budgets of firms in these industries.

Nonprofits as for-profits in disguise

All three of these theories assume that nonprofits and for-profits are different, and in particular that nonprofits offer more output either due to the altruism of their owners or their community. But are nonprofit and for-profit firms truly different, with different types of ownership, motivations, and ideals?

A fourth theory argues that nonprofit firms may just be for-profit firms in disguise (Brickley and Van Horn 2002). Recall that nonprofit firms are not permitted to have shareholders or generate positive monetary profits. This theory argues that owners and employees of the firm are effectively shareholders who capture the rents that would have been declared as profits by a for-profit firm. The "profits" are distributed not as stock dividends but rather as higher wages or non-monetary benefits like access to the company fleet. Under this theory, firms decide whether to organize as a for-profit or a nonprofit to maximize net returns to owners, shareholders, or employees based on the tradeoffs listed in Table 6.2 (?).

Lakdawalla and Philipson (1998) argue nonprofit status is actually a way for profit-maximizing firms to gain experience before switching to for-profit status. Fledgling firms initially organize as nonprofits and use the government tax breaks to lower operating costs. At this point, the inexperienced firm cannot generate substantial profits, so the costs of organizing as a nonprofit are small. Meanwhile, tax breaks enable them to expand output, which offers them experience and opportunities for learning by doing.

Once enough learning is accumulated and the firm can produce output more efficiently than its competitors, it may then switch to for-profit status to realize the newly possible profits. This hypothesis also explains why nonprofit and for-profit firms coexist in the hospital industry. The mixed production occurs because firms are at different stages of learning by doing.

Table 6.3. *Summary of theories for the existence of nonprofits.*

Theory	Argument
Government failure	Nonprofits exist to satisfy the demand for charity care above and beyond what the government provides
Altruistic motives	Some entrepreneurs have altruistic preferences (e.g. maximizing output, not profits) and organize nonprofits to achieve them
Asymmetric information	Nonprofits exist because donors cannot observe how for-profits will use their donations and do not trust them
For-profits in disguise	Nonprofits are actually profit-maximizing firms taking advantage of the legal benefits of nonprofit status

6.5 The relationship between hospitals and payers

Lastly, we discuss the economics of how hospitals are paid. In nationalized systems such as the UK and Sweden, the government decides how to fund hospitals. But in systems with private parties, payers typically negotiate with hospitals to decide the bill. We first introduce the idiosyncratic way that hospitals charge for their services in the US and then how those hospitals are actually paid. In Chapter 16 we discuss hospital payment in nationalized health systems in more detail.

The hospital bill

Hospitals bill for procedures according to a list of prices known as the charge description master or chargemaster. Each hospital manages its own chargemaster, and prices can vary tremendously from hospital to hospital, even within one region. In 2004, the chargemaster price for a chest X-ray ranged from $120 at San Francisco General to as much as $1,519 at Modesto Doctors Hospital (see Figure 6.3).

	SCRIPPS MEMORIAL LA JOLLA, San Diego	SUTTER GENERAL, Sacramento	UC DAVIS, Sacramento	SAN FRANCISCO GENERAL, San Francisco	DOCTORS, Modesto	CEDARS-SINAL, Los Angeles	WEST HILLS HOSPITAL, West Hills
Chest X-ray (two views, basic)	$120.90	$790	$451.50	$120	$1,519	$412.90	$396.77
Complete blood count	$47	$234	$166	$150	$547.30	$165.80	$172.42
Comprehensive metabolic panel	$196.60	$743	$451**	$97	$1,732.95	$576	$387.18
CT-scan, head/brain (without contrast)	$881.90	$2,807	$2,868	$950	$6.599	$4,037.61	$2,474.95
Percocet* (or Oxycodone hydrochloride and acetaminophen) one tablet, 5-325 mg	$11.44	$26.79	$15	$6.68	$35.50	$6.50	$27.86
Tylenol* (or acetaminophen) one tablet, 325 mg	$7.06	No charge	$1	$5.50	No charge	12 cents	$3.28

*Hospitals carry generic version, name brand, or both   ** Represents the added total of 14 tests that make up the comprehensive metabolic panel
Sources: Scripps Memorial La Jolla; Sutter General; UC Davis Health Systems; San Francisco General; Doctors Medical Center; Cedars Sinal Health Systems; West Hills Hospital and Medical Center

Figure 6.3. *Prices for common procedures from California chargemasters in 2004.*

Source: Lagnado (2004). Reproduced with permission.

The list prices from these chargemasters, however, do not necessarily correspond to the amount that insurers or patients are actually charged. Private insurance firms as well as Medicare and Medicaid usually negotiate large discounts from hospitals, so the prices they pay are typically much lower than the chargemaster amounts. On the other hand, uninsured patients lack the market power to negotiate such discounts and can receive the full brunt of the chargemaster fees (Reinhardt 2006).

An article from *The Wall Street Journal* from 2004 relates the case of an uninsured Virginian patient who received a bill of $29,500 for a cardiac catheterization, a stent procedure, and a one-night stay in the hospital. In comparison, Medicare would have reimbursed $15,000 for the same procedure and Virginia's Medicaid only $6,000 (Lagnado 2004). This example of higher charges for an uninsured patient is not singular. In 2004 on average, the prices charged to the uninsured were about 150% more than the charges Medicare recognized, and this gap had been growing since 1984 (Anderson 2007).

Even in the case of the uninsured, what hospitals charge and what patients pay may still be different. Partially, this may be due to the inability of some uninsured to finance the full bill. But increasingly in recent years, spurred on by negative publicity, hospitals have been more proactive in providing discounts to the uninsured (Tompkins et al. 2006). For example, the Henry Ford Hospital System in Detroit, Michigan, charges uninsured patients $1,650 for a colonoscopy even though the estimated total cost is $2,750 (Henry Ford Health System 2012).

While different hospitals may charge different prices according to their own chargemaster, a single hospital can also charge different insurers different prices for the same procedure. The payment received by the hospital from a specific insurer for each procedure or group of procedures is typically determined through an annual negotiation between the hospital and insurer. The resulting price schedule can depend greatly on the bargaining position of hospitals, so the same hospital might bill different insurers very differently (Ginsburg 2010).

For example, "star" hospitals such as Massachusetts General Hospital in Boston and the Cleveland Clinic in Ohio command higher payments from insurers because of their stronger bargaining position. If insurers were to balk at these high bills and deny their customers coverage at these hospitals, many enrollees would switch to other insurers that do cover the star hospitals. For similar reasons, hospital systems that negotiate as blocs can also extract more from insurers, because they can control supply for a larger region. Evidence from US hospitals between 2002 and 2003 supports these hypotheses. Star hospitals earned $6,700 more per patient than non-star providers, and hospitals in systems generated $180,000 higher monthly profits than standalone hospitals. The latter finding may explain a recent movement toward hospital mergers (Ho 2009).

Uncompensated care

Chargemasters describe how much patients and their insurers are charged for medical care, but it does not always reflect how much hospitals are paid for procedures. For example, for some uninsured patients, even a discounted bill may be too costly to bear. If not paid, the care for these patients goes **uncompensated**.

Definition | **6.5**

Uncompensated care: hospital costs that are not covered by out-of-pocket payments, public insurance, or private insurance.

Studies indicate that as much as 6–7% of hospital expenditures are uncompensated. One study estimates that uncompensated care for the non-elderly in the US totaled $49.4 billion from 1996 to 1998, and Medicare estimates uncompensated care for the whole population reached $20.8 billion in 1999 (Hadley and Holahan 2003).

Who pays for uncompensated care? The answer is not "nobody," of course. Hospital bills that go unpaid must be either taken out of hospital profits, subsidized (explicitly or implicitly) by the government, or passed on in the form of higher prices to other customers. It seems likely that each of these players – Medicare, Medicaid, local and state governments, hospital shareholders, and other, non-indigent hospital customers – absorbs at least some of the costs of uncompensated care (Hadley and Holahan 2003).

In the US, both Medicaid and state governments provide explicit subsidies for uncompensated care. Medicaid disproportionate share (DSH) payments are given to hospitals that provide substantial uncompensated care. These payments can serve as an incentive for hospitals to increase their indigent care (Duggan 2000). Certain state governments also levy taxes on insurance payments to hospitals to fund a program dedicated to medical education and uncompensated care (Vladeck 2006).

Additionally, Medicare and some local governments make payments that are ostensibly for other purposes but effectively help defray the cost of uncompensated care. Like Medicaid, Medicare has a DSH program with payments allotted to hospitals serving low-income Medicare beneficiaries. Because Medicare beneficiaries, by definition, all have insurance coverage, this is not explicitly a subsidy for uncompensated care, but the same hospitals that tend to serve low-income Medicare beneficiaries also tend to accumulate the greatest number of unpaid bills.

Cost-shifting

More generally, even for care that is not uncompensated, hospitals may be engaging in *cost-shifting*, using richer recipients to subsidize poorer recipients of care. This hypothesis, also known as *cross-subsidization*, implies that patients with health insurance pay more for hospital care than the uninsured do. This practice is not at all novel. As early as 1958, health economist Reuben Kessel advanced the hypothesis that hospitals charge the rich more in order to finance the health costs of the poor (Kessel 1958). In the words of one surgeon:

> I don't feel that I am robbing the rich because I charge them more when I know they can well afford it; the sliding scale is just as democratic as the income tax.
> I operated today upon two people for the same surgical condition – one a widow whom I charged \$50, the other a banker whom I charged \$250. I let the widow set her own fee. I charged the banker an amount which he probably carries around in his wallet to entertain his business friends.
>
> (Seham 1956 p. 22)

Researchers have also tried to determine the extent of cost-shifting in hospital payments. Cost-shifting is hard to observe or measure because it is rarely explicit, so researchers focused on uncovering indirect evidence of cross-subsidization. For example, David et al. (2011) study the reaction of hospitals in Colorado and Arizona that face new local competition from cardiac specialty centers. Because cardiology and cardiovascular treatment is a major source of net revenue for the typical community hospital, increased competition from specialty centers is likely to reduce profits significantly. The study found that hospitals facing new competition reduced their provision of psychiatric services, substance abuse care, and trauma care. These are relatively unprofitable services that tend to be offered disproportionately to the uninsured population and often result in unpaid bills. This is suggestive evidence that hospitals use profits from lucrative services to subsidize uncompensated care.

If cross-subsidization is happening, which payers are subsidizing which others? Melnick and Fonkych (2008) study billing and payment data from California hospitals between 2001 and 2005. To compare the relative financial contributions of different payers, they calculate a *collection ratio*: revenue actually collected divided by the total chargemaster bill (their results for 2005 are listed in Table 6.4). The collection ratios for all groups – the privately insured, the uninsured, and those covered by Medicare or Medicaid – are far below

Table 6.4. *Collection ratio at California hospitals by insurance type, 2005.*

Insurance type	Collection ratio*
Private insurance	38%
No insurance	29%
Medicare	27%
Medi-Cal (California Medicaid)	23%

* The collection ratio is defined as the total revenue actually collected by the hospital divided by the official chargemaster bill for the procedures performed. These two numbers tend to differ due to negotiated discounts, patient bankruptcy, inability to pay, or refusal to pay.

Source: Data from Melnick and Fonkych (2008) analysis of Office of Statewide Health Planning and Development (OSHPD) Annual Hospital Financial Data.

100%, which means that hospitals collect far less for each procedure on average than the chargemaster would suggest. Additionally, the evidence that the collection ratio of those with private insurance is greater than among other groups suggests that patients with private insurance may be cross-subsidizing uninsured patients and patients with Medicare or Medicaid. Separate studies agree that cross-subsidization occurs in hospitals but argue that the effect tends to be small generally except in markets with less competition (Frakt 2011; Robinson 2011).

Meanwhile, in countries where the government pays for all medical care, such as the United Kingdom and Sweden, cost-shifting occurs well before the hospital visit. In these systems, hospital payments come not directly from patients at the point of service but instead from tax revenues. Progressive tax systems ensure that the burden of funding health care falls more on the wealthy than the poor.

6.6   Conclusion

Though hospitals may not have been the place to find effective cures at the start of the twentieth century, they are now technological marvels. Conditions that were once impossible to treat are now routinely cured, and surgeries that used to be unimaginable are now commonplace.

The technological advances of hospitals have not come cheaply: expenditures have exploded around the world. Some of the rise in costs reflects improvements in technology that are expensive but worthwhile, but a portion may be the result of hospital market power, the medical arms race, and the conflicting incentives of doctors and hospital administrators.

In efforts to constrain these costs, governments have adopted various policies that address the problems of market power, the positive and negative effects of market competition, and concerns about equity. We examine closely the tradeoffs different countries make in Chapters 15 through 17.

6.7   Exercises

Comprehension questions

Indicate whether the statement is true or false, and justify your answer. Be sure to cite evidence from the chapter and state any additional assumptions you may need.

1 Hospital admission rates have dropped in the past two decades.
2 There were more hospitals in the US in the late 1990s than there were in 1940; the largest source of growth has been among for-profit hospitals.
3 The average length of hospital stays in the US has remained flat after a sharp decline in the 1980s.
4 Higher values of the Herfindahl–Hirschman Index indicate higher levels of competition in those markets.
5 The hospital's experience with cardiac catheterization is at least as important as the cardiologist's experience in reducing complication rates following percutaneous coronary intervention (PCI).
6 Nonprofit firms can legally raise funds by issuing stock.

7 Consider the following theory due to Arrow (1963): nonprofits exist because for-profit firms are less trustworthy in the performance of actions that are hard to observe. According to this theory, government regulations requiring hospitals to report data on outcomes should lead to a lower share of nonprofit production in the hospital industry.

8 Medical arms races, since they are a form of private competition, lead to socially optimal levels of technology acquisition by hospitals.

9 Uncompensated care in the United States is almost entirely covered by government programs like Medicare and Medicaid.

10 Doctors are typically direct employees of hospitals in the US, whereas in the UK, they do most of their work in private practice settings.

11 In a DRG payment system, hospitals receive payment according to the number of services rendered.

Analytical problems

14 **Learning by doing.** Suppose a hospital is planning how many patients to treat over the next two years. One key factor the hospital needs to consider in its planning is that hospitals that see many patients in one year have lower costs of care in subsequent years. Let p be the price of hospital care, let q_1 be the number of patients the hospital treats in year 1, let q_2 be the number of patients the hospital treats in year 2, and let c_1 and c_2 be the hospital's per-patient cost in years 1 and 2. The hospital's profits over the two-year period are

$$\Pi = (p_1 - c_1)q_1 + (p_2 - c_2)q_2$$

The hospital takes p_1 and p_2 as fixed and they choose q_1 and q_2 to maximize profits, Π.

a Suppose, as a warm-up exercise, that there is no learning by doing, and that the unit cost functions are $c_1 = \frac{q_1}{2}$ and $c_2 = \frac{q_2}{2}$. Is the cost of caring for patients increasing or decreasing in the number of patients seen? Derive the supply function in periods 1 and 2 for the hospital. [*Hint:* Substitute the unit cost functions into the profit functions and take the derivative of Π with respect to q_1 and q_2.]

b Let us introduce learning by doing into the problem. Now, the unit costs in period 2 are lower if the hospital has a higher number of patients seen in period 1. As we have seen in this chapter, there is a lot of evidence that suggests that such learning by doing by hospitals does in fact happen. The unit cost function in period 1 is still $c_1 = \frac{q_1}{2}$, but the unit cost function in period 2 now depends also on the number of patients seen in period 1: $c_2 = \frac{q_2}{2q_1}$. Derive the supply function in periods 1 and 2 for the hospital. [*Hint:* Solve first for the optimal q_2 taking q_1 as given. Then use your question for q_2^* in your expression for q_1^*.]

c Should the hospital see more or fewer patients in period 1 if there is learning by doing?

15 **Herfindahl–Hirschman indexing.** The Herfindahl–Hirschman Index, H, gives economists a way of measuring how much competition there is in a market. Suppose

that there are N hospitals in a market, each with s_i percent of the market share, where $\sum_{i=1}^{N} s_i = 1$. Recall that the index is defined as follows:

$$H = \sum_{i=1}^{N} s_i^2$$

a   Suppose that there are $N = 10$ firms in a market, and each of them has an equal share of the market, so that $s_i = \frac{1}{N} = \frac{1}{10}$ for each firm. What is the value of the Herfindahl–Hirschman Index in this market?

b   Suppose instead that one firm in this market dominates such that it has 90% of the market share, while the remaining nine firms each have an equal share of the remainder. What is the value of the Herfindahl–Hirschman Index in this case? Do increases in H represent an increase or a decrease in competition?

c   What is the largest value H can take? When is H equal to this number?

d   Now suppose a new firm enters the market and pulls away market share from each of the incumbent firms such that $s_i = \frac{1}{11}$. Would you say that competition has increased with the entry of the new firm into the market? Calculate the value of H after the firm has entered.

e   Under perfect competition, there are an infinity of firms in the market, each with an infinitesimal market share. What is the value of H in a perfectly competitive market?

16 **Medical arms race.** Consider a two-hospital town with hospitals unimaginatively named A and B. The hospitals are considering installing a new imaging machine to attract more patients. The population of the town is small enough that it really only needs one of these machines. Purchasing a machine costs $1,000.

- If both hospitals install a machine, each earns $800 in revenue.
- If only one hospital installs a machine, that hospital earns $1,800 in revenue. The other hospital loses $300 in revenue as patients switch to the other hospital.
- If neither hospital installs a machine, then revenue does not change for either one.

a   Consider hospital A's decision to buy one of these fancy new machines. A's profits will depend on what B decides to do. Suppose hospital B buys a machine. How much will A earn if it also decides to buy a machine? How much will A earn if it does not? What should A do if B buys a machine?

b   Now consider A's optimal choice if B decides not to buy a machine. How much will A earn if it buys a machine? How much will A earn if it does not? What is A's best response if B does not buy a machine?

c   We assume that the hospitals make their decisions about the imaging machine concurrently, so this interaction can be modeled as a simultaneous-move game.

		Hospital B	
		Buy	Do not buy
Hospital A	Buy	A_{11}, B_{11}	A_{12}, B_{12}
	Do not buy	A_{21}, B_{21}	A_{22}, B_{22}

where A_{11} and B_{11} are hospital A's and B's respective payoffs when both hospitals install the imaging technology. Fill in this game payoff matrix.

d   Hospitals A and B both act to maximize profits. What do you predict will happen in this market? Will the socially optimal outcome – only one machine is purchased in the town – happen? [*Note:* This type of game is commonly known as a Prisoner's Dilemma.]

e   Suppose hospitals A and B share an owner who maximizes joint profits rather than individual ones. What do you predict will happen?

f   In this case, is hospital competition good for welfare? What other information, if any, would you need to make an assessment?

Essay questions

17 Below is the abstract of a recent National Bureau of Economic Research working paper entitled "Can governments do it better? Merger mania and hospital outcomes in the English NHS" by Martin Gaynor, Mauro Laudicella, and Carol Propper (2011).

The literature on mergers between private hospitals suggests that such mergers often produce little benefit. Despite this, the UK government has pursued an active policy of hospital mergers. These mergers are initiated by a regulator, acting on behalf of the public, and justified on the grounds that merger will improve outcomes. We examine whether this promise is met. We exploit the fact that between 1997 and 2006 in England around half the short term general hospitals were involved in a merger, but that politics means that selection for a merger may be random with respect to future performance. We examine the impact of mergers on a large set of outcomes including financial performance, productivity, waiting times and clinical quality and find little evidence that mergers achieved gains other than a reduction in activity. In addition, mergers reduce the scope for competition between hospitals.

a   In the UK, most hospitals are owned by the government, rather than privately held. In a setting where most hospitals are not owned by the government (such as in the US), what effect do you predict that hospital mergers would have on the price of hospital care?

b   Can you think of reasons why hospital mergers might lead to improvements in the quality of care for a given level of inputs (which is one measure of hospital productivity)?

c   How might the fact that a hospital is run by the government in the UK change your prediction about the effect of hospital mergers on productivity?

18 Below is the abstract of a recent National Bureau of Economic Research working paper entitled "Human capital and organizational performance: evidence from the health care sector" by Ann Bartel, Ciaran Phibbs, Nancy Beaulieu, and Patricia Stone (2011):

This paper contributes to the literature on the relationship between human capital and organizational performance. We use detailed longitudinal monthly data on nursing units in the Veterans Administration hospital system to identify how the human capital (general, hospital-specific and unit or team-specific) of the nursing team on the unit affects patients' outcomes. Since we use monthly, not annual, data, we are able to avoid the omitted variable bias and endogeneity bias that could result when annual data are used. Nurse staffing levels, general human capital, and unit-specific human capital have positive and significant effects on patient outcomes while the use of contract nurses, who have less specific capital than regular staff nurses, negatively impacts patient outcomes. Policies that would increase the specific human capital of the nursing staff are found to be cost-effective.

General human capital includes the sorts of broad skills that people might learn during schooling; these sorts of skills apply to many kinds of work settings. By contrast, *specific* human capital includes the sorts of skills and knowledge that someone might learn while working on the job. Such skills cannot readily be translated to other jobs within the hospital, or even to the same job at another hospital. Why might contract nurses, who are typically hired for short periods of time by hospitals to fill unexpected scheduling holes, tend to have negative impacts on patient outcomes? Speculate about the sorts of specific human capital that might give regular nurses an advantage over contract nurses in helping patients. Can this help explain the positive volume–outcome relationship observed in hospitals?

Students can find answers to the comprehension questions and lecturers can access an Instructor Manual with guideline answers to the analytical problems and essay questions at **www.palgrave.com/economics/bht**.

III INFORMATION ECONOMICS

7 Demand for insurance 126

8 Adverse selection: Akerlof's market for lemons 141

9 Adverse selection: the Rothschild–Stiglitz model 162

10 Adverse selection in real markets 184

11 Moral hazard 203

7 DEMAND FOR INSURANCE

Many people have been told since their youth that gambling is an unwise activity, only to be dabbled in for entertainment purposes, if at all. But buying health insurance is actually a form of gambling. Take life insurance, for instance – a term life insurance contract is a bet that you will die before some fixed date. To win, you must die early.

Despite warnings about the dangers of gambling, life insurance is, in many circumstances, a wise choice. The reason why buying insurance may be wise is that it is a bet that *reduces* uncertainty. Insurance is a hedge against risk, against the possibility of bad outcomes. But nothing is costless: purchasing insurance means forfeiting income in good times. The homeowner who pays monthly for fire

Buying health insurance is akin to placing a bet that you will become sick and need medical care.
Credit: © Sashkin – Fotolia.com.

insurance for the fire that never occurs might have been better off spending that income elsewhere. The individual who buys health insurance but never visits the hospital loses out on that income.

What drives the demand for insurance seems to be fear of the unknown. We want to understand what causes people to be afraid of the unknown in the first place. The story economists tell has little to do with the psychology or biology of fear. It has more to do with the mundane topic of declining marginal utility of income.

7.1 Declining marginal utility of income

In this section, we introduce the simplest possible model that illustrates the notion of risk aversion and the demand for insurance. In this model, an individual cares about the income she earns and nothing else. As always, we model preferences by defining a utility function, and in this case the utility function will have a single input – income I. While this is certainly unrealistic, it is all that is necessary to demonstrate risk aversion.

What properties should the individual's utility function $U(I)$ have? First, utility should increase with income; that is, the first derivative of the utility function is positive:

$$U'(I) > 0 \tag{7.1}$$

A second property of this individual's preferences is that her marginal utility of income is declining in income. This means that the first dollar the individual has is very valuable to her, because an income of one dollar ($I = 1$) is much better than an income of zero dollars ($I = 0$). But if the individual is already a millionaire, gaining an extra dollar means very little to her. Empirically, these preferences seem to be very common. This second property is equivalent to the second derivative of the utility function being negative:

$$U''(I) < 0 \tag{7.2}$$

Figure 7.1 graphs a utility function with both of these properties. Utility is increasing with income, but at a declining rate. While this figure may seem simple, it turns out to be the key to understanding why the individual is risk averse, why she might demand insurance, and what sort of insurance contracts she prefers. Indeed, that there is a relationship between declining marginal utility of income and risk aversion is a key insight of modern economics.

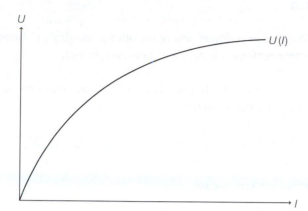

Figure 7.1. *An income–utility diagram.*

7.2   Uncertainty

Our next step is to model uncertainty. Again, our strategy is to build the simplest possible model that accomplishes our task. In this case, suppose that the individual faces a possibility of becoming sick. She does not know whether she will become sick, but she knows the probability of sickness is $p \in (0, 1)$. Consequently, her probability of staying healthy is $1 - p$. She also knows that if she does get sick, medical bills and missed work will reduce her income considerably. Let I_S be her income if she does get sick, and let $I_H > I_S$ be her income if she remains healthy.

Whenever there is uncertainty, it is important to have ways of summarizing all the possible outcomes in a concise way. One such summary is the **expected value**.

Definition | **7.1**

The **expected value** of a random variable X, $E[X]$, is the sum of all the possible outcomes of X weighted by each outcome's probability. If the outcomes are $X = x_1$, $X = x_2, \ldots, X = x_n$, and the probabilities for each outcome are $p_1, p_2, \ldots, p_n$ respectively, then

$$E[X] = p_1 x_1 + p_2 x_2 + \cdots + p_n x_n \tag{7.3}$$

$E[X]$ is also sometimes called the **mean** of X.

In the individual's case, the formula for expected value of her income, $E[I]$, is simple. There are only two possible outcomes for I and we know the probabilities associated with each:

$$E[I]_p = p I_S + (1 - p) I_H \tag{7.4}$$

One feature of equation (7.4) is that expected income depends critically on p, the probability of illness. As getting sick becomes more likely, p rises and the weight given to I_S in the formula for $E[I]$ increases. As we would expect, rising p translates to a reduced expected income.

7.3   Risk aversion

Suppose we conduct an experiment where we offer a starving graduate student a choice between two possible options, a lottery and a certain payout:

A: a lottery that awards $500 with probability 0.5 and $0 with probability 0.5.
B: a check for $250 with probability 1.

It is easy to see that the expected value of both the lottery and the certain payout is $250:

$$E[I]_p = pI_S + (1-p)I_H$$

$$E[I_A] = 0.5(500) + 0.5(0) = \$250 \tag{7.5}$$

$$E[I_B] = 1(250) = \$250.$$

Despite the fact that both lotteries provide the same expected income, studies reliably find that most people prefer certain payouts like (B) over uncertain lotteries like (A). If a starving graduate student says he prefers option (B) in the above example, what does that imply about his utility function? To answer this question, we need to define **expected utility** for a lottery or uncertain outcome. Like expected income, expected utility is an average over all states of the world, weighted by the probability of each state.

Definition	7.2

The **expected utility** from a random payout X, $E[U(X)]$, is the sum of the utility from each of the possible outcomes, weighted by each outcome's probability. If the outcomes are $X = x_1, X = x_2, \ldots, X = x_n$, and the probabilities for each outcome are $p_1, p_2, \ldots, p_n$ respectively, then

$$E[U(X)] = p_1 U(x_1) + p_2 U(x_2) + \cdots + p_n U(x_n) \tag{7.6}$$

The starving student's preference for option (B) over option (A) implies that his expected utility from (B), $E[U(B)]$, is greater than his expected utility from (A), $E[U(A)]$:

$$E[U(B)] \geq E[U(A)] \tag{7.7}$$

$$U(\$250) \geq 0.5 \cdot U(\$500) + 0.5 \cdot U(\$0)$$

In this case, the starving student prefers the more certain payout over the less certain one, even though the expected value of those two options is equal. We say that the student is acting in a **risk-averse** manner over the choices available.

The situation that the individual who might get sick faces is similar to the lottery in option (A) in that her income I is a random variable. She gains a high income ($I = I_H$) if she stays healthy, and a low income ($I = I_S$) if she is sick. Furthermore, she is uncertain about which outcome will happen, though she knows the probability of becoming sick is p. Her expected utility $E[U(I)]_p$ in this situation is:

$$E[U(I)]_p = pU(I_S) + (1-p)U(I_H) \tag{7.8}$$

Figure 7.2 shows how expected utility changes as the probability of sickness changes. Consider the extreme case where the individual is sick with certainty, so the probability of sickness is $p = 1$. It should be clear from equation (7.8) that when $p = 1$, $E[U(I)] = U(I_S)$. In Figure 7.2, we label this point S. At that point, the individual's expected utility equals the utility she gains from a certain income of I_S. Similarly, if the individual has no chance of becoming sick, $p = 0$, her income is I_H with certainty, and her utility is $U(I_H)$. We label this point H in the figure.

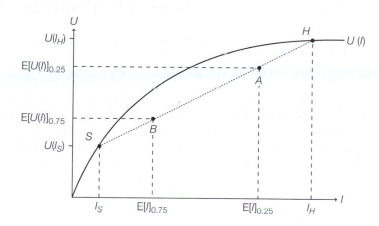

Figure 7.2. *Expected utility from income for different probabilities of sickness.*

What if her probability of illness lies somewhere between 0 and 1? In that case, her expected utility falls on a line segment between S and H in Figure 7.2. One way to see this is to consider equation (7.8) again. Think of $U(I_S)$ and $U(I_H)$ as fixed numbers, since changes in p have no effect on those quantities. Therefore, equation (7.8) is a linear function in p. As p increases from 0 to 1, the weight placed on $U(I_S)$ increases and the weight placed on $U(I_H)$ decreases.

For instance, when $p = 0.25$, the individual's expected utility is shown at point A, a quarter of the way along the line segment between H to S. The individual's expected income at this point is:

$$E[I]_{0.25} = 0.25 \cdot I_S + (1 - 0.25) \cdot I_H$$

and her utility at this point is $E[U(I)]_{0.25}$. Similarly, point B represents her expected income and expected utility when $p = 0.75$. We can calculate these quantities for any p by moving along the line segment HS.

Expected utility vs. expected income

The important fact to notice is that we do not read her expected utility off the income–utility curve, but instead off the line segment HS. Figure 7.3 illustrates this distinction in

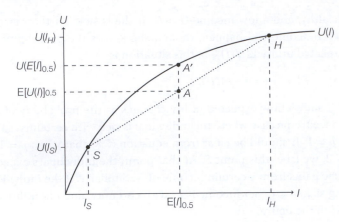

Figure 7.3. *Risk-averse individuals want to limit uncertainty. Achieving* $E[I]$ *with certainty is better than receiving the expected utility of a coin flip between* I_H *or* I_S. *Therefore,* $U(E[I]_{0.5}) > E[U(I)]_{0.5}$.

the case when $p = 0.5$. The individual's expected income and expected utility from the sickness lottery are:

$$E[I]_{0.5} = 0.5 \cdot I_S + (1 - 0.5) \cdot I_H$$

$$E[U(I)]_{0.5} = 0.5 \cdot U(I_S) + (1 - 0.5) \cdot U(I_H)$$

In Figure 7.3, the resulting point is labeled A and falls on the line segment HS. This point corresponds to the *expected utility from income* of $E[U(I)]_{0.5}$. This is not to be confused with the *utility from expected income* $U(E[I]_{0.5})$, which corresponds to point A'. This value is the utility that would result if the individual could earn $E[I]_{0.5}$ with certainty. Just like the starving student, the individual gains more utility from the certain outcome than the uncertain outcome. This statement implies that she is risk-averse.

Definition | **7.3**

Risk aversion in the utility–income model:
   The following statements are equivalent:

- The individual prefers a certain outcome to an uncertain outcome with the same expected income.
- The individual prefers the utility she would get from her expected income to the expected utility she will get from her actual (uncertain) income.
- $U(E[I]) > E[U(I)]$.
- The individual is risk-averse.

Notice that these statements are all true because the utility–income curve is concave. The geometry of the utility–income curve guarantees that the curve always lies above the line segment HS for any value of I. The individual always gains more utility from a certain outcome than an uncertain outcome with the same expected income. This holds true as long as there is some uncertainty; $0 < p < 1$. Recall that we modeled the individual's utility curve as concave in the first place in order to reflect her declining marginal utility from income (see equation (7.2)). We see now that risk aversion follows directly from this assumption.

While the theory we describe here is intuitively appealing since it relies on standard notions from probability theory, even within economics there is considerable controversy over whether the model accurately describes how people make decisions under uncertainty. Perhaps not surprisingly, people often reason in strange ways when they make decisions in face of the unknown. Psychologists have developed an elaborate story, known as prospect theory, that describes the distortions in reasoning that occur when people think about uncertain outcomes. We will leave that part of the story for later, in Chapter 23, because it builds on the simpler model of expected utility maximization that we describe in this chapter.

7.4   Uncertainty and insurance

In a world with affordable time travel, health insurance would serve no purpose.

Credit: Allen Cox.

In our model, a person is either fully well or fully sick but never halfway between. This means that individuals cannot achieve the higher utility at A' from Figure 7.3 on their own, even though risk-averse people would prefer it. A risk-averse individual seeking to achieve A' would need to somehow send money from one potential self in the world where she stays healthy to her other potential self in the world where she becomes sick. She cannot do this herself without some sort of time machine, but she has another option: insurance. As we will see, an insurance contract functions by transferring money from the well state to the sick state.

A basic insurance contract

The individual approaches a health insurance company that offers a policy with the following features:

- The individual pays an upfront cost r regardless of whether she stays healthy or becomes ill. The payment r is known as the *insurance premium*.
- If the individual becomes ill, she receives a payout q.
- If the individual remains healthy, she receives nothing from the insurance company (not even a refund of the insurance premium r).

Here we return to the notion that buying an insurance contract amounts to a bet. The individual is betting the insurance company that she will be sick. If she falls ill, she "wins" the bet and receives payout q. But if she stays healthy, she "loses" the bet and receives nothing in return for the premium paid. For a risk-averse individual, this bet may be wise, because it allows the individual to hedge against illness and reduce uncertainty about her final income. Though she is just as likely to fall ill as before, the financial burden of illness is lower. The insurance does not make her healthier, but it can make her happier.

Let I'_H and I'_S represent the individual's income in the healthy and sick states of the world with the insurance contract. These quantities will be functions of I_H and I_S, as well as the parameters of the insurance contract: the premium r and payout q. Her incomes in the two states are thus

$$\text{Healthy: } I'_H = I_H - r$$

$$\text{Sick: } I'_S = I_S - r + q$$

(7.9)

Recall that the individual's goal in buying insurance was to achieve an income of $E[I]_p$ with certainty, whether she is healthy or sick. What the individual would like most is

$$E[I]_p = I'_H = I'_S$$

(7.10)

An insurance contract that fulfills equation (7.10) is said to be *actuarially fair, full insurance*. We discuss these terms in more detail shortly.

Let us consider an insurance contract X with the following parameters. In this contract, assume the individual receives the difference between her healthy income and sick income if she is sick: $q = I_H - I_S$. In addition, assume that the premium is set such that the contract represents a fair bet: $r = pq$. On average, the individual neither gains nor loses income from this contact.

The following algebra shows that with contract X, the individual's income is $E[I]_p$ regardless of whether she turns out to be healthy or sick. In each column we start with equation (7.9) and substitute in the parameters of this insurance contract; in the second line, we substitute $r = pq$; in the third line, we substitute $q = I_H - I_S$.

■ **Healthy state**

$$I'_H = I_H - r$$
$$= I_H - pq$$
$$= I_H - p(I_H - I_S)$$
$$= pI_S + (1 - p)I_H$$
$$I'_H = E[I]_p$$

■ **Sick state**

$$I'_S = I_S - r + q$$
$$= I_S - pq + q$$
$$= I_S - p(I_H - I_S) + (I_H - I_S)$$
$$= pI_S + (1 - p)I_H$$
$$I'_S = E[I]_p$$

With this contract, the individual can receive $E[I]_p$ with certainty. This enables her to achieve points on the utility function, like A', in Figure 7.3, whereas before she was only able to achieve points on line segment HS below the utility–income curve. With the insurance contract, the individual's utility increases even though her income does not. The insurance contract creates utility seemingly out of nowhere; simply by reducing uncertainty, the insurance contract can make the risk-averse individual better off.

The nature of the insurance contract is that the individual loses income in the healthy state ($I_H > I'_H$) and gains income in the sick state ($I_S < I'_S$) relative to the state of no insurance. This is the sense in which the insurance contract acts as an instrument that transfers income from the healthy state of the world to the sick state. The risk-averse individual willingly sacrifices some good times in the healthy state to ease the bad times in the sick state.

Fair and unfair insurance

Consider now the same insurance contract we have been discussing from the point of view of the insurance company. Let $E[\Pi]$ be the expected profits that the insurer makes from offering a contract with premium r and payout q to any customer with probability of sickness p. If the customer actually stays healthy, the firm earns r dollars. On the other hand, if the customer falls ill, the firm still receives the premium r but loses the payout q. By applying the formula for expected value (see equation (7.3)), we find:

$$E[\Pi(p,q,r)] = (1-p)r + p(r-q)$$

$$\qquad\qquad = r - pq \qquad\qquad\qquad\qquad\qquad (7.11)$$

In a perfectly competitive insurance market, profits will equal zero. Just like in any competitive market, if profits were positive, new entrants would compete away those profits until all the firms left in the market would be making zero profits. If the profits were negative, then the insurer is giving money away to customers in the long run and will go out of business. Firms leave the market until profits reach zero. Setting expected profits to zero in equation (7.11) implies $r = pq$. This condition is known as **actuarial fairness**.

Definition | **7.4**

Actuarially fair insurance contract: an insurance contract which yields zero profit in expectation; also called **fair insurance**:

$$E[\Pi(p,q,r)] = 0 \qquad \Longrightarrow \qquad r = pq \qquad\qquad (7.12)$$

An insurance contract which yields positive profits is called **unfair insurance**:

$$E[\Pi(p,q,r)] > 0 \qquad \Longrightarrow \qquad r > pq \qquad\qquad (7.13)$$

When insurance is fair, in a sense, it is also free. The customer's expected income does not change from buying the contract, so she effectively pays nothing for it. Despite the fact that the premium r is positive in an actuarially fair contract, the *price* is actually zero. Thus, we reach the counter-intuitive conclusion that the premium associated with an insurance contract is not its price.

In the real world, of course, nothing is free, and insurance markets are not perfectly competitive. Insurance companies make some positive profits on the contracts they sell, so there must exist insurance contracts with positive prices that consumers actually purchase. An insurance contract with a positive expected profit for the insurer is called an **actuarially unfair contract**. Applying the firm's profit equation (equation (7.11)), we find that the profit-making insurer must set premiums r above the expected payout pq:

$$E[\Pi(p,q,r)] > 0 \qquad \Longrightarrow \qquad r > pq \qquad\qquad (7.14)$$

The difference between the premium r and expected payout pq is analogous to the price of the contract and determines the change in expected income. The higher r rises above pq, the pricier the contract is and the more *unfair* it becomes. Risk-averse consumers may still be willing to pay positive prices for unfair insurance contracts if doing so sufficiently reduces their uncertainty. But there is a limit to the price even risk-averse customers will pay for additional certainty, as we discuss in Section 7.5.

Full and partial insurance

So far we have examined insurance contracts where the insured individual ends up with the same income in the sick state and the healthy state, $I_S' = I_H'$. This property is known as **state independence**, because the individual's income no longer depends on her health status. An insurance contract that achieves state independence completely eliminates income uncertainty and is called a **full insurance contract**.

Not all insurance contracts are full, however. An insurance contract can be designed that reduces income uncertainty without completely eliminating it. Under **partial insurance**, income in the sick state even with insurance is still lower than income in the healthy state ($I'_S < I'_H$), but some income is still transferred from the healthy to the sick.

Definition | **7.5**

Full insurance contract: an insurance contract that achieves state independence; income in all states is equal:

$$I'_S = I'_H$$

Partial insurance contract: an insurance contract that is state-dependent; income in the sick state is still less than income in the healthy state:

$$I'_S < I'_H$$

Just as we derived the premium r in the cases of actuarially fair and unfair insurance, we can derive the payout q in the cases of full and partial insurance. We rely on the state-independence property of full insurance and the state-dependence property of partial insurance:

■ **Full insurance**	■ **Partial insurance**
$I'_S = I'_H$	$I'_S < I'_H$
$I_S - r + q = I_H - r$	$I_S - r + q < I_H - r$
$I_S + q = I_H$	$I_S + q < I_H$
$q = I_H - I_S$	$q < I_H - I_S$

The size of the payout q determines the fullness of the insurance contract. A contract with a payout that fully covers the spread between I_H and I_S is full, while contracts with payouts that do not fully cover this difference are partial. The closer an insurance contract's payout q comes to equaling $I_H - I_S$, the fuller we say that contract is.

Just as we think of the fairness of a contract as its effective price, we can think of the fullness of a contract as its effective *quantity*. Fuller contracts offer higher quantities of insurance, in the sense that they provide greater income certainty and produce greater expected utility.

Figure 7.4 compares an individual's income and utility under three different insurance contracts that are all actuarially fair but vary in their degree of fullness:

- **No insurance:** the individual receives either I_S or I_H, and has expected utility at A.
- **Partial insurance:** the individual receives either I^P_S or I^P_H, and has expected utility at A^P.
- **Full insurance:** the individual receives both I^F and utility at A^F with certainty.

From Figure 7.4 we see that the expected utility from full insurance at A^F is highest, followed by utility from partial insurance A^P and then no insurance A. The income uncertainty the individual faces is largest in the case of no insurance: she receives either I_H

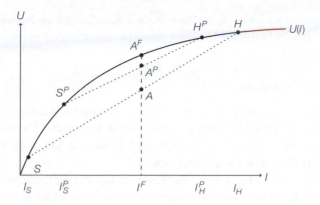

Figure 7.4. *Comparing full-fair, partial-fair, and no insurance.*

or I_S, which may be significantly different. Partial insurance lowers her uncertainty but does not eliminate it altogether since I_S^P is still less than I_H^P. Only with the highest quantity of insurance – full insurance – does the individual reach state independence and fully eliminate income uncertainty.

7.5   Comparing insurance contracts

So far we have defined actuarially fair insurance contracts and full insurance contracts separately. In fact, insurance contracts are defined by the extent to which they are both fair and full. Table 7.1 shows how various combinations of premium r and payout pq result in different types of insurance contracts. Of course, there is an infinitude of partial contracts, unfair contracts, and every possible interaction between the two. The four-way classification in Table 7.1 is a convenient way to study and compare the different contracts.

Table 7.1. *Premium and generosity of different insurance contracts.*

	Fair	Unfair
Full	$r = pq$ $q = I_H - I_S$	$r > pq$ $q = I_H - I_S$
Partial	$r = pq$ $q < I_H - I_S$	$r > pq$ $q < I_H - I_S$

The contract's parameters r and q determine its level of fairness and fullness for any particular individual with given values of p, I_H, and I_S. At a fixed level of fairness (which we can think of as a fixed price), full insurance is preferable to partial insurance because it provides certainty about income. At a fixed level of fullness (or a fixed quantity), however, fair insurance is preferable because it costs less than unfair insurance and delivers the same benefit.

These two rules imply that insurance that is both fair and full (the upper-left quadrant in Table 7.1) is always preferable to anything else. Accordingly, we term this the **ideal contract** because it is the best attainable contract from the consumer's point of view. Whenever the individual is offered a choice between the ideal contract and a non-ideal one, she chooses the former. But when she is offered a choice between two non-ideal contracts, she can only decide between them by a closer comparison of her expected utilities under each.

Two non-ideal contracts

Consider a market with only two health insurance contracts being offered: contract P which is fair but partial, and contract F which is full but unfair. Because neither is ideal, we cannot say which contract is the better choice for any potential customer until we evaluate her expected utility under each option.

Figure 7.5 depicts the situation of an individual considering these two contracts. In this example, we define a full-but-unfair contract A^F that offers a higher expected utility than the partial-but-fair A^P. Although contract F is unfair and thus more expensive in terms of expected income, its fullness makes it worth the added cost. For a risk-averse individual with this utility function, the reduction in uncertainty warrants paying an actuarially unfair price.

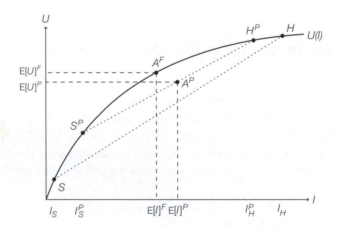

Figure 7.5. *Two non-ideal contracts, A^P and A^F.*

But there is still a limit to how much the individual is willing to pay, even for full insurance. As the unfair-but-full contract F becomes progressively more unfair, it moves left on the income–utility diagram, representing a gradual decline in expected income. If the unfair-but-full contract becomes too unfair, the individual's expected utility will drop to below her expected utility from the fair-but-partial contract. Graphically, this occurs when $E[U]^F$ falls lower than $E[U]^P$. At that point, the individual prefers contract P to contract F.

We can determine the highest degree of unfairness that the customer is willing to tolerate before switching to the fair-but-partial contract. Figure 7.6 illustrates two contracts such that expected utility from both is equal. The first contract P is the same fair-but-partial contract that we considered before. The second contract F' is an unfair-but-full contract that leaves the customer indifferent between P and F'. That is, $E[U]^{F'} = E[U]^P$.

F' is more unfair than contract F in Figure 7.6; it provides a lower expected utility and income. The individual prefers P to any contract more unfair than F', because P then gives higher expected utility. So $E[I]^P - E[I]^{F'}$ is the most that the individual is willing to pay to eliminate uncertainty when the partial insurance contract P is available.

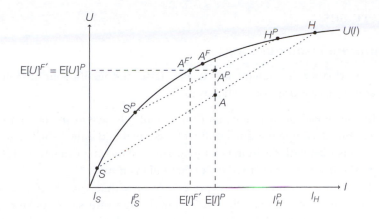

Figure 7.6. *A partial-fair contract* A^P *and a full-unfair contract* AF' *offering the same utility.*

7.6   Conclusion

It is surprising how far diminishing marginal utility of income goes in explaining the demand for insurance and risk aversion. The theory applies beyond income to many other decisions that people make under uncertainty. Any good or item that has a higher marginal value when you have a little of it than when you have a lot can be the subject of a similar analysis:

The forecast is calling for hail – hopefully this farmer has another plot of land somewhere in a better climate. Credit: © smereka – Fotolia.com.

- Mid-twentieth-century singer and actress Marlene Dietrich was famous for her trademark long legs. The insurance exchange Lloyd's of London organized an insurance policy that would pay out $1,000,000 in case her legs came to harm.

- In medieval Europe, peasants who faced climatological uncertainty sought to reduce risk. Crop yields were "susceptible to a lack of rainfall, too much rainfall, a flooding creek, frost, bugs, molds, and all other manner of shocks" (Bekar 2000). Peasants hedged against uncertainty by scattering their holdings in hills and valleys with different microclimates. They were willing to travel long roads between different parcels to reduce risk of total crop failure.

- One hypothesized reason for large family sizes in developing countries is high infant mortality risk. According to this hypothesis, children serve as insurance against the vicissitudes of old age. The elderly do not want to be left childless after they are no longer able to work productively. Raising many children may be expensive, but serves as a hedge against this risk.

Whether the subject is health insurance, Marlene Dietrich's legs, horticultural strategies in medieval Europe, or family planning in poverty-stricken Mozambique, the basic logic of hedging bets is the same. People are consistently willing to sacrifice utility in the good state in exchange for utility in the bad state. Because we are naturally risk-averse about so many things, insurance is an essential economic tool that arises wherever uncertainty exists.

7.7   Exercises

Comprehension questions

Indicate whether the statement is true or false, and justify your answer. Be sure to state any additional assumptions you may need.

1 In the model of insurance and uncertainty discussed in the chapter, an individual exhibits declining marginal utility of income if and only if she is risk-averse.

2 A consumer with declining marginal utility of income will never prefer actuarially fair, partial insurance to actuarially unfair, full insurance.

3 Risk-averse consumers always prefer insurance that is actuarially fair but not full to full insurance that is actuarially unfair – but the opposite is true for risk-loving consumers.

4 There are no possible utility functions in which a person is indifferent between actuarially fair, full insurance and actuarially fair, partial insurance.

5 A risk-averse individual prefers a certain outcome to an uncertain outcome with the same expected income.

6 Insurance represents a transfer of wealth from healthy states to sick states.

7 When insurance is fair, in a sense, it is also free.

8 Under partial insurance, income in the sick state with insurance is higher than income in the healthy state.

9 In an actuarially fair insurance contract, the insurance premium equals the probability of sickness times the payout amount.

Analytical problems

10 Consider an individual whose utility function over income I is $U(I)$, where U is increasing smoothly in I ($U' > 0$) and *convex* ($U'' > 0$).
   a Draw a utility function in U–I space that fits this description.
   b Explain the connection between U'' and risk aversion.
   c True or false: this individual prefers no insurance to (I_S, I_H) to an actuarially fair, full contract.

11 Assume that Jay discovers, to his dismay, that his 2014 healthy-state income will be lower than his 2013 healthy-state income, but that his sick-state income I_S is unchanged from 2013 to 2014. Assume that his healthy-state income in 2013 is I_H, and his healthy-state income in 2014 is $I_H - \Delta$. Assume $0 < p < 1$.
   a What is the difference between Jay's expected income in 2014, $E[I_{14}]$, and his expected income in 2013, $E[I_{13}]$?
   b Assume that a local insurance firm designed an ideal insurance contract for Jay in 2013 – that is, one that was actuarially fair and full that year. They now want to adjust the contract so that it remains ideal for Jay in 2014. How will the premium r change, if at all? How will the payout q change, if at all? Interpret these changes in terms of the concepts of price and quantity.
   c Suppose Jay finds a stipulation in the fine print of his contract that the premium and payout cannot change for five years. The firm gnashes its teeth and admits it cannot legally change the contract set in 2013. Describe how full and fair this contract will be for Jay in 2014. Would Jay prefer to be healthy or sick, assuming he buys the contract and that his utility is determined by his income level?

12 Now consider a different insurance company that does not have the inclination to tailor contracts specifically to individuals. Instead, it will offer a "standard contract" with the premium $r = \$100$ and payout $q = \$500$ to anyone who will purchase it.

   a Peter has healthy-state income $I_H = \$500$ and sick-state income $I_S = \$0$. He has probability of illness $p = 0.1$. Is the standard contract fair and/or full for Peter? If he ends up getting sick, what will his final income be?

   b Tim has $I_H = \$500$ and $I_S = \$0$, but a probability of illness $p = 0.2$, higher than Peter's. Is the standard contract fair and/or full for Tim? How does purchasing the standard contract affect Tim's expected income?

   c Jay has $I_H = \$1,000$ and $I_S = \$0$, with probability of illness $p = 0.2$. Is the standard contract fair and/or full for Jay?

   d Suppose there is a customer named Ronald for whom the standard contract is partial and actuarially unfair in the insurance company's favor. Give a set of possible values for Ronald's I_H, I_S, and p. Recall that we always assume $I_H > I_S$.

   e Now suppose that we have learned that Ronald's $I_S = \$200$, but we do not know the value of his healthy-state income, or his probability of falling ill. Derive an upper bound for p and a lower bound for I_H.

   f True or false: if we assume all four individuals are risk-averse, then we know that Tim has the most to gain by taking up the contract. Justify your answer.

13 Consider an individual whose utility function over income I is $U(I)$, where U is increasing smoothly in I and is concave (in other words, our basic assumptions throughout this chapter). Let $I_S = 0$ be this person's income if he is sick, let $I_H > 0$ be his income if he is healthy, let p be his probability of being sick, let $E[I]$ be expected income, and let $E[U]$ be his expected utility when he has no insurance.

   a Write down algebraic expressions for both $E[I]$ and $E[U]$ in terms of the other parameters of the model.

   b Consider a full insurance product that guarantees this individual $E[I]$. Create a diagram in U–I space. Draw the individual's utility curve and the lines representing I_S, I_H, and $E[I]$. Then draw and label a line segment that corresponds to the utility gain, ΔU, from buying this insurance product. Draw and label another line segment, M, which corresponds to the consumer surplus from the purchase of insurance (that is, the monetary value of the utility gain from buying insurance).

   c Derive an algebraic expression for M. [*Hint:* you may assume that U is invertible and its inverse is U^{-1}.]

   d Draw a graph plotting how M changes as p (the probability of being sick) varies between 0 and 1. [*Hint:* draw a coordinate plane with p on the x-axis and M on the y-axis.] Describe intuitively why this graph has the shape that it does.

14 Now consider another individual who is risk-loving instead of risk-averse.

   a Is $U(I)$ concave or convex?

   b Suppose this person is offered an actuarially fair insurance product that guarantees her a certain income, $E[I]$. Graph the consumer surplus this person receives from buying this insurance as p, the probability of being sick, varies from 0 to 1. You should plot p on the horizontal axis and consumer surplus on the vertical axis.

   c Suppose, finally, that this person is offered a subsidy (perhaps from her parents) for buying insurance so that, if she buys insurance, she will be guaranteed an income $\gamma E[I]$, where $\gamma > 1$. With the subsidy, insurance is now actuarially unfair in her favor. Graph how her consumer surplus (M) changes as p, the probability of being sick, varies from 0 to 1. [*Hint:* draw a coordinate plane with p on the x-axis and M on the y-axis.] Based on this graph, under what conditions is she least likely to buy the subsidized insurance?

Essay questions

15 Health insurance is normally seen as a good that is most valuable to sick people, since health expenditures are highest for the sick. Yet, in the basic insurance model discussed in this chapter, actuarially fair health insurance is worth nothing to people who are *certain* to become sick ($p = 1$). Why does the standard model produce this result? How is this different from the way real-world insurance markets work?

16 In the basic model of insurance, income is the only input into a person's utility. This is obviously not realistic. If we relax our assumption that utility is determined only by income levels, can any insurance contract provide *full* protection against the possibility of becoming severely ill? Give examples of risks associated with becoming sick that are not typically covered by formal health insurance. Can you think of ways that people informally insure against these "uninsurable" risks?

Students can find answers to the comprehension questions and lecturers can access an Instructor Manual with guideline answers to the analytical problems and essay questions at **www.palgrave.com/economics/bht**.

8 ADVERSE SELECTION: AKERLOF'S MARKET FOR LEMONS

Consider a man who walks into a life insurance office, asking for a million dollar policy against dying tomorrow. He tells the insurance agent that he does not smoke or drink, and by all appearances seems to the agent like a perfectly healthy young man. The policy the man wants will only last a day – if he dies tomorrow, the insurance company will owe his heirs a million dollars. The insurance agent faces two questions. Should the company provide coverage to this man at all, and if so how much should the man be charged as a premium?

The savvy insurance agent realizes that there must be something wrong in this situation. The man insists that he is healthy and wants the policy "just in case," but if that is true, then why does he want such a generous policy over such a short period of time? He must be hiding something important, the insurance agent reasons, something that will put him at significant danger of dying tomorrow. Though the insurance agent can never directly observe the potential customer's risk of dying, the very fact that the customer wants to buy this unusual policy provides evidence that the customer is likely to die tomorrow.

It will be difficult to find a good price for this contract, as well. Suppose the agent offers this insurance for an astronomical price. If the customer is still willing to take the contract at this high price, this is further evidence that the man is sure of his fate, and might cause the agent to retract her offer and demand an even higher price.

The main problem inhibiting trade in this story is that the insurance agent and the potential customer do not have equal access to a key piece of information – the customer's health risks. The customer is in a much better position to observe this fact, and he has a strong incentive to represent himself as healthier than he actually is, since healthier customers will tend to be charged a lower premium for the policy. This asymmetry in the information between the buyer and the seller makes it difficult to write insurance contracts that benefit both the buyer and the seller. As we will see, insurance markets work best when buyers and sellers are identically knowledgeable about the probability of different outcomes but identically ignorant about which outcome will occur.

In Chapter 7, both the insured individual and the insurance company knew in advance the individual's probability of sickness and could set premiums and payouts accordingly. Typically though, insurance firms and customers do not share identical knowledge. Firms, which view customers from a distance, might have trouble judging who is likely to stay healthy and who is likely to get sick. Meanwhile, customers familiar with their own medical history and unhealthy habits have intimate knowledge of their own risk.

There are thus two related concepts to analyze in the market for insurance: uncertainty and information. As we have seen in the last chapter, uncertainty by itself does not impede the market from functioning well. A theme of this chapter is that **asymmetric information** about that uncertainty can pose a more existential threat to the market. The major problem is that the party with more information has incentive to misrepresent himself to obtain better terms in the transaction – in other words, to lie about his position. The party with less information anticipates this dishonesty and takes action to protect herself.

Definition	8.1

Information asymmetry: a situation in which agents in a potential economic transaction do not have the same information about the quality of the good being transacted.

The used-car market is the standard context to start exploring these themes. This market is sometimes known as the "market for lemons," because defective used cars are known colloquially as lemons. Misrepresentation is common in this market, which is notorious for seedy salesmen and suspect merchandise. Even though used cars and insurance contracts are very different things, the lessons about asymmetric information that we learn here can be applied readily to insurance markets.

8.1   The intuition behind the market for lemons

Imagine a well-functioning used-car market. Sellers advertise prices for old cars they no longer want, while potential buyers scour websites and classified ads looking for good deals. If they find a potential match, the buyers visit the sellers and examine the vehicle for sale. They kick the tires, peer under the hood, or take the car for a test drive in hopes of assessing the vehicle's condition.

Let us suppose that these simple diagnostic techniques are sufficient to uncover any problems. Buyers who open the hood of their potential new ride will notice if critical car parts are missing, or are held together with duct tape. Then the seller and buyer have identical information about the quality of each car, so the price of each car adjusts to reflect its specific quality. This market will function well.

Nobel prize-winning economist George Akerlof imagined what would happen if the used-car market described above suffered from information asymmetry (Akerlof 1970). Sellers know all about the problems that their cars have, but crucially *buyers do not*. Buyers can test-drive cars all they want, but they cannot make a confident quality assessment.

If any cars are to sell at all in this market, they must all sell at the same price. To show this, we argue that a market for used cars with two prices must converge to a single price. Suppose that there are two cars in this market, one for sale at a high price P' and one for sale at a low price $P < P'$. Since they cannot tell the difference between the two cars, buyers consider the two cars as identical and they would never pay the higher price. Hence, only the car at the lower price has any chance of selling. And as a result, the seller at P' must lower his price to P to have a chance of finding a buyer.

From the previous paragraph, we can conclude that any cars that do sell must sell at exactly the same price. The next step is to see if any cars sell at all at a single price P. We will show that, under certain conditions, for this P no cars will sell. And since P was selected arbitrarily, we can assert that there is no P under these conditions such that cars will sell.

The lot of used cars do not all have the same quality. The well-maintained ones are worth much more than P, but the rickety ones are worth much less. If P is the market price, not all cars reach the market. The sellers who own cars worth more than P will not want to put their cars on sale at all. Thus, the high-quality cars are withdrawn from the market, leaving only the low-quality ones. This is an example of **adverse selection**, which causes the market to unravel.

Definition | **8.2**

Adverse selection: the oversupply of low-quality goods, products, or contracts that results when there is asymmetric information. For instance, if a supplier of a product has better information about product quality than a buyer, then the highest-quality products will not be offered.

Now we have price P, where the highest-quality cars have been withdrawn from the market by their sellers. Consider the remaining cars. There is a distribution of value amongst these cars, and the most valuable of them will be worth at most P. Thus, the average value of the remaining cars is less than P. Buyers thus know that they would be purchasing a car worth much less than P, so unless the market price declines, buyers will refuse to purchase any cars.

A typical interaction between an Akerlofian buyer and an Akerlofian seller.

Credit: Allen Cox.

Suppose a new price establishes itself below P. The same exact argument outlined above applies again. Sellers withdraw the top-quality cars, and as a result, the average worth of the cars remaining on the market falls further. Realizing that the market price still exceeds average value, buyers respond by refusing to purchase. With each new price drop and subsequent round of adverse selection, the car quality in this market continues to degrade until only the lowest-quality goods are still on the market. Depending on the exact utility function of buyers and sellers, even those may not sell.

It should be clear, at least at an intuitive level, why the market for lemons can fail under asymmetric information. Sellers cannot guarantee to buyers the quality of the cars they are selling, and sellers of low-quality cars have incentive to masquerade as high-quality sellers. The market fails because of a lack of incentives for honesty; instead, having the information advantage gives the sellers incentive to misrepresent the quality of their cars.

8.2   A formal statement of the Akerlof model

The intuitive story of the market for lemons should be clear at this point, but there are many nuances and limitations to this argument that only become clear with a more formal treatment. For instance, does the market still fall apart if buyers value cars so much that they are willing to pay top dollar for even the lowest-quality cars? Careful study of this formal treatment will help build the reader's intuition about the effects of adverse selection.

In addition, it will enable the reader to apply the logic of the Akerlof model to related situations and ask questions about the effects of potential government policies. The extensions we address later in this chapter include: What if the government introduced a price ceiling in this market? What would be the effect of a law that forbade low-quality cars from being placed on the market? Under these conditions, can the market work? The formal apparatus we develop next will enable us to answer these questions.

Seller and buyer utility functions

In the model, both sellers and buyers seek to maximize their own utility. At the beginning of the model, before any trades have taken place, each buyer and seller owns a set of cars, which we label 1 through n. Each car has exactly one owner. Of course, no one lives on cars alone; both buyers and sellers also derive utility from other goods, which we will call M.

Let the utility that a seller derives from the set of cars he owns and the other goods he consumes be U_S. Let the utility that a buyer derives from the set of cars she owns and the other goods she consumes be U_B. To keep things simple, we assume that buyers and sellers have the following utility functions:

$$U_S = \sum_{j=1}^{n} X_j + M$$

$$U_B = \sum_{j=1}^{n} \frac{3}{2} X_j + M$$

(8.1)

where X_i is the quality of the ith car owned by a buyer or seller. We will assume throughout that the price of a unit of other goods M is fixed at \$1. This presentation of the analysis of the market for lemons follows Akerlof's presentation in his classic 1970 paper.

Notice that these functions differ in one important way: a buyer values a car of given quality at 50% more than a seller would value the exact same car. The difference makes sense because buyers naturally desire cars more than sellers do – that is why the buyers are buying and the sellers selling. Additionally, these utility specifications imply that buyers and sellers are risk-neutral with respect to uncertainty about car quality. Doubling car quality, for example, exactly doubles the contribution of car quality to utility. In later sections, we introduce different utility functions.

Distribution of car quality

Sellers own cars of varying quality. For now, we assume that car quality X is uniformly distributed on a scale between 0 and 100:

$$X \sim Uniform(0, 100)$$

Because of the nature of the uniform distribution, cars owned by sellers are equally likely to have quality level 3.14, 70, 99.999, or anything in between 0 and 100. Additionally, there is a $(100 - q)$% likelihood that the quality exceeds q for any q from 0 to 100. Figure 8.1 shows the distribution of car quality.

Information assumptions

In introductory economics, we tend to study markets where both buyers and sellers share the same information about the quality of goods they are trading. In that setting, students should recall, the market price clears the market by equating supply and demand. In a market for used cars of varying quality with perfect information, each car of a given quality

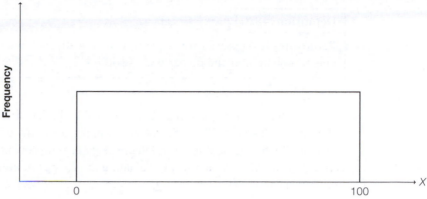

Figure 8.1. *The distribution of car quality.*

level is its own market, with its own market-clearing price. Higher-quality cars sell at higher prices than lower-quality cars because buyers value them more.

One of the authors owned a lemon that looked much like this back in 1985. The undercarriage was extensively rusted, the window hand-cranks had fallen off, and the car stalled on every other left turn. Even clueless Akerlofian car buyers would have been able to detect that $X_i \approx 0$. Credit: © WoGi – Fotolia.com.

In Akerlof's model of the market for lemons, however, buyers and sellers do not share the same information. Sellers know the quality of their cars; over time, they have observed how well their cars have been maintained, whether they suffered in any accidents, how they perform in cold weather, and whether anyone has vomited all over the back seat. But buyers know none of this and consequently cannot assess the true quality of any particular car.

But buyers are not uninformed; they know the form of the utility functions of the sellers. They also know the distribution of cars available for sale – how many cars of each quality level there are. They understand how the sellers react to changes in the prevailing price in the market. For instance, they understand that sellers will withdraw the highest-quality cars if the price does not justify selling. Therefore, the buyers know the distribution of cars actually placed on the market by the sellers at any given price. In other words, they understand how adverse selection works.

Recall that in the standard market, each car of a different quality level essentially represented its own market. In Akerlof's model, though, all the cars in this market are indistinguishable to buyers. It is one big market and all the cars must share the single price *P*. No buyer would pay more than *P* for any car because good cars and lemons appear identical and paying more does not lower the probability of buying a lemon. This is actually a general property of markets with asymmetric information: goods of varying quality that would otherwise be in separate "markets" are lumped together in a single market with a single price.

When do cars sell?

Under asymmetric information, our goal is to find out if the market functions as well as it does under symmetric information. That is: do all trades that would be Pareto-improving actually occur?

> **Definition | 8.3**
>
> **Pareto-improvement:** a transaction or reallocation of resources that leaves at least one party better off and no party worse off.

Our strategy is to propose a candidate price P and ask which cars remain on the market at that price. Then we will see if buyers are willing to buy any of the remaining cars. We try every candidate price and see at which prices Pareto-improving, mutually beneficial trades actually occur. We will do this by evaluating the change in utility due to a transaction for both buyers and sellers.

Which cars will sellers offer?

In order for a seller to be willing to sell a car at price P, the utility from selling the car must exceed the value of the car to the seller. Before any cars are sold, the seller's utility was

$$U_S(\text{before}) = \sum_{j=1}^{n} X_j + M$$

Suppose that a seller sells car 1 with quality level X_1. In this transaction, the seller loses X_i units of utility but gains P dollars with which he buys P units of M, and hence P units of utility. So his utility after selling is

$$U_S(\text{after}) = \sum_{j=1}^{n} X_j - X_1 + M + P$$

The change in seller's utility ΔU_S from selling car 1 is

$$\Delta U_S = U_S(\text{after}) - U_S(\text{before})$$
$$= P - X_1 \tag{8.2}$$

Sellers put cars on the market if their utility increases from doing so. As we can see from equation (8.2), sellers gain utility from selling if and only if $\Delta U_S \geq 0$, which implies and is implied by $X_1 \leq P$. This means the car is offered on the market only if the quality level is less than or equal to the single price. In other words, this price serves as an upper bound on the quality of cars offered in the market.

For what follows, we need a bit of notation to define the set of cars put on the market at any P. Let $\Omega(P)$ be the set of all cars still on offer in the market at price P, which coincides with the set of cars with quality less than or equal to P:

$$\Omega(P) = \{i | X_i \leq P\} \tag{8.3}$$

Figure 8.2 illustrates the situation with price P. In the figure, the shaded area to the right of the vertical price line represents the cars withdrawn from the market because their value is so high that sellers would lose utility from selling them at P. The unshaded area to the left of the vertical price line is the set of cars that are left on the market, or $\Omega(P)$ as defined in Equation (8.3). These cars all have quality less than P.

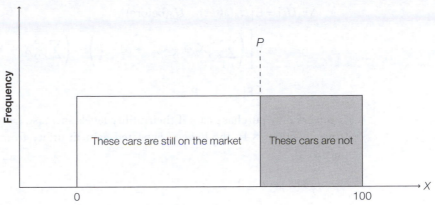

Figure 8.2. *Adverse selection in the used-car market. The highest-quality cars are not offered for sale.*

When will buyers buy?

We have established which cars are offered by sellers when the market price is P. To determine if transactions take place, we must also analyze the behavior of buyers.

At a given price P, a buyer is only willing to buy car i if her utility increases from doing so. From the buyer's point of view, the quality of the car she gets is uncertain. But it is drawn from a distribution that she does know, the distribution of $\Omega(P)$; that is, the set of cars remaining on the market after sellers have withdrawn the cars whose quality exceeds the selling price. So buyers have to make the decision to buy based on their expected utility from buying a car drawn from this set. They hope to get the best car available but may instead end up buying the worst.

If a buyer purchases a car, it will be her $(n+1)$th car, so we will label it car $n+1$ with quality level X_{n+1}. In this potential transaction, she will lose $\$P$ with certainty and hence P units of other goods M (since each unit of other goods costs $\$1$). In exchange, she receives a car of unknown quality.

To decide whether this is a good trade *ex ante*, the buyer evaluates all the possible levels of X_{n+1} and thinks about the resulting utility from the best car, the worst car, and everything in between for all the cars in $\Omega(P)$. She knows to ignore the cars in the shaded area in Figure 8.2 because there is no chance the car she purchases will be from that region.

Before the potential transaction, the buyer's utility (equation (8.1)) is

$$U_B(\text{before}) = \sum_{j=1}^{n} \frac{3}{2} X_j + M$$

Given our specification of the buyer's utility, the buyer would gain $3/2 X_{n+1}$ utility units from purchasing this car, and would lose P units of M. After buying car $n+1$, her utility would be

$$U_B(\text{after}) = \sum_{j=1}^{n} \frac{3}{2} X_j + \frac{3}{2} X_{n+1} + M - P$$

But the buyer does not know the actual value of X_{n+1}, and hence cannot compute $U_B(\text{after})$. However, since she knows $\Omega(P)$ and the distribution of cars on the market given $\Omega(P)$, she can calculate her *expected* utility from buying the car. The change in her expected utility is

$$\Delta \mathrm{E}[U_B] = \mathrm{E}\left[U_B(\text{after}) - U_B(\text{before})\right]$$

$$= \mathrm{E}\left[\left(\sum_{j=1}^{n} \frac{3}{2}X_j + \frac{3}{2}X_{n+1} + M - P\right) - \left(\sum_{j=1}^{n} \frac{3}{2}X_j + M\right)\right] \tag{8.4}$$

$$= \frac{3}{2}\mathrm{E}[X_{n+1}] - P$$

Buyers only purchase cars if their utility levels increase from doing so. As we can see from equation (8.4), the buyers' expected gain in utility from buying is positive if and only if

$$\frac{3}{2}\mathrm{E}[X_i] - P \geq 0$$

$$\frac{3}{2}\mathrm{E}[X_i] \geq P \tag{8.5}$$

Another way to interpret this condition is that the expected marginal benefit of the purchase (the additional expected utility from car $n+1$ with quality X_{n+1}) must outweigh the marginal cost of buying it, P. Keep in mind that this expectation is computed with respect to the cars that are actually offered on the market, $\Omega(P)$, given that the sellers withhold the best cars.

The market unravels

Now that we have the conditions for the sellers selling and the buyers buying, we are ready to assess this market's ability to match these buyers and sellers at prices that induce them to trade. In this section, we consider a numerical example to make clear exactly how the market unravels.

Arbitrarily, we first assume a candidate price of $P = \$50$. At this price, equation (8.2) implies that only cars with quality $X_i \leq 50$ reach the market. This is the effect of adverse selection.

Figure 8.3 illustrates the situation in this market. This figure is just like Figure 8.2 except that we have chosen a specific value of P. Since the distribution of car quality is uniform to begin with, the distribution of car quality conditional on the set of cars that sellers actually sell, $\Omega(50)$, will also be uniform. This is a property of uniform random variables. So the cars remaining on the market are uniformly distributed in quality from 0 to 50.

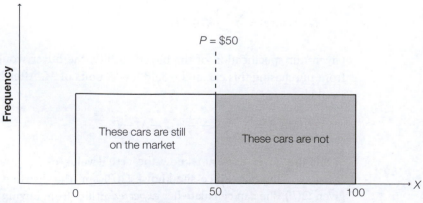

Figure 8.3. *Adverse selection in the used-car market with* P= $50.

At this point, since we know what cars are offered on the market, we are ready to determine whether any buyers will purchase them. To do so, we must evaluate equation (8.5) at $P = \$50$. This equation calls for us to calculate the expected value of the random variable X_{n+1}, which has a uniform distribution. Equation (8.6) contains this formula.

For a uniform random variable X which varies from a to b, the formula for the expectation of X is

$$E[X] = \frac{b+a}{2} \qquad\qquad (8.6)$$

Applying this formula, taking a as the worst possible car quality and b as the best possible car quality, we find that the average quality of cars remaining on the market when $P = \$50$ is 25:

$$E[X_{n+1}] = \frac{50+0}{2} = 25$$

How do buyers evaluate this distribution of cars that are on the market? We can calculate their expected change in utility from buying car $n+1$ by applying the last line of equation (8.4):

$$
\begin{aligned}
E[\Delta U_B] &= \frac{3}{2} E[X_{n+1}] - P \\
&= \frac{3}{2} \cdot 25 - 50 \qquad\qquad (8.7) \\
&= 37.5 - 50 \\
&= -12.5
\end{aligned}
$$

The buyers know that the average quality of cars still on offer in this market is 25. At this average quality level, it does not make sense for them to buy because P is 50. This means that a buyer is being asked to yield 50 units of utility for a car they expect to value at 37.5 utility units.

This is not a good trade for the buyers; their expected change in utility is negative.

Why not just find a better price?

No car sells if $P = \$50$, but are there other prices that could induce trades between buyers and sellers? Unfortunately, the answer is no in this example; it turns out that if we pick *any* value for P, the market runs into the same dead end.

First assume any value of $P \geq \$100$. All cars will be offered, but any such price is too high to satisfy any buyers, because the expected car quality $E[X_i]$ is 50. So the expected utility from buying a car is 75, lower than the costs of purchasing it.

Therefore, the only hope is $P < \$100$. But in that case the average quality of cars on the market is $P/2$ by the formula for the mean of a random uniform variable from equation (8.6):

$$E[X_{n+1}] = \frac{P+0}{2} = \frac{P}{2}$$

The change in a buyer's utility, should she buy a car at price P, is given by equation (8.4):

$$E[\Delta U_B] = \frac{3}{2} \times \frac{P}{2} - P = -\frac{1}{4}P$$

So for any price less than 100, buyers will face the following choice. They can give up P in exchange for a car that can be expected to give them only $\frac{3}{4}P$ worth of utility. No matter the price P, this market unravels.

8.3   The adverse selection death spiral

Now we switch our focus to a health insurance market that actually looks quite similar to the used-car market we just studied. First, we must make a few assumptions about the way this market functions to bring it in line with the very simplified world of the Akerlof model.

Assumptions

- Each customer i has an expected amount of health care costs over the course of the year X_i.
- An insurance company offers a single policy with an annual premium P. This full-insurance policy covers all health care costs incurred during the year.
- Customers are risk-neutral. Customer i will purchase insurance if and only if P is less than his expected health care costs X_i.
- The insurers are not allowed to discriminate between healthy and sick, and must contract with any customer willing to pay the premium. They have no way to exclude more sickly customers from purchasing insurance.
- Expected customer health care costs X_i are distributed independently and uniformly in the population:

$$X_i \sim Uniform[\$0, \$20{,}000]$$

Take a second to compare this market with Akerlof's market for used cars. You will see that an extended analogy can be drawn. The "cars" here are the customers' bodies, and the "sellers" are the customers trying to convince the "buyers" (insurance companies) that the "cars" are healthy and unlikely to break down. Just as a high-quality car is worth paying a high price, a high-quality body should only be charged a low premium. And just as high-quality cars leave the market when a universal price is set, high-quality bodies will leave the market when a universal premium is set.

Suppose that the insurance company offers a contract with a premium $P = \$10{,}000$ in 2013. Half of the customers do not purchase insurance because their expected health costs are less than the premium. Just as it was not worthwhile for sellers with high-quality cars to enter the market in the Akerlof universe, it is not worthwhile for relatively healthy people to buy health insurance in this market. The sickly customers, on the other hand – the ones with expected health care costs exceeding \$10,000 – sign up as quickly as possible (see Figure 8.4). For these high-risk customers, this insurance contract is a great deal.

What happens to the insurance company's books? Adverse selection ensures that the insurer will lose money. The company collects \$10,000 from each customer, but pays an average of \$15,000 for each customer's health care. This means the insurance company suffers an expected loss of \$5,000 per customer.

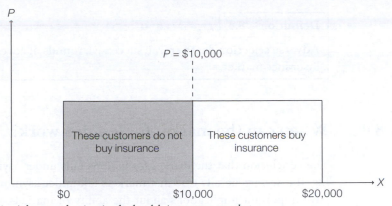

Figure 8.4. *Adverse selection in the health insurance market.*

After a round of mid-level executive downsizing at the insurance firm, consultants recommend raising premiums to $P = \$15,000$ for 2014. If each customer costs the insurer $15,000, the new premium should balance the company's cash flow. Right?

Unfortunately, the consultants are wrong; they neglect the fact that adverse selection will continue. Of the remaining enrollees, the healthier among them exit the plan, while the sicker, more expensive, customers sign on for another year of coverage. This time, the selection is even more adverse than before – only the sickest of the sick enroll. Now prices have risen, fewer people are choosing to buy insurance, and the insurance company is still unprofitable (see Figure 8.5).

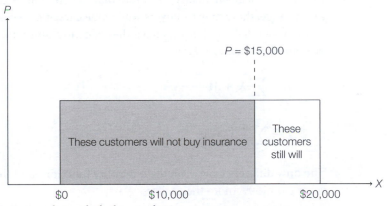

Figure 8.5. *A second round of adverse selection.*

Now the company collects $15,000 from each customer. And while some customers cost slightly less or more than expected, collectively they average $17,500 in insurance claims. This means the insurance company still loses $2,500 per customer.

With each successive correction by the insurance company, the premium increases, subscription drops, and the remaining pool of customers gets smaller and sicker. This cyclical phenomenon is called an **adverse selection death spiral**. It concludes with an Akerlofian market collapse – as the insurance company eventually learns, it cannot make a profit with any premium in this market. In Chapter 10, we will see evidence of real-life adverse selection death spirals that happened just about like this.

> **Definition | 8.4**
>
> **Adverse selection death spiral:** successive rounds of adverse selection that destroy an insurance market.

8.4   When can the market for lemons work?

The conclusion that the market for lemons fails under asymmetric information is striking. If it were generally true that markets fail under asymmetric information, that would have important implications about the ability of markets to facilitate Pareto-improving trades. However, the model as we presented it depends on strong assumptions about the utility of the buyers, the utility of the sellers, the distribution of car quality, and the institutional setting, including the legal rules under which the market functions. If some of these assumptions are relaxed, the market for lemons may function, though not as well as in perfect competition when buyers and sellers have the same information about the cars. The goal of this section is to explore how robust the Akerlof model is to changes in these assumptions, and by extension to explore whether health insurance markets can be saved from the adverse selection death spiral.

What if buyers value cars very highly?

In the utility functions for buyers and sellers that we presented in equation (8.1), buyers valued a car of given quality 50% more than sellers. This is clearly an arbitrary assumption; for instance, there may be buyers who value cars at considerably higher margins.

Suppose sellers and buyers have the following utility functions instead of the ones we presented in equation (8.1):

$$U_S = \sum_{j=1}^{n} X_j + M$$

$$U_B = \sum_{j=1}^{n} \frac{5}{2} X_j + M$$

(8.8)

The only difference between the old utility functions and the new ones is that buyers now value cars 150% more than sellers.

We start again, as usual, with a candidate price P. Because the sellers' utility functions have not changed, their behavior is the same as before. The set of cars they place on the market will still be $\Omega(P)$, and is still characterized by $X_i < P$ (see equations (8.2) and (8.3)). In the numerical example above, where $P = \$50$, the set of the cars offered on the market would still range in quality from 0 to 50, where the average quality of cars is still 25.

We turn next to buyers. Their behavior *does* change, since they now have a different utility function. They value cars on the market more, even though the distribution of car quality and average car quality have not changed. We must reexamine equation (8.4), reproduced here:

$$\Delta E[U_B] = E\left[U_B(\text{after}) - U_B(\text{before})\right]$$

After plugging in the buyers' new utility function, we obtain

$$\Delta E[U_B] = E\left[U_B(\text{after}) - U_B(\text{before})\right]$$

$$= E\left[\left(\sum_{j=1}^{n}\frac{5}{2}X_j + \frac{5}{2}X_{n+1} + M - P\right) - \left(\sum_{j=1}^{n}\frac{5}{2}X_j + M\right)\right] \qquad (8.9)$$

$$= \frac{5}{2}E\left[X_{n+1}\right] - P$$

which implies that buyers will purchase cars when

$$\frac{5}{2}E\left[X_{n+1}\right] - P \geq 0$$

$$\frac{5}{2}E\left[X_{n+1}\right] \geq P \qquad (8.10)$$

Will this condition be satisfied for our candidate price P? Recall that since we started with a uniform distribution of car quality, even after the sellers withhold the top-quality cars, the distribution of cars in $\Omega(P)$ will still be uniform. We can calculate the expected value of car quality in $\Omega(P)$ using equation (8.6):

$$E\left[X_{n+1}\right] = \frac{P+0}{2} = \frac{P}{2}$$

Given this average car quality, the change in utility from purchasing a car is

$$\Delta U_B = \frac{5}{2} \cdot E\left[X_{n+1}\right] - P$$

$$= \frac{5}{2} \cdot \frac{P}{2} - P \qquad (8.11)$$

$$= \frac{1}{4}P > 0$$

These buyers gain utility from buying a used car on this market, *almost no matter the price*, even though they are fully aware that sellers withhold the top-quality cars. Actually, there is a price above which buyers no longer gain utility from buying a car. What is it and how does that change with the maximum quality of cars? With the buyers' utility function? Exercise 9 addresses these questions.

What if the government sets a price ceiling?

Governments often intervene in insurance markets by regulating the prices at which insurers can sell and by requiring certain kinds of risk-pooling. We say more about this in future chapters, but in this context, we can imagine a similar government intervention. Suppose a consumer-protection agency decides to set a price ceiling in the market for lemons in an attempt to protect buyers from being gouged by unscrupulous sellers. What effect does this price ceiling have on the market?

Surprisingly, the answer is almost none. To see this, consider again the case where buyers' utility is given by

$$U_B = \sum_{j=1}^{n}\frac{3}{2}X_j + M$$

where they value any given car 50% more than sellers. In this case, the price ceiling does not change the logic of adverse selection at all. Sellers cannot charge more than the ceiling price, so suppose that sellers charge some price less than the ceiling. They will withhold the top-quality cars just as before – in fact, the price ceiling ensures that the best cars (those more valuable than the price ceiling) never reach the market under any circumstances. Buyers know this and, as before, value the typical car on the market less than the price, and the market collapses again.

Suppose instead that buyers value any given car 150% more than sellers, as in the previous example. In that example, buyers were always willing to purchase cars, almost regardless of the price. The price ceiling does not change that logic at all. The only thing it affects is $\Omega(P)$ – the set of cars that sellers bring to the market.

In neither case does the price ceiling benefit buyers, and in some cases, may actually harm them. In the second example, where buyers value cars very highly, the price ceiling forces sellers to leave the highest-quality cars off the market. Those cars may have found buyers who would have benefited from a sale, even at a high price. Meanwhile, the other buyers in this example are unaffected by the price ceiling. This is a good example of an economic inefficiency induced by a well-meaning reform.

What if there is a minimum guaranteed car quality?

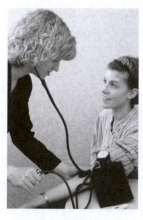

Many life insurance companies will physically examine potential customers before insuring them. They do this for the same reason that used-car buyers scrutinize the repair histories of the cars they might buy.
Credit: PhotoDisc.

In many industries where the form of adverse selection we have been talking about exists, private groups have formed to address the market failure caused by information asymmetry. For instance, there are companies that will, for a fee, provide potential buyers with the complete repair history of any used car in the US. Additionally, government agencies sometimes fill the market's information gap by requiring sellers to disclose problems to buyers or by enforcing a minimum standard of quality. The Food and Drug Administration, for instance, requires that new drugs meet a minimum quality standard before allowing pharmaceutical companies to place them on the market. The Akerlof model has implications for the efficacy of such interventions.

Suppose the state government passes a law banning the sales of cars with quality $X_i < 10$. Our goal is to see whether there are any prices at which transactions do occur. Suppose we have a candidate price P. Given the sellers' utility function in equation (8.1), sellers will place all cars i of quality between $10 and P on the market.

Figure 8.6 illustrates this new situation. The shaded areas represent cars that are not placed on the market, while the unshaded area represents cars that are offered for sale. Cars with quality less than 10 do not reach the market due to the new law. And as usual, sellers with cars of quality greater than P withhold their cars from the market. This means $\Omega(P)$ has both a lower and an upper bound:

$$\Omega(P) = \{i \,|\, 10 \leq X_i \leq P\} \tag{8.12}$$

It should be clear that P must be greater or equal to $10, otherwise $\Omega(P)$ is the empty set and no cars would be offered on the market.

We find the new average quality of cars on the market by applying the formula for the mean of a uniform distribution (equation (8.6)):

$$E[X_i] = \frac{P+10}{2}$$

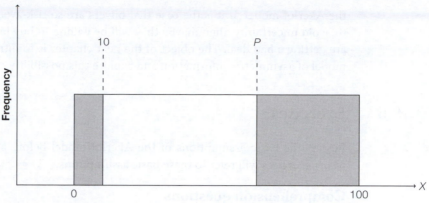

Figure 8.6. *Adverse selection in the used-car market with a guaranteed minimum car quality. Cars with quality $X_i < 10$ are prohibited from being offered on the market.*

In this market, we will consider only buyers who value a given car 50% more than sellers. The change in utility to a buyer from purchasing a car is (equation (8.4)):

$$\Delta U_B = \frac{3}{2} \cdot E[X_i] - P$$
$$= \frac{3}{2} \cdot \frac{P+10}{2} - P \qquad (8.13)$$
$$= \frac{15}{2} - \frac{1}{4}P$$

implying that buyers will purchase cars so long as

$$\Delta U_B = \frac{15}{2} - \frac{1}{4}P \geq 0$$
$$30 - P \geq 0 \qquad (8.14)$$
$$30 \geq P$$

For prices between $10 and $30, sellers place on the market cars of quality between 10 and P. Buyers buy those cars because their utility increases from doing so. Therefore, this minimum-quality floor guarantees a range of prices where the market can function, even though it does not completely solve the market failure associated with adverse selection.

8.5   Conclusion

We have seen that asymmetric information can upend the used-car market, but it is important to note that all this talk about used cars is highly pertinent to insurance markets. Wherever asymmetric information is lurking, such as in transactions between a seemingly healthy person and an insurance agent, markets can unravel and fail. This is not to say that markets with asymmetric information will automatically fail. Remember, if buyers care enough about a product or if there are credible minimum-quality guarantees, the Akerlof market does not unravel.

It is important to remember that the Akerlof model is very simple, and abstracts away from risk aversion altogether to focus on uncertainty and asymmetric information. This is not an irrelevant omission. Introducing risk aversion may overturn the major results of the Akerlof model. If it is the case that buyers are so risk-averse that they are desperate to avoid uncertainty, then maybe they will be willing to buy insurance even though they are getting a bad deal. The object of the next chapter is to introduce risk aversion into a model of asymmetric information and explore this possibility.

8.6   Exercises

Review the basic assumptions of the Akerlof model before answering these questions. Many exercises will refer to these basic assumptions.

Comprehension questions

Indicate whether the statement is true or false, and justify your answer. Be sure to state any additional assumptions you may need.

1   In the Akerlof model, suppose that the price of used cars is P and the quality of used cars (X) held by sellers varies between 0 and 100. Suppose further that sellers' utility is given by

$$U_S = M + a \sum_i^n X_i$$

where M is the number of units of video games, which sell at \$1 per game, and a is a utility function parameter that is strictly less than one ($a < 1$). Then sellers will offer cars with quality $X_i = P$ on the market.

2   In the model, buyers know the utility function of sellers, but do not know anything about the general quality of cars for sale.

3   If buyers care sufficiently more about cars than do sellers, then there are prices at which transactions can occur. In that scenario, there is no longer any adverse selection (although there still may be some information asymmetry).

4   The Akerlof model indicates that government intervention is the only way to solve the adverse selection problem.

5   If the quality of cars is normally distributed rather than uniformly distributed, the market will not unravel.

6   Ultimately, the market unravels because buyers are risk-averse. If buyers were risk-neutral, there would always be prices at which cars would sell.

Analytical problems

7   Review the basic assumptions of the Akerlof model. Assume that, in this market, the quality of cars X_i is distributed as follows:

$$X_i \sim Uniform[q_1, q_2]$$

Note that in the discussion above, we analyzed the version of the Akerlof model where $q_1 = 0$ and $q_2 = 100$.

a   Let $q_1 = 0$ and $q_2 = 50$. Will any cars sell in this market? Explain your reasoning carefully.

b   Let $q_1 = 0$ and $q_2 = 200$. Will any cars sell in this market? Explain your reasoning carefully. Does raising the *maximum* quality of cars that sellers possess have any effect on predictions of the model? Explain why or why not.

   c Let $q_1 = 50$ and $q_2 = 100$. Will any cars sell in this market? Explain your reasoning carefully. Does raising the *minimum* quality of cars that sellers possess have any effect on predictions of the model? Explain why or why not.

8 In Section 8.4 we studied the case of a government-mandated ban on the sale of low-quality cars. Review the basic assumptions of the Akerlof model, assume that car quality X_i is distributed uniformly from 0 to 100, and assume that the buyer and seller utility functions are as originally supposed in equation (8.1).

   a Let the government-mandated minimum quality be denoted as B. If $B = 50$, this means car i can only be offered on the market if $X_i \geq 50$. What is the range of prices, if any, that would allow transactions if $B = 50$?

   b What if $B = 90$? $B = 5$?

   c Find the smallest B for which you can still find prices that will allow transactions to occur. If there is no minimum, explain why not.

9 Consider again the example where buyers value cars much more than sellers. We assume again that

$$U_S = \sum_{j=1}^{n} X_j + M$$

$$U_B = \sum_{j=1}^{n} \frac{5}{2} X_j + M \tag{8.15}$$

Recall that, under these assumptions, any price P such that $\$0 < P \leq \$100$ induced at least some sales.

   a Will there be any transactions if $P = \$150$? Why or why not?

   b What is the maximum price P at which at least some transactions will occur?

   c Suppose instead that the buyer and seller utility functions are given by

$$U_S = \sum_{j=1}^{n} X_j + M$$

$$U_B = \sum_{j=1}^{n} h X_j + M \tag{8.16}$$

where h reflects how much more buyers value cars than sellers. What is the maximum price at which at least some transactions will occur, in terms of h?

   d Assume further that the utility functions are still given by equation (8.16), but that car quality X is distributed as follows:

$$X_i \sim Uniform[0, G]$$

where $G > 100$ is a distribution parameter. Now, what is the maximum price at which at least some transactions will occur, in terms of h and G?

   e Interpret your findings about how the market's functioning changes with h and G in non-mathematical terms.

10 Assume that instead of a uniform distribution, in this market, the quality of cars X follows a triangle distribution from 0 to 100 as depicted in Figure 8.7.

Given this new distribution, the formula for expected value of X conditional on an upper bound P is

$$E[X_i | \Omega(P)] = \frac{2}{3} P \tag{8.17}$$

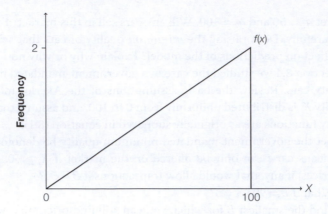

Figure 8.7. *A triangle distribution.*

We assume the original seller and buyer utility specifications:

$$U_S = \sum_{j=1}^{n} X_j + M$$

$$U_B = \sum_{j=1}^{n} \frac{3}{2} X_j + M$$

a First assume $P = \$50$. Will any cars sell in this market?

b What is the range of prices for which cars will sell?

c Describe in qualitative terms how the triangle distribution is different from the uniform distribution we assumed earlier. Do the sellers possess more high-quality cars or low-quality cars? How does this allow the market to function even in the face of asymmetric information?

d Use the formula for conditional expectation below to derive equation (8.17). Note that $f(x)$ is the probability density function and $F_X(x)$ is the cumulative distribution function for the triangle distribution above.

$$E[X_i | \Omega(P)] = \int_0^P \frac{x f(x)}{F_X(P)} dx$$

e Now assume a different triangle distribution for car quality X as depicted in Figure 8.8. Without doing any calculations, predict whether the market will unravel. Justify your answer.

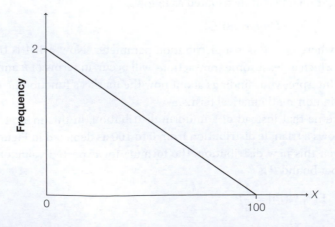

Figure 8.8. *Alternate triangle distribution.*

11 Suppose a local car dealership is offering an inspection service that can perfectly deter-mine the quality of any car on the market. The dealership is trying to determine how much it will be able to charge for this procedure. Review the original assumptions about the Akerlof model. Specifically, we assume the buyer and seller utilities from equation (8.1), that car quality X is distributed uniformly from 0 to 100, and that the prevailing price $P = 50$.

   a   Due to adverse selection, only some of the cars remain on the market ($\Omega(P)$). How are these cars distributed, and what is their average quality?

   b   Suppose a buyer picks a car i at random from the cars still available on the market, and thinks about whether to purchase it. What is her expected change in utility from this transaction?

   c   Even though her *expected* change in utility is negative, there is a possibility that she picked a relatively high-quality car and that her actual change in utility would be positive. What is the lowest value of X_i such that this will happen, and what is the probability that X_i is at least this high?

   d   Now suppose the local car dealership decides to offer this buyer its inspection service for free, before she decides whether to purchase the car. She resolves to purchase car i if it will increase her utility, and refrain from purchasing it if it will not increase her utility. Now, what is her expected change in utility from this trans-action, considering that we do not yet know whether the car will be good enough to purchase? How does this differ from your answer in Exercise 11(b)?

   e   How much will the dealership be able to charge for the inspection service, assum-ing the price remains at $50 and that all other assumptions are constant? Justify your answer.

   f   Imagine that word about the inspection service gets out to everyone in the mar-ket, including sellers. How will sellers with high-quality cars react? How will sellers with low-quality cars react? Will there be any adverse selection in the market?

12 We assume again the original assumptions of the Akerlof model, but now alter the information assumptions in this exercise. Now assume that *neither* buyers nor sellers have information about specific car quality, although each group knows the distribution of X_i as before.

   a   Assume that there is a market equilibrium price of $P = 80$. What set of cars will be *offered* in this market? In other words, what is $\Omega(80)$ under these assumptions?

   b   Does adverse selection occur in this situation?

   c   Derive a more general expression for $\Omega(P)$. For any given P, what is the set of cars that will be offered?

   d   What is the range of P for which at least some cars will be offered and at least some cars will be purchased? Remember that sales do happen when buyers and sellers are indifferent.

13 **Thirdhand car markets.** Consider now two sequential used-car markets. The first is a market for secondhand cars (one previous owner). The second is a market for thirdhand cars (two previous owners).

   In the first market, there are two types of traders: *Original Owners* and *Original Buyers*. Original Owners own all the cars and have the following utility function:

$$U = M + \sum_{j=1}^{n} ax_j$$

where M is the amount of non-car goods consumed, x_j is the quality level of the jth car, and a is a parameter in the utility function.

Original Buyers own no cars and have the following utility function:

$$U = M + \sum_{j=1}^{n} bx_j$$

where again M is the amount of non-car goods consumed, x_j is the quality level of the jth car, and b is a parameter in the utility function.

There is a uniform distribution over the quality of all cars, with

$$x_j \sim Uniform[0, 100]$$

Let P_1 be the price of used cars put up for sale by Original Owners in equilibrium. Original Owners know the quality of the cars they are selling, but Original Buyers only know the average quality of the cars on the market. Original Buyers know the utility function of the Original Owners.

a   What will be the average quality of cars offered on the market by Original Owners under these conditions, as a function of P_1 and a?

b   For what values of b will Original Buyers be willing to buy the cars, as a function a?

c   Suppose b satisfies the condition you found in the previous question, and some cars are sold from the Original Owners to the Original Buyers. Now the second market takes place. The Original Buyers become Secondhand Owners and they are in a thirdhand car market with new buyers, which we call Secondhand Buyers. The Secondhand Buyers know all about the first market for secondhand cars. The Secondhand Owners, after driving around their new cars, have learned the quality of the cars, but the Secondhand Buyers only know the average quality of the cars on the market. The Secondhand Buyers own no cars and have the following utility function:

$$U = M + \sum_{j=1}^{n} cx_j$$

where c is a parameter in the utility function. Let P_2 be the price of used cars put up for sale by Secondhand Owners in equilibrium. For what values of c will Secondhand Buyers be willing to buy the cars, as a function of b?

d   Suppose $b = 3$. For what price P_2 will the cars available on the thirdhand car market be uniformly distributed between 0 and 50?

e   Suppose also that $c = 5$. Will the Secondhand Buyers buy any cars in equilibrium if car quality is distributed uniformly between 0 and 100?

(Question courtesy of Kyna Fong, Stanford University)

Essay questions

14 Assume that the market for lemons has unraveled, as it did in several of the above examples. Who is *harmed* by the existence of asymmetric information? Who is *helped*?

15 How can we be sure that the price P is the same for all vehicles? Why can't sellers with excellent cars not simply advertise their high car quality and charge higher prices?

16 The Akerlof model can be used to model the health insurance market. In this market, which party is analogous to car buyers? Which party is analogous to car sellers? What would it mean for the health insurance market to unravel?

17 What happens when we *reverse* the information assumptions in the Akerlof model? Let us assume that buyers have perfect information about car quality, and that sellers have no information about the quality of any specific car (although they do know the distribution of car quality). Assume that all other basic assumptions apply as usual, including the buyer and seller utility functions (equation (8.1)).

a   Explain how these information assumptions might be possible in certain circumstances. What sorts of goods would likely have markets that feature these counter-intuitive assumptions?

b   Imagine that you are a car seller who owns car i with quality X_i (unknown to you). What strategy could you pursue to sell the car in such a way that your utility increases?

c   Does adverse selection occur in this market?

Students can find answers to the comprehension questions and lecturers can access an Instructor Manual with guideline answers to the analytical problems and essay questions at **www.palgrave.com/economics/bht**.

9 ADVERSE SELECTION: THE ROTHSCHILD–STIGLITZ MODEL

We have examined Akerlof's model of the market for lemons, which illuminates the destructive potential of asymmetric information in a transactional market. We have also examined the underlying structure of risk aversion, and analyzed insurance contracts to determine the expected amount of utility they will yield. Economists Michael Rothschild and Joseph Stiglitz developed a model that puts these two insights together (Rothschild and Stiglitz 1976). Our goal in this chapter is to describe this model and present its conclusions about how insurance markets deal with adverse selection.

9.1   The I_H–I_S space

We start by developing a framework to display multiple insurance contracts simultaneously and intuitively. Consider Figure 9.1(a), an example of the income–utility diagram we developed in Chapter 7. Using this diagram, it is fairly easy to evaluate a single insurance contract to see if it is utility-enhancing when compared with the uninsured state. But once we try to examine more than one insurance contract at a time, the graph quickly becomes illegible.

One way around the problem of displaying multiple contracts is to plot the same insurance contracts on different axes. We let each axis plot income in one state of the world: healthy on the horizontal axis and sick on the vertical axis. These quantities are both plotted along the income axis in Figure 9.1(a), but in Figure 9.1(b) I_H and I_S are set perpendicular to one another. The chief insight here is that insurance contracts transfer income from the healthy state of the world to the unhealthy. By plotting I_S and I_H in the same space, we can better visualize the transfers that different contracts imply.

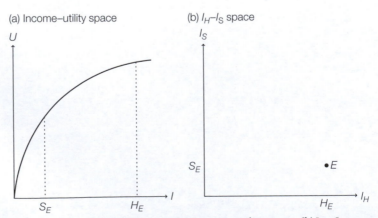

Figure 9.1. *Symmetry between two diagrams. (a) Income–utility space. (b)* I_H–I_S *space.*

As can be seen in Figure 9.1(a), the individual receives an income of H_E if she remains healthy and an income of S_E if she becomes sick, assuming no insurance. We call the point $E = (H_E, S_E)$ the individual's **endowment**. In Figure 9.1(b), the endowment E is plotted in the I_H–I_S space. The endowment point E reflects all the information about the individual's income in the healthy and sick states.

The same graph can also be used to represent income in various states of the world for an individual who is insured. Let H_C and S_C represent income in the healthy and sick states for the same individual with partial insurance contract C. Figure 9.2(a) shows this partial insurance contract in the familiar income–utility space. Figure 9.2(b) more concisely shows this contract as a single point I and contains the same information about the insured individual's possible income levels under partial insurance.

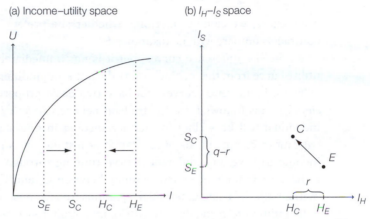

Figure 9.2. *Symmetry between two diagrams, part II. (a) Income–utility space. (b) I_H–I_S space.*

Again, Figure 9.2(a) and Figure 9.2(b) depict the exact same information. A single point in I_H–I_S space concisely summarizes any insurance contract. The horizontal distance between H_E and H_C shows the premium r, whereas the vertical distance between S_C and S_E equals the payout net premium $q - r$. Later, we will find that in this space it is easy to see whether any given insurance contract is fair or unfair, full or partial.

9.2   Indifference curves in I_H–I_S space

Our next job is to introduce utility into the I_H–I_S space. This is easy in the income–utility space from Chapter 7, since utility is plotted on the vertical axis in that space. In the I_H–I_S space, though, we must introduce indifference curves to compare potential insurance contracts.

Figure 9.3 shows the endowment point and four potential insurance contracts C_1 to C_4. Even without knowing much about the individual's preferences, we make some evaluations about the relative utility from these contracts. Consider, for instance, the difference between contracts C_1 and C_2. Both contracts result in the same sick-state income a, but contract C_2 gives a higher healthy-state income than does C_1. As long as the individual prefers more income to less, she always prefers C_2 to C_1. For similar reasons, the individual always prefers C_1 to C_3. Still, without further information about the individual's

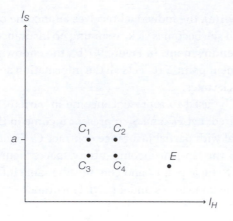

Figure 9.3. C_1 *through* C_4 *represent four insurance contract offerings alongside the endowment point* E. *For anyone who values income,* C_1 *is strictly better than* C_3, *and* C_4 *is better than* C_3. C_2 *is better than all three other contracts, but further knowledge about the individual's preferences is necessary to compare between* C_1 *and* C_4 *as well as between insurance and no insurance* E.

preferences, we cannot determine whether she prefers C_1 to C_4, or how any of these contracts compare with no insurance E.

We need indifference curves, but it is not immediately obvious how to translate the utility curve from the income–utility diagram into indifference curves in I_H–I_S space.

These indifference curves will have two basic properties. First, they are *downward-sloping*. This follows from the tradeoff between I_H and I_S in an insurance contract. An individual will be willing to sacrifice income in one state only if she is compensated with more income in the other state. For instance, it is possible for someone who likes income to have an indifference curve running through C_1 and C_4, but never possible to have an indifference curve running between C_2 and C_3. This fact can also be proved mathematically using differential equations (see Exercise 17).

In addition to being downward-sloping, indifference curves are also **convex** whenever consumers are risk-averse. In other words, they are steeply downward-sloping at low levels of I_H but flatten out at higher levels of I_H. Convex indifference curves imply that I_H and I_S are substitutes, but not perfect ones. The individual is willing to trade off some I_H for I_S and vice versa but prefers to maintain at least moderate levels of both. This is a natural consequence of risk aversion (see Exercise 17 for a mathematical proof).[1]

Figure 9.4 displays two downward-sloping and convex indifference curves in the I_H–I_S space. Indifference curve U_1 shows that the individual is indifferent between points C_1, C_4,

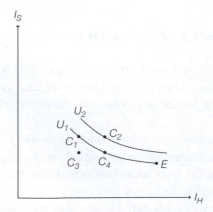

Figure 9.4. *Sample indifference curves for a risk-averse insurance consumer.*

---

1 Recall from Chapter 7 that a concave utility function implies risk aversion. A concave utility function also implies convex indifference curves.

and E. Meanwhile, C_2 is clearly preferred to the endowment point, since C_2 is on a higher indifference curve U_2.

At this point, we can compare multiple insurance contracts, draw indifference curves, and determine which insurance contracts are preferable to which others. But it is still not easy to figure out which insurance contracts are full or fair. This determination was straightforward in the income–utility model; can we do the same in I_H–I_S space?

9.3   The full-insurance line

The *full-insurance line* is an important landmark in I_H–I_S space. By definition, a full-insurance contract is one that achieves state independence, $I_H = I_S$. A fully insured individual is guaranteed the same income whether she is sick or healthy. The 45° line defined by the equation $I_H = I_S$ is pictured in Figure 9.5 and covers the range of all full-insurance contracts. Any insurance contract not on this line cannot be a full-insurance contract, because $I_H \neq I_S$.

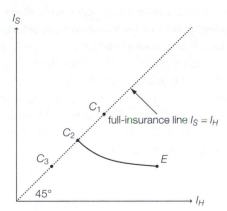

Figure 9.5. C_1, C_2, and C_3 *are full-insurance contracts, because they achieve state independence,* $I_H = I_S$. *Any contract on the 45° line fulfills this property, so we call it the full-insurance line.*

In Figure 9.5, three insurance contracts are displayed. All fit the definition of full insurance, because $I_H = I_S$ in every case. But the three contracts offer different levels of utility. C_1 is preferable to C_2, which is preferable to C_3. In fact, the individual's indifference curve indicates that she is indifferent between C_2 and E, and prefers E to C_3. In Section 9.4, we show that these preferences are driven by the fact that C_3 is more unfair than C_2, and C_2 is more unfair than C_1.

9.4   The zero-profit line

Just as there is a line characterizing all full-insurance contracts in the I_H–I_S space, there is also a line characterizing all actuarially fair contracts.

The actuarial fairness of a contract depends on the probability, p, that the individual falls ill. If the individual is very likely to be sick, a certain set of contracts with high premiums and low payouts will be actuarially fair. If the individual is very likely to be healthy, a different set of contracts with low premiums and high payouts will be fair.

Suppose an individual with probability of sickness p starts with an income at endowment point $E = (H_E, S_E)$. Her income without insurance is H_E if she is healthy, and S_E if she falls ill. Consider an arbitrary insurance contract that moves the individual to a point

(H_C, S_C). This contract is actuarially fair if the insurer's expected profit from this contract is zero (or equivalently if the customer's change in expected income is zero). The insurer gains $H_E - H_C$ if the individual stays healthy, but loses $S_C - S_E$ if she becomes sick. In expected value, the insurer makes zero profit if

$$p(S_C - S_E) = (1 - p)(H_E - H_C) \qquad (9.1)$$

This expresses the same actuarial-fairness condition from Chapter 7, except that $H_E - H_C$ is the premium r and $S_C - S_E$ is payout net premium $q - r$.

Rearranging equation (9.1) yields

$$S_C = \frac{1 - p}{p} \cdot (H_E - H_C) + S_E$$

We have been considering an arbitrary contract $C = (H_C, S_C)$, but this equation plots out the set of contracts that has zero profit for the insurer. If we replace the contract with an arbitrary actuarially fair contract (I_H, I_S), the condition would still hold:

$$I_S = \frac{1 - p}{p} \cdot (H_E - I_H) + S_E \qquad (9.2)$$

This equation defines a **zero-profit line** in I_H–I_S space with slope $^{1-p}/_p$. The line will always run through the endowment point E, which confirms our intuition that the endowment point uninsurance is actuarially fair. Importantly, the zero-profit line's slope changes with p; a more sickly person with higher p has a flatter slope than a less sickly person with a lower p. By contrast, the slope of the full-insurance line does not change with p.

Figure 9.6 shows an example of a zero-profit line in I_H–I_S space. In this figure, three actuarially fair insurance contracts are displayed, alongside the endowment contract E. The other contracts are all preferable to E – any contract with fair insurance, whether partial or full, will be preferred to the endowment point.

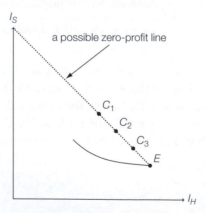

Figure 9.6. *Contracts on the zero-profit line generate zero profit for the insurer in expectation. Equivalently, contracts on this line like C_1, C_2, and C_3 are actuarially fair. The particular slope of the zero-profit line depends on the purchaser's probability of sickness p – the higher this probability, the flatter the zero-profit line.*

Also consider the insurance company's preferences. Just as consumers generally prefer actuarially fair insurance to unfair insurance, insurance companies prefer the opposite. They like the profitable, actuarially unfair contracts better than zero-profit actuarially fair contracts. In the I_H–I_S space, contracts in the zone southwest of the zero-profit line make positive profits, and contracts in the northeast zone make negative profits. Figure 9.7 demonstrates why this is so.

Consider contracts C_1, C_2, and C_3. C_2 is on the zero-profit line and hence makes zero profit. C_1 charges the same premium $H_E - H_C$ as C_2 but pays out less, since $S_{C_2} > S_{C_1}$.

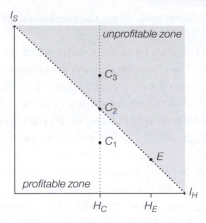

Figure 9.7. *Contracts* C_1, C_2, *and* C_3 *all result in the same healthy-state income* H_C, *so premiums for all three are equal,* $r = H_E - H_C$. *But the insurance payout is highest for the* C_3 *and lowest for* C_1. *This provides intuition for why unprofitable contracts for insurers are northeast of the zero-profit line and profitable contracts are southwest.*

This is true for all contracts in the southwest zone; one can always find a contract on the zero-profit line that requires the same premium but offers a higher payout. Thus, contracts in this region always make positive profits for the insurer. Similarly, contracts in the northeast region like C_3 always make negative profits for the insurer, because these contracts pay out more for the same premium.

9.5   The feasible contract wedge

Our next task is to determine where in the I_H–I_S space insurance companies and customers would be happy to meet and do business. The insurance market unravels if there are no contracts that mutually benefit both companies and customers.

So far, we have discussed the full-insurance line, the zero-profit line, and indifference curves – for now, we focus on the indifference curve passing through the endowment point. These lines and curves divide up the I_H–I_S space into four regions, labeled R_1, R_2, R_3, and F in Figure 9.8. In which of these regions, if any, can contracts be offered and accepted?

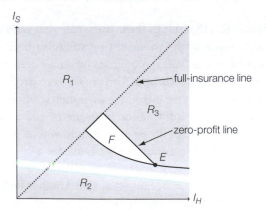

Figure 9.8. *The feasible contract wedge.*

- Region R_1 is home to contracts that represent overfull insurance. In other words, these contracts pay out more to customers if they get sick than if they stay healthy: $I_S > I_H$. These contracts could theoretically exist but seem implausible for risk-averse individuals. Overinsurance of this sort reintroduces uncertainty that risk-averse individuals would never seek. Thus, the market will produce no contracts in region R_1.

- Region R_2 contains contracts that all lie to the southwest of the indifference curve passing through E. Therefore, the customers always prefer uninsurance to any contract offered in this region. These contracts cost so much and offer so little in return that uninsurance is preferable. No successful contract can exist here.
- Region R_3 contains only unprofitable insurance contracts as it lies entirely northeast of the zero-profit line (see Figure 9.7). No insurance company would be willing to offer insurance contracts here.
- This leaves region F. It is labeled the *feasible contract wedge* because it is the only region where contracts can exist. All the contracts in the feasible contract wedge are at least weakly preferable to E and represent positive (or at least zero) profits. Note that all points on the edge of the wedge are feasible as well.

9.6   Finding an equilibrium

Identifying the set of feasible contracts is a step toward determining whether contracts will actually sell in this market. Next, we need to define an **equilibrium** in this market. A market equilibrium satisfies three conditions: consumers maximize utility, firms maximize profits, and no new firm can enter the market without incurring negative profits. We formalize these conditions below.

Definition | **9.1**

A set of contracts is in **equilibrium** if:

1 all individuals select the contract in the equilibrium set that offers the most utility;
2 no contract in the set earns negative profits for the firm offering it;
3 there exists no contract or set of contracts outside the equilibrium set that, if offered, would attract customers *and* earn at least zero profit.

Any set of insurance contracts that fulfills these three rules is a valid equilibrium. At this point, it may be unclear to readers why we need to distinguish between the second and third equilibrium conditions. In the typical model of consumer demand, these conditions are combined into a single one: in equilibrium, firms make zero profit. As we will see, this distinction becomes important when we introduce asymmetric information.

Let us consider the case with no information asymmetry and a homogeneous set of consumers, all alike with probability of illness p and endowment point E. Any potential equilibrium must live in the feasible contract wedge; consider a contract α in that region (Figure 9.9). Is α an equilibrium?

All consumers would buy contract α, because it lies on a higher indifference curve than E. Thus, α satisfies the first equilibrium condition.

Furthermore, α lies southwest of the zero-profit line, so it generates positive profits for the insurance company. Thus, α satisfies the second equilibrium condition.

However, α does not meet the third equilibrium condition: there is an opening for a different insurance company to offer a profitable contract that induces all the customers to switch from α. Such a contract would necessarily be located between U_α and the

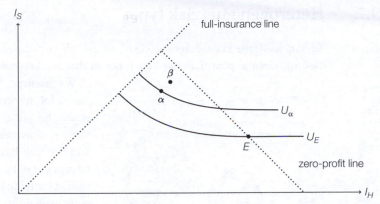

Figure 9.9. *When only contract α is available, it satisfies the first two conditions of equilibrium. But if contract β is offered, purchasers all shift away from α, and β would earn positive profits. Hence, α fails the third equilibrium condition.*

zero-profit line, say at *β* in Figure 9.9. If a second insurance company were to offer *β*, the consumers would switch from *α* to *β*. Hence, *α* is not in the stable equilibrium set.

The same logic reveals that *β* cannot be an equilibrium contract either. As long as the proposed contract lies in the interior of the feasible contract wedge, an enterprising insurance company can offer a different contract that makes positive profits.

Only when an actuarially fair, full-insurance contract is offered (Ω) are the equilibrium conditions satisfied (Figure 9.10). Consumers maximize utility by selecting Ω, the insurance company makes zero profit, and no insurance company can steal away customers without offering a negative-profit contract.

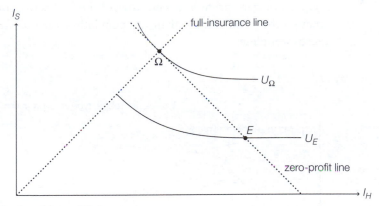

Figure 9.10. *A stable equilibrium.*

Note that the customer's utility curve is tangent to the zero-profit line at Ω. It can be shown that this condition must hold true for any full-insurance contract – we know the zero-profit line and indifference curves will always be tangent at the full-insurance line for any consumer with any risk level and any set of risk-averse preferences. This tangency at the zero-profit and full-insurance intersection reflects the fact that actuarially fair and full insurance is the most ideal insurance from the consumer's point of view. And as we have shown, the market with homogeneous customers produces this ideal contract in equilibrium.

9.7   Heterogeneous risk types

So far, we have considered a world where all consumers are identical. We relax this assumption and postulate two risk types in this market: **robust** and **frail**.

We assume that these two types actually have a lot in common. Both types of individuals share the same income–utility curve and the same endowment point. However, the robust and the frail have different probabilities of illness p. Let p_r be the probability of illness for all robust individuals, and let $p_f > p_r$ be the analogous probability for all the frail individuals. As their names suggest, the robust individuals are less likely than frail individuals to become sick.

Earlier we noted that the slope of the zero-profit line is dependent on probability of sickness. There will be different zero-profit lines for the robust and for the frail individuals. Because $p_r < p_f$, the robust zero-profit line is steeper than the frail zero-profit line (see

An old adage holds that zebras can't change their stripes – but insurance seekers can disguise their risk type in the Rothschild–Stiglitz model.

Credit: Allen Cox.

equation (9.1)). Figure 9.11 plots these zero-profit lines in I_H–I_S space.

There are two types of individuals in this market, so the market-wide probability of falling sick p_{avg} is an average of p_r and p_f, weighted by the fraction of each type in the population. Thus, the slope of the *population* zero-profit line depends on the composition of the overall population. If there are many frail individuals, for example, the population zero-profit line tends toward the frail zero-profit line. Conversely, if there are many robust individuals, then the population zero-profit line tends toward the robust zero-profit line.

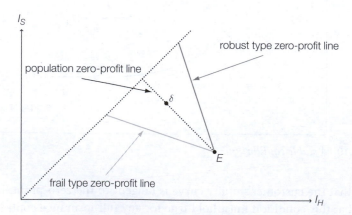

Figure 9.11. *A possible contract δ and the zero-profit lines of different risk types.*

Figure 9.11 depicts a contract δ that lies on the population zero-profit line. If the entire population, robust and frail, adopts this contract, then the firm makes zero profit. If robust individuals adopt the contract and the frail refrain, then the firm makes positive profits, since δ is to the southwest of the *robust* zero-profit line. Conversely, if only frail individuals adopt the contract, then the firm makes negative profits, since δ is to the northeast of the *frail* zero-profit line. Whether or not this contract is profitable depends on who takes it up.

9.8   Indifference curves for the robust and the frail

Despite the fact that everyone in the population, robust and frail, has the same income–utility curve, the two types of individuals have different expected incomes and different expected utilities. One consequence of this fact is that each type has its own distinct set of indifference curves in I_H–I_S space. All risk-averse individuals would be happy to trade income in the healthy state for income in the sick state. But robust individuals are more likely to end up healthy, so they place a relatively higher value on I_H than do frail individuals.

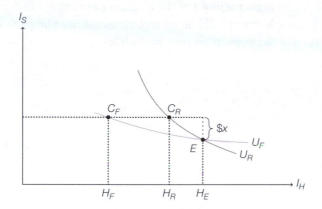

Figure 9.12. *The indifference curves of the robust individuals* U_R *are steeper than the indifference curves of the frail individuals* U_F. *That steepness means that for an identical gain in sick-state income* x, *robust individuals are willing to sacrifice less healthy-state income than frail individuals are.*

Figures 9.12 and 9.13 illustrate how robust and frail individuals value the tradeoff between I_H and I_S differently. We plot a pair of sample indifference curves, one for the robust individuals and one for the frail individuals.

Consider an insurance contract that pays out $x in the sick state. How much income in the healthy state would the two types of customers be willing to pay in exchange for receiving x if sick? The robust individual would be willing to pay at most $H_E - H_R$ in the healthy state in exchange for x. This tradeoff leaves the robust individuals with the same utility they would receive at E. Because frail individuals value income in the sick state more than the robust individuals, they would be willing to pay up to $H_E - H_F$, more than robust individuals would.

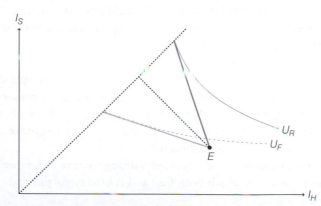

Figure 9.13. *In the figure, we plot the robust indifference curve that is tangent to the robust zero-profit line on the full-insurance line, as well as the analogous frail indifference curve. These tangency points represent each risk type's own ideal contract.*

While Figure 9.12 shows the robust and frail indifference curves that intersect at E, we could conduct a similar analysis at any point in the $I_H - I_S$ space. In fact, it can be shown that any robust indifference curve crosses every frail indifference curve exactly once, and vice versa. This is called the **single-crossing property** and is a consequence of the definition of expected utility.

9.9   Information asymmetry and the pooling equilibrium

Suppose insurance companies are perfectly able to tell the robust and frail individuals apart, and are legally allowed to exclude certain risk types from certain contracts. Figure 9.14 depicts the stable equilibrium, with each risk type contracting at their respective ideal insurance points, Ω_1 and Ω_2. Frail customers would prefer to switch from Ω_1 to Ω_2, because Ω_2 yields higher utility, but the insurance company can deny them. If the frail were allowed to switch, they would do so and the insurance company would lose money (Ω_2 falls northeast of the population zero-profit line).

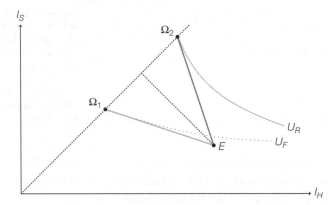

Figure 9.14. *Stable equilibrium with heterogeneous customers and perfect information.*

In this case where insurers can distinguish robust and frail types, the insurance market functions well. Both risk types purchase their own ideal contract. This is known as the *symmetric information equilibrium*. This is analogous to the situation in the Akerlof model where cars have heterogeneous quality, but the buyers and sellers have the same, symmetric information. Each car is priced according to its own quality, and all cars sell.

What happens if insurance companies, like clueless Akerlofian used-car buyers, cannot tell the difference between robust and frail individuals? In practice, this means insurers cannot restrict any type of person from buying any contract; all offered contracts must be available to everyone, or not offered at all. Insurers are no longer able to forbid the frail type from adopting contracts designed for the robust.

In this case, all the frail customers, previously trapped at Ω_1, would disguise themselves as robust and sign up for Ω_2. It makes sense for these frail customers to lie about their health – it allows them to get a better deal on insurance. As we have seen, if they do successfully masquerade themselves, the insurance companies make negative profits, so this outcome cannot occur in equilibrium.

From a policy perspective, there is often a desire to have risk types pool together in a single insurance policy, in which both frail and robust types pay the same premium and receive the same payout if sick. This is known as a pooled contract, and an equilibrium consisting of this pooled contract is known as a **pooling equilibrium**.

Definition | **9.2**

Pooling equilibrium: a contract that attracts both robust and frail customers and simultaneously satisfies the equilibrium conditions.

Let us propose a candidate pooling contract α in Figure 9.15. Any possible pooling equilibrium must rest on the population zero-profit line. If α lies to the right of the zero-profit line, then the firm loses money. If it lies to the left, then other insurance firms could enter and make money.

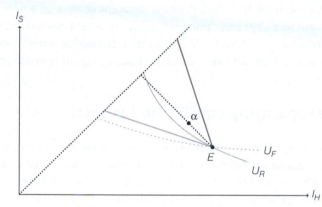

Figure 9.15. *A hypothesized pooling equilibrium.*

The contract α satisfies the first condition of equilibrium because both robust and frail types choose α over E. The second condition is satisfied because both robust and frail types choose α, and it is on the population zero-profit line. Therefore, the firm makes zero profit.

The third condition, however, is not satisfied. Figure 9.16 shows the robust and frail indifference curves that pass through α. Because the curves have different slopes, they form a triangular region that a crafty insurance company can exploit.

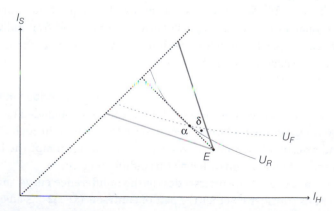

Figure 9.16. *The pooling equilibrium is destroyed.*

Suppose a different company offered an insurance contract at δ. Who would it attract? It is above the robust indifference curve that passes through α, so naturally the robust individuals would happily switch to δ. Meanwhile, the frail individuals choose to stay at α because their utility level is higher there than at δ.

Thus, we have a case of adverse selection. The contract δ differentially attracts the robust individuals but leaves the frail individuals at α. This is good for the company offering δ. Because the expected payouts to the robust individuals are low, the firm makes positive profits (δ is to the southwest of the robust zero-profit line). Meanwhile, the differential selection adversely affects the firm that was offering α. Now only the frail individuals most likely to be sick choose α, which drives up the company's expected payouts and makes α unprofitable (α is to the northeast of the frail zero-profit line).

We picked α as a candidate pooling equilibrium, but, as we have seen, it is not an equilibrium at all. Our choice of α was not in any way special – we selected an arbitrary point on the population zero-profit line, which we established as the only place a pooling equilibrium could exist. If we had started with a different candidate point α' somewhere else on the zero-profit line, the same argument would have held. Because of the relative shapes of the indifference curves, there will always be a triangular zone where an enterprising company can offer a contract like δ. Thus, no pooling equilibrium can exist.

9.10   Finding a separating equilibrium (sometimes)

While a pooling equilibrium can never exist in this model, a different kind of equilibrium, called a **separating equilibrium**, can sometimes exist. This equilibrium separates the robust and frail types not by discriminating against them directly, but instead by offering different contracts that appeal specifically to each. Since the insurance companies cannot distinguish between the two risk types, this is their only hope of separating them.

Definition	9.3

Separating equilibrium: a set of two contracts that satisfies the equilibrium conditions, one that attracts robust customers and one that attracts frail customers.

We have already seen a separating equilibrium under the assumption of perfect information in Figure 9.14. We have also seen that this equilibrium breaks down if the insurance companies cannot distinguish between robust and frail individuals. The equilibrium falls apart specifically when the frail customers flee Ω_1 for the much-preferred contract Ω_2. This suggests we might be able to create a stable equilibrium if we just make Ω_2 less attractive to the frail types – so unattractive that Ω_1 looks good by comparison.

Let us try to construct an equilibrium using the strategy described in the previous paragraph. Ω_1 belongs in this equilibrium set, but Ω_2 cannot be included because it breaks the equilibrium. Consider the frail indifference curve that passes through Ω_1 (Figure 9.17). In order to find a second insurance contract Ω_3 that will not tempt the frail individuals to leave Ω_1, we need to put Ω_3 on or below this indifference curve.

Suppose we place Ω_3 at the intersection of the indifference curve and the robust zero-profit line. Let us consider whether the pair of contracts (Ω_1, Ω_3) is an equilibrium.

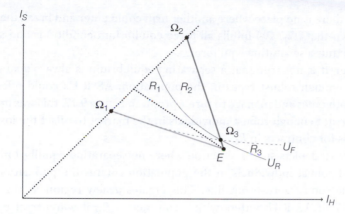

Figure 9.17. *In search of a separating equilibrium.*

The frail types are indifferent between Ω_1 to Ω_3, since both lie on a single frail indifference curve. We assume that the frail types choose Ω_1 over Ω_3 since they are indifferent between the two.[2] At the same time, the robust types prefer Ω_3 to Ω_1.

It may be counter-intuitive that the frail individuals pass up Ω_3, which is actuarially unfair in their favor. The explanation is that, while Ω_3 is a lower-price insurance contract, it provides only a small quantity of insurance; it is far from full. The frail types, who are very likely to become ill, prefer Ω_1, which is expensive but full insurance.

So, does the pair (Ω_1, Ω_3) satisfy the definition of equilibrium? As we have seen, each risk type maximizes its own utility over the available alternatives; the two risk types voluntarily separate themselves between the two contracts. Because those contracts lie on the risk types' respective zero-profit lines, the insurance firm makes zero profit on each contract. The only question is whether another company can enter the market, steal away some or all of the customers, and earn at least zero profit. If a company can do this, the equilibrium breaks down.

Suppose another firm called Adverse-Selection-R-Us enters with a contract in the region labeled R_1 in Figure 9.17 in an attempt to disrupt the market. The reader should be able to see that any such contract would attract the frail individuals but not the robust ones. Those contracts would therefore be unprofitable for the entering firm, so no such contract would invalidate the proposed equilibrium (Ω_1, Ω_3).

Suppose AS-R-Us instead enters with a contract in region R_2. Both frail and robust risk types would choose such a contract over their existing ones. However, any such contract would lose money; the entirety of R_2 is to the northeast of the population zero-profit line. While AS-R-Us makes money off its robust customers with this contract, frequent payouts to the frail customers result in overall negative expected profits.

Increasingly desperate, AS-R-Us turns to region R_3. Contracts in this region do successfully skim the robust customers away from the original firm. When we considered the pooling equilibrium, this skimming was sufficient to make the contract profitable and break the equilibrium. This is not the case for the proposed separating equilibrium. Because Ω_3 is already zero-profit for robust individuals, anything more generous (like the contracts in R_3) will be unprofitable for AS-R-Us.

---

2 We can assume that the frail types will take Ω_1 over Ω_3 even though they lie on the same indifference curve. We are allowed to do this because we can always imagine moving Ω_3 very slightly to make it strictly inferior. Analytically, it is often simpler to just assume that the frail individuals in question will do what we want when they are actually indifferent between multiple alternatives.

In fact, there is no place where another firm could enter and break the equilibrium. We have shown that (Ω_1, Ω_3) fulfills all three equilibrium conditions and separates the risk types; it is thus a separating equilibrium.

However, it is not true that a separating equilibrium is always guaranteed to exist. If there are enough robust types in the population, AS-R-Us could offer a contract that attracts both types and manage to turn a profit. In Figure 9.17, this was impossible because there were not enough robust individuals in the market to offset the losses from the frail individuals for contracts in R_2.

Figure 9.18 depicts such a situation where no separating equilibrium exists. The large number of robust individuals in the population rotates the population zero-profit line toward the robust zero-profit line. This creates a new region R_4 that did not exist in Figure 9.17. If AS-R-Us enters with a contract in R_4, it will attract both types of customers – frail types who are willing to give up full insurance to get lower premiums, and robust types who are willing to give up actuarially fair insurance to get something closer to full coverage. Since contracts in R_4 are profitable, the candidate separating equilibrium (Ω_1, Ω_3) fails under these circumstances.

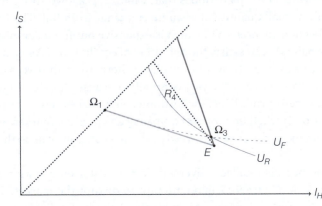

Figure 9.18. *A separating equilibrium breaking down.*

The Rothschild–Stiglitz model thus predicts a separating equilibrium only when the robust population is small enough relative to the whole population. Like the Akerlof market, this market is hindered by asymmetric information and can only function under particular circumstances. Even when it does function, it does not perform as well as it could with symmetric information.

So far, we have found two separating equilibria: one when we assumed symmetric information and that insurers could discriminate on the basis of health (Ω_1, Ω_2) and one when we assumed asymmetric information (Ω_1, Ω_3). Figure 9.19 depicts the two equilibria and the indifference curves that pass through their contracts.

In both the symmetric and asymmetric information cases, the frail types purchase *the same* insurance contract. One might think that frail types would suffer if insurance companies developed a technique, such as a genetic test, to differentiate them from the robust types. But the Rothschild–Stiglitz model implies that frail types are indifferent to whether insurance companies can distinguish them from the robust.

Instead, it is the robust individuals who have the most at stake. When insurers can distinguish between the two types of customers, they can offer an exclusive contract to the robust that features actuarially fair, full insurance (Ω_2) – the ideal contract for robust

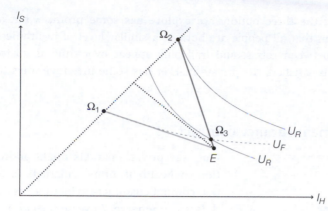

Figure 9.19. *Comparing separating equilibria.*

individuals. When insurers cannot discriminate on the basis of risk type, they cannot afford to offer this attractive, ideal contract because the frail individuals will masquerade as robust. So the robust individuals are left with a low-quantity insurance contract (Ω_3) that falls substantially below full insurance.

In this sense, the frail individuals exert a negative externality on the robust merely by the fact of their existence. Because the potential exists for frail individuals to poison the insurance pool, insurers must severely limit the quantity of insurance available to robust individuals.

9.11   Can markets solve adverse selection?

Suppose that we live in a world where everyone is risk-averse, but different people face different levels of risk. Let us also assume that the bad side-effect of insurance, moral hazard, is at most a minor problem that is outweighed by the benefits of insurance (see Chapter 11). Under these conditions, it is socially optimal for everyone to be fully insured.

If a society wants to ensure that all of its members have full insurance coverage, how would it go about accomplishing that goal? The two models of adverse selection we have studied indicate that adverse selection can sometimes cause markets to unravel or disappear altogether. An insurance market with asymmetric information like the one described in the Rothschild–Stiglitz model has trouble producing a "good" outcome if a society wants full insurance for all. Even in a separating equilibrium where both robust and frail customers can buy welfare-enhancing insurance, robust customers are quantity constrained and cannot insure fully.

If we assume a goal of universal full insurance, there are a few ways it could be accomplished. A government could force everyone to buy an insurance contract at the intersection of the full insurance line and the population zero-profit line. This would result in discount insurance for the frail but also actuarially unfair insurance for the robust. In practice, most policy attempts focus on this sort of strategy: mandating people of different risk levels to form a single insurance pool. Nationalized health insurance and insurance mandates, which we will read much more about in Chapter 15, both represent attempts to defeat adverse selection by essentially outlawing it.

In the remainder of this chapter, we consider ways in which private markets may be able to solve the adverse selection problem without forcing people to pool against their will. Each of the three options we explore has some promise, but all are predicated on the notion that all people are born at a similar level of healthiness and that health differences between robust and frail only appear over time as customers age. If this assumption is satisfied, the private market has some inventive ways to combat adverse selection.

The lifetime insurance contract

...The water seems just fine to me.....

Insurance Co.

In$urance Pool

A lifetime health insurance pool with robust and frail participants – really just one big happy family.

Credit: Allen Cox.

One way private markets might address adverse selection in health insurance markets is to offer contracts that commit customers to lifetime insurance *before* health differences emerge. Adverse selection depends on information asymmetry, but what if the information advantage that people have over health insurers only develops over time? Young insurance customers may not know any more about their future risks than insurance companies (we will see an example of this in Chapter 10). If risk type only becomes apparent later in life, lifetime insurance contracts could induce young people to pool together before the robust types realize how robust they are.

A lifetime insurance contract would feature a prearranged premium schedule that may vary over time but does not depend on subsequent health developments. In other words, an 18-year-old who signs such a contract knows what he will pay in premiums every year for the rest of his life, no matter if he is diagnosed with a chronic disease or if he is perfectly healthy. Such contracts would provide insurance against both health risk and the risk of becoming frail.

This arrangement has a weakness, though: it creates some antagonistic relationships once different risk levels become apparent. Imagine two 18-year-old customers, Peter and Tim, who both appear perfectly healthy. They both want to purchase lifetime insurance policies because the policies will protect against health risks this year *and* also against the risk of higher premiums in future years.

Now imagine that thirty years have passed, and it has become clear that Peter is actually much healthier than Tim. Tim has developed hypertension and hypercholesterolemia, while Peter is unusually healthy for a 50-year-old. The insurance company still receives the same premium from the two customers, but pays dramatically more for Tim's frequent checkups and prescription drugs.

The insurance company would like to dump Tim but is contractually obligated to keep paying his medical bills without raising his premium. Similarly, Peter would like to dump the insurance company, because he is healthy but still paying high premiums to cover Tim's costs. The commitment aspect of the insurance contract signed thirty years ago is the only thing holding this insurance pool together.

A contractual arrangement like this may be legally fragile, as courts in the US and many other countries have historically been unwilling to hold customers to these sorts of lifetime binding contracts. The contract is the only thing keeping Peter in the pool, so if courts do not enforce it then this pool unravels just like any other. The lifetime nature of the contract also prevents competition from flourishing, because these two customers are stuck with their insurer for life and no other insurer can compete for them.

The guaranteed renewable contract

Pauly et al. (1995) propose a similar scheme: the *guaranteed renewable contract*, which is cleverly designed so that both risk types will actually want to remain in the contract of their own volition, and no commitment is required. The guaranteed renewable contract works by frontloading premium payments, shifting premiums into the younger years when Peter and Tim still do not know who will stay healthy and who will be ill.

In the guaranteed renewable contract, the premiums are set to fall gradually over time. By the time Tim is significantly sicker than Peter, both are paying low premiums and neither wants to leave. Effectively, the younger versions of Peter and Tim pay ahead of time for most of the costs that both of them will incur later in life. Rather than having the 50-year-old Peter subsidizing the 50-year-old Tim, the younger version of both subsidize whoever turns out to be sick later in life.

Because at their young age they do not yet know who will be generating those costs, Peter and Tim are both willing to pay high premiums while they are young. Rather than a legally binding commitment, it is these high upfront premiums that effectively lock in customers. Hendel and Lizzeri (2003) find that many life insurance contracts in the US do in fact feature frontloading with premiums that gradually decrease over time relative to mortality risk.

The Cochrane lifetime contract

Cochrane (1995) proposes a similar solution that has the added feature of allowing customers to move between insurers, which fosters greater competition. In his scheme, each insurer offers actuarially fair contracts that are renegotiated yearly. These contracts cover health costs and also provide *premium insurance* – insurance against higher future premiums (that is, against the risk of becoming frail).

If a customer with a Cochrane lifetime contract is diagnosed with cancer, she not only receives reimbursement for her immediate health care costs but also a lump sum payment covering the higher premiums she will inevitably have to pay in future years. Next year her actuarially fair premiums will be much higher, but she will be able to afford them thanks to her lump sum payment from the previous year. By providing both same-year health insurance and future-year premium insurance, the market becomes much more mobile and competitive. Sick customers are not tied to their current insurers because they have the money to afford actuarially fair premiums anywhere.

9.12   Conclusion

Economic models must provide sharp predictions in order to be testable in the real world and useful in guiding policy. The Rothschild–Stiglitz model makes two such predictions.

First, no pooling equilibrium can exist: robust individuals will never voluntarily subsidize frail individuals in an insurance market, even if both types are risk-averse. Insurance markets are well designed to pool risk among people with similar risk profiles, but not across populations with differing risk profiles.

Second, if a separating equilibrium exists, frail individuals will be fully insured, but pay a high premium per unit of coverage. Robust individuals will be partially insured, but pay a lower premium appropriate to their health risk. Insurance companies will never offer bulk discounting – in fact, they offer the opposite.

In the next chapter, we examine the empirical evidence that tests these two predictions in real-world insurance markets. Our discussion will cover chain-smoking teachers, terminal AIDS patients, and frail college professors.

9.13 Exercises

Review the basic assumptions of the Rothschild–Stiglitz model before answering these questions. Many exercises will refer to these basic assumptions.

Comprehension questions

Indicate whether the statement is true or false, and justify your answer. Be sure to state any additional assumptions you may need.

1 In a Rothschild–Stiglitz model with asymmetric information and heterogeneous risk types, the frail population would be worse off if insurance companies were suddenly able to distinguish between the two types of customers, because they could no longer pretend to be healthy.

2 The Rothschild–Stiglitz model predicts that people who own life insurance should have fewer unobserved traits (that is, unobserved by insurance companies) that lead to a higher risk of death when compared against people with the same level of income but who do not own life insurance.

3 In a Rothschild–Stiglitz model separating equilibrium, there is a volume discount for insurance purchases – those who choose to buy more insurance pay a lower per-unit price for it.

4 In a Rothschild–Stiglitz model separating equilibrium, low-risk consumers of insurance are quantity constrained. They cannot buy as much insurance as they want because the insurance company is worried it will lose money on them.

5 Under certain circumstances in the Rothschild–Stiglitz model, a separating equilibrium cannot exist.

6 In the Rothschild–Stiglitz model, an individual who is offered a choice between full insurance and no insurance will always choose full insurance if they are risk-averse.

7 A pooling equilibrium can exist if the contract being offered lies on the same indifference curve as the endowment point of the robust population.

8 Under the typical assumptions of the Rothschild–Stiglitz model, there is nothing that an insurance company can do to distinguish between robust and frail customers.

9 Private markets are powerless to combat adverse selection, so the only solution is a government-mandated insurance contract.

10 The main advantage of a Cochrane insurance contract over a guaranteed renewable contract is that it does not rely on a legally unenforceable binding lifetime commitment.

Analytical problems

11 A medical test that an insurance company could use to distinguish between high- and low-risk types would create an equilibrium in which both high- and low-risk types

could have full insurance. Sketch a brief proof using a diagram. Why is this equilibrium *not* an equilibrium under the normal information asymmetry assumptions?
Show which of the three equilibrium criteria does not hold.

12 Consider Figure 9.20.

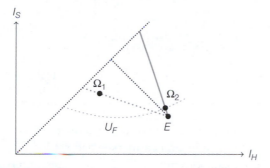

Figure 9.20. *Candidate separating
equilibrium.*

a Explain why the frail-type indifference curve pictured, U_F, is *not* a valid indifference curve.
b Draw your own version of this figure and label two contracts, A and B. Draw the
   two contracts such that:
   ● contract A is strictly better than B, with more income in both states of the
     world, and
   ● the customer with the pictured indifference curve nonetheless prefers contract
     B to contract A.
c Draw a valid version of a frail-type indifference curve that intersects Ω_1, Ω_2, and
   the full-insurance line.
d Is (Ω_1, Ω_2) a valid separating equilibrium? Defend your answer.
13 **A tax on healthy people.** Consider the basic Rothschild–Stiglitz model with asym-
    metric information and robust and frail customers.
    a Suppose the government imposes a Wellness Tax, $\tau > 0$, on robust and frail types
       but collects on this tax only when they are healthy (that is, there is no tax if they
       turn out to be sick). Will a separating equilibrium still be possible? Draw a version
       of the Rothschild–Stiglitz diagram to support your answer.
    b Will a separating equilibrium be possible if the tax $\tau > 0$ is imposed on all
       customers in both sick and healthy states? Again, support your answer graphically.
14 Review Figure 9.18, which depicts a separating equilibrium breaking down. In this
    figure, the separating equilibrium breaks down because the zero-profit line is too far
    to the right. But this is not the only way that a separating equilibrium can fail.
    a Draw a version of the Rothschild–Stiglitz model where a separating equilibrium
       holds, but just barely (the robust-type indifference curve should almost touch the
       aggregate zero profit line).
    b Imagine that all the robust types in the insurance market suddenly become much
       more risk-averse. How would this change the shape of their indifference curves?
       Show how this change can unravel the separating equilibrium.
15 **The Rothschild–Stiglitz model and its discontents.** Imagine policymakers in the
    fictional nation of Pcoria are trying to create a Pcorian National Insurance Program
    (PNIP) that will bring full insurance to all the citizens of Pcoria.

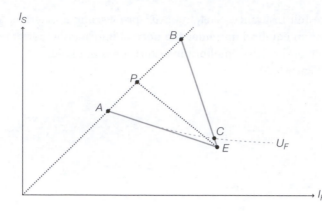

Figure 9.21. *A Rothschild–Stiglitz diagram of the Pcorian insurance market.*

a   Figure 9.21 depicts the current state of the insurance market in Pcoria before the plan is implemented. The insurance market had settled into a separating equilibrium at (A, C). Explain why no insurance company enters with a contract at point B.

b   Draw your own version of the Pcorian Rothschild–Stiglitz diagram and draw a robust-type indifference curve that passes through point C. Remember that the separating equilibrium is valid, so make sure your indifference curve does not contradict that assumption.

c   Suppose PNIP establishes a new national pooling contract at point P, and bans any private insurance company from offering any other contract. Assume both frail and robust consumers decide to join the contract at P. Draw another robust-type indifference curve through P that is consistent with this assumption.

d   Is this policy change a Pareto-improvement?

e   A robust Pcorian citizen named Hercules sues PNIP because he says the new insurance rules are harming him. Due to the explosive nature of the case, it goes straight to the Pcorian Supreme Court. The chief justice asks Hercules how PNIP could possibly be harming him if he went from having barely any insurance (point C) to full insurance (point P). How should Hercules respond?

f   The Pcorian Supreme Court issues an opinion that the ban on private insurance is unconstitutional, but that the PNIP can continue to operate. Hercules decides to go into business for himself and start a health insurance company. Where can he place his new contract so that it skims off the robust Pcorians, leaves the frail Pcorians in the PNIP, and makes a profit? Draw his contract (point Z) on your diagram.

g   Suppose Hercules is successful. The PNIP starts losing billions of dollars a year and is shut down by the Pcorian government. For a moment, Hercules's contract Z is the only contract available. Is there any place that a new insurance company can enter and earn positive profits?

16 **Genetic testing**. After the fiasco with the Pcorian National Insurance Program (see Exercise 15), a Pcorian senator proposes a new policy that will go to a referendum of voters in the next election. Below is the text of the referendum.

> *Proposition 99*: All Pcorians will submit to be genetically tested to see if they are frail or robust. If they are frail, they will receive a Frailness Compensation Payment of \$1. Compensation payments will be funded through a tax that will be divided equally between all Pcorians, robust and frail.

You can assume that the genetic test costs nothing and is perfect at distinguishing frail and robust people. Under current law, genetic testing for the purposes of insurance contract underwriting is strictly illegal in Pcoria.

a   Assume that all Pcorians will vote to maximize their own utility, and that their utility is totally determined by their healthy-state and sick-state incomes. Which Pcorians will vote for the proposition?

b   Explain how Proposition 99 can be thought of as a Coasian transfer. What property rights are being sold in this situation, and by whom? (Review Chapter 20 for our discussion of Coasian transfers.)

c   A privacy watchdog group called Anonymity sues to prevent the genetic testing from taking place. They claim that Proposition 99 harms frail Pcorians. Explain why they are wrong if utility is totally a function of income. Explain also why they might be right if utility is not determined wholly by income.

17   In this exercise, we will formally show the two properties of indifference curves in I_H–I_S space we discussed in Section 9.2. To prove that indifference curves are downward-sloping, we calculate the slope of the indifference curves dI_S/dI_H directly. Recall that the individual with income I_H in the healthy state and I_S in the sick state, and with probability p of becoming sick, has an expected utility $E[U]_p$ of

$$E[U]_p = pU(I_S) + (1 - p)U(I_H) \tag{9.3}$$

a   Take the total derivative of $E[U]_p$. This will give a formula explaining how changes in I_H and I_S contribute to changes in $E[U]_p$.

b   Because indifference curves, by definition, connect points with constant utility, set $dE[U]_p$ equal to 0 and then solve for $\dfrac{dI_S}{dI_H}$.

c   Using what you know about the signs of p, $U'(I_H)$, and $U'(I_S)$, prove that the sign of $\dfrac{dI_S}{dI_H}$ is negative.

d   A curve is convex in I_H–I_S space if its second derivative is positive everywhere. Derive the second derivative of the indifference curves by taking the derivative of your expression for $\dfrac{dI_S}{dI_H}$ with respect to I_H.

e   Using what you know about the signs of p, $U'(I)$, and $U''(I)$, prove that your expression for the second derivative is positive everywhere.

Essay questions

18   One major premise of the Rothschild–Stiglitz model is that there is a perfectly competitive market for health insurance. Suppose instead that the market is not perfectly competitive, and in fact competitor firms have a hard time entering the market. Could a pooling equilibrium occur in this case? What is it about competition that prevents pooling in the Rothschild–Stiglitz model? No formal proof is necessary, but do make your reasoning clear. Evaluate the following statement: competition in health insurance markets is harmful.

Students can find answers to the comprehension questions and lecturers can access an Instructor Manual with guideline answers to the analytical problems and essay questions at **www.palgrave.com/economics/bht**.

10 ADVERSE SELECTION IN REAL MARKETS

BASE jumpers leaping off a tall building. BASE is an acronym for Building, Antenna, Span, and Earth, which are the types of objects such jumpers leap from with no more than a parachute. One study estimates a BASE jumper fatality rate of one in sixty (Westman et al. 2008). Credit: © Xof711 – Fotolia.com.

Imagine that you run a family-owned life insurance company in a small town. You know most of your customers personally and are comfortable offering good rates; you are confident your neighbors will not try to cheat you or submit fraudulent claims. You can truthfully advertise as having the lowest rates for miles around. Your typical product is a $1 million life insurance policy taken out by a middle-aged parent to protect his or her children in the event of an early death.

Then one day a hale and handsome stranger arrives in town. He is young and seems to be perfectly healthy, but his first stop in town is the offices of your life insurance company. He explains that he is a single parent and has several children that he wants to provide for in the case of his death. Then he asks to buy a life insurance policy with $100 million worth of coverage. Since he is buying so much, he explains, he is hoping he can get a volume discount, and only pay 50 times as much as the customers with $1 million policies.

Is this a great opportunity to sell a ton of insurance, or is this customer bad news? Most real-life insurance actuaries would probably run away from this customer as fast as they can; if a healthy-looking stranger asks for a lot of life insurance, there may be reason to suspect he knows something you do not know. For example, maybe he is a professional BASE jumper with an upcoming jump into the Grand Canyon, or he is a politician who has recently hired hitmen to assassinate him.[1]

A smart insurance company recognizing its information disadvantage would be wary of such a customer. You, as an insurance agent, could do a number of things to prevent being ripped off. You might charge him more per dollar of insurance, reject his application, or require that he undergo a thorough physical examination before agreeing to a contract.

In the previous two chapters, we have seen stark predictions about the failure of insurance markets in the face of asymmetric information. When there are information asymmetries, insurers always have to worry that the riskiest customers are naturally the most attracted to a given insurance policy. Models predict that *adverse selection* has the power to compromise or even destroy markets, and yet there are countless examples of functioning insurance markets throughout the world. After all, used-car markets do exist despite Akerlof's prediction that they might unravel. In this chapter, we search

---

1 This latter example is derived from the plot of the 1998 political satire *Bulworth*. Suicidal US Senator Jay Bulworth takes out a $10 million life insurance policy moments before hiring his own hitmen.

for evidence of adverse selection in real markets and see how markets and governments address its presence.

10.1   Predictions of asymmetric information models

The models of adverse selection that we discussed in the previous chapters – the Akerlof model of the market for lemons and the Rothschild–Stiglitz model with robust and frail insurance customers – make some specific predictions about how real-world insurance markets should look.

A positive correlation between risk and coverage

The most basic prediction of the models of asymmetric information is adverse selection itself. In a market where insurers cannot assess risk type of customers accurately, high-risk insurance customers should be more likely to participate in insurance markets because average contracts represent a good deal for them. These high-risk customers are analogous to the low-quality cars flooding Akerlof's used-car market when the quality of cars cannot be observed.

Thus, a positive correlation between risk levels and insurance coverage – that is, a finding that high-risk people are more likely to be covered by insurance or have more coverage – would be evidence of adverse selection (Cohen and Siegelman 2010). Recall that the main prediction of the Rothschild–Stiglitz model is a separating equilibrium in which the high-risk types have full insurance and the low-risk types have incomplete insurance. Researchers studying a separating equilibrium such as one shown in Figure 10.1 would observe positive correlation between risk levels and insurance coverage.

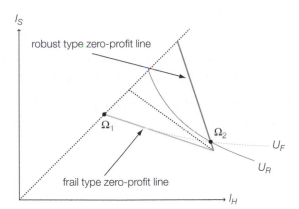

Figure 10.1. *The separating equilibrium in the Rothschild–Stiglitz model. It features a positive correlation between risk and coverage (because frail types have more insurance than robust types) and bulk markups (because those customers with more insurance pay a higher per-unit premium).*

One problem with this empirical strategy is that measuring risk can be difficult. The theories of asymmetric information all refer to the inherent riskiness of a customer *before* buying insurance. Economists refer to this as the customer's **ex ante** risk. But as we will discuss extensively in Chapter 11, the purchase of insurance may actually increase the risk the insurance firm faces in covering the policyholder (for example, by inducing reckless behavior or extra doctor visits) above the *ex ante* risk. This post-purchase elevated risk is known as the customer's **ex post** risk.

> **Definition | 10.1**
>
> *Ex ante* **risk**: the inherent riskiness of a customer before he buys an insurance policy against that risk.
>
> *Ex post* **risk**: the riskiness of a customer after he buys an insurance policy against that risk. *Ex post* risk is almost always greater than the corresponding *ex ante* risk because of moral hazard.

Researchers typically measure risk by analyzing insurance claims or health care expenditure levels. These claims and expenditures are proxies for *ex post* risk, rather than *ex ante* risk. Unfortunately, researchers are typically unable to measure *ex ante* risk directly, so they rely on measures of *ex post* risk, which are easier to observe. Even if there is truly no correlation between *ex ante* risk and coverage – that is, no adverse selection – moral hazard could confound the results by inducing a positive correlation between *ex post* risk and coverage. Hence, any positive correlation between *ex post* risk and coverage must be interpreted in light of the possibility of moral hazard.

Bulk markups

Most markets for commodities like consumer goods or industrial materials feature **bulk discounts**: lower per-unit prices for larger purchases. These lower prices often reflect the fact that large purchases help defray fixed costs. If each transaction at a store or shipment to a warehouse costs a small amount above and beyond the price of raw materials, suppliers will use discounts to encourage purchasers to buy in bulk. By contrast, the Rothschild–Stiglitz model predicts just the opposite: **bulk markups**.

> **Definition | 10.2**
>
> **Bulk discount:** a lower per-unit price for a larger purchase of a commodity. These lower prices often reflect the fact that large purchases help defray fixed costs.
>
> **Bulk markup**: a higher per-unit price for a larger purchase of a commodity. Rarely seen in other markets, these higher prices are a tactic for combating adverse selection in insurance markets.

Bulk markups are a response to adverse selection. In the Rothschild–Stiglitz model, frail customers are more likely to get sick and more interested in high levels of insurance. If an insurance company offers each additional unit of insurance at the same price, frail customers would buy more insurance than robust customers and bankrupt the firm. In insurance markets, high demand by a single customer is a sign of high risk (recall the seemingly healthy insurance customer from the beginning of this chapter). In the Rothschild–Stiglitz separating equilibrium, firms use bulk markups to ensure that unhealthy customers who demand high-volume insurance pay disproportionately more (see Figure 10.1).

The adverse selection death spiral

One implication of the Rothschild–Stiglitz model is that pooling between different risk types cannot survive in the market in the long run. But in real-life insurance markets, such insurance pools do form. In nearly all of these cases there is some sort of inducement, such as a legal mandate or a subsidy, that keeps the low-risk types from dropping out of the pool. In the absence of such inducement, successive rounds of adverse selection can lead to a devastating phenomenon known as the *adverse selection death spiral* (see Section 8.3).

Three predictions of the asymmetric information models

1 There will be a **positive correlation** between riskiness and insurance coverage. Customers who are *more* likely to rack up insurance expenditures should be *more* likely to have insurance policies.

2 Insurers will use **bulk markups** in their pricing strategies. Customers with more insurance coverage should have not only higher premiums but higher *per-unit* premiums.

3 Pooling between different risk types will cause an **adverse selection death spiral** which unravels the pool, absent an inducement that keeps low-risk types in the pool.

10.2 Adverse selection in health insurance

How important a problem is adverse selection in real-world insurance markets? Does adverse selection occur at all and, if so, is it a minor nuisance or a major market failure that fosters uninsurance and under-insurance?

Adverse selection is predicated on the ability of customers to accurately gauge their own risk better than insurers can and to act on this information asymmetry. Evidence from the RAND Health Insurance Experiment indicates that customers are indeed capable of this. As part of the RAND HIE, participants were asked to make predictions of their own health care costs for the coming year, as well as their willingness to purchase a (hypothetical) insurance policy to supplement their randomly assigned plan (Marquis and Phelps 1987).[2] Families with high predicted costs were more likely to want a supplemental insurance contract and actually did incur significantly higher health care costs in the following year. Evidently, the participants were good at predicting their own future health care costs: the correlation between expected health care costs and actual costs was about 0.4.

Most worrisome from the perspective of insurance companies was the participants' ability to accurately forecast higher costs that could not have been predicted simply by demographic factors like age. This means that the RAND HIE participants would have had a real information advantage over insurance companies that could only observe basic demographic information about their customers.

It is little surprise, then, that studies conducted in many different health insurance settings find a positive risk-coverage correlation. Risk pools studied include:

---

2 See Chapter 2 for a much more detailed explanation of the RAND HIE.

- elderly Medicare beneficiaries (Brown and Finkelstein 2009);
- Dutch families seeking supplemental private insurance (van de Ven and van Vliet 1995);
- Harvard professors and staff (Cutler and Zeckhauser 1998);
- low-income Mexican families (Spenkuch 2012);
- young graduates joining the American workforce (Cardon and Hendel 2001).

These studies and others show that the first of our three predictions is confirmed in many different health insurance markets.

The Harvard University death spiral

Because an adverse selection death spiral is a phenomenon that encompasses an entire market and unfolds slowly, it can be hard to observe in data. Harvard health economist David Cutler studied a change to the structure of employee health insurance at Harvard University and found evidence of a real-life death spiral (Cutler and Reber 1998).

In 1994, Harvard University employed about 10,000 people full time. As part of their employee benefits, all had access to low-cost, low-benefit HMO[3] plans as well as a higher-cost PPO[4] plan from Blue Cross Blue Shield. Plan premiums and enrollment had been relatively stable for many years; in 1994, about 18% of employees elected to pay more for the PPO. That year, a round of budget cuts at Harvard compelled administrators to reduce the employer subsidy for the PPO plan for the 1995 fiscal year. While the PPO only cost employees $361 more than the HMO in 1994, it would cost $731 more in 1995.

The PPO subsidy cut spurred an exodus from the PPO plan. While the majority of PPO enrollees did not switch to an HMO plan ("PPO stayers"), hundreds of them did switch ("PPO leavers") and the PPO enrollment rate declined from 18% to 14% in 1995. The selection of employees out of the plan was decidedly non-random. Harvard employees who anticipated more health care expenses were more likely to remain in PPO despite the price increase. PPO stayers were older on average – much more likely to be over 60 years of age – and their medical expenses were commensurately higher. Even adjusting for age, expenses were 6% higher among PPO stayers than PPO leavers.

The new, smaller PPO customer pool was less healthy on average in 1995, and as a result the PPO was more expensive to maintain on a per-customer basis. The insurer promptly raised premiums for 1996: Harvard employees would now have to pay $1,414 to enroll in the PPO rather than the HMO. Another round of adverse selection ensued, worse than the year before. PPO stayers in 1996 were again much older than PPO leavers and incurred 9% more in age-adjusted health care costs. By 1997, only the highest-risk Harvard employees remained in the PPO, and Harvard was forced to abandon the plan. Figure 10.2 illustrates the death spiral at Harvard.

While the Harvard case is one of the cleanest examples of an adverse selection death spiral in action, other examples have been found in other contexts.

In the mid-1990s, the state of New Jersey revised the rules governing its individual health insurance market, which caters to people who do not have insurance through their employer or the government. The new rules forbade insurers from offering different

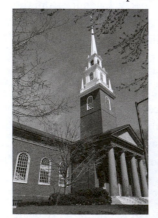

The Memorial Church on Harvard Yard. Harvard's stellar academic reputation survived the havoc of the 1995–96 death spiral. Credit: © Yevgenia Gorbulsky ~ Fotolia.com.

---

3 Health Maintenance Organization.
4 Preferred Provider Organization.

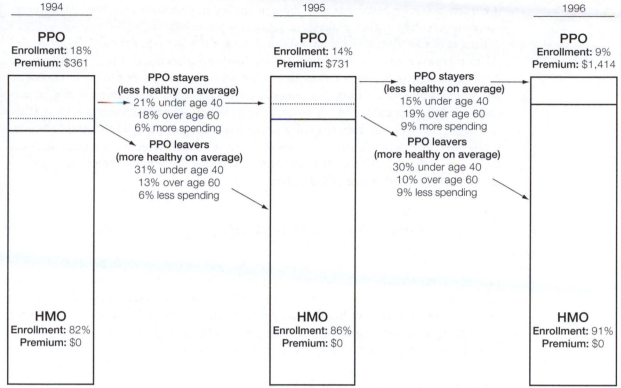

Figure 10.2. *Illustration of the adverse selection death spiral at Harvard.*

Source: Data from Cutler and Zeckhauser (1998).

contracts to different people and mandated a slate of plans ranging in generosity from low-benefit HMOs to high-benefit indemnity plans.

Starting in 1996, enrollment in the plans began declining precipitously and premiums began rising. At the same time, the average age of people covered under individual insurance rose faster than the average age of New Jersey workers (Monheit et al. 2004). All these trends – increasing premiums, decreasing enrollment, and riskier enrollees – suggest a death spiral dynamic in New Jersey's individual health insurance market. Older studies find the same death spiral signature in the Federal Employee Health Benefits Program during the early 1980s and the University of California employee health insurance network during the mid-1990s (Price and Mays 1985; Buchmueller 1998).

The evidence against adverse selection

Not every study has found evidence consistent with the positive risk-coverage correlation hypothesis in health insurance markets. Cardon and Hendel (2001), who study a nationally representative dataset of US workers and their employer-sponsored health insurance options, do find that health care costs and coverage are positively correlated. But this correlation disappears when costs are adjusted for easily observed factors like age, race, and gender. The implication is that employees do not have an information advantage over insurers. Adverse selection does exist in this context, but only as an artifact of policies that forbid insurers from discriminating on the basis of demographic factors. This conclusion, if correct more generally, has very different policy implications than the risk-coverage correlation found by other studies.

Fang et al. (2008) study a health insurance market that actually exhibits a *negative* correlation between risk and coverage. Among Medicare beneficiaries in the US, it is the healthier beneficiaries, rather than the sicker ones, who disproportionately choose to purchase a supplemental insurance policy known as Medigap. Seniors who choose to purchase Medigap incur about $4,000 *less* in annual medical expenses on average. Thus, there is a negative correlation between risk and coverage. Fang et al. argue that this "advantageous selection" occurs because seniors with greater cognitive ability are both healthier and more likely to purchase Medigap. Apparently, this effect more than offsets adverse selection in this market (see Section 10.4).

10.3   Adverse selection in other markets

The theory of adverse selection is a general one that can in principle be applied to any market – recall that the main motivating example in Akerlof (1970) is the used-car market. In fact, the way that asymmetric information alters different markets depends on details unique to each market. For health economists, it pays to study adverse selection in other markets because the lessons learned often apply to traditional health insurance markets and tell us about the limits of the theory of adverse selection.

Automobile insurance markets

In most countries, some minimal threshold of car insurance is required for everyone behind a steering wheel. The barest policy covers liability for damages wrought by the policyholder to other vehicles, but policyholders can purchase additional policies that cover damages to their own cars as well. The theory of adverse selection predicts that high-risk drivers are the ones who purchase the higher amounts of the supplemental insurance coverage.

Chiappori and Salanie (2000) study rookie French drivers with one to three years of driving experience. They gather all the information – such as age, profession, and driving record – that the insurer knows about each driver before setting premiums. Controlling for all these factors, they find no correlation between risk and coverage. Counter to the predictions of the adverse selection model, people more likely to get into accidents do not purchase more insurance coverage.

One proposed explanation for their finding is that adverse selection rides on asymmetric information, and novice drivers lack the experience to develop information advantages over insurers. If so, evidence of adverse selection might still appear among more experienced drivers. Cohen (2005), studying Israeli drivers between 1995 and 1999, finds evidence supporting this explanation. Over this period, experienced drivers who purchased more complete coverage tended to report more accident claims, but there was no correlation between claims and insurance type for drivers with less than three years of experience.

Another wrinkle in the Israeli car insurance market created an opening for adverse selection. In that market, the accident record of a driver with one insurer was inaccessible to other insurers. This meant that drivers with spotty track records could switch insurers and leave their bad driving history behind. If insurers cannot deduce from observable characteristics such as age which new customers are fleeing bad records, there is an information asymmetry between the new applicants and the insurance companies. Cohen (2005) finds that drivers who filed a claim in the last year were the ones most likely to switch insurers by the year's end.

The adverse selection result found in the Israeli market for car insurance does not hold everywhere though. For example, Saito (2006) does not find a positive risk-coverage correlation for either new or experienced drivers in Japan. In neither group do higher-risk drivers have higher rates of coverage. Similarly, Dionne et al. (2001) find no correlation between risk and auto insurance coverage in the Canadian province of Quebec.

Life insurance markets

Life insurance also presents a ready market for testing the predictions of the adverse selection model. Policyholders pay premiums for the rest of the term of the policy, and their beneficiaries only receive the insurance payout upon the policyholder's death. Thus, buying life insurance makes more sense when the end of life is near. From the insurer's perspective, the more profitable customers are ones with long life expectancies, and the high-mortality-risk individuals should be avoided or charged high premiums. But the adverse selection model predicts that if customers know their mortality risk better than insurers do, the life insurance market should be dominated by the sickly, not the well. Contrary to these predictions, Cawley and Philipson (1999) study mortality data in the US and find that life insurance holders tend to live longer. McCarthy and Mitchell (2010) find similar evidence in the UK and Japan.

These results are inconsistent with the predictions of the asymmetric information models, but there may be another interpretation. Because the high-mortality-risk policyholders are by definition more likely to die, low-risk people tend to be over-represented in a cross-section sample of living policyholders. This would bias findings to suggest that a higher percentage of policyholders are low risk than actually are. Figure 10.3 illustrates this possible bias.

Consider five people, three of whom know themselves to be in poor health and purchase life insurance at $t = 0$. The two healthier individuals forgo insurance coverage. At $t = 1$, one of the unhealthy policyholders dies. A second policyholder dies at $t = 4$, but the last one is lucky enough to live through $t = 7$. Of the two uninsured people, one survives the entire time, but the other dies at $t = 5$.

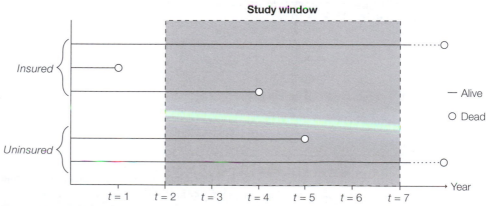

Figure 10.3. *Left censoring bias identified by He (2009).*

A study only tracking people between $t = 2$ and $t = 7$ would find mortality rates of 50% for both uninsured and insured groups. It would conclude that there is no positive risk-coverage correlation and, hence, no adverse selection. Yet, as shown in Figure 10.3, the mortality risk among the insured is actually 67%, higher than the uninsured mortality rate. The hypothetical study overlooks the policyholder who dies at $t = 1$ and misjudges mortality risk as a result. He (2009) claims many studies testing for adverse selection in life insurance markets do not observe early deaths prior to the observational window of the study. If so, these studies may miss evidence of adverse selection.

Using the same Health and Retirement Study dataset of biennial health information from 1992 to 2004, He (2009) concludes contrary to earlier studies that over a given time period, there is a positive correlation between risk and coverage. Over a six-year time period, those who died were 49% more likely to have life insurance at the beginning of the period than those who survived through all six years. She avoids the over-representation problem by considering only potential new life insurance customers in 1992 and 1994, and tracking them over a 12-year time horizon. By comparison, Cawley and Philipson (1999) use a five-year window.

He's finding, however, does not explain the presence of bulk discounting in the life insurance market found by Cawley and Philipson (1999). Figure 10.4 shows premium cost per dollar of life insurance coverage offered by the Teachers Insurance and Annuity Association (TIAA). Clearly, life insurance is more expensive for the elderly than the youthful, and for smokers than non-smokers. But the graph also shows that TIAA offers bulk discounting: the more dollars of coverage the policyholder buys, the less expensive each unit of coverage costs. Rather than becoming suspicious of teachers who want large policies (recall the man from the introduction), TIAA actually offers them a discount. Such bulk discounting is inconsistent with the separating equilibrium predicted by the Rothschild–Stiglitz model.

The finding suggests that not all the predictions of the simple adverse selection model have been borne out in the market for life insurance. These results imply that insurers are skilled at predicting life expectancy and hence at underwriting mortality risk. If the information asymmetry is overcome, insurers could prevent high-risk, unprofitable people from buying cheap policies and only sell to low-risk individuals. This would explain

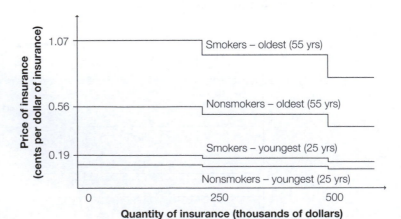

Figure 10.4. *Premium cost per dollar unit of life insurance coverage.*

Source: Cawley and Philipson (1999). Reproduced with permission from American Economic Association.

the negative risk-coverage correlation, and also explain why insurers like the TIAA could afford to offer bulk discounting.

Viatical settlement markets

The possibility of adverse selection is not limited to insurance markets; the theory may also apply in *reverse insurance* markets as well. One prominent example of a reverse insurance market is the viatical settlements market. In this market, people who already own a life insurance policy sell their policies to third parties known as viatical firms, who buy the right to collect on the original policy when the seller dies.

In the early 1990s, the viatical settlements market was dominated by HIV patients. There was not yet an effective treatment for AIDS available, and the typical HIV patient was a young gay man, with no children to inherit his life insurance payout. Consider an HIV patient in need of a potentially life-saving treatment. Penniless, he cannot afford the treatment, but he does own a life insurance plan valued at $10,000. There is no way of claiming the life insurance payout until he dies (in which case, the money hardly helps him), but a viatical firm is willing to buy his life insurance policy. The viatical firm offers him an immediate payout of $5,000 in exchange for being named the policy's sole beneficiary. The viatical firm then waits for the HIV patient to die, at which point it collects the full $10,000.

The term viatical *comes from the Latin word* viaticum, *literally "sustenance for the road." It was customary among the ancient Greeks and Romans to place a coin in the mouth of the dead (in order to bribe the ferryman Charon for the journey across the river Styx). Credit: stocksnapper – iStockphoto.com.*

Morbid as this transaction seems, both parties may benefit. Although an HIV diagnosis is bad news, it does have one beneficial side-effect for a patient with life insurance. Because the patient's life expectancy has dropped and the payout of the policy will come earlier, the policy has become more valuable. By selling the policy to a viatical firm, the patient can access the increased equity in his policy while he is still alive. The HIV patient gains the liquidity he needs to pay for his treatment or any other use. The viatical firm, depending on how much it pays for the policy and how long the original policyholder ends up living, may stand to make a profit on the transaction.

The policy buyer (the viatical firm) is taking a bet on the insured person's life expectancy. If the policy seller lives a long, healthy life, then the viatical firm cannot collect the life insurance's payout for years to come and would have been better off investing its money elsewhere. Meanwhile, the policy seller is betting that he will survive for a while. If the policy seller knows he is going to die soon but he cannot convince any viatical firms of this prognosis, the settlement offer will be too low to justify selling. He is better off borrowing money and leaving his heirs to repay the loan with their inheritance.

There is an information asymmetry in the viatical settlements market if policy sellers know their life expectancy more accurately than viatical firms can estimate. If in fact sellers hold this information advantage, models of asymmetric information predict that only the individuals who are healthier than the viatical firms think they are will agree to sell their life insurance policies.

Contrary to this prediction, empirical evidence from the US in the early 1990s shows no sign of adverse selection in the viatical settlements market. During this period, a diagnosis of HIV/AIDS augured death within a few years or even sooner. The HIV virus attacks a particular kind of white blood cell, called a CD4 T-cell, which is important for immune system function. As the patient grows sicker and sicker, CD4 levels decline at a predictable rate. With a simple blood test, viatical firms could measure CD4 levels and thereby accurately forecast life expectancies. Since the firm and the policy seller have effectively the same information about the seller's life expectancy, there is no information asymmetry and hence no adverse selection (Bhattacharya et al. 2004).

In the mid-1990s, a new type of treatment for HIV called highly active anti-retroviral therapy (HAART) was discovered. This new treatment, which extended life expectancies of HIV patients dramatically, was a fantastic development for HIV patients. But for viatical firms, especially those holding policies, the introduction of HAART was akin to the Black Tuesday stock market crash of 1929. The price of viatical settlements plummeted as equity in these life insurance contracts suddenly evaporated. Another consequence of HAART was that it made life expectancy forecasting for HIV patients more difficult for firms. CD4 levels alone no longer sufficed to accurately predict life expectancy. HAART thereby introduced a potential information asymmetry into the market. Perhaps as a consequence, the number of viatical transactions in the US fell from 2,623 in 1995 to just 226 in 2001 (Bhattacharya et al. 2009).

Long-term care insurance markets

Paying for nursing home care is difficult for most elderly patients. Insurance for the elderly rarely covers the high cost of these facilities (the 2002 annual rate for a semi-private room in the US was $50,000). Since life expectancies have been increasing throughout the developed world, the financial bill for such long-term care can be overwhelming. The potentially high costs of nursing home care and the uncertainty associated with it make long-term care insurance (LTCI) attractive. But in fact, the market for long-term care insurance has not taken off; only 10% of elderly Americans carry any (Finkelstein and McGarry 2006). One possible explanation for why long-term care insurance is not more popular is the presence of adverse selection.

Using data on self-reported probability of entering a nursing home, Finkelstein and McGarry (2006) find that customers for long-term care insurance in the US have private information about their likelihood of ending up in a nursing home. This evidence alone suggests that insurance providers are vulnerable to information asymmetry.

Yet, despite finding information asymmetry between policy buyers and insurers, Finkelstein and McGarry do *not* find positive risk-coverage correlation in the long-term care insurance market in their dataset of US retirees – the insured are no more likely to enter nursing homes than the uninsured are. This contradicts the predictions of the asymmetric information models despite the presence of private information.

The researchers investigate whether there may be another selection bias besides health risk that offsets the effect of adverse selection. While the theory of asymmetric information predicts that risky individuals are more likely to need nursing home care and demand more long-term care insurance, there may be other reasons why *less* risky customers would tend to buy more insurance.

Risk aversion may be one such reason. Risk-averse people are both more likely to buy insurance and more likely to take precautions to protect their health. That is, the risk-averse simultaneously tend to buy insurance more and file fewer insurance claims. For example, Finkelstein and McGarry find that seat-belt wearers, who tend to be risk-averse, are less likely to enter a nursing home but also more likely to purchase long-term care insurance.

The risk preference of potential customers can drive a negative correlation between health risk and insurance coverage. If this negative correlation offsets the positive risk-coverage correlation due to adverse selection, then there will be no correlation between health risk and insurance coverage. Finkelstein and McGarry (2006) conclude that these dueling selection biases balance each other out in the long-term care insurance market, which reconciles their finding of information asymmetry with no positive risk-coverage correlation.

This finding suggests that adverse selection is not the reason that so few people carry long-term care insurance. Pauly (1990) posits an alternative explanation that has nothing to do with information asymmetries. Very often, long-term nursing home care serves as a substitute for in-home care by the children of the elderly. Having long-term care insurance decreases the effective price of nursing home care to the children. By not buying long-term care insurance, seniors increase the chance that their children will opt to care for them instead. The desire of elderly parents to be cared for by family rather than strangers may depress the demand for long-term care insurance.

10.4   What prevents adverse selection?

Despite the attention given to the prospect of adverse selection, empirical studies do not consistently find adverse selection at work in all insurance markets. Cohen and Siegelman (2010) outline several reasons for why adverse selection is not omnipresent. There are at least four possible reasons:

- customers misperceive their own risk;
- customers do not act on their private information;
- insurers can accurately observe customer risks;
- selection on other factors (like risk aversion or cognitive ability) overcomes adverse selection on health risks.

Consumers misperceive their own risk

The extent of adverse selection in a market hinges on the degree of information asymmetry between consumers and insurers. But in certain markets, there may not actually be an asymmetry at all. For example, Cohen (2005) argues that novice drivers with only one to three years of driving experience do not yet know how risky they are and so do not differentially demand insurance on that basis. Even seasoned drivers may not predict their risk accurately. A survey of American and Swedish students found that 88% of the American students and 77% of the Swedish believed they were safer than the median driver (Svenson 1981).

Similar examples of misperceived risk occur in health. According to a survey of the elderly in the US, male respondents aged 85 to 89 report a subjective probability of reaching age 100 of 31%, even though objective life tables show that only about 3.4% actually will. Younger females were more pessimistic about their life expectancies: only 51% of females aged 70 to 74 thought they would reach 85, though life tables reported a 57% survival rate (Hurd et al. 2001).

Consumers do not act on their private information

Even when potential insurance buyers can evaluate their own risks better than insurance companies, adverse selection is not a given. There may be behavioral reasons why consumers do not capitalize on their information advantage. Pauly et al. (2003) write that "real consumers, after all, have more on their minds than paying attention to small bargains in insurance markets."

A related possibility is that consumers may not be cognizant of the value of their information advantage. For example, even though car owners have very good information about how many miles they will drive in the coming year, insurers do not. In any given year, people who drive more are more likely to get into accidents, so those who expect to drive more should demand more generous insurance. Yet studies show that miles driven is not a predictor of insurance coverage (Cohen and Siegelman 2010). So even though an information asymmetry may exist, adverse selection does not emerge because consumers fail to take advantage.

Insurers can accurately predict risk

The threat of adverse selection may also be checked if insurers can accurately assess the risk of policy buyers. For example, the CD4 T-cell counts were a strong predictor of mortality risk for HIV patients during the early 1990s, so viatical firms could readily and accurately evaluate a potential customer's mortality risk. Other research finds that insurers may be even better than their middle-aged customers at predicting whether the customers will eventually need nursing home care (Finkelstein and McGarry 2006). And Hendren (2012) finds that insurers are good at assessing the risk profiles of potential customers as long as they are still relatively healthy and have not yet been diagnosed with a chronic disease.

If insurers are adept at assessing the risk of potential policy buyers, then they can risk-adjust premiums correctly. This is analogous to the Rothschild–Stiglitz symmetric information equilibrium where both risk types are fully insured with different premiums.

Insurers can also take preemptive measures to cull potential high-risk customers through tactical targeting of robust, low-risk customers. Neuman et al. (1998) study the marketing strategies of a group of American insurance firms serving the elderly and highlight their strategy to attract healthy customers. Advertisements showcased physically active seniors pursuing outdoor activities, while avoiding pictures of people with walkers or in wheelchairs. Nearly a third of the information seminars held by these insurance firms were hosted in buildings without wheelchair access, which discouraged those with disabilities from attending and enrolling. Information in ads mentioning that customers could not be refused based on health status was mostly relegated to fine print in font sometimes smaller than the minimum size recommended for materials intended for the elderly. See Section 17.2 for more about this strategy, which is called *risk selection*.

Advantageous selection

There are myriad factors that influence whether someone buys insurance – income, bequest motives, superstitions, or anything else that moves demand. If privately observed health risks are the dominant consideration, then selection into insurance will be adverse from the perspective of the insurer. If other considerations like risk aversion offset this particular selection mechanism, then the selection is no longer adverse. It may even be **advantageous selection** if healthy people are the ones who disproportionately purchase insurance.

Definition	10.3

Advantageous selection: a phenomenon where less-risky people are *more* likely to purchase insurance or buy more complete insurance than more-risky people. This may occur because less-risky people are more risk-averse, wealthier, or better able to understand the benefits of insurance.

We have already seen at least two examples of advantageous selection in this chapter. Fang et al. (2008) show that cognitive ability is positively correlated with Medigap purchase and negatively correlated with health expenditures. This may be because smarter consumers better understand the benefits of insurance or they can find better deals on the market. This creates a negative correlation between insurance coverage and risk.

A second example is Finkelstein and McGarry's 2006 study of long-term care insurance. They find that heterogeneous tastes for risk may cause a negative risk-coverage correlation, an effect known as *preference-based selection*. In our theoretical examples up until now, we have assumed that potential insurance buyers have heterogeneous risk types but homogeneous risk preferences. In other words, people have different inherent likelihoods of becoming sick or being involved in a car accident, but everyone has the same tendency to take precautions. Now we consider the opposite assumption: all potential insurance customers have the same risk types but different risk preferences. So while everyone has the same inherent risk level, the more risk-averse take more precautions and also gain more utility from insurance.[5]

In this model of homogeneous risk types and heterogeneous risk preferences, the predictions of the asymmetric models from Section 10.1 are *reversed* (De Meza and Webb 2001).

In reality, neither health risk nor risk preferences is likely to be homogeneous, so both adverse and preference-based selections may occur in the same market. The result may be stable pooling equilibria. For example, the high-risk and the very risk-averse low-risk may pool together, with the risk-averse knowingly cross-subsidizing care for the high-risk. If their risk aversion is sufficiently strong, these extra costs are not enough to unravel the equilibrium.

10.5   Conclusion

The early theoretical models of adverse selection such as those by Akerlof (Chapter 8) and Rothschild and Stiglitz (Chapter 9) predict that insurance markets cannot function

---

5 See Chapter 7 for a formal model of the relationship between risk aversion and utility from insurance.

well or at all in the presence of asymmetric information. And, in fact, sometimes real-world markets function poorly because of adverse selection – recall the death spiral in the market for health insurance at Harvard.

As we have seen, however, some insurance markets show no evidence of adverse selection. This is despite the fact that information asymmetries abound – people often hold private information and attempt to exploit their information advantage. Markets are clearly more resilient in the face of asymmetric information than those early theories would predict.

Nevertheless, those theories provide an important backdrop for understanding why markets are structured the way they are. Sometimes markets create incentives for people to reveal their private information; for instance, many life insurance sellers require a physical examination by a doctor before issuing a contract. The insurer assumes, probably correctly, that someone who rejects being examined has something to hide. In other cases, two different markets are linked together in such a way that the welfare harms from adverse selection – uninsurance and under-insurance – are mitigated. For instance, tying together the market for health insurance and the labor market can (at least partially) solve adverse selection. Thus, asymmetric information serves to shape markets, even when evidence of adverse selection is non-existent.

One major goal of social policy is to encourage pooling between the people of high health risk and the people of low risk. Adverse selection poses a major challenge for the market to accomplish this goal. As we will see in Chapters 15 through Chapter 18, different governments have taken various approaches to this challenge. Adverse selection is integral to understanding which of these policies will work and which policies will fail.

10.6   Exercises

Comprehension questions

Indicate whether the statement is true, false, or unclear, and justify your answer. Be sure to cite evidence from the chapter and state any additional assumptions you may need.

1 One of the major predictions of the Rothschild–Stiglitz model is a positive correlation between risk and insurance coverage. This has never been observed in practice due to the confounding influence of moral hazard.

2 On average, observed mortality rates are higher for people who buy life insurance than for people who do not. This is best taken as evidence in favor of adverse selection in life insurance markets.

3 In some markets, adverse selection develops over time as customers learn about their own risk levels.

4 Although a firm prediction of Akerlof's model, the adverse selection death spiral has never been observed in practice.

5 *Ex post* risk is typically much lower than *ex ante* risk because uncertainty is largely eliminated by the purchase of an insurance contract.

6 Cawley and Philipson (1999) find that, in life insurance markets, there is a bulk discount (that is, people buying larger policies pay lower per unit prices). They conclude that this finding is inconsistent with the Rothschild–Stiglitz model.

7 Consider an HIV patient who recently started HAART therapy and whose health is improving rapidly as a result. Viatical settlement firms will offer him more money for his life insurance policy than they would have before he started HAART because his health outlook is much better.

8 The fact that high-risk customers are usually less risk-averse than low-risk customers helps counteract adverse selection.

Analytical problems

9 Consider Table 10.1, which has data on insurance status and medical expenditures for different types of professors at Adverse Selection University (ASU). In 2014, every employee of ASU was offered a full insurance contract at no premium. In 2015, ASU charged any employee who wanted to keep health insurance a $4,000 premium. As a result, all history professors dropped their coverage in 2015. Assume that the underlying health of ASU professors did not change much from year to year.

  a Is there evidence of moral hazard in this market? How do you know?

  b Is there evidence of adverse selection in this market? How do you know?

  c Explain how moral hazard and adverse selection combine to create a positive risk-coverage correlation in this market.

  d Could the data exhibit a positive risk-coverage correlation if one of these elements were absent? How does this complicate researchers' efforts to find evidence of adverse selection?

Table 10.1. *Information from the human resources department at ASU.*

	2014		2015	
	Insured?	Average expenditures	Insured?	Average expenditures
Economics professors	Yes	$5,000	Yes	$5,000
History professors	Yes	$3,000	No	$2,000

10 Employer sponsored insurance. Consider a Rothschild–Stiglitz model of adverse selection in which there are two types of people (robust and frail) who work for a single employer, BHT Inc. Both types of people are risk-averse in income and have utility function of wealth

$$U(W) = 1 - \exp\left(-\frac{W}{500}\right)$$

During any given year, the probability of becoming ill for the robust and frail is given by $p_{frail} = 0.2$, and $p_{robust} = 0.1$. If a person falls ill, the cost of treatment (that is, **damages**) is $200. BHT Inc. is deciding whether to offer their workers insurance. The firm is assumed to be risk-neutral.

Each worker pays BHT a **premium** at the beginning of the year, and if the worker falls ill, the insurer will pay the worker some amount of **coverage**. When they decide whether to buy insurance, workers know if they are robust or frail (though they do not know if they will fall ill during the year), but neither BHT Inc. nor BHT Insurance Co. can observe any worker's health status. Workers will, of course, misrepresent their type if it is in their interest to do so.

The firm decides what insurance plan (coverage and premium) to offer workers, and workers decide whether to purchase the plan or not by maximizing their expected utility. All workers have $1,000 in initial wealth.

a   BHT first proposes a contract for robust workers. The contract offers full coverage of the damages (that is, an individual receives $200 if he falls ill). What is the maximum premium BHT could price the contract, so that it remains attractive for robust people? Would selling this contract (at the maximum premium) to robust people be a good decision for BHT? You can ignore frail workers for this part of the question.

b   BHT decides to price the Total Coverage for Robust People contract at a premium of $23. Would frail people want to buy this contract? If a frail person bought this contract by pretending to be robust, on average, would BHT make or lose money?

c   To avoid this adverse selection, BHT Inc. thinks of designing a total coverage contract for frail workers. What is the maximum premium frail workers would be willing to pay for this contract?

d   If only frail workers buy the contract, what is the minimum premium BHT Inc. could charge for a full insurance contract to just break even? Would frail people want to buy this contract? Would robust people want to buy it?

e   BHT decides to launch two contracts: Total Coverage and Minimal Coverage. The characteristics of both contracts are given in Table 10.2. Workers choose between total coverage, minimal coverage, and no coverage.

Table 10.2. *BHT-sponsored insurance contracts.*

	Total Coverage	Minimal Coverage
Payout if ill	$200	$25
Premium	$43	$3

(i)   Do frail workers prefer total coverage, minimal coverage, or no coverage? [*Hint:* Calculate the expected utility from each option to four decimal places.]

(ii) Do robust workers prefer total coverage, minimal coverage, or no coverage?

(iii) Suppose BHT Inc. has 100 workers, of which 75 are frail and 25 are robust. What is the firm's expected profits from offering these two contracts?

f   In order for insurance to be sold, the insurer must be more risk-neutral than the customers. In this case, we assumed that the firm is risk-neutral, while the workers are risk-averse. Could the insurance market still function if we assumed that the firm also had utility function $U(W) = 1 - \exp\left(-\frac{W}{500}\right)$? [*Hint:* The answer is yes. Why?]

(Question courtesy of Professor Elisa Long, Yale University)

Essay questions

11 In the early 2000s, the state of Massachusetts in the US implemented a health reform aimed at enrolling people without health insurance into an insurance plan. The reform required people without health insurance (at least those who could afford it) to buy insurance, and put in place penalties on those who nevertheless chose not to buy

insurance. Below is the abstract of a recent National Bureau of Economic Research working paper entitled "Health reform, health insurance, and selection: estimating selection into health insurance using the Massachusetts health reform" by Martin Hackmann, Jonathan Kolstad, and Amanda Kowalski (2012). The authors conducted a study of the effects of the Massachusetts reform. They write:

> We implement an empirical test for selection into health insurance using changes in coverage induced by the introduction of mandated health insurance in Massachusetts. Our test examines changes in the cost of the newly insured relative to those who were insured prior to the reform. We find that counties with larger increases in insurance coverage over the reform period face the smallest increase in average hospital costs for the insured population...

a   Is this evidence consistent with the predictions of the Rothschild–Stiglitz model? In other words, is this evidence consistent or inconsistent with adverse selection into insurance before the Massachusetts health reform? Explain why or why not. [*Hint*: Think about the types of people who enrolled in insurance as a result of the mandate.]

b   In the context of the Rothschild–Stiglitz model of adverse selection, what effect does mandating health insurance have on the utility of the robust people in the model? [*Hint*: Be careful to distinguish the cases of pooled and actuarially fairly priced insurance.]

12   Below is an excerpt from the abstract of a recent National Bureau of Economic Research working paper entitled "Adverse selection and switching costs in health insurance markets: when nudging hurts" by Benjamin Handel (2011):

> This paper investigates consumer switching costs in the context of health insurance markets, where adverse selection is a potential concern . . . We present descriptive results to show that (i) switching costs are large and (ii) adverse selection is present. To formalize this analysis we develop and estimate a choice model that jointly quantifies switching costs, risk preferences, and *ex ante* health risk. We use these estimates to study the welfare impact of an information provision policy that nudges consumers toward better decisions by reducing switching costs. This policy increases welfare in a naive setting where insurance plan prices are held fixed. However, when insurance prices change endogenously to reflect updated enrollee risk pools, the same policy substantially exacerbates adverse selection and reduces consumer welfare, doubling the existing welfare loss from adverse selection.

a   Handel finds that providing information about health insurance plans to people can exacerbate adverse selection. Explain how barriers to switching health insurance plans can partially solve the adverse selection problem in health insurance.

b   In Handel's model, reducing plan-switching costs actually makes people worse off. Explain how the utility of people in the market might decrease if these costs are reduced. Are robust types harmed? Are frail types harmed?

13   The private market for long-term nursing home care is small in the US – only about 10% of the elderly population hold a long-term care insurance policy, despite the substantial financial risk associated with needing such care. Jeffrey Brown and Amy

Finkelstein (2007) argue in the *Journal of Public Economics* that market failure due to adverse selection cannot provide a complete explanation for the small fraction of the American population that is covered by long-term care insurance:

> Long-term care represents one of the largest uninsured financial risks facing the elderly in the United States. We present evidence of supply side market failures in the private long-term care insurance market. In particular, the typical policy purchased exhibits premiums marked up substantially above expected benefits. It also provides very limited coverage relative to the total expenditure risk. However, we present additional evidence suggesting that the existence of supply side market failures is unlikely, by itself, to be sufficient to explain the very small size of the private long-term care insurance market. In particular, we find enormous gender differences in pricing that do not translate into differences in coverage, and we show that more comprehensive policies are widely available, if seldom purchased, at similar loads to purchased policies. This suggests that factors limiting demand for insurance are also likely to be important in this market.

a How would adverse selection arise in the market for long-term care insurance? How would moral hazard arise?

b What is a typical substitute for long-term nursing care for the elderly population? What might a family without the financial resources to pay for formal nursing home care do when an elderly member becomes unable to take care of herself? Why might the grown children of an elderly person who is at risk for needing long-term care insurance want their parent to have long-term care insurance?

c What government programs are available to cover long-term care expenditures? Are these programs available to everyone in your country? [*Hint*: Answering this question may require searching online government resources for information that is not in this book.] Can the availability of such government programs affect the demand for private long-term care insurance by families who are currently ineligible for government-financed long-term care insurance?

Students can find answers to the comprehension questions and lecturers can access an Instructor Manual with guideline answers to the analytical problems and essay questions at **www.palgrave.com/economics/bht**.

11 MORAL HAZARD

One day, three co-workers named Jay, Peter, and Tim win a free hang-gliding lesson in a workplace raffle. When the day of the lesson arrives, Tim and Peter have been laid off from their jobs and have lost their health insurance. As a consequence, Tim decides that he will just watch the lesson from the safety of the cliff's edge; he fears that he will face major hospital bills if he has a hang-gliding accident, and has no insurance to help pay. He is not a major enthusiast for extreme sports anyway, so he is happy to give up his free lesson to someone else.

Peter has also lost health insurance coverage, but hang-gliding is his passion. Ever since he won the raffle, he has been watching hang-gliding YouTube videos and reading up on the latest news from the world of hang-gliding. He decides the thrill of actually going hang-gliding is well worth the risk of a catastrophic accident that might obliterate his savings.

Hang-gliding rental companies thrive on moral hazard.
Credit: © Steven Paine – Fotolia.com.

Jay, meanwhile, still has his job and retains his health insurance. He has not been anxiously counting down the days until the lesson like Peter has, but because he knows his health insurance will cover every penny of his hospital bills in the case of an accident, he barely thinks twice when the instructor straps him into his hang-glider.

Unfortunately, Peter and Jay get caught in an updraft as soon as they leap from the cliff, and crash to the ground as Tim looks on in horror. After a harrowing medivac helicopter ride, Jay and Peter are laid up in traction at the local hospital. Each has broken nearly every bone in his body; with a traditional regimen of painkillers and bedrest, it will take them months to recuperate.

Fortunately, a local drug company has recently concocted a magical elixir called Bone-Gro that can repair broken bones in a matter of minutes. Peter is excited to hear of this remedy, which will save him months of being stuck in bed with nothing to do. But he is crestfallen to hear that the price of the treatment is an eye-popping $100,000. Peter *could* afford the treatment, barely, but he decides it is not worth spending most of his remaining savings on Bone-Gro.

When Jay hears about Bone-Gro, by contrast, he jumps at the chance. He does not even inquire as to the cost, because the doctors inform him that his insurance will pay 100% of the bill. Despite his painful accident, Jay is back to work in just a few days. Peter, meanwhile, spends the next few months immobilized in bed, reading books about the famous hang-gliders of yore.

This story might seem like merely a cautionary tale against hang-gliding, but it is actually a parable about health insurance and its unfortunate by-product, *moral hazard*. In our context, moral hazard occurs whenever health insurance causes people to take greater risks with their health, or causes them to consume more health care than they would otherwise. On one level, Jay's broken bones were caused by an untimely gust of wind. But on another level they were actually *caused by his health insurance policy*, which encouraged him to do something risky that he otherwise would not have done. Likewise,

Jay's expensive Bone-Gro treatment was only administered because Jay knew his health insurance would foot the bill. Ultimately, everyone in Jay's insurance pool pays for his risky decisions – just as he pays for theirs.

In Chapter 7, we learned how health insurance can generate utility for consumers by reducing painful uncertainty. In this chapter we discuss moral hazard, the major downside of health insurance. As we will see, balancing the benefit of risk reduction against the costs of moral hazard is a major concern of health policy, and will be a prominent theme in Chapters 15 through 19, where we discuss national health policy and national health insurance.

11.1   What is moral hazard?

The term **moral hazard** was coined by insurers in the nineteenth century. The earliest known mention of moral hazard is from an 1862 handbook for insurance actuaries called *The Practice of Fire Underwriting* (Baker 1996). The author used the term to distinguish between *natural* hazards that cause fire (like lightning strikes) and *moral* hazards like carelessness that can lead to fire and are the result of decisions by humans. Over time, the term has come to encompass all the risky changes in behavior that result from insurance coverage.

Definition	11.1

Moral hazard: the tendency for insurance against loss to reduce incentives to prevent or minimize the cost of loss (Baker 1996).

Each case of moral hazard follows a simple pattern:

1 An individual faces some risk of a bad event X, and his actions can increase or decrease its likelihood.
2 The individual buys an insurance contract that will help pay some or all of the costs of X if it occurs. The price of X to the individual is now lower – this *price distortion* means the individual does not face all the consequences of his actions.
3 In response to the price distortion, the individual changes his behavior in a way that increases the chances of X or increases the costs of recovering from X.
4 The insurance company cannot observe this behavior change, because there is an *information asymmetry*. Otherwise the contract would have been written to discourage or penalize the riskier behavior.
5 The individual's riskier behavior creates a social loss, because the costly event X occurs more than it would have without insurance.

Consider the case of hang-gliding accidents, which we discussed above. Event X in this case is a broken bone resulting from a hang-gliding accident. Someone with insurance certainly has some control over how likely X is – for instance, he can eliminate the risk of X entirely by refusing to go hang-gliding (1). Health insurance will typically pay most of the hospital bills associated with a broken bone, so having health insurance means the cost of breaking a bone while hang-gliding is not as high (2). Knowing this, health insurance customers may have less incentive to protect against broken bones, and some will be more likely to go hang-gliding, or go hang-gliding more often; this obviously increases the chances of suffering a broken bone (3). Insurance companies cannot afford to hire spies to follow their customers around and see how often they are hang-gliding, so they cannot include a stipulation in the contract like an extra charge for people who go hang-gliding several times a week (4). As a result, bones are broken more often than they would be if the health insurance contract did not exist. This means society must devote time and effort to healing the "extra" bones that broke as a result of moral hazard (5).

Any instance of moral hazard involves a price distortion, price sensitivity, and asymmetric information. If one of these elements is not present in a particular context, moral hazard cannot exist. What could have prevented the moral hazard in our example?

Removing the price distortion would have worked; if the insurance company refused to pay for all hang-gliding-related injuries, then Jay would have faced the full consequences of his actions and he would have done the optimal amount of hang-gliding.

If Jay were not sensitive to the price of a hang-gliding accident, that would also have eliminated moral hazard. If Jay cared much more about the pain and recovery time of an accident than its financial cost, his behavior would not change even when his insurance company agreed to cover all financial costs of broken bones.

Finally, if there were no information asymmetry, the insurance company could observe everything Jay did and adjust its policy accordingly. It could charge him a small fee every time he strapped on his hang-gliding equipment, and even penalize him for playing distracting games on his cell phone during the critical pre-flight safety lecture. If the insurance company truly observes everything and can price every risky decision, Jay will only take the risks that are truly worth it to him.

Note that step (3) above allows for two different types of behavior changes. First, the insured individual may take fewer precautions or pursue reckless activities that increase the risk that the insured event X actually occurs. This is known as *ex ante* **moral hazard**, because it occurs before the insured event. In our health insurance parable, this occurred when Jay decided to get in the hang-glider.

But with health insurance, there is another opportunity for moral hazard after an injury or disease has occurred. After the insurable event has occurred, the insurer will help pay the costs of recovery, so the insured person has less reason to be frugal. Instead, he can demand a higher quantity of more expensive treatment than he would have without insurance. This change in behavior due to the price distortion is called *ex post* **moral hazard** because it occurs after the insured event. In our story, this happened when Jay opted for the expensive Bone-Gro treatment that he would not have chosen if he had had to pay for it all himself.

Definition	11.2

Ex ante **moral hazard:** behavior changes that occur before an insured event happens and make that event more likely. Examples include skipping the flu vaccine, consuming artery-clogging cheeseburgers, and going hang-gliding.

Ex post **moral hazard:** behavior changes that occur after an insured event happens and make recovering from that event more expensive. Examples include opting for knee-replacement surgery over painkillers or taking an expensive drug like Bone-Gro rather than a more inexpensive remedy.

The social loss of moral hazard occurs when the insurance company pays for extra procedures and treatments that would not have been needed were it not for moral hazard. But the insurance company does not simply eat these losses and go bankrupt; instead, these extra costs are passed on to all customers in the insurance pool. Ultimately, each instance of moral hazard anywhere in the insurance pool results in slightly higher premiums for everyone in the pool. In practice, moral hazard means that everyone in an insurance pool has to pay for each other's risky decisions and overconsumption of medical care.

11.2   A graphical representation of moral hazard

Consider an individual who loves cheeseburgers but is at risk of a heart attack. If he does not have insurance, the cost of each cheeseburger to him includes both the price of the burger and the increased chance of a heart attack. But with insurance that covers all of his health care costs, the effective cost of each cheeseburger declines, since the insurer picks up the costs of heart attack care.

Figure 11.1 illustrates how moral hazard in this case leads to social loss. With insurance, the effective price to the individual of each cheeseburger falls from P_U to P_I, and his consumption of cheeseburgers spikes from Q_U to Q_I. Point A is the socially efficient equilibrium where the individual perfectly balances the marginal cost and benefit of each additional cheeseburger. Point B is the privately efficient outcome with insurance where the individual perfectly balances the marginal benefit of each cheeseburger against the insurance-subsidized price he actually faces.

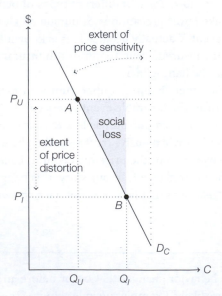

Figure 11.1. *The basic analysis of social loss caused by moral hazard.*

The social loss (represented by the shaded triangle in the figure) is a result of *ex ante* moral hazard. In this case, social loss takes the form of extra money, labor, time, and effort that other people expend on caring for individuals who have eaten more cheeseburgers than is optimal – that is, more than they would have eaten if they had to pay the full price. Just like a fancy steak dinner that is only worth ordering when someone else is paying the check, or an upgrade to a first-class ticket that only makes sense if your company is covering it, extra cheeseburgers consumed between points Q_U and Q_I result in more costs than they are truly worth.

The vertical distance between P_U and P_I shows the *extent of price distortion*. This distance affects the social loss from moral hazard; a small price distortion cannot induce much moral hazard, even if the demand curve is relatively elastic. The angle between the demand curve D_C and the vertical represents the *extent of price sensitivity*. The larger this angle is, the more responsive behavior is to price distortions and the larger the social loss from moral hazard. Relatively inelastic demand for cheeseburgers would imply a small angle and minimal moral hazard; relatively elastic demand for cheeseburgers would imply a large angle and major moral hazard.

Varying price distortion and price sensitivity

In Figure 11.2, we vary the extent of price distortion and the degree of price sensitivity to demonstrate how they combine to create social loss. In Figure 11.2(a), the price distortion and price sensitivity are both quite high. Insured individuals bear very little of the cost of their heart attack treatments, and since they are quite price-sensitive they respond with even more frequent trips to the local burger joint. This results in a large social loss. In Figure 11.2(b), the price distortion and price sensitivity are minimal. Insured individuals bear most of the cost of their cheeseburgers, and their demand for burgers is not very sensitive to prices anyway. In this case, there is still moral hazard but it produces a much smaller social loss.

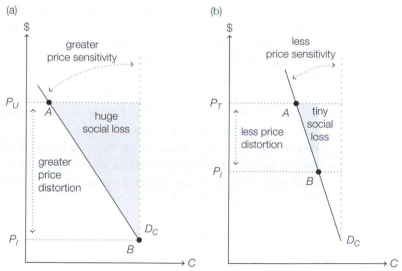

Figure 11.2. *Varying the extent of price distortion and price sensitivity affects the social loss from moral hazard.*

Figure 11.2 makes clear that price distortions and price sensitivity are multiplicative, not additive. The greater the price distortion, the more damaging is each extra bit of price sensitivity. Likewise, the greater the price sensitivity, the more costly is each marginal increase in price distortion. Finally, if there is either no price distortion *or* no price sensitivity, then moral hazard does not occur and social loss is zero.

How much moral hazard is there?

In practice, what determines the magnitude of moral hazard for any given insurance contract? As we saw in the previous section, the major determinants of moral hazard are price distortion and price sensitivity.

The extent of price distortion is a function of the *completeness* of the insurance (see Chapter 7). If a health insurance contract is full, for example, any health problem will not affect the customer's income. This means the (financial) price of any injury or illness is zero, so the price distortion can be large. In a partial insurance contract, by contrast, the customer must pay a positive amount out of pocket for care, so medical care is not completely free to them. This means the price distortion is smaller, and the moral hazard is commensurately less severe.

The extent of price sensitivity (also known by the term price *elasticity*) depends mostly on the nature of the risk being insured, and how controllable it may be. Some risks are basically impossible to control and are never the result of carelessness; these are called natural hazards. For example, your risk of developing certain genetic diseases is entirely out of your control and may be determined before you are born. At the other end of the spectrum are controllable risks like cutting yourself with a knife while slicing a bagel or making an error on your taxes: these are almost completely avoidable if you are careful enough. In between are risks like suffering a heart attack or being involved in a car accident, which are the result of both natural hazards (like a genetic predisposition to heart attacks, or maniacal drivers on the roadways) and individual choices (like eating cheeseburgers every day or driving at twice the speed limit).

Insurance against different types of risks tends to create different amounts of moral hazard. An insurance policy against developing Huntington's disease (a rare disease determined entirely by one's genetic makeup) will not induce moral hazard because it does not affect the insured party's actions or decisions. Put another way, this contract will not create any new instances of Huntington's disease.

An insurance policy that fully protects against tax errors, however, would likely result in some very sloppy tax returns because the insured party has little to gain from taking care – in other words, the demand for laziness is quite responsive to price. Such insurance contracts would literally create more tax errors.

Meanwhile, policies covering car accidents or heart attacks lie somewhere in between, because insured parties have substantial, but not total, control over outcomes.

In Section 11.4 we survey empirical measures of moral hazard in different insurance contexts, including the RAND Health Insurance Experiment.

The role of asymmetric information

We have already seen how price distortions and behavioral changes are necessary conditions for moral hazard, but the presence of asymmetric information is a necessary criterion as well. Almost any type of externality can be modeled in the same way we modeled a customer's overconsumption of cheeseburgers in Figure 11.1, but only externalities arising from asymmetric information qualify as true moral hazard.

The information asymmetries that give rise to *ex ante* and *ex post* moral hazard are not identical. First, consider *ex ante* moral hazard. As we discussed in Section 11.1, Jay's hang-gliding injury might have been prevented if his insurance company had charged him a fee every time he did anything dangerous, thereby deterring him from hang-gliding in the first place. In practice, though, this sort of insurance contract is not feasible, because it would involve insurance companies hiring spies to continuously monitor their customers and report back whenever any customer takes any risk. While that is obviously unrealistic, some insurance companies do take some steps to monitor the behavior of their customers and provide incentive for less risky behavior (see Section 11.3).

This same information asymmetry does not exist when it comes to medical treatment – an insurance company actually does know the details about every medical service and procedure administered. So *ex post* moral hazard is driven by a slightly different information asymmetry concerning the *necessity* of any given medical treatment. If a patient visits her doctor twenty times in one year, is it because she is frequently getting sick and seeking treatment or is it because she knows the visits are free and swings by the doctor's office whenever she has a papercut because they have really nice band-aids? If a patient opts for knee replacement surgery, is it because his joint pain is truly debilitating or is it because the surgery is marginally better than painkillers and costs him just the same?

This information asymmetry, unlike the one discussed above, could actually be eliminated pretty easily in principle. If the insurance company charged customers the full prices for their medical care, it would quickly determine which patients really needed expensive treatment and which patients were just taking advantage of artificially low prices. The only problem with this strategy is it defeats the entire purpose of insurance, which is designed to reduce expenses in the case of illness or injury.

Moral hazard due to insurance occurs if and only if three conditions hold:

- the cost of a risky or wasteful action to an individual is reduced, usually as a consequence of insurance
- asymmetric information prevents an insurer from adequately pricing the action
- that individual responds to the price distortion by changing his behavior, taking more risks or demanding more covered goods and services.

11.3   How to limit moral hazard

Insurers include provisions in their contracts that attempt to mitigate the effect of moral hazard. Recall that the extent of moral hazard depends on both how sensitive demand is to price and the amount of price distortion caused by insurance. Insurers cannot alter their customers' price sensitivity, which is a property of consumers' demand functions, but they do have ways to reduce the price distortion due to insurance. We discuss several common devices that insurers use to reduce moral hazard: coinsurance, copayment, deductibles, gatekeepers, and monitoring.

Cost-sharing: coinsurance and copayment

Suppose an insurer offers a full insurance plan that covers all medical bills for its enrollees. In this case, the marginal cost of health care to each consumer is zero, and each consumer will demand all the health care that provides him any positive utility at all. Even a procedure that costs the insurer millions but provides him only minimal utility, he demands. This is the standard case of moral hazard in health insurance.

Coinsurance and **copayment** are two insurance contract provisions that maintain positive marginal costs for the insured. Enrollees who face coinsurance must pay a fixed percentage of their bill, while those who face copayment pay a fixed amount known as a *copay* for each episode of care.

An insurance customer on a plan with coinsurance might have to pay 20% of any medical bills, while the insurer funds the remaining 80%. In a copayment plan, each visit to the doctor might cost $25, regardless of whether the visit is a routine checkup or involves expensive diagnostic tests. Cost-sharing means that a customer's wealth level will vary depending on his health outcomes, so contracts with cost-sharing do not provide full insurance by definition. These plans are analogous to the partial insurance plans discussed in Chapter 7.

Definition	11.3

Coinsurance: insurance provision in which enrollees pay a *percentage* of each medical bill, and the insurer covers the remaining portion.

Copayment: insurance provision in which enrollees pay a fixed amount, called a *copay*, for each medical episode and the insurer covers all the costs above this copay.

Figure 11.3 illustrates how cost-sharing plans can reduce moral hazard. If the individual is uninsured, he consumes at point Q_U. Every unit of medical care he consumes provides at least as much marginal benefit as marginal cost. If the individual subscribes to a full insurance policy, the marginal costs of medical care from the insured person's point of view fall to zero. Then his effective demand curve is D_F and he consumes at point Q_A, shown in Figure 11.3(a). In Figure 11.3(b), the firm institutes a copay of P_C, which becomes the effective price for each episode of care. Reading off his demand curve, we find that this reduces the consumer's demand to Q_B.

By contrast, a coinsurance plan rotates the insured individual's demand outward (Figure 11.3(c)). Imagine the consumer starts at full insurance – 0% coinsurance. His demand curve is then vertical since he faces no out-of-pocket costs for any services he consumes. The insurer pays 100% of the bill, and graphically the demand curve becomes

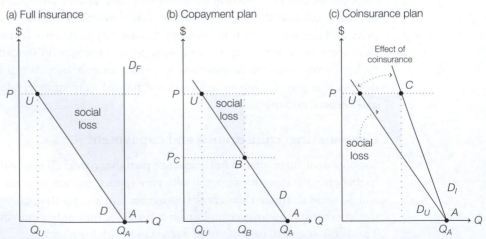

Figure 11.3. *Social loss from different insurance plans. (a) Full insurance. (b) Copayment plan. (c) Coinsurance plan.*

a vertical line over point A. As coinsurance rises, out-of-pocket prices become closer and closer to actual prices, and the demand curve rotates back toward the uninsured demand curve D_U. At the extreme, coinsurance of 100% is equivalent to no insurance.

In Figures 11.3(b) and 11.3(c), the imposition of either a copay or coinsurance increases the marginal cost of additional medical care to the consumer and lowers the quantity demanded. This reduces social loss at the expense of increasing uncertainty faced by consumers who are no longer fully insured.

Deductibles

In addition to coinsurance and copayment, insurers also sometimes include **deductibles** as part of their offered plans (in British English known as an 'excess'). Deductibles set minimal levels of expenses below which the insurer does not help reimburse medical expenses. For example, a person insured with a deductible of $1,000 pays for his first thousand dollars of health care expenditures out-of-pocket. His insurance policy then helps pay for expenses beyond the thousandth dollar. Depending on the policy, deductibles may apply to an individual episode of care or over an entire year of expenditures.

Deductibles may be paired with coinsurance or copayments in the same policy. Figure 11.4 shows the relationship between total medical care expenses and out-of-pocket expenditures for a health insurance policy with 33% coinsurance, a deductible of Ω, and full insurance for catastrophic care expenses above Ψ. For the first Ω dollars of medical care, the insured individual pays the whole price, so the slope m in this region equals 1. However, each dollar of medical care above Ω only costs the customer $0.33 because his coinsurance has now taken effect. The slope in this region is therefore only 0.33. Lastly, this hypothetical policy provides full insurance for catastrophic care, which we model as care above Ψ. For care beyond Ψ, the individual pays nothing out of pocket, so $m = 0$ in the rightmost region.

Requiring insurance enrollees to pay a deductible can limit or eliminate the moral hazard from insurance. Figure 11.5(a) shows an insurance policy with an initial deductible Ω_a and a copay of P_C once the deductible is reached. There is effectively no insurance coverage for all $Q < \Omega_a$ because of the deductible. Because the individual's demand is too low to reach the high deductible Ω_a, the insured person only demands Q_U. There is no price distortion and no moral hazard.

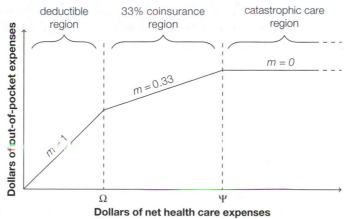

Figure 11.4. *The relationship between out-of-pocket expenses and total medical expenditures for a 33% coinsurance policy with a deductible of Ω and full insurance for catastrophic care.*

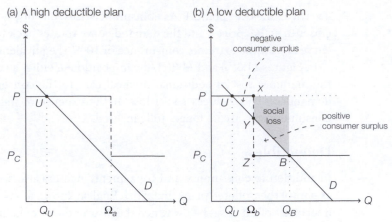

Figure 11.5. *Graphical analysis of insurance policies with deductibles and copayments. (a) A high deductible plan. (b) A low deductible plan.*

However, if the deductible is low enough, moral hazard may still persist. Consider an insurance policy with the same copay P_C but a much lower deductible $\Omega_b < \Omega_a$ as shown in Figure 11.5(b). The insured person's demand curve intersects his out-of-pocket price curve twice, once at U and once at B.

Recall that the demand curve captures the individual's marginal benefit from each additional unit of health care. For the units consumed between Q_U and Ω_b, the price P he pays exceeds the marginal benefit, so he loses consumer surplus on these purchases, a loss measured by the triangle UXY. However, the individual pays only the copay P_C for any units consumed beyond the deductible Ω_b. So the quantity purchased between Ω_b and Q_B yields a positive consumer surplus the size of triangle YZB. If this benefit (triangle YZB) exceeds the negative surplus (triangle UXY), then the insured person consumes Q_B of medical care.

This additional consumption from Q_U to Q_B is induced by moral hazard and the price distortion creates a social loss, shown by the gray area in Figure 11.5(b). However, notice that this social loss is less than the social loss would have been without the deductible Ω_b. In fact, the difference in social loss as a result of combining the copay policy with a deductible is exactly the area of triangle UXY or the negative consumer surplus from a deductible.

Like coinsurance and copayments, deductibles detract from the fullness of insurance contracts and therefore limit the utility gained by consumers from insurance. Lower deductibles mean fuller insurance but also more danger of moral hazard, so policies with lower deductibles tend to charge higher premiums.

Monitoring and gatekeeping

Other tactics for reducing moral hazard involve confronting information asymmetry head on. Some insurance companies try to observe and guide the preventative measures their customers take, while others choose to supervise the medical care that customers receive.

Motivation and incentive programs for customers are two ways that insurers and employers encourage healthy habits to reduce eventual health costs. Kaiser Permanente, a major American insurer, has a program called *Thrive* that encourages enrollees to exercise and stay healthy. Its website offers online yoga courses, motivational tips for dieting,

Doing yoga can save people money with their insurance companies because it proves they are not taking full advantage of moral hazard.
Credit: ImageSource.

and a tool to find local farmer's markets. Employers who must cover health care costs also offer money to reduce *ex ante* moral hazard. Stanford University, for instance, provides employees with an annual cash payment if they complete a number of tasks including a fitness test, a visit with a nutritionist, and an on-campus athletic class.

Once enrollees fall sick and visit the doctor, many managed care organizations (MCOs) use *gatekeeping* practices to manage health care expenditures and limit *ex post* moral hazard. A typical system involves a primary care physician to assess patients and decide how much care they really need. If a patient comes in with a headache, the insurance-company doctor might send her away with only a prescription for painkillers, rather than refer her for the costly CT scan she might have sought without gatekeeping. Gatekeeping tactics can substantially reduce unnecessary medical procedures – although they also have the potential to prevent patients from receiving needed care. See Chapter 18 for much more about managed care organizations.

11.4 Evidence of moral hazard in health insurance

How big a problem is moral hazard in real-world insurance markets? If insurance customers do not react to price distortions the way we would expect, or if insurers have less of an information disadvantage than we thought, moral hazard may be at most a minor problem for insurers and induce little social loss.

Moral hazard is quite difficult to study empirically. Researchers suffer from the same information asymmetry that prevents insurers from eliminating moral hazard: behavior changes are very hard to observe. But a few careful studies, most of which use randomization to determine the effect of health insurance coverage on behavior, do find credible evidence of moral hazard.

In this section, we draw on evidence from three health insurance experiments, two of which we discussed in Chapter 2. There, we introduced the RAND Health Insurance Experiment (HIE), and the Oregon Medicaid Study. The RAND HIE randomly assigned non-elderly families in six US cities into different insurance plans of varying coinsurance levels. It lasted for several years and covered almost 6,000 people. In the Oregon Medicaid Study, winners of a random lottery in 2008 received the right to enroll in Oregon's Medicaid program, whereas lottery losers did not.

We will also study Seguro Popular en Salud, a government-sponsored insurance program for low-income Mexican citizens. Due to budget constraints, this program was initially piloted in only a handful of cities in Mexico, while some nearby cities did not receive treatment. But because of political considerations, the assignment of cities to treatment and control groups might not have been completely random. Nonetheless, several economists have treated the Seguro Popular roll-out as a natural health insurance experiment (Spenkuch 2012).

Ex ante moral hazard

Ex ante moral hazard occurs when those with insurance coverage take more risks. There is some indirect evidence from the RAND HIE suggesting that enrollees with more generous insurance are indeed more reckless with their health. Table 11.1 displays diagnosis rates for participants on free plans (full insurance) and participants on cost-sharing plans (partial insurance). Patients with full insurance were 25% more likely to appear at the doctor's office or hospital with a broken bone or dislocated joint, 18% more likely to present with some other serious trauma, and 35% more likely to be hospitalized for drug or alcohol abuse.

"What happens in Vegas, stays in Vegas" according to a recent tourism promotion. In practice, what happens in Vegas ends up contributing to everyone else's health insurance premiums. Credit: © Andy – Fotolia.com.

This is suggestive evidence that full insurance induces *ex ante* moral hazard, specifically behavior that results in acute hospitalizations such as hang-gliding, rugby, or frequent trips to Las Vegas. But it is also possible that this effect is entirely driven by ex post moral hazard – perhaps fully insured individuals are no more likely to suffer acute trauma, just more likely to show up at the hospital for treatment because it is cheaper for them, or more likely to show up with very minor versions of these injuries. This *ex post* moral hazard explanation seems unlikely for these diagnosis categories though; as we saw in Chapter 2, patients are not very sensitive to price when it comes to acute medical problems that require immediate attention.

Two non-randomized observational studies from outside the United States provide split evidence on the existence of *ex ante* moral hazard. Consider the case of Ghana, where malaria is the leading cause of morbidity and mortality, and accounts for about 38% of the country's outpatient visits and 36% of its admissions into health care facilities (Yilma et al. 2012). In examining the impact of health insurance on malaria prevention efforts in Ghana, Yilma and colleagues found that insured households tend to have fewer members sleeping under treated mosquito nets than uninsured households. While there is disutility associated with contracting malaria for the insured and uninsured alike, having health insurance appears to decrease the cost of malaria treatment relative to burdensome preventative measures, such as sleeping under bed nets.

Courbage and Coulon (2004) examined preventative measures in the UK and instead find little evidence that superior health insurance coverage (specifically, private insurance) is associated with risk-taking. For example, those with private health insurance in the UK

Table 11.1. *Evidence of* ex ante *moral hazard from the RAND HIE.*

Diagnosis	Annual visits per 10,000 enrollees		Ratio of free to cost-sharing
	Free plan	Cost-sharing plans	
Fracture/dislocation	168	134	125%
Misc. serious trauma	67	57	118%
Acute alcohol/drug related	27	20	135%

Source: Data from Table 5.3 in Newhouse (1993). With permission from RAND.

appear to smoke less often and engage in sporting activities more frequently than those who rely on public insurance. This may indicate that *ex ante* moral hazard does not exist among this population. Alternatively, it may simply be that people who opt for private insurance differ from those who rely on public insurance. For example, they may be more risk-averse, and consequently more likely to both purchase private insurance and maintain healthier behaviors than their counterparts with public insurance.

The case of preventative health care is trickier. If we observed that people randomly assigned to full insurance coverage were less likely to use preventative care, we could point to that as an instance of *ex ante* moral hazard – those people are taking more risks with their health because they know insurance has them covered. But what if instead we observed that those people were using *more* preventative care, because the insurance company covers most of those costs as well? That would seem like an example of *ex post* moral hazard resulting from health care overconsumption. There are examples of both phenomena in the data.

Low-income Mexicans whose villages were randomly included in the Seguro Popular program tended to seek less preventative care than their compatriots who were randomly assigned to uninsurance. Seguro Popular enrollees were less likely than non-enrollees to get a flu shot or receive cancer screenings, even though medical care was cheaper and more accessible for enrollees. This is evidence that the uninsured low-income Mexicans were more invested in preventative care, probably because getting sick without insurance is worse than getting sick with insurance. If in fact insurance did cause this reduction in preventative care, this finding is good evidence of *ex ante* moral hazard.

By contrast, the RAND and Oregon studies find no evidence that insured people sought less preventative care like vaccinations or mammograms (Table 11.2). Those with more insurance coverage tended to use more preventative care, probably because it was cheaper for them. Together, these studies suggest that both *ex ante* and *ex post* moral hazard effects arise when preventative care is covered by insurance.

Table 11.2. *Preventative care test frequency in the Oregon Medicaid Experiment.*

	Serum cholesterol[a]	Serum glucose[b]	Mammogram[c]	Pap test[d]
Lottery winners	73.9%	69.4%	48.5%	58.9%
Lottery losers	62.5%**	60.4%**	29.8%**	40.6%**

[a] High serum cholesterol levels or hypercholesterolemia can cause heart disease and strokes.
[b] High fasting serum glucose levels are an indicator of Type II diabetes.
[c] Mammograms are a screening test for breast cancer, recommended for women over 40. Mammogram use data was collected only for this group of women.
[d] The Papanicolaou test also known as the Pap smear or Pap test is a screening exam for cervical cancer. Pap test data was collected only for women.
** Indicates statistically significant difference from lottery winners at the $p = 1\%$ level.

Source: Amy Finkelstein et al. (2012) The Oregon Health Insurance Experiment: evidence from the first year, *Quarterly Journal of Economics*, 127(3): 1057–1106, Supplementary Data. With permission from Oxford University Press.

Ex post moral hazard

Studies are better able to observe *ex post* moral hazard than *ex ante* moral hazard in health insurance. While *ex ante* moral hazard is usually reflected in personal behaviors that are hard to observe (none of these studies recorded data on how often individual participants washed their hands, for example), *ex post* moral hazard can be identified by comparing groups with different insurance coverage levels and studying detailed records of what treatments or benefits the participants receive. For example, Guinnane and Streb (2011) examined moral hazard in late nineteenth and early twentieth century Germany, and found that German miners feigned illness at greater rates when participating in pooled sickness funds. Moreover, they found that the extent of such feigned illnesses was positively correlated with the generosity of funds' sick pay provisions.

Another study of *ex post* moral hazard occurred at Stanford University in April 1967, after university administrators increased the coinsurance rate of the university-provided health insurance. Stanford's faculty and staff who previously received free outpatient care at the Palo Alto Medical Clinic were suddenly required to pay a 25% coinsurance rate. In this natural experiment, the control group comprised Stanford employees before 1967, and the treatment group consisted of the same employees after the policy change who had to pay more for doctor's visits. Compared with the control group, the treatment group visited the doctor 24% less often (Scitovsky and Snyder 1972; Scitovsky and McCall 1977).

The randomized health experiments also show clear evidence of *ex post* moral hazard. As shown in Table 11.3, higher rates of coinsurance in the RAND HIE were associated with fewer outpatient episodes and lower probability of an inpatient visit. These are the same patterns we examined in Chapter 2 when we established the sloping demand curve for health care.

Table 11.3. *Evidence from the RAND HIE.*

Plan by coinsurance	No. of outpatient episodes	Probability of inpatient visit	Probability of emergency care
Free	2.99	10.3%	22%
25%	2.32	8.8%	19%
50%	2.11	8.3%	20%
95%	1.90	7.8%	15%
Elasticity	−0.17	−0.14	

Source: Data from Keeler et al. (1988) and Newhouse (1993). With permission from RAND.

Those in the Oregon Medicaid study exhibited similar behavior. Lottery winners with the opportunity of enrolling in the state-sponsored insurance tended to use outpatient care more than lottery losers (Table 11.4). But like the RAND HIE, the Oregon Medicaid study also shows that more urgent care is typically less price-elastic. Demand for outpatient care is more downward-sloping than demand for inpatient care for both experimental groups. The use of inpatient care and emergency care is not significantly different between lottery winners and lottery losers in the Oregon Medicaid study.

Table 11.4. *Health care utilization in the past six months, Oregon Medicaid Experiment.*

Group	% with outpatient visit	% with inpatient visit	% with emergency care
Lottery winners	78.6	8.0	28.3
Lottery losers	57.4**	7.2	26.1

**Indictes statistically significant difference from lottery winners at the $p = 1\%$ level.

Source: Amy Finkelstein et al. (2012) The Oregon Health Insurance Experiment: evidence from the first year, *Quarterly Journal of Economics*, 127(3): 1057–1106, Supplementary Data. With permission from Oxford University Press.

If the increased use of health care due to lower prices improved health status, then the evidence found by both the RAND HIE and the Oregon Medicaid Experiment might not be indications of moral hazard but rather of efficient use. Yet neither study found significant differences in mortality rates as a result of different levels of insurance. In fact, of 23 health metrics tracked by the RAND HIE, only three – blood pressure, myopia, and presbyopia – improved with better insurance. See Chapter 2 for a more detailed account of these findings.

There is also evidence of *ex post* moral hazard in other countries. Ortmann (2011), using data from Germany's small private health insurance industry, examines the impact of deductible size on expenditures for outpatient services. His model suggests that deductibles in Germany are associated with significant cost savings, up to 35% of total outpatient expenditures. Interestingly, Ortmann also finds that introducing a deductible can lead to reductions in health insurance premiums that actually exceed the amount of the deductible, leading to a decline in total payments for all customers. This is evidence that curbing moral hazard in this way does indeed save money for everyone by decreasing the total amount of health care consumed.

Devlin et al. (2011) finds evidence that one type of insurance can create moral hazard for a different type of service. All Canadian residents have access to free appointments with a primary care physician, but only some Canadians have prescription drug coverage (often obtained through an employer or parent). They find that those who rarely visit the doctor start visiting the doctor much more often when they obtain prescription drug coverage. They speculate that this is because patients begin to substitute prescription drugs for over-the-counter drugs when they no longer have to pay their full price.

Another study from Australia provides a counter-example. Eldridge et al. (2010) analyze data from the Australian National Health Survey and study those who opt to pay for private insurance that grants them access to more luxurious private hospitals. These patients receive perks like private rooms and their choice of doctor, so they might be expected to take advantage of these luxuries and extend their hospital stays. However, these patients did not seem to stay in the hospital any longer than otherwise similar patients who stayed in public hospitals.

The lack of moral hazard in this instance might be explained if the non-financial costs of a night in the hospital weigh more heavily on patients' minds than financial costs. If spending a night in the hospital is a fairly miserable experience even if it is free, then patients will seek to be discharged as soon as possible and will not react much to price changes. Recall that moral hazard disappears if consumers are not price-sensitive (see Section 11.2).

11.5   The tradeoff between moral hazard and risk reduction

Moral hazard is a by-product of insurance contracts, and it creates social loss. So the obvious public policy question is whether insurance policies that create moral hazard should be permitted at all. As we have seen, moral hazard creates a kind of externality, because the costs of each person's risky decisions are borne by other people in the insurance pool. Is an insurance contract that creates more broken bones and more cases of the flu all that different from a factory that is dumping pollution into the atmosphere, for example? And if not, should the provision of insurance be taxed or even banned?

As we explored at length in Chapter 7, an insurance contract provides positive welfare gains that may offset the harm from moral hazard. Risk-averse individuals gain utility from insurance, because it lowers the uncertainty they face. The more full their insurance is, the more utility the contract confers.

So while limiting the provision of insurance through taxes or quotas might seem like an efficient way to reduce moral hazard, it also creates a different social loss by limiting the benefits of insurance. The joint presence of uncertainty and asymmetric information creates a tradeoff between moral hazard and risk exposure. More insurance means more social loss from moral hazard, but less insurance means more social loss from exposure to risk. The optimal insurance contract will be designed to perfectly balance this tradeoff (Pauly 1974). The economist Mark Pauly is credited with this important insight, and the model that follows is based on his 1974 paper on optimal insurance.

Figure 11.6 shows a view of health insurance in a hypothetical world *without* moral hazard. In this case, a population's rate of illness p does not depend on the fullness of insurance coverage. Note that the bold line – which represents the relationship between p and insurance fullness – is flat. This reflects the lack of moral hazard; by assumption, the level of insurance does not influence the rate of illness among the insured population.

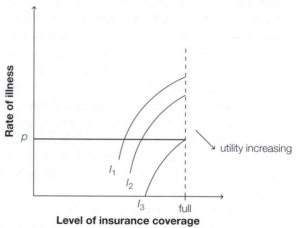

Figure 11.6. *The relationship between insurance coverage and probability of sickness in a world* without *moral hazard.*

The indifference curves $I_1, I_2,$ and I_3 represent different levels of utility for different combinations of insurance coverage and illness rates. Risk-averse individuals prefer lower probabilities of illness and fuller insurance, so utility is increasing toward the graph's lower-right corner. This means the utility of I_3 exceeds the utility of I_2, and I_2 is preferable to I_1. The figure confirms what we already know: fuller insurance increases consumer utility and full insurance maximizes it. A full-insurance contract would be optimal in this environment because it minimizes risk exposure (and there is no moral hazard to worry about).

But in a world *with* moral hazard, the rate of illness p is not independent of the amount of insurance purchased. Instead, insurance coverage may induce recklessness, as people take less preventative care or adopt new dangerous hobbies. They know their insurance will lessen any costs of illness or injury. In the world of moral hazard, a person's probability

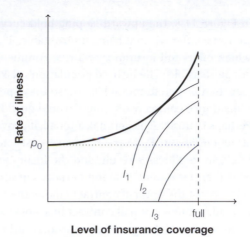

Figure 11.7. *The relationship between insurance coverage and probability of sickness in a world with* moral hazard.

of sickness p increases with the fullness of insurance. This is reflected in the shape of the bold line in Figure 11.7, which is not flat like it was in the previous figure.

In this world, full insurance may no longer be optimal. To see why, we must think about how the rate of illness affects the price of insurance. In order to avoid bankruptcy, an insurance company whose customers tend to get sick more often needs to charge higher premiums to compensate. If we assume that insurance markets are competitive and profits are zero, then insurance company premiums should be proportional to the rate of illness among customers. Remember that actuarially fair premiums are increasing linearly with the probability of illness. As this probability grows, so does the actuarially fair premium in Figure 11.8. As a result, we can replace the rate of illness with the premium per unit of coverage on the vertical axis without changing the graph.

Figure 11.7 illustrates the principle that moral hazard causes higher insurance premiums for everyone. Note that we treat the *premium per unit* of coverage in an insurance contract as its price; it does not make sense to compare the premium of a full contract and a partial contract without adjusting for how full it is.

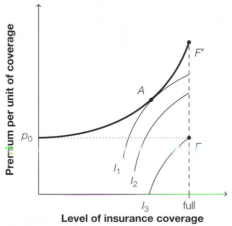

Figure 11.8. *The locus of feasible contracts in a world with moral hazard.*

In Figure 11.8, the upward-sloping bold curve represents the set of contracts that an insurer may offer without being unprofitable. This means that the full-insurance contract F, which offers full insurance at a rate commensurate with the uninsured illness rate, is no longer feasible. The insured population's risk of sickness under full insurance is much higher than p_0 due to moral hazard, so the expected insurance claims exceed premiums. Any insurance company offering F would quickly collapse into bankruptcy.

Perhaps contract F' is optimal; after all, it provides full insurance and it is on the feasible contract curve. But F' is very expensive; customers face no financial consequences if they get sick, more illnesses result, and the insurance company must crank up premiums to pay for their treatment. The indifference curves indicate that, even though this contract is full, it is not the optimal contract among the feasible options.

Instead, the new optimal contract in a world with moral hazard is at A. Given the set of feasible contracts, A maximizes consumer utility and social welfare. However, compared with the (now unattainable) contract F, contract A charges higher per-unit premiums and offers a lower quantity of insurance. The drop in the utility represented by indifference curve I_3 and curve I_1 represents the social loss caused by moral hazard.

Moral hazard makes insurance more expensive than it "should" be – that is, more expensive than it would be if no one adjusted their behavior to take insurance coverage into account. But insurance is often so valuable that some insurance, even a partial contract, is still worth it. The Pauly model of optimal insurance illustrates this tradeoff and helps us determine the precise magnitude of the loss from moral hazard.

Optimal insurance in private markets

The optimal insurance contract A maximizes welfare, so it also minimizes the net social loss from moral hazard and uninsurance. Ideally, all health insurance contracts would sit at this optimal point. This might occur in private markets for health insurance, given their self-correcting nature. Suppose a firm offers an insurance policy α in Figure 11.9. In that case, if another firm were to offer a different contract that is even slightly fuller than α, customers would flock to that contract and leave α, even though the new contract has higher premiums. Graphically, this is because the new contract lies on a higher indifference curve than α.

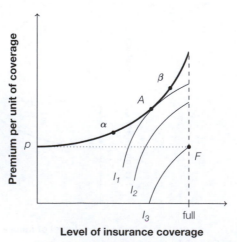

Figure 11.9. *Three insurance contracts* α, β, *and A in a world with moral hazard.*

For similar reasons, an insurance contract of β is not stable. Any contract that is slightly less full than β but charges lower premiums would yield a higher consumer utility, so contract β would never be purchased. The feedback mechanism of customer demand ensures that private, perfectly competitive insurance markets eventually find the utility-maximizing contract A.

This feedback mechanism relies on the tacit assumption that everyone in the population has identical preferences, identical rates of illness, and hence that there is no adverse selection (see Chapter 9). In a world with *both* moral hazard and adverse selection – which is, unfortunately, the world we live in – this analysis is much more complicated. But this simple example shows that, in principle, moral hazard in private health insurance is a private problem. If you are not in an insurance pool with someone, their moral hazard does not affect you. And if you *are* in an insurance pool with someone, then the costs of their moral hazard must not outweigh the benefits of insurance (otherwise, you would not be in a voluntary arrangement with them).

Optimal insurance in public markets

By contrast, the threat of social loss from moral hazard looms large in the *public* provision of insurance. If a government were to offer full insurance, the resulting moral hazard would cause health care expenditures to balloon. And unlike with private insurance, citizens cannot leave these insurance plans in protest, so they must pay higher premiums in the form of higher taxes. The involuntary nature of national insurance means that people whose insurance costs outweigh their benefits cannot leave the pool, so choosing the optimal level of insurance that minimizes social loss becomes a vital policy question.

Empirically, national health insurance systems tend to be quite generous, with fewer charges for patients and more comprehensive care. In the language of Chapter 7, national health insurance tends to be more full than private insurance. This is certainly the case in the US, where the Medicare insurance program for the elderly covers a broad array of services and charges patients minimal amounts for their care. Sapelli and Vial (2003) find that the Chilean public insurance system is similar, and that moral hazard among Chilean workers is greater with public insurance than with private insurance.

Though moral hazard is a significant problem with national insurance, national insurance is popular and appealing in many countries, in part because it can solve the problem of adverse selection. It is also popular as a means of achieving the goal of universal coverage that many countries have. Hence, moral hazard does not mean that governments should never offer public insurance. Instead, governments that provide national insurance must navigate the tradeoff between the social loss from moral hazard and the social loss from uninsurance. See Chapter 15 for more.

11.6   The upside of moral hazard?

While moral hazard is usually thought of as a scourge that should be minimized or eliminated, economists have identified at least two ways in which *ex post* moral hazard may be a good thing. Recall that *ex post* moral hazard occurs whenever insured people consume more health care than they would if they faced the full price. This is usually a bad thing, because it indicates that people are consuming care they do not consider valuable enough to pay for on their own. But in cases when people underestimate the care they need, or simply cannot afford care that they value highly, this type of overconsumption may be beneficial.

Extra preventative care

In Chapter 2 and Section 11.4, we saw evidence from the RAND HIE and the Oregon Medicaid Experiment that lower prices induce patients to seek more medical care, including more preventative care. Although sometimes it is the uninsured customers who actually consume more preventative care (like the uninsured Ghanaians who were more likely to use mosquito bed nets), there is good evidence that insurance coverage generally promotes preventative care.

We normally think of preventative care as a great investment, and doctors and public health workers are constantly reminding patients to get vaccinations, annual checkups, and cancer screenings. But customers should consume the optimal amount of preventative care at full price, in which case any increased use of preventative care is too much of a good thing, and is an example of wasteful moral hazard.

Then again, what if people routinely consume less preventative care than they "should"? This could result from ignorance of the benefits of preventative care, or an inability to correctly judge the likelihood of rare events like breast cancer. If this is the case, and if people systematically seek too little preventative care, then the moral hazard that arises from health insurance might actually correct for these mistakes and bring preventative care up to efficient levels. This would represent a deviation from the tenets of welfare economics, which holds that people can and do maximize their utility and achieve the best outcome they can given their constraints. In Chapters 23 and 24 we explore these behavioral economic ideas in greater detail.

The income effect

Health insurance provides a beneficial income effect to customers in addition to risk reduction (Nyman 2004). A comprehensive insurance policy puts an incredibly expensive kidney replacement surgery or chemotherapy treatment within reach of families with modest means. This effectively makes sick insurance customers much richer than they would be without insurance.

Consider an uninsured individual with total assets of $20,000, who gets diagnosed with cancer. A course of chemotherapy treatment will cost $300,000 out of pocket. It will also provide $1,000,000 worth of benefit to the patient. Unfortunately, he cannot afford the treatment and cannot get access to credit for a loan, so he goes without.

Now imagine the same individual gets diagnosed with cancer but *does* have insurance. Thanks to his insurance plan, chemotherapy treatment will only cost him $3,000 out of pocket, and will still provide the same large benefit. In this situation, he decides to go forward with chemotherapy. Essentially, the insurance contract turns him into a much richer man who can afford an expensive treatment.

In this case, insurance does induce a behavior change, so it might fall under our definition of moral hazard. But at the same time, it is socially beneficial because someone gets access to a treatment that is well worth it. This is fundamentally different from the social loss that happens when the insured person buys more prescription sunglasses than he would have without insurance, or eats more cheeseburgers because heart attack care is covered by insurance.

The possibility of efficient moral hazard means that the optimal contract is more full than if the income effect is ignored. When we account for the full benefits of insurance, including risk reduction *and* the income effect, the optimal level of insurance is higher than Figure 11.8 indicates. Nyman (1999) argues that this income effect is substantial and that insurance contracts should be more full because not all moral hazard is inefficient. Several economists agree that this income effect does exist, but estimate it to be somewhat small empirically (Blomqvist 2001; Manning and Marquis 2001).

11.7   Conclusion

It is impossible to understand the way health insurance works without an understanding of moral hazard. Every insurance scheme, private and public, throughout the world, must cope with the problem. The existence of moral hazard explains why it is so difficult for both markets and governments to provide full financial insurance against health risks. Insurance products in real markets are always necessarily incomplete because of moral hazard – they include cost-sharing provisions, such as coinsurance, and restrictions such as gatekeepers for specialty care. Similarly, even nominally free insurance with no cost-sharing by patients (like the national insurance programs provided in some countries) is restricted by the existence of queues for some services.

At bottom, the difficulty is that insurance companies and governments do not have enough information about the behavior of insured individuals and of health care providers. It is effectively impossible for a third-party insurer to tell whether someone eschews jogging or jumping jacks because she has health insurance. It is also difficult, though perhaps not impossible, for insurers to distinguish between a medically justified surgery, and a redundant test for an unlikely condition that serves little medical purpose.

For private insurers, being able to tell the difference between appropriate and inappropriate care may mean that they can charge lower premiums than their competitors. For governments, being able to distinguish proper care may mean lower tax rates and electoral success. The stakes in combating moral hazard are high for both private and public entities.

The adoption of new technologies by providers poses a particular challenge, since untried and expensive technologies create more opportunities for moral hazard to flourish. In Chapter 14, we discuss cost-effectiveness analysis, which is the primary tool that many insurers and governments use to measure the worth of new technologies.

11.8   Exercises

Comprehension questions

Indicate whether the statement is true, false, or unclear, and justify your answer. Be sure to cite evidence from the chapter and state any additional assumptions you may need.

1   When the price elasticity of demand for health care is zero, health insurance coverage induces no moral hazard.
2   An uninsured patient who incessantly visits his doctor because he always thinks he is getting sick is an example of moral hazard.

3 A woman who uses her fireplace only after she buys homeowner's insurance is an example of moral hazard.

4 A previously uninsured man who enrolls in his workplace health insurance plan after being diagnosed with multiple sclerosis is an example of moral hazard.

5 Pauly (1974) shows that the socially optimal level of insurance in a market is either full or none, depending on whether moral hazard or risk aversion predominates.

6 Besides the common practice of charging copayments, health insurers have no successful strategies for combating moral hazard.

7 If a health insurance company could somehow monitor everything a customer does and thinks, it could create a full-insurance contract with no moral hazard.

8 It would be easy for private health insurers to eliminate moral hazard by redesigning insurance contracts, but they are prevented from doing so by strict government regulations (at least in most developed countries).

9 Moral hazard is mostly a problem in countries with universal insurance programs like the UK.

10 The fact that more free-plan participants logged ER visits for broken bones than cost-sharing plan participants in the RAND Health Insurance Experiment is evidence of moral hazard.

11 An all-you-can-eat buffet is a classic example of moral hazard, because a price distortion induces overconsumption.

Analytical problems

12 **Faustian health economics**. Consider Figure 11.10, which shows the locus of feasible contracts for the population of the nation of Pcoria.

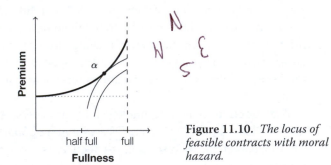

Figure 11.10. *The locus of feasible contracts with moral hazard.*

a In which corner of this diagram (northeast, southeast, northwest, or southwest) is utility highest for consumers? What prevents insurance companies from offering contracts in this corner?

b On your own version of Figure 11.10, plot new points to represent where the market would be under (i) a nationally mandated *full* insurance policy and (ii) an insurance ban.

c Would a nationally mandated full insurance policy be optimal for Pcoria? What about an insurance ban?

d Suppose the devil approaches the newly elected President of Pcoria with an unusual bargain. He offers to magically eliminate moral hazard, but in return Pcoria must forbid contracts that are more than half full. On a new version of this figure, draw a new locus of the contracts that would be feasible if the President takes the devil's bargain.

e Should the President take the devil's bargain? Why or why not?

f The indifference curves in Figure 11.10 represent one possible set of preferences for Pcorian society. On a new figure, draw an alternative set of indifference curves such that the bargain is a good deal relative to the status quo.

g Which type of society is more likely to accept the devil's bargain: one that is relatively risk-neutral or one that is relatively risk-averse? Explain why your answer makes intuitive sense.

13 **Exotic indifference curves.** Consider Figure 11.10, which shows the locus of feasible contracts for the population of the nation of Pcoria. The indifference curves are concave, which represents the fact that consumers want full insurance but also want low premiums.

a Suppose now that the indifference curves are horizontal. What does this imply about Pcorian preferences? What is the optimal level of insurance under this scenario?

b Suppose now that the indifference curves are vertical. What does this imply about Pcorian preferences? What is the optimal level of insurance under this scenario?

14 **Imperfect competition and moral hazard.** Some economists have argued that moral hazard and monopolistic health care markets are two socially inefficient problems that partially cancel each other out.

a Relative to the optimal level of health care Q^*, how much health care is provided in the presence of moral hazard? Assume perfectly competitive health care markets.

b Relative to the optimal level of health care Q^*, how much health care is provided in the presence of monopolistic health care markets? Assume no moral hazard.

c Write a one-sentence defense of the argument that moral hazard and imperfectly competitive health care markets could combine to provide a good level of health care provision Q.

d Gaynor and Vogt (2000) contend that this argument is not quite right. Draw your own version of the Pauly tradeoff diagram (Figure 11.8) with a locus of feasible contracts under moral hazard and perfect competition in the health care market. Now draw a new focus of insurance contracts under imperfect competition. [*Hint*: Imperfect competition raises price levels, so per-unit premiums will now be higher than before at every insurance level.]

e Draw a plausible set of indifference curves that shows the optimal contract under perfect competition A^* and the optimal contract under imperfect competition A'.

f How would you refute the argument you made in Exercise 14(c)?

15 **Fun with cost-sharing.** An important distinction in health insurance is between the *list* price (P_L) and *out-of-pocket* price (P_P) of a medical good or service. The list price is the official price that the provider charges the insurance company, while the out-of-pocket price is the price that the insurance customer faces. Sometimes, the out-of-pocket price depends on the list price.

a Draw a set of axes with *list* price P_L on the y-axis and quantity Q on the x-axis (you will want to make your graph nice and big, because you will be adding several demand curves).

b Suppose a consumer's demand for a particular medical procedure is $Q = 100 - P_P$. Draw her demand curve in P_L–Q space under the assumption of no insurance and label it D_1. You will have to think about the relationship between P_L and P_P to draw it correctly.

c   Now assume the same consumer is fully insured. Think about how this affects the relationship between P_L and P_P and draw a full-insurance demand curve in $P_L–Q$ space. Label this curve D_2.

d   Now assume the consumer is part of a partial insurance plan with a coinsurance provision. Her insurance pays 50% of all medical expenses. Consider again the relationship between P_L and P_P and plot a coinsurance-plan demand curve in $P_L–Q$ space. Label this curve D_3.

e   Finally, assume the consumer is part of a partial insurance plan with a copayment provision. Her insurance pays all expenses above and beyond her copayment of $25 for each unit of Q. Consider again the relationship between P_L and P_P and plot a copayment-plan demand curve in $P_L–Q$ space. Label this curve D_4.

16 **More fun with cost-sharing.** (You may want to review Exercise 15 before proceeding, although it is not necessary.) A consumer's demand for a medical service is

$$Q = 100 - P_P$$

where P_P is the out-of-pocket price she actually faces. She is considering four different insurance options: uninsurance, full insurance, a 50% coinsurance plan, and a copayment plan with a $25 copay.

a   Assume this service has a list price of $P_L = \$70$. Calculate Q under each insurance plan.

b   Calculate the amount of social loss under each insurance plan.

c   Derive a general expression for social loss as a function of x and P_L, where x is the copay amount under a copayment plan. For simplicity's sake, assume $x < P_L$.

d   Derive a general expression for social loss as a function of y and P_L, where y is the coinsurance rate.

Essay questions

17 Long-term disability (LTD) insurance policies cover workers who become disabled and can no longer perform their job functions. Workers who think they qualify as disabled can submit a claim to their employer for LTD payments to replace their lost wages.

Below is an excerpt of the abstract of a recent NBER working paper entitled "Moral hazard and claims deterrence in private disability insurance" by David Autor, Mark Duggan, and Jonathan Gruber (2012):

> We provide a detailed analysis of the incidence, duration and determinants of claims made on private Long Term Disability (LTD) policies using a database of approximately 10,000 policies and 1 million workers from a major LTD insurer. . . . [W]e find that a higher [wage] replacement rate and a shorter waiting time to benefits receipt . . . significantly increase the likelihood that workers claim LTD.

a   Higher disability claim rates when LTD benefits are more favorable may be an instance of moral hazard. Any instance of moral hazard involves a price distortion, a behavior response, and an information asymmetry. What is the price distortion in this example?

    b What is the purported behavior response?

    c What is the nature of the information asymmetry? Explain what would happen if this information asymmetry did not exist.

    d If the higher wage replacement rate and shorter waiting time policies had been applied randomly to different workers in this sample, then the finding would be convincing evidence of moral hazard. Explain how the same result could have been found even if in fact there was no moral hazard (that is, no behavior response to the price distortion)?

18 Below is an excerpt of the abstract of a recent journal article entitled "Do social connections reduce moral hazard? Evidence from the New York City taxi industry" by C. Kirabo Jackson and Henry Schneider (2011):

> We investigate the role of social networks in aligning the incentives of agents in settings with incomplete contracts. We study the New York City taxi industry where taxis are often leased and lessee-drivers have worse driving outcomes [like gas overuse and accidents] than owner-drivers due to a moral hazard associated with incomplete contracts. We find that ... drivers leasing from members of their country-of-birth community exhibit significantly reduced effects of moral hazard ...

    a Draw an analogy between health insurance and taxi leasing in terms of moral hazard. In each case, highlight the price distortion, the behavior change due to price sensitivity, the information asymmetry, and the form of the social loss.

    b The researchers find that moral hazard is reduced when lessor and lessee share a country of birth (most lessors and lessees in the NYC taxi industry are immigrants to the US, so participants in the market come from many different countries).

    c The researchers find that the effect seems to be due to social sanctions against drivers with bad outcomes. Does this mechanism operate through price distortions, price sensitivity, or information asymmetries?

Students can find answers to the comprehension questions and lecturers can access an Instructor Manual with guideline answers to the analytical problems and essay questions at **www.palgrave.com/economics/bht**.

IV ECONOMICS OF HEALTH INNOVATION

12 Pharmaceuticals and the
   economics of innovation   230

13 Technology and the price of
   health care   255

14 Health technology
   assessment   278

12 PHARMACEUTICALS AND THE ECONOMICS OF INNOVATION

There is evidence that the ancient Egyptians were cataloging medicinal plants and herbs as early as 1500 BCE. Credit: © Morphart – Fotolia.com.

Since antiquity, humans have made use of naturally occurring substances to soothe aches and pains and treat some diseases. While most old-fashioned treatments like exorcism and bloodletting have fallen into disuse, doctors in developing countries still sometimes use a substance called quinine – first discovered centuries ago in the bark of the cinchona tree – to combat malaria. Other chemicals derived from tree bark or common plants and discovered to have medicinal properties have been used by humans for ages.

But pharmacology, the study of chemical substances used to treat ailments, could not properly be called an industry until the late nineteenth century. Around that time, a German chemical company called Bayer was experimenting with a compound called salicylic acid, which is found in the bark of the willow tree. Trial and error over the years had shown the extract of willow tree bark to be an effective painkiller and fever reducer, but it also produced ulcers and upset stomachs (Scherer 2010). If a company could figure out how to alter salicylic acid to eliminate side-effects while retaining its medicinal power, that company stood to make a lot of money.

In 1899, Bayer introduced a new pill containing acetylsalicylic acid, a close chemical cousin of salicylic acid with milder side-effects. Marketed under the more pronounce-able name aspirin, the drug became a worldwide success and is still widely used today. In the century since aspirin's development, a massive worldwide pharmaceutical industry has emerged and created thousands of new drugs to treat diseases ranging from acne to zygomycosis.

Drug development today has evolved a more formal methodology, as scientific and technological advancements have uncovered knowledge about both the mechanisms of disease and the human body's response. But even today, drug development is far from certain – a proposed drug that treats one condition effectively can trigger lethal side-effects in another part of the body. As a result, drug developers need to test their drugs extensively for adverse effects, a process that can cost hundreds of millions of dollars.

Pharmaceutical innovations, costly as they may be, have shown a capacity to massively promote social welfare. New drug developments between 1986 and 2001 extended average life expectancy in the US by a week each year (Lichtenberg 2005). Recognizing these health benefits, governments attempt to foster more research by offering patents or direct financial rewards for new drugs or vaccines.

The modern pharmaceutical industry is tightly regulated, and decisions about how to regulate the industry involve several distinct tradeoffs. Patent protections increase incentives for innovation but also restrict access to drugs by enabling higher drug prices. Drug regulatory agencies like the US Food and Drug Administration (FDA) work to keep the drug supply safe but impose significant costs on pharmaceutical companies that are passed on to consumers. In this chapter, we explore the modern pharmaceutical industry and analyze the tradeoffs implicit in the policies governments use to control it.

12.1   The life cycle of a drug

Producing a drug that is shown to be safe to use in humans and effective at treating a disease is a Herculean task. First, scientists sort through hundreds or even thousands of candidate molecules searching for a chemical entity promising enough to test in animals. They may use computer models to predict what sort of molecules are the right shape to bind with a certain protein, or alter known drugs that work well but have undesirable side-effects. Sometimes, researchers simply try every new chemical entity they can find, hoping for success. Suppose that scientists at a drug company have isolated a molecule called *BHTn*1, which they believe may be a breakthrough treatment for carpal tunnel syndrome.

Next, the drug enters animal trials and, if those prove successful, preliminary trials begin in healthy humans. The drug company is not yet looking for signs that *BHTn*1 can cure or prevent disease; these trials simply establish that the drug is not detrimental to the health of living things. If successful there, the drug is put to the test in a major clinical trial with humans who are actually suffering from carpal tunnel syndrome. The drug company hopes that the clinical trial, which may take several years and cost tens of millions of dollars, will provide statistical evidence that the new chemical entity is both safe and effective at treating carpal tunnel syndrome (or maybe some other ailment discovered along the way).

If all goes well, the drug company submits a new drug application to the US FDA with a meticulous report of its clinical trial results. As long as the drug does not seem to be causing adverse health reactions and proves effective, the FDA will approve it for sale in the US. If *BHTn*1 makes it this far, it has beaten some long odds: according to one estimate, fewer than 1 in 5,000 new chemical entities researched by major drug companies ever make it to market (Gambardella 1995).

By this point, the arduous process of discovering, isolating, and (especially) testing a new chemical entity has cost the drug company dearly. If *BHTn*1 is typical, the drug company has already invested over $100 million in its creation, as well as many millions on *BHTn*1's cousins that never even made it to market.

Now, the drug company has the opportunity to recoup all of those expenses and more. It is aided by the patent system, which provides the drug company with a temporary legal monopoly on the production and sale of *BHTn*1. Once the drug is patented in the US, the company has 17 years before its patent expires; during that time, it is protected from competition and can earn potentially massive economic profits from its monopoly. Returns are not immediate or guaranteed though; the drug needs to establish itself in the market and get the attention of prescribing doctors. It may not be the only drug that treats carpal tunnel syndrome, so it may need to compete with other companies with similar products.

Once the patent expires, other companies are free to produce their own versions of *BHTn*1 and sell it at whatever price they wish. These new drugs from other companies, called *generics*, can encroach significantly on a drug company's profits. Before long, the company will need to find revenue from other drugs to remain profitable.

The demand for different types of drugs is an important consideration in the innovation process. If carpal tunnel syndrome is waning but there is an increase in smartphone-induced thumb numbness (SITN), the drug company will alter its research agenda accordingly. Demand-responsive research and development (R&D) work of this sort, called *induced innovation*, is a focus of policymakers trying to steer research towards neglected diseases.

12.2   The uncertainty and costs of drug development

The first step in the lengthy process of bringing a new drug to market is the search for a new molecule with possible therapeutic properties. Through the mid-1900s, this step largely consisted of broad trial-and-error screenings. One report found that the US pharmaceutical industry in 1970 tested over 700,000 substances in animals, of which only about a thousand were promising enough to pass into human trials (Schwartzman 1976). This trial-and-error methodology gradually gave way in the late 1970s to a "rational drug design" approach that relied on better scientific understanding of the role of proteins in the human body (Scherer 2000; Henderson and Cockburn 1994).

As technologies such as X-ray crystallography matured, researchers were able to visualize the molecular structure of proteins and invading organisms. Drug developers use this knowledge to search for specific molecules shaped to bind with proteins, cell walls, or other biological structures. Even more recent advances in computer modeling enable researchers to predict how proteins fold and how potential drugs can modify the behavior of biological systems.

Still, the search for potential drugs remains difficult and far from certain. In 1994, one American biotechnology company designed 367 different molecular variants in hopes of finding one that might prevent graft-versus-host disease in organ transplant recipients. Unfortunately, none of the variants was successful (Werth 1995).

Once pharmaceutical firms identify a new chemical entity and test the drug in animals, the drug developer can apply for clinical testing on humans. For US pharmaceutical firms, the drug needs to pass three increasingly strenuous human testing phases before it can be placed on the market:

- **Phase I**: Researchers administer the drug to a small cohort of healthy volunteers. Starting with low dosages that were previously shown to be safe in animals, the researchers test the safety of increasingly large doses. Their main goal is to confirm the safety of the drug in humans. The average duration is two years.
- **Phase II**: Researchers administer the drug to a cohort of patients with the condition the drug is intended to treat. Having shown the drug is safe in healthy patients, they are looking to establish the safe dose in unhealthy patients and an early indication that the drug has the intended therapeutic effect. Phase II typically lasts two years.
- **Phase III**: Researchers conduct randomized double-blind trials in many different centers often with over a thousand test subjects. The results of these trials must show that the drug is effective at treating at least one disease or condition to gain FDA approval. This phase can last three or four years and can cost tens of millions of dollars.

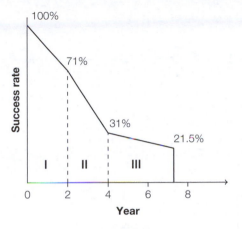

Figure 12.1. *Cumulative success rate of drugs entering the three clinical FDA approval phases. Phase durations are approximate.*

Source: DiMasi et al. (2003). Copyright (2003), with permission from Elsevier.

Many promising drug candidates are winnowed out during the testing process. DiMasi et al. (2003) find that only 21.5% of drugs that enter Phase I pass Phase III, with the largest attrition occurring in Phase II (see Figure 12.1). When we think of drug innovation we tend to picture scientists in white lab coats experimenting with mysterious chemicals, but these lengthy clinical trials are a major aspect of drug research and often the most expensive phase of it. In the words of one American pharmaceutical CEO, "we're in the business of selling statistical information, not drugs."

Not only are the returns from pharmaceutical R&D highly uncertain, but the costs of drug development can be remarkably high. Estimates of the average cost of bringing a drug to market between 1970 and 2000 range between $92 million and $883.6 million. While these estimates do vary greatly, the consensus is that the costs of developing new drugs have risen dramatically over time (Morgan et al. 2011).

Together, the high costs of pharmaceutical R&D and the uncertainty of financial profitability mean that drug developers rely heavily on the success of a few blockbuster drugs to fund the costly amounts of R&D necessary to find their products. Grabowski and Vernon (1990) study a sample of drugs introduced between 1970 and 1979 and find that only the top deciles of drugs made more than the average costs to R&D, highlighting the importance of outliers to financial well-being of the pharmaceutical industry (see Figure 12.2).

Given all these uncertainties that pharmaceutical firms face – identifying a viable new drug, passing it through phases of testing, and then marketing the drug to consumers – as well as the high costs of R&D, it may seem surprising that much R&D happens at all. The next section discusses the importance of patents in creating economic incentives that make pharmaceutical companies willing to face such uncertainty and put up the astronomical funds required for R&D.

12.3   Patents

The previous section chronicled the high costs of pharmaceutical innovation. Presumably, these investments must earn substantial returns to justify the continuing spending by firms on pharmaceutical R&D. To ensure that drug developers can successfully capitalize on their research, governments often award the developers exclusive rights in the form of **patents** to manufacture their drug as a monopoly for a limited time.

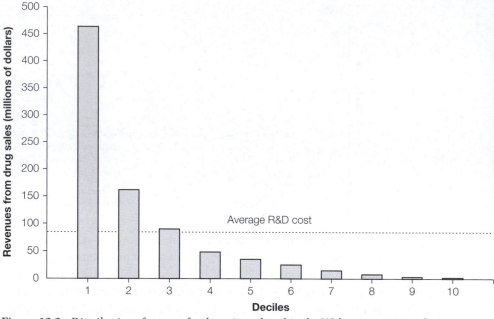

Figure 12.2. *Distribution of returns for drugs introduced in the US between 1970 and 1979.*

Source: Figure 5 republished with permission of *Management Science*, from H. Grabowski and J. Vernon (1990). A new look at the returns and risks to pharmaceutical R&D, *Management Science*, 36(7): 804–21; permission conveyed through Copyright Clearance Center, Inc.

Definition	12.1

Patent: government-sanctioned monopoly in a limited market, usually for one specific idea, algorithm, or product. Patents are typically awarded to the first person or firm that invents a new technology.

Without the protection of patents, drug developers could not recover the costs of their research. Consider a pharmaceutical firm searching for a new drug by painstakingly testing molecules for possible medical benefits. After years of false starts and millions in costs, it discovers a vaccine for the common cold. The firm next spends millions more organizing clinical trials to gain regulatory approval. Finally, after several years of development, the drug enters the market and earns profits for a year.

Suppose this firm is operating in a country without a patent system. By the second year, another firm notices this lucrative opportunity, back-engineers the vaccine formula, replicates it exactly, and enters the market with its *generic* knock-off drug. This second firm invests a small amount in research to replicate the drug and free-rides on the vast R&D expenses shouldered by the drug's original developer. Since the drug was already proven safe and efficacious, the imitator skips the expensive approval process and enters the market immediately. With comparatively trifling fixed costs, it can afford to charge much lower prices for the drug. And as more and more manufacturers enter the market, they compete away any possible profits, and the original firm may end up with little to show for all its R&D.

Anticipating the entry of generic drug makers, the original vaccine innovator likely would never have invested millions in the R&D process to begin with. The vaccine would never have been developed, and consumers would still routinely suffer colds every winter. Allowing firms temporary monopoly profits under a patent system is a way to induce investments in costly pharmaceutical R&D.

Depending on the length of the patent and the market demand, the pharmaceutical firm may successfully recover all its R&D costs and generate economic profits. Once the patent expires, however, the patent holder loses its monopoly, and identical copies of the drug, known as generics, can enter the market. As the barriers to entry fall, the market becomes competitive and future profits should be competed away.

The importance of patents to the pharmaceutical industry cannot be overstated. One survey of R&D officials in the US reported that without patent protection, pharmaceutical innovation between 1981 and 1983 would have fallen by 65%, much higher than the economy-wide average (Mansfield 1986). Similar results were found when surveying R&D managers in the UK. Economists Taylor and Silberston estimated that pharmaceutical R&D expenditures would have fallen 64% without patent protection, compared to just 8% in other industries (Grabowski 2002).

The reason that patent protection is comparatively so important for pharmaceutical innovation is that the vast majority of pharmaceutical R&D goes toward discovering information about the health effects of various molecules. Not only is the chemical formula of a new drug important, but so is proof that the drug is effective. The knowledge generated by Phase I, II, and III testing can cost tens of millions to uncover, but once uncovered, can readily be converted into a marketable drug. Without patents, other firms can free-ride on the information found by innovators and synthesize their own generics. The marginal costs of manufacturing a chemical compound tends to be very low (Caves et al. 1991).

By comparison, having knowledge of the materials used to construct the Boeing 787 Dreamliner is far from sufficient to actually duplicate a version of the plane. In addition to a huge construction factory, an imitator would need an understanding of integrated electronic systems, aerodynamics, and mechanical engineering (Scherer 2010). Unlike with drugs, both fixed and marginal costs of building Dreamliners are very high. The relative ease of imitating a drug once the drug's chemical makeup is known makes the pharmaceutical industry particularly vulnerable to generics and especially dependent on patent protection.

Analeptic drugs like modafinil (the chemical in Provigil) combat sleepiness and are often prescribed to patients who must work long, sleepless shifts. The French military tested modafinil on its pilots and found they could stay awake for days at a time with only a small decrease in performance. Credit: © npology – Fotolia.com

The tradeoff between consumer surplus and innovation

By temporarily protecting drug companies from price competition, a patent system preserves the financial incentives for drug developers to invest in R&D and invent new drugs for the future. These innovations benefit future consumers, protecting their health and extending their life expectancy. But in exchange for these future benefits, costs are imposed on today's consumers in the form of higher – and for some people, unaffordable – drug prices. The optimal length of patent protection is a policy question that balances the future benefits from innovation against the present costs of high monopoly prices.

Even if policymakers decide that the benefits of innovation justify the costs of a strict patent regime, strengthening patent protection too much may actually stunt innovation. A drug company will be deterred from developing an improved version of its old drug as long as the old drug is still under patent, because it does not want to compete with itself. For example, the drug company Cephalon had little incentive to develop a new analeptic drug while its old one, Provigil, still dominated the market. Coincidentally or not, it patented a new analeptic drug called Nuvigil just as its Provigil patent was about to expire.

Similarly, stricter patents also may deter *subsequent innovation*. This type of research, which builds directly on the research of others, is risky if subsequent innovators could be sued for infringing on the patent of the original developer (Gallini 2002). Hence, the relationship between the strength of patents and the rate of innovation likely resembles an inverted-U, as shown in Figure 12.3 (Horowitz and Lai 1996).

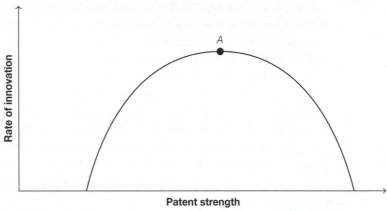

Figure 12.3. *Relationship between patent strength and the rate of innovation.*

Different intellectual property regimes may lie on different parts of this curve. One US study suggests that American pharmaceutical patent protection may be too weak (Goldman et al. 2011). Currently, American law stipulates that generic manufacturers cannot use the clinical trial data obtained by the original drug developer to apply for FDA approval in the first five years after the drug's introduction. The researchers estimated that drug developers would earn an average of 5% more per drug, and develop 228 additional drugs between 2020 and 2060, if they could just maintain data exclusivity on new drugs for seven more years. This increased innovation, they argue, would extend the expected life expectancy of people turning 55 in 2050 by 1.7 months.

The implication of the model built by Goldman et al. (2011) in their study is that patent policy should be designed to maximize the rate of innovation (that is, to achieve point *A* in Figure 12.3). In other words, the benefits due to innovation are sufficiently high to justify the tradeoff of higher costs to consumers. However, dramatically extending patent life may increase producer surplus at the expense of consumer surplus. Furthermore, insurance coverage may induce overuse of expensive new drugs, which is socially inefficient. Point *A* may not be socially optimal if we also take into account these equity and cost-effectiveness concerns.

Patents in developing countries

Developing countries approach the patent policy tradeoff differently. For them, the costs of a stronger patent environment are higher, since monopolistic pricing weighs more heavily on poorer populations and may halt access to drugs altogether. The benefits of stronger patents are also less important, because these countries lack the purchasing power necessary to affect the research agenda of multinational drug developers.

We have previously discussed that the marginal costs of drug production are low. Why would drug manufacturers be unwilling to sell even their patented drugs at a low price in developing countries, as long as that price exceeds the marginal costs of production? Even as a profit-maximizing monopoly, the drug company would be willing to part with its goods at any price above marginal cost. This would be a form of *price discrimination*, in which drug companies would charge high prices in countries like the US where people have high willingness to pay, and low prices in poorer countries.

Nor would offering drugs at lower prices in developing countries stall innovation. Instead, price discrimination between rich and poor countries increases the overall profits of drug companies and actually makes drug development more lucrative. If this pricing strategy were implemented widely, we would expect to observe a strong positive correlation between a country's average drug price and per-capita income.

Yet evidence from world drug markets does not exhibit this correlation. Examining 1998 pricing data, Maskus (2001) finds a weak overall correlation, and for certain drugs, a negative correlation – the price of those drugs was higher in low-income countries than in high-income ones. More recent studies have similarly found that patients are often, though not always, charged higher prices for non-generic drugs. In some cases, those drugs are not offered in the developing country at all (Cameron et al. 2009).

One reason price discrimination is not widespread is political controversy. One US Senator in a 1982 congressional hearing confronted a vaccine manufacturer about charging the US government three times as much as it charged foreign countries. In response, the drug company canceled its future bids to supply vaccines to the United Nations Children's Fund (UNICEF) in order to protect its access to the lucrative US market (Mitchell et al. 1993). When all nations clamor for the same low price, then pharmaceutical markets become a tragedy of the commons. No country wants to pay higher costs to cover the expensive R&D process, so ultimately all prices must be equally high or drug development stops.

However, the primary explanation for why drug manufacturers do not offer lower prices to low-income countries is the fear of *price leakages*. That is, if a drug costs $1 per pill in country A but $5 in country B, a third party can arbitrage the market by buying pills at $1, exporting them to country B, and then selling them there at $4 a pill. Countries like the US have outlawed the reimportation of drugs for sale in order to protect the drug companies' patent monopolies in their domestic market.

Despite the ban, black market reimportation still occurs. Pharmaceutical companies take private measures to thwart price leakage. One strategy employed by Gilead pharmaceuticals, which makes drugs to treat HIV/AIDS, is to manufacture pills in different colors or shapes to sell in Africa and the rest of the world. The different colors make black market reimportation much easier to detect. Ultimately, however, the only way to guarantee the elimination of price leakage is to eliminate the price differentials that motivate reimportation. Many pharmaceutical firms follow this strategy, setting price differentials small enough to stop price leakages (Danzon and Towse 2003).

Drug developers are also often reluctant to offer their drugs in developing countries because they lack strong patent laws. In countries with weak or nonexistent patent protections, generic drug makers can flood the market and deprive innovators of profits. This has been the case in India, which has developed a thriving generic pharmaceutical industry. Pharmaceutical companies hoping to protect their innovations have pressured their governments to threaten trade sanctions against countries without patent laws. This pressure became the impetus in the Uruguay Round trade negotiations in 1994, which mandated that all members of the World Trade Organization implement 20-year patent protections for pharmaceutical products by 2016 (Scherer 2000).

The effect of the Uruguay Round agreement is still to be determined. Proponents argue that extending intellectual property right protection offers greater incentive for drug companies to develop drugs for tropical diseases prevalent in developing countries but rare in developed ones, but others disagree. Lanjouw (1998), studying the Indian economy, argues that income levels there limit the potential pharmaceutical profits from the country, so even stronger patent protections may not provide sufficient motivation for drug developers to pursue R&D for India-specific drugs. Similarly, the low potential profits might deter international drug companies from offering their products in India at all. If so, the effect of the Uruguay Round agreement is to deprive the Indian drug market of generics without providing enough incentives for patent-holders to offer their own drugs.

Thus, strengthening patent protection alone may not be sufficient to galvanize pharmaceutical innovation. Where per-capita income is low, even monopoly returns may not be enough to justify costly R&D, with or without intellectual property recognition. For similar reasons, price controls for drugs constrain the potential profits by pharmaceutical companies and might therefore stymie drug development. For example, pharmaceutical R&D in Italy did not rise after the country legalized patents for drug products in 1982 (Weisburst and Scherer 1995). One hypothesis is that stringent price controls there may have sapped pharmaceutical interest in R&D, even with the arrival of patent protections. We next turn to discussing the effect of price controls on the pharmaceutical market.

Price controls

Markets for pharmaceuticals, in addition to being controlled by patent systems, are often regulated by price controls. A common form of price control is a price ceiling set by the government. Firms are legally prohibited from selling drugs above specified prices that vary from drug to drug. In countries like the UK and Canada where the government is the primary provider of health care, these price controls take the form of prices that the government has negotiated with drug companies (Kanavos 2003). Large buyers like universal insurance programs and US Medicare have monopsony buying power that counters the monopoly seller power of patent-holding drug companies.

It is unsurprising that the typical sale price of pharmaceutical products is lower in places with national price controls than in the US. For instance, Atella et al. (2012) compare the price per milligram of all patented drugs that were sold in common in the US and Italy in 2006. They hypothesize that there should be a stark contrast, because Italy has a strict national price control regime while prices in the US are mostly unregulated. Figure 12.4 shows the resulting distribution of drug prices in Italy and the US. In Italy, there are many more inexpensive drugs and many fewer expensive ones. On average, the price of drugs in the US is nearly twice the price of drugs in Italy.

As we have seen, the ability to charge monopoly prices (protected by patents) is the main motivation for drug manufacturers to embark on the costly drug development

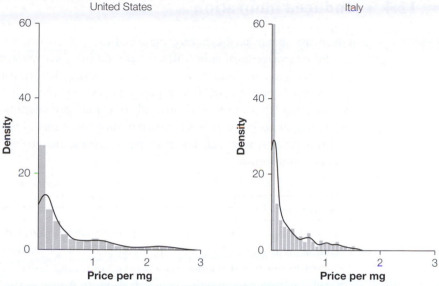

Figure 12.4. *Distribution of drug prices in the US and Italy.*

Source: Atella et al. (2012). Based on data from the Italian National Agency for Drug Administration and Control Prices (AIFA) and the US Medical Expenditure Panel Survey (MEPS).

process at all. Drug price controls undercut the effects of patents; they keep innovative firms from charging monopoly prices and concomitantly limit the incentive to research new drugs. Price controls and patents work in opposite ways, trading off between consumer access to existing drugs and incentives for developing new drugs.

As we have seen, the market for prescription drugs is international in scope. Drug companies devote their research to areas of highest potential worldwide profit, not just in their local economy. Suppose for the sake of example that Americans and Italians suffer from different ailments and require different drugs. Profit-seeking pharmaceutical companies will invest expensive R&D in researching the conditions that Americans have, because their monopoly profits in the US are unrestrained by price controls. On the other hand, drug companies might ignore the afflictions of Italian patients, because even successful drugs sold there may not recover the costs of development.

Of course, our assumption that Italians and Americans demand completely different drugs is not accurate. Developed countries are afflicted with the same costly diseases – cancer, diabetes, heart disease, hypertension, among others – and need the same drugs. Hence, Italian patients benefit from the innovation spurred by profits from the lucrative American markets. But American patients suffer from the price controls instituted by the Italian government. They receive no discount on their drugs, while the overall rate of innovation falls slightly due to the Italian price controls.

A price control in one country imposes a negative externality on everyone outside that country. At the extreme, if every country on Earth were to adopt binding price controls, there would be little financial incentive to develop and research new drugs. Due to its size and lack of broad price controls, the US pharmaceutical market offers the most financial incentives and dominates the attention of innovating drug companies. Other countries with strong price controls rely on these incentives offered by the US for a steady stream of drug advancements (Danzon et al. 2005).

12.4   Induced innovation

Given the somewhat haphazard nature of drug discovery, we might wonder how successful pharmaceutical companies are at focusing their research on producing the most profitable drugs. If companies are capable of steering their research agendas to take advantage of profit opportunities, then public policy interventions like incentives to discover certain drug types can work. If instead companies are stumbling around in the dark and producing drugs more or less at random, then these sort of inducements are at best useless and at worst wasteful. The response by researchers to profit opportunities is called **induced innovation**.

Definition	12.2

Induced innovation: discoveries that result when innovators change their research agenda in response to profit opportunities. For pharmaceutical companies, profit opportunities might include the outbreak of a new disease that lacks a vaccine or a rapidly aging population that demands drugs to treat diseases of old age.

There is good evidence that induced innovation in the pharmaceutical industry does occur. Several studies find that drug companies respond to both natural market forces and artificial government incentives by tailoring their research accordingly. Acemoglu and Linn (2004) study new drugs approved by the FDA between 1970 and 2000. They hypothesize that if innovation is nonrandom, companies respond to changing demographic trends by channeling research efforts toward age groups that are growing in size. Conversely, if innovation is mostly a random process, drug approval patterns would have no relation to demographic trends.

To test this hypothesis, Acemoglu and Linn first develop a classification system dividing the universe of new drugs approved by the FDA into 33 therapeutic categories, a sample of which is listed in Table 12.1. Then they use drug purchasing data to create an age profile for the user populations in different therapeutic categories. For example, the age profiles of antibiotic users and glaucoma medicine users are very different; over 40% of antibiotic expenditures are for patients under 30, whereas the typical glaucoma patient is in her 70s or 80s. In essence, their methodology categorizes drugs into those aimed at young people, middle-aged people, and elderly people.

Using this classification, the researchers study which types of drugs are approved each year. Between 1970 and 1975, for example, about 30% of new drugs were in therapeutic categories that principally served people between 30 and 60. Acemoglu and Linn compare this data to demographic information about the relative size of these age groups in the American population. They find that innovation is surprisingly responsive to changes in market size. A 1% increase in the size of a market leads to a corresponding 1% increase in new drug approvals in that market. The increase is partly accounted for by new generic drugs but it also represents real innovation in the form of new chemical entities.

Figure 12.5 shows a summary of these results for broad age categories. One can clearly see the shift in drug innovation from drugs for the under-30 demographic to drugs in the middle-age demographic as the baby boomers age over the course of the study window.

Table 12.1. *Sample of drug categories with age range of principal users.*

Therapeutic category	Principal age group	Share of expenditures by principal group
Antibiotics	under 30	41%*
Anorexants[a]	under 30	52%
Topical otics[b]	under 30	41%
Antivirals	30–60	91%
Antidepressants	30–60	70%
Contraceptives	30–60	52%
Antitussives/cold remedies	30–60	57%
Anticoagulants	over 60	80%
Anabolic steroids	over 60	77%
Glaucoma	over 60	85%
Movement disorders	over 60	74%
Vascular sedatives	over 60	64%

* Share of expenditures in a particular drug category by members of the principal group. For instance, 41% of all antibiotic expenditures were for patients under 30.
[a] An anorexant is an appetite suppressant.
[b] A topical otic is an antibiotic or other drug applied topically inside the ear.

Source: Based on Appendix 2 from D. Acemoglu and J. Linn (2004). Market size in innovation: theory and evidence from the pharmaceutical industry. *Quarterly Journal of Economics*, 119(3): 1049–1090, by permission of Oxford University Press.

By 2000, about 40% of new drugs were in therapeutic categories that principally served people between 30 and 60. Innovation in antivirals and antidepressants had sped up, while innovation in antibiotics and anorexants had slowed down.

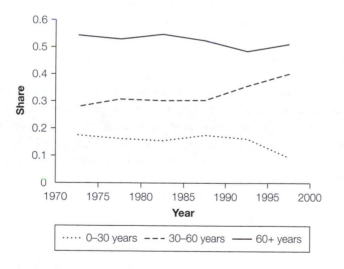

Figure 12.5. *Distribution of newly approved drugs by approximate target age demographic, 1970–2000.*

Source: Figure III from D. Acemoglu and J. Linn (2004). Market size in innovation: theory and evidence from the pharmaceutical industry. Quarterly Journal of Economics, 119(3): 1049–1090, by permission of Oxford University Press.

Bhattacharya and Packalen (2012) examine a different measure of innovation – publications in medical journals – and find that nonprofit innovators like university scientists also seem to respond to population demand for cures and treatment. They show that topics in academic pharmaceutical research track closely with changing disease prevalence. For instance, as obesity rates rose in the American population, researchers shifted their agenda toward understanding the physiological basis of obesity.

Induced innovation is not limited to natural market forces like age or disease dynamics. In the 1990s, three major policy decisions regarding vaccinations greatly increased the return to research on six vaccine-preventable diseases: Hepatitis B, influenza, polio, diphtheria–tetanus, measles–mumps–rubella, and pertussis (Finkelstein 2004). As a result, the number of new clinical trials for vaccines against these six diseases more than doubled. Finklestein estimates that every $1 increase in expected vaccine demand induced a 6 cent increase in annual research spending on these conditions. Similarly, Blume-Kohout and Sood (2008) find that expanded coverage of prescription drugs under Medicare in the US attracted new innovation in drugs for the elderly.

In countries where strict price controls exist and profits for pharmaceutical firms are not as apparent, induced innovation is created through increased reimbursement rates for drugs that are more cost-effective. Pharmaceutical companies that create more beneficial drugs for society will be rewarded with more generous reimbursement rates and therefore more profits. Finland, for example, bases reimbursement of available drugs on economic evaluations (Mossialos et al. 2004).

Innovation by academic and public institutions

Induced innovation occurs when pharmaceutical companies tilt their research toward areas of high profit opportunity. It may also occur when university or government researchers pursue topics that are scientifically interesting or affect the lives of large numbers of people (Bhattacharya and Packalen 2012).

The story of penicillin presents an illustrative example. In 1928, a professor at the University of London named Alexander Fleming was researching the *staphylococcus* bacteria in his lab at St Mary's Hospital. Before leaving for a brief vacation, he left his Petri dishes of bacteria stacked in a corner. Upon his return, he noticed a fungus growing in his samples that seemed to contain the spread of bacteria. Fortunately, Fleming did not trash the contaminated samples, and his article the next year in the British *Journal of Experimental Pathology* became the first scientific publication about penicillin.

Fleming's penicillin was not yet safe for use in humans. Oxford University's Howard Florey and Ernst Boris later discovered the techniques needed to transform penicillin into a medical marvel. In the late 1930s, they identified its chemical structure and found a way to stabilize it for testing in humans, just in time for World War II.

The Allied Powers were eager to manufacture enough of this wonder drug to send to the war front, and the US Department of Agriculture developed an industrial process to mass-produce penicillin. The department shared this technology with 20 drug companies in order to rapidly build up the supply of the drug. After the war, these firms were allowed to use the technology to continue producing penicillin and leverage their learnings to develop further medical advancements (Scherer 2010).

The innovation of penicillin, thus, was achieved mostly through the research of several public institutions rather than private drug companies. These researchers were less motivated by the opportunity for profit and more by the chance to help large numbers of people and gain scientific fame. Though private pharmaceutical firms did later commit resources to design the many descendants of penicillin, the costly R&D for the original penicillin was done primarily by scientists on the payroll of universities and government labs.

Today, the link between public institutions and pharmaceutical innovation is closer than ever. The amount of US taxpayer dollars directed toward health research in 1999 was four times the inflation-adjusted amount spent in 1970 (Cockburn and Henderson 2000). In 2006, America's National Institute of Health (NIH) allocated $28 billion in grants for health-related research, compared with $34 billion in R&D investment by private drug companies (Scherer 2010).

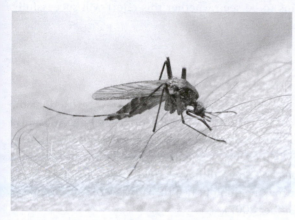

As was the case with penicillin, the research advances made in universities, government labs, and other not-for-profit research centers with public funds often contribute directly to actual drug innovations. Toole (2011) estimates that each 1% increase in the stock of basic public research dollars induces a 1.8% increase in new drug applications.

Tropical diseases and orphan drugs

Governments have tried to harness the power of induced innovation to direct research efforts toward diseases that they believe should receive more research attention. Two classes of disease often ignored by major pharmaceutical companies are tropical diseases and **orphan diseases**.

The anopheles mosquito, which carries malaria. During World War II and the Vietnam War, when American soldiers were deployed to tropical locales, the US Army worked furiously to develop effective malaria treatments. Once the Vietnam War ended, malaria research mostly ceased. Credit: © Kletr – Fotolia.com.

Definition	12.3

Orphan disease: a rare disease that receives little or no research attention from major drug companies. In the US an orphan disease is defined as one that afflicts fewer than 200,000 people (about 1 out of every 1,500 Americans).

Tropical diseases like malaria and yellow fever used to be common in the US but are now mostly found in parts of Africa and Asia. Because incomes are low in the afflicted countries, and American pharmaceutical consumers are the source of almost all profits for drug companies, working on solutions for tropical diseases is not lucrative. A Doctors Without Borders study found that barely 1% of new drugs on the world pharmaceutical market between 1975 and 1999 were intended to treat tropical diseases. Likewise, orphan diseases receive little attention from drug companies because the demand for cures is quite limited (Scherer 2010).

The Orphan Drug Act of 1983 was a result of lobbying efforts by advocates frustrated with the lack of innovation for the treatment of orphan diseases. The Act provides a tax reimbursement for 50% of clinical trial expenses incurred in the testing of a drug for an orphan disease. The aim of this Act was to induce innovation in this moribund pharmaceutical sector: before 1983, only 36 drugs had ever been approved by the FDA for orphan diseases.

The Act spurred significant new innovation on drugs for rare diseases; the number of new clinical trials for rare diseases increased by 69% in the years after the Orphan Drug Act (Yin 2008). There is also evidence that Americans with rare diseases have seen significant increases in longevity since 1983 (Lichtenberg and Waldfogel 2003).

Likewise, recent international humanitarian efforts have tried to create inducements for innovation in drugs for tropical diseases. In 2006, a consortium of developed countries endorsed a different approach to induce innovation (Scherer 2010). The effort specified three diseases – HIV/AIDS, malaria, and tuberculosis – that are commonplace in developing countries but rare in the US. The countries pledged to purchase 200 million doses of an effective vaccine developed for any of these diseases at $15 per dose, a total commitment of $3 billion for each disease. It remains to be seen whether this effort will successfully lead to vaccines for these deadly diseases.

12.5   Regulation of the pharmaceutical industry

In the nineteenth century and the early twentieth century, there were few restrictions on drug manufacturing or sales. Drugs available for sale were not complicated pharmaceuticals that took hundreds of millions of dollars to develop, nor were they tested strenuously for safety or efficacy. Instead, most medicines were concoctions of alcohol and unusual ingredients that worked through the placebo effect if they worked at all. Traveling salesmen who hawked exotic solutions while making dubious health claims were commonplace during this period, at least in the US (Graber 2007).

However, even then the pharmaceutical market was not entirely unregulated. As of 1875, chemists and druggists in the UK were required to register with the government in order to sell substances classified as poison (Penn 1979). Starting in the late 1930s, drugs were only allowed onto the American market if they had been certified as safe in drug trials by the US Food and Drug Administration (Sherman and Strauss 1986). This last regulation was a major difference between the American and European pharmaceutical markets: back then, drugs generally did not need to be proven safe before going on sale in Europe.

This permissive regime lasted until the early 1960s, when an international medical scandal inspired governments around the world to tighten controls on the pharmaceutical market.

The story of thalidomide

In October 1960, pediatricians from all over West Germany descended on the town of Kassel for a routine meeting. When two doctors at the meeting presented on unusual cases of phocomelia – underdeveloped limbs in newborns – most doctors in the audience had never seen anything like it before (Smithells and Newman 1992).

Almost a year later, a German medical journal published a note from a pediatrician named Dr Wiedemann. He reported an unprecedented outbreak of phocomelia among his patients (13 newborns afflicted within a ten-month period), and the journal received dozens of replies reporting over a hundred more cases throughout western Europe. This tragic development was especially alarming because phocomelia was a very rare disorder thought to be solely an inherited condition. Why the sudden and violent spike in birth defects among infants born to healthy parents?

Scarcely two months later, in November 1961, the outbreak was linked to the recently introduced sedative and painkiller thalidomide. Thalidomide, which had gone on sale in Germany and England in the late 1950s and was widely available in many countries, was frequently prescribed to combat insomnia and nausea. Specifically, it was often given to pregnant women suffering morning sickness. In the late fall of 1961, thalidomide was pulled from druggists' shelves almost everywhere it was available. Nine months later, the epidemic was over and phocomelia rates had returned to their typical very low levels (Burgio 1981).

Thalidomide caused birth defects in more than 10,000 newborns, mostly in Germany, and the associated scandal became a media sensation all over Europe. But the scandal went almost unnoticed in the US. Thalidomide had *not* yet been approved for sale in the US or France by the time its connection with birth defects was discovered, and it had not been available in drug stores in those countries at any point. American and French regulators, such as the FDA's Dr Frances Kelsey, were concerned about some preliminary evidence that thalidomide could cause peripheral neuropathy – numbness in the fingers and toes – although no one foresaw the link to phocomelia. As a result, American newborns were almost entirely unaffected (Sherman and Strauss 1986).

Meanwhile, Estes Kefauver, a prominent US senator from Tennessee, was trying to drum up support for a controversial new bill to control drug prices and enhance the FDA's power to regulate both the safety and efficacy of new drugs. In the summer of 1962, the bill was stalled in Congress. Kefauver's staff leaped on the thalidomide scandal and the story of Frances Kelsey. After a conscious attempt by Kefauver and his staff to promote the story, the scandal finally became a major news item in America, inspiring investigative journalism and an endless string of editorials about drug controls.

Suddenly, Kefauver's bill started moving through Congress. The epidemic of birth defects inspired a popular outcry for tighter controls of pharmaceuticals. When the bill – eventually titled the Kefauver–Harris Amendment – became law in 1962, it granted the FDA broad new powers to regulate drugs. Drug companies had to demonstrate that their offerings were not only safe but also efficacious through evidence from randomized clinical trials. In 1968, the passage of the Medicines Act in the UK ushered in similar changes there: drugs became subject to regulatory approval and pharmaceutical companies had to show that their offerings were safe and effective (Penn 1979). As European nations have become more integrated, the European Medicines Agency (EMA) has assumed the role of regulating the safety and efficacy of drugs.

How did the Kefauver–Harris Amendment impact the burgeoning US pharmaceutical industry? Establishing tougher regulatory standards for drugs involves a tradeoff. If done effectively, regulation makes the marketplace for drugs safer and less wasteful, because drugs that are dangerous or useless are shut out of the market. But it also discourages research investment and requires companies to complete Phase II and Phase III trials to establish efficacy, which often costs millions of dollars. Stricter regulation also results in higher prices for the drugs that do reach the market.

Peltzman (1973) finds evidence that the 1962 reforms significantly depressed the number of new chemical entities introduced each year in the American pharmaceutical market. Figure 12.6 plots the number of new drugs actually introduced after 1962 (solid line) alongside the number predicted by Peltzman's model in the absence of the new regulations (dashed line). Apparently, the tougher standards limited the entrance of new drugs into the marketplace. Another study estimates that the Kefauver–Harris Amendment approximately doubled the cost of bringing a new chemical entity to market (Grabowski and Vernon 1992).

Do these results mean that the FDA is effectively protecting public health? Or does it mean that the FDA merely hinders new drug development? The evidence could be consistent with both stories. Suppose that the drugs that the FDA kept off the market after

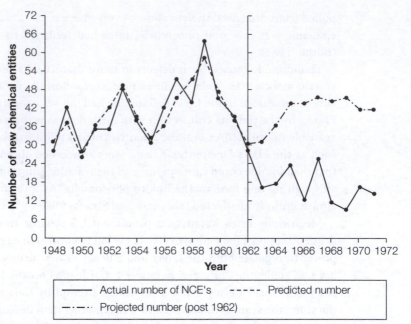

Figure 12.6. *Predicted and actual number of new chemical entities (NCEs) before and after the 1962 Kefauver–Harris Amendment.*

Source: Figure 1 from S. Peltzman (1973). An evaluation of consumer protection legislation: the 1962 Drug Amendments. *Journal of Political Economy*, 81(5): 1049, reproduced with permission. *Journal of Political Economy* © 1973 The University of Chicago Press.

1962 were mostly ineffective and would have wasted consumers' money. Suppose further that the agency was able to screen the bad drugs out with minimal expense. Then the new regulations may have been worth the cost of delayed approval and lengthy clinical trials.

But if effective drugs were prevented from reaching the marketplace, or were significantly more expensive as a result of FDA reporting requirements, then the regulations may be counterproductive. Peltzman estimates that the regulations provide some benefits in the form of reduced expenditures on ineffective drugs, but they are ultimately not cost-effective. He calculates that the Kefauver–Harris Amendment effectively imposed a net 5–10% tax on American pharmaceutical consumers during the 1962–1971 period.

Type I and Type II error

The Peltzman finding highlights the tradeoff between a more permissive FDA and a more restrictive one. The problem the FDA faces is that simply examining the structure of a molecule is not sufficient to establish whether a drug is safe or effective. There may be people for whom the drug is safe, and others for whom the drug is dangerous. For instance, thalidomide is safe for HIV patients with wasting syndrome but unsafe for expectant mothers and their unborn children.

A regulatory agency aiming to distinguish good drugs from bad must formulate a process or test that results in a decision for each candidate drug. No test, however, can be perfect. A more permissive standard allows more dangerous drugs to go to market, but a more restrictive standard keeps more good drugs off the market. These two unfavorable outcomes are called **Type I error** and **Type II error**, respectively.

Definition | **12.4**

Type I error: a false positive decision. In this context, a Type I error occurs when a bad drug gets approved for sale.

Type II error: a false negative decision. In this context, a Type II error occurs when a good drug gets rejected and does not go on the market.

The approval of Vioxx, a painkiller that was later implicated in a number of cardiac arrests and strokes and taken off the market in 2004, is an example of a recent Type I error by the FDA. Type II errors are harder to observe, but a good example is the delay in approving timolol, a beta blocker that helps to prevent a second heart attack after a patient has had his first. Gieringer (1985) estimates that as many as 70,000 preventable heart attack deaths occurred in the US during the lag between the first evidence of timolol's effectiveness and its eventual approval in 1981.

Some errors are inevitable because the process that distinguishes between good and bad drugs is imperfect. The FDA and other modern regulatory agencies rely on the results of clinical trials to decide which drugs to approve. Data from Phase III trials does help determine when a drug is effective and safe, but it never generates complete information about a drug. Sometimes dangerous side-effects do not surface during testing, or the treatment group happens to be unusually resistant to the drug being tested. Alternatively, the clinical trial may not have included members of some subpopulations (like patients with rare diseases) who may especially benefit or be harmed by the drug. Under these conditions, regulators are bound to err from time to time.

Figure 12.7 illustrates the quandary of drug regulators. Imagine that each candidate drug is tested and receives a single score, T, that provides an imperfect estimate of how beneficial it will be. We can think of this as a summary score of the drug's performance during Phase II and III trials. The probability distributions of T for bad drugs (those that should not be approved) and good drugs (those that should be approved) are shown in the figure. Because the test is not perfect, the distributions overlap; a few bad drugs will score higher than a few good drugs – even though the good drugs are truly better.

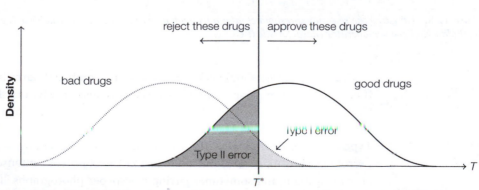

Figure 12.7. *The probability distribution of* T *for good drugs and bad drugs. Drugs that score higher than* T* *are approved, while drugs that score lower than* T* *are rejected.*

Drug regulators have to decide which drugs to approve and reject. If the test scores are the only information available, their best strategy is to pick a threshold T^*, approve drugs which score higher than T^*, and reject all other drugs. If the good-drug and bad-drug distributions overlap like they do in Figure 12.7, any choice for T^* unavoidably creates some error. The particular threshold depicted in the figure results in some Type I error (light gray region) and some Type II error (dark gray region).

Now imagine a thalidomide-type scandal where a dangerous drug is approved and causes a widely publicized epidemic of blindness. Drug regulators might respond to the political uproar by becoming more conservative about approving marginal drugs. This corresponds in the model to a rightward shift in the vertical threshold approval line. Perhaps drug regulators increase the threshold from T_1^* to T_3^* (Figure 12.8(a)). Whereas at T_1^* all good drugs were approved along with many bad ones, at T_3^* some good drugs are rejected while fewer bad drugs are approved. In other words, raising the threshold reduces Type I error and the chance of another scandal, but it comes at the cost of increasing Type II error.

The selection of any threshold involves a tradeoff between the two types of error. We can virtually eliminate the possibility of harmful drugs being approved (Type I error) if we raise T^* enough, but that would also keep a larger fraction of good drugs off the market (Type II error). Figure 12.8(a) illustrates five different possible thresholds and the rate of Type I and II error generated by each. A *receiver-operator characteristic* curve plots the tradeoff between Type I and II error rates (Figure 12.8(b)).

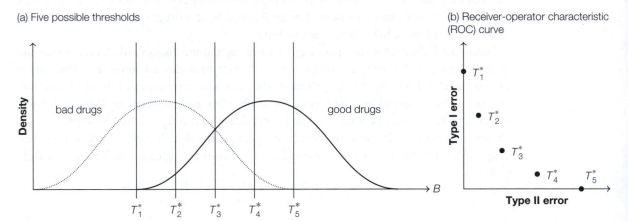

Figure 12.8. *Adjusting the rejection threshold creates a tradeoff between Type I error and Type II error. (a) Five possible thresholds. (b) Receiver-operator characteristic (ROC) curve.*

Ideally, regulators should act to minimize the combined harm from Type I and Type II errors. From the perspective of total social welfare, regulators should not care which type of error was the source of a particular harm, but instead focus on making the right tradeoff to minimize overall harm. But, in fact, regulators probably have incentive to avoid Type I error more than Type II error because it generates more negative publicity. Type I errors like the approval of thalidomide and Vioxx provoke intense scrutiny in the form of investigations and sometimes jarring newspaper photographs. Type II errors like the delay in approval of beta blockers often receive little attention and are not discovered until years later.

Controlling access to drugs

The power of the FDA and EMA to bar drugs deemed unsafe or ineffective is not the only restriction on drug markets. While some mild drugs like painkillers, antiseptics, and topical medications are sold freely to any buyers – "over-the-counter drugs" – most drugs and especially the most profitable ones are available by prescription only.

When a government appoints an agency like the FDA to determine which drugs are allowed to be sold, it trades off the safety of the drugs on the market against access to the full panoply of potential pharmaceutical products. There is a similar tradeoff between safety and access when a government institutes prescription controls.

In this case, the decision to vest prescription power in doctors instead of pharmacists (or even patients themselves) is intended to increase safety by discouraging unsafe or unsupervised use of powerful substances. Doctors are presumably knowledgeable about both the drugs they are prescribing and their patients' medical histories. This knowledge leads to better outcomes than if patients were to pick drugs for themselves (Crawford and Shum 2005). But this restriction inevitably makes drugs more expensive in terms of access and transaction costs. If a patient has to schedule an appointment and visit a doctor's office before she can pay for a drug that she knows will benefit her, the prescription control acts like a tax on her purchase.

Another, related type of regulation is limits on direct-to-consumer (DTC) advertising for pharmaceutical products. In most developed nations, including Canada and the UK, direct-to-consumer print, TV, or web advertising is illegal or tightly controlled. This means pharmaceutical companies are not free to advertise their great new medicines to prospective customers; they must instead convince doctors to prescribe them for patients. In the US, by contrast, direct-to-consumer advertising is allowed, although ads must conform to FDA guidelines about the disclosure of side-effects and risks.

As with any regulation, DTC restrictions involve a tradeoff. Permitting DTC advertising allows consumers free access to information that could make them aware of important new remedies, and there is evidence that consumers themselves tend to oppose restrictions on DTC advertising (Berndt 2005). But if these drugs are expensive and no more effective than cheaper alternatives, persuasive advertisements can drive up health care costs and exacerbate moral hazard. DTC ads also tend to put a strain on doctor–patient relationships when patients begin clamoring for drugs they do not understand to treat conditions they do not in fact have (Hoffman 1999).

There is one more reason why restricting access to some drugs can be beneficial. As we will see in Chapter 20, antibiotic resistance is a growing concern, and improper antibiotic drug use can generate substantial negative externalities. By restricting access to antibiotics, governments hope to decrease unnecessary antibiotic use that can help breed drug-resistant bacteria.

12.6   Conclusion

Barely a century has passed since aspirin was developed, but in that short time pharmaceutical innovation has grown into a massive and heavily regulated industry. This innovation has undoubtedly saved lives, but it also contributes to the skyrocketing costs of health care. A key debate in insurance policy is the extent to which new drugs should be covered.

The evolution of aspirin provides a good example. Aspirin was originally marketed as a painkiller when it was introduced in 1899. But during the 1960s researchers began to notice that aspirin had an anti-clotting effect. Now, one of the main uses of aspirin is to prevent and treat heart attacks.

Aspirin has been joined in this market by Plavix, a newer anti-clotting medication that was one of the world's most profitable drugs in 2010. Some have questioned whether Plavix and aspirin together are more effective at preventing heart attacks than aspirin alone, but no one denies that Plavix is much more expensive – each Plavix pill costs more than a whole bottle of aspirin (Bhatt et al. 2006).

This debate about Plavix highlights one of the thorniest issues that societies must confront: balancing the costs and benefits of medical discoveries, especially when the costs and benefits are measured in human lives. In Chapters 13 and 14, we explore the effect of innovation in the health care sector and attempts by governments and insurers to balance the costs and benefits of using new technologies.

12.7   Exercises

Comprehension questions

Indicate whether each statement is true or false, and justify your answer. Be sure to cite evidence from the chapter and state any additional assumptions you may need.

1 In the US, drug companies receive a patent of 100 years for each drug they develop. This allows them a prolonged legal monopoly on the sale of that drug.
2 Phase III clinical trials are a minor part of the drug development process in the US.
3 If a government wishes to maximize the rate of pharmaceutical innovation, it should offer non-expiring patents to drug companies.
4 Price controls decrease the innovation rate for drugs but make existing drugs more affordable.
5 The US government has harnessed the power of induced innovation to create cures for orphan diseases.
6 Most economists think that innovation is *not* random, and that pharmaceutical companies can steer their research toward profit opportunities.
7 After passage of the Kefauver–Harris Amendment in 1962, the number of new chemical entities introduced into the US market by pharmaceutical companies dropped substantially.
8 The Food and Drug Administration (FDA) decides whether to approve a drug for use in the US based in part on whether each drug is cost-effective in the treatment of some disease.
9 Phase II drug trials are conducted on animals, while Phase III drug trials are conducted on healthy volunteers. Both are required for FDA approval.
10 The approval of Vioxx, a painkiller that was taken off the market in 2004 because it was implicated in several cardiac arrests, is an example of Type I error by the Food and Drug Administration.

Analytical problems

11 Suppose there is a test, ϕ, that yields the distribution of test outcomes for good drugs and bad drugs seen in Figure 12.9. In this case, is it possible to create a rule for

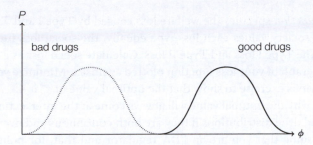

Figure 12.9. *Bad drug and good drug distributions for Exercise 11.*

accepting and rejecting drugs that yields no Type I or Type II error? If so, be sure to show this threshold rule explicitly on the graph above. If not, explain why this is impossible.

12 Explain why the following statement is true, or provide a counter-example: A receiver-operator characteristic curve, which plots the Type I error of a test against the Type II error from that same test, always slopes downward. See Figure 12.8(b) for an example of this kind of curve.

13 **Loss function.** Suppose there is a test, x, that yields the distribution of test outcomes for good drugs and bad drugs shown in Figure 12.10. The bad drug curve $b(x)$ is defined as

$$b(x) = \begin{cases} 1, & \text{if } 1 \le x \le 5 \\ 0, & \text{otherwise} \end{cases}$$

while the good drug curve $g(x)$ is defined as follows:

$$g(x) = \begin{cases} x - 3, & \text{if } 3 \le x \le 10 \\ 0, & \text{otherwise} \end{cases}$$

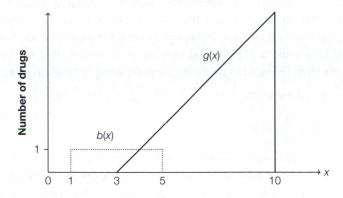

Figure 12.10. *Bad drug and good drug distributions for Exercise 13.*

a Let x^* be the drug acceptance threshold. Let "total Type I loss" equal the total area under the bad-drug curve to the right of x^*. It captures the number of bad drugs approved with this drug acceptance threshold. Write down an equation for total Type I loss as a function x^*. The function $L_1(x^*)$ should indicate how much total Type I loss there is for any value of x^*.

b Now write down a function for total Type II loss as a function of x^*. This function $L_2(x^*)$ should give the number of good drugs not approved given threshold x^*.

c   A *loss function* specifies the welfare loss caused by Type I and Type II error. If we assume society values each loss type equally, the social loss function will be the sum of the Type I loss and Type II loss. Calculate social loss as a function of x^*.

d   Draw a graph of your loss function plotted against x. Minimize your function from the previous exercise to show that the optimal value of x^* is 4.

e   Explain why the optimal value will always come at the intersection of the bad drug and good drug distributions if they are both continuous and overlapping.

f   Now assume that you are an FDA regulator and that, for political reasons, you regard Type I error to be twice as harmful as Type II error. Rewrite your loss function to reflect these preferences and find the FDA optimal value for x^*.

g   How much total welfare loss is induced if the FDA picks its optimal threshold instead of society's optimal threshold? Calculate your answer using society's loss function, not the FDA's.

14 **Establishing a new drug in the market.** Bhattacharya and Vogt (2003) study the pricing strategies of pharmaceutical companies that bring new drugs to market. They observe that new drugs often debut at relatively low prices and get more expensive over time. They interpret this strategy as an attempt by the drug company to establish its drug in the minds of doctors and patients before trying to extract monopolistic profits.

Recall our fictional drug for carpal tunnel syndrome called *BHTn*1 which was introduced in Section 12.1.

a   Suppose demand for the new drug is

$$Q = 1,000 - P$$

where P is the price that the monopolistic firm sets. What price will the firm choose to maximize profits $\Pi = PQ$? We assume the cost of producing the drug is negligible throughout this problem.

b   Now suppose that Bhattacharya and Vogt are on to something when they say that drug companies must manage the stock of knowledge about their drug. Imagine a two-period model where the drug company is trying to maximize the sum of profits over two periods. In the first period, the monopolistic firm will price low to build buzz about *BHTn*1, and in the second period the firm will capitalize on its popularity. Demand in year 1 (Q_1) and demand in year 2 (Q_2) are as follows:

$$Q_1 = 100 - 5P_1$$

$$Q_2 = \frac{Q_1}{10} \cdot (100 - 5P_2)$$

(12.1)

Note that demand in year 2 is a function of sales in year 1. Find the sequence of prices P_1, P_2 that the firm chooses to maximize profits $\Pi = P_1 Q_1 + P_2 Q_2$. [*Hint*: Use backward induction. Start with year 2, considering the output in year 1 as given. Then find the year 1 output that maximizes total profit.]

c   Explain intuitively why your results do or do not match up with the Bhattacharya–Vogt hypothesis.

d   Now assume that the company, if it follows your pricing strategy, will earn $P_1 Q_1$ in the first year and $P_2 Q_2$ in every subsequent year while it still holds a patent and can price like a monopolist. Afterwards generic versions of *BHTn*1 will flood the market and it will earn no more profits. If the company has to invest $60,000 in year 0 to discover the drug, would a 17-year monopoly be long enough for the firm to invest in researching the drug? Assume no discounting.

e What if the discount rate is 5%?

15 **Price controls and induced innovation**. Suppose that drugs can be assigned a value W from 0 to 100 that indicates their quality. Perhaps a drug with $W = 1$ is a hangnail medication that barely works, while a drug with $W = 99$ is a life-saving cancer treatment. In general, suppose the annual demand for drug i in the nation of Pcoria is

$$Q_i = W_i - P_i$$

where W_i is the quality of drug i and P_i is its price.

a Assume that a company has a one-year patent on drug j with quality W_j. What is the profit-maximizing price P_j that the company will charge if it is free to choose its own price, as a function of quality? Assume that the drug costs nothing to manufacture.

b How much profit does the company make on the drug in its one-year patent period as a function of W_j?

c Suppose the drug discovery process at Drugs-R-Us Inc. works as follows: Drugs-R-Us decides to invest a certain amount of money I_k in creating a new drug k, and the new drug is likely to have higher quality W_k if the company invests more money. Assume for all new drugs that

$$W_k = 13I_k^{\frac{1}{4}}$$

where I_k is the amount of money invested in drug k. Assume the firm can only make profits during its one-year patent period. Find the profit-maximizing investment I^* that Drugs-R-Us will make on each drug.

d Now suppose that Pcoria implements a price control because the impoverished citizens of Pcoria do not have access to the best medicines. The Supreme Pcoria Drug Council rules that any drug with $W_i > 50$ must be made available for only $25 per unit. What is the optimal investment for Drugs-R-Us under these rules? What happens to average drug quality as a result?

e Suppose that there was a blockbuster drug with $W = 100$ already in existence before the price controls. How much extra consumer surplus do Pcorians enjoy on this drug due to the price controls compared with the unrestrained monopoly pricing regime? Answer this question graphically.

f What are the costs and benefits of any price control initiative like this? Why might it matter if other nations have citizens with the same ailments that the Pcorians have?

Essay questions

16 The 1992 drama film *Lorenzo's Oil* is based on the true story of Lorenzo Odone, who was diagnosed with a hereditary orphan disease called adrenoleukodystrophy (ALD). His diagnosis induced his parents to research the disease intensively, interview scientists who had studied the disease, and convince a small pharmaceutical manufacturer in England to make a few doses of an experimental drug. Explain why there are so many more drugs available to treat acne than the typical orphan disease, and discuss any government efforts that benefit people afflicted by rare diseases.

17 Compare the tradeoff implicit in allowing the FDA to regulate pharmaceutical markets with the tradeoff implicit in allowing the American Medical Association to restrict the supply of doctors in the US (see Chapter 5).

18 **Policy prescriptions**. List the costs and benefits of the following hypothetical policies.

a The US government offers a $5 billion prize to the first drug company that develops a cure for Alzheimer's disease.

b The patent length for drugs to treat fatal diseases is reduced to five years, and all current patents for such drugs that are already more than five years old instantly expire.

c The European Medicines Agency announces that it will instantly approve new drug applications that have shown any promise in treating Creutzfeldt-Jakob disease (also known as mad cow disease), even if there are safety concerns or if the evidence of efficacy is not conclusive.

d The US government allows patients to write themselves prescriptions on weekends, when physicians are typically not available.

Students can find answers to the comprehension questions and lecturers can access an Instructor Manual with guideline answers to the analytical problems and essay questions at **www.palgrave.com/economics/bht**.

(13) TECHNOLOGY AND THE PRICE OF HEALTH CARE

The da Vinci Surgical System, a robot controlled remotely by surgeons, was approved for use in the US in 2000.
Credit: With permission from Intuitive Surgical.

Rising health care costs are a major topic in the news, but there is nothing new about them. Health care costs have actually been increasing much faster than inflation for decades. In 1960, for example, the typical American spent a twentieth of her income on medical care. But today about a sixth of the American economy is spent on medical care. In 2010, for example, Americans spent a total of $2.6 trillion on health care alone (this is equivalent to $8,402 per person). Throughout the 1980s, 1990s, and most of the 2000s, American health care spending increased much faster than inflation (Martin et al. 2012). Figure 13.1 plots the explosive rise of the health care sector in the US.

Similarly aggressive growth has been happening in other developed countries. Table 13.1 shows the rate of adoption of expensive technologies such as MRI machines, CT scanners, and linear accelerators for radiation therapy. In nearly every case, adoption increased between 1997 and 2007.

Why are expenditures for medical goods and services increasing so much faster than expenditures on other goods and services like hamburgers and haircuts? The first step to answering this question is determining whether this increase in expenditures reflects

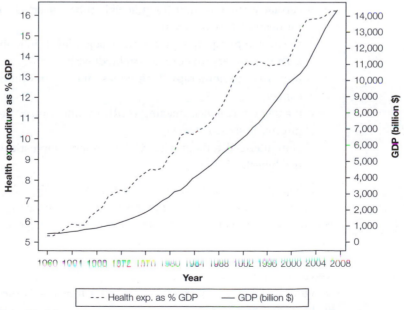

Figure 13.1. *Health care expenditures as a proportion of US GDP, 1960 to the present.*

Source: Data from OECD Health Data 2012 – Frequently Requested Data. © OECD (2012) URL: http://www.oecd.org/health/healthpoliciesanddata/oecdhealthdata2012.htm

Table 13.1. *Technology adoption by nation per million people.*

Country	No. of MRI units[a] 1997	No. of MRI units[a] 2007	No. of CT scanners[b] 1997	No. of CT scanners[b] 2007	Radiation therapy equipment 1997	Radiation therapy equipment 2007
Australia	3.5	5.1	23.2	56.0	4.9	7.8
Austria	8.5	17.7	25.2	30.0	3.8	4.8
Canada	1.8	6.7	8.2	12.7	–	–
Iceland	7.4	19.3	14.8	32.1	14.8	12.8
Italy	4.1	18.5	14.8	30.1	2.4	5.4
South Korea	5.1	16.0	21.0	37.1	3.8	5.1
US	13.5	26.6	24.1	34.3	–	–

[a] Magnetic resonance imaging machines (MRIs).
[b] Computed tomography scanners (CT scanners).

Source: Data from OECD Health Data 2012 – Frequently Requested Data. © OECD (2012) URL: http://www.oecd.org/health/healthpoliciesanddata/oecdhealthdata2012.htm.

price increases, or instead reflects increases in quantity. Maybe people simply consume *more* medical care as incomes rise or as the population ages and needs more care.

Technological change, too, could help explain this increase in expenditures. New technologies are often expensive, and myriad medical innovations have been introduced in the past decades. Consider the following incomplete list of recent medical advances, which gives a flavor of the range and significance of these improvements:

- laparoscopic surgery (minimally invasive surgery with miniature cameras);
- beta blockers (drugs to reduce blood pressure);
- statins (drugs to reduce cholesterol);
- cardiac catheterization (long flexible tubes inserted to unclog the coronary artery for heart disease patients);
- the insulin pump (to regulate blood sugar levels in diabetic patients);
- laser eye surgery (to cure nearsightedness);
- improved radiotherapy techniques and chemotherapeutic regimens (to treat cancer);
- magnetic resonance imaging (MRI) scanners (uses powerful magnets to visualize internal body structures);
- computerized tomography (CT) scanners (sophisticated three-dimensional X-ray machines).

Perhaps prices in the medical care sector are actually *falling* and the seemingly ominous trend outlined above is the happy result of new life-saving technologies being adopted. When new technologies get created, it is natural to expect an increase in overall health care expenditures as they come into use.

After surveying the many factors that might be leading health care costs to increase, Newhouse (1992) concludes that technological change – not monopolistic hospitals, not an aging population, not more generous insurance – is the biggest driver of increasing health care expenditures.

In the first half of this chapter, we point to changing technologies for the treatment of a number of diseases, ranging from Hodgkin lymphoma to clinical depression, that have served to increase total expenditures but also seem to have reduced the price of health. If this story is true more broadly, it means that increased health care expenditures are a good sign of innovation in medical care and improved patient welfare.

But the arrival of gleaming new technologies in hospitals and doctors' offices is not unambiguously good news for medical consumers. In the second half of this chapter, we discuss the phenomenon of *technology overuse*, and the way that expensive new treatments and therapies can create new opportunities for moral hazard. Unlike in most markets – where innovation is almost always a blessing – technological advances can actually do more harm than good in insurance markets where moral hazard is always present.

13.1   Technology and the rise in medical expenditures

It is easy to think about rising health care costs as synonymous with rising health care prices, but these two things are not equivalent. When we speak of "health care costs," we really mean *total health expenditures*. There is a simple way to think about the rise in medical expenditure E, which is motivated by the following basic formula:

$$E = P \cdot Q$$

where E is expenditure on medical care, P is the price of medical care and Q is the quantity of medical care. Expenditure is the product of the price and quantity, so the evidence of rapidly increasing medical care expenditures can be explained in two ways:

- *Prices are going up, due to . . .*
  - **increased resource costs**: If syringes or band-aids are getting more expensive, or if surgeons and nurses are commanding higher wages, prices will rise at hospitals and outpatient clinics.
  - **less competitive markets**: If hospital mergers, for example, have made the market for health care more monopolistic, prices will increase.
  - **expensive new technology**: If modern medical care routinely incorporates new, expensive technologies like MRI machines and linear accelerators for radiation therapy, the price of treating many ailments will rise.
- *Quantity demanded is going up, due to . . .*
  - **an aging population**: As people get older and sicker, they demand more medical services than they did before.
  - **a richer population**: Because health care is a normal good, rising incomes also lead to more health care consumption.
  - **more insurance coverage**: More insurance reduces the out-of-pocket price to patients of more medical care, leading to more demand.
  - **the increasing *quality* of medical care**: If, as technology improves, each dollar spent on health care generates a higher marginal health benefit, then demand for health care will increase.
  - **new types of health care coming into existence**: If new technologies are invented but do not completely replace old treatment methods, people will demand both and more health care will be consumed overall.

If the increase in medical expenditures is driven by increases in price P, then this trend does in fact harm health care consumers. If health is getting more expensive to produce (due to resource constraints, a lack of competition, or some other combination of the factors listed above), then people will either have to cut back on health care or spend more money to stay healthy.

If instead the increase in medical expenditures is mostly driven by increases in quantity Q, then the trend toward higher medical expenditures does not necessarily imply that people are worse off as a result. Instead, it may mean that consumers feel that extra spending on health care is worth it – perhaps technological advancements have made health expenditures more worthwhile. However, it could also mean that people are spending more on unnecessary care due to moral hazard.

Measuring medical inflation with a price index

A price index can be used to measure **medical inflation**, which is the price change of medical goods and services over time. All else equal, rising prices reduce consumer welfare, because consumers cannot achieve as much utility with the same income as they could before. Governments publish **medical care consumer price indices** (CPI) that track the changing prices of medical goods and services. Unlike the expenditure data in Figure 13.1, the CPI captures only price changes and not quantity changes.

Definition	13.1

Medical inflation: a rise in the price level for medical goods and services. A **medical care consumer price index** (CPI) is an estimate of medical inflation.

In the last thirty years, the US medical care CPI has remained consistently higher than overall inflation (Figure 13.2). This is evidence that the rise in medical expenditures is explained at least in part by rising prices, not just by rising demand or the emergence of new and expensive technologies.

Ideally, a price index provides an answer to the following question: How much more does it cost this year to achieve the *same utility* I achieved last year? In other words,

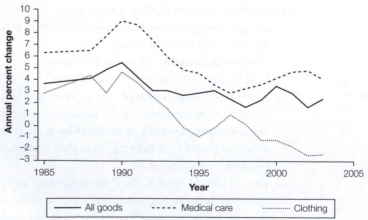

Figure 13.2. *Annual change in various price indices, 1985–2003. The US medical care CPI grew faster than the general US CPI every year from 1985 to 2003.*

Source: US Bureau of Labor Statistics.

it indicates how much more expensive it is for the economy to generate utility for consumers. A price index is therefore a measure of welfare. A rising medical price index is an indicator of decreasing welfare for health care consumers, because it costs more to achieve to the same health level. An ideal price index would give a perfect measure of how changing prices affect welfare, but such an index is impossible to construct because utility is never directly observable.

Instead, economists rely on indices that are more feasible to measure called *Laspeyres* price indices. A medical care CPI, which is a Laspeyres price index, answers a slightly different but related question: How much more does it cost this year to buy the *same things* I bought last year?

This price index is calculated by creating a "bundle" of goods and services that approximates the typical consumer's yearly medical care purchases. In a given year, the average American consumer receives a certain number of vaccinations, spends a certain amount of time at the dentist's office or in the hospital, and buys a certain number of prescription drugs. By tallying up the total cost of this representative fixed bundle each year, we can determine how price levels are changing across the entire health care sector. Changes in a Laspeyres price index reflect changes in price rather than merely expenditures, because the size and composition of the bundle is fixed between consecutive years.

Equation (13.1) illustrates the basic mathematics of a Laspeyres price index like the medical care CPI. Suppose for simplicity that there are only two goods in the bundle, A and B. Let (q_0^A, q_0^B) and (p_0^A, p_0^B) represent yesterday's quantities and prices of A and B, and let (p_1^A, p_1^B) represent today's new prices for the same pair of goods.

The Laspeyres index I_{CPI} is the ratio of the price of yesterday's goods at today's prices to the price of yesterday's goods at yesterday's prices:

$$I_{CPI} = \frac{p_1^A q_0^A + p_1^B q_0^B}{p_0^A q_0^A + p_0^B q_0^B} \tag{13.1}$$

This type of index is not a perfect measure of how price changes affect utility, but it is easy to calculate and often gives a good approximation of the welfare effects of price changes. If a Laspeyres price index rises by 5%, then consumers are approximately 5% worse off because the things they want to consume are 5% more expensive.

The Laspeyres price index becomes a bad approximation, however, when the goods that are included in the original bundle change subtly from year to year. A blood transfusion, for example, might seem like the same good in 1960 and 2013, but modern blood transfusions are much safer due to improved screening techniques for infectious blood-borne diseases such as HIV and viral hepatitis (Cutler et al. 1998). A night's stay at the hospital, which the medical care CPI treats as a homogeneous commodity, might also become more valuable over time with the incorporation of new technologies like blood oxygen monitors and automatically adjustable beds.

A simple Laspeyres price index also fails to account for the advent of completely new medical technologies. Due to continual medical care innovation, the bundle of goods consumers purchase is not fixed from year to year but instead constantly evolving. In the 1700s, the typical medical care consumer bundle might have included five leeches, a tourniquet, and some medicinal herbs. Today, the typical bundle consists predominantly of goods and services invented in the last hundred years, like laparoscopic surgery, insulin pumps, and blood pressure medication. In the case of medical care, the mix of goods and services purchased by consumers is dramatically different from what it was even ten or twenty years ago.

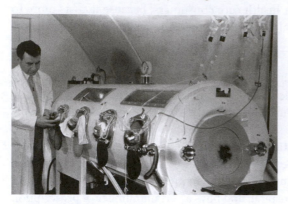

New medical technologies often supplant existing technologies, for example when the advent of the polio vaccine rendered the iron lung virtually obsolete for polio treatment. The prices of those old goods are thus no longer relevant to the welfare of the medical care consumer, while the prices of the new inventions (missing from the bundle) are quite relevant. The simple Laspeyres price index is unable to account for rapidly evolving markets and might dramatically underestimate welfare changes over time if new medical technologies are making consumers better off.

An Emerson iron lung, which was once state-of-the-art technology for treating diaphragmatic paralysis due to polio. A patient would lie in the chamber, and oscillations in air pressure would help her to inhale and exhale. Credit: Center for Disease Control and Prevention – Public Health Image Library.

Hodgkin's lymphoma and peptic ulcers

Two examples illustrate how the introduction of new technology exposes shortcomings in the bundle-based approach to measuring the welfare effects of price changes.

Hodgkin's lymphoma is a cancer of the lymph nodes, and one of the most common types of cancer seen in young people between the ages of 15 and 25. Because Hodgkin's is a relatively slow-moving and localized cancer, it is easier to treat with a targeted approach than most other cancers. Using modern radiation therapy and chemotherapeutic techniques, doctors can aggressively target affected lymph nodes. Treatment success rates are high: of the thousands of Americans diagnosed with early-stage Hodgkin's lymphoma between 2001 and 2007, nearly 90% were still alive five years after their diagnosis (National Cancer Institute 2012).

The statistics were much bleaker for those diagnosed with Hodgkin's lymphoma in the 1950s. At that time, radiation and chemotherapy techniques were still in their infancy, and only a few pioneering doctors had applied radiation therapy to Hodgkin's cases (Mukherjee 2010). As a result, people diagnosed with Hodgkin's lymphoma were mostly treated with palliative care designed to keep patients comfortable as the cancer progressed. In this era, only about 15% of people with Hodgkin's survived five years after diagnosis (Lacher 1985).

Hodgkin's care in the 1950s was inexpensive but produced almost no survival benefit. Hodgkin's care today is relatively expensive (a full course of chemotherapy can cost $50,000 or so in the US) but yields substantial health benefits. Because modern treatment is so effective, millions are spent every year on treating the disease; Hodgkin's expenditures have skyrocketed since the 1950s.

Has treating Hodgkin's lymphoma become "more expensive" since 1950? It is true that expenditures on treatment have increased, and radiation is definitely more expensive than 1950s-era palliative care. But Hodgkin's care in 1950 and Hodgkin's care now are not really the same thing, so comparing their prices is not meaningful. Consider the difference in the price of Hodgkin's care and the price of a Hodgkin's *cure*. The price of care has increased, but largely because the standard of care has vastly improved. The price of a Hodgkin's cure, meanwhile, has plummeted. A cure for Hodgkin's lymphoma did not exist in 1950, and was purchased by none of the people who might have demanded it.

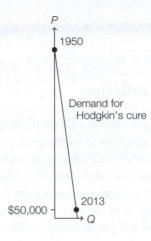

Figure 13.3. *As the price of a cure for Hodgkin's lymphoma fell from practically infinite in 1950 to affordable in 2013, expenditures on Hodgkin's treatment increased. If a good is not available at any price during a certain period (because it has not been invented yet, for instance), we consider its price to be the price that would induce zero demand; not even one person would want to buy it at this hypothetical price. For goods or services with highly inelastic demand, this price is effectively indistinguishable from ∞. In this sense, a Hodgkin's cure cost $∞ in 1950.*

Even the wealthiest people in the world could not purchase a cure back then. We can say that the price for a Hodgkin's cure in 1950 was so high that demand was zero (see Figure 13.3).

Increased chocolate consumption by people with peptic ulcers is a subtle sign of the decreasing price of ulcer treatment. Credit: © *Natika – Fotolia.com.*

There is a similar story to be told about changing standards of care for the treatment of peptic ulcers in the 1990s. Peptic ulcers are erosions in the lining of the esophagus, stomach, or small intestine that can be extremely painful due to the acidity of the stomach. Through the early 1990s, conventional medical understanding held that peptic ulcers resulted from stress and from eating certain types of foods. When peptic ulcers arose, people were treated with a combination of dietary restrictions – spicy foods and chocolate were often forbidden – and in extreme cases, invasive surgery to remove part of the vagus nerve. The vagus nerve is responsible for signaling the stomach to produce acid, which can exacerbate the damage from peptic ulcers and prevent healing.

In the 1980s, Robin Warren and his student Barry Marshall, two medical researchers working in Australia, proved that the vast majority of ulcers are actually attributable to the bacteria *Helicobacter plyori*. In order to convince skeptical colleagues, Marshall drank a petri dish full of *H. plyori* and, sure enough, developed terrible ulcers within a few days. The self-experimentation was cut short when his wife threatened to evict him from the house (nausea and halitosis are two major symptoms of peptic ulcers), but the discovery did earn him and his colleague the 2005 Nobel prize in medicine (Weyden et al. 2005). In the years since, the strategy for treating peptic ulcers has been transformed. Ulcer patients are now first put on antibiotics; partial vagotomies are undertaken only as a last resort and have become very rare. Medical dietary restrictions for ulcer patients are also mostly a thing of the past.

As with Hodgkin's lymphoma, this more effective set of treatments has led to increased expenditures on peptic ulcer treatment. Whereas ulcer patients in a previous generation suffered with persistent peptic sores and no chocolate to soothe the pain, ulcer patients today take antibiotics that often eliminate the problem entirely. Yet again, this increase in expenditures masks the fact that the price of *curing* a peptic ulcer has fallen since the 1980s.

13.2   New technology and medical inflation

In the Grossman model, we treated health care not as a direct input into the utility function but instead as a tool that helps people generate something they value: health. Cutler et al. (1998) propose adopting this mindset when considering measures of medical inflation. Rather than consider the changing price of medical care – which itself is evolving so quickly that these price comparisons are sometimes meaningless – they consider the changing price of *health*. With this strategy, they develop an alternate price index that accounts for both the effects of new technology and the continually increasing quality of medical care.

The price of heart attack survival

Cutler et al. (1998) focus on a specific question to build their price index: What is the price of survival after a heart attack, and how has it changed over time? They analyze a Medicare dataset with records of nearly all the acute myocardial infarctions (AMIs), commonly referred to as heart attacks, that occurred in the elderly population in the US between 1984 and 1991. Over this time span, the average cost of treating an AMI – which includes the input costs of goods like alcohol swabs and beta blocker medications and services like open-heart surgery and prescription refills – rose steadily and faster than inflation (see Table 13.2). The cost of treating an AMI rose 32%, from $11,175 to $14,772 (both figures are put in 1991 dollars to account for economy-wide inflation).

This increase in the price of heart attack care is quite substantial. A naive, Laspeyres-type price index that measures the changing price of a specific bundle of goods used in AMI treatment might indicate that heart attack patients were worse off in 1991 than in 1984. The problem with this interpretation is that, because of improving AMI treatment

Table 13.2. *Life expectancy of AMI patients in the US Medicare system and average costs of AMI treatment over time (in constant 1991 dollars).*

Year	Life expectancy (years)	Costs ($)
1984	5 $\frac{2}{12}$	11,175
1985	5 $\frac{4}{12}$	11,691
1986	5 $\frac{4}{12}$	11,998
1987	5 $\frac{5}{12}$	12,253
1988	5 $\frac{6}{12}$	12,725
1989	5 $\frac{8}{12}$	13,019
1990	5 $\frac{9}{12}$	13,623
1991	5 $\frac{10}{12}$	14,772

Source: D. Cutler, M. B. McClellan, J. Newhouse, and D. Remler, (1998). Are medical prices declining? Evidence from heart attack treatments. *Quarterly Journal of Economics*, 113(4): 991–1024. Reproduced by permission of Oxford University Press.

technology, a Laspeyres price index is an unreliable measure of the welfare effects of price changes.

Heart attack treatment changed in many ways between 1984 and 1991. The use of open-heart surgery expanded and surgical teams mastered techniques for keeping patients stable during surgery. Aspirin was discovered to have a life-saving effect on patients experiencing an AMI. Improvements in emergency response technology meant that more heart attack victims had a chance to be seen by surgeons before it was too late. A new technology called the intra-aortic balloon pump, which did not exist in 1984, was introduced to help the heart pump blood into coronary arteries during a heart attack. And coronary angiography matured, improving physicians' ability to visualize blood clots in the coronary arteries and treat patients accordingly.

Contrary to the assumption of the Laspeyres price index that the AMI treatment bundle remained static between 1984 and 1991, innovations in the intervening years changed the quality of heart attack care. Using the most basic measure of treatment quality – average years of survival after the AMI – Cutler et al. (1998) find that AMI treatment improved significantly during this period. The typical heart attack victim in 1984 lived for five years and two months after his heart attack, while the typical heart attack victim in 1991 lived about five years and ten months (a 13% improvement). Life expectancy in the general elderly population in the US only increased by about four months in this interval, so about half of this eight-month increase can plausibly be attributed to improved technologies for treating heart attack victims.

So Medicare paid more for heart attack services in 1991 than in 1984, but its enrollees received many more months of life in exchange. Cutler et al. (1998) construct an alternate price index for post-AMI survival that takes both of these factors into account. Their cost of living (COL) index compares the cost of reaching a baseline level of utility in 1984 with the cost of reaching that same level of utility in later years when heart attack care was better but more expensive.[1] The COL index answers the question about whether patients should prefer today's heart attack care at today's prices or yesterday's care at yesterday's prices.

If this COL index goes up over time, it indicates that achieving the same amount of post-heart-attack survival (which is approximately equivalent to achieving the same utility level) is more expensive in 1991 than 1984. This would happen if the increased cost of treatment outweighed the marginal improvement in survival. If the COL index increases, it could be a sign that there is a shortage of surgeons or that oxygen masks are getting more expensive. It could also be a sign that moral hazard is increasing with the availability of new, expensive technologies. Because Medicare enrollees face very low marginal costs for extra services, they might demand superfluous technologies that increase costs but barely improve survival.

If the COL index is going down over time, on the other hand, it indicates that the same amount of survival is actually cheaper in 1991 than in 1984, even though heart attack care expenditures have risen. This would happen if the increased cost of treatment was outweighed by the marginal improvement in survival among heart attack patients.

---

1 The term "cost of living index" traditionally refers to any general measure of inflation for everyday consumer goods, but in this context it takes on a double meaning.

A falling COL index either indicates falling resource prices – maybe oxygen masks are actually getting cheaper, so equivalent care can be delivered more cheaply – or improved technology that allows patients to get more health out of each dollar spent on medical care.

Under an assumption that people value additional years of survival at $25,000/year, Cutler et al. (1998) find that the COL index declined by an average of 0.5% each year from 1984 to 1991.[2] Over the seven-year period, the cost of heart attack survival fell by roughly 3.4%. This means that it only took about 96.6% as much money in 1991 as it did in 1984 to achieve an average 1984 post-AMI outcome. Technological improvements in heart attack care allowed consumers (or, in this case, Medicare) to stretch their dollars farther in 1991 than in 1984. In this case at least, the welfare of heart attack patients improved during this period despite apparently rising prices.

Other studies of medical inflation: cancer and depression

Several other studies use a similar approach to calculate the effect of new technology on welfare. Bhattacharya et al. (2012), for example, examine spending and survival outcomes for Medicare patients with four types of cancer during two intervals, 1987–94 and 2000–04. This period saw massive innovation in cancer care, including new radiation techniques like intensity-modulated radiation therapy and chemotherapeutic agents such as Avastin for colorectal cancer and Provege for prostate cancer. Unsurprisingly, expenditures on cancer treatment rose significantly during this period as well, so a careful analysis is needed to determine whether cancer survival actually got cheaper over this span.

Medicare outcomes data shows that the cost of living during the first period (1987–94) rose for some cancers but not others. A woman diagnosed with stage 1 breast cancer in 1994 cost Medicare $16,600 more than her counterpart diagnosed in 1987 did, and her life expectancy was actually 2.6 years *less*. But a man diagnosed with stage 1 prostate cancer in 1994 could expect to live about ten months longer than his counterpart from 1987, and treating his cancer was only about $990 more expensive. The 2000–04 period was even better for cancer patients; there were cost-of-living decreases for breast, prostate, lung, and colorectal cancers.

Survival is not the only health outcome that can be measured this way. Berndt et al. (2002) use the same approach to measure changes in the price of curing clinical depression between 1991 and 1996. This period overlapped with a major transition in the preferred therapy for depression patients from trycyclic drugs common in the 1970s to a new generation of selective serotonin re-uptake inhibitors (SSRIs) like Prozac and Zoloft. SSRIs are both more expensive and more effective than the older drugs, and consequently expenditures on depression treatment increased rapidly during this period.

In order to determine whether these cost increases were worthwhile, the researchers use the Hamilton depression rating scale (HDRS), which is a clinical measure of the extent of depression symptoms. Individuals who score 18 or higher on the HDRS are considered to have major clinical depression. Berndt et al. define partial remission as an HDRS score of 12 or less for a previously depressed person. They find that the price of a partial remission fell by 17% between 1991 and 1996 as the new SSRIs slowly supplanted the older drugs.

---

2   See Chapter 14 for more on the contentious practice of valuing life in monetary terms.

13.3   Technology overuse: the Dartmouth Atlas

We have seen that better technology for treating cancer, heart attack, and depression has lowered the price of better health despite rising health expenditures. But this does not mean that technological advancements are always a boon for patients – they may be used inappropriately in some cases or be too expensive to justify their use in other cases. There may be some technological advancements that are more effective at improving patient outcomes than others. For example, aspirin for heart attack patients is a cheap way to dissolve clots that cause coronary ischemia. On the other hand, Plavix, a modern anti-clotting medication, may be marginally more effective but also costs much more.

The Dartmouth Atlas is a project started at Dartmouth College in New Hampshire that tracks Medicare spending across the US. The Dartmouth researchers split the country into 307 different regions and tally expenditures for elderly Medicare enrollees with nine different medical conditions.

The two most important findings from the Dartmouth Atlas are the following:

- The care patients receive varies tremendously depending on where each patient lives. These treatment differences across regions persist even for similar patients with the same condition (Fisher et al. 2003b).
- In general, more expensive treatment does not correlate with better outcomes (Fisher et al. 2003a).

The evidence that health outcomes do not improve as a result of higher spending suggests that some of the expenditures may be wasteful. In a typical market, a new technology is *never* a bad thing: either it will be inefficient and go unused (causing no harm), or it will be efficient and supplant other technologies. But in the market for health care, insurance coverage and information asymmetries may lead to moral hazard and technological overuse, as new technologies may be used frequently even if they are not very efficient.

Evidence from the Dartmouth Atlas has spurred scrutiny into how public health care dollars are spent and has generated policy proposals on how to limit technological overuse. In Chapter 14, we study the process by which governments and private insurers evaluate new technologies and decide whether they are worth using.

Variations in Medicare spending

The Dartmouth Atlas Project (2008) analyzes Medicare spending by patients suffering from at least one of nine chronic conditions in the last two years of their life. These conditions listed in Table 13.3 account for nine out of ten deaths among the Medicare population. Spending during the last two years for these patients makes up 32% of Medicare's budget.

Table 13.3. *Chronic conditions tracked in the Dartmouth Atlas.*

congestive heart failure	peripheral vascular disease
chronic lung disease	diabetes
cancer	chronic liver disease
coronary artery disease	dementia
renal failure	

Between 1999 and 2005, Medicare patients in their last two years of life incurred $46,412 in medical expenses on average. But there was considerable regional variation: in the highest spending state, New Jersey, Medicare spent on average $59,379 per patient, almost double the average amount spent in North Dakota.

At the city level, there was even greater variance in Medicare spending. The average two-year bill for Medicare patients in Miami, Florida, was $83,504, while patients in La Crosse, Wisconsin, cost Medicare only $36,949 on average in their last two years of life. Large variations persisted even within cities. The most expensive hospital in Los Angeles cost more than twice as much as the city's cheapest hospital (Dartmouth Atlas Project 2008). Figure 13.4 shows the vast variation in average per capita Medicare spending for these patients.

Lack of correlation between spending and health

We would hope that Medicare is getting something valuable for its money in the high-spending regions like New Jersey and Miami, Florida. But health outcomes for patients in these regions do not appear to be consistently better than health outcomes in low-spending regions, despite the staggering discrepancy in spending. Fisher et al. (2003b) find that Medicare patients in high-spending regions do not report better health status in surveys relative to patients in low-spending regions. There is also not a significant difference in overall five-year mortality rates between high-spending and low-spending regions. In fact, for certain conditions like hip fracture, colon cancer, and AMI, mortality risks actually appeared to be growing with health care expenditures.

Thus, the variation in per capita Medicare expenditures across regions does not correlate with better general health status or lower mortality rates.

13.4   Theories to explain the Dartmouth findings

In the face of the tremendous variation in Medicare expenditures shown in Figure 13.4, and the apparent absence of health benefits from higher spending, researchers have tried to explain why the variations exist. Understanding the source of the variation can tell us whether technology – and health care dollars in general – is being used optimally.

One point of view is that whatever medical care is appropriate in one region is also appropriate in another, so medical practice should be the same everywhere. In this view, the existence of variation in spending without variation in health outcomes is evidence of inefficient care that should be eliminated. Another point of view is that different regions require different kinds of medical care. In this view, variations are due to local conditions and might, but do not necessarily, imply wasteful spending or technology overuse.

To make clear these different viewpoints, consider the case of La Crosse, Wisconsin, and Miami, Florida. Medicare enrollees in Miami suffering from any of the nine conditions from Table 13.3 incurred an average of $83,504 in spending during their last two years of life. Meanwhile, the same types of patients in La Crosse cost Medicare only $36,949 on average during their last two years. Despite this sizeable spending discrepancy, Medicare enrollees in La Crosse were just as healthy as those in Miami.

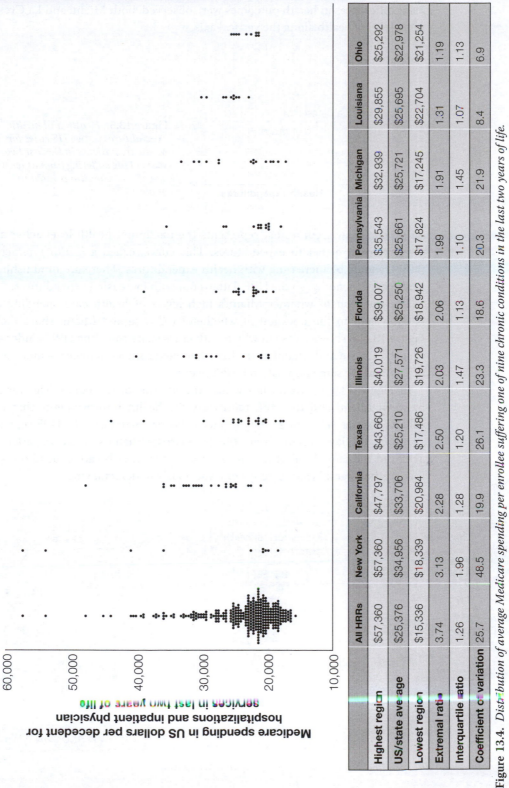

	All HRRs	New York	California	Texas	Illinois	Florida	Pennsylvania	Michigan	Louisiana	Ohio
Highest region	$57,360	$57,360	$47,797	$43,660	$40,019	$39,007	$35,543	$32,939	$29,855	$25,292
US/state average	$25,376	$34,956	$33,706	$25,210	$27,571	$25,250	$25,661	$25,721	$25,695	$22,978
Lowest region	$15,336	$18,339	$20,984	$17,486	$19,726	$18,942	$17,824	$17,245	$22,704	$21,254
Extremal ratio	3.74	3.13	2.28	2.50	2.03	2.06	1.99	1.91	1.31	1.19
Interquartile ratio	1.26	1.96	1.28	1.20	1.47	1.13	1.10	1.45	1.07	1.13
Coefficient of variation	25.7	48.5	19.9	26.1	23.3	18.6	20.3	21.9	8.4	6.9

Medicare spending in US dollars per decedent for hospitalizations and inpatient physician services in last two years of life

Figure 13.4. *Distribution of average Medicare spending per enrollee suffering one of nine chronic conditions in the last two years of life.*

Source: Dartmouth Atlas Project (2008). With permission of the Dartmouth Institute.

Figure 13.5 plots health and health care expenditures for the two cities. Since no significant differences in health outcomes were observed, both Miami and La Crosse share the same level of health along the vertical axis.

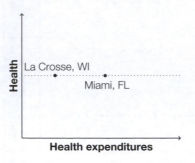

Figure 13.5. *Health and health expenditures in two US cities for Medicare patients in the last two years of life suffering from at least one of nine conditions listed in Table 13.3.*

We can draw a curve that represents the maximum health level achievable for each given amount of health expenditures. This curve, called a *health production function* (HPF), should be increasing with health expenditures. There are diminishing returns to health care spending, so the HPF flattens out with increasing expenditures.

The question of whether Miami's high levels of health care spending are wasteful is equivalent to the question of whether La Crosse and Miami share the same HPF. Figure 13.6(a) shows a case in which both cities share the same HPF. Under this assumption, La Crosse and Miami share the same medical technologies, similar medical input prices, and the same population health needs.

In Figure 13.6(a), Miami lies within the interior of the curve. The vertical distance between Miami and the HPF represents the health improvements that Miami could achieve for free. The horizontal distance between Miami and the HPF represents wasted spending. If Miami has the same HPF as La Crosse, then its Medicare patients could have achieved the same level of health for much lower health care expenditures. Under this theory, the Miami health care system is seriously underachieving.

One theory to explain the spending disparity between Florida and Wisconsin.

Credit: Allen Cox.

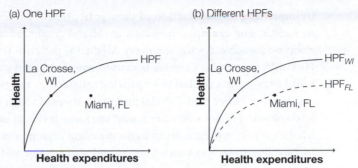

Figure 13.6. *Possible health production functions for La Crosse, WI and Miami, FL. (a) Same HPF. (b) Different HPFs.*

Alternatively, Miami and La Crosse may have different HPFs, as illustrated in Figure 13.6(b). If so, both cities may be investing in health optimally given their local characteristics and constraints. Unlike the case of only one HPF, there is no way the Medicare patients in Miami could improve their health without spending more money. If Figure 13.6(b) is accurate, then there must be something about Miami which makes it harder to produce health there. Under this assumption, the variations in spending do not represent wasteful spending or technology overuse.

Do local characteristics explain spending variation?

The relevant policy question is determining whether Figure 13.6(a) or Figure 13.6(b) is more accurate: Are Miami and La Crosse on the same health production function or are they on different ones? If they do lie on different curves, forcing Miami to reduce their Medicare spending to the same level as La Crosse might drastically harm patients there, rather than just eliminating wasteful care. We outline five theories that would suggest that the HPFs are different in different regions and share the evidence for each one.

Differing input costs

Different locations have different costs of living. For instance, surgeons command higher salaries in Miami, Florida, than in La Crosse, Wisconsin. Medicare reimburses health care providers differently based on the higher costs of surgeons in Miami. One hypothesis posits that the variation in price of health care explains the variation in Medicare spending. But empirical studies have shown that adjusting for local prices reduces the geographic variation in per-patient Medicare expenditures only slightly (Gottlieb et al. 2010). Furthermore, the price hypothesis does not help us understand why variations in spending persist at the more local level. For example, this hypothesis fails to explain why the cost of care for the last two years of life in Los Angeles can range between $61,239 and $130,992 at different hospitals only a few miles apart.

Differing hospital amenities

Even though mortality risk and some health outcomes do not appear lower for hospitals with high expenditures, there may still be differences in the quality of care that explain variations in spending. Perhaps higher-spending hospitals devote more resources to improving the satisfaction of their patients, even if those resources do not contribute to health. For example, hospitals in Miami might offer more comfortable beds or an always-accessible doctor for every Medicare patient. This theory suggests that Miami's HPF differs from La Crosse's because some Medicare expenditures in Miami go toward reimbursing costs related to improving satisfaction but not health.

However, Fisher et al. (2003a) find that patients in high-spending regions and patients in low-spending regions actually report the same levels of satisfaction with their hospitals in Medicare surveys. Patients in high-spending regions even reported slightly worse access to care due to longer waiting times and a lower percentage of patients having a regular source of care. Similarly, Wennberg et al. (2009) find that inpatient satisfaction is negatively correlated with the amount of Medicare spending. Thus, hospitals in high-spending regions do not appear to be offering better health care amenities that could explain the variation in spending.

Differing medical malpractice environments

Another theory is that hospitals in regions with a higher rate of medical malpractice suits practice more defensive medicine. This would explain the higher volume of health services in high-expenditure regions without much improvement in health outcomes. Yet this theory also does not explain why so much variation exists within the same state, where medical malpractice environment laws are uniform (Gawande 2009).

Differing health habits

Fuchs (1975) relates the story of Nevada and Utah, two neighboring states in the western US. At the time, the states were demographically similar, with similar median income levels, education levels, and urbanization rates. Yet Nevadans were significantly less healthy than Utahns, with strikingly higher rates of infant mortality, liver failure, and lung cancer. Fuchs attributed this pattern to the fact that Utahns, unlike Nevadans, tend to be devout Mormons, eschew tobacco and alcohol, and enjoy very stable family lives.

In theory, disparities in health habits driven by cultural differences could explain some of the Atlas findings. If there is something about the culture of Miami that is hazardous to the health of local residents, then it is not so surprising that Medicare must spend more on its residents than those residing in Wisconsin. But then again, the Atlas expenditure data is on a per-person basis, which means that higher rates of disease cannot explain the disparity.

Differing levels of illness severity

More likely, the variation in expenditures reflects differing levels of illness severity in different regions (Bach 2010). The Dartmouth Atlas treats all diabetic patients as if they were all equally ill before treatment, but perhaps the diabetics in La Crosse, Wisconsin, had better controlled blood sugar levels than the diabetics in Miami, Florida. Then the variation in spending would be warranted.

This hypothesis would also explain the evidence that there are no health outcome differences between high-expenditure and low-expenditure regions – the patients who are sicker to begin with require more health services to reach a health level comparable to the less sickly patients. If so, Miami lies on a lower HPF than La Crosse, because its patients tend to be sicker than La Crosse's (Bach et al. 2004).

The Dartmouth researchers do control for some elements of severity such as cancer stage and the presence of other diseases such as hypertension. And there is evidence that even patients with similar levels of severity can receive very different levels of care. If so, spending variations would persist even among regions with the same distributions of patient illness.

Wennberg et al. (2004) track health care procedures for a group of Medicare enrollees with solid tumor cancers, congestive heart failure (CHF), or chronic obstructive pulmonary disease (COPD) at 77 academic medical centers. The researchers had access to patient chart data, which allowed them to measure disease severity. Even when accounting for patient chart data, they find that variations remained in how much care hospitals gave each patient (though patient outcomes did not seem to vary with spending). For example, the number of physician visits varied more than 400% for cancer and CHF patients and more than 650% for COPD patients. So the researchers conclude that even patients suffering similarly severe ailments can receive very different levels of treatment.

These theories seem insufficient for explaining all of the variation in Medicare expenditures found by the Dartmouth Atlas researchers. Some evidence, particularly differing levels of initial health in different regions, does suggest that regions have distinctive local traits that cause them to lie on their own HPFs. But the Dartmouth Atlas researchers argue that those local differences do not account for all the documented variation in Medicare expenditures. According to their argument, the HPFs of Miami and La Crosse may not perfectly coincide, but they are not sufficiently separated to explain the vast difference in expenditures (see Figure 13.7).

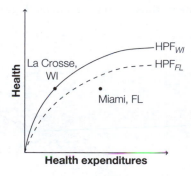

Figure 13.7. *HPFs according to Dartmouth Atlas researchers.*

So the vast differences in Medicare spending between regions are mostly due neither to local variation in patient characteristics nor to improved health outcomes for high spenders. If high-expenditure regions such as Miami, Florida, are indeed spending at suboptimal points according to their HPF, what causes them to reach that point?

The Dartmouth Atlas researchers argue that half of the variation in Medicare expenditures is the result of supply-sensitive care, which we discuss next and which is in many ways just another form of moral hazard.

Supply-sensitive care and moral hazard

Supply-sensitive care refers to health services whose use depends greatly on the supply or availability of that service. For example, a doctor's reliance on MRI diagnostic testing may depend on how accessible an MRI machine is to him. The physician who has his own imaging machine is more likely to request tests than the doctor who has to refer patients to an outside hospital (Baker 2010).

Definition	13.2

Supply-sensitive care: health services whose use depends greatly on the supply or availability of that service.

Supply-sensitive care can also include hospitalizations and stays in an intensive care unit. The more beds a hospital has, the more willing it is to allow patients to stay overnight for monitoring or additional testing. Even some surgeries may be supply-sensitive. For example, Macinko et al. (2011) finds that greater private and nonprofit hospital bed densities in Brazil are associated with higher hospitalization rates. There is also evidence that the performance of select medical procedures in Brazil is supply-sensitive in private and nonprofit hospital settings (but not in public sector hospitals). Thus, with supply-sensitive health care, doctors with laparoscopic cameras may overuse them even though the surgery might yield only small benefits, because they believe laparoscopic surgeries are minimally invasive and the hospital is already equipped to perform laparoscopic surgeries.

If the demand for care is indeed sensitive to supply, then we would expect hospitals with many resources to also have large expenditures, whether or not patients are especially sick and actually need those extra resources. Figure 13.8 plots the relationship

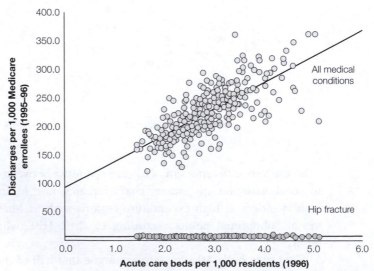

Figure 13.8. *Relationship between health care use and supply of hospital beds in various US regions.*

Source: Dartmouth Atlas Project (2008). With permission of the Dartmouth Institute.

between the number of hospital beds per 1,000 residents and the number of hospital discharges per 1,000 Medicare enrollees in that region. The strong positive correlation for overall medical conditions supports the hypothesis that care is supply-sensitive, especially given evidence that severity does not seem to be driving the correlation (Dartmouth Atlas Project 2008).

Figure 13.8 also reveals that there is little correlation between number of hospital beds and health care demand for hip fracture patients. The Dartmouth Atlas researchers argue that diagnoses of hip fractures are unambiguous and physicians everywhere agree about the best way to treat it. As a result, there is little room for physician discretion, and so, the demand for hip fracture care is determined only by the incidence of fractures and not by the number of hospital beds. Hence, situations where treatment is unambiguous, like hip fractures, are not as susceptible to supply-sensitive care.

However, for situations where there is less consensus about optimal medical treatment, different physicians may take very different actions. For example, there is no consensus that vena cava filters are a good way to prevent pulmonary embolisms (blood clots in the lung). But doctors in high-spending regions are more likely to apply this expensive treatment than doctors in low-spending regions (Dartmouth Atlas Project 2008). Perhaps the culture of medical practice in certain regions leads doctors to spare no expense in treating patients, which in turn leads to higher expenditures (Wennberg 1984).

The concept of supply-sensitive care is closely related to the idea of physician-induced demand (PID) discussed in Chapter 5. The information asymmetry between physicians and patients as well as the asymmetry between physicians and insurers offers significant room for physician discretion. And doctors with more accessible resources – hospital beds, imaging machines, medical specialists – are more likely to employ them.

Supply-sensitive care is a form of moral hazard. Up to now we have discussed moral hazard as excess care demanded by insurance enrollees, because they face low out-of-pocket costs for health care. In the case of supply-sensitive care, physicians cause moral hazard by recommending care that is expensive but only marginally useful. Patients, knowing that their insurers are footing the bill, accept their physicians' recommendations because the marginal benefits outweigh their out-of-pocket costs.

The loss from moral hazard can be exacerbated in two ways: more hospital resources and new expensive technologies. In resource-rich hospitals with innumerable hospital wings and all the latest medical machinery, doctors may prescribe more MRI scans, more overnight stays, more surgeries, and more specialist referrals than would be socially optimal.

A related explanation for the variation in hospital spending is variations in local medical culture. There is good evidence that physician culture matters. One natural experiment showed that variation can even persist within the *same* hospital with two distinct physician cultures. Doyle et al. (2010) study a single large hospital affiliated with two different medical schools and two different groups of physicians. In this hospital, both groups share the same supply of beds, nurses, facilities, and medical technology. Patients, upon entering the hospital, were randomly assigned to be treated by doctors either from Program A or from Program B, where Program A physicians were from a top-tier medical school, while Program B physicians were from a mid-tier medical school.

Compared with physicians from Program B, doctors in Program A tended to perform fewer diagnostic testing, so their patients cost on average 10% less. But patient mortality and health status did not differ between the two medical programs.

One policy implication of the Dartmouth Atlas findings is that evidence-based medical practice guidelines should be developed more extensively and better promulgated. The Dartmouth researchers argue that best practice standards, which exist in the case of hip fractures but not for many other diagnoses, could curtail rising health costs by changing physician culture and reining in supply-sensitive care in outlier regions like Miami.

But developing comprehensive standards of practice for the wide variety of medical conditions and complications is a massive task. And this policy approach must also confront the difficulty of altering physician behavior. Physician decision-making is affected by a number of factors including education, their style of practice, patient wishes, and local malpractice environments in addition to the physician's own financial incentives (Eisenberg 1985; Grol 1992; Solomon et al. 1998).

13.5   Conclusion

In this chapter, we have seen two seemingly opposing views of technological change in medicine. In one view, the development of new technologies has provided an enormous boon to medical consumers, making people healthier and extending their lives. The past decades have seen enormous scientific and technological progress on the treatment of AMIs, Hodgkin's lymphoma, depression, and countless other diseases, and people's lives are undoubtedly better as a result. The first view speaks to the transformative power of new scientific discovery and its application in medicine. Murphy and Topel (2006) estimate that the life-extending technologies implemented between 1970 and 2000 in the US alone were worth an additional $3.2 trillion per year not accounted for in traditional GDP calculations. The *average* value of technological change is thus incredibly high.

In the opposing view, the dissemination of new medical technologies has greatly contributed to the rapid rise in health expenditures in the developed world (Newhouse 1992). This view, by contrast, highlights the difficulty of using new technology efficiently in an environment where insured patients are shielded from paying most of the costs of their care. If care is free to patients at the point of service, they have every incentive to demand every technology that improves their health, regardless of the costs imposed to others in the same health insurance plan.

At least in part, it is moral hazard that explains why it costs so much to treat the same medical condition in two different regions of the US, even if the two areas have similar population health needs. Because of moral hazard, both patients and providers demand the adoption of new technologies, even if the *marginal* value of the new technology is low relative to other uses of the money.

Though these views seem to contradict one another, both are simultaneously true. The first view means that the *average* returns to new technology are high, while the second means that the *marginal* value of new technologies is low. For both private insurers and public insurers, the fundamental policy challenge is to distinguish between technologies of high and low marginal value. Insurers that decline to fund valuable technologies risk backlash at the polls (in the case of public insurance) or losses to competing health plans (in the case of private insurance). In the next chapter, we discuss cost-effectiveness analysis, which is a key tool that insurers use to decide which new technologies should be funded.

13.6   Exercises

Comprehension questions

Indicate whether each statement is true or false, and justify your answer. Be sure to cite evidence from the chapter and state any additional assumptions you make.

1 A Laspeyres price index of health care inflation typically overestimates year-to-year increases in the price of health.
2 The price of curing Hodgkin's disease has risen substantially between 1950 and 2000.
3 The fact that total expenditures on heart attack care increased between 1984 and 1991 is good evidence that the price of surviving a heart attack increased.
4 The Dartmouth Atlas research project finds that health care spending varied widely between different American cities in the early 2000s, and that Medicare enrollees in high-spending cities were a lot healthier as a result.
5 The Dartmouth Atlas results are proof that health is easier and/or cheaper to produce in some American cities than others.
6 High health care expenditures in certain cities and states have been interpreted as evidence for supply-sensitive care and heterogeneous local medical cultures.
7 If Medicare patients in Boston are paying more per capita for a hip replacement than Medicare patients in Boise for the same procedure, but health outcomes are exactly equal, then this is evidence that Boston is wasteful in their health spending.
8 One reason why total health expenditures are rising is because of an aging population.

Analytical problems

9 **Fun with price indices.** Suppose that your utility function over health care (h) and other goods (c) is given by $U(h, c)$ and that you have a fixed income of $100. (Assume that the indifference curves of your utility function bear the usual convex shape.) Each year, you choose h and c to maximize your utility subject to a budget constraint:

$$p_h h + p_c c = Y$$

where p_h is the price of health care, p_c is the price of other goods, and Y is your income.

   In year 1, the price of health care is $1, while the price of other goods is $2. At these prices, you demand 30 units of health care and 35 units of other goods. In year 2, your utility function and your income do not change, but prices do. Health care becomes more expensive at $1.50, while other goods become cheaper at $1.50. At these prices, you demand 20 units of health care.

   a   Assuming you spend all your income in year 2, how many units of other goods do you buy?
   b   Draw a graph with your demand for health care on the horizontal axis and your demand for other goods on the vertical axis. On this graph, draw your budget constraints in year 1 and in year 2. On these budget lines, indicate your demand points for h and c in year 1 and year 2. Also draw concave indifference curves tangent the points in year 1 and year 2 that represent your demand. Label the indifference curves U_1 and U_2.
   c   Do the price changes leave you better off, worse off, or the same as before? Is this result just for the indifference curves you drew, or will it hold for any set of convex indifference curves?

    d Draw a budget constraint that answers the question: *How much income do you need this year to buy the same bundle of goods from last year?* In other words, draw a budget constraint with a slope that reflects year 2 prices but that intersects the year 1 bundle.

    e Either geometrically or algebraically, use this budget constraint to calculate the Laspeyres price index; that is, the amount of money you need to buy the year 1 bundle in year 2, divided by the money you paid for it in year 1.

    f Now draw a budget constraint that answers the question: *How much income do you need this year to get to the same level of utility from last year?* In other words, draw a budget constraint with a slope that reflects year 2 prices that lies tangent to U_1.

    g Does the Laspeyres price index overstate or understate the welfare effect of the price changes?

Assume now that you draw utility not only from health care (h) and other goods (c) but also from futuristic health care (f). Futuristic health care did not exist in year 1 or year 2; it was as though the price was so high that you demanded none of it. In year 3, futuristic health care is invented and the price is \$10 per unit of f. Meanwhile, the prices of h and c both double to \$3.

    h Calculate a Laspeyres price index for the changes from year 2 to year 3. Remember to use the bundle of goods from year 2.

    i According to your result from the previous question, are you better off in year 2 or year 3 (assuming constant income)?

    j In year 3, you purchase 5 units of f and 10 units of h. Explain how you might actually have more utility in year 3 than year 2 despite the Laspeyres price index result.

    k How did your total health care expenditures (on both h and f) change from year 2 to year 3?

    l Explain why you cannot use this result to conclude that health care is getting more expensive or less expensive.

10 **HIV survival and the introduction of HAART**. In a journal article, Philipson and Jena (2006) study HIV survival and expenditures. Figure 13.9 shows trends in HIV survival and HIV expenditures in the US.

    a Figure 13.9(a) shows that HIV survival after diagnosis improved dramatically over a twenty-year period. Propose three explanations for this fact, one involving pharmaceutical innovation, one involving improved HIV screening, and one involving demographic changes in the at-risk population. It is okay if these explanations do not reflect actual historical developments, but they should explain why survival after diagnosis might be improving over time.

    b Suppose now that these curves have been adjusted for screening and demographics, and that the survival improvement is entirely a reflection of technological change (such as the introduction of HAART, an effective AIDS drug that boosts immune function, in 1994). Explain why we do not have enough information in Figure 13.9(a) to determine if the improvements in HIV longevity were cost-effective.

    c Figure 13.9(b) shows that expenditures on HIV treatment rose rapidly during approximately the same period. Is this evidence that the price of HAART was

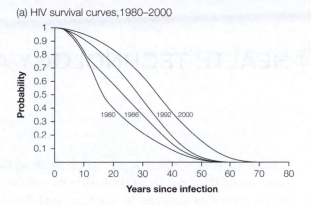

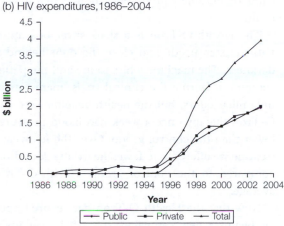

Figure 13.9. *Trends in HIV survival and expenditures in the US. (a) HIV survival curves, 1980–2000. (b) HIV expenditures, 1986–2004.*

Source: Figures 3 and 4 from Philipson and Jena (2006). Reproduced with permission of De Gruyter.

increasing during this time? Is it evidence that the cost of survival was increasing during this time?

d   Suppose Philipson and Jena analyze the numbers and find that the survival improvements depicted in Figure 13.9(a) are outweighed by the increased expenditures depicted in Figure 13.9(b). Assume that AIDS patients are well informed about the costs and benefits of the new technologies. Why would they overspend on HIV treatments that are not worth it?

e   In actuality, the researchers found that the technology improvements during this period such as HAART were massively beneficial to HIV patients, and that the survival gains far outweighed the increased cost of treatment. How do you square this statement with the fact that the price of treating HIV was increasing steadily over this period?

Students can find answers to the comprehension questions and lecturers can access an Instructor Manual with guideline answers to the analytical problems and essay questions at **www.palgrave.com/economics/bht.**

HEALTH TECHNOLOGY ASSESSMENT

A medical device company is putting the finishing touches to its latest product. The company, Moral Hazard R Us, specializes in creating medical devices of dubious value that it sells at exorbitant markups. Its latest accomplishment, the Health-O-Tron, is the latest in a line of amazingly profitable products that never seem to do much to improve anyone's health.

The Health-O-Tron is a sleek silver box approximately the size of a phone booth. Patients step inside and close the door behind them, finding themselves in complete darkness. The machine whirs to life and the patients are zapped with mysterious hypersonic rays. During the clinical trials, many participants reported light-headedness and unfamiliar odors. But the health benefits were clear: patients who submitted to Health-O-Tron therapy once a week had blood pressure and cholesterol levels that were 0.1% lower than the control group. Over the five-year span of the clinical trial, those on the treatment suffered one fewer heart attack and one fewer stroke per thousand patients, compared to the control group. Health-O-Tron patients also lived 0.1% longer on average.

Now that the Health-O-Tron has secured approval from the FDA, Moral Hazard R Us begins a new campaign. Its goal is to convince major insurers to cover the costs of treatment – it has set the price of one session in the Health-O-Tron at $100,000, as each machine requires enormous amounts of electricity, a full-time staff of nurses to tend to patients, and a team of expert technicians to prevent meltdowns. Without insurance coverage, few individuals will be willing to pay the costs of weekly treatment out of pocket. But if they have insurance that will pay for the cost of treatment, many patients will flock to the Health-O-Tron which has definite (if small) health benefits.

The Health-O-Tron is any insurance company's worst nightmare: it provides small health benefits at an astronomical cost, and will drive up insurance premiums for all customers. In this example, the insurance companies should identify the Health-O-Tron as not very cost-effective (especially if they know Moral Hazard R Us's reputation). But insurers have to evaluate thousands of new technologies every year, none of which are quite as conspicuously terrible as the Health-O-Tron. Each time a company designs a new medical device, or a pharmaceutical company rolls out a new drug, insurance companies and governments need to decide whether the new technology is a life-saving marvel or just the next incarnation of the Health-O-Tron.

This practice of evaluating new medical advances is called health technology assessment (HTA) and it can generate enormous controversy; in fact, health technology assessment is so controversial that it is illegal for US Medicare to use HTA in its decision-making. That HTA is a source of contention is no surprise, because lives hang in the balance whenever cost-effectiveness decisions are made. If either private or public insurers decide not to cover an expensive cancer medication, then it becomes unaffordable for a large group of people whose lives may have been saved by it. Making these decisions involves implicitly or explicitly placing a monetary value on human life. Such valuations of life are philosophically contentious and politically explosive.

HTA encompasses two different types of analysis. This chapter first introduces *cost-effectiveness analysis*, which is the science of comparing the costs and benefits of different medical treatments. Then we proceed to discuss *cost–benefit analysis*, which is used to choose optimally from among different treatments by creating an explicit tradeoff between money and health.

14.1 Cost-effectiveness analysis

The first step in health technology assessment is to measure the costs and benefits of a health technology. The term "technology" should be interpreted broadly – technologies studied as part of HTA include new pharmaceutical products, new methods for doing a particular surgery, or a new machine that helps doctors screen for a disease. The process of painstakingly measuring the costs and benefits of each alternative treatment for a condition is called **cost-effectiveness analysis**.

Definition | **14.1**

Cost-effectiveness analysis (CEA): the process of measuring the costs and health benefits of various medical treatments, procedures, or therapies.

The goal of any cost-effectiveness study is to compare multiple therapies or strategies that can be used to treat the same disease or condition. Sometimes the multiple treatment options are alike and have similar costs and benefits – like two pills with different medications that treat the same psychiatric disorder. Sometimes the treatment options are entirely dissimilar – like palliative care at a hospice versus experimental surgery inside an MRI scanner. In that case, the cost and benefit of each choice may vary tremendously, and it is not obvious how to compare them.

In some instances, one treatment is unambiguously superior to the other. If one treatment is both cheaper and more effective than a second treatment, then the second treatment is said to be **dominated** by the first. If a certain drug or therapy is dominated by some other treatment, then it never makes sense to use that treatment. The dominated treatment is unequivocally worse than the alternative because the alternative treatment provides more health for less money.

Definition | **14.2**

Dominated treatment: a treatment that is both more expensive and less effective than some other treatment. It is never optimal to use a dominated treatment because there is a more effective and cheaper alternative available.

When one treatment dominates another, it makes life simple for patients, doctors, and insurers: everyone agrees on which course of treatment is preferable. But comparing two non-dominated options is trickier, because it requires patients, providers, and payers to weigh health benefits against monetary costs.

ICER: the incremental cost-effectiveness ratio

The heart of cost-effectiveness analysis is the **incremental cost-effectiveness ratio (ICER)**, which provides a comparison between any two treatment options that are not dominated. If neither treatment is dominant, one treatment must be both more expensive and more effective.

Definition | **14.3**

Incremental cost-effectiveness ratio (ICER): the ratio of the incremental costs of pursuing one treatment over another to the incremental benefits of that treatment. The formula for an ICER is given by equation (14.1).

Consider two treatments for the same disease, A and B. A is both more expensive and more effective than B, so neither treatment dominates the other. The ICER of using A over B is

$$\text{ICER}_{A,B} = \frac{C_A - C_B}{E_A - E_B} > 0 \tag{14.1}$$

where:

- C_A and C_B are the respective costs of treatments A and B, and
- E_A and E_B are the respective health outcomes of treatments A and B.

The formula for the ICER is simply the ratio of the difference in costs to the difference in health outcomes. As long as neither treatment dominates the other, the ICER between the two will always be positive.

Typically, costs are expressed in dollars and represent the financial costs of treatment, although sometimes other costs like time and travel expenses are also considered. Health outcomes are often defined in terms of additional years of life, although the relevant measure may vary depending on the application. The health benefits of medical treatments can range from extending life (open heart surgery) to relieving pain (morphine) to avoiding complications from a disease (insulin therapy for diabetics).

Cost-effectiveness in action: HIV screening and lead poisoning

How much money and time should doctors spend screening patients for unusual diseases? Early detection saves lives in the cases of cancer, diabetes, HIV, and many other diseases. But screening indiscriminately can also be expensive and harms patients who are wrongly diagnosed, so it is not always obvious how aggressive doctors should be in screening their patients. Cost-effectiveness analysis helps us answer this question.

Imagine two health clinics across the street from each other in a big city where exactly 1% of the population has HIV. At the first clinic, the doctors use a strategy called *targeted screening*: they only test patients for HIV if they are showing symptoms of AIDS, or are part of a high-risk population like intravenous drug users. They miss a few cases of HIV that could have been caught earlier, but they save patients money on tests that would have been negative 99% of the time.

At the second clinic, the doctors are more aggressive. They use a strategy called *universal screening*, which means they test every last patient who walks in the door for HIV, whether they report AIDS symptoms, cold symptoms, or a broken leg. Naturally this is more expensive than targeted screening, but every once in a while it leads to early detection of an HIV case. This is great news for patients because they can start taking anti-retroviral drugs immediately and forestall immune system decline.

Which strategy is superior? Sanders et al. (2005) examine both strategies using real-world HIV survival data and a simulation model. They find that neither strategy is dominated: universal screening is more expensive, and it leads to a higher average life expectancy for patients. Table 14.1 presents their cost and health outcome estimates.

Table 14.1. *Comparison of strategies for HIV screening.*

Treatment strategy	Cost per patient	Average life expectancy
Targeted screening	$51,517	21.063 years
Universal screening	$51,850	21.073 years

Source: Data from Table 3 in Sanders et al. (2005).

The cost listed is the total cost of HIV screening and treatment divided by the total number of patients at each clinic. This cost is averaged over all patients, not just those with HIV, because the decision about whether to screen applies to all patients. Universal screening is more expensive than targeted screening both because of the cost of the HIV test itself and because cases are discovered earlier, which leads to more expenditures on doctors' visits and prescription drugs than would have occurred otherwise. Of course, for healthy people, HIV treatment costs are $0, but the few actual HIV patients are very expensive to treat.

The ICER for universal screening over targeted screening is

$$\text{ICER}_{u,t} = \frac{\$51,850 - \$51,517}{21.073 \text{ years} - 21.063 \text{ years}} = \frac{\$333}{3.92 \text{ days}} = \$84.95/\text{day of life}$$

Lead poisoning often arises when infants eat the peeling paint off the walls in old houses and apartments. Lead additives in paint were banned in the United States in 1977. In recent years, the lead additive ban has been credited with plummeting crime statistics and soaring high-school graduation rates.
Credit: © The Power of Forever Photography – iStockphoto.com.

This ICER essentially provides a price for generating extra days of life for patients with universal screening. If the clinic that uses targeted screening switches to universal screening, it could "buy" extra days of life expectancy for about $85 each. If this tradeoff is worthwhile, then universal screening is optimal.

Note that the ICER by itself does not make a determination about which treatment is optimal; it simply indicates exactly how expensive a health improvement is in monetary terms. An ICER is a positive fact about costs and benefits of two different treatments, not a normative judgment about which treatment is better.

Cost-effectiveness analysis is not limited to measuring the costs of extending life. For instance, lead poisoning among children is typically not fatal, so mortality risk is not a relevant outcome for comparing two lead poisoning treatments. Instead, Glotzer et al. (1995) study the impact of two different treatment strategies on reading disability rates. They find that the more aggressive treatment is both more expensive and more effective (Table 14.2).

Table 14.2. *Comparison of two lead poisoning treatments.*

Treatment strategy	Cost of treatment	Prob. of reading disability
Conservative treatment	$786	35.3%
Aggressive treatment	$1,778	21.6%

Source: Data from Table 1 in Glotzer et al. (1995).

The ICER for the aggressive treatment over the conservative treatment is

$$\text{ICER}_{Agg,\ Cons} = \frac{\$1,778 - \$786}{0.353 - 0.216} = \$7,241/\text{reading disability}$$

If avoiding a case of reading disability is worth at least $7,241, then the aggressive treatment is a cost-effective way to reduce the rate of reading disability in lead-poisoned children. Again, the ICER does not indicate whether this is a worthwhile proposition; it merely reports the monetary price of improving health using a particular treatment.

14.2   Evaluating multiple treatments: the cost-effectiveness frontier

Imagine a new, deadly disease called bhtitis. If only one drug were available to treat this disease, cost-effectiveness analysis is easy. Suppose the costs of the drug are C_{drug} and the benefits (measured in terms of life expectancy) are E_{drug}. We could find an ICER by comparing the costs and benefits of using the drug with the costs and benefits of doing nothing:

$$\text{ICER}_{drug,nothing} = \frac{C_{drug} - 0}{E_{drug} - 0} = \frac{C_{drug}}{E_{drug}} \tag{14.2}$$

This formulation assumes that the treatment option of doing nothing is costless and leads to instant death. But this assumption is rarely accurate. Most diseases do not kill you right away, so the effectiveness of doing nothing is not zero. Also, "doing nothing" might actually involve some real costs, such as painkillers or hospice care. But if those assumptions of zero cost and instant death do hold in the case of bhtitis, equation (14.2) is valid. The resulting value indicates how costly it is to extend life with this drug. Physicians and patients can use this ICER to help decide whether the drug is worth using.

In actual practice, the situation is typically more complicated than comparing between the only drug on the market and instant death. Assume instead that there are ten different drugs that treat bhtitis and these drugs are mutually exclusive – patients who take multiple drugs may suffer deadly side-effects. Table 14.3 lists the results of careful cost-effectiveness studies that have determined the costs and associated health effects of each drug. Health effects in this case are measured in terms of life expectancy. In Section 14.4, we discuss various other measures of health effects in some detail.

When comparing more than two drugs, ICER analysis seems quite complicated. If drug A has an ICER of $40,000 over doing nothing, drug C has an ICER of $60,000 over drug A, and drug G has an ICER of $107,692 over drug B, it is far from clear which of the three drugs is preferable. The situation is even more complicated, because there are 10 total treatment strategies (including no treatment) for a total of 45 pairwise comparisons. Would we have to calculate 45 ICERs and then painstakingly compare them with each other? Even after doing that, how would we determine the most cost-effective drug of all?

Table 14.3. *Various drug therapies for bhtitis.*

Treatment regimen	Total cost (TC)	Life expectancy (LE)	Cost per extra year of life (TC/LE)
No treatment	$0	0.0	–
Drug A	$40,000	1.0	$40,000
Drug B	$80,000	0.2	$400,000
Drug C	$160,000	3.0	$53,333
Drug D	$220,000	2.0	$110,000
Drug E	$260,000	1.0	$260,000
Drug F	$280,000	0.2	$1,400,000
Drug G	$320,000	2.8	$114,286
Drug H	$360,000	3.4	$105,882
Drug I	$400,000	3.4	$117,647

It seems more intuitive to compare these drugs by simply dividing the costs of each drug by their health effects, just as we did in equation (14.2). This appears to tell us how expensive it is to extend life with each drug, and dramatically simplifies the ten-way comparison. The decision rule would be simple: always pick the drug with the lowest cost per year of life. In the case of bhtitis, drug A appears to be the most cost-effective, because it produces life years most cheaply: each year costs only $40,000. But as we will see, this method for comparing drugs is incorrect.

The trouble with average cost-effectiveness ratios

When we compare a treatment with a hypothetical alternative with no costs and instant death, we are actually calculating an *average cost-effectiveness ratio* (ACER), not an ICER. The average cost-effectiveness ratio is the ratio of the costs of pursuing a treatment to the health effect of that treatment. For a treatment T, the ACER is

$$\text{ACER}_T = \frac{C_T}{E_T} \tag{14.3}$$

where C_T is the cost of T, and E_T is the health effect of T. The last column in Table 14.3 lists the ACER for each drug.

Comparing the ACERs of different treatment options, intuitive though it may be, will not typically reveal all the cost-effective drugs. Consider, for example, a comparison between drug A and drug C. Drug A has the lower ACER, so it seems like it must be more cost-effective than drug C. But now consider the ICER between the two:

$$\text{ICER}_{C,A} = \frac{C_C - C_A}{E_C - E_A} = \frac{\$160,000 - \$40,000}{3.0 - 1.0} = \$60,000/\text{year}$$

This ICER is high, but not so high that A is definitely preferable to C. If someone values life at more than $60,000 per year, then drug C is better than drug A, because it produces more years of life at a relatively low price. The misleading comparison of ACERs showed that drug A was always more cost-effective than drug C, but a calculation of the ICER shows that drug C may sometimes be more cost-effective.

The cost-effectiveness frontier

In order to find all of the **potentially cost-effective** treatments, we must compare every drug to every other drug to figure out which treatments are dominated. This task is made easier with a graphical approach that allows us to construct a curve called a **cost-effectiveness frontier (CEF)**. This frontier shows the subset of treatment strategies which are not dominated by any other treatment.

Definition | 14.4

Cost-effectiveness frontier (CEF): a subset of treatment strategies for a condition that is not dominated by any other treatment. Any treatment on the CEF is said to be **potentially cost-effective**.

   Treatments that are *not* on the cost-effectiveness frontier are **dominated** by at least one other treatment on the CEF, so they are *not* cost-effective.

Our first step is to graph the costs and health effects of the various possible treatments for bhtitis. We label the option of doing nothing as treatment 0. Figure 14.1 plots the nine drugs from Table 14.3, along with treatment 0.

Simply examining Figure 14.1 tells us a lot about these different treatments. Recall that a treatment is *dominated* if another treatment is both cheaper and more effective. Graphically, a treatment is dominated if any treatment lies to its northwest. In Figure 14.1, many treatments are dominated: drug *B* is dominated by drug *A*, drug *D* is dominated by drug *C*, and drug *F* is dominated by drug *E*, among others.

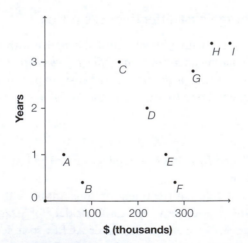

Figure 14.1. *Several possible treatment options for bhtitis.*

In order to draw a cost-effectiveness frontier, we connect the points that are not dominated and ignore the points that are dominated. The result is the curve in Figure 14.2, which connects treatments 0, *A*, *C*, and *H*.

It is clear why most points are not on the CEF; drug *F*, for example, is dominated by several other drugs. But it is less clear why we discard drug *I* as well. A close inspection of drug *I* reveals that it is dominated by drug *H*, because it provides exactly the same health effect but costs more money. Even though *H* does not lie to the northwest of *I*, *I* is still dominated.

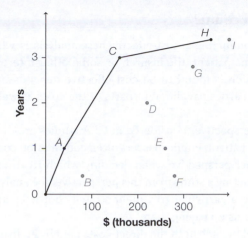

Figure 14.2. *Cost-effectiveness frontier (CEF) for bhtitis.*

The CEF simplifies the comparison between treatments by identifying which drugs are dominated. Cost-effectiveness analysts can then rule out the dominated drugs (which should never be used anyway) and focus only on treatment options that are non-dominated.

The slope of the line segment between any two points also has a ready interpretation: it is equal to the inverse of the ICER of those two treatments (see Figure 14.3). This link between the ICER and the slope of the CEF will be helpful when we decide which of the potentially cost-effective treatments is best to use.

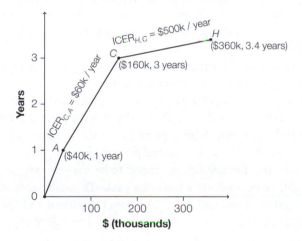

Figure 14.3. *The ICER of any pair of treatments is the inverse of the slope of the line segment between them.*

14.3   Measuring costs

The mathematics of cost-effectiveness is simple. Once we know the costs and health effects of all the treatments, we can calculate their ICERs, plot the CEF, and identify the potentially cost-effective treatments. But the result is only meaningful if we use the true Cs and Es in this calculation. Should long-term costs for future medical problems be included in the cost calculations for treating a heart attack? What is the best measure of a medicine's effectiveness – years of survival, disability avoidance, or something else entirely? Answering these questions and calculating values for C and E in equation (14.1) is the practical challenge of cost-effectiveness analysis.

Whose costs should count?

The first question in conducting a cost-effectiveness analysis is whose perspective the analysis should take – the patient, the insurer, or some other interested party. Whether any particular intervention is found to be cost-effective depends upon the perspective taken because different parties pay different parts of the costs as well as accrue different parts of the benefits.

The most common perspectives considered in CEA studies are those of a hypothetical "social planner" and of a patient. Public insurers often commission cost-effectiveness analyses from a social planner perspective when deciding which treatment strategies should be covered. When conducting a study from this perspective, the analyst should include *all* the costs associated with a particular treatment strategy borne by anyone in society, no matter who ultimately ends up paying them.

Thus, the costs should include both the direct costs paid by an insurer as well as by the patient for the care received. If the treatment induces the patient to miss work, then the costs should include the monetary value of the lost work time, even if it is the patient's employer who bears those costs. Similarly, if the treatment strategy requires the help of family members to care for the patient, the family's lost leisure time should be included as a cost.

There is one exception to this rule of counting all of the costs. If the treatment includes prescription drugs and other inputs that are priced at monopoly levels, only the marginal costs of the drug should be counted. The money paid above marginal cost for drugs is accrued to the producer of the drug as monopoly profits (Cutler 2010). So while the monopoly profits are a loss to the payer, they are an equal-sized gain to the drug company's shareholders. From a social planner's perspective, the net cost of using the drug is only its marginal cost of production.

Studies that instead take the patient perspective should only include costs of the treatment that are directly borne by the patient, but not costs borne by others such as employers or family members. Chief among these costs to be included are the out-of-pocket costs for the treatment itself. These will typically be higher if the patient is uninsured than if the patient is insured, though cost-sharing provisions such as copayments and deductibles increase the out-of-pocket costs that insured patients face.

There is no guarantee that a treatment found to be cost-effective from the social planner perspective will be cost-effective from the patient's perspective, since the costs may differ in the two studies. As we will see, CEAs from the patient and the social planner will diverge if there is moral hazard induced by insurance coverage. They may also diverge if a treatment has a positive or negative externality (see Chapter 20).

Which costs should count?

Cost-effectiveness analysts must also make decisions about which costs to include in the analysis. A simple story demonstrates the ambiguities of cost accounting. Suppose a national insurance system is facing the decision of whether to provide coverage for an incredible new treatment for lung cancer. The treatment works so well that it even cures patients with late-stage lung cancer. In addition to being incredibly effective, the treatment is cheap to produce and to administer. A complete course of treatment costs a mere $1,000. If ever there were a treatment that ought to be covered, this is it: the direct costs of the treatment are low and the benefits are high relative to alternative lung cancer treatments which, by contrast, are expensive and ineffective.

Suppose, however, that the treatment can only be administered at one hospital in the world, located in the remote reaches of the Gobi Desert. Additionally, the treatment is extremely uncomfortable and time-consuming, as it requires patients to lie curled up inside a small chamber for ten courses of ten hours each. As a result, lung cancer patients seeking this treatment must travel a long way, and must incur significant non-pecuniary costs to actually undergo treatment. It makes sense to count such costs in a cost-effectiveness analysis if the analysis is undertaken from the point of view of the social planner or the patient (Garber and Phelps 1997). Those related non-medical costs require real resources to be expended and would not have been necessary if an alternative treatment had been chosen.

It is more difficult to answer how future costs should be counted against a candidate treatment. If this miraculous lung cancer treatment is covered by insurance, many cancer patients will survive much longer than they would otherwise have done. Those patients now have some chance of suffering heart attacks next year which will be expensive to treat. If the miracle treatment is not covered, the cancer patients would not have survived and the heart attacks would never happen. Should the extra heart attack costs be counted against the new cancer treatment? If so, then the miracle lung cancer treatment is more costly than it first appeared. While most economists agree that future costs should be considered in CEA, there is debate over what kinds of future costs should be included (Meltzer 1997; Garber and Phelps 1997; Lee 2008).

Even when researchers agree which future costs should be considered, the actual estimation of these future costs can be difficult. It requires researchers to forecast the likelihood and costs of all possible health contingencies. But a comprehensive accounting of all contingencies is impossible, so, in practice, most cost-effectiveness analyses simplify the calculation of costs to include only a subset of possibilities (Weinstein and Manning 1997). Given that all real-world health technology assessments must be performed with limited information about the consequences of any given decision, this simplification seems like a reasonable compromise.

14.4   Measuring effectiveness

To decide if a drug is potentially cost-effective, we must correctly account not only for its costs, but also for its health benefits. This involves choosing an appropriate health outcome to measure (such as survival) and quantifying the effect of the candidate treatments on this outcome. In the two examples we covered in Section 14.1, E was defined in terms of days of life expectancy and cases of reading disability. But health effects can also be measured in happiness, pain, sick days, physical mobility, and any other aspect of health that people value.

Suppose that in a certain CEA study, "effectiveness" is defined as the increase in life expectancy. Then treatments are evaluated only on the basis of their ability to extend life. But how would this study value a palliative drug like morphine that does not extend life but makes disease more bearable? More pointedly, would a surgery that doubles life expectancy but causes paralysis be considered more effective than a drug that has no side-effects but adds only one year of life?

Clearly, people value not only the number of years they live but also their health condition during those years. Any measure of effectiveness used in CEA therefore should also capture health-related quality of life (Dolan 2000). The most commonly used approach to combine quality of life and life expectancy into a single index is the **quality-adjusted life years** (QALY) approach.

Definition | **14.5**

Quality-adjusted life year (QALY): a unit of life expectancy that is adjusted for the quality of life during those years. QALYs are commonly used in cost-effectiveness analysis as a measure of health benefit.

In a QALY calculation, each year of life receives a *quality weight q* between 0 and 1 that reflects the quality of that life year. Years with a weight of 0 are equivalent to death, whereas years spent in full health are assigned a weight of 1. In practice, almost every year lived is weighted somewhere in between 0 and 1. Because these weights indicate how enjoyable a year is, they are also known as *health utilities*.

The number of QALYs derived over a certain time span is the weighted sum of the quality weights and duration lived at that weight. For example, a patient receives the same number of QALYs from living two years at $q = 0.5$ (with chronic cough and insomnia, say), from four years at $q = 0.25$ (confined to a wheelchair, perhaps), and from one year with full health $q = 1$.

Formally, the calculation of QALYs is the discounted sum of the product quality weights q of each year times the likelihood of survival to each year. For someone with current age t_0 and the potential of living at most to age Z, the quality-adjusted life expectancy (QALE) is the number of years people expect to live weighted by the discounted quality of life in each of those years. In other words, the QALE is the number of QALYs a person expects to live:

$$\text{QALE} = \sum_{t=t_0}^{Z} \delta^{t-t_0} q_t P_t \tag{14.4}$$

where P_t is the probability of surviving to each year t, q_t is the quality weight, and δ is the time-discounting factor. If there is no time discounting ($\delta = 1$) and if each year of life is lived in full health ($q = 1$), then the formula for QALE is identical to the formula for life expectancy.

A related measure of quality-adjusted life expectancy is the *disability-adjusted life years* (DALY). DALYs measure health *lost* compared with a benchmark, whereas QALYs measure health *gained* from a treatment. Because they measure health outcomes as losses, DALYs are commonly used to measure the effect of epidemics or health crises. For example, Krishnamoorthy et al. (2009) report that the 2006 chikungunya epidemic in India caused a total loss of 25,588 DALYs across about 1.39 million cases.

Calculating a QALE requires estimating three pieces of information: a time-discount factor δ, the probability P_t of surviving to each year t, and the quality of life q_t for each year. Typically CEA studies assume a time-discount rate of between 3% and 5% (Weinstein et al. 1996). The probability P_t of surviving to year t is based on mortality data from studies of the effects of adopting the various treatments.

Measuring the quality of life q_t is contentious. One reason why measurement of q is inherently difficult is because it involves comparing health conditions that are entirely dissimilar. How should the following three conditions be ranked: being wheelchair-bound, becoming blind, or losing ten years of life? Another debate revolves around the perspective of the respondents: who is in the best position to judge these conditions? Healthy people, paraplegics, and the blind might have very different opinions about the relative desirability of these different health states.

Survey methods for measuring quality weights

There are several survey methods that researchers use to measure quality weights q (Torrance 1986). One straightforward approach is to survey a broad sample of people and ask them how they feel about different health conditions.

- **Visual analogue scale** (VAS). The VAS approach asks respondents to rate health outcomes between 0 and 100, where 0 represents the worst imaginable health state and 100 represents the best. Respondents mark where different health states lie on a scale similar to the one in Figure 14.4.

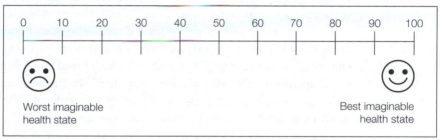

Figure 14.4. *Example visual analogue scale (VAS).*

The VAS approach is appealing because it is simple to administer and easy for respondents to understand. But many economists dislike the VAS because it does not require survey respondents to think about tradeoffs between different health states. Instead, survey-takers are asked to consider health states one at a time. The result is a ranking of health states that does not necessarily reflect the intensity of their preferences. For example, if a respondent is asked to rank three health states, there is a tendency to spread them evenly by marking them at 25, 50, and 75, even if the first two are much worse than the third (Dolan 2000).

Instead, economists typically prefer two other strategies that attempt to uncover preferences by asking respondents to choose between two options. These two strategies are known as the *standard gamble* and the *time tradeoff*:

- **Standard gamble** (SG). The SG approach offers respondents two options: a health state H with certainty, or a gamble between perfect health and death. This option allows respondents to achieve perfect health with probability p or death with probability $(1 - p)$. Researchers offer respondents different versions of this gamble with different values for p. The probability p which makes respondents indifferent between the certain option and the gamble is the estimated quality weight q of health condition H.
- **Time tradeoff** (TTO). Like the SG approach, the TTO method asks respondents to choose between two options: either living for t years with a health state H before dying, or living for a shorter amount of time τ in full health and then dying. As with

SG, researchers offer different versions of this tradeoff with different values of τ. For the length of time τ^* such that respondents are indifferent between the two options, the estimated quality weight of health state H is the ratio τ^*/t.

Both SG and TTO methods rely on the same underlying strategy: they pose hypothetical tradeoffs to find the full-health equivalent for any health state. For any health state H, the SG approach finds the gamble between full health and death that yields utility equal to H. The TTO approach finds the number of years of full health necessary to match the utility from t years with H.

No method measures utility from health states directly. The SG approach may be affected by risk aversion. Even if a person views the health state H as worse than others, she may be more likely to choose the certain outcome if she is particularly risk-averse. We also discuss evidence from behavioral economics in Chapter 23 that people respond in counter-intuitive ways to uncertain gambles like the SG. The TTO approach may be similarly biased if τ^* is a function of age. If utility from full health diminishes with age, then older respondents may systematically need fewer years of full health than younger respondents to match the utility from t years of living in health state H.

These biases mean that the estimated quality weights obtained from different survey methods will differ, even if the ordering of preferences over multiple health conditions is consistent across surveys (Read et al. 1984; Bleichrodt and Johannesson 1997). Figure 14.5 shows quality weight estimates for a sample of health conditions obtained through three different methods for the same group of 69 respondents. All three graphs show similar ordering patterns across conditions, but the quality weight estimates vary vastly. The SG estimates tend to be higher than the TTO estimates for the same condition, while the VAS estimates are spread out evenly between 0 and 1. A number of other studies have also found that SG estimates tend to be higher than TTO estimates (Bleichrodt and Johannesson 1997; Lenert et al. 1998; Bleichrodt 2002). In Chapter 23, we discuss how behavioral deviations from our typical definitions of rationality can explain these differences as well as undermine the reliability of survey approaches for estimating quality weights.

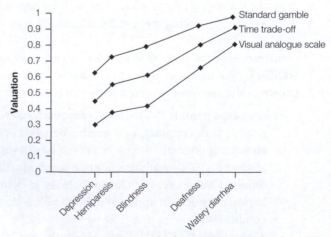

Figure 14.5. *Average quality weight estimates for five conditions under three different estimation methods.*

Source: Data from Salomon and Murray (2004).

Table 14.4. *Summary of survey methods for QALY quality weight.*

Method	Description
Visual analogue scale (VAS)	Questionnaire respondents score health conditions on a thermometer-like scale from 0, the worst imaginable health state, to 100, the best imaginable health state.
Standard gamble (SG)	For any health condition H, questionnaire respondents choose between having H with certainty or a gamble with probability p of full health and probability $(1 - p)$ of death.
Time tradeoff (TTO)	For any health condition H, questionnaire respondents choose between having x years of condition H before dying or fewer years in perfect health before dying.

Table 14.4 summarizes some of the methods used for the estimation of QALY quality weights.

Whose opinion matters in QALY surveys?

Picking the survey method, however, is just part of the debate about quality weights. The next step is choosing the right population to receive the survey. Estimates about quality weights may differ widely depending on the survey audience. Part of the reason that estimates vary is that the surveys pose difficult hypothetical questions. Healthy people may be unequipped to judge their hypothetical quality of life with a disability. For example, a sighted person may have a lot of trouble imagining what life would be like blind.

One approach known as the *Delphi method* involves asking a panel of medical experts to estimate what they believe the quality weights for various health states should be. Like the Oracle of Delphi, this Delphic panel tries to divine the preferences of the broader population. This approach is appealing because the experts have taken care of many patients with the given disorder and observed their quality of life. But this method is prone to weigh the concerns of doctors over the concerns of patients. For instance, patient comfort may be overlooked in Delphic estimates of quality weights (Jachuck et al. 1982).

If a healthy population is unequipped to imagine the quality of life in health states they have not experienced, and a panel of experts is unlikely to ably represent the preferences of patients, then perhaps the best strategy is to survey actual patients with the disease. For example, only the teen covered with acne can truly appreciate the effect of his condition on his quality of life.

The Oracle of Delphi was the priestess at the Temple of Apollo in ancient Greece. Her job was to give prophetic answers to impossible questions. Supplicants underwent a long journey along the Sacred Way to prepare to speak to the Oracle. Credit: © ollirg – Fotolia.com.

One problem with this approach, though, is that people seem adept at adapting to their health states and finding ways of coping with complications. As a result, survey responses from actual patients may understate the suffering of their conditions, because they have found a way to manage the most difficult hardships. In confirmation of this hypothesis of habit formation, Dolan (1996) finds that people in poorer health generally report higher quality of life assessments for the same health states than members of the general public do.

No matter which group is surveyed – healthy populations, expert panels, or sick patients – the resulting estimates will reflect that group's point of view over the point of view of others, so there is no perfect group of survey respondents. The influential 1996 Panel on Cost Effectiveness in Health and Medicine proposed that when the general public is paying for health care, CEA should defer to the judgments of the general public

(Gold et al. 1996) because experts may not be able to reflect the preferences of a broad population.

14.5   Cost–benefit analysis: picking the optimal treatment

Up until now, we have shied away from the question of assigning a value to life years or other health outcomes. We have merely plotted a cost-effectiveness frontier (CEF) to identify the set of *potentially* cost-effective treatments. Cost-effectiveness analysis makes no judgment about whether more expensive treatments on the frontier are worth it (though it does identify treatment strategies inside the frontier as not worthwhile).

Cost–benefit analysis (CBA) takes the additional step of assigning a value to health benefits in monetary terms. CBA allows us to pick an optimal treatment from the list of potentially cost-effective treatments. In other words, cost–benefit analysis allows us to determine which single treatment is most **cost-effective**. This is where the dispassionate mathematics of cost-effectiveness ends and the contentious practice of life valuation begins.

In Section 14.6, we will discuss in more detail the methods researchers use to derive an estimate of the value of life, as well as the limitations of these methods. For the purposes of this section, we will take as given that people have an estimate of the value of life, though of course there is bound to be disagreement among reasonable people about what that value should be.

Definition	14.6

Cost–benefit analysis (CBA): the process of choosing an optimal treatment among the potentially cost-effective ones, given a certain monetary value for each unit of health effect. This optimal treatment is **cost-effective** for a person or agency with that valuation.

When we place a monetary value on each life year or quality-adjusted life year, we implicitly create a set of indifference curves that can be plotted in the same space as the CEF from Figure 14.3. Let us assume that a person values each QALY at $100,000. As a result, the indifference curves are sloped as to indicate indifference between one additional quality-adjusted life year and $100,000. Below we plot this set of indifference curves and find a tangency point with the CEF for bhtitis (Figure 14.6). Under this assumption, the cost-effective treatment for a patient stricken with bhtitis is drug C.

Consider a bhtitis victim without insurance who also values each QALY at $100,000. Because he is uninsured and pays the full cost of treatment, he optimizes by picking drug C. He takes the three additional QALYs that drug C provides for only $160,000. He forgoes the extra 0.4 QALYs he could get with drug H, which would cost $200,000 more than drug C. Drug H would only be worth it if he values extra QALYs at $200,000 ÷ 0.4 = $500,000.

Another way to say this is that the ICER between drug C and drug H is $500,000, which exceeds the value he places on a QALY. Instead of buying those extra 0.4 years, he would rather save his money and bequeath it to his children (or maybe spend it on a year-long cruise of the seven seas). Based on his valuation of a life year, this is a good decision for him. This cost-effectiveness analysis was done from the perspective of the uninsured patient; we discuss next how the analysis changes with insurance coverage.

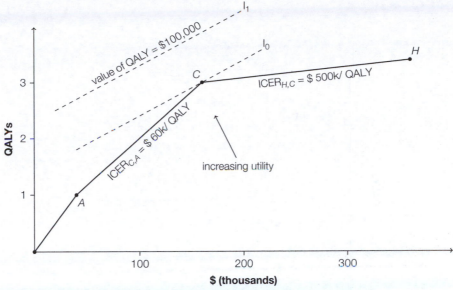

Figure 14.6. *Tangency between indifference curves and the CEF at point C.*

The impact of insurance

Consider the same bhtitis victim with the same valuation of a quality-adjusted life year, but now with a generous insurance package that covers 90% of his medical expenses. His insurer does not use health technology assessment and is willing to cover any and all treatments – even dominated ones and ones that are not cost-effective. The insurance coverage lowers the man's out-of-pocket price per QALY. Because he only has to pay 10% of any treatment, drug C now costs $10\% \times \$160{,}000 = \$16{,}000$ for three QALYs and drug H costs only $10\% \times \$360{,}000 = \$36{,}000$ for 3.4 QALYs. Figure 14.7 depicts the new cost-effectiveness frontier from the insured person's perspective as a result of insurance. H' represents the cost and health benefits of drug H with an insurance plan that covers 90% of medical costs.

Notice that with insurance the person optimally chooses drug H, whereas without insurance he would have opted for the cheaper (but less effective) drug C. This is a typical example of moral hazard. When the bhtitis victim had to pay his own way, he decided the slightly more effective drug H was not worth the extra costs. The ICER of drug H with respect to drug C is $\$500{,}000$/QALY, while he only valued life at $\$100{,}000$ per QALY. But when his insurance kicked in, the patient opted instead for drug H, which costs *him* only $\$20{,}000$ extra. The additional costs of drug H are shared by everyone in the patient's insurance pool. In this way, insurance encourages technology overuse and the development of highly inefficient innovations like the Health-O-Tron.

Rationing

Insurance companies and national insurance programs are cognizant of the problem of technology overuse. In Chapter 11, we discussed various techniques that companies use to reduce moral hazard, including higher rates of coinsurance, the use of deductibles, and gatekeeping. But we omitted a major technique that is relevant to cost-effectiveness analysis: rationing.

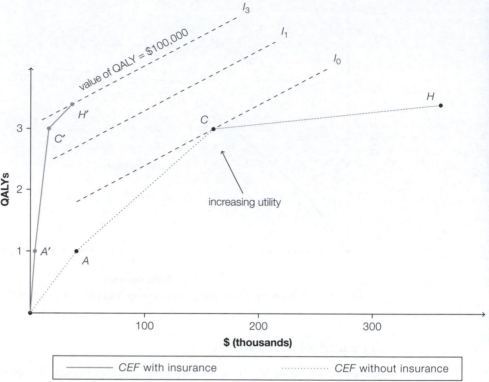

Figure 14.7. *Tangency between indifference curves and the CEF at point H′ due to insurance.*

Definition	14.7

Rationing: any method for allocating a scarce resource other than prices.

Rationing is commonly employed by governments during wartime. In these situations, the military is consuming most of the resources, so basic necessities of life like food and clothing become very scarce on the home front. If competitive prices prevailed, food and other basic goods may become prohibitively expensive and much of the population would starve. A law that restricts each family from buying more than one chicken, one loaf of bread, and one stick of butter per week is a form of rationing. This system ensures that everyone in the population has access to adequate food, even though it frustrates those who could otherwise afford more.

In a typical market, prices serve the role of making sure that scarce resources are allocated efficiently. In a sense, everyday goods like gasoline and breakfast cereal are "rationed" by price: people cannot receive an unlimited amount of gasoline because they must pay for each gallon and do not have unlimited budgets. But insurance markets are different. Prices of medical care are artificially low by design and do a poor job of limiting the use of scarce medical resources like hospital beds and a surgeon's time. Insurers and governments can use rationing to reduce moral hazard without raising prices.

Private insurance companies, and sometimes national insurance programs like the UK's National Health Service (NHS), decline to pay for certain treatments that are deemed not cost-effective. In the case of bhtitis, an insurance company that covers 90% of patient expenditures might decline to cover drug H. Wealthier patients and those who place a greater value on their health can still purchase drug H with their own money of course, but the insurance company is only willing to cover 90% of expenses for drug A and drug C. Our hypothetical customer would likely respond by choosing drug C, which is what he would have chosen anyway without insurance. This is a compromise solution: the patient does not get the best treatment money can buy, but he does get the treatment that he would have chosen without insurance and gets it at a steep discount.

For example, in an effort to cut health care spending in the 1990s, the Czech Republic created a commission to regulate medical treatments that utilize the most expensive technologies and drugs (such as cochlear implants, pacemakers, and *in vitro* fertilization) (Krízová and Simek 2002). Based on a review of the professional indications for treatment, including the health, social, and psychological situation of the patient, the commission either withholds or issues approval for the procedure. In the case of cochlear implants, the commission may consider such factors as the patient's educational prospects and his family's commitment to ensuing therapeutic and rehabilitative efforts. While there are no explicit age limits associated with specific treatments, some of the more expensive operations (such as hip replacements) are typically conducted on younger patients – who are expected to lead more physically active lifestyles and have more future years of life to enjoy the benefits – while older patients are slated to receive less expensive alternative therapies.

The whole reason researchers study valuation of a year of life or the appropriate quality weight for a disability is because companies and governments need to make life-and-death decisions on the patient's behalf. If people paid full prices for health care and made their own decisions about whether to get treatment A, C, or H, we would not need to measure QALYs and the value of a life year because customers would make socially optimal decisions on their own. This is why governments do not feel compelled to research the valuations of video games; we leave it up to people to decide whether to buy video games with their own money.

In the case of health insurance, though, customers do not make socially optimal decisions because prices are distorted. Moral hazard justifies cost-effectiveness analysis, which in turn necessitates research into quality weights and life valuation. Without such research, companies and policymakers could never figure out which treatments are worth covering from a social planner's perspective.

Although rationing is understandably contentious, it might nevertheless be optimal for insurance customers. Rationing can drastically reduce overall health costs and allows for lower premiums (or a lower tax burden in the case of public insurance). Consider Figure 14.8, which depicts the tradeoff between moral hazard and risk. The contract at α is full insurance and induces the most moral hazard; this is the case where an insurance company is willing to cover any treatment, including ones like drug H that do not produce much health benefit. The contract at β is partial insurance with rationing, perhaps a contract that does not cover cost-ineffective treatments like drug H but still covers treatments like drug C.

The indifference curves in this figure suggest that customers are actually happy to live with rationing in insurance, since curve I_0 generates the greatest feasible utility. Rationing reduces the fullness of insurance because there are some moments – when they catch bhtitis, for instance – when rationing will prevent them from enjoying extra years of life they could have had with drug H. But rationing also saves customers from having to pay for *everyone else's* ineffective drugs. Sometimes, those savings are enough to make rationing

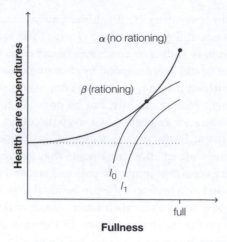

Figure 14.8. *Rationing and moral hazard.*

appealing. Moving from α to β leads to worse health and fewer QALYs, but the money saved on health care costs can be spent on other things that are more valuable.

In order to actually decide whether this decrease in health expenditures is worth it, we need some measure of the value of life. Figure 14.6 depicted indifference curves that implied that people valued each quality-adjusted life year at $100,000. If this figure underestimates the true value of life, then some socially optimal treatments will not be covered. If this figure is instead an overestimate, there will be substantial harm from moral hazard even after rationing is imposed.

14.6   Valuing life

How much is your life worth to you right now? Perhaps you think it is infinite or cannot be valued economically. No amount of money could convince you to give up your life right now. But if your valuation of life were truly infinite, you would make some odd decisions. For example, suppose an eccentric benefactor left you a million dollars in a suitcase across the street. To reach it, you must cross the street and run a small risk of being fatally hit by a bus in the crosswalk. If your valuation of life is truly infinite, you would forgo the million dollars without thinking twice.

Of course, such behavior is rightly seen as overly cautious. Most, if not all, people would venture across the street for a million dollars. This action implies that the valuation of life is not infinite. Suppose the risk of getting hit by a bus if you cross the street was 1%. Then by dodging incoming traffic to collect your bounty, you have implicitly valued your life as being worth at most $1 million $\div 0.01 = \$100$ million dollars. You might protest indignantly that your life is worth far more – but if your life is so valuable, why did you risk a 1% chance of losing it in order to gain "only" $1 million? This value places an upper bound on your **value of statistical life**.

Definition   14.8

Value of statistical life (VSL): a monetary measure of how a life should be valued for the purposes of cost–benefit analysis.

VSL is not intended to measure how much a person would be willing to pay in exchange for life nor how much he would accept in exchange for certain death. That is, even if someone has a VSL of $5 million, that does not mean he would be willing to drop dead in exchange for that amount. Instead, VSL is used to measure how valuable or how costly *small changes* in mortality risk are. A vaccination campaign that lowers the probability of death by 1 percentage point in a population of a hundred people is equivalent, statistically speaking, to a campaign that saves one life with certainty. By seeing how much people value that campaign, we can estimate how much people value that hypothetical life saved. A person's VSL varies as his risk tolerance varies, so we expect it to be a function of country, age, income, and health among other variables.

Estimating the value of life

The cost-effectiveness frontier helps us find the best treatments for a given budget, but it is agnostic about how much we should be willing to spend to obtain more life years or QALYs. In other words, how much is a QALY worth? When are more expensive and more effective treatments worth their higher cost? These questions weigh on the coverage decisions of both private and public insurers, and economists have devised several methods to try to estimate the value of life based on the actions of people and governments.

Attempts to estimate the value of life rely primarily on three sources: labor market choices, product purchase decisions, and government policies. The first two kinds of studies infer VSL from tradeoffs between money and risk. By finding the amount of money necessary to compensate people for accepting higher risk, or the amount of money people are willing to pay to reduce risk, researchers can uncover how much individuals value a statistical life. The third technique involves looking at policy deci-

A fishing trawler off the coast of Alaska. The Discovery Channel's Deadliest Catch *follows a fleet of fishermen searching for Alaskan king crabs in the Bering Sea. By modeling the willingness of these fishermen to fish during colder years when the risk of hypothermia is more acute and wages are greater, Schnier et al. (2009) estimate their VSL to be about $4 million.* Credit: © sergeytimofeev – Fotolia.com.

sions and new laws to infer how much governments value lives saved or years of life gained.

Consider a hypothetical worker named Jay with two potential job prospects. He can either work for the local hospital restocking drugs and other medical instruments or he can work for the nearby nuclear power plant. Let us further assume that the human capital necessary for both jobs is the same, and, in fact, the actual labor he would do is similar at both locations. The main difference is that at the hospital Jay might catch the flu on occasion, but the risk of a fatal injury is relatively low. At the nuclear plant, however, he would be constantly endangered by powerful machinery and exposed to hazardous beta particles. The chances of fatal injury and the likelihood of terminal cancer are both much higher at the power plant.

In order to attract Jay to the more hazardous job, the power plant would need to offer him more money than the hospital. The extra wages are known as the *risk premium*, and for a certain wage differential, Jay is exactly indifferent between the hospital job and the nuclear power plant position.

If researchers can learn both the risk premium and the difference in risks, then they can estimate how much the worker values his life. This is the labor market strategy for estimating VSLs (Viscusi 1993). For example, a worker who would be just willing to take a job with a 1% higher fatal injury risk for $50,000 more in wages has a VSL of $50,000 ÷ 0.01 = $5 million. Most studies of the US labor market using this approach estimate VSLs of between $5 and $12 million dollars (Viscusi 2003).

Though this approach is conceptually simple, it is difficult to implement in practice because it is hard to find two different jobs that are identical except for levels of mortality hazard. This can be problematic, since there are people who accept riskier jobs for the same wages because they value something else about that job. For example, Red Cross workers eagerly travel to war-ravaged regions for humanitarian causes. Likewise, a strong sense of civic duty compels firefighters to rush into burning buildings.

Neither firefighters nor Red Cross workers need high-risk premiums to attract them to their dangerous jobs. So applying this labor market strategy for estimating VSLs for these workers might underestimate their VSL. For example, Low and McPheters (1983) find that the VSL for American police officers between 1972 and 1975 was just $584,249, lower than other estimates of VSL at the time. If these police officers had counterfactually entered different jobs with similarly high levels of risk but which were not as psychically rewarding, they would likely have demanded much higher wages, and estimates of their VSL would be correspondingly higher.

Another problem with the labor market approach is that the competitive labor market sets wages based on the preferences of the marginal worker, not the average worker. Consider a Dubai window-washing company attempting to hire exactly one worker for the dangerous task of climbing and cleaning the Burj Khalifa. The company raises the wage just high enough to attract the window-washer who values his life the least in all Dubai. As a result, the workers who take dangerous jobs are necessarily less risk-averse than the general population. So estimates of VSLs based on the wages of these most risk-loving workers do not generalize to the population at large.

Another concern is the difficulty of defining and measuring risk. Most studies use recent average fatality count data as a proxy for occupational risk. But there is debate about how to account for the risk of *nonfatal* accidents. If the risk premium also compensates for the possibility of nonfatal injuries, then the labor market estimation strategy may be overestimating the VSL (Viscusi 2003).

Lastly, these studies assume that the workers understand the risk associated with their daily labor. But if workers consistently misjudge this risk, then the wages would not reflect the willingness to accept greater risk. To account for this, some studies have included not only industry average fatality rates but also measures of workers' self-reported risk assessments (Viscusi 1979; Duncan and Holmlund 1983). Nevertheless, it is well documented in the literature that people have difficulties in understanding and evaluating risk, even in life-and-death settings such as this. In Chapter 23, we discuss an alternative approach that behavioral economists have taken to understanding decision-making under uncertainty.

The labor market approach uses data on how much more people must be paid in order to accept a riskier job. Similarly, the product purchase approach studies how much people pay for goods and services that reduce risk – for example, smoke detectors, bicycle helmets, or a more expensive house in a safer neighborhood.

Jenkins et al. (2001) use price data for children's bike helmets to estimate the VSL for kids. The decision to wear a helmet indicates a judgment that the risk reduction of head trauma from bike accidents is worth the cost of buying helmets. So the researchers can use the prices of bike helmets to estimate a lower bound for the value of the risk reduction and use that to calculate a lower bound for the VSL of helmet-wearers.

Jenkins et al. estimate that the VSL was at least $2.7 million for children aged 5–9, $2.6 million for children aged 10–14, and at least $4.0 million for adults aged 20–59. Of course, children rarely buy their own helmets, so the VSL calculated for youth probably reflects the valuation of their parents more than themselves (Hammitt and Haninger 2010). Moreover, the evidence that VSL is higher for 5–9-year-olds may be an indication that parents are especially risk-averse about their younger children.

One additional benchmark that researchers have used to estimate VSL is to examine the implicit value that governments have placed on life years in their policymaking decisions. For example, in 1972, the US passed an amendment expanding Medicare to guarantee kidney dialysis to all patients under 65 with end-stage renal disease. Without kidney dialysis, the toxins that healthy kidneys are capable of filtering build up in the bloodstream and ultimately poison the patient. Kidney dialysis has been estimated to cost $50,000 per QALY (Klarman et al. 1968; Winkelmayer et al. 2002). Since there is near-universal consensus that kidney dialysis is a worthwhile treatment, the passage of the Medicare amendment suggests that a QALY is worth *at least* $50,000 to American taxpayers (Weinstein 2005).

The policy uses of VSL estimates

VSLs are routinely used to decide whether life-saving regulations are worthwhile. Regulations are often judged on whether the value of reduced mortality outweighs the costs. For example, the US Food and Drug Administration (FDA) valued each statistical life at $2.7 million when evaluating a 1996 policy that criminalized the sale of tobacco to children (Viscusi 2003). VSL estimates are also used by environmental, health, transportation, and other regulatory agencies whose actions may save or cost lives. Table 14.5 lists the actual VSL estimates used by a number of US regulatory bodies.

Table 14.5. *VSL estimates used by American regulatory agencies.*

Year of study	Regulatory agency	VSL (millions of 2008 dollars)
1985	Federal Aviation Administration	$1.2
1990	Federal Aviation Administration	$2.5
1995	Consumer Product Safety Commission	$6.9
1996	Food and Drug Administration	$3.3
2000	Consumer Product Safety Commission	$6.2
2000	Department of Transportation	$3.9 – $6.2
2000	Environmental Protection Agency	$7.8
2006	Food and Drug Administration	$5.3 – $6.8
2006	Environmental Protection Agency	$8.5
2007	Department of Homeland Security	$3.1 – $6.2
2008	Environmental Protection Agency	$6.8

Source: Developed from data in Viscusi (2010) and Viscusi (2003).

One way to interpret the variation in Table 14.5 is that the US government values a life lost in a plane crash less than a life lost to food poisoning. The large variation in VSLs used across agencies is not unique to the US. One Canadian regulatory agency used a range of VSLs from $1.7 to $5.7 million to study a regulation on tobacco sales. Regulatory bodies in the UK, however, do not explicitly use VSL estimates, likely due to the large variation in estimates from the relatively few UK studies (Viscusi 2003).

Another reason for the variation in VSL measures shown in Table 14.5 is that regulations affect different demographic groups. For example, the US Federal Aviation Administration (FAA) has argued that because airplane passengers tend to be more affluent and therefore have higher VSLs, the FAA should use a higher VSL than the rest of the Department of Transportation uses. Since a higher VSL means more benefit from the same reduction in risk, a higher VSL for the FAA would increase the calculated benefit from their regulatory policies.

On the other hand, policies that use lower VSLs for certain demographics have been viewed as morally repugnant. For example, in 2003, the US Environmental Protection Agency (EPA) decided to use a lower VSL for people above the age of 65. This decision provoked political backlash, since the agency was explicitly valuing the lives of older people less than those of younger people. This backlash ultimately led the EPA to repeal its decision and revert to treating younger and older people equally (Viscusi 2010).

Table 14.5 also reveals that VSL has been increasing over time, partially as the result of improved estimation strategies and the expected consequence of improved standard of living and longer life expectancies. Hall and Jones (2004) argue that the rise in VSL also explains the growth in health care expenditures. In fact, according to their model, health care spending is still inefficiently low and should grow to 30% of GDP or more in the US by 2050. Similarly, Murphy and Topel (2006) argue that the world is much richer than GDP estimates would suggest because of rising life expectancies.

The vast VSL literature aids the task of cost-effectiveness analysis by providing guidance on how much people value life and how much they would pay to decrease the risk of dying. VSL estimates can be used to construct estimates for how much people value gains in health and then how much people value a QALY. For example, it is feasible to calculate the average value of a QALY for a group of people with average life expectancy of 40 years and VSL of $4 million. We would need to apply the time-discounting factor and estimate the quality weight for each of those 40 years. Doing so would allow us to determine not only the willingness to pay per QALY but also what the optimal treatment is.

14.7   Conclusion

Health technology assessment is a vital tool that both public and private insurers use to control moral hazard. If insurers pledged to fully reimburse all medical procedures, then patients and doctors would demand even the most minimally effective treatments like the Health-O-Tron. Health care spending would skyrocket with little patient benefit.

Insurers cannot cover every single new technology, nor can they refuse to cover all new procedures or else their customers would revolt. Instead, most insurers choose to be selective about which procedures to cover. Cost-effectiveness analysis and cost–benefit analysis are tools that many insurers use to make these decisions.

But the history of HTA is littered with controversy, and efforts to apply it to public policy settings have provoked backlash. In 1989, the state of Oregon wanted to expand the percentage of low-income residents covered by the public insurance program Medicaid. Because of its limited budget, the only way to expand coverage was to limit the set of procedures it would pay for.

The Oregon Medicaid program studied more than 700 costly medical treatments and diagnoses. Using cost-effectiveness analysis and input from the public and physicians,

Medicaid administrators generated a priority list of the treatments. At the top were very cost-effective treatments such as emergency care for severe head trauma. Near the bottom were treatments deemed less cost-effective such as *in vitro* fertilization and radial keratotomy for nearsighted people (Bodenheimer 1997).

In the first year of the program, Oregon Medicaid could only afford to reimburse the top 587 procedures. So head trauma victims still received care, but infertile women and myopic people were out of luck. The list drew outraged accusations of rationing care for the very poor and complaints from patient advocacy organizations.

Private insurers have also drawn criticism for rationing care. In the late 1980s, a radical new treatment for late-stage cancer was gaining popularity. Autologous bone marrow transplantation is a complex procedure that involves harvesting bone marrow from sick patients and preserving it for later. Doctors then subject patients to searingly high levels of toxic chemotherapy. This chemotherapy kills cancer cells but also destroys bone marrow cells along with the patient's immune system. After chemotherapy is complete, the patient is reinjected with her own healthy bone marrow, which rebuilds her immune system (Mukherjee 2010).

In the early 1990s, most private insurers in the US were unwilling to cover autologous bone marrow transplantation, which could cost up to $400,000 and had yet to demonstrate benefit in any controlled clinical trials. After a few high-profile cases where young mothers with breast cancer were denied coverage by their insurers, several states enacted laws requiring insurers to cover transplantation. In one notable instance, protesters picketed the offices of HealthNet, a Californian insurer that had denied coverage for a local woman with breast cancer.

Coverage decisions informed by cost-effectiveness analyses can lead to very public and acrimonious protest. Yet all insurers must enact some limitations on coverage in order to curtail the consequences of moral hazard. In coming chapters, we discuss various strategies governments use to navigate the path between insurance coverage and moral hazard (Sorenson et al. 2008a). Some insurers, like the UK's National Health Service, explicitly use cost–benefit analysis (Sorenson et al. 2008b). Others, like America's Medicare program, are legally proscribed from considering cost in making coverage decisions. As we will see in Chapter 18, this contributes to the high costs of US medical care.

14.8   Exercises

Comprehension questions

Indicate whether each statement is true or false, and justify your answer. Be sure to state any additional assumptions you may need.

1 A dominated treatment is one that is less cost-effective than another treatment (even though it may produce better medical outcomes).

2 Both ICERs and ACERs compare two drugs on the basis of both cost and medical efficacy.

3 If a medical screening technique is perfect at detecting a disease before it develops and is able to prevent the disease from occurring, it must be cost-effective.

4 An ICER value indicates which of two treatment options is better.

5 The cost-effectiveness frontier (CEF) shows the subset of treatment strategies which are not dominated by any other treatment.

6 The results of any CEA analysis depend on the perspective taken, but analyses from the perspectives of the patient and a social planner will never differ.

7 There are several survey methods that health services researchers use to measure quality of life under different diseases.

8 Medical experts are ideal candidates for providing estimates of the quality weights associated with various health states.

9 Cost–benefit analysis (CBA) allows us to pick an optimal treatment from the list of potentially cost-effective treatments.

10 The value of statistical life (VSL) is a measure of how much money someone would be willing to accept in exchange for dying.

11 Studies of labor market choices and product purchase decisions infer VSL from tradeoffs between money and risk.

12 Empirically, VSL estimates vary widely by country, income, age, and gender.

13 Cost–benefit analysis is used to determine which medicines and treatments US Medicare will cover.

Analytical problems

14 Traders from the faraway nation of Chplandia have brought infected goods to market in the capital of Pcoria. As a result, a new infectious disease called chpitis is spreading through the Pcorian population. Chpitis is not fatal, but leaves victims severely disfigured for the remainder of their lives. Throughout this problem, assume no discounting of future years.

   a The Pcorian government surveys victims to determine how burdensome chpitis is. Respondents claim they are indifferent between living six years without chpitis and living ten years covered with chpitis scars. Most respondents explain that they face a major social stigma in Pcoria's schools and workplaces. What is the implied quality weight q for a year lived in the aftermath of a chpitis infection?

   b Now assume that a drug company has developed an ointment that can be used to treat chpitis sores and reduce scarring. Surveys indicate that the ointment, which costs $10,000 for a full course of treatment, can improve quality of life from 0.6 to 0.7 for chpitis survivors. What is the ICER for taking the ointment over doing nothing for the typical chpitis victim (a 20-year-old)? Assume that life expectancy in Pcoria is 70 years.

   c Assume that everyone in Pcoria agrees that a QALY is worth $5,000. Will a 20-year-old chpitis victim decide to get the ointment, which costs $10,000? What about a 60-year-old chpitis patient? What about a 69-year-old chpitis patient?

   d Suppose that the Pcorian government enrolls all its citizens in the Universal Insurance Program which pays (with 10% coinsurance) for any treatment. So the ointment costs patients only $1,000 out of pocket. Will a 20-year-old chpitis victim still decide to get the ointment? What about a 60-year-old chpitis patient? What about a 69-year-old chpitis patient?

15 Suppose Jay has been experiencing back pain, and has four options for treatment (Table 14.6).

   a Plot these four treatments on cost–pain reduction axes. Create a cost-effectiveness frontier by connecting potentially cost-effective treatments.

Table 14.6. *Potential therapies for back pain.*

Treatment regimen	Total cost	Pain reduction
Do nothing	$0	0 units
Chair cushion	$100	20 units
Cortisone injections	$700	25 units
Acupuncture	$1,000	50 units

b   Calculate the ICER between cortisone injections and a chair cushion, and between acupuncture and cortisone injections.

c   Assume that indifference curves in this space are linear. Interpret this assumption.

d   Find the range of valuations for a pain reduction unit that Jay would need in order to pick cortisone injections as the cost-effective treatment. Explain your answer.

e   Under this assumption of linearity, is it possible to draw indifference curves such that cortisone injections will be cost-effective?

f   Relaxing this assumption, draw an indifference curve such that cortisone injections are preferred to all other treatments. Describe the preferences that your indifference curves imply.

Essay questions

16 Jachuck et al. (1982) report on an analysis of a certain drug designed to reduce hypertension (high blood pressure). Such hypotensive drugs are frequently effective but are also linked to side-effects like irritability, a decline in energy, and a loss of sexual interest. Seventy-five patients with mild hypertension were put on hypotensive drugs and their progress was monitored by doctors and relatives (typically spouses). Suppose that everyone agrees that the quality weight for hypertension is $q = 0.8$. That is, one year spent with mild hypertension is equivalent to 0.8 years of full health.

a   When asked to rate the treated patients as improved, worse, or unchanged, the doctors rated all 75 patients as "improved." Meanwhile, the spouses rated 74 of the 75 patients as "worse." Why might spouses and doctors differ in their opinions about the effect of undertaking hypotensive therapy?

b   Explain why the drugs might be a dominated treatment, and indicate what other treatment(s) might dominate it.

c   Make a one-sentence argument for each of two viewpoints:
   ● The doctors' opinions should be used to determine how beneficial hypotensive drugs are for the purposes of CEA.
   ● The spouses' opinions should be used to determine how beneficial hypotensive drugs are for the purposes of CEA.

d   Suppose that everyone agrees that the quality weight for hypotensive therapy is $q = 0.6$, which is less than the quality weight for living with hypertension ($q = 0.8$). And we know that hypotensive therapy costs more than no treatment. Can we conclude that hypotensive therapy is dominated? What other information would we need? When would we conclude that hypotensive treatment is *not* dominated?

17 A company developing an artificial retina to help the blind see is trying to determine the quality of life for blind people.

- The company first surveys a group of sighted people using a time tradeoff (TTO) approach. The results indicate that being blind should be assigned a quality weight of $q = 0.4$.
- The company then surveys a group of people who recently became blind due to accidents or glaucoma. The results indicate that being blind should be assigned a quality weight of $q = 0.1$.
- Finally, the company surveys a group of people who were not born blind but became blind over twenty years ago. The results indicate that being blind should be assigned a quality weight of $q = 0.9$.

a   Explain why these three approaches might return different quality of life estimates. Why might people who have lived with blindness for a long time rate their quality of life so much higher than people who have only recently become blind?

b   For a cost-effectiveness study of a drug that may, as a side-effect, result in blindness, which of these quality weight measures is most appropriate?

c   Now suppose researchers are measuring the cost-effectiveness of artificial retinas, which may be able to restore sight to the blind. Does this change your answer about which quality of life measure to use?

Students can find answers to the comprehension questions and lecturers can access an Instructor Manual with guideline answers to the analytical problems and essay questions at **www.palgrave.com/economics/bht**.

V HEALTH POLICY

15 The health policy
    conundrum   306

16 The Beveridge model:
    nationalized health care   328

17 The Bismarck model: social
    health insurance   354

18 The American model   372

19 Population aging and the
    future of health policy   402

15 THE HEALTH POLICY CONUNDRUM

In the first 14 chapters of this book, we highlighted several problems that arise in both health care markets and health insurance markets.

Hospital markets can be vulnerable to oligopolies that raise prices and make care unaffordable. Perverse incentives may motivate doctors to recommend wasteful care for patients or lobby hospitals to install fanciful new medical devices of questionable value.

Health insurance markets, meanwhile, malfunction in the face of asymmetric information. If adverse selection is severe, insurance markets may collapse altogether, leaving much of the population uninsured. And when people do manage to become insured, moral hazard makes health care less efficient and more expensive.

In most sectors of the economy, the problem of using resources in the most effective way is left for private industry to solve – private firms compete to provide consumers with high-quality food, electronics, and entertainment at the lowest possible prices. But health care markets are different. Because they face so many market imperfections, and because many people feel that health is a special kind of good that should be accessible to all, governments have long been much more involved in health care than in other markets.

In this chapter we discuss the menu of policies available to different countries. These policies run the gamut from private market solutions that prioritize efficiency to public sector initiatives that emphasize equity. In the following chapters, we highlight three main health system models – each of which uses a different combination of these policies – and discuss the virtues and drawbacks of each approach. Our theme throughout is that every available policy entails a tradeoff, and that there are no perfect solutions to the health policy conundrum.

15.1   Arrow's impossibility theorem

The task of designing a national health system is at its heart an optimization problem, not dissimilar to the task of an individual in the Grossman model (see Chapter 3). Societies must decide how much time and money they want to spend on improving their health, and how much time and money they want to spend on other national priorities – like education, the military, and the environment. Once they have made this determination, they must also chart an optimal strategy for achieving that level of health in the cheapest and most efficient manner.

This analogy between an individual and a society is not quite right though. A society – composed of many people – is fundamentally different from a single person. Each person is presumed to have consistent and transitive preferences. Suppose an individual prefers eating a cookie to watching TV, and prefers watching TV to exercising. If she has *transitive* preferences, then she also prefers eating a cookie to exercising. If, instead, she prefers exercising to eating a cookie, then she has *circular* preferences and it is unclear which of these three activities is optimal (or even if there is an optimum at all).

Without transitive preferences, welfare economics falls apart. Transitive preferences are a necessary assumption for utility maximization and optimal choice to have meaning. Luckily for economics, transitivity seems like a very natural assumption, and much of the field is built upon it. However, in a shocking 1951 paper, economist Ken Arrow (1921–) proved that societies do not necessarily have transitive preferences, even when everyone in them does (Arrow 1951). His finding is known as **Arrow's impossibility theorem**.

The proof of the theorem is involved and technical,[1] but we illustrate the basic idea with an example from the turbulent political culture of our fictional nation of Pcoria. Pcorian political discourse is dominated by three major political parties: the Federal Democrats, the Social Libertarians, and the Enviro-Greens. Pcoria's population is split between three types of voters – students, workers, and retirees – who each make up exactly one third of the electorate. The members of each group share identical political preferences, which happen to differ from the political preferences of the other two groups (see Table 15.1).

Table 15.1. *Voter preferences in Pcoria.*

Voter type	1st choice	2nd choice	3rd choice
Students	Fed Dems	Soc Libs	Enviro-Greens
Workers	Enviro-Greens	Fed Dems	Soc Libs
Retirees	Soc Libs	Enviro-Greens	Fed Dems

Any single Pcorian voter has a transitive set of preferences over the three political parties. But what is Pcoria's society-wide preference ordering among the three parties? Since Pcoria is a democracy, all of its citizens have an equal say in determining the ordering of the political parties. Two-thirds of the population – the workers and students – prefer the Fed Dems to the Soc Libs. So it is clear that society prefers the Fed Dems to the Soc Libs. Similarly, the workers and the retirees prefer the Enviro-Greens to the Fed Dems. Thus, society prefers Enviro-Greens to the Fed Dems and, by transitivity, prefers the Enviro-Greens to the Soc Libs as well.

But this analysis is flawed. The Enviro-Greens are supposedly Pcoria's single preferred party, but two-thirds of Pcoria – students and retirees – would rather see the Soc Libs in power. Thus, Pcoria prefers Enviro-Greens to the Fed Dems, Fed Dems to the Soc Libs, and Soc Libs to the Enviro-Greens as well. Even though each individual member of society has transitive preferences, the preferences of Pcoria as a whole are circular.

In this sense, it is not always meaningful to speak of what a society "wants" or a society "prefers." If each of the three Pcorian political parties has a starkly different set of health policies, who is to say which option is best for Pcoria?

15.2   The health policy trilemma

Arrow's impossibility theorem says it does not make sense to speak of an "optimal" health policy for a country because societies do not always have a set of preferences that can be optimized in the traditional sense. Nevertheless, political decisions do occur and various

---

1 Interested students can find an elegant proof in Sen (1979).

national health policies have emerged. In this book, we assess these policies by analyzing how well they meet three broad goals: health, wealth, and equity. These assessments cannot reveal which nation's health policy, if any, is "optimal," but they allow us to study the tradeoffs inherent in health policy.

The first two goals, health and wealth, are familiar from the Grossman model, where an individual has one fundamental tradeoff to think about: health versus other goods. Societies trying to determine their health policy have to consider not only that tradeoff, but also another set of tradeoffs between different groups within society. Many in society would be willing to sacrifice health or other goods to ensure better outcomes for the worst-off. Achieving fairness or *equity* in health access and outcomes is the third goal of health policy.

Figure 15.1 depicts the three-pronged tradeoff inherent in health policy. In an ideal world, all three goals would be attainable at once: people would live long, healthy lives; pay very little for health care; and this happy state of affairs would be available to everyone in society.

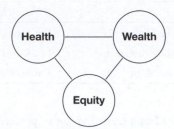

Figure 15.1. *The health policy trilemma.*

In practice, though, it is impossible to have everything. Any attempt by a nation to move closer to one of these three goals necessarily involves a tradeoff that moves that nation further away from some other goal. Any hypothetical policy X that effectively combats adverse selection and increases equity, for example, would either increase costs or lower health at least for some. That there are tradeoffs between these three goals should not be surprising. If all three goals could be met simultaneously, health policy would not be a source of endless political acrimony – nor would it be interesting or important to study.

Furthermore, people disagree about how important each item in Figure 15.1 is. Some countries may value social equity very highly, and be willing to pay more in taxes to achieve it. Others may place a higher premium on health, and be willing to countenance more moral hazard or monopoly pricing to secure it. The variation we see in health policies across the world is not necessarily an indication that some governments are getting it right and others are getting it wrong. Instead, the variation reflects the fact that different nations have different preferences and face different constraints.

The health policy optimization problem is difficult because health care markets suffer from a number of pathologies that we have studied throughout this book. Table 15.2 lists

Artist's conception of a perfect health care system.

Credit: Allen Cox.

Table 15.2. *Pathologies present in health care markets.*

Adverse selection	*Monopolistic suppliers*
Moral hazard	*Health disparities*

the four main pathologies that make the goals in Figure 15.1 harder to achieve. There are ways to combat each pathology, but of course each solution leads to a new set of problems. Often, policy debates come down to the question of which of these pathologies we are more willing to live with.

What follows is an introduction to the most important policy choices that societies must make. Without exception, each policy choice involves a tradeoff between the different items in Figure 15.1 so none is obviously right or obviously wrong. We present these policies as answers to the three broad questions that any national health care system must answer:

- How should insurance markets work?
- How should moral hazard be controlled in public insurance?
- How should health care provider markets (like the markets for hospital services, pharmaceuticals, and physicians) be regulated?

While each country has its own unique system, most developed countries have settled on one of three broad approaches to health policy, which we call the *Beveridge, Bismarck,* and *American models.* In Chapters 16, 17, and 18, we explore each model in detail and see how various countries answer these questions in different ways.

15.3   How should health insurance markets work?

In Chapters 8, 9, and 10, we detailed the problem of adverse selection. Adverse selection arises because of asymmetric information between insurers and their customers, and has the potential to destroy or severely limit private health insurance markets. In addition, even in a well-functioning private market without adverse selection, the poor may struggle to afford health insurance. One of the principal decisions any society makes in shaping its health care system is: How should the government address uninsurance?

This decision, like all the decisions we will discuss in this chapter, entails a fundamental tradeoff. While governments can and do intervene to provide insurance to the uninsured, such interventions create their own problems.

Completely private insurance

The simplest policy option is to maintain completely private health insurance markets. This is the scenario we studied in the basic version of the Rothschild–Stiglitz model. That model predicts that in private markets, only the frailest customers are insured fully and much of the population is underinsured (this is a separating equilibrium). Under certain conditions, a completely private market can unravel completely, leading to uninsurance for everyone – just as in the Akerlof model for used cars.

This option minimizes government involvement in insurance markets, but it results in maximal adverse selection. Taxpayers are happy with their low tax bills, but many citizens cannot buy full insurance. Instead they fret about the medical bills they might rack up if they hurt themselves or develop a life-threatening disease. In practice, no developed country has completely private health insurance markets.

Universal public insurance

At the opposite end of the policy spectrum is *universal public insurance*. As the name would suggest, health insurance under this policy is universal – that is, everyone in a certain population is covered; and public – it is run and administered by the government. Universal public insurance is the policy of many developed countries, including the UK, Canada, and others. Because the government provides everyone with health insurance and pays for almost all medical bills, these systems are known as *single-payer* systems.

This policy option is appealing because it sidesteps adverse selection and ends uninsurance. Figure 15.2 depicts the single-payer system in the Rothschild–Stiglitz model. In a private insurance market, insurance contract α is unsustainable because it will be undercut by a contract like δ that skims off the robust customers. But if the government offers contract α and requires everyone to take it, everyone is fully insured, and there is no additional demand for more insurance.

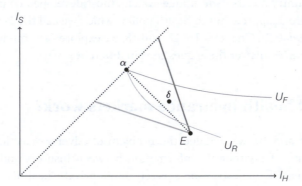

Figure 15.2. *Universal public insurance in the simplified Rothschild–Stiglitz model with only frail and robust citizens. Insurance contract α may be one such contract where everyone receives full insurance. Robust citizens may prefer contract δ, but the government forbids it from being offered, which protects the national insurance plan from unraveling.*

It is possible that some adverse selection could still exist under universal public insurance, but only if a robust Dane (say) decided to take the extreme step of emigrating from Denmark simply because he did not want to contribute his tax money to the public insurance system. This sort of adverse selection may occur every so often among the super-rich, but does not seriously undermine any national insurance system.

Universal public insurance also furthers the goal of equity. Private insurance markets often result in some uninsurance, which can leave some members of society without affordable access to health care if they are diagnosed with cancer or diabetes. Universal public insurance ensures that everyone in a society is covered and can access a similar standard of care. Wealthy people may still receive better treatment at nicer hospitals, but no one goes without coverage in a universal public system.

While this policy effectively combats adverse selection and promotes equity, it does not come without costs. Rather than formally charge all citizens for insurance contracts, most nations with public insurance simply offer it "for free" but increase taxes to fund the insurance program. Higher tax rates are one cost of public insurance but they may not be the sole cost. Most government taxes – like income taxes and sales taxes – distort behavior by discouraging labor and commerce, so the entire economy becomes less efficient as a result.

Some also argue that universal public insurance is more efficient than private insurance markets because of low overhead costs. In private insurance markets, money is spent by private firms competing with each other, advertising, trying to find customers, and trying to avoid sick customers. A universal public system is logistically much simpler, because everyone must sign up for insurance and there is no need to advertise or search for customers. This alternative can thereby reduce non-health-related costs incurred by insurers.

However, public insurance creates another sort of headache for policymakers. Public insurance program administrators must take steps to control moral hazard, which can explode the government budget if left unchecked. With private insurance contracts, it is private insurers that make the difficult and often unpopular choices about what copays to charge, what deductibles to impose, and which inefficient new technologies not to cover. But when insurance becomes public, these agonizing decisions become the responsibility of lawmakers, who must answer to angry voters averse to benefit cuts. We discuss the policymaking dilemma of moral hazard control in detail in Section 15.4.

A variant of this policy option is *selective* universal public insurance. This occurs when universal public insurance is offered to a partial segment of the population, such as military veterans (the Veterans Health Administration in the US) or the elderly (Medicare in the US and *Roken* in Japan). Selective universal public insurance may be particularly effective if adverse selection is singularly acute in one subpopulation.

Compulsory insurance

An alternative policy route to achieving full insurance that does not require the government to serve as an insurer is an insurance mandate. A mandate, which is a legal requirement that everyone in a population purchases an insurance contract, confronts adverse selection by effectively banning it. Even robust customers who would prefer to opt out are legally required to buy into the system. Japan, Germany, and Switzerland are among the countries that feature some sort of compulsory mandate policy.

A mandate can function in a purely private market and does not necessarily involve the government in providing insurance or paying for health care. But a mandate is not a magical solution; it is not free for governments and does not absolve them of all regulation of the market. A mandate can be an expensive option because health insurance itself can be expensive, and many citizens may not be able to afford it even if they are legally bound to do so.

In light of this complication, mandates are either coupled with subsidies to poor households that could not reasonably afford coverage on their own, or paid for with payroll taxes (so that higher-income customers pay proportionately more). These subsidies or taxes can be nearly as expensive as providing universal public insurance in the first place.

A mandate must also be carefully defined or it may be completely ineffective. Suppose a nation imposes a mandate on each citizen to purchase health insurance, but does not specify how full the insurance must be. Under this policy, adverse selection might resurface. Health insurance firms could offer new mini-insurance plans that provide negligible coverage for a small premium. This would be an ideal product for robust customers who do not really want to buy full-fledged health insurance, and an adverse-selection death spiral could result. To prevent this, mandates must specify what characteristics an insurance contract must meet. Making these determinations requires policymakers to become deeply involved in private health insurance markets, and may be as much of a political challenge as designing a universal public system.

An insurance mandate can also induce *risk selection* on the part of insurers. Risk selection is the flipside of adverse selection – it occurs when insurers seek out the healthiest people to insure, leaving the sickest without insurance or on a last-resort public plan. In Chapter 17 we discuss policy responses to address risk selection in the compulsory-insurance systems of Germany and Switzerland.

Employer-sponsored insurance

The final strategy we discuss for combating adverse selection within private insurance markets is an employer-sponsored insurance system. Under such a system, employers are required or encouraged to offer a private insurance contract to all of their employees. Because the typical company has a range of healthy and sick employees, the insurance company loses money on some sick employees but recoups money from the healthy employees.

Rather than legally compelling robust customers to pool with their frail compatriots (as in the case of universal insurance), an employer-sponsored insurance system can induce robust people to voluntarily pool with their frail co-workers. Employer-sponsored plans, not the government, are the primary source of insurance in the US.

As we will see in Chapter 18, job-specific human capital provides a strong incentive for healthy employees with a low risk of illness to pool with high-risk, unhealthy employees. Through a workplace insurance pool, a healthy 55-year-old pays for the higher health care bill of her 55-year-old co-worker who seems healthy but actually suffers from diabetes and high blood pressure. Though she may not want to provide this subsidy to her colleague, it may not be worth finding a new job just to avoid paying it.

Employer-sponsored insurance is a private solution to the adverse selection problem, but it is only a partial solution. Certain populations – like children and retirees – do not generally have jobs and cannot participate in this system. An employer-sponsored insurance system also generates its own problems by distorting labor markets and complicating the process of switching jobs. We discuss this problem, termed *job lock*, in detail in Chapter 18.

Means-tested health insurance

Another insurance option for a country without universal coverage is means-tested insurance, which provides subsidized health care to the poor. Medicaid in the US and Couverture maladie universelle (CMU) complémentaire in France are prominent examples of means-tested insurance. Subsidized insurance is not primarily intended to combat adverse selection, but instead to improve equity by providing health care to those who could not afford it otherwise.

The costs of providing or expanding subsidized health insurance for the poor are basically identical to the costs of expanding public health insurance in other ways: higher tax burdens and greater moral hazard.

15.4   How should moral hazard be controlled?

In a completely private health insurance market, the task of controlling moral hazard falls to private firms. As we discussed in Chapters 11 and 14, insurers have a wealth of tools with which to combat moral hazard: charging coinsurance, copayments, and deductibles; gatekeeping specialty care; and using cost-effectiveness analysis to decide which treatments and procedures not to cover. Each of these tools makes insurance contracts less full, but also reduces costs by reining in moral hazard. Remember that customers in private insurance markets actually want some degree of moral hazard control, because it makes health insurance much more affordable.

In a private market, it is also up to private insurers to compete for customers by offering the optimal mix of insurance coverage and moral hazard control. But when governments enter the insurance business, lawmakers and policymakers assume responsibility for these tough decisions. The experience of many countries has shown that moral hazard control is controversial and politically treacherous.

Figure 15.3 illustrates the dilemma of moral hazard. Suppose a country establishes a new, generous public insurance system. The new government insurance is completely full: it covers every last cent of medical expenditures that its enrollees incur, and is willing to pay for any treatment, no matter how ineffective. The country's citizens do not think twice about visiting the doctor for minor ailments, and always opt for the latest medical technologies to treat their aches and pains. In short, this is a system with moral hazard run amok.

Figure 15.3. *Given moral hazard, the optimal contract is β.*

This full, public insurance contract lies at point α in the figure. Recall that completely full insurance is typically not optimal because moral hazard makes it so expensive. If we assume the nation's populace has typical preferences about risk and health care costs, its indifference curves might look something like those in the figure. In that case, contract α is far from optimal. This new insurance program improves the health of the covered populace, but it comes at a high cost. Financing all these extra checkups and surgeries requires the government to hunt for funding, and the resulting tax increases will be very large.

The government could improve matters by curtailing its insurance program slightly. Perhaps by charging a copay for basic checkups or refusing to pay for cost-ineffective drugs, the government could move its insurance program to β. This would make the insurance somewhat less generous – and make the populace somewhat less healthy – but it would also substantially decrease costs for taxpayers. According to the indifference curves in Figure 15.3, the move from α to β would be a good tradeoff.

Sapelli and Vial (2003) further suggest that countries with mixed public and private health insurance systems may face greater levels of moral hazard than countries with just one type of insurance, as people tend to self-select into the type of insurance that presents them with the lowest costs of care. Accordingly, people with higher incomes will opt for private health insurance (as they have a higher opportunity cost for the time they must spend in public queues), while the poor will opt for public insurance (as rationing by price is more costly for them than rationing by queues).

Of course, real-life policymakers do not have a neatly labeled diagram like Figure 15.3 to use as a guide. Figuring out the exact shape of the moral hazard curve and the relevant indifference curves is difficult, so policymakers must make some educated guesses about how best to manage moral hazard in any public insurance program. The rest of this section outlines the three major tools policymakers have at their disposal to control moral hazard.

Cost-effectiveness analysis

Probably the single most important cost containment technique is cost-effectiveness analysis (CEA). As we discussed in Chapter 14, CEA entails gathering information about treatment options and determining which treatments can produce the most additional health for the least cost. In this context, "health" is usually measured in quality-adjusted life years (QALYs). Based on its performance, each treatment – whether it is a drug, a new kind of surgery, or a new screening technique – is assigned an incremental cost-effectiveness ratio (ICER). An ICER indicates how expensive it is to produce an additional QALY with a treatment compared with the next best treatment.

Once a government has found ICERs for various treatments, it can decline to cover treatments with large ICERs. If a cancer drug has an ICER of $10,000, for example, it can produce extra years of life relatively cheaply and would probably be covered by government insurance. But if a new kind of expensive, open-heart surgery has an ICER of $1,000,000, the government may decline to cover that treatment because it is not a very efficient use of health care dollars.

Some public health insurance programs operate in exactly this way. In the UK, an agency called the National Institute for Clinical Excellence (NICE) evaluates the cost effectiveness of different treatment options and decides which treatments the National Health Service (NHS) will cover. Similar cost effectiveness practices are used when making treatment coverage decisions in Canada, Australia, and other European nations (Neumann et al. 2005).

CEA limits moral hazard by reducing spending on the sort of inefficient, costly treatments that patients would only want if their insurance pays. But CEA also makes the public health insurance contract less full for patients, because some services are no longer covered. As Figure 15.3 shows, this tradeoff can be worthwhile because it makes the entire system cheaper.

But denying coverage for some treatments may be unappealing for political reasons. Suppose a promising new chemotherapy is developed that might alleviate the suffering of – or even extend the lives of – people with otherwise incurable cancers. If a government decides that the regimen is not cost-effective and denies coverage, that decision saves money for taxpayers. But these savings come at the expense of cancer victims whose lives could have been prolonged if the government had approved the drug.

Clearly, any decision to deny life-saving treatment to dying patients in the name of saving money is bound to stir up political controversy. While some governments have embraced CEA, others have reacted by shunning it altogether. US Medicare, for example, is forbidden by law from using CEA in its coverage decisions (Neumann et al. 2005). Medicare covers any medically effective treatment, no matter how expensive. This strategy obviates gut-wrenching decisions about treating sick patients, but it also allows moral hazard to flourish.

Cost-sharing

Another technique for combating moral hazard is cost-sharing through the use of deductibles, coinsurance, and copayments. These are out-of-pocket costs that insured patients pay when they receive health care. Public insurance is sometimes offered without any cost-sharing; in Canada and the UK patients pay nothing for health care at the point of service. This is popular with enrollees but does nothing to control moral hazard, as patients do not have to take the cost of their health care into account at all when demanding treatment.

Other government insurance programs embrace cost-sharing as a way to control moral hazard. The US Medicare system does not cover patient costs fully; as of 2012, Medicare enrollees must pay the first $1,156 dollars of expenses for each hospital visit and the first $140 of outpatient clinic expenses each year. They must also start paying $289 per day once a hospital stay lasts longer than 60 days. This forces enrollees to economize somewhat or purchase supplemental private insurance. Cost-sharing controls moral hazard in a way that is sometimes more politically palatable than CEA. But it also makes health care less accessible for patients.

Gatekeeping and queuing

Yet another strategy for controlling costs and keeping moral hazard in check is gatekeeping. Gatekeeping usually entails a tiered system of doctors whom patients must visit in a specified order. In order to see a specialist, patients must first visit their primary care physician (sometimes called a general practitioner or GP) who certifies the need for a specialist appointment. This keeps costs down by eliminating frivolous appointments and reserving specialists to focus on patients who truly need care.

Gatekeeping in health care systems can regulate the flow of patients when demand outstrips supply. In systems where patients do not face any price for health care, this alternative means of managing demand is crucial. Credit: © Christian Delbert – Fotolia.com.

In addition to gatekeeping, public insurance systems also attempt to control costs by limiting the total number of specialists available. Sometimes, this tactic is explicit; government-run health care systems may simply hire fewer cardiologists or oncologists to work at their clinics and hospitals. Even in countries with private hospitals and doctors, public insurance systems can limit the number of specialists by setting low reimbursement rates for specialist appointments. These low compensation rates discourage doctors from becoming specialists in the first place.

When demand for specialists' services outstrips supply, queues result. Patients must wait their turn, sometimes for several months, if they want to see specialist doctors or undergo elective surgery. In a private system, queues do not exist for long because new doctors enter the market and serve any patients willing to pay for care. But when there is not free entry for doctors (in the case of government-run hospitals) or when the government insurer can set and enforce low prices (in the case of universal public insurance), queues persist. Usually queues are a sign of a market inefficiency. But in the presence of moral hazard, queues might instead be an indication of inflated demand. If so, then limiting the number of specialists might be saving money without sacrificing health. Almost every country with public insurance uses gatekeepers and health care queues to some extent.

To see how gatekeeping and queues work together, imagine an elderly citizen who feels a persistent ache in her knee. The matter is not an emergency, so she must first visit her primary care doctor. From the time she calls to schedule an appointment, she must wait several weeks to get in the door. Once the primary care doctor sees her and recommends a knee replacement, she joins a new queue to consult with a knee replacement specialist. Months later, she visits that doctor and is cleared for surgery. At this point, she enters a third queue and waits several more months until her scheduled surgery date. At no point did she have to pay anything for her surgery, but she had to clear several logistical hurdles, make arrangements with an array of different doctors, and wait nearly a year for care.

The hassle of waiting in line constitutes a non-financial cost that patients must "pay" when they want care. Queues can replace financial cost-sharing arrangements as a way to limit moral hazard. A queue-based system may be more equitable than a cost-sharing system if it means that rich or poor alike must wait in the same line for care. But as with any attempt to contain costs, queuing systems risk provoking political backlash from angry constituents tired of waiting in line. We study gatekeeping and queuing in greater detail in Chapter 16.

Prospective payment and diagnosis-related groups

The traditional method for paying for health care was *retrospective payments*. Such payments were made after services were rendered, and the amount paid depended on how much health care was received. This is the same way that payments are made in other markets: restaurants charge their customers based on how much food they end up ordering, and car mechanics bill based on how many hours of labor were used to fix a vehicle. The fee-for-service model, a prime example of retrospective payment for health care, was very common among health insurance plans in the 1960s and 1970s.

In a fee-for-service system, doctors would not have reason to deny patients any kind of service even if it were astronomically expensive. This system fosters trust between patients and doctors, but creates incentives for physician-induced demand. An alternative system designed to reduce moral hazard is *prospective payments*. Under a prospective payment system, payments are made to doctors or hospitals *before* any health care is actually delivered. Charges are based not on what procedures are performed, but instead on the condition of the patient who is admitted.

A prospective-payments system pays hospitals a fixed amount for treating any heart attack patient, regardless of what expensive techniques they use to treat him or how many hours the surgeons must work. This gives hospitals incentive to economize in their treatment of heart attack patients, because they no longer receive payments for doing extra work or performing extra procedures (Herwartz and Strumann 2012). Because payments are typically based on a patient's diagnosis upon entering the hospital, such a payment scheme is called *diagnosis-related groups* (DRGs).

Since the early 1980s, governments around the world have embraced prospective payment schemes as an effective way to reduce moral hazard and physician-induced demand. But prospective payment systems do not come without a price. The end of fee-for-service has turned some doctor–patient relationships adversarial by making health care providers partly responsible for containing costs.

15.5   How should health care provision be regulated?

In Chapter 6, we discussed the problems of market power in the hospital industry. In a private market with high barriers to entry, hospitals may wield market power as oligopolists. However, increasing the number of competitors does not necessarily lead to a better outcome because it may result in inefficient quality competition and perhaps a medical arms race.

Unlike with typical markets, governments have two opposing concerns in regulating hospital markets. They want to foster competition to prevent oligopolistic pricing, but they also want to eliminate the sort of inefficient competition that leads to the adoption of unnecessary medical technologies. Empirically, increased competitiveness is both negatively and positively correlated with mortality rates in different contexts (Kessler and McClellan 2000; Gowrisankaran and Town 2003).

The third question is thus how best to regulate the provision of health care. Different governments have embraced different approaches to this problem. Some have nationalized their entire health care systems so that hospitals are government-run and physicians are government employees. Others have maintained mostly private provision but retained some safeguards such as anti-trust laws and physician licensure rules.

The different approaches all aim to further the goals of health, wealth, and equity. But as is the case with health insurance, every policy involves trading off one goal for another.

Publicly provided health care

One approach to the problems of market power and inefficient quality competition is to nationalize health care provision. With this approach, hospitals are government-run and financed by taxes, and physicians are employed by the government. Within such a system, hospitals do not "compete" as they would in a private market, so problems of market power and inefficient competition do not arise. Almost all the health care providers in the UK, Canada, and Sweden, for instance, are public.

If hospital market power or inefficient quality competition are sufficiently severe, then nationalizing the hospital industry could reduce the costs of medical care and ideally improve the quality of care. Prices at previously oligopolistic hospitals should decline as long as the public hospitals choose not to exercise their market power. Nationalization also gives governments more control over the provision of care, so they can address underprovision of care more directly.

Similarly, nationalizing the hospital industry also limits inefficient quality competition. Unlike in a private market, hospitals are not competing to attract more patients, since public firms do not claim profits like private ones. As a result, no hospital has incentive to install socially wasteful medical equipment in order to gain more customers.

So in theory, publicly provided health care could offer lower costs and better care than private hospital markets. Empirically, countries with nationalized systems do seem better at controlling health care costs. Their success is likely related to the fact that countries with public hospitals also tend to have single-payer health insurance. In these systems, the government controls both the provision and the payment of health care. As a result, these governments have incentive to maintain low costs (as the payer) and the means to do so (as the provider).

The UK and Sweden, two countries with universal public insurance and public hospitals, devoted only 7–8% of GDP to health care in 2007. By comparison, France and Germany, which have some private providers, spent 11% of their GDP on health care (Or et al. 2010). In America, where private hospitals predominate, health care expenditures topped 15%.

However, the common charge against government-run hospitals is that they offer lower-quality care. Such contentious claims are difficult to substantiate, because quality itself is so difficult to assess. One measure of quality might be life expectancy, but many other factors besides health care determine how long people live. There are countless plausible measures of care quality, such as cancer survival rates, infant mortality rates, and life expectancy of the elderly. Empirically, comparisons of these measures between countries with nationalized hospitals and those with private hospitals are inconclusive (Or et al. 2010).

In addition, the concept of health care quality can include more than just the success rates of surgeries or treatments. It can also include the doctor's bedside manner, the cleanliness of the hospital, and the waiting time for procedures. These inputs may not alter mortality rates or life expectancy, but nonetheless affect people's satisfaction with their health care experiences. Empirically, countries with public hospitals face long queues, which creates long waiting times for their patients.

Previously, we discussed the existence of long queues as a moral hazard control measure, but long waiting times could also be evidence of welfare loss and patient harm. If people who really need care are stuck waiting in line, then the queues are symptomatic of a shortage in the supply of health care. Evidence that people waiting in long queues for care are sometimes willing to pay for quicker care suggests that patients waiting in queues are not always seeking superfluous care. Apparently, queues also restrict access to valuable medical care. We discuss this evidence in greater detail in Chapter 16.

Are long waiting times and other inefficiencies inevitable in public hospital systems? One hypothesis is that systems with public provision are fundamentally less efficient than private markets. Governments are vulnerable to agency problems, because government workers may have less incentive than private workers to ensure the success of their hospital.

Government workers with high job security and no financial stake in improved operations have less incentive than private workers to fix inefficient systems or respond to patient complaints. As a result, a public hospital may be less likely to adopt innovative medical technologies or streamline operations that could reduce long queues. Government-run systems are also vulnerable to corruption and lobbying. If these agency problems are severe, a nationalized system may be more inefficient than the oligopolistic free market it supplants.

Even if a government-run system is transparent and its civil servants work diligently in the public interest, it lacks clear feedback mechanisms to correct it if it is not succeeding. Private hospitals that waste money or fail to please customers will lose business. Public hospitals that waste money or fail to please customers may continue to receive full funding each year, so there is less punishment for operating inefficiently.

In theory, elections can be an opportunity for voters to judge the performance of the government and "fire" the ruling party if it is running the system poorly. But this feedback is noisy because elections are infrequent, voters are not fully informed, and, as the Arrow impossibility theorem suggests, elections cannot fully capture the preferences of society.

Private hospital markets

At the opposite end of the policy spectrum is private provision of health care. For instance, most hospitals in the US, Germany, France, and Japan are privately run. This approach allows for competition among hospitals and preserves the incentives for hospitals to operate efficiently. As a result, long queues are rarely a concern in countries with systems of private provision. Instead, these countries can suffer the dual maladies of too little competition (oligopoly) and too much competition (medical arms race).

In private markets, too little competition leads to market power and the accompanying social loss due to high prices and underprovision. Cognizant of this threat, countries with private hospital markets are usually vigilant about preventing anticompetitive behavior. For example, the US Federal Trade Commission, the German Bundeskartellamt, and the Dutch Nederlandse Mededingingsautoriteit have all moved to block hospital mergers in recent decades. Some countries are more aggressive about blocking mergers than others, but common across all is the goal of limiting market power in hospital markets (US Department of Justice, Federal Trade Commission 2004; Varkevisser and Schut 2009).

Too much competition can also be a problem in hospital markets. In most private markets, "too much" competition is never a worry; firms exit the market until supply and demand equilibrate. But the health care market is different due to information asymmetries between doctors and patients and the ubiquity of insurance. Too much competition can exacerbate inefficient quality competition, lead to a medical arms race, and drastically increase the costs of health care (see Section 6.3).

In many of the nations with private hospitals, high health care expenditures have become a political issue, especially since public insurance pays for much or all of the rising costs. In response, some governments have enacted reforms to restrain competition and avert wasteful spending.

For example, state governments within the US have passed Certificate of Need (CON) laws that restrict the entry and expansion of hospitals. If a new hospital wants to establish itself or an existing one wants to add a new wing, it must first submit justification to a state agency, which reviews the application to determine whether the addition furthers the goals of the community. CON laws are intended to reduce inefficient quality competition and curb the medical arms race. If CON laws are successful, areas with stricter limits on hospital expansion should have lower health care expenditures without sacrificing patient outcomes. Empirical studies have found ambiguous effects (Popescu et al. 2006; DiSesa et al. 2006; Ho 2004).

Another concern with private hospital markets is that some populations – like the poor and uninsured – lack access to care. One policy is to give tax breaks to nonprofit hospitals, which historically have attended to the poor and the vulnerable. The US, France, and Germany all have robust nonprofit hospital sectors. To the degree that nonprofits do in fact offer more charity care and charge lower prices, their presence promotes equity.

Additionally, virtually all developed countries requires that hospitals provide emergency care to incoming patients regardless of their citizenship status or their ability to pay. These requirements, encoded in "last resort" laws, ensure everyone has access to ambulatory services and a minimum level of care. But once patients are stabilized, the legal obligation typically ends and the hospital is free to discharge them.

Last resort laws promote equity by ensuring a minimum level of care for everyone, but they also impose costs. In the US, for instance, hospitals are not reimbursed by

Table 15.3. *The benefits and costs of various national health policies.*

Policy option	Examples	Benefit	Cost
How do health insurance markets work?			
Completely private insurance	-	No government involvement in insurance markets; lower **taxes**	Susceptible to **adverse selection**; reduces **equity**
Private insurance mandate	US, Japan, Switzerland	Can reduce **adverse selection**	Curtails **choice**
Employer-sponsored private insurance	US, Japan, Switzerland	Reduces **adverse selection**	Potential **job lock**; reduces **equity**
Universal public coverage (single payer)	UK, Canada, Sweden, Norway	Eliminates **adverse selection**; promotes **equity**	Potential **moral hazard**; higher **taxes**
Means-tested insurance	Medicaid in the US, Kokuhu in Japan	Promotes **equity**	Potential **moral hazard**; higher **taxes**
How can moral hazard be controlled?			
Cost-sharing (copays or deductibles)	US Medicare, France	Reduces **moral hazard**	Reduces **equity**
Zero cost-sharing for hospital services	UK, Canada	Promotes **equity**	Higher potential **moral hazard**
Cost-effectiveness analysis	NICE in England, Oregon Medicaid Priority List, Canada's Common Drug Review	Reduces **moral hazard**	Restricts **access to health care**
Gatekeeping	England, Canada, Norway, Sweden, US Medicare Advantage	Reduces **moral hazard**	Restricts **access to health care**
How is health care provision regulated?			
Unregulated, private care	-	Removes government from health care	Reduces **equity**; possible unlicensed doctors
Private hospitals with anti-trust law	US	Limits government involvement	Reduces **equity**; potential **medical arms race**
Private care with price controls	Japan, Switzerland	Promotes **equity**	Large government involvement
Government-run hospitals and clinics	England, Sweden, Norway	Promotes **equity**; no **medical arms race**	Large government involvement; higher **taxes**
"Last resort" laws	US	Promotes **equity**	Higher **taxes**

the government for last-resort care. In order to fund it, hospitals must shift these costs onto other patients with insurance, so such laws drive up costs for everyone. Sometimes, this added financial pressure has led hospitals to shut down their emergency wards to evade the burden of providing last resort care. This is an unintended and undesirable consequence of the pursuit for greater equity (Lee 2004).

Government-set prices

Another way to address both the cost and equity problems in private health care markets is the imposition of strict price controls. By setting prices, governments aim to prevent private providers from exercising any market power they may have and to keep health care affordable.

Japan provides a prominent example of a government setting prices for private hospitals and clinics. Korosho, the Ministry of Health, Labor, and Welfare, sets uniform reimbursement schedules for all medical procedures, in negotiation with the Japanese Medical Association. For a given procedure, like an appendectomy or a hip replacement, hospitals receive the same fee regardless of whether the patient is rich or poor and regardless of whether an experienced hospital or a relatively new hospital conducted the surgery.

In theory, such price controls should contain hospital costs, but government-set prices could also induce some perverse incentives. Unless the prices are set properly, the procedures priced below marginal costs may not be offered to patients by their providers, while the most profitable services may be over-offered. In this way, a market with government-set prices can suffer a set of inefficiencies similar to markets with government-run hospitals. We discuss health systems with government-set prices further in Section 17.3.

Table 15.3 lists several policies along with their costs and benefits. We discuss each of these policies more in the next three chapters, which cover the three major types of health systems in the developed world.

15.6   Comparing national health policies

In the next three chapters, we look at three different models for addressing the health policy conundrum:

- **The Beveridge model** (Chapter 16). This model features single-payer insurance, public control of health care provision, and health care available to patients for free. In this model, health care is a good provided by the government and paid for with tax revenue (just like schools or libraries). Equity is a primary consideration of this model, with an emphasis on equal access to care regardless of ability to pay. The Beveridge model is named for Sir William Beveridge, who proposed an outline for the new health care system put into place in the UK after World War II. Today, Canada, Sweden, Australia, and the UK are all prominent examples of Beveridge countries.
- **The Bismarck model** (Chapter 17). This model features universal insurance, but with private insurers playing a major role. The Bismarck model allows substantial private health care provision, but health care services are heavily regulated with price controls. The Bismarck model is named for Otto von Bismarck, who established the first national universal insurance program in Germany in the 1880s. Japan, Germany, France, and Switzerland are major examples of Bismarck countries.

The Bismarck model occupies a middle ground between the Beveridge model and the American model.

- **The American model** (Chapter 18). This model, unique to the US, features private markets in a central role. Insurance markets and hospital markets are dominated by private firms. Universal insurance is not provided or mandated, and a portion of the population is uninsured. In practice, the American health care system also incorporates some major Beveridge and Bismarck elements: Medicare, which provides generous and universal coverage to Americans over age 65, and Medicaid, which provides free or nearly free coverage for the poor. This set of policy choices reflects a political emphasis on individual choice for patients and doctors, but also a concern for equity. Health care reform passed in 2010 will move the American system closer to the Bismarck model, but it will retain many unique characteristics.

As we will see, these nations take starkly different approaches to the fundamental health policy dilemmas of adverse selection, moral hazard, health inequality, and monopolistic competition. No country fits precisely under one model – indeed, every country's policies incorporate ideas from each of the three models in some way – but this typology provides a good way to start thinking about the panoply of national health care systems (Reid 2010).

Health, wealth, and equity outcomes

How best to judge and compare each country's decisions? The simplest possible evaluative tool would be a comparison of per capita health expenditures and resulting health levels (perhaps quantified in terms of a summary measure such as life expectancy or QALYs). These two numbers would serve as a kind of report card for a national health economy: Which country is making the best, most efficient health policy choices?

Figure 15.4 plots health expenditures against life expectancy in 2009 from a sample of developed countries. The figure also plots the best fitting curve through these points. Compared with this curve, the US achieves lower life expectancy than would be predicted

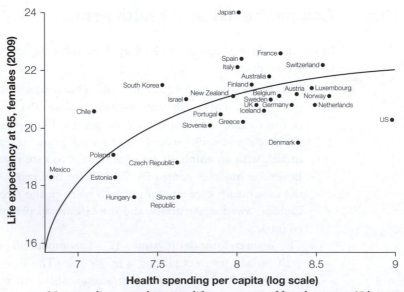

Figure 15.4. *Health expenditures and average life expectancy of females at age 65 by country.*

Source: Data from OECD, Life expectancy at birth, females; and Total expenditure on health per capita. http://www.oecd.org.statistics/.

by its health expenditures, while Japan and Switzerland, for instance, achieve higher life expectancy at a much lower cost.

From this sort of analysis, one might conclude that the US is doing a poor job of stewarding its health care system, while European countries like the UK and France, and East Asian countries like Japan and South Korea, are doing a more satisfactory job. But this analysis is far too simplistic: it assumes both that every country can achieve the same point and furthermore that every country wants to achieve the same point.

There may be several flaws in those assumptions. What if different countries have different inherent levels of health? Or what if people in different countries value health differently? Finally, what if countries differ in how much health inequality exists? If countries differ in any of these ways, then Figure 15.4 is insufficient to render judgment on the effectiveness of health systems in different countries.

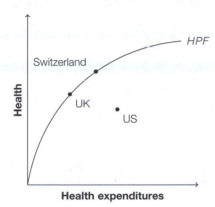

Figure 15.5. *Three health economies.*

Lifestyle differences may be to blame for some of the apparent disparity in Figure 15.5. The average American drives about twice as much each year as the average European. Credit: Photo Disc/Getty Images.

Consider Figure 15.5, a stylized comparison of the health economy in three countries with three different health care policies, the US, the UK, and Switzerland. The curve labeled *HPF* is the health production frontier; it indicates how much health each society can produce with a given amount of spending. Which of these countries is doing the best job optimizing its health economy? As we will see, this type of figure does not contain enough information to answer that question.

Differing inherent levels of health

First, we compare the US with Switzerland and the UK. It seems like Figure 15.5 implies that the US must be mismanaging its health economy, squandering its resources and producing little return. Perhaps the US Medicare system is spending a lot of money on patients in their last days of life, or the uninsured population is neglecting preventative care and incurring massive emergency room bills as a result.

A country that is below its own health production frontier is said to be *productively inefficient* since it could spend less on health care and achieve the same health outcomes, or spend the same on health care and achieve better health outcomes (Garber and Skinner 2008).

But the main problem in interpreting cross-country differences in health expenditures is the same problem we saw in Chapter 13 when interpreting health outcome differences within the US. It is not clear whether all the countries share the same health production frontier (with some countries like the US inefficiently below the frontier) or whether the US is on a completely different HPF from the European countries.

One possibility is that the US and the other countries have different populations with different inherent health states; this would explain how the countries have different HPFs. Americans may prefer fast food while Europeans prefer sit-down meals. Americans are more likely to drive to work, while Europeans may be more likely to bike in the open air. International differences in life expectancy may be explained largely by behavioral, cultural, and lifestyle differences across countries (Michaud et al. 2009).

This argument is depicted in Figure 15.6, where the US sits on a different HPF. In this scenario, the US is doing as well as it can, given its inherent unhealthiness.

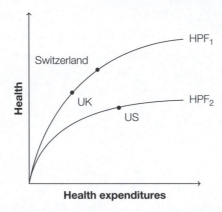

Figure 15.6. *Three health economies, two* HPFs.

Differing preferences for health

Next, let us consider the different positions of Switzerland and the UK. If Figure 15.6 is accurate, then both are situated on their shared HPF, so neither is productively inefficient. Switzerland is spending more money but is also the healthier for it. Which country is doing a better job of managing its health economy?

Even if a country is productively efficient, and hence on its own health production frontier, this fact does not imply that the country is spending the optimal amount of money on health care. It is possible, for example, that the marginal dollar spent on education or parks produces more utility for the population than the marginal dollar spent on health care. Such a country is said to be *allocatively inefficient* since it spends too much on health care relative to other productive activities (Garber and Skinner 2008). Since the country is on its health production frontier, shifting money to other activities will reduce health, but increase the overall welfare of the population. The opposite is also possible – the country on its health production frontier spends too little on health care and too much on other activities.

It may actually be the case that each nation in Figure 15.6 is pursuing its own, optimal course. Just as with the Grossman model, nations must choose how much to invest in health and how much to invest in the home good. If the Swiss care a little bit more about being healthy than the British, then their positions in Figure 15.6 might both be optimal.

Differing health equity

Health inequality may also create an illusion of inefficiency. Countries whose subpopulations vary widely in income levels or in their preferences for unhealthy habits may appear to be productively inefficient on average, even though each individual subpopulation within the country is on the health production frontier.

Figure 15.7 plots the health production frontier of a country consisting of two populations – a poorer population, A, and a richer population, B. We assume, for purposes of illustration, that population A optimally chooses a lower level of health care expenditures and lower optimal health level than population B. Such an assumption could be justified if in terms of the Grossman model, the marginal efficiency of health investment is lower for people with lower income. In Figure 15.7 populations A and B are both on the health production frontier – neither population is productively inefficient in its health care expenditures.

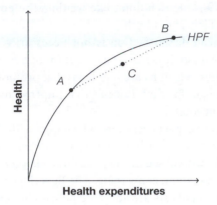

Figure 15.7. *Separate optima for population subgroups.*

Point C shows the aggregate average life expectancy of the entire population (both A and B) plotted against the per person health expenditures of the entire population. Point C lies on the chord connecting points A and B. Since the health production frontier is concave, point C necessarily lies inside the health production frontier. An analysis that ignores the heterogeneity of income within each country will mistakenly conclude that the country as a whole is productively inefficient in its health expenditures, even though no population subgroup within the country is itself productively inefficient.

One further explanation for the apparent productive inefficiency of the US in Figure 15.5 is that its population is more heterogeneous in income and health insurance coverage than other developed countries (Garber and Skinner 2008). Whether or not this is a separate problem that should be addressed in itself, it certainly makes the US look worse in an aggregate efficiency analysis.

15.7   Conclusion

Though health policy can look like a complicated mess, in one sense, at least, it is simple. One of the major themes of this book is that information is a precious commodity and people – patients, doctors, insurers alike – use it to their advantage when they can. In Chapter 9, we have seen that the inability of insurers to accurately observe people's health status can lead to a failure of the market to provide health insurance. In Chapter 11, we have seen that hidden information can lead to the overuse of inefficient services.

While government policy can address some of the problems created by information asymmetries, as we have, it is impossible to solve them all simultaneously. As we discuss in the upcoming chapters, countries that have adopted policies that solve the adverse selection problem face a significant challenge in controlling moral hazard. By contrast, in part because its health policy does not adequately solve the adverse selection problem, the US population has a large number of people without health insurance coverage.

Given all of the difficult tradeoffs inherent in health policy, we should hardly be surprised by the results of a 1999 study that surveyed respondents in Australia, Canada, New Zealand, the UK, and the US. According to the survey, a majority of people in every country was dissatisfied with their country's health care system (Donelan et al. 1999). In the words of Wildavsky (1979), "the rich don't like waiting, the poor don't like high prices, and the middle class complain about both."

This apparent widespread dissatisfaction is not necessarily a sign that policymakers everywhere are doing a bad job. It is maybe a reflection of how entrenched the trilemma is. There are no free lunches in health care – policies that promote equity either cost more or force people to wait longer for care. Policies that improve hospital efficiency result in higher taxes or sacrifice on equity.

It is probably too much to expect everyone to be happy with their health care system – people fundamentally disagree about how the tradeoffs implicit in the trilemma should be navigated. Despite this, we will see in the next three chapters that health policy in the developed world is, to some extent, converging. The Beveridge countries with a large government role in the provision of care are adopting policies aimed at introducing elements of private competition among their public providers. The Bismarck countries, in which the government mandates and heavily regulates the provision of health insurance but allows private provision, are moving to include ideas used in Beveridge systems to control costs. And finally, the US is starting to borrow more elements from Bismarck health care systems.

15.8   Exercises

Comprehension questions

Indicate whether each statement is true or false, and justify your answer. Be sure to state any additional assumptions you may need.

1 If members of a society have transitive preferences, then that society as a whole must also have transitive preferences.
2 The goal of health policy is to maximize health, wealth, and equity.
3 Health systems focused on promoting equity typically have purely private insurance markets.
4 Insurance mandates do little to combat the problem of adverse selection.
5 Cost-sharing is used to combat moral hazard at the expense of equity.
6 Queues can help to equitably reduce moral hazard.

7 Prospective payment systems align the interests of doctors and their patients.

8 There is no such thing as "too much competition" in the private hospital market.

9 A country operating below its own health production frontier is said to be productively inefficient.

10 If a country is productively efficient and hence on its own health production frontier, it is spending the optimal amount of money on health care.

11 If health disparities exist within a country, then it cannot be operating on its health production frontier.

Students can find answers to the comprehension questions and lecturers can access an Instructor Manual with guideline answers to the analytical problems and essay questions at **www.palgrave.com/economics/bht**.

16 THE BEVERIDGE MODEL: NATIONALIZED HEALTH CARE

In the late 1940s, the UK and much of the rest of Europe were recovering from the ravages of World War II. Soldiers were returning from the front lines and igniting a historic baby boom. Aid from the US in the form of the Marshall Plan was helping to rebuild Europe and restore its economic strength. After nearly two decades of worldwide depression and war, Britons finally had reason to feel optimistic.

In the midst of these massive changes, a new government had come to power in the UK. The Labour Party under Prime Minister Clement Atlee based its domestic agenda on an ambitious plan laid out by economist William Beveridge during the war. The plan, titled *Report of the Inter-Departmental Committee on Social Insurance and Allied Services*, was an outline for a new social compact defined by shared sacrifice and a notion of solidarity between countrymen (Abel-Smith 1992). The health care system that would eventually grow out of the plan had three defining features:

- *Universal, single-payer insurance:* All citizens automatically receive insurance coverage through the government. This insurance is financed though taxes rather than premiums, so no one has to pay anything to enroll.
- *Public health care provision:* The government runs hospitals and clinics, and hires doctors, nurses, and managers to provide care. The government determines when and where hospitals will be built or expanded, and decides how many doctors and specialists will be working at each hospital.
- *Free care:* Care is provided for free (or at very low cost) at government hospitals and clinics. Patients are not responsible for any premiums, deductibles, or coinsurance. There are exceptions for certain kinds of care (typically prescription drugs, eye care, and dentistry).

After a long political debate about reshaping the entire British health system, Parliament passed the National Health Services Bill in 1946, which transformed health care delivery in the UK. Over 1,500 hospitals owned by private organizations, religious institutions, and local governments were nationalized by the legislation, and longstanding local insurance boards were abolished. The bill also established the National Health Service (NHS), a new hospital system based on tenets of the Beveridge Report that would begin operations on July 5, 1948.

Although initially opposed by doctors who wanted to maintain professional autonomy and patients wary of government meddling, the NHS soon became a popular institution. The NHS blueprint, with some variations, was later adopted by many countries in the British Commonwealth (Canada, Australia, New Zealand) and Scandinavia (Sweden, Norway, Denmark) (Klein 2010). In Section 16.1 we describe several of the largest Beveridge systems in greater detail.

In the *Beveridge model*, health care is a good provided by the government and paid for with tax revenue, just like schools or libraries. A key priority of the Beveridge model is eliminating price rationing of health care. In 1944, future British Ministry of Health official Sir John Hawton described the proposed NHS system as one where patients would receive services irrespective of class: "their getting [health care services] shall not depend on whether they can pay for them, or any other factor irrelevant to the real need – the real need being to bring the country's full resources to bear on reducing ill-health and promoting good health in all its citizens" (Klein 2010). Indeed, the 2009 NHS Constitution affirms the guiding principle that health care access "is based on clinical need, not an individual's ability to pay" (National Health Service 2012).

Instead, the government provides health care for free at the point of service to all eligible citizens or residents. The Beveridge model aims to eliminate most or all of the situations where a patient must choose between her money and her health. This is a worthy goal, but it creates its own challenge: How should scarce health care resources be allocated without price rationing?

16.1   A brief tour of the Beveridge world

In the years since 1948, many nations around the world have remade their health care systems in the Beveridge mold. These countries do not have identical health care systems, and none of these systems, not even the UK's, represents a perfect embodiment of Beveridge's vision. Still, these systems are similar in that they all feature nationwide single-payer insurance, public providers, and (largely) free care. They all make use of gatekeepers and have queues to allocate care. The systems tend to differ on two major points: how they allow for competition and how they try to contain costs. Below, we describe four of the largest Beveridge systems.

The UK

The health care system in the UK has changed somewhat since 1948, but the basic outline of the system conforms to the Beveridge model. Patients receive free care at government hospitals and clinics run by the National Health Service (NHS). Private hospitals and clinics do exist, but they fill mostly a niche role in the overall health care system. Hospital staff and doctors are salaried employees working directly for the government, while most general practitioners (GPs) are contractors who work in both the public and private systems. Each country within the UK has its own locally administered program with its own rules; for most of this chapter we focus on the largest system: the NHS in England.

Almost every type of health care is provided for free – exceptions include prescription drugs, dentistry, and eye care – and the system is financed primarily through tax receipts. Queuing is a major aspect of the British health care system, although wait times have declined in recent years as the NHS has taken steps to introduce elements of competition into its hospital system. The NHS also includes an agency called the National Institute for Clinical Excellence (NICE) that uses cost-effectiveness analysis to make recommendations to the NHS about which new medicines and procedures are worth covering (Bodenheimer and Grumbach 2009).

Sweden

As with the health care system in the UK, the government plays a dominant role in the Swedish health care system. While there is a small parallel system of private health care providers, the national and regional governments finance the vast bulk of medical expenditures in Sweden – by some estimates about 97% of all health care dollars (Glenngard et al. 2005). Sweden is divided into 20 county councils, each of which maintains the primary responsibility for financing and administering the regional health care systems. The county councils have the authority to collect income taxes, and in fact finance about 70% of government health care expenditures, with the national government financing the remainder (Harrison and Calltorp 2000; Fotaki 2007).

Hospitals are mostly government-run and doctors are mostly employed by the government. While there are some private providers, they are required to contract with the county councils, which regulate the prices private providers can charge and what services they can offer.

Patients face modest cost-sharing requirements. For instance, there is an annual deductible for prescription medication of about $250. There are also small copayments for doctor visits and hospitalizations, but the annual deductible is low for these services – only about $100. National boards such as the Swedish Council on Technology Assessment in Health Care and the Dental and Pharmaceutical Benefits Board make recommendations about the coverage of new drugs and medical devices based in part on cost-effectiveness studies to county councils. The councils in turn make decisions about coverage of the new technologies and reimbursements to providers on the basis of the recommendations.

Australia

The Australian health care system features a national hospital and provider network called Medicare (it shares the same name with both the American insurance program and the Canadian health system). Australian patients can receive free care from Medicare hospitals and doctors, which are financed with taxpayer funds.

Unlike the UK's NHS, Australian Medicare coexists with a robust private hospital sector. When patients are admitted to a hospital they choose whether to be treated by Medicare (for free) or by private doctors (for a fee). Increasingly, these sectors are distinguished by how much new technology they adopt, because Medicare is more cautious about installing new expensive technologies like MRI machines (Peabody et al. 1996; Raftery 2010)

Canada

The Canadian health care system is organized around the government insurance plan, also called Medicare. While there are federal laws mandating minimum standards of care, Medicare is largely administered by the 13 provincial and territorial governments. Traditionally, the provincial Medicare systems set an operating budget for each hospital, decide reimbursement rates for physicians working outside hospitals, and set prices for drugs.

The Canadian Health Act requires each province's Medicare program to provide most types of care for free, except dental care and drugs. Nevertheless, each province has set up its own pharmaceutical insurance program. In some provinces it is universal, while in others it is only available to certain groups like the elderly or the low-income. Canada is not quite a traditional Beveridge system because hospitals and doctors are nominally private, nonprofit institutions. But because their budgets are set entirely by the government, they effectively act as public enterprises (Grootendorst 2002; Detsky and Naylor 2003; McMahon et al. 2006).

16.2   Rationing health care without prices

Scarce resources – like gasoline, tickets to a crucial football match, apartments in a fancy neighborhood, or health care – are not plentiful enough for everyone to have as much as they want. Every economy faces two fundamental questions: How much of a good should be produced, and who should get it?

Private markets use prices to answer these questions. Scarce resources go to those willing and able to pay the most for them. This is known as *price rationing*. Price is a sieve for differentiating people who really value a good and those who do not. Market failures can distort the results of private markets, but at least the prices help the market allocate resources somewhat efficiently.

But the nature of price rationing is that the rich wield an advantage over the poor. For certain goods like concert tickets, designer jeans, and private yachts, this is largely uncontroversial. Such luxury goods provide incentives for people to work and earn money. However, for other goods such as education and basic dietary needs, market outcomes in which the poor remain uneducated and hungry – in part, because they might perhaps choose to spend their limited resources on other things – are broadly seen as unacceptable. Public schools and food stamp programs ensure that everyone has a basic access to both. Goods with this property are known as *merit goods*.

Health care is treated as a merit good in developed nations. For example, there exist public insurance programs to provide care for the elderly and indigent in every developed nation. But the Beveridge model goes further and organizes health policy around the idea that all citizens should have equal access to health care, regardless of their personal wealth.

The Beveridge model is designed to eliminate price rationing by making health care available to everyone at no cost. But no health system can magically make health care "free." Someone must pay for alcohol swabs, medical machinery, hospital beds, and physicians' time. Beveridge countries typically finance health care through general taxation rather than patient fees. Thus, although health care is not free, basic health services are equally accessible to rich and poor alike. In most cases, at least some residual price rationing still exists; patients in both the UK and Canada pay out of pocket for prescription drugs and dental care, for example.

A system dedicated to avoiding prices faces a difficult challenge in deciding how much health care should be produced and who should get it. The notable characteristics of health care systems in Beveridge countries – queues, rationing, and initiatives to promote competition – all represent attempts to meet that challenge.

16.3   Queuing

Suppose a public hospital is opening up a new cardiology department. After considering the size of the town, the prevalence of heart conditions in the population, and the cost of employing a new doctor, the government decides to staff two cardiologists at the hospital. These two cardiologists can only see so many patients per day, so it is possible that demand will outstrip supply.

In a system where the price of care is allowed to float, the out-of-pocket price of health care will increase to reduce demand. Simultaneously, the wages of providers in the market could increase to attract the entry of more suppliers. These equilibrating forces will continue until supply and demand are equated. As a result, health systems with floating prices and open labor markets tend not to exhibit queues.

However, in Beveridge countries, neither of these equilibrating forces are allowed to operate freely. Price rationing is not permitted as a matter of principle, so out-of-pocket prices are constrained to zero. Also, the salaries of new doctors are limited by fixed budgets. These restrictions promote the goals of equity and cost containment, but they prevent supply and demand from equilibrating. When there are only a few doctors but many patients, queues expand and patient waiting times – the time between referral and appointment – can reach months or even years.

In March 1990, the median waiting time for inpatients in the English NHS was five months. Over 20% of patients had waiting times of longer than a year (Department of Health 2011). Waiting times have declined dramatically in recent years, at least in part due to policy changes designed to reduce queues, but queues remain a concern in Beveridge countries. A 2001 phone survey revealed that 38% of respondents in the UK, 27% in Canada, and 23% in Australia had been waiting more than four months for treatment (Blendon et al. 2002). In 2010, the median waiting time for Canadian patients was over two months (Barua et al. 2010).

The effect of these waiting times on long-term health is unclear, because research on the topic is scarce. Two studies on hip fracture surgery found that longer waiting times in England and Canada did not increase surgery-related mortality. But the studies did not examine longer-term outcomes such as life expectancy or quality of life (Hamilton and Bramley-Harker 1999; Hamilton et al. 2000).

One reason why long waiting times might not adversely affect health is that doctors triage the most urgently ill patients to be treated first. For example, in 2010, waiting times were over six weeks for elective cardiac surgery but less than one week for urgent cardiac surgery. Similarly, patients needing orthopedic surgery waited much longer than those needing cancer care (Barua et al. 2010).

Even if long waiting times do not directly kill patients, they can still make patients very unhappy and prolong painful conditions. In the 1990s, as queue lengths grew and attracted more scrutiny from the press, satisfaction with the English NHS plummeted. In every Beveridge country, queue lengths remain a contentious political issue.

Pros and cons of queues

Queues are usually perceived negatively, but they may serve some desirable social purposes. Queues promote social solidarity by equitably distributing medical care when the budget is finite. Rather than allocating care based on the ability to pay, queues allocate care based on the patient's spot in line.

In addition, queues can serve as a means of limiting moral hazard. Long waiting times may deter patients indifferent between treatment and home-care. These patients may opt not to join long lists for surgeries, or once they are on the list, drop out during the lengthy wait (Cullis and Jones 1986). For example, a mail survey of 757 people on a waiting list for orthopedic surgery at a large British general hospital revealed 17% no longer wanted the surgery, while 9% had moved away, and 5% had died. Another 9% had already received treatment; only 48% of people on the waiting list still actually wanted treatment (Donaldson et al. 1984).

This is evidence of the rationing power of long waiting times. Moreover, if the patients who dropped out of the queue were ones for whom surgery was not that valuable in the first place, the long queue saved money without sacrificing much patient health.

On the other hand, long waiting times harm people for whom care is extremely valuable. These patients suffer prolonged pain as they wait weeks or months for treatment. During the wait, they also risk developing new conditions that render the intended surgery futile. Perhaps the 52% of patients who dropped out of the orthopedic surgery queue needed surgery originally. But during their wait, their health deteriorated to a point where they could no longer be helped. But had the queue been shorter, they would have received surgery earlier and possibly avoided the subsequent decline in health.

Thus, long queues may be an effective means of limiting moral hazard, but they can also be symptomatic of insufficient supply. We next introduce a simple model of queuing to illustrate the tradeoffs implicit in reducing queues. Later we discuss actual efforts by Beveridge countries to reduce waiting times.

Optimal queue length

Consider a country with an iconic Beveridge system – all health care is publicly provided and publicly financed, and medical care is free at the point of service to all citizens. Suppose one hospital's orthopedic department has a long waiting list for knee replacements. Right now, the queue has eight patients waiting to be seen by the single orthopedic surgeon on staff (see Figure 16.1).

Figure 16.1. *A basic queue with no price rationing. For patients labeled either* U *or* U_p, *treatment would be useful; they would receive substantial health benefits. But for patients labeled* W, *treatment would be wasteful, since cheaper alternatives could deliver comparable outcomes.*

The patients are not all the same. All eight of them have arthritic knees and feel pain when they walk, but some are in more pain than others. Those in extreme pain would benefit substantially from knee replacement surgery to replace the painful arthritic joint with one made of zirconium and polyethylene. But patients in less pain could ease their knee problems with a cheaper regimen of physical therapy or steroid injections. For this latter group, the marginal benefit of costly knee replacement over other less expensive treatments is low.

Figure 16.1 labels patients in the waiting list for whom surgery would be useful as U and patients for whom knee replacement surgery would be wasteful as W. Patients labeled U_p also receive high benefit from surgery, but are poor and would not be able to afford knee replacement surgery if they had to pay for the treatment themselves.

Patients are treated on a first-come, first-served basis. In our example, the surgeon sees a low-benefit W-patient before several high-benefit U-patients. This inefficiency arises because knee replacements are free for everyone. Patients for whom care is only marginally valuable nevertheless join waiting lists, since they do not fully internalize the costs of surgery. They receive a small benefit, one that justifies the pain of having their knee sliced open and the opportunity costs of their hospital stay. But the benefits do not justify the financial costs of the treatment shouldered by the government.

Of course, the threat of moral hazard is present in all markets with insurance, but it may be particularly severe in countries with Beveridge systems, because they lack price rationing. Long queues may be the result of excess demand from moral hazard when the price of care to the consumer is zero.

Suppose instead that patients had to pay an out-of-pocket fee θ for the knee replacement. This copayment covers only a small portion of the overall surgery cost but is greater than zero. θ is small compared with the benefit for U-patients who are in extreme pain. But the fee might dissuade patients for whom knee replacement surgery is only slightly better than physical therapy or steroid injections.

Figure 16.2 shows the effects of price rationing. Those for whom surgery would be wasteful, the W-patients, exit the queue, leaving just those for whom surgery would be useful, the U-patients. Thus, price rationing can reduce the number of wasteful surgeries conducted and ensure that only people who really needed knee replacement surgery received care sooner (Felder 2008; Gravelle and Siciliani 2008b).

Figure 16.2. *Price rationing.*

However, Figure 16.2 also reveals that price rationing can deprive low-income people of valuable care. In our example, charging the copayment also dislodged U_p patients from the queue, not because the surgery was worthless to them, but because θ may have been too expensive to pay. Price rationing undermines solidarity, a core tenet in Beveridge countries, which is why price rationing is used sparingly. This choice means that one potent method for reducing queues is unavailable.

An empirical question remains about the composition of queues. Figure 16.1 displayed a hypothetical queue with a mix of U-patients and W-patients. But it may instead be that patients in the queue are all type U.

This could happen if the health system employs effective *gatekeepers* – GPs who screen patients and decide whether to refer them to specialists (Forrest 2003). In the case of knee pain, the GPs order diagnostic imaging to assess the extent of arthritic degeneration. Ideally, the GPs could distinguish the U-patients from the W-patients on the basis of X-rays, and prevent W-patients from clogging the queues by declining to recommend them for surgery (Figure 16.3).

Figure 16.3. *Hypothetical queue in a health system with perfect gatekeeping.*

If GPs can perfectly distinguish between U- and W-patients, persistent queues would suggest an inefficient shortage in the supply of providers. People in need of care are being forced to wait, so the government should hire more orthopedic surgeons to treat them.

However, gatekeeping is never perfect. Diagnostic tools are imprecise, so some W-patients may appear to be good candidates for surgery, even though in reality they are not. Moreover, ailing patients may insist on what they believe is the best care and pressure their GPs to refer them for surgery.

Another hypothesis offered by Lindsay and Feigenbaum (1984) is that people's demand for treatment can decay over time. In our example, patients may join the end of the queue truly needing a knee replacement. But as they wait, exercise and weight loss may improve their knee function, or they acclimate to the pain of their condition. In either case, the benefit from knee replacement surgery has fallen, so the previously U-patients have become W-patients. This second hypothesis suggests that queues will contain W-patients, even with effective gatekeeping and minimal moral hazard.

Thus, the optimal length of queues is partly determined by the effectiveness of gatekeepers. If gatekeeping is perfectly effective, then all patients referred for surgery should receive prompt treatment. In this case, any persistence of long waiting times indicates that there are insufficient providers delivering valuable medical care. The government should invest more resources in hospital beds and surgeons so that waiting times are minimal.

However, if gatekeeping cannot perfectly distinguish between patient types – due to either asymmetric information or demand decay – then long waiting times are not necessarily a sign of system malfunctioning. Current providers may be conducting the efficient number of procedures. But the allocation of their services is inefficient because some treatment goes to low-benefit W-patients instead of high-benefit U-patients. In this case, the optimal queue length depends on the tradeoff between wasteful spending on W-patients and delayed care for U-patients. Reducing queue length improves access for U-patients at the cost of wasting more money on the W-patients.

Estimates of the welfare loss from queuing

Various strategies have been used to estimate the disutility from waiting times for non-urgent surgeries. Propper (1990, 1995b) asks English patients how much they would be willing to pay, hypothetically, for immediate treatment compared with waiting in a queue. She estimates a month's reduction in waiting times to be worth about £50 in 1991 terms (about $80). Using a slightly different hypothetical question, Johannesson et al. (1998) estimate that Swedish patients value a month's reduction in waiting times at about $160.

Another way to estimate the value of reduced waiting times is to observe the decisions of English patients to bypass public queues by paying for private care. Using this method, Cullis and Jones (1986) calculate that the value of a month's reduction in waiting times in the NHS was about £115 in 1986 prices. The estimates are higher than Propper's perhaps because they also capture quality differences between private and public care. If private care is perceived as better, then the value of private care includes not just shorter waits but also higher-quality treatment.

A third method involves studying the tradeoff patients make between waiting times and travel distance in choosing hospitals. If the psychological costs of waiting are high, then we would expect patients to be willing to travel to distant hospitals to reduce their

Not all queues are necessarily inefficient. Sometimes queues arise naturally in the private sector as ways to reduce labor costs (banks), smooth out manufacturing demand (iPhone waitlists), or even advertise a business ("world famous" restaurants with lines out the door). They also arise in private health care systems.
Credit: © cbsva – Fotolia.com.

wait. Monstad et al. (2006) studies Norwegian hip replacement patients and finds that though queue length affects patients' choice of hospitals, travel distance matters more. Sivey (2012) studies cataract patients in England and finds the same result: patients seem willing to accept longer waiting times in exchange for shorter journeys.

This difference in weights placed on waiting times and travel times may reflect the difference in opportunity costs. Driving even an extra hour to hospital means an hour not spent collecting wages, reading, or watching television. However, an additional week in a patient queue does not preempt any of these activities (Culyer and Cullis 1976).

Socioeconomic status and queuing

One of the key metrics of the performance of any health care system is how difficult it is for people at the low end of the socioeconomic status (SES) spectrum to obtain appropriate and timely care. Indeed, one of the main reasons for the enduring popularity of Beveridge systems in countries that have adopted them is that such systems are widely seen to promote equal access to care to people of all SES levels (though perhaps not equal health care outcomes – see Chapter 4). Long queues by their nature reduce ready access to health care, and if poorer or less well-educated people are forced to wait longer, then queues reduce equity and threaten social solidarity.

The empirical evidence about queue length in the UK suggests that, at least for elective surgeries, less well-educated people and poorer people do in fact wait longer. For instance, Laudicella et al. (2012) finds that within the NHS, well-educated patients wait about 9% to 14% less than poorly-educated patients. Their results suggest that this increased waiting does not happen because better-educated patients select different hospitals to attend. Rather, they argue that these waiting-time differences arise after patients have picked or been assigned a hospital. Similarly, Propper et al. (2005) find better-educated arthritis patients receive more actual care than do less well-educated arthritis patients.

Shorter waiting times for high SES patients are a common feature throughout Europe for non-emergency procedures in both Beveridge- and Bismark-style systems (though waiting times tend to be shorter in the latter systems). In an analysis of nationally representative data from nine European countries, Siciliani and Verzulli (2009) find that for non-emergent surgeries, highly educated patients wait 48% less in Sweden and 66% less in Denmark. They find similar reductions in waiting times for better-educated patients seeking specialist consultations.

In Norway, patients seeking elective medical procedures (that is, patients who are not facing an imminent emergency) are assigned into priority groups on the basis of their medical diagnosis. Age, sex, and socioeconomic status are not explicit parts of the algorithm to assign patient priority, but Carlsen and Kaarboe (2010a) find that women and older patients are more likely to fall into a low-priority group, and hence wait longer for care. In a separate study, Carlsen and Kaarboe (2010b) find longer waiting times for less well-educated patients seeking elective care or outpatient care, though they find no income differences in waiting times.

Queue-reduction policies

Widespread dissatisfaction with long waiting times has motivated governments to try to shorten queues. During one period between 1992 and 1996, England, Norway, Sweden,

Denmark, and New Zealand all promulgated target waiting times for at least some subset of patients. To reach these targets, the countries adopted a variety of different queue-reduction policies (Hanning 1996; Siciliani and Hurst 2005).

One set of policies focuses on reducing the demand for care. For example, gatekeeping works to reduce queues by controlling the inflow of patients and limiting the demand for specialist services.

A more aggressive gatekeeping strategy entails increasing the eligibility threshold for surgery – only the patients in dire need of surgery receive it. Stricter eligibility thresholds for services reduce demand for queues but restrict access to care and may disgruntle patients who are not cleared for surgery. GPs may also react negatively if they are responsible for turning patients down and managing the resulting backlash. Nonetheless, New Zealand employed this strategy to successfully reduce patient waiting times between 1999 and 2001 (Siciliani and Hurst 2005).

Other strategies focus on expanding the supply of care. Perhaps the most straightforward of these policies is simply to increase the number of hospitals and doctors in the system. More capacity for treating patients would naturally decrease waiting times, as long as the greater availability of resources does not itself increase patient demand (Martin and Smith 1999). England, for example, nearly doubled its total hospital budget in a four-year span between 2001 and 2005 in order to lower waiting times (Willcox et al. 2007).

But constructing new hospitals or expanding existing ones can be time-consuming and expensive. Another way to quickly increase supply is to contract the care of publicly insured patients out to private providers. But this option could induce perverse incentives if there are doctors working simultaneously in public and private hospitals. If their private practice is more lucrative, then doctors may adopt strategies that increase public waiting times to encourage more patients to switch (Iversen 1997; Barros and Olivella 2005). For instance, doctors might work at a more leisurely pace when serving public patients or allow patients to stay longer in hospital beds. Partially as a result of this fear, some countries limit the ability of doctors to work within both systems. Others have even sent their publicly insured patients abroad to hospitals in foreign countries to avoid the conflict of interest for doctors at home (van Ackere and Smith 1999).

Employing more health care providers, either public or private, requires increasing budgets. Other policies seek to improve the productivity of existing providers without increasing expenditures, often by restructuring the way public hospitals and doctors are compensated for care. Traditionally, governments compensated hospitals with fixed budgets, which did not reward hospitals for treating more patients. As a result, hospitals may have incentive to admit as few patients as possible, which leaves patients languishing in queues.

Iversen (1993) outlines another perverse incentive to maintain longer queues. Previously, some governments interpreted long waiting times at hospitals as a sign of distress that signaled a need for more resources. Governments responded by directing more resources to these hospitals. Efficient hospitals with short queues were passed over for additional funding in the next year's budgeting, creating a de facto penalty for treating people expeditiously.

Having recognized this problem, many Beveridge countries now reward hospitals with shorter waiting times by granting them financial bonuses and greater autonomy for hospital administrators (Siciliani and Hurst 2005). But this change creates a new perverse incentive for hospitals to lower waiting times by any means possible. Rather than treating patients more efficiently, these hospitals could simply expel patients from queues for illegitimate reasons. Waiting times would decline but patients would suffer; access to care would be worse than before.

To confront this potential problem, governments have increasingly moved away from fixed budgeting. Instead, alternative compensation plans, such as payment by procedure or by diagnosis, tie hospital revenue to the number of patients treated. Such reforms have been implemented recently by several Beveridge nations including England and Canada (Siciliani and Hurst 2005). If successful, the changes will not only encourage hospitals to treat more patients but also induce improvements in the efficiency of treating each one. We discuss the changing payment plans more in Section 16.5.

Lastly, hospitals can reduce the waiting time for at least some patients by prioritizing patients within the queue. Patients with the highest need or who would benefit the most receive the surgery first, while the more marginal patients are pushed back in line. Just as with gatekeeping, the success of such a strategy hinges on the ability of providers to distinguish between high-need and low-need patients, and triage them appropriately (Gravelle and Siciliani 2008a).

Governments typically adopt a combination of all of these tactics and apply them to different degrees, so isolating the effect of individual policies is difficult (Iversen and Siciliani 2011). Countries have found differing levels of success in reducing waiting times for health care.

England has been particularly successful in reaching its waiting time targets. In March 1990, 21% of inpatients treated in England's NHS suffered waiting times of over a year. By March 2000, that fraction had dropped to under 5%. And by March 2010, under 1% of inpatients treated had waiting times of over six months. Over the same two decades, the median waiting time fell from 19.2 weeks to 4.3 (Department of Health 2011).

Moreover, the reductions in queue lengths seem not to have come at the cost of reduced equity; the decline in public waiting times was shared across populations of differing socioeconomic status (Cooper et al. 2009). There is, however, some concern that English patients with private insurance have advantageous access to care (Dimakou et al. 2008). England's overall success seems to be a combination of dramatically increased public funding, strong emphasis on aggressive targets, greater patient choice of both public and private hospitals, and rewards for more efficient providers (Willcox et al. 2007).

Januleviciute et al. (2010) analyze the effect of a prioritization strategy in Norway. They conclude that while prioritization did successfully reduce waiting times for low priority cases (that is, patients who have conditions that are deemed to be less severely ill, or who are seeking treatments that are cost-ineffective), the strategy actually increased waiting times for higher priority patients. They argue that establishing whether a patient is low or high priority requires referring physicians to transmit detailed information to hospital-based doctors. This additional cost of referring patients to specialists differentially increased the waiting times for high priority patients more than it did for low priority patients.

Meanwhile, in Canada, waiting times have grown substantially in every province between 1993 and 2010. The median waiting time to see a specialist after GP referral for patients nationwide rose from 3.7 weeks in 1993 to 8.9 weeks in 2010. The increase in waiting time was particularly pronounced for certain types of care. For instance, the median wait to see an ophthalmologist was 4.5 weeks in 1993 but 11.7 weeks in 2010. The median wait to see an orthopedic surgeon similarly grew from 8.1 weeks to 17.1 weeks (Barua et al. 2010). These worsening waiting times have drawn continual media attention and remain a pressing political issue (CBC 2012).

16.4   Health technology assessment

Before the 1980s, formal standardized cost-effectiveness analysis (CEA) was not a part of any Beveridge system. Decisions to deny coverage for expensive or ineffective care – if they occurred at all – were haphazard, decentralized, and inconsistent (Sorenson et al. 2008a; Newdick 2007). This changed gradually during the 1990s as more and more national health care systems adopted cost-effectiveness techniques to confront rising costs, often at the urging of health economists (Fuchs 1996). Today, CEA is used in various ways to help make coverage decisions in the large Beveridge model countries: England, Sweden, Australia, and Canada (Sorenson et al. 2008a; Anell 2004; Neumann 2005).

In each country, agencies staffed with full-time analysts have been established to make coverage recommendations and decisions. These agencies use cost–benefit analysis to determine what new technologies and pharmaceuticals to provide under national health plans. Governments will not pay for new technologies and pharmaceuticals that are judged to be too expensive relative to their benefit.

The decision-making procedure is complex and takes into account not only cost-effectiveness but also other criteria like the number of patients affected, the clinical safety of the treatment, and any public health impact. Scores of stakeholders are usually consulted, including academics, doctors, ethicists, and health economists (Sorenson et al. 2008a; Banta et al. 2009). This complex and regimented governmental process is often called **health technology assessment (HTA)** to distinguish it from CEA studies undertaken by researchers. (See Chapter 14 for an introduction to HTA).

Definition	16.1

Health technology assessment (HTA): the practice of evaluating new health technologies for the purpose of deciding what a public insurance plan will cover. Cost-effectiveness is usually a major decision criterion in HTA, but there are other important criteria such as the number of people affected, the clinical safety of the treatment, public health, and equity.

CEA and HTA are not unique to the Beveridge countries; both public and private insurance plans in other countries routinely make similar coverage decisions as new technologies are unveiled. But HTA takes on a larger policy relevance in Beveridge countries because the government pays for and delivers most health care. In Beveridge systems, governments must make the tense decisions about whether to deny coverage of new chemotherapeutic drugs or robotic surgeries that could save the lives of some patients in order to fund more cost-effective care.

Why HTA?

Two main factors motivated the establishment of centralized HTA systems: soaring health care costs and inconsistent HTA implemented at the sub-national level.

Rising health care costs in the 1980s and 1990s, especially for drugs, alerted policymakers to the fact that they could no longer afford to cover pay for all care without raising taxes or curtailing other, non-health-related government functions (Klein 1998; Pearson and Rawlins 2005; Raftery 2010). Policymakers and politicians in many Beveridge systems

Unfortunately, the postcode lottery did not yet exist when Jane Austen was writing her penetrating novels about English society.

Credit: Allen Cox.

slowly became convinced that placing limits on exceedingly expensive care would be an effective way to constrain rising costs.

Another motivation for centralizing HTA decisions was to equalize access to medical technologies for all patients. Traditionally, health technology assessment was conducted at the local level, often without a uniform, regimented process. For instance, up until 2002, each Canadian province maintained its own prescription drug plan and performed its own assessment of new prescription drugs. This system led to needless duplication of basic administrative tasks and created unpopular disparities in drug availability across provincial borders (McMahon et al. 2006; Anis et al. 2001).

Prior to 1999, the HTA process in the UK was even more decentralized. There, local commissioners and hospitals would make decisions on what drugs and procedures to offer, often based only on their local budgetary constraints and perhaps a cursory review of the clinical literature (Newdick 2007).

This decentralized decision-making regime led to inconsistencies in drug availability across regions, and sometimes even within towns or neighborhoods. The British press dubbed this the "postcode lottery," because patients were either granted or denied care depending on where they lived. A patient's street address determined which hospital she could go to, which doctors she could see, and ultimately what care she received (Pearson and Rawlins 2005).

An article in the *Guardian* in 2000 highlighted the case of a Lancashire man who had suffered several heart attacks and whose local hospital declined to perform a new kind of laser heart surgery that may have helped improve blood flow to his heart muscle (Boseley 2000). Only two hospitals in all of the UK performed the procedure at the time. The doctors at one of these hospitals, St Thomas's hospital in London, pronounced him "eminently suitable" for the procedure, but his local health authority denied it. Had he lived in London near St Thomas's, he likely would have received the surgery.

The rise of centralized HTA

Although HTA in its earliest forms dates back to the 1970s, it only became formalized on a national scale in the 1980s and 1990s. First in Sweden and Norway, and then eventually across the Beveridge world, national governments established agencies to oversee and implement HTA (Banta et al. 2009). In some countries these agencies play merely an advisory role, while in others they have the power to deny coverage for new drugs and other technologies.

Both the postcode lottery and the broader issue of rising costs motivated the UK National Health Service to establish the National Institute for Health and Clinical Excellence (NICE) in 1999. NICE was created with the authority to provide guidance on the use of new technologies and drugs. As of 2005, its guidance became binding for all providers in England and Wales; doctors and hospitals must now agree to provide any procedure or drug that NICE approves, and cannot provide procedures or drugs that NICE rejects (Pearson and Rawlins 2005; Sorenson et al. 2008b).

NICE assesses only those technologies likely to have a large budgetary impact. Local care trusts have the authority to make decisions about the drugs and technologies that the NHS does not review. But local providers must still abide by NICE's recommendations. The introduction of NICE has helped to standardize the availability of care across England and Wales and alleviated some of the controversy surrounding the postcode lottery (Morgan et al. 2006).

NICE is probably the world's most prominent HTA agency, but it has counterparts in many Beveridge nations. The Pharmaceutical Benefits Advisory Committee (PBAC) in Australia and the Pharmaceutical Management Agency in New Zealand, like NICE, have the authority to deny coverage for cost-ineffective drugs (Raftery 2010).

Australia in particular has pioneered greater use of HTA. Its drug assessment agency, PBAC, was founded in 1992 in the early days of the HTA revolution. Its earliest HTA efforts date to the 1980s, when the National Health Technology Advisory Panel was formed to study the expensive new technologies – like MRI and bone mineral densitometry – that were being rapidly adopted in Australia's private hospitals (Peabody et al. 1996).

In other countries, HTA agencies only have the power to provide non-binding recommendations to local health authorities which have the ultimate say in what drugs and technologies to cover. In Sweden, the Council for Technology Assessment in Health Care (SBU) evaluates new technologies and screening techniques, while the Pharmaceutical Benefits Board (LFN) uses CEA to make reimbursement decisions about new drugs (Jonsson et al. 2001; Anell 2004). The Canadian Agency for Drugs and Technologies in Health (CADTH) plays a similar role in that country (McMahon et al. 2006). Though non-binding, the recommendations of these central agencies are usually respected by local decision-makers.

Controversy surrounding HTA

HTA agencies are charged with making tough decisions that determine who shall live. Inevitably, their decisions will antagonize some patients and their families. NICE has been criticized for inconsistent decision-making, lack of transparency, and unclear decision criteria (Kmietowicz 2001). In addition, NICE's decisions have been ignored by some local health authorities despite their legally binding nature, which allows some postcode disparities to persist (Sorenson et al. 2008b).

NICE responded to some of this criticism when it released a manual of internal guidelines that it uses to reach internal decisions. These guidelines explicitly invoke CEA, quality-of-life evaluation, and an assumed discount rate of 3.5%. NICE generally considers an intervention to be cost-effective if its incremental cost-effectiveness ratio (ICER) is less than £20,000, but that there "should be increasingly strong reasons" to endorse more expensive treatments with ICERs greater than £30,000 (NICE 2007).

These steps to increase transparency have done little to quell the ongoing conflict about whether HTA should occur at all. The story of the drug Avastin illustrates the political peril of using CEA to deny care. Avastin, a drug introduced by Roche Labs and approved for use in Europe in 2005, was shown to prolong life by an average of six weeks in patients with advanced colorectal cancer. In some cases, it reversed tumor growth enough to allow for potentially life-saving surgery.

But each course of treatment cost £20,800, and NICE ruled in 2010 that the drug was too expensive to be covered by the NHS. In the words of NICE's chief executive, "we have to be confident that the benefits justify the considerable cost of this drug." Patients in England with colorectal cancer can no longer receive Avastin unless they seek care outside the public system. This move drew widespread criticism and accusations that NICE was placing a value on human life (Pidd 2010).

Despite periodic controversies along these lines, most of the nations in the Beveridge world have come to terms with rationing care through HTA. This acceptance is not universal, though. US Medicare, the world's largest public insurance plan by expenditure, is forbidden by law from denying coverage based on CEA (see Chapter 18.)

16.5   Competition in Beveridge systems

Many of the ailments affecting health systems in Beveridge nations do not arise in nations with more competitive, privatized systems like the US. For all the problems of the American system, long queues for health care are rarely a concern. Many Beveridge nations have experimented with introducing competitive elements into both the financing and the provision of health care. These reforms seek to maintain the solidarity goal of the Beveridge model, while striving to better align the incentives of hospitals for the delivery of efficient care.

The reforms have met with resistance and, in some cases, have even been withdrawn. Some have voiced accusations that permitting competition in the market undermines equitable access to care. And some evidence suggests that the initial round of reforms in England reduced health care quality. Nonetheless, nearly every Beveridge country continues to experiment with initiatives to inject competition into the hospital sector, such as allowing private competition and increasing patient choice.

The appeal of competition

The appeal of adding private elements to health care is easiest to understand in the setting of long waiting times. In completely private markets, long queues rarely arise, and if they do, are quickly dissipated, because firms with excess demand can raise prices to equilibrate supply and demand. And even if firms cannot raise prices, perhaps due to a government-imposed price ceiling, new firms can enter the market to fulfill the unmet demand.

However, in public health care systems, patients do not typically pay out of pocket for care, so beleaguered hospitals with long lists of waiting patients lack the ability to raise the price patients face. The government also controls the entry and exit of hospitals, so potential new providers cannot readily enter to reduce queues. Thus, the market-based remedies for long queues are unavailable in countries with public provision.

Hospital competition has the potential to improve patient outcomes by motivating doctors and hospital administrators to provide better care for patients. But in some cases, it could also lead to higher health care prices due to oligopolistic power by provider, which are ultimately borne by taxpayers in Beveridge systems. In Chapter 6, we discussed the mixed empirical evidence on the tradeoff between the benefits of allowing hospital competition and the costs of oligopoly power in health care markets.

Historically, Beveridge systems tightly constricted any competition between hospitals. For example, English patients were usually matched to a hospital according to street address. This was the infamous "postcode lottery." In this setting, patients do not choose their source of care, so public hospitals have no ability to compete for more patients. And under fixed budgets, in which revenue is independent of quantity, public hospitals have no financial incentive to attract more patients in the first place.

Under this system, incumbent hospitals worry neither about the threat of entry by new hospitals nor about any increased efficiency by rivals. Thus, they lack real incentives to develop and achieve efficiency gains that could expedite patient intake. So lack of competition, at least in theory, stunts innovation by hospitals and fosters long waiting times. These potential benefits have motivated the tentative adoption of limited competition in Beveridge countries.

Uneasiness with private markets

If competition is such an appealing feature, why not just permit private health care markets in the first place? In fact, many Beveridge countries do have a parallel private health care system alongside the large government-run and financed public system (Colombo and Tapay 2004). Even in the UK, the birthplace of the Beveridge model, private spending comprised 10.5% of total expenditures in 1980 and the fraction grew to 17.8% in 2000 (OECD 2011).

A small portion of these private expenditures in the UK reflects copayments for services like dental care and drugs not fully covered by the NHS. But the vast majority comes from people with private insurance, paying for care at private hospitals or on a private basis at public hospitals. Queues are typically much shorter or non-existent in the private system, because private hospitals are free to ration by price. Though some of the care includes procedures denied by NICE and not covered by the NHS, the private system sometimes duplicates the care covered by the NHS. So even though the UK embraces the Beveridge model, it has a parallel private health care system (Tuohy et al. 2004).

One theorized benefit to having a parallel private system is that it could alleviate long waiting times if some public demand shifts to the private side. Empirical evidence seems to reject this hypothesis, however. Besley et al. (1998) find that areas in England with more private insurance coverage tended to have longer waiting times, even after accounting for demographic differences. Martin and Smith (1999) find that length of stay in public hospitals was higher in areas with more private facilities.

These findings make sense if the private system siphons resources away from the public sector to treat patients on the private side (Brekke and Sorgard 2007). Or, perhaps, physicians serving in both private and public workplaces concentrate on their more lucrative private practice to the detriment of their public sector work (see Section 16.3). Either way, this is evidence that a parallel private system does not necessarily alleviate queues (Marchand and Schroyen 2005; Oliver 2005).

A parallel private system may also undermine the Beveridge ideal of equal access to care for rich and poor alike. Naturally, private care tends to be purchased by those with higher incomes who are able to pay the private insurance premiums (Propper 2000; Regidor et al. 2008). By signing up for private insurance, these wealthier patients are paying to skip long public queues and gain quicker access to care.

Furthermore, as richer patients increasingly buy private health care and no longer need public hospitals, their political support for government health agencies may wane. They may even support politicians who advocate cuts in the public health system. This would further widen the gap in health care access between the wealthy and the poor (Tuohy et al. 2004).

For these reasons, among others, some Canadian provinces effectively outlawed private insurance by banning private carriers from financing any of the same procedures covered by Canada Medicare (Flood and Archibald 2001). These bans were largely struck down by the Canadian Supreme Court in the 2005 case *Chaoulli v. Quebec*. The province of Quebec responded by allowing limited parallel coverage but also sought to simultaneously lower the appeal of private care by redoubling efforts to cap waiting times for public care (Flood and Thomas 2010).

Even private insurance coverage of care denied by public agencies has met with uneasiness within Beveridge countries. For example, Syrett (2010) argues that English patients who choose to "step out" of the NHS by buying care denied by NICE should be excluded from all future NHS care. According to him, the ability of some to afford care that others cannot violates the tenet of the NHS Constitution that access to health care should be determined by health status and nothing else.

Tuohy et al. (2004) offer one more detrimental effect of allowing the private purchase of care declared cost-ineffective by public agencies. If such care is also more profitable, then medical research firms will steer their work toward these markets, with less motivation to develop cost-effective care. As a result of induced innovation, the development of new treatments available to public patients stalls, while more and more expensive but comparatively ineffective treatments are introduced. Once again, equity is harmed as new health technologies are disproportionately offered to richer patients over poorer ones.

For the most part, Beveridge countries have been wary of both private insurance and private provision, largely because of the potential rise of inequities in health care access (Hunter 2009). One exception is Australia, a Beveridge nation which has actively encouraged enrollment in private health insurance. The Australian government permits private insurers to exist, but it maintains tight regulations on premiums and reimbursements to doctors and hospitals. The government also subsidizes enrollment in private insurance to improve access for the low-income population (Peabody et al. 1996; Tuohy et al. 2004).

However, even in Australia, the coexistence of private and public health systems has proven difficult to maintain. The fraction of the population with private health insurance was 80% in 1970, 50% in 1984, and 30% in 1998 (Hall et al. 1999; Willcox 2001). This unraveling may be evidence of an adverse selection death spiral, which drove the government to increase subsidies and regulations around 1999. These reforms spurred some re-adoption of private insurance, but concerns about adverse selection continue to motivate government policies even today (Paolucci et al. 2008; Hall 2010).

16.6   Injecting competition

Despite the wariness with which private markets for health care are regarded, the benefits of competition are still enticing, especially when waiting times are long. For instance, long waiting times in the UK motivated a major reform in 1991. Since then, other Beveridge nations have also experimented with quasi-private market reforms in both the public financing and the public provision of health care.

NHS internal market

Prior to 1991, hospitals received fixed budgets from the NHS, which were based on their previous year's budget plus growth. This fixed budget system meant hospital administrators could readily predict their overall revenue but had diminished incentive to treat more patients or develop more efficient systems.

In 1991, the ruling Conservative Party in the UK passed a set of reforms to introduce competition between health care suppliers. The reforms introduced regional purchasers responsible for buying basic and elective care from public hospitals for people in their region. The purchasers had limited tax funds from the government, so they had incentive to negotiate cheaper contracts with hospitals. The lower the price, the more hospitals they could afford to contract with and the more patients they could afford to treat. The NHS also rewarded purchasers who achieved shorter waiting times for their constituents.

On the supplier side, hospitals no longer received fixed budgets from the NHS; instead, they needed to win contracts with the purchasers to receive revenue. This buyer–seller relationship between hospitals and government purchasers was known as the NHS internal market.

In order for individual hospitals to win contracts, they needed to offer competitive prices and short queues to the purchasers. Since the 1991 reforms also mandated that these prices be equal to average costs, hospitals needed to reduce costs in order to earn their operating budgets. In theory, these incentives to lower costs arising from competition for contracts could induce improvements in hospital efficiency (Propper 1995a).

However, Propper et al. (2008) argue that one problem with these reforms is that reliable data on health care quality was unavailable. Purchasers could observe each hospital's prices and waiting times but did not know the mortality rates or other relevant clinical information. So the competition between public hospitals revolved around cost and queue length but not quality. Consequently, competition may have motivated hospitals to sacrifice patient outcomes to achieve the cost and waiting time reductions necessary to woo purchasers.

There is evidence that the NHS internal market did not suffer just such a "race to the bottom" as hospitals skimped on quality of care in order to push down costs and waiting time. Propper et al. (2008) find that after the reforms were introduced, areas with greater concentration of hospitals had higher mortality rates than areas with only a few hospitals. Hospitals in closer proximity to one another presumably faced more pressure to compete for purchaser contracts.

Waiting times did decline on average a little more than three weeks per patient at these hospitals. But Propper et al. find that the benefit of reduced queue lengths did not offset the welfare loss from heightened mortality. Valuing each year of life lost at £30,000 and each month of waiting time reduction at £95, they calculate that the costs of reduced life expectancy from heart attacks outweighed the benefits of queue reduction by a ratio of 3 to 1.

Prices, patient choice, and hospital autonomy

The UK's initial experimentation with competition within the NHS ended in 1997, as the Labour Party came into power. The delineation between purchasers and providers remained, but instead of competition, a mindset of cooperative planning was adopted (Ham 1996).

Continued apprehension about high waiting times, however, led to further experimentation. From 2002 to 2008, three large reforms were rolled out that expanded competition much more ambitiously than the internal market of 1991–1997. At the same time, the English NHS authorities increased health care funding and allowed NHS patients to seek treatment at private hospitals.

The three main initiatives of England's second wave of market-based reforms from 2002 to 2008 were:

- moving hospitals away from global budgets to a "payment by results" system;
- giving patients freedom to choose between providers;
- allowing hospital administrators greater autonomy in managing their hospitals.

Crucially, unlike the previous round of reforms, the 2002–2008 reforms set uniform prices for all hospitals with the "payment by results" system. Hospitals, public and private alike, could compete only on quality, not price. This avoids the "race to the bottom" that occurred in 1991–1997. Since prices are uniform, private and public practices are equally lucrative, so doctors are also less likely to neglect public sector patients. And expanding patient choice means hospitals compete for patients directly, rather than through intermediary purchasers.

Cooper et al. (2011) find that hospitals have improved their quality of care since 2006 as a result of the new round of reforms. They find that the reforms saved 300 heart attack patients each year. Since heart attacks comprise only 0.5% of NHS admissions, the total number of lives saved by the reforms could be much greater. Waiting times also declined precipitously over this period, suggesting another benefit from these pro-competitive reforms (Gaynor et al. 2010).

Moving away from global budgets

Historically, hospitals in the Beveridge model received their funding in the form of budgets from the government. These budgets, known as *global budgets*, were typically negotiated between the government and each individual hospital each year based on the previous year's costs adjusted for inflation. In exchange for their funding, public hospitals offered approved services free for patients. But the hospital's budget was fixed and independent of the number of patients actually treated. Since it did not depend on number of patients treated, a system of global budgets was a means of strict cost containment (Raftery et al. 1996). This appeal of global budgets explains some of the motivation for why, for example, most of Canada's hospitals still operate on global budgets. But even Canadian policymakers are considering moving to a different funding system (Sutherland 2011).

Part of what is spurring health systems to move away from global budgets is that the disassociation between revenue and number of patients under global budgets can create some perverse incentives. A hospital close to exhausting its budget may want to slow its rate of patient intake in order to avoid overspending. As a result, that hospital may keep inpatients in beds longer to avoid admitting new patients (Peabody et al. 1996). Moreover, if budgets are based on past expenditures, then inefficient hospitals are actually rewarded for their higher costs. Efficient providers, on the other hand, are effectively punished with lower budgets (Barnum et al. 1995).

In general, a system of hospital budgets may not deliver the proper incentives for providers to improve productivity. The fear of stunting hospital innovation, amplified by the problem of long queue lengths, has motivated many Beveridge nations to move away from global budgets toward operating on an activity-based basis.

England's NHS started its move away from global budgets in 2004 with the rollout of its "payment by results" program. Its bundles of services are known as *health resource groups* (HRGs). Under the HRG payment system, services are typically grouped based on both patient diagnosis and actual procedure, such that the resource costs of each service in the bundle are similar. The hospital receives the price associated with the bundle each time it conducts a procedure within the bundle. Hospitals receive larger payments if the patient requires more complicated or costly procedures.

Charing Cross Hospital in London is part of the Imperial College Healthcare NHS Trust.

An alternative system of payment, known as diagnosis-related groups (DRGs), is used to pay hospitals in the US, Sweden, and other countries. DRGs are often compared to HRGs because, under the DRG payment system, hospitals receive a payment based on the patient's condition at the time of hospital admission. However, unlike HRGs, DRG payments, by and large, are based only on diagnosis and not on what happens during the hospital stay. DRGs are thus described as *prospective*, since the hospital's reimbursement is set once an admitting diagnosis is made, before any procedure is conducted. This seemingly minor distinction fundamentally differentiates the economic incentives created by DRGs and HRGs. We discuss DRGs in greater depth in Chapter 18, but for the rest of this section, we focus on HRGs under England's NHS.

With HRGs, a hospital's income is partly linked to the volume of services provided. This alleviates some of the perverse incentives due to global hospital budgets. Providers that care for more patients receive more revenue, so more productive and lower-cost hospitals earn more than inefficient ones. Even if their greater net revenue cannot be taken home as profits by executives of the public hospitals, the additional funds may be reinvested into medical technologies and supplies that enhance the prestige of the hospital and its administrators. Thus, shifting from global budgets to activity-based compensation may motivate hospitals to improve their efficiency, potentially reducing costs and patient waiting times (Mannion et al. 2008).

But policies to implement HRGs may backfire if the price of each bundle of medical services is set improperly (Street and Maynard 2007). These price bundles determine how much the government reimburses the hospital, and if they are set too low – that is, below marginal cost – then providers may avoid offering underpriced services to avoid losing money. Conversely, providers may *over*-offer medical services with excessively generous remuneration. In either case, the result will be worse patient outcomes.

This fear underlies the importance of accurately setting reimbursement prices for HRGs, but the actual calculation of the rates is not at all straightforward (Hearnden and Tennent 2008). The price for an HRG is calculated based on the average hospital costs across all NHS hospital trusts for providing those procedures over the previous two years. But the tabulation of average costs is difficult, because it is often unclear how costs indirectly related to patient care, such as pharmacist hours and building maintenance, should be included.

In addition, the very categorization of services into HRGs can be problematic. Consider two patients who arrive at a hospital with the same condition and needing the same treatment. One may be much older and in poorer health than the other and consequently require much more attention. If that additional attention is expensive, then folding the treatments of both patients into the same HRG obscures the actual costs of that treatment. To address this concern, the definition of an HRG considers the patient's age and gender in addition to diagnosis and length of hospital stay (Epstein and Mason 2006).

One further concern with HRGs is that hospitals may cut corners to derive extra financial rewards. They may offer patients reduced services in order to lower costs. If so, what appears to be (and is rewarded as) increased efficiency may just be evidence of profiteering hospitals. Thus, moving away from global budgets has the potential to worsen patient outcomes. Despite these concerns, some empirical evidence suggests that England's "payment by results" (PbR) program, which introduced HRG pricing, increased provider efficiency without sacrificing patient health.

Farrar et al. (2009) use the phased roll-out of England's PbR as a natural experiment. The introduction of HRGs led to lower operating costs, while simultaneously the volume of treated patients increased. In-hospital mortality, 30-day post-surgical mortality, and emergency readmission rates did not differ significantly between hospitals with global budgets and those under PbR. Though these measures are imperfect proxies for hospital quality, these results suggest that PbR may have averted some of the negative consequences of shifting hospital reimbursement to activity-based funding.

Opening up patient choice

Moving to a system of payment by results ties hospital revenue to the number of patients seen. However, the policy goal of higher quality hospitals competing to attract patients cannot succeed if patients are not permitted to choose between hospitals.

Recall that in the postcode-lottery era, patients were assigned to a specific hospital based on their street address and, with limited exception, could not switch providers. Under this historical design, a system of HRGs is similar to one with global budgets. Since the number of potential patients is fixed, hospitals only have a limited incentive to improve their efficiency and to compete and gather potential gains from fee-for-service reimbursement.

This link between patient choice and hospital competition is the reason why many Beveridge countries have expanded patient choice of providers. Sweden and Norway liberalized patient choice in the early 2000s, and a similar policy went into effect in England in 2006 after being piloted in a few local areas. Starting in January 2006, GPs under England's NHS were required to offer their patients a choice of at least four different providers whenever referring them for hospital care. And by mid-2008, patients were granted free choice of any NHS provider nationwide (Dixon et al. 2010).

Enabling patient choice has the potential to improve hospital services through competition in several ways. The first is that patient choice may motivate hospitals to perform well in order to protect their reputation or gain prestige. Doctors and hospital staff want to be recognized as the best, and they hope to compete for patients with the hospital from the next town over. Interviews revealed a widespread desire among hospital officials that their hospitals become known as a good place for specific kinds of surgery (Dixon et al. 2010).

Opening up patient choice therefore also improves patient outcomes if the threat of patients switching to better providers motivates hospitals to improve. However, this argument requires that patients can differentiate among providers and make good decisions about their health care (Luft et al. 1990). But it may be that choices about medical care are difficult to make, and Rice (2001) argues that people may not be cognitively equipped for the complexity of those choices.

Scitovsky (1976) draws a comparison of patients choosing their own health care to customers eating at a Chinese restaurant with a long and esoteric dinner menu. Diners unfamiliar with the cuisine may gravitate to the dishes they know and miss out on better-tasting alternatives. If health care is like this Chinese menu, then allowing free patient choice may result in suboptimal decision-making. However, the presence of GPs in Beveridge systems undermines the analogy with the Chinese restaurant. Even in the presence of free patient choice, a medical expert continues to guide patients in choosing the right medical procedure and restrain them from demanding cost-ineffective care.

Patients, therefore, do not necessarily choose *what* medical care to receive, but they do choose *where* to receive that care. This decision too is difficult – how well are patients equipped to assess different hospitals and select the "best" one? They may receive advice from neighbors about treatment from this hospital or that one, but anecdotal evaluations may be easily biased.

To address these concerns, England's NHS established a website called "NHS Choices." The website reports data about each hospital, including mortality rates, history of antibiotic-resistant bacterial infections, food quality, availability of parking, and reviews from previous patients. This information, in theory, could enable patients to make improved decisions about their health care.

The site is effective only if it reflects actual hospital quality. But physician and staff performance itself is difficult to measure. Statistics like mortality rates are noisy, since they reflect not only quality but also the risk types of patients at the hospital (Lilford and Pronovost 2010). For instance providers treating riskier cases may appear to have high mortality rates, even if they have lower preventable deaths than other hospitals. Partially as a result of these worries, NHS Choices also reports broad surveys of hospital staffs about the quality of care at their hospital.

One concern is that richer and better educated people may be better able to take advantage of the choices available to them. For instance, Ringard (2012) studies the outcome of 2001 reforms that opened patient choice of hospitals in Norway. Using a survey of patients, he finds the likelihood of a patient actively choosing a hospital increases with education level. On the other hand, the 2002 London Patient Choice (LPC) project found no relationship between socioeconomic status and patients actively choosing hospitals (Coulter et al. 2005).

If indeed, as evidence from Norway suggests, patient choice is used more by the better-educated, then opening up patient choice may allow inequities in health care access to develop, undermining the Beveridge ideal of equity (Barr et al. 2008). Due to this fear, decisions by England's NHS to expand patient choice have provoked significant rancor (Hunter 2009). While allowing patients to choose their own providers may reduce waiting times and improve hospital quality, its potential negative impact on equity poses a significant tradeoff in Beveridge countries (Fotaki 2007).

Increasing managerial autonomy

Before the 2002–2007 reforms, the English government centrally guided the resource allocations of all public hospitals. They regulated the number of surgeons, number of nurses, number of beds, and even the number of syringes. So individual hospital managers lacked full freedom to improve efficiency, even if they had ideas about how to do so. While patient choice and PbR gave hospitals incentives to improve efficiency, hospital managers could not act on these incentives without greater autonomy. The reforms relaxed government control over the operations of public hospitals. This gave hospital managers the agency to adapt to local market conditions and attract more patients.

To enable even greater innovation, the government allowed high-performing hospitals to become a new type of entity, known as a *Foundation Trust*. Foundation Trusts are given greater autonomy over both their operations and how they distribute their extra revenues. Foundation Trusts are similar to private hospitals, except they are audited by an independent non-governmental agency known as Monitor (Garber 2011).

Empirically, the question remains whether providing public hospitals with private incentives and the autonomy to act based on those incentives improves welfare. Bloom et al. (2010) offer one answer based on an assessment of management quality at public hospitals in the NHS system after reform. They survey doctors and managers about managerial and operational practices at a sample of 100 English hospitals with acute care services. The survey topics ranged from how patients flowed through the hospital's physical space to how employees were chosen for promotion. Based on the responses, they assigned each hospital a subjective management quality score.

Bloom et al. find that hospitals with better management had lower mortality rates for heart attack patients. Furthermore, they find a positive correlation between hospital competition and hospital management quality. The reforms apparently opened a pathway from increased competition to better hospital management and, ultimately, to better patient outcomes.

Despite this encouraging evidence about hospital management, the consequences of the reforms have not been uniformly positive. One chilling example is the case of Mid Staffordshire. In March 2008, the Mid Staffordshire hospital trust was promoted to Foundation Trust status largely on the basis of their low costs. At the time, only a small fraction of hospitals received Foundation Trust status, which is viewed as a mark of distinction.

But a year earlier, the Healthcare Commission, which conducts annual reviews of public hospitals, had noticed evidence that patient mortality rates at Mid Staffordshire were higher than at comparable hospitals. Unsure if the elevated mortality might have been due to a statistical anomaly or bad reporting, the Commission requested further data. Mid Staffordshire claimed that the earlier data was faulty, but the new data they provided only raised more suspicion. In April 2008, only a month after Foundation Trust status was granted, the Healthcare Commission launched a formal investigation into Mid Staffordshire.

The investigation found that mortality rates were indeed higher for emergency patients at the Mid Staffordshire hospital trust. It revealed a dangerously understaffed hospital, where the untrained reception staff sometimes stepped in to triage emergency patients when doctors were unavailable (Healthcare Commission 2009).

Those findings motivated a full public inquiry under Queen's Counsel Robert Francis. The Francis inquiry corroborated the findings of the Healthcare Commission and also unveiled sordid stories of patients being left with soiled clothing and bedding. Family members visiting loved ones in the hospital reportedly had to bathe their relatives and even launder dirty bedsheets at home themselves. Some disabled patients who were unable to feed themselves were brought food but given no assistance in eating it. Other patients reported not being served certain meals entirely. Overall, the Francis inquiry describe a hospital with a skeleton staff and a callous disregard for patients (Francis 2010).

One lesson of the Mid Staffordshire scandal is that a "race to the bottom" may still arise even with unfettered patient choice if quality monitoring is absent or lenient. The NHS had approved the Mid Staffordshire Foundation Trust application based largely on its cost savings without carefully scrutinizing its patient outcomes (Klein 2009). The website NHS Choices now publishes mortality data for all public hospitals in the hope that patients will better hold hospitals accountable (Donnelly 2009).

16.7   Conclusion

Of the three elements of the health policy trilemma we first described in Chapter 15 – health, wealth, and equity – equity has been the element that countries embracing the Beveridge model have focused most intently. While these systems have not eliminated differences in health outcomes between different classes and groups (see Chapter 4), they do promote social solidarity by guaranteeing that citizens need not worry about how rich they are if they fall ill.

However, increasing concerns about long queues and cost control have recently pushed Beveridge nations to adopt policies typical of countries following the Bismarck model. None of these reforms have proceeded without controversy, and the effect of the most recent round of reforms remains a topic of intense research. The rubric for judging these reforms will be how much they improve patient outcomes and control costs without harming equity.

It is likely that this experimentation by Beveridge nations will continue in the years to come. As health care becomes more expensive due to longer life expectancies and newer technologies, the question of allocating health care resources while minimizing price rationing will require continued attention.

As we discuss in the next chapter, countries following the Bismarck model have also experimented by importing some components from the Beveridge model. Notably, both Germany and France recently added voluntary gatekeepers to their health care systems in an effort to control costs. While we have categorized different countries under different models, economic realities – how best to provide high-quality health care for all at a reasonable cost – may be nudging the two models closer together.

16.8   Exercises

Comprehension questions

Indicate whether each statement is true or false, and justify your answer. Be sure to cite evidence from the chapter and state any additional assumptions you may need.

1 There are no out-of-pocket costs (i.e. coinsurance, copayments, premiums, deductibles, etc.) for patients being treated by health providers in the UK, at least for most types of care.
2 Beveridge countries typically feature single-payer insurance.
3 A difference between Canada and most Beveridge countries is that hospitals and doctors in Canada are private, nonprofit entities.
4 Queuing care is never optimal because it increases wait times and provides no concomitant benefit.
5 Price rationing helps remove patients who do not really need treatment from queue lines.
6 In a typical Beveridge system, patients are able to enter queues to see specialists automatically.
7 NICE conducts health technology assessments for the UK, but the NHS is not authorized to use their analyses to make decisions about what health care is actually available.
8 Patients in the UK have historically been unable to choose their health care provider, but recent reforms have created options for patient choice.
9 The NHS internal market require regional purchasers to negotiate contracts with hospitals for efficient patient care.
10 One hundred percent of health expenditures in Beveridge countries is publicly financed.
11 There is great emphasis in the Beveridge model on equitable care for all; therefore it is illegal for private insurance to be sold.

Essay questions

12 In a typical competitive market (not in health care), how does competition work to promote the efficiency of organizations operating in the market? What are the consequences for an organization (and its employees) that fails to operate efficiently in a competitive market? What are the consequences for a hospital that fails to operate efficiently in the NHS internal market? In what ways are the incentives providers face in the NHS system similar to those for private firms in a competitive industry? In what ways are the incentives different?

13 The existence of a parallel private health care system within a broader public Beveridge system provides an opportunity for patients who are unhappy with the service they receive in the public system. Since higher income people are more likely to have the resources to pay for private treatment than lower income people, many favor restricting the parallel private market on equity grounds. Consider a Beveridge country that abuts another country with a large private health care market (Canada would be a great example). How effective can restrictions on a parallel private health care system be in promoting equity in this context? How effective can such restrictions be when such outside private options are not available?

14 Leaving equity issues aside, can the existence of a parallel private market for health care directly harm people who can only afford to get their care from the public system?

15 In the US, public insurers such as Medicare are forbidden by law from applying formal health technology assessments – and in particular, cost-effectiveness analyses – in deciding whether to cover new health technologies, no matter how expensive. By contrast, in Beveridge countries, centralized health technology assessment is required before the public health care system will cover expensive new technologies. What is the nature of the social costs associated with covering a new technology in a Beveridge public health care system? What is the nature of the social costs associated with *not* covering a new technology in such a system? What economic problem does centralized health technology assessment partially address?

Students can find answers to the comprehension questions and lecturers can access an Instructor Manual with guideline answers to the analytical problems and essay questions at **www.palgrave.com/economics/bht**.

17) THE BISMARCK MODEL: SOCIAL HEALTH INSURANCE

The signing of the Treaty of Frankfurt in 1871 at the opulent Palace of Versailles signaled an end to the Franco-Prussian War and a new age for the recently unified kingdom of Germany. The German-speaking states and principalities of central Europe had finally been united politically under the leadership of masterful Prussian politician and statesman Otto von Bismarck, who was appointed by the Kaiser to be the first Chancellor of modern Germany.

Bismarck had much to contend with in his new country, including restless ethnic minorities, disgruntled factory workers, an economic depression, and a major cultural schism between Catholics and Protestants. But one of the biggest threats to his political rule was the rise of socialism in Germany. In 1871, when the first Imperial Diet was elected, the Socialist Party received only about 3% of the vote and earned only two seats. But by 1877, the Socialists held twelve seats and were an aggressive and growing political force (Dawson 1912).

In keeping with his philosophy of realpolitik, Bismarck hoped to co-opt the Socialist political agenda and earn the support of the workers employed in Germany's rapidly growing industrial sector. In 1881, he introduced a popular new policy designed to undermine support for the Socialists: universal sickness insurance (Hennock 2007).

Otto von Bismarck (1815–98), first Chancellor of unified Germany and namesake of the Bismarck model.
Credit: © Erica Guilane-Nachez – Fotolia.com.

The idea was not new in Germany. For centuries, miners in Prussia could join mutual aid societies or sickness funds called *Knappschaftskasse*. These funds operated by collecting a small portion of each miner's wages, and then disbursing the proceeds to sick and injured workers to cover some of their lost wages and sometimes to provide basic medical care (Dawson 1912; Guinnane and Streb 2011). While not health insurance in the modern sense, the funds did protect miners from the risk of poverty arising from sickness or accidents. Starting in 1854, membership of the *Knappschaftskasse* became mandatory; all workers at a mine were required to pay into the system, and all would be cared for if they fell ill (Companje et al. 2009).

Sickness and accident funds became increasingly popular, and Bismarck's legislation served to establish mandatory sickness funds and accident insurance. The passage of Bismarck's 1883 insurance bill is considered a foundational moment in the history of the welfare state (Dawson 1912; Hennock 2007). While health insurance was extended at first only to workers in some industries, over time the government adopted policies that extended coverage to workers in other industries, dependents of workers, and eventually the whole population (Amelung et al. 2003).

As in Germany, Japanese politicians adopted a universal insurance program piecemeal as a way to counter the popularity of left-wing political parties. Health insurance was first extended to workers with the passage of the 1922 Health Insurance Law, which extended compulsory sickness funds to manufacturing and mining employees. The 1938 National

Health Insurance Act further extended health care benefits to the self-employed (mainly fishermen and farmers) and their families, and resulted in the formation of national health insurance societies. In 1958, the National Health Insurance Law was passed, guaranteeing health insurance to all Japanese citizens. Other East Asian nations like South Korea and Taiwan followed Japan's lead in the late twentieth century (Eggleston and Hsieh 2004).

Many of the health care systems of continental Europe, such as those in France, Switzerland, and the Netherlands, were also first implemented as ways to insure subsets of the working population, and thus share the same beginnings as the German and Japanese systems. While any generalization of the health policy of so many countries is necessarily inexact, the countries that follow the *Bismarck model* share a few key traits (Hassenteufel 2007):

- *Universal insurance:* All or nearly all of the population have health insurance coverage either through a plan sponsored by an employer or through the government. While the employer-sponsored health insurance schemes tend to be nominally private, they are heavily regulated by the government.
- *Community rating:* The financing of health insurance coverage is primarily through payroll and other taxes, rather than through insurance premiums based on the health risk of the insured person. This sort of financing arrangement means that healthier people in the population with low expected medical spending subsidize the care of the sicker people who have high expected medical spending.
- *Regulated private health care provision:* Hospitals tend to be privately run, and physicians are not public employees. However, prices in the medical care sector are set by the government in consultation with doctors and hospital managers.

The set of policies that comprise the Bismarck model reflect two major values: solidarity and economic liberty (Rodwin 2003). The poorest and sickest members of society are supported by the system, which subsidizes health insurance for those who are least able to afford it. This subsidy is paid for by the wealthiest and healthiest, who pay high taxes and actuarially unfair premiums to keep the system afloat. However, unlike in the Beveridge model, patients and doctors are at liberty to make fundamental economic choices, such as which hospital to visit or where to open a new clinic. Ultimately, the Bismarck model achieves a kind of compromise between the nationalized health systems of the Beveridge world and the relatively unregulated system in place in the US.

17.1   A brief tour of the Bismarck world

While every Bismarck health system shares the defining traits of the model (universal insurance, community rating, regulated private providers), each nation takes a slightly different approach to supervising insurance markets and controlling the provision of health care. Below, we introduce six major Bismarck systems and briefly outline each system's particular character.

The countries that have adopted a Bismarck health care system tend to have higher national health care expenditures compared with the Beveridge countries (Simonet 2010; Thomson et al. 2011). Health policy in the Bismark countries tends to focus on ways to control health expenditures, rather than on ways to alleviate queues.

Germany

Health insurance in Germany is divided into two broad classes: statutory health insurance (SHI) and private health insurance (PHI). All Germans who earn less than a high-income threshold (€50,850 in 2012) are required to sign up for a statutory health insurance plan. People earning above that amount, as well as some civil servants, may opt for private health insurance over statutory insurance, but may not choose to be uninsured. Once patients choose to enter the private health insurance market, they may not return to the public system.

Originally, SHI plans were tied to employment and targeted at blue-collar workers. Richer, white-collar ones were supposed to be able to purchase their own insurance or health care. However, in 1996, a set of reforms dramatically expanded the choices available to patients, loosening the link between employment and the SHI plan. Since then, Germans have had the option of choosing among all available statutory health plans, including plans run by other companies or faraway states. While the statutory plans are nominally private, nonprofit entities, they are extensively regulated and effectively publicly run. They are required to accept all patients, regardless of their medical histories, and cannot charge differential rates to sicker customers. This strategy for strictly regulating an insurance market is called managed competition, so Germany is said to have a managed-competition health insurance market.

Premiums to finance the SHI companies are collected as payroll taxes, and vary only with income. This means that high-income patients pay more for coverage, but sick patients do not. SHI serves as a vehicle for both the rich to subsidize the poor and the healthy to subsidize the sick, and insures patients against both health risk and classification risk. This redistribution is sustained by an ongoing political appetite for solidarity (Hinrichs 1995).

Patients and insurers are free to choose their health care providers, who can compete to attract them by providing high-quality care. But health care providers cannot compete on price; price schedules for doctors and hospitals are negotiated annually between the insurers and providers. This philosophy of self-regulation by industry members rather than the German government is known as *Selbstverwaltung* (Lungen and Lapsley 2003).

Switzerland

Historically, the Swiss health system did not feature universal insurance and did not provide much in the way of subsidies; of all the western European countries, its system most closely resembled the American health system. In 1996, however, insurance became universal and subsidies were established for low-income people to afford private insurance plans. Today, the Swiss system closely resembles the German system: insurers are heavily regulated and compete to attract customers who are required to purchase some form of coverage (Okma et al. 2010; Thomson et al. 2011).

Switzerland is also notable for pioneering managed care plans, like health maintenance organizations (HMOs) that became popular in the US during the 1990s (see Section 18.2). Among European countries, Switzerland led the way in allowing insurers to offer plans with managed care features (Okma et al. 2010).

Switzerland still faces several health policy challenges. In recent years, subsidies have failed to keep up with rising insurance premiums and vast disparities in premiums between regions have appeared (Bolgiani et al. 2006; Okma et al. 2010). Additionally, policymakers have struggled to combat risk selection, which occurs when insurance companies compete for the healthiest customers and try to evade sick customers (van de Ven 2011).

The Netherlands

The evolution of the Dutch health system followed a path similar to that of the Swiss system. In the 1970s, the system was fairly unregulated, with no price controls and fee-for-service payments to physicians. Rising costs during this period motivated policymakers to reexamine these choices. The Health Care Prices Act of 1982 gave the government greater control over physician reimbursement rates, and fee-for-service reimbursement for public patients ended in 1983.

The health insurance market also resembles the managed-competition model in Germany. In 1992, the Dutch system introduced patient choice and subsequent reforms have firmly established a managed-competition framework (van de Ven and Schut 2008). Unlike in Germany, though, insurance is financed jointly by payroll contributions and additional premiums. As in Switzerland, there are subsidies for low-income households, defined in the Netherlands as those that would have to pay more than 6.5% of their income for insurance (Turquet 2012).

Israel

The Israeli health system features a managed-competition model reminiscent of the German, Swiss, and Dutch systems. The 1995 National Health Insurance Law established the current system, but with only four sickness funds (as opposed to the hundreds that operate in the other Bismarck countries). The 1995 law also defined a universal standard basket of services that every sickness fund must provide to customers. As in most other Bismarck countries, the government has the authority to set hospital and physician fee schedules for the entire country.

Japan

Unlike most other Bismarck health systems, Japan's system is not centered around a managed-competition market where patients can choose their insurers. Instead, the system retains the characteristics of its beginnings with a strong emphasis on employer-based financing of health care. The type of company one works for determines the insurance society to which one belongs and the financial contributions one must make. The five basic insurance types are as follows:

- *Seikan* refers to government-managed health insurance that covers the employees of small and medium-sized companies and their dependents.
- *Kenpo* refers to society-managed health insurance that covers workers employed by larger firms and the workers' dependents. Companies such as Toshiba, Honda, and Sony maintain their own Kenpo societies. There are about 1,700 Kenpo associations in Japan.
- *Kyosai* covers public employees, both national and local, as well as private school teachers, staff, and their dependents.
- *Kokuho* covers the self-employed, retirees, and their dependents, and anyone else who does not otherwise qualify for health insurance.
- *Roken* is a special pooling fund for the elderly.

As with other Bismarck systems, there exists significant cross-subsidization both within and across pools. All pools are community rated, so premium payments do not depend on individual health but the overall health of everyone in the pool. This means that the healthy subsidize the sick within each pool.

Additionally, an extensive and explicit cross-subsidization scheme occurs across different pools like the Kenpo, Roken, and Kokuho plans. The Kenpo plans that cover employees of larger firms tend to be the richest, because they cover high-income individuals who tend to be relatively young. Meanwhile, the Roken and Kokuho plans cover lower-income people and those who are elderly and unemployed. Under the cross-subsidization scheme, Kenpo enrollees pay extra in taxes to help cover the costs of Roken and Kokuho members.

In other aspects, the Japanese system more closely resembles its Bismarck counterparts. Patients are not assigned to doctors or hospitals, and can visit whichever provider they wish. Hospitals are nominally nonprofit but are owned by physicians and are effectively for-profit entities. The actions of health care providers are constrained by strict price controls negotiated by the Japanese government and the Japanese Medical Association (JMA).

France

Health insurance in France has been universal since the 1970s, and today the vast majority of the French population is covered by a large sickness fund for salaried workers called the Caisse nationale de l'assurance maladie des travailleurs salariés (CNAMTS). Much smaller funds cover other specific groups of the French population, such as farmers and agricultural workers. French workers do not have a choice between plans, but all plans are more or less identical. The plans cannot charge additional premiums and their benefit packages are largely specified by the government (Rodwin 2003).

There is a large degree of choice, though, when it comes to selecting a doctor. This freedom is treasured by patients who know they can always switch doctors or even go straight to a specialist or a hospital if they desire (Hassenteufel 2007). France is notable for its modest coverage of ambulatory services, and cost-sharing can rise to as high as 40% for some basic physician services. As a consequence, there is a robust private supplemental insurance sector that covers copayments for these services. In 1999, the government established CMU Complémentaire, a program that covers copayments for low-income patients who cannot afford private supplemental insurance (Turquet 2012).

France's health care providers are paid directly by their patients under a fee-for-service system, where patients are later reimbursed by their health insurance funds for a portion of their expenses (Chevreul et al. 2010). The national reimbursement rates are negotiated annually between insurance funds and doctor and nurse unions, but all final negotiations must be approved by the government (Hassenteufel 2007). Reimbursement amounts typically range between 60% and 80% depending on the type of care and medical condition being treated. Exceptions are made in public hospitals and for certain populations who cannot explicitly pay providers the full price of treatment. In these special cases, the government directly pays health care providers the reimbursement for care, leaving only a copayment for the patient (Green and Irvine 2001).

Because patients pay costs of care upfront, this ensures patients the freedom to choose between different providers while also allowing physicians to freely prescribe and practice medicine.

17.2   Health insurance markets in the Bismarck model

In health care systems that follow the Beveridge model, all citizens are automatically enrolled in free public insurance. Adverse selection is not an issue, because there is no choice of plan. Nobody has the option to leave the public insurance plan for another one. All must pay taxes to support it, even if they purchase additional coverage through private insurers. Unless healthy citizens decide to leave the country permanently, they have no choice but to subsidize their unhealthy compatriots.

Bismarck systems, by contrast, are not immune to adverse selection. The compulsory nature of insurance enrollment prevents the worst of adverse selection; people are prevented from leaving the pool when they are healthy. This guarantees that there are always healthy people paying into the system to subsidize care for the sick. But if people can choose among several insurance plans within a Bismarck system, adverse selection can still appear. Below, we describe the unusual mechanics of the compulsory market for health insurance in the Bismarck model and discuss its vulnerabilities.

Managed competition

Today, the health insurance markets in most Bismarck countries follow a managed-competition model resembling the system described by Enthoven (1993). Multiple non-profit insurance funds offer health insurance in a nationwide market that is constrained by four major rules:

- **Minimum standards:** Every insurance contract is required to meet a minimal standard of care; often a central governmental body will enumerate a list of procedures or treatments that all plans are required to cover. There are also limits on copayments and deductibles.
- **Open enrollment:** Insurers may not reject any eligible customers, even if they are unhealthy and certain to cost the insurer dearly.
- **Community rating:** Insurers cannot set premiums using **risk rating**; instead they must be **community rated**. This means that individual customers cannot be charged differentially even if they are likely to be more expensive.
- **Compulsory participation:** Customers are mandated to have (and pay for) insurance coverage at all times. This is a means of limiting adverse selection. Without it, people could go without insurance most of the time and then sign up for coverage only when they fell ill.

Definition | 17.1

Risk rating: charging different premiums to different customers based on their individual risk of needing health care. The alternative is **community rating**, which entails charging everyone in an insurance pool an identical premium. Depending on the insurance program, the pool could consist of a few workers at one company or millions of people across a large geographical area.

These insurance plans are financed primarily through payroll taxes (that is, proportional taxes on income), rather than premiums on individual customers. This financing is part of the community rating, since taxes vary only on the basis of income, not any other factor.

Imagine three workers: a healthy young man, a pregnant woman with two children, and an older man with diabetes and high blood pressure, all earning the same annual salary and part of the same insurance pool. Each owes the same payroll tax even though their expected health care costs may differ greatly. This community rating system, where the healthy subsidize the sick, is a hallmark of the Bismarck model of social health insurance.

Payroll financing of health insurance also promotes equity by ensuring that low-income, unemployed, or retired workers receive an automatic discount on their health insurance. Put another way, no one is ever too poor to afford health insurance because rates adjust based on income. In many European countries, payroll contributions for health insurance are limited to a certain percentage of an employee's income. Unemployed workers with no income can simply join any open plan for free.

Unlike private insurers, the insurers in the Bismarck model are not for-profit corporations but rather regulated, nonprofit entities called "sickness funds." In Germany, for instance, these funds are effectively owned by their enrollees. If a German sickness fund has a good year – that is, if its enrollees incur low medical expenditures – the enrollees receive a partial refund of the payroll contributions they paid in. In bad years, enrollees face a surcharge at the end of the year to make up the difference.

The highly regulated insurance market described above ensures that everyone can access affordable health insurance coverage, which is central to the philosophy of the Bismarck model. But it is also vulnerable to two potentially costly problems: adverse selection and its cousin, risk selection.

Risk selection

While adverse selection concerns the behavior of insurance *customers*, risk selection concerns the behavior of insurance companies. Risk selection occurs when insurers seek to enroll low-risk customers and seek to avoid high-risk customers. This practice, also known as "cream skimming," is motivated by a desire to reduce the expected expenditures of the pool (see Chapter 10).

At first it seems like risk selection would be easy. Recruiters could visit university campuses to sign up young, healthy customers while making sure never to advertise in nursing homes. However, risk selection is not so easy in Bismarck systems because it is illegal to refuse any customers. Often, the key to risk selection for a sickness fund is ensuring that sick people never ask for coverage in the first place.

There are several tactics available to insurance funds hoping to engage in risk selection. Anecdotal evidence, especially from Germany and Switzerland, suggests that such attempts are widespread (van de Ven et al. 2003). These range from the questionable:

- advertising specifically to certain groups;
- switching to a managed care model that discourages sick customers;

. . . to the controversial:

- closing offices in high-cost regions;
- rewarding agents who identify sick customers and foist them off onto other plans;
- selectively reminding unprofitable customers that they are allowed to switch funds at any time;

. . . to the downright illegal:

- ignoring inquiries from certain consumers;
- flatly rejecting potential customers;
- holding information sessions or sign-ups in buildings that are not accessible to the disabled;
- intentionally providing deficient health care to sick customers in the hope of chasing them away.

Open enrollment is key to making managed competition work, but it creates an antagonistic relationship between sickness funds and their least healthy enrollees. Not only does risk selection put sick customers in a disadvantaged position, it is also purely wasteful from a social perspective. Any time, money or ingenuity that is devoted toward risk selection cannot be used to improve patient care. And *someone* will end up covering the sick customers anyway due to the universal mandate, so even the most intense risk selection efforts do not save any money for the system as a whole (van de Ven 2011).

The extent of risk selection in practice is uncertain, since it is almost impossible to observe directly. A study by van de Ven et al. (2007) finds suggestive evidence of risk selection in Belgium, the Netherlands, Germany, Switzerland, and Israel during the mid-2000s, although Nuscheler and Knaus (2005) question the existence of true risk selection in Germany.

One particularly egregious example of risk selection. There is no evidence that any sickness funds actually use fiery moats to weed out applicants.

Credit: Allen Cox.

Eliminating risk selection

Luckily, risk selection can be confronted. One straightforward option is an *ex-post cost-based compensation* scheme. This involves establishing a national fund to re-insure the various sickness funds. Under such a system, unlucky sickness funds that end up with sicker customers and higher expenditures are reimbursed with transfers from the lucky funds that had healthier customers and lower expenditures (Swartz 2003).

If unlucky firms are compensated for 100% of their higher-than-average costs, the motivation to perform risk selection disappears. Insurers can recruit customers confident that, at the end of the year, no patient will be any more or less expensive than any other. Funds know they will be reimbursed for any customer who incurs more expenditures than the average customer.

This solution completely erases risk selection, but it also lessens the incentive for insurance funds to operate efficiently. If insurance funds are confident in the knowledge that all of their enrollees' expenses will be paid by the other insurance funds, they have little reason to economize on care (Newhouse 1996).

Another option for avoiding risk selection is a related compensation scheme known as **risk adjustment**. Risk adjustment also entails the establishment of a central fund to manage transfers between sickness funds. However, under risk adjustment, transfers are based on *ex ante* risk assessments and not actual cost outcomes. Insurance funds that draw unhealthy customers are reimbursed based on how expensive their customers are expected to be, not on how expensive they actually are (Dow and Fulton 2010; van de Ven 2011).

Definition	17.2

Risk adjustment: the practice of compensating sickness funds with high-risk customers using payments from funds with low-risk customers. Compensation payments are based on predicted costs, not actual health expenditures.

The *Gesundheitsfonds* ("health fund") is the government-run risk adjustment mechanism for German sickness funds. It determines payments based on the composition of each fund's pool of enrollees, who are stratified by age, sex, disability, and 80 costly diseases like diabetes, high blood pressure, and epilepsy.

To make the process of risk adjustment more concrete, consider a sickness fund with a 52-year-old diabetic customer. His contribution into the fund is based only on his income, but he will be much more expensive to treat than the average enrollee. At the end of the year, analysts at the *Gesundheitsfonds* calculate the average annual health expenditures of all 52-year-old diabetic men across Germany. This is a measure of how much this customer "should" have cost the fund during the year. They compare this with the average for all people across Germany, and compensate the sickness fund for the difference. If the average German costs €5,000 to treat but the average 52-year-old diabetic man costs €12,000 to treat, the sickness fund would receive a check for €7,000 to compensate it for the burden of treating this high-risk patient.

A risk-adjustment scheme reduces the incentive for cream skimming because high-risk customers are no longer necessarily unprofitable. It simultaneously maintains incentives for efficient care because the insurance fund keeps the difference if it manages to treat its 52-year-old diabetic man for less than €12,000. In fact, if an insurance fund learns how to effectively control costs for a certain disease and routinely spends less than the national average, it can actually make money by enrolling sick people.

But if the risk-adjustment scheme is not perfect – that is, if the central fund does not fully compensate insurance funds for certain types of risks – risk selection will continue. This is a problem in countries that use a limited set of criteria for determining risks. In Switzerland before 2012, for example, the expected cost for each patient was judged solely on age, sex, and region. This left ample motivation for risk selection, because old people with high blood pressure (for example) cost more than old people in good health, but the firms did not receive any extra credit for enrolling them. A similarly incomplete risk-adjustment system existed in Germany before 2002 (Busse 2004; van de Ven et al. 2007).

Switzerland and other nations are moving towards more complete risk-adjustment systems to reduce cream skimming. Starting in 2012, for example, Swiss insurance funds received extra compensation if their enrollees were hospitalized in the previous year.

Adverse selection in compulsory insurance markets

While successful risk-compensation schemes can reduce the problem of risk selection, they do not solve the problem of adverse selection. Risk adjustment affects the incentives of insurance funds but does not directly affect enrollees. The familiar problem of adverse selection could still arise if frail customers disproportionately enroll in certain funds that provide the most generous coverage. This could result in a separating equilibrium as predicted by the Rothschild–Stiglitz model or even an adverse selection death spiral (see Chapters 9 and 10).

Community-rated insurance markets in both Switzerland and South Africa show evidence of separating equilibria. In Switzerland, sicker patients ended up in generous insurance funds with high premiums, and healthy patients ended up in insurance funds with high deductibles but lower premiums (Geoffard et al. 2006; van de Ven et al. 2007). In South Africa, younger patients were differentially attracted to medical savings account plans with weaker insurance coverage, which fragmented risk pooling and created a separating equilibrium (McLeod and Grobler 2010).

Separating equilibrium outcomes can be undesirable on a number of levels. First, they create a welfare loss for the robust patients who would prefer more generous insurance. More generous insurance cannot be offered though, for fear that unobservably sick customers will flock to it. Second, it represents a failure of solidarity, because sick patients are stuck paying high premiums and are not subsidized by their healthier counterparts.

Finally, adverse selection can become extremely destabilizing if firms are not allowed to adjust their premiums at all (as is the case in Israel). In that context, no fund has any desire to gain a reputation as a good caretaker of the sick. Such a fund would be mobbed by sick patients and would have no way to raise premiums to compensate. If these new customers were unobservably sick and the fund could not receive reimbursement through risk adjustment, then bankruptcy would ensue. In the face of adverse selection and fixed premiums, insurers simply have no incentive to provide quality care for the sick (van de Ven et al. 2007).

Bismarck systems have two main ways to combat adverse selection and avoid these bad outcomes. The first option is simple: deny customers the right to choose their insurers in the first place. This is the policy in Japan, which does not have a managed-competition system like Germany or Switzerland but instead a collection of closed funds. Every Japanese citizen is assigned to an insurance fund based on his or her employment status, age, and location. Most are covered through employer-based plans (if they work at large firms) or a government-run plan for employees at small firms. Coverage is still universal because anyone who does not have access to employer-based insurance or retiree insurance is eligible to enroll in the safety-net general insurance program called *Kokuho*. This was also the policy option in place in Germany before 1996, when the previously closed system was opened for the first time.

The second antidote to adverse selection within a managed market is to restrict product differentiation. If insurance funds cannot distinguish themselves significantly from competitors, then there will be little to motivate adverse selection by customers, and less inequality if a separating equilibrium does emerge. Germany can be said to use this policy, because statutory insurance funds are limited in how they can differentiate themselves (Lisac et al. 2010). There is also a generous minimum standard that every fund must meet, which prevents an adverse selection death spiral from taking hold. Nevertheless, the option for richer patients to opt out of statutory health insurance for private insurance means some adverse selection still exists in Germany (Thomson and Mossialos 2006).

17.3   Containing costs with price controls

As we have seen, the markets for hospital and physician services can suffer from imperfections – such as oligopoly power and medical arms races – that lead to inefficiently high prices and over enthusiastic adoption of new medical technology. In the US, where private provider markets predominate, these problems are partially to blame for health care prices that are the highest in the world (Gerdtham 1991).

In principle, oligopoly power can be countered if insurers band together and form a monopsony that can drive prices down. Furthermore, insurers can carefully set reimbursement rates to deter the adoption of cost-ineffective medical technologies. However, in practice, private insurers are not always successful in driving down provider costs or deterring wasteful care in market-based systems such as the US (Vladeck and Rice 2009).

Given that health insurance coverage is universal in the Bismarck model, it is even more important to keep health care prices low. To avoid unaffordably high health care expenditures and to limit the need for taxes to publicly finance it, countries have adopted policies to explicitly control the price of health care.

While the Beveridge countries approach this same problem by nationalizing health care provision, the Bismarck countries instead maintain private markets. Each nation has instituted a system of negotiated price controls, enforced by the government, that applies to all health care transactions in the country. Fee schedules have the potential to rein in oligopoly power and inappropriate technology adoption, but they may also lead doctors to make medically questionable decisions when treating their patients.

Negotiating fee schedules

Setting prices in the medical care sector is a complicated endeavor since the range of possible medical activities is so varied. A price schedule must reflect the relative value of seeing a patient for a routine checkup, performing heart bypass surgery, diagnosing a fever of unknown origin, and many other activities requiring medically specific knowledge.

Usually, this task is accomplished by a private market with free-floating prices capable of aggregating information about the preferences and constraints of all participants. When prices are instead set by fiat, a small group of people must do their best to approximate how a well-functioning market would set prices (Hayek 1945).

In Bismarck health systems in practice, prices are set periodically through negotiations between medical professionals and payers. In each country, the parties invited to the negotiating table are slightly different. In Germany, for instance, the two mandatory associations of doctors and nurses negotiate with the sickness funds that will pay them for care. In Japan, by contrast, the Japanese Medical Association negotiates directly with the government.

Both private and public providers are bound by these price negotiations, and must charge these prices, no more and no less. Hence, fee schedules can be used as leverage by policymakers to influence and alter the behavior of health care providers. Manipulation of the fee schedule serves as one of the primary mechanisms by which governments regulate the supply of medical services, the use of care, and the level of aggregate health care spending.

Under the Japanese system, all medical facilities are reimbursed for medical services according to the official uniform fee schedule *shinryo hoshu*. Each year, the Japanese Ministry of Health, Labor, and Welfare (known as *Korosho*) sets the price list in negotiation with the Japanese Medical Association (JMA). The price list delineates the reimbursement amounts that doctors and hospitals receive for performing procedures, prescribing drugs, and all other patient care activities. The fee schedule is incredibly detailed; it specifies the price of every conceivable medical procedure that the government has decided the insurance funds must cover. The schedule also includes regional adjustments so that doctors practicing in high cost-of-living areas like Tokyo receive more than their counterparts in Hokkaido.

Germany has a similar national fee schedule for medical services. Unlike in Japan, where the government plays a direct role in the setting of prices, in Germany the sickness funds and providers negotiate with each other to set prices. The German Federal Joint Committee plays a role in facilitating this negotiation, but does not have the authority to set prices itself. Decisions about which new technologies the sickness funds will cover are also determined in these negotiations. Even providers who care for patients with private insurance (rather than German statutory insurance) are paid under the common negotiated fee schedule (Schreyögg et al. 2006).

Though the level of direct government involvement varies, other countries with the Bismarck model also set health care prices on the basis of negotiations that apply to all health care transactions in the country. In France, health care prices are set as the result of negotiations between doctors' trade unions and sickness funds. However, the French government wields veto power, and a representative from the government participates directly in the negotiations (Hassenteufel 2007). In Switzerland, providers negotiate fees with a consortium of all insurers known as the Santesuisse, while the Ministry of Health codifies the results of these negotiations into fee schedules for health care that apply across the country (Okma et al. 2010).

Clinical distortions

The process for setting prices would ideally result in a price for each activity equal to its marginal costs of production. For governments, this is more or less an impossible task because of the difficulty of measuring the marginal costs of care provision with any degree of accuracy. Marginal costs are also changing over time with the development of new technologies and with new provider arrangements. Additionally, groups with a stake in the outcome of the negotiations will seek to influence the ultimate price list. In practice, government agencies that are given the responsibility of setting prices are constrained by limited information, political pressures, and the overriding need to keep health care budgets at manageable levels.

Inevitably, the process of government price-setting produces some prices that do not match the actual marginal costs and benefits of care. These administered prices can introduce distortions in the way that doctors elect to treat their patients. Suppose a doctor is caring for an end-stage renal disease patient whose kidneys have failed. The doctor has two choices for treating the patient: kidney dialysis thrice weekly or a kidney transplant surgery followed with immunosuppresant drugs for the rest of the patient's life. Clinical experience has shown that a transplant produces a better quality of life over the long run.

If we assume the lifetime costs of each course of treatment are identical, then referring the patient for a transplant is the clinically sound decision.

But what if a government price-setting agency, perhaps influenced by their recent week-long resort vacation paid for by dialysis industry lobbyists, sets a much higher reimbursement rate for dialysis than for a kidney transplant? In that case, the doctor would have a financial incentive to prescribe care that is not clinically optimal. This problem recurs whenever there are two or more clinically defensible treatments that may be used in the same situation. If the government sets prices incorrectly for even one of those treatments, clinical distortions will arise.

Despite these theoretical problems, every Bismarck health system sets some prices centrally, mainly as a way to limit public expenditures on health care. Additionally, the US Medicare program for the elderly sets a list of prices every year that it is willing to pay to physicians and hospitals. As a result, both the Bismarck health systems and US Medicare are subject to clinical distortions due to government price setting. (Although the US does not follow the Bismarck model itself, the Medicare program shares some similarities to the Bismarck system for one particular population.)

The literature on the clinical distortions induced by price controls is voluminous. Here, we focus on two examples, one where prices are set too high – the case of payments to physicians for drug prescribing and dispensing in Japan – and one where prices are set too low – the case of payments for cochlear implants in the US.

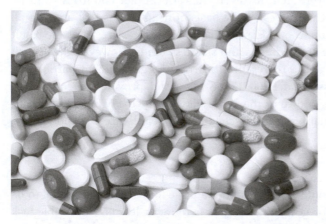

In Japan, official prices for most pharmaceuticals are deliberately set higher than the actual purchasing price charged by drug companies (Yoshikawa et al. 1991). This provides a fixed profit margin for hospitals and clinics, which (unlike in Europe and the US) are permitted to sell the pharmaceuticals they prescribe directly to patients. This long-standing gap between purchase and sale price for drugs is known as *yakka saeki* or the "doctor's margin." Predictably, the prospect of easy profits distorts the prescribing practices of Japanese doctors. Rodwin and Okamoto (2000) find that Japanese physicians often opt to sell higher-priced drugs, to the point where Japanese pharmaceutical expenditures constituted nearly 30% of all health care spending in 1993. By contrast, this figure was only 11% that same year in the US.

A deluge of pills, tablets, and capsules: the natural economic consequence of the yakka saeki. In 1991, the Japanese spent about three times as much on prescription drugs as Americans. Credit: © pxlsjpeg – Fotolia.com.

Prices that are set too low can be just as harmful as prices set too high. The story of cochlear implantation, a technology introduced in the mid-1990s to restore hearing to the deaf, provides a good case study of how low reimbursement rates can slow the adoption of useful technology.

A common cause of deafness is damage to the hair cells that line the cochlea, a structure of the inner ear. These cells help transform vibrations entering the ear into neural signals the brain can understand as sound. Cochlear implantation involves surgically inserting a small electronic device into the inner ear that performs the functions of the damaged hair cells. Cost-effectiveness studies have found that cochlear implants are a relatively inexpensive way to improve quality of life in both adults and children (Cheng 1999; Cheng et al. 2000).

When the technology was first developed, both the US Medicare and Medicaid systems priced the reimbursement for the surgical procedure at very low levels (Garber et al. 2002). Any doctor performing a cochlear implantation would have to buy an expensive implant and perform the difficult surgery, only to be reimbursed at a rate less than the cost of the device itself. As a result, only a limited number of deaf people had the implants placed in the US. This was a particular concern for deaf children, because placement of the implant early in life results in better speech and hearing outcomes than if the placement is delayed. By contrast, in Japan, the cochlear implantation was reimbursed at a higher level in the *shinryo hoshu* (the national fee schedule), so the technology spread much more rapidly in Japan than in the US (Kim 2008).

Limiting access to specialists and new technologies

In addition to price schedules, countries with Bismarck health systems have introduced other mechanisms to control the public burden of health care costs, including gatekeeping access to specialists and formal health technology assessment (HTA). These policies, already common in the Beveridge model, where the government provides health care directly, are a relatively recent addition to the Bismarck model.

Traditionally, Bismarck countries have permitted patients to seek care from whichever providers they want, and have permitted patients to seek care from specialists even without a recommendation from a primary care doctor. This has started to change in recent years. Both France and Germany, for example, have imposed gatekeeping reforms. Like gatekeepers in the UK, French and German gatekeepers are physicians who manage the referrals of patients to specialists and other hospital services. But unlike in the UK, both the French and German gatekeeping systems are voluntary for patients. Patients can avoid gatekeepers and go straight to specialists if they pay a small fee, so the reforms are known as "soft gatekeeping" (Or et al. 2010).

Another approach recently imported from the Beveridge model is the centralized control of HTA. In recent years, many Bismarck countries have moved to incorporate formal HTA into their health care systems in order to limit the use of wasteful technologies (Koch et al. 2009).

In 2004, Germany established the Institute for Quality and Efficiency in Health Care (IQWiG) to advise the Federal Joint Committee on the effectiveness of new medical technologies (Busse and Riesberg 2004). Unlike the UK's HTA agency (NICE), IQWiG does not conduct any independent cost-effectiveness analyses, but relies instead on independent assessments conducted elsewhere. IQWiG has no formal authority to deny coverage of even the most inefficient new technologies, although German sickness funds can independently choose to do so on the basis of IQWiG's findings. Even that power is limited though, because insurers may only refuse to cover a new technology on the basis of cost if there already exists an alternative technology that is at least as effective as the new one (Nasser and Sawicki 2009).

The introduction of formal HTA has proved a controversial addition to the Bismarck model, and not every country has adopted it. In Japan, for instance, there is no formal HTA performed by government at all (Oliver 2003; Hisashige 2009). Similarly, Switzerland has no publicly financed health technology agency. Despite the lack of formal HTA agencies in these countries, studies of the cost-effectiveness of new technologies conducted elsewhere are an important input in both price negotiations and technology adoption decisions by insurance societies.

Table 17.1. *Health care technology utilization in select countries following different health policy models in 2010.*

Country	Doctor visits per capita	MRI exams (per thousand population)	CT exams (per thousand population)	MRI machines (per million population)	CT scanner machines (per million population)
Beveridge nations					
Australia	6.5	23.0	93.0	5.6	42.8
Canada	5.5	46.7	126.9	8.2	14.2
Denmark	4.6	57.5	105.2	15.4	27.6
UK	5.0	40.8	76.4	5.9	8.2
Bismarck nations					
France	6.7	60.2	145.4	7.0	11.8
Germany	8.9	95.2	117.1	10.3	17.7
Israel	6.2	18.1	127.2	2.0	9.2
Japan	13.1	–	–	43.1	97.3
Netherlands	6.6	49.1	66.0	12.2	12.3
Other nations					
United States	3.9	97.7	265.0	31.6	40.7

Source: Data from OECD Health Data 2012 – Frequently Requested Data. © OECD (2012) URL: http://www.oecd.org/health/healthpoliciesanddata/oecdhealthdata2012.htm.

Table 17.1 shows the adoption rate of CT machines and MRI machines in selected Beveridge and Bismarck countries, as well as in the US. These two particular innovations, both of which are used to aid in the diagnosis of an incredible variety of conditions, are prime examples of expensive technologies that are becoming more widespread in modern health systems. This data provides some indication of how successful each country has been in controlling the advance of such medical innovations.

On average, patients in Bismarck nations visit the doctor more often and receive more MRI and CT scans than their counterparts in Beveridge nations. The hospitals in Bismarck nations also tend to make more capital investments in these machines (which can cost more than $1 million each) than hospitals in the Beveridge countries. While there are some exceptions to each trend, generally the data suggests that Beveridge nations have done more to resist the proliferation of these technologies. This does not necessarily indicate that Beveridge nations are doing a better job of providing care – perhaps the patients there would benefit from improved access to MRI scans – but it does suggest that attempts to limit technology use in Beveridge countries have succeeded.

17.4   Conclusion

As politicians and officials in Beveridge and Bismarck countries consider future health care reforms, a question naturally arises: how do the Beveridge and Bismarck models compare? As we discussed in Chapter 15, this question is not easy to answer. But we can glean some clues by examining spending levels and health outcomes in countries implementing each model.

Table 17.2. *Health care spending as a percentage of GDP in select countries following different health policy models in 2010.*

Country	Spending (% of GDP)
Beveridge nations	
Australia	9.1
Canada	11.4
Sweden	9.6
Norway	9.4
UK	9.6
Bismarck nations	
France	11.6
Germany	11.6
Israel	7.9
Japan	9.5
Netherlands	12.0
Other nations	
United States	17.6

Source: Data from OECD Health Data 2012 – Frequently Requested Data. © OECD (2012) URL: http://www.oecd.org/health/healthpoliciesanddata/oecdhealthdata2012.htm.

Spending data from recent years indicates that the Beveridge systems in Europe spend less on health care than the Bismarck systems in Europe, although the pattern worldwide is more equivocal (see Table 17.2). But tradeoffs are unavoidable, so it is little surprise to learn that Beveridge countries are also slightly less healthy than Bismarck countries, at least by some common measures. In 2006, the UK spent only 9.6% of GDP on health care, but performed worse than many other OECD countries on several health measures. For example, its five-year survival rate for breast cancer patients was 69.8%, ten points lower than France's. Its neo-natal death per thousand live births rate was 3.5, higher than either France or Germany.

On the other hand, Sweden, another system with nationalized hospitals and relatively low health care spending, performed better than both France and Germany on the same metrics. This may be because its system is particularly efficient or innovative, or may be simply because it has a healthier population to begin with. Regardless, this exception indicates that broad generalizations about the merits of the various models can be dangerous.

In the last two chapters, we have highlighted the differences between the Beveridge and Bismarck systems. Beveridge systems emphasize equity and equal access to care, while Bismarck systems emphasize patient choice and provider competition. But we must remember that no country perfectly embodies either model in its policies; in fact, every country has adopted some elements of both. Recent reforms in Beveridge countries have focused on increasing choice for patients and competition between providers. Meanwhile, recent reforms in Bismarck countries have introduced gatekeeping and managed-care tactics that restrict patient choice in certain ways. In short, the Beveridge and Bismarck models seem to be moving closer together, and may one day even be hard to distinguish (Or et al. 2010; Hassenteufel 2007).

In the next chapter, we study the American model, which is still quite distinct from the egalitarian Beveridge–Bismarck synthesis that prevails in Europe and East Asia. Even more than the Bismarck model, the American model emphasizes free choice for patients and free markets in health care provision but does not feature universal insurance coverage.

17.5   Exercises

Comprehension questions

Indicate whether each statement is true or false, and justify your answer. Be sure to cite evidence from the chapter and state any additional assumptions you may need.

1 Sickness funds in Bismarck health care systems are publicly administered and financed.
2 Bismarck nations tend to have higher national health care expenditures than Beveridge countries.
3 Universal health care in Bismarck countries emphasizes equity of care for all individuals, regardless of social and economic circumstances. The sale of private supplemental insurance is prohibited.
4 There is an emphasis on managed competition in the Bismarck model.
5 Even though it is illegal for sickness funds to deny coverage to individuals, insurers still often engage in risk selection.
6 Physicians have no say in what prices to charge their patients.
7 Patients in France typically pay all their health fees directly to the doctor and are later reimbursed by their insurance fund.
8 One way that Bismarck nations control costs is through government-set prices for care.
9 Every Bismarck country has over a hundred sickness funds for patients to choose from, which distinguishes them from Beveridge countries.
10 Health insurance coverage is primarily financed through payroll and other taxes.
11 People in Bismarck countries tend to visit the doctor and receive more CT and MRI scans than people who live in Beveridge countries.
12 Even though health insurance is universal, citizens can choose whether or not they are insured.
13 Like the Beveridge model, there are no real cost controls in the Bismarck model, therefore long queues are a problem.
14 Bismarck countries have all had universal insurance for at least 40 years.
15 Patients in Bismarck model countries are able to choose which health care provider they see.
16 Patients are charged premiums based on their risk rating.
17 Like NICE in the UK, Germany has an entity that advises sickness funds on the cost-effectiveness of new technologies.

Essay questions

18 In a paper entitled "How do consumers motivate experts? Reputational incentives in an auto repair market," University of Chicago economist Tom Hubbard (2002) studies the market for vehicle emission inspections. In California, automobile owners are required at regular intervals to have their cars checked by registered mechanics to see whether the cars pollute the air in excessive amounts. Owners of cars that fail the test

are required to pay for repairs until the car tests at an acceptable level of emissions. Often, the same repair shop that diagnoses excessive emissions provides the services required to repair the problem. This market is in some ways similar to the market for physician services – in both markets experts both diagnose a problem and then provide treatment aimed at curing the diagnosed problem. In both markets, experts may have an incentive to "over-diagnose" problems and then profit from providing marginally necessary services. Just as in Bismarck health care systems, prices for both diagnostic and repair services are set annually by a process in which governmental authorities play a vital role.

Hubbard's main conclusion in his paper is that "consumers are 30 percent more likely to return to a firm at which they previously passed than to one at which they previously failed and that demand is sensitive to a firm's failure rate across all consumers. These and other results suggest that demand incentives are strong in this market because consumers believe that firms differ greatly in their consumer friendliness and are skeptical even about those they choose." To what extent can physicians' reputations serve as a limitation on the sorts of clinical distortions that we discuss in Section 17.3? Can patients accurately observe whether a doctor is acting on an incentive to provide profitable but marginally necessary services? Does the fact that many patients tend to develop a long-term relationship with the same primary care physician help alleviate patient fears of clinical distortions? Does the fact that in many cases, many *different* physicians provide diagnostic services and treatments help?

Students can find answers to the comprehension questions and lecturers can access an Instructor Manual with guideline answers to the analytical problems and essay questions at **www.palgrave.com/economics/bht**.

18 THE AMERICAN MODEL

In 1943, during the depths of World War II, the US Congress passed emergency economic measures designed to sustain the war effort and prevent ruinous inflation. Wages were frozen at their existing levels and employers barred from raising them, even for exemplary employees. Many employers adapted to the wage freeze by offering employees health insurance as a non-wage perk. Unlike salary, health insurance benefits were not technically considered wages for the purposes of the wartime emergency regulations. With this rule, Congress unwittingly laid the groundwork for the modern-day system of employer-sponsored insurance in the US (Lyke 2008).

After the war ended and the wage freezes were lifted, President Harry Truman made a push for universal health insurance as part of his Fair Deal agenda in 1949. His proposal would have eliminated involuntary uninsurance by establishing a national health insurance plan open to all. If Truman's plan had been adopted, America's modern health system might have resembled the Bismarck model (see Chapter 17).

Despite widespread public support for the basic notion of promoting health equity, Truman's plan was defeated (Blendon and Benson 2001). Historians attribute the plan's demise to the effective lobbying efforts of the American Medical Association (AMA) for the plan's demise. In the aftermath of this defeat, universal insurance advocates tried again with a proposal more limited in scope: health insurance for the elderly. The elderly were particularly disadvantaged by the dominance of employer-sponsored health insurance, because most elderly Americans were retired and could not access insurance through work. Obtaining insurance outside the employer insurance market was difficult and expensive, and periodic adverse selection death spirals ensured that most elderly people could not afford coverage (Ball 1995; Marmor 2000).

In the 1960s, President Lyndon Johnson adopted the plan to cover the elderly, rebranded as Medicare, as part of his Great Society – a set of domestic policy proposals organized around a theme of promoting equity. After the Democratic Party's landslide victories in the Presidential and Congressional elections of 1964, Medicare was enacted along with Medicaid, a similar program designed to extend free insurance coverage to the poor (Blumenthal 2008).

Employer-based health insurance, together with Medicare and Medicaid, form a patchwork health system that is fundamentally different from the Beveridge and Bismarck models discussed in previous chapters. Unlike every other developed country, the US lacks universal guaranteed insurance for all citizens, and some people have no health insurance. Nevertheless, most Americans find insurance coverage through one of these three avenues: employer-based insurance, Medicare, or Medicaid. This unique system, which we term the American model, is characterized by the following:

- *Private health insurance markets:* The non-elderly and non-poor seek insurance on the private market, which is centered around employer-based health insurance pools. Individual health insurance is also available, but that market is smaller and vulnerable to adverse selection.

- *Partial universal health insurance:* Subsidized universal health insurance is provided to two vulnerable subpopulations: the elderly (through Medicare) and the poor (through Medicaid).
- *Private health care provision:* Most hospitals and doctor's clinics are private, although federal and local governments do run some hospitals. While there is some antitrust regulation, there are few legal restrictions on where doctors can practice and hospitals can open. There are also no direct price controls enforced by the government; doctors and hospitals can charge whatever prices the market will bear.

The unique structure of the American model reflects a political preference for free choice. With a few important exceptions, insured American patients can choose to visit whichever doctor they want, and can receive treatment at whatever hospital they want. They can choose how generous an insurance plan they want, or even choose to go without insurance at all. Meanwhile, providers are free to offer any medical service, regardless of its cost-effectiveness, and may charge any price they choose.

While most people in the US are insured and have excellent access to care, there is also a large group – numbering 50 million people or more – who are not covered by insurance at all. In March 2010, a new law called the Patient Protection and Affordable Care Act (PPACA) was passed to address the problem of uninsurance. When it is fully implemented in 2014, the law will extend health insurance coverage to over 35 million people who would otherwise be uninsured. The law accomplishes this with an expansion of public insurance and a mandate requiring those not otherwise insured to buy insurance on the private market. As we will see, this mix of private and public insurance is a hallmark of the American model.

18.1   Employer-sponsored health insurance

Today, most non-elderly Americans who are insured receive coverage either through their employer or through the employer-sponsored plan of a spouse or parent. This insurance is by no means "free" insurance, since coverage is actually part of the worker's total compensation package. If an employee is worth $50,000 to his employer, then the employer cannot afford to pay him $50,000 as well as pay for his health insurance. The phenomenon of insurance costs coming out of the worker's wages is known as *wage pass-through*. So for the same type of job and skill level, jobs without employer-sponsored insurance plans will offer higher salaries than jobs with them.

Nevertheless, jobs with health insurance plans are still appealing for a number of reasons. First, the employer provision of health insurance yields an income tax break for employees. The forgone wages that went into paying insurance premiums never reached the employee, so they are not taxed as income. On the other hand, if the employer did not sponsor a health insurance plan, then worker's income would be slightly higher, but the increase would be taxed and he would have to buy health insurance himself on the private market. Ultimately, his bank account balance may be lower than it would be if his job had just provided health insurance in the first place.

In addition, there is no guarantee that everyone will be able to buy insurance through the individual health insurance market. Adverse selection can cause that market to unravel since it may be difficult for insurers in that market to assess the health status of potential enrollees (see Chapter 10).

Employer-sponsored insurance combats adverse selection by providing a reason for employees to pool together. Consider a firm called BHT Enterprises with four employees, two of whom are young and two of whom are old. The younger employees have lower expected health care costs than the older two. But one of the young employees has frequent migraines that increase his health costs compared with his young counterpart. Meanwhile, one of the two senior employees is unusually healthy for his age, since he enjoys spending his leisure time training for triathlons.

Crucially, the employer does know about all the health risks of his employees. Age is readily observable – that is, information about age is symmetric between employer and employee. But the employer does not observe the migraines or the triathlon training sessions. So there is also asymmetric information that employees know about their health and BHT Enterprises does not.

Since BHT cannot observe health risk but can observe age, it "charges" the older employees more for health insurance than the younger employees. Wage pass-through effectively separates the young and old employees into different pools. The older triathlete subsidizes the insurance of the other older employee, and the young migraine suffering worker is subsidized by the other, healthy, young worker. Both healthy employees have an incentive to find an employer who does not hire unhealthy employees.

The existence of *firm-specific human capital* can help keep these pools from unraveling even though employees have health risks that are difficult to observe, as we will discuss. Employer-sponsored health insurance can thus partially solve the adverse selection problem. However, the tendency for employer-sponsored insurance to bind employees to their employers may induce a different problem known as *job lock*.

Wage pass-through

As we just described, employer-sponsored insurance is not a free job perk; the cost of premiums are taken out of the worker's wages. Suppose our example firm BHT Enterprises pays a monthly insurance premium of $4,000 for all four of its employees. The insurer charges the firm a lump sum bill and the medical records are sealed, so the employer cannot distinguish which of its employees is placing the greatest burden on its insurance. But, of course, the firm suspects that its older employees cost more than its younger ones. Based on actuarial data sets, the firm guesses that the two young employees each cost $500 in premiums, while the two elderly ones each cost $1,500.

Suppose that BHT Enterprises tried to pool all four of its employees, so that the $4,000 premium bill is split evenly. Everyone forgoes exactly $1,000 in monthly wages. If the younger employees realize that the firm is doing this, then they also realize that they are overpaying for insurance and subsidizing health care for their older co-workers. Disgruntled, the younger employees may seek outside employment.

A rival firm Acme Inc offers the young employees another deal. Rather than pooling them together with sicker ones, Acme Inc offers young employees their own pool. This means that since young employees each cost the firm $500 in premiums, they forgo only $500 in wages. As a result, the two young employees could earn $500 more at Acme Inc than at BHT Enterprises. No young employee would ever work at BHT Enterprises again.

Realizing this, BHT Enterprises would be unlikely to pool all its employees in a single pool. Instead, like Acme Inc, it would use wage pass-through to "charge" older employees more for their health insurance (through forgone wages). Meanwhile, the younger laborers pay less, so they are less tempted to leave for other firms.

As a result of the differential wage pass-through, the BHT Enterprises insurance plan splits into separate insurance pools for the young and the old. All four employees still receive the same insurance coverage, but the older two employees "pay" $1,500 for it and the younger two only $500. In this system, the older employees do not enjoy subsidies from their younger colleagues, even if nominally the employer charges its employees equally for insurance. Differential wage pass-through is not limited to age differences but can occur whenever employers can observe elevated health risks among their employees.

Technically, passing lower wages through to sicker workers is illegal in the US. The Americans with Disabilities Act of 1991 prohibits firms from discriminating against the sick or disabled, especially in hiring and salary decisions. But wage discrimination is difficult to detect, and there is evidence that people who have higher expected medical expenditures do earn less.

Gruber (1994) studies the response to a 1976 federal law in the US that mandated maternity care coverage for employer-sponsored insurance plans. The change meant that insurers had to start paying for health care costs related to pregnancy, childbirth, and maternity leave. As a result, premiums rose for businesses with many female employees of childbearing age. On the other hand, businesses whose employees were all 60-year-old men were unaffected, because their employees and their spouses did not have any maternity-related health care costs.

The wage pass-through hypothesis predicts that the wages of young women would rise more slowly than they otherwise would have in the years after the law passed. The extra maternity care costs that insurers had to cover would be passed right back to those employees most likely to incur them. The wages of other types of workers – men and women too old to bear children – would be unaffected. The data confirms these predictions: women of childbearing age saw their salaries fall in the years after 1976 relative to both men and older women.

Bhattacharya and Bundorf (2009) find more evidence of wage pass-through by comparing the wages of obese workers with the wages of their thinner co-workers. There is good evidence that obese workers earn less per hour than their thinner colleagues in Europe and the US (Cawley 2004; Brunello et al. 2009). This finding is surprisingly robust and does not appear to be explained by differences between obese and thinner workers in their education, age, or training. Most often, economists attribute the obesity wage gap to discrimination against the obese. Occasionally, economists argue that in some workplaces (think of the modeling industry), non-obese workers are legitimately more productive than obese workers.

But another possible explanation for the obesity wage gap is that obese and thin workers are in different insurance pools and effectively pay different premiums. According to this explanation, obese workers who receive insurance through their employers pay for their higher health care expenditures in the form of lower wages.

Consider two groups of workers: one group with health insurance provided by their employer and one group without. The left panel of Figure 18.1 shows wage paths for a nationally representative group of American workers with employer-sponsored health insurance. The workers in this survey were between 24 and 31 years old in 1989 and were tracked over the next 14 years. As expected, the obese workers earned less than thinner workers, and the gap grew as the cohort aged and became more likely to require medical care. By 2003, the insured obese workers earned nearly $4.60 less per hour than the insured non-obese workers. This wage gap is at least as big as the expected difference in medical expenditures between obese and thin workers.

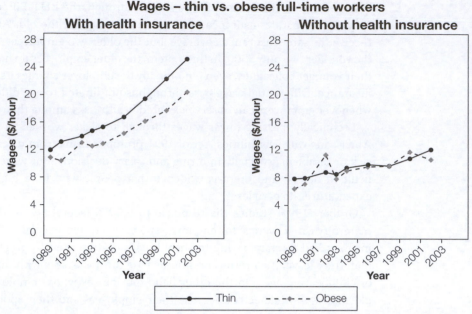

Figure 18.1. *Obesity wage differential. In jobs that provide health insurance, obese workers earn less than thinner workers and gain smaller raises over time. By contrast, in jobs without health insurance, obese and thin workers earn the same wages on average. The obesity wage differential may thus be evidence of wage pass-through.*

Source: Bhattacharya and Bundorf (2009).

By contrast, the right panel of Figure 18.1 shows wage paths for the group without employer-sponsored health insurance. For this group, the obesity wage gap *never develops* – thin and obese workers earn about the same, on average, throughout the study. This pattern of results is exactly what one would expect if it is wage pass-through, not discrimination, driving the wage differential.

In each of these examples, wage pass-through depends on the ability of employers to observe the risk-types of their employees. An employee's age, gender, and weight are easy for managers to observe. When health information is symmetric between employees and employers, sicker employees pay more for health insurance.

But what about unobservable conditions like hypertension? A family history of breast cancer? Other latent genetic conditions? When health information is asymmetric, healthy employees end up pooling with unhealthy ones because firms do not know which employees should receive lower wages. Usually such pooling would unravel due to adverse selection, with healthy enrollees exiting the pool. But the existence of job-specific human capital allows employer–provider insurance pools to survive.

Firm-specific human capital

Recall that the adverse selection problem has to do with differences in *unobservable* risk. In the Rothschild–Stiglitz model, the "robust" and "frail" health insurance customers were indistinguishable because they seemed equally healthy to insurers. If robust and frail people could be told apart easily – if all frail people were elderly and all robust people were young, for example – then adverse selection would not unravel insurance markets because information asymmetry would not exist.

Instead, adverse selection takes place when people who appear equally healthy on the outside – like the two young employees working at BHT Enterprises – actually have two very different risk-types. Wage pass-through separates the employees into different groups according to observable risks. But what is to keep those pools from unraveling due to unobservable health differences?

Even though one is healthier than the other, both young employees lose the same amount in wages as a result of wage pass-through. Similarly, both older workers receive the same wage, though one is a triathlete and has lower expected health care costs. In both pools, the more robust employee subsidizes the frailer one (Figure 18.2).

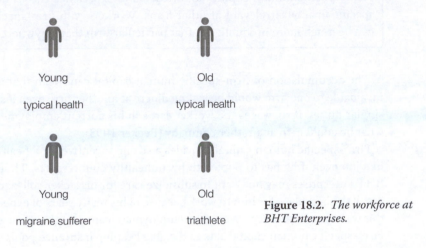

Young
typical health

Old
typical health

Young
migraine sufferer

Old
triathlete

Figure 18.2. *The workforce at BHT Enterprises.*

According to the Akerlof model, these pools should unravel. Robust employees will leave their respective pools, because they are being overcharged for health insurance. As was the case with individual insurance markets, when the robust types leave, average health care costs will grow, causing premiums to increase. This catalyzes another round of adverse selection and another premium increase. Employer-sponsored health insurance will suffer from the problem of adverse selection, unless robust employees can be convinced not to leave their pool.

The endurance of employer-sponsored insurance in the US suggests that there is some motive that keeps employees attached to their insurance pools. The reason is that enrollment in insurance is tied to employment. Most employers do not allow their workers to opt out of paying for their company's insurance plan. They can choose to decline coverage, but a portion of their wages still goes toward funding the firm's insurance premium. Workers can only withdraw from the employer plans by quitting their jobs completely. As long as the disincentive to quit is high enough, the employer-sponsored insurance plan is protected from unraveling.

Why would robust employees stay in their jobs, even when they realize they might be subsidizing their frailer co-workers? If the robust workers could find a desirable job elsewhere where they do not subsidize frailer colleagues, then they would have every incentive to leave their original job. In that case, robust employees migrate to firms with only healthy employees or firms without insurance. As the healthier employees exit their firms, the burden of insurance on other employees increases through greater wage pass-through. Eventually, employer-sponsored health insurance unravels, because the firm is left with only unobservably sick employees.

However, if finding alternative, attractive opportunities is difficult, then the adverse selection problem could be mitigated. One plausible reason why finding alternative employment may be difficult is the existence of **firm-specific human capital**. This kind of capital refers to knowledge gained from experience working with a particular firm that is highly relevant there but irrelevant at other companies. Hence, the human capital is firm-specific.

Definition	18.1

Firm-specific human capital: knowledge and experience that is highly relevant at a specific firm but irrelevant at other firms. Workers with firm-specific human capital can be much more productive at that particular firm than anywhere else.

The accumulation of firm-specific human capital can mean that an employee who is invaluable to one firm would be just mediocre at another firm even if she were performing similar duties. If so, wages the worker earns in his current employment would far exceed what he could earn at another company (Becker 1993).

Firm-specific human capital provides a strong incentive for a healthy employee to stay in a job even if he has to pool with his unhealthy counterparts. Though the triathlete in BHT Enterprises may not want to subsidize care for his sicker colleague, BHT Enterprises is still the best place for him to work because of his many years of experience at the firm. In this way, tying insurance coverage to employment can solve the adverse selection problem. Firm-specific human capital acts as the glue keeping insurance pools together.

The need for firm-specific human capital in maintaining insurance pools may explain why firms in industries with high turnover rates do not typically provide health insurance. At those firms, pooling is harder to sustain, because there is nothing to counteract the effects of adverse selection due to more robust employees exiting the pool. On the other hand, the firms that rely on workers with firm-specific human capital are more likely to provide health insurance (Bhattacharya and Vogt 2006; Amelung et al. 2003).

Job lock

As we have discussed, the success of employer-sponsored insurance in mitigating the adverse selection problem depends on its ability to keep healthy and unhealthy workers together on the same insurance plan. And this in turn depends on the strength of job-specific human capital to reduce the appeal of leaving the company. In one way, tying employer-sponsored health insurance to employment is good, because it combats adverse selection. But tying the two together can also be bad, because it distorts labor markets by hindering job mobility.

Consider a worker at a job which provides employer-sponsored health insurance. Despite working at his current company for years, he would be a better fit for a new job opportunity elsewhere. He is unhappy and could be more productive – and better paid – at another company.

However, in the previous year, the worker became confined to a wheelchair due to a progressive case of multiple sclerosis (MS). He anticipates high health care costs, but, fortunately, his current company's insurance plan covers MS-related care. Despite his higher health care costs, his wages have not been cut by wage pass-through. This may be because wages are sticky downward – that is, resistant to reductions once set (Hall 2005). Moreover, reducing a worker's wages immediately after a disease diagnosis may be a legal liability in a discrimination lawsuit (DeLeire 2000). As a result, the worker's wages may not change, even though the burden he places on the company's health insurance bill has increased.

Suppose the worker still wants to switch jobs. The insurance from his new job might still offer to cover his MS care. But his new employers, when negotiating his new salary, observe his wheelchair and lower his offered wage to compensate for the anticipated rise in health care premiums. Unlike a wage reduction at his current job, the sickness-related wage discrimination is difficult to observe, because the employers can argue that the lower wage is due to being new at the firm and not his MS.

Thus, the potential employers offer the worker a lower salary than his current one, even though his productivity is higher there. This lower offer deters the worker from switching jobs, and he stays – unhappily and inefficiently – at his current one. This confluence of employer-sponsored health insurance, wage pass-through, and sticky wages is known as *job lock*.

The agony of job lock.

Credit: Allen Cox.

Even in the absence of sticky wages, job lock may persist if insurers can, for a time, refuse coverage for expensive pre-existing conditions – ones diagnosed before insurance coverage began. Our example worker was diagnosed with MS while he was with his current firm, so the employer-sponsored insurance plan was obligated to cover his MS-related care. On the other hand, a new insurer at a new employer would view the MS as a pre-existing condition, since it was diagnosed before enrollment. It may deny coverage for his MS, at least for the first year or two.

Under this scenario, switching jobs could be prohibitively costly – the worker would have to pay out-of-pocket for medication and expensive physical therapy. Staying with his current firm, though, allows the worker to keep his current insurance, which is obligated to cover his MS. Thus, employer-sponsored health insurance and the insurer's denial of coverage on pre-existing conditions would also lock the worker in his current job.

Through job lock, employer-sponsored health insurance distorts labor markets and thus can reduce social welfare. Our example worker would be more productive at a different job than he is at his current one, so it would be socially efficient for him to switch. But job lock discourages him from doing so. Society, as a result, misses out on the productivity gain from him switching to a more productive job. From data on American employees in 1987, Madrian (1994) estimates that job lock reduces voluntary employee turnover rate by 25%. In a back-of-the-envelope calculation, Gruber and Madrian (2004) estimate that the total cost of job lock in the US is modest, less than 0.1% of GDP.

One of the reasons why the social loss from job lock is modest may be the result of policies aimed at mitigating the harm of job lock. The Consolidated Omnibus Budget Reconciliation (COBRA) Act of 1985 mandates that firms offer former employees the opportunity to continue in their employer-sponsored health insurance plan temporarily after their termination. Workers have to pay the insurance premium themselves but can typically maintain the plan for up to 18 months. By temporarily decoupling insurance coverage from employment, COBRA eases job mobility.

18.2   The managed care alternative

One of the virtues of a private market in health insurance is that innovators can come up with new ways of doing things. Insurance companies that are not state-run must compete for customers, and this competition can inspire new ideas that save money and make health insurance more efficient. The biggest new idea in health insurance in the last few decades has been *managed care*. As we will see, the philosophy of managed care revolutionized private health insurance in the US and inspired governments around the world to change their public insurance systems as well.

The rise of managed care

In the middle of the twentieth century and even into the 1980s, the American private insurance market was dominated by *indemnity* insurance. This type of insurance is better known as *fee-for-service (FFS)* because it operates on the very simple principle that customers receive health care, and then the insurance company pays the doctor or hospital a fee for each service rendered. Customers would typically be responsible for a deductible and a copayment, but otherwise there were few restrictions. It was up to customers and doctors to decide what care was needed, and payment was based on a tally of whatever services were performed. Coverage for specific treatments was rarely if ever denied, even for expensive regimes that provided only small medical benefits.

The FFS model did not do much to contain moral hazard and provided ample incentive for physician-induced demand. Patients could seek superfluous treatments confident that their insurer would cover most of the bill. Doctors knew that they would be paid for each blood test, X-ray, and surgery they ordered, and some ordered as many procedures as they could get away with. As a result, FFS insurers paid for a lot of unnecessary care, and plans were expensive and inefficient.

But not every insurance plan worked this way. One exceptional plan began as a communal insurance pool for workers in the shipyards of Richmond, California, during World War II. Shipping magnate Henry Kaiser had won several federal contracts to build Liberty warships. At the peak of the war effort, 50,000 workers had flooded into the local area, and the populations of nearby counties had exploded.

Medical care was hard to come by, so Kaiser adopted a solution that had worked for him in the past: charge workers a premium for health care, and then deliver it to them and their families directly through company-owned clinics and hospitals. To run the plan, Kaiser appointed physician-entrepreneur Sidney Garfield, who had administered similar plans at Kaiser's earlier construction projects in Washington state and Southern California. After the war, employment at the shipyards dwindled, and Garfield began marketing the Kaiser plan to the public. Today, Kaiser Permanente is one of the most prominent managed care plans in the US (Hendricks 1991, 1993; Mechanic 2004).

The Kaiser plan was not the first of its kind, but it featured several aspects that would have been unfamiliar to most of its new customers. Insured patients were only reimbursed for treatment at Kaiser-owned and operated hospitals and clinics, and saw doctors and nurses who were employed exclusively by Kaiser Permanente. The insurance would not pay for appointments with doctors outside the group and would not pay for specialist appointments unless first approved by a Kaiser primary care physician (Hendricks 1991).

Unlike with the FFS arrangement, Kaiser's doctors were salaried and had no incentive to order superfluous tests. In fact, doctors were explicitly responsible for thinking economically and containing costs. As a result, Kaiser faced complaints and legal challenges from the American Medical Association, which accused it of "corporatizing" medicine (Hendricks 1991).

The Kaiser plan is emblematic of the managed care movement. It features gatekeeping tactics, vertical integration of insurance and health care provision, and replaces the FFS system with salaried doctors. Patient outcomes and health care expenditures are also monitored to ensure that only cost-effective care is provided. If the patient demands cost-ineffective care, like an expensive drug or an ineffective surgery, that care may not be covered. Patients may appeal denial decisions to an arbitration but there is no guarantee that all treatments will be covered (Studdert et al. 1999). These managed care strategies aim to reduce moral hazard, reduce physician-induced demand, and consequently reduce health care costs.

Definition 18.2

Managed care: health insurance plans that use tactics intended to reduce moral hazard and physician-induced demand; if successful in reducing health expenditures, plans can charge lower premiums.

These tactics include:

- **gatekeeping** – patients can only visit specialists or surgeons after receiving approval from a primary care doctor;
- **coverage networks and vertical integration** – patients can only receive care from a specified list of providers, who are sometimes direct employees of the managed care organization;
- **monitoring** – doctors and hospitals are monitored for costs and health outcomes;
- **salaries and fixed payments** – the insurer pays a fixed amount for care; not fee-for-service;
- **denials of coverage** – care may not be covered if it is not cost-effective.

In the decades after Kaiser Permanente was founded, more insurers began offering managed care plans. Customers and policymakers alike took notice of their apparent cost savings. A 1973 federal law called the Health Maintenance Organization Act removed potential legal roadblocks for managed care plans and provided other tax incentives to encourage adoption. It also established the term *health maintenance organization* (HMO) to denote vertically integrated managed care organizations like Kaiser Permanente.

Another type of managed care option is the *preferred provider organization* (PPO), which also gained popularity during this period. A PPO is a less restrictive version of a HMO that does not integrate insurer and provider. Instead, the insurer restricts patients to a list of preferred providers where they can seek care. Like HMO, the PPO requires patients to go through gatekeepers. It also monitors doctors and hospitals closely by tracking expenditures and health outcomes. If a provider fails to treat its patients in a cost-effective manner, it risks being dropped from the preferred provider list and losing customers.

Gradually, consumers and employers began migrating from expensive FFS insurers toward cheaper HMO and PPO plans. During the 1990s and 2000s, HMOs and PPOs drove the FFS model nearly to extinction. In 1988, 27% of Americans with private insurance subscribed to plans with managed care elements instead of more traditional FFS plans. By 1996, that figure had risen to 73%, and by 2008 it was 98% (see Figure 18.3).

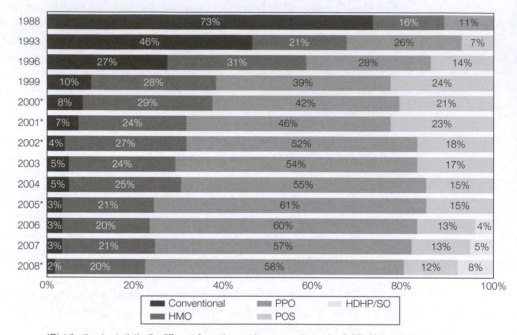

*Distribution is statistically different from the previous year shown (p<0.05). No statistical tests were conducted for years prior to 1999. No statistical tests are conducted between 2005 and 2006 due to the addition of HDHP/SO as a new plan type in 2006.

Figure 18.3. *Distribution of US private health insurance customers by plan type.*

Note: The "conventional" plans are fee-for-service plans. HDHP/SO and POS plans are less common types of managed care plans that are not discussed in this chapter.

Source: Reproduced with permission from Employer Health Benefits 2012 Annual Survey (no. 8345), The Henry J. Kaiser Family Foundation and HRET, September 2012.

Does managed care work?

As managed care became increasingly popular in the 1990s, it spawned an outburst of research trying to determine whether managed care is better for patients than traditional fee-for-service insurance. The research focuses on two questions: does managed care make health care cheaper, and does it keep people healthy?

In a review of evidence from thirty studies in the 1990s, Gottfried and Sloan (2002) show that there is no systematic difference in health outcomes between managed care organizations and FFS plans. Instead, the evidence appears mixed across different health outcomes. For example, managed care patients with unstable angina and breast cancer fared better than their counterparts on FFS plans, but stroke victims on managed care plans fared worse. There is some stronger evidence that vulnerable populations (including the elderly, the poor, and those who are already severely ill) are worse off under managed care.

Evidence on cost savings is less equivocal: it seems that managed care organizations do keep costs lower. In general, managed care patients are hospitalized less often and undergo fewer expensive tests (Baker 2002). There is also evidence that managed care has slowed the proliferation of expensive technologies like MRI machines (Baker 2001).

One important caveat is that managed care plans tend to attract healthier customers due to adverse selection. The logic of adverse selection suggests that unobservably healthy customers opt for cheaper plans that offer less comprehensive insurance. If this is the case, managed care might appear to be reducing costs not because of the tactics listed in Definition 18.2, but simply because their customers are healthier (Baker 2002).

An interesting side note is that academic researchers who study managed care professionally are less likely to personally enroll in managed care plans themselves. In a survey of 17 academic institutions, Studdert et al. (2002) find that managed care experts were significantly less likely to enroll in an HMO than philosophers, mathematicians, and law professors.

The backlash against HMOs

The managed care revolution had another effect on the American health care system. Some of the strategies employed by managed care organizations included gatekeeping and restrictive networks, and the acronym "HMO" became something of a dirty word in American political discourse and even in popular culture. A 2001 survey found that Americans held the managed care industry in very low esteem; its unpopularity was second only to the tobacco industry (Mechanic 2004). Even as managed care enrollment increased throughout the 1990s and 2000s, HMO enrollment actually peaked in 1996 and declined thereafter (Figure 18.3).

The backlash against HMOs became a cultural phenomenon that even appeared on the silver screen. The 1999 film John Q *tells the story of a father whose son is denied a heart transplant by his HMO. He responds by taking a hospital hostage and demanding that his son receive the surgery. The 1997 hit* As Good As It Gets *also features a stingy HMO.   Credit. Brand X Pictures.*

In the FFS era, doctors had no reason to deny patients any kind of service because the costs were too high. While ineffective at controlling moral hazard, this system fostered trust between patients and doctors, and freed patients from having to worry about economic considerations entering their doctor's thinking. But the introduction of HMOs turned some doctor–patient relationships adversarial by making doctors partly responsible for containing costs. This introduced a note of distrust – patients now had to worry that their doctors might prioritize reducing costs over improving their patients' health (Starr 1982).

HMOs also became notorious for refusing to pay for some care for sick patients. Cancer patients or AIDS patients who wanted to try experimental treatments or cost-ineffective drugs were occasionally denied coverage, and some of these incidents received intense media attention and became a rallying point for politicians and activists (Remler et al. 1997). In the late 1990s, many state governments instituted reforms and regulations to combat some of the perceived parsimony of HMOs.

Despite the backlash, public insurance plans in the US and around the world have also adopted or maintained some of the same tactics pioneered by HMOs. US Medicare has ended FFS payments to hospitals, France and Germany have embraced gatekeeping rules,

Switzerland has experimented extensively with HMOs, and several single-payer systems have adopted explicit cost-effectiveness measures (Forrest 2003; Lehmann and Zweifel 2004; Schreyögg et al. 2006). Moreover, the backlash itself is coming to be seen in a new light. Subsequent research has shown that HMOs remain popular among Medicaid and Medicare enrollees, low-income groups, and in regions with high health care costs (Marquis et al. 2004).

18.3 Medicare: universal coverage for the elderly and the severely disabled

Medicare is the major government insurance program for the elderly that was enacted in 1965. Prior to that time, retirees were hard-pressed to find health insurance coverage, because they could not access employer-sponsored insurance and the individual market was extremely expensive (Ball 1995). With the introduction of Medicare, seniors were assured affordable access to health insurance, regardless of their wealth or health status.

Medicare provides insurance coverage for 48 million elderly and disabled people (as of 2012), so it is little surprise that the program is very expensive. In 2011, it represented over 15% of the US federal budget, totalling $549 billion in health expenditures. This makes Medicare the world's largest insurer by expenditures, and by far the biggest payer in the American health system. This means that Medicare has significant power in the market for health care services, and private insurers often follow its lead when it comes to pricing and coverage decisions. Although enormously popular with enrollees, its future is in doubt as health care costs continue their rapid rise.

Structure

In part because of the history of its implementation, the structure of Medicare is a farrago of four parts:

- **Part A** pays for enrollees' hospital care.
- **Part B** pays for outpatient care and physician services.
- **Part C** provides an option for Medicare enrollees to receive their health insurance from a private plan (typically a plan with managed care features) rather than through the government.
- **Part D** was implemented in 2006 and pays for prescription drugs for enrollees.

Part A

Every American citizen over age 65 is eligible to enroll in Medicare Part A. Severely disabled Americans who have been out of work for at least two years are also eligible to enroll, but these enrollees make up only a small share of the Medicare population. Part A also covers patients with end-stage renal disease who need regular kidney dialysis to survive. For those enrolled in Medicare Part A, the government pays most of the costs related to hospitalizations and short stays in skilled nursing facilities. Part A was implemented with the passage of the Medicare enabling act in 1965.

As of 2012, there was a premium of $375 per month for Medicare Part A, but the vast majority of enrollees are exempt. Those who have worked in the US for at least ten years and paid the requisite Medicare taxes while they were working do not need to pay any premium. The spouses of these workers, along with all severely disabled enrollees, are also exempt.

Part B

Eligibility for Medicare Part B is determined in exactly the same way as for Part A. Unlike Part A, however, all eligible people must pay a premium of about $100 per month, though wealthier enrollees face higher premiums. For those enrolled in Part B, the government pays for physicians' services and outpatient visits, as well as for certain injectable drugs, like morphine or chemotherapeutic agents, given to patients during hospital stays.

Part C

Medicare Part C, also known as Medicare Advantage, is an optional private system that replaces the other parts of Medicare for those enrollees who opt for it. It was first implemented in 1997. Rather than the government directly insuring enrollees, Medicare contracts with a private Medicare Advantage insurer of the patient's choice. Most Medicare Advantage plans are organized like HMOs, with gatekeepers and provider networks.

Over 10 million people, nearly a quarter of all Medicare enrollees, receive insurance through Part C (Jaffe 2009). Participation varies substantially by region, depending on the availability of local Medicare Advantage plans. Nearly half of Medicare enrollees opt for Part C in California (where HMOs are plentiful), but enrollees in some rural areas have no Part C plans available.

If an enrollee opts for Part C, the government pays the insurer a fixed amount each year. In exchange, the company is responsible for covering any services that traditional Medicare would cover. Medicare Advantage insurers can attract customers by offering additional services, lower copayments, or lower premiums.

Medicare pays a risk-adjusted amount to the private insurer for each enrollee's participation and also pays more for individuals who live in counties with high health expenditures. Part C is intended to save money by privatizing insurance care for some enrollees. But in practice, it costs the government more to cover patients through Medicare Advantage than it would to cover them directly through traditional Medicare (Brown et al. 2011; Kronick 2009). This overpayment happens largely because the premiums government pays to Part C insurers can be generous compared with the expected expenditures of healthy enrollees. One consequence of this overpayment is that Part C plans tend to target their marketing toward more healthy enrollees, creating adverse selection for the traditional (Parts A and B) Medicare plan.

Part D

The newest part of Medicare, Part D, provides an optional prescription drug benefit to Medicare enrollees. Prior to the introduction of Part D in 2006, only 75% of elderly Americans had prescription drug insurance, and then only through supplemental plans. Within one year of its introduction, over 90% of elderly Americans had prescription drug coverage (Levy and DeLeire 2009).

Like Medicare Advantage, Part D coverage is administered by private insurance companies. The insurance companies charge enrollees a premium for these plans, but a Medicare subsidy covers most of that cost. The companies offer insurance packages that vary in cost-sharing levels, as well as the set of covered drugs.

For a private insurer to offer a Part D plan, the government requires that the insurer offer consumers at least one standard plan that meets certain minimum standards for generosity. For instance, the standard plan cannot have coinsurance rates above a maximum permissible level; that is, the plan cannot require enrollees to pay more than a pre-specified fraction of their prescription drug costs. Private plans often offer more generous coverage than the standard plan, and they also compete with each other on the premiums that they charge to enrollees (Joyce and Lau 2009).

Financing

Medicare is expensive because it covers elderly people who are less healthy than the general population and tend to demand lots of medical care. It also reimburses for any procedure that is shown to be medically effective, irrespective of cost.

Despite this great expense, one of the main principles that underlie Medicare financing is that the premiums paid by Medicare enrollees should be much less than actuarially fair premiums would be. For most enrollees, there is no premium charged for Medicare Part A at all. And though enrollees do pay some premiums for the other parts of Medicare as well as coinsurance and deductibles, premiums and cost-sharing paid for only 16% of the costs of Medicare in 2011 (Medicare Board of Trustees 2012).

The rest is paid for by taxes, mostly from people still in the workforce and not yet eligible for Medicare. Workers and their employers finance Medicare Part A by jointly paying a payroll tax totaling 2.9% of every worker's income. In 2013, this is scheduled to increase to 3.8% for income above $200,000 per year. The other parts of Medicare are financed through general federal revenues. The primary source of monies is individual income taxes and corporate income taxes.

Is Medicare progressive or regressive?

One of the main arguments for government provision of health insurance is to promote more equitable access to expensive health care. Whether any particular program actually does promote equity in practice is an empirical question that depends both on who bears the burden of financing the program and on who receives the benefits from the program. A *progressive* program benefits poorer people more than the rich, while a *regressive* program benefits the rich more than the poor.

In the US the fact that poorer people die at earlier ages than richer people (see Chapter 4) means that the latter have more time to receive Social Security pension benefits (Garrett 1995). However, over their lifetime, richer people also tend to pay more in taxes. Researchers have come to different conclusions regarding whether US Social Security is progressive or regressive. Coronado et al. (2011) argue that if people have a low discount rate, then the system is progressive.

Calculating whether the US Medicare system is regressive or progressive is difficult because expenditures on health care depend on both health status and income. Poorer people tend to be less healthy than richer people and so have higher health expenditures, all else being equal. Also, income taxes, which finance parts of Medicare, are progressive since the rich pay higher rates. Together, these facts make Medicare more progressive, because poorer people pay less and benefit more. However, the poor do not live as long as the rich, and richer people tend to spend more on any given health condition than the poor. This makes Medicare more regressive. Thus, judging Medicare's overall progressivity requires a complete accounting of all of these facts (Bhattacharya and Lakdawalla 2006).

McClellan and Skinner (2006) analyze the progressivity of Medicare by calculating its lifetime net present value from the point of view of an 18-year-old. They proxy lifetime wealth with neighborhood income levels: those living in high-income neighborhoods are considered rich. Those people tend to consume more health care resources than people of equivalent health living in a poorer neighborhood. Based on this preliminary analysis, they conclude that Medicare is regressive, since it provides a higher net present value for richer people than it does for poorer people.

However, this initial analysis does not include the welfare benefits of risk reduction due to Medicare. McClellan and Skinner (2006) argue that prior to Medicare's introduction in 1965, the burden of uninsurance and underinsurance fell most heavily on poorer elderly; richer people were better able to find insurance in an incomplete market. By completing the market, Medicare's universal insurance coverage disproportionately benefits the poor. The poor seem to benefit more from the security of Medicare coverage, even if they tend to use less health care. McClellan and Skinner ultimately conclude that Medicare is progressive for this reason.

Cost control in Medicare

Medicare includes a number of mechanisms designed to mitigate moral hazard and control costs. In both Medicare Parts A and B, patients face modest cost-sharing requirements, including deductibles and copayments for outpatient visits and hospital stays longer than 60 days. However, most Medicare enrollees also purchase private supplemental insurance, called Medigap plans, which pay for enrollees' deductibles and copayments. While this reduces the financial risk borne by Medicare enrollees, such plans undercut the moral hazard mitigation effects of cost-sharing (Wolfe and Goddeeris 1991; Coulson et al. 1995).

A more significant cost control mechanism is the diagnosis related group (DRG) system, first introduced in 1984 as a new method by which Medicare pays hospitals and subsequently adopted by many public insurance plans around the world. Under the system, Medicare pays a fixed amount to hospitals based upon the *diagnosis* the patient has when admitted to the hospital, rather than on how many days the patient stays in the hospital or on what particular medical services the patient receives while there.

For particularly difficult patients with many comorbid conditions, hospitals may be eligible for an additional fixed payment (called an "outlier" payment). Payments are also adjusted upward for hospitals located in high-income or urban areas, and also for hospitals that serve a high volume of low-income patients (Brady et al. 2001).

The DRG system of hospital payment transfers risk from the government to hospitals. Hospitals partially internalize the costs of patient care because they are paid the same whether the patient receives one MRI scan or two. The aim of this policy is to eliminate any incentive for hospitals to provide unnecessarily expensive care to patients. Medicare pays the same amount to a hospital for a patient admitted with a heart attack, no matter which services the patient receives during the stay. Because of this, the hospital has every

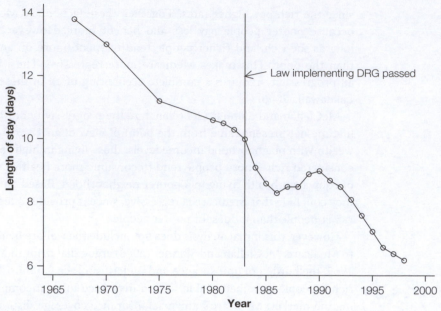

Figure 18.4. *Average hospital length of stay in the US fell more sharply after the diagnosis related group (DRG) system went into effect.*

Source: Authors' calculations using data from the AHA Hospital Statistics database.

incentive to care for the patient efficiently and keep any margin as profit. One consequence of this incentive is that the DRG system contributed to the reduction in the average length of stay at American hospitals in the years after it was introduced (Figure 18.4).

However, hospitals do face other constraints that limit how much they can cut services. For instance, if a hospital responds by eschewing all expensive care – even valuable services – it risks losing patients to other hospitals. It also alienates doctors who want to provide their patients with high-quality care (Harris 1977).

Some opposed the adoption of DRGs because they feared patients would suffer if hospitals became overly concerned with cutting costs. Cutler (1995) finds no long-run change in inpatient mortality as a result of the introduction of DRGs. However, he did find that mortality increased temporarily at a subset of hospitals during the transition to the DRG system in 1984. The hospitals that faced the steepest decline in payments due to DRG pricing had the worst short-run outcomes. Presumably, these were the hospitals that had splurged the most on patient care in the pre-DRG era and faced the biggest challenge in adjusting to the new payment scheme.

By contrast, physicians are paid on an FFS basis using a system known as the resource-based relative value scale (RBRVS). In this system, each unit of physician labor is priced based on the skill, time, energy, and resources needed to provide that unit. For example, a routine office visit (procedure code 99213) is valued at 1.7 relative value units (RVUs). In 2009, each RVU was reimbursed at a rate of $36.0666, so the routine office visit earned the doctor $61.31. A more complicated procedure, such as lancing a leg hematoma (procedure code 27603), is valued at 12.99 RVUs. That procedure would earn the doctor $468.51. Medicare compensates doctors according to how many RVUs they accumulate, so they have incentive to order treatments and procedures that are highly valued by Medicare and relatively inexpensive to perform (Robinson 2001).

Finally, there is a major cost control tool that Medicare is prohibited from using: cost-effectiveness analysis (see Chapter 14). Medicare's authorizing legislation states that Medicare cannot pay for "items and services that are not reasonable and necessary for the diagnosis or treatment of illness or injury." Before 1989, "reasonable and necessary" was interpreted by Medicare as "safe, effective, non-investigational, and appropriate." In other words, any treatment that was proven effective in scientific studies – regardless of cost – would be covered by Medicare (Neumann 2005).

In 1989, the agency that administers Medicare proposed changing the interpretation of "reasonable and necessary" so that CEA could be used to help determine what treatments to cover. Officials argued that it was not "reasonable" for Medicare to pay for treatments that produced little health benefit at enormous cost. These proposed rule changes met stiff resistance in Congress and from industry groups, and were never adopted. Today, Medicare continues to pay billions of dollars annually for expensive procedures like lung-volume reduction surgery, left ventricular assist devices, and positron-emission tomography that are restricted in countries that base coverage decisions on CEA (Neumann et al. 2005).

It seems likely that Medicare could reap substantial budgetary savings from CEA, but so far there has been little political will to introduce CEA into Medicare's coverage determination. In the coming decades, rising costs may force policymakers – and voters – to revisit the issue (Gold et al. 2007).

18.4 Medicaid: subsidized coverage for the poor

Medicaid is the other major public insurance program that was created alongside Medicare in 1965. Medicaid provides highly subsidized insurance coverage to low-income families who have no insurance and would not be able to afford it on the open market. Medicaid was heralded as an effort to improve health equity in the US by providing free and low-cost care to the poorest members of society.

Structure and financing

Unlike Medicare, which is run by the US federal government and administered uniformly across the United States, Medicaid is run jointly by the federal government and state governments. State governments have wide latitude to set budgets, determine eligibility rules, and decide how generous their local Medicaid program will be. As a consequence, Medicaid coverage and generosity can vary substantially from state to state. Medicaid spending comprises about 15% of state budgets on average, second only to education spending in most states (Geo 2011). The federal government matches state expenditures to help states finance Medicaid, but it also mandates minimum levels of coverage and eligibility.

In all states, Medicaid provides free or nearly free coverage to those who are eligible and enroll. In 2009, Medicaid covered 62.5 million people – about a fifth of the US population – and its expenses totaled about $400 billion nationwide. This spending amounted to about $5,500 per enrollee, much less than average expenditures for Medicare and private insurers (Kai 2012). Copayments for prescription drugs and physician services are typically nominal (under $10) for most enrollees, while copayments for hospital visits can range up to $50 or $100 (Kai 2012). Because these out-of-pocket payments by enrollees are low by design, almost all Medicaid expenses are paid for with taxpayer dollars.

Low income alone does not qualify one for Medicaid in most states. Various other factors including marital status, number of children, pregnancy, disability, health, and immigration status are also taken into account and can affect eligibility. In general, able-bodied individuals without children are not eligible for coverage, no matter how low their incomes are.

The recent 2010 health care reform expanded the eligibility requirements to include people at higher income levels – up to 133% of the federal poverty line from 100%. We provide more details about the changes in Medicaid due to the health reform act later in the chapter.

Cost control in Medicaid

Cost-sharing burdens for Medicaid enrollees are typically very low, so Medicaid programs must contain costs and curb moral hazard with a combination of eligibility and coverage restrictions. Each state is responsible for financing a share of its Medicaid bill, so it relies on these restrictions to control state spending. States do face some constraints; the federal government sets minimum eligibility thresholds that depend on income and family structure. Poor families with dependent children, for instance, must be eligible for enrollment. States are free to expand Medicaid eligibility beyond this core group, but they are also at liberty to maintain strict limits on Medicaid eligibility.

Another major way that states control Medicaid expenditures is by setting reimbursement rates at a low level. A doctor treating a Medicaid patient can expect only a fraction of the payment she would get for seeing a privately insured patient with the exact same health condition. One consequence of these low reimbursements is that Medicaid patients can have trouble finding a regular source of care, as many doctors choose not to accept Medicaid patients. Weissman et al. (2008), for instance, find that 24% of low-income individuals in the US report a lack of access to physician services due to the high costs of care, even in states with generous Medicaid coverage.

An audit study run in 2002 illustrates the difficulty of securing timely health care with Medicaid insurance. Asplin et al. (2005) employed two sets of research assistants to contact 499 clinics nationwide and ask for a doctor's appointment. The research assistants posed as patients who had recently been seen in an emergency room and requested a follow-up appointment within the week. They each pretended to have one of three urgent conditions requiring immediate attention: pneumonia, very high blood pressure, or symptoms of ectopic pregnancy.

The two sets of research assistants reported the exact same background story and the exact same set of symptoms to each clinic, but one group claimed to be insured by Medicaid while the other group claimed to be insured privately. While 64% of the privately insured research assistants were able to schedule appointments within one week, only 34% of the Medicaid-insured research assistants were able to receive similar appointments.

States also control costs by restricting the set of prescription drugs that are available to Medicaid enrollees, and again by setting reimbursement rates at a low level. The list of drugs available – known as a formulary – often excludes expensive branded drugs when generic alternatives are available. Unsurprisingly, Coughlin et al. (2005) find that Medicaid enrollees have less access to prescription drugs than their counterparts with private insurance. However, unlike some other researchers, they do not find any differences in access to physician services and hospital care.

Access to health care for the poor can be quite uneven across states as a result of differing eligibility rules and reimbursement rates. Bhattacharya et al. (2003) highlight the case of HIV patients on Medicaid in the mid-1990s. At the time, the best treatment to control the consequences of HIV was called highly active anti-retroviral therapy (HAART). HAART treatment consists of a cocktail of drugs which act together to limit the advance of HIV. HAART is expensive (it cost about $13,000 a year in 1997) so Medicaid is usually the only way for the poor to obtain it.

In 1997, some states made all low-income HIV-positive patients eligible for Medicaid and covered the full set of drugs that comprised HAART. But in other states, copayments for treatment were high or some of the HAART drugs were not covered at all. In yet other states, HIV patients could qualify for free care, but only once they became extremely poor and extremely sick. Unsurprisingly, HIV mortality was higher in states with stingier Medicaid programs. In the years since 1997, coverage for HAART within Medicaid has become much more generous and comprehensive nationwide.

Some states have experimented with other forms of cost containment, including explicit cost effective analysis – unlike Medicare, Medicaid plans are not prohibited from using CEA. One high-profile cost containment initiative is the Oregon Medicaid List. In 1991, the Oregon Health Plan devised a ranking of more than 700 medical procedures by priority. The priority list drew on input from four sources: town hall meetings with the general public, quality of life surveys with random citizens, treatment cost and effectiveness ratings by physicians, and the judgment of the Oregon Health Care planning commission (Kaplan 1994). In the first year the list was in effect, the administrators decided they could afford to cover only the top 587 procedures, so Oregon's Medicaid plan stopped paying for its enrollees to receive low-priority procedures like *in vitro* fertilization and radial keratotomy (Bodenheimer 1997).

The plan immediately drew accusations of rationing. Future Vice-President Al Gore criticized it for "[rationing] health care to [Oregon's] poorest women and children." In 1992, the Oregon Medicaid proposal was rejected by the US federal government. In particular, Oregon's Health Plan was considered illegal because the plan discriminated against people with disabilities by valuing their lives less (see Chapter 14 for more about valuing life). An altered proposal without an explicit quality-of-life component was approved and went into effect in 1994. Despite initial opposition, the plan succeeded in reducing costs and saved enough money to significantly expand Medicaid eligibility (Oberlander 2006).

Work disincentive effects of Medicaid

While Medicaid certainly improves health equity, it also reduces economic efficiency. This is because Medicaid is a means-tested program, so eligibility depends on income (and a few other factors). Medicaid eligibility rules create a disincentive to work as hard as possible, because rising incomes can mean disqualification from Medicaid.

Consider Jay, a manual laborer who can only manage to find odd jobs in his neighborhood due to a bad recession. His annual income is far below the federal poverty line, so he is eligible for Medicaid coverage in his state. This is fortunate for him, because Medicaid is the only way that he can afford the expensive medicines he needs to control his diabetes and chronic back pain. If he loses Medicaid coverage, he would have to pay thousands of dollars each year out of pocket for the drugs that keep him healthy.

When the recession ends, construction jobs become plentiful and contractors are offering attractive wages – but no health insurance – to anyone willing to work. Jay considers taking some of those jobs, but he knows that if he works full time his income will rise above the poverty line and he will lose Medicaid coverage. If the Medicaid benefits are worth more to Jay than the income from extra hours of work would be, Jay has no reason to increase his labor output. Even if the prospective income slightly exceeds the value of Medicaid, the prospect of reduced leisure time may be enough to dissuade him. He can instead opt to work a light schedule, rest his back, and have Medicaid pay for his prescription drugs.

To formalize Jay's choice, let:

- L be the number of hours Jay works each year,
- w be his wage,
- M be the quantity of health care that Jay consumes, and
- p the price of each unit of health care.

Jay's income I is

$$I = wL \tag{18.1}$$

and his total assets A are the sum of his income and the value of Medicaid to him:

$$A = I + pM \tag{18.2}$$

Figure 18.5 depicts the labor market decision of a low-income worker like Jay. The solid line indicates the total assets (wage plus Medicaid benefits) that Jay earns as a function of L, and the slope of this line reflects his wage.

The indifference curves represent Jay's tastes for assets and leisure. Since Jay prefers having more assets and more leisure, utility is increasing to the northwest in this figure. Jay prefers any point on indifference curve U_1 to points on indifference curve U_0. The positive slope of the indifference curves reflects Jay's tradeoff between assets and leisure.

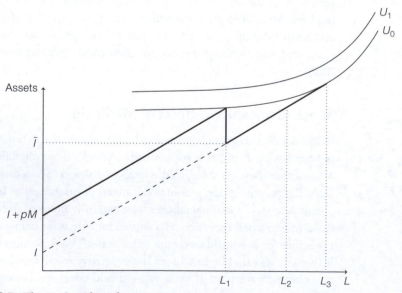

Figure 18.5. *The Medicaid notch.*

In the figure, $\bar{I}$ is the income threshold for Medicaid eligibility. If $I > \bar{I}$, Jay loses eligibility for Medicaid. The moment Jay's income exceeds $\bar{I}$, which happens when Jay works more than L_1 hours, he loses pM worth of assets. This creates a cleft in the solid line called the *Medicaid notch*. The presence of this notch creates a perverse labor incentive for Jay.

Would Jay ever choose to work between L_1 and L_2 hours per year? He has the same total assets at L_1 and L_2, but at L_2 he works more hours. Since he likes leisure, he is better off working L_1 hours and collecting Medicaid benefits. In fact, he will never choose to work between L_1 and L_3 hours per year. His indifference curve indicates that the extra leisure he enjoys at L_1 is more appealing than the additional income he would earn between L_2 and L_3.

Without the Medicaid notch, workers like Jay would work more. The Medicaid notch represents a social loss because it is an indication that human capital that could be effectively put to use is instead sitting idle. Yelowitz (1995) finds that several reforms in the early 1990s designed to decrease the work disincentive effects of Medicaid succeeded in increasing the labor force participation of poor women.

18.5   Uninsurance

Together, the government and the private sector provide health insurance to hundreds of millions of people in the US. As we have seen, most full-time workers, including their spouses and children, are covered through employer-sponsored private insurance. Elderly and disabled individuals are covered through the Medicare program, which is financed and run by the federal government. Poor people are covered through the Medicaid program, which is financed and run by both state and federal governments. Children are insured either through their parents' insurance or through a public program called State Child Health Insurance Program (SCHIP).

But there is no guarantee of health insurance coverage provided by the government to all citizens, and there are many who do not fall into any of the categories mentioned above and have no affordable source of insurance coverage. In theory, anyone without insurance could buy private insurance on the individual market. However, the premiums for signing on to such health insurance are often very high, and only a small fraction end up signing on to non-employer-based private health insurance. The remainder, who number about 50–60 million people as of 2012, are not covered by any health insurance program and are termed "uninsured." The uninsured can still pay for medical care out of pocket, but they face the risk of catastrophic health bills and often end up deferring care until it becomes an emergency (Hadley and Holahan 2003). The persistence of uninsurance has been one of the main drivers of health policy reform in the US.

Figure 18.6 reports the findings of the 2010 National Health Interview Survey, a nationally representative survey that collects information about insurance coverage in the US. The rate of uninsurance depends on how the term is defined; about 60 million Americans (20%) were uninsured for at least part of 2010, but only 36 million (12%) were without insurance for the entire year (Cohen et al. 2011). The latter group is sometimes called chronically uninsured, and may consist of kinds of people very different from those who are merely uninsured for a brief spell.

Some uninsurance is voluntary; a large segment of the uninsured population consists of young people who are fairly healthy and see no reason to seek health insurance.

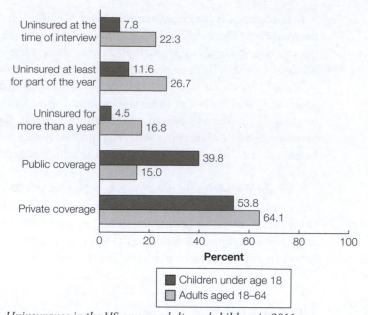

Figure 18.6. *Uninsurance in the US among adults and children in 2011.*

Source: Figure 1 of Cohen et al. (2011). Based on estimates from the US National Health Interview Survey, CDC.

Uninsurance was near 34% among the 19–25 age group in 2010. A different segment of the uninsured population is only momentarily uninsured; oftentimes these people are between jobs or about to enroll in a public insurance program.

However, there are others who desire insurance coverage but have no prospects of obtaining it anytime soon. These people tend to be long-term unemployed or working jobs that do not offer health insurance. Farber and Levy (2000) find that these sorts of jobs – which tend to be "peripheral" jobs that are part-time or involve high turnover – have become increasingly common in the US labor market in recent years.

Those without insurance through their employer have the option of seeking coverage on the individual insurance market, but adverse selection is largely unchecked in these markets (recall the example of the adverse selection death spiral in the individual insurance market in New Jersey from Chapter 10). Insurance through the individual market can be unaffordable for even middle-class families.

Uninsurance is problematic for several reasons. First, evidence from the Oregon Medicaid Experiment suggests that uninsurance can be hazardous to one's health (see Chapter 2). Second, Chapter 7 shows that insurance provides useful risk reduction; the uninsured population faces unpleasant and costly health-related financial risks that people with insurance do not need to worry about. Finally, widespread uninsurance is considered a failure of equity, since vulnerable populations are typically the least likely to be insured.

18.6   2010 health reform

In March 2010, a health care reform law called the *Patient Protection and Affordable Care Act (PPACA)* was passed by the US Congress. This law, colloquially known as "Obamacare," was designed to address the ongoing problem of uninsurance. Starting in 2014,

PPACA will extend insurance coverage to about 35 million people who would otherwise be uninsured.

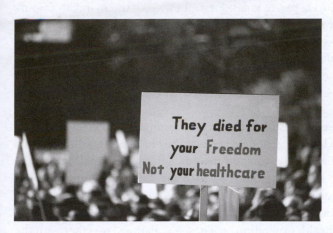

In some ways, PPACA represents a shift of the American model toward the Bismarck and Beveridge models; free insurance for the poor will be expanded, insurance coverage will be mandated for almost all citizens, and many will receive subsidies to purchase insurance. At the same time, the American model will retain many of its defining characteristics, even after PPACA is implemented fully in 2014 (barring repeal or changes to the law). Private insurers and employer-sponsored insurance will still play large roles in the health care system, and private health care providers will still be able to set their own prices and innovate without direction from the government. Though PPACA is a far-reaching law with thousands of separate provisions, we focus here on three major parts of the law that will affect insurance coverage in the US.

Health care policy changes tend to arouse political passions, and PPACA was no exception. The law nearly died in Congress after a series of protests swept across the country in the summer of 2009. Credit: Wayne Howard – iStockphoto.com.

Medicaid expansion

The law expands Medicaid dramatically, covering about 17 million additional people by making eligibility requirements less restrictive (Elmendorf 2011). Traditionally, only poor families and single parents with children qualified for Medicaid coverage. After PPACA, Medicaid will become available to all American citizens under a certain income threshold (about $15,000 in 2014), even if they are single and do not have any children. Care for these people will be financed partly by the federal government and partly by states, with minimal cost-sharing and no premiums paid by enrollees.

The individual mandate and health insurance exchanges

The second major part of PPACA is the requirement that all citizens purchase private health insurance if they do not have health insurance available through another source. The law requires each state to establish a private health insurance marketplace called an "exchange." The law sets numerous regulations for private insurance products sold on the exchange, including minimum levels of required coverage for particular services (such as maternity benefits) and maximum levels of cost-sharing. The government also rates each insurance product on the basis of its generosity, designating each plan as gold, silver, or bronze.

Insurance products offered on these exchanges will be expensive; a typical insurance plan for a family of four could cost about $12,000. Given that the law mandates that people buy such coverage, this could impose a significant hardship on even middle-class families. To address this concern, the law provides substantial subsidies, adjusted for household income level, to people who purchase insurance on the exchange (Holtz-Eakin and Smith 2010). For instance, a family of four who earn $31,500 (133% of the federal poverty line) per year will qualify for a $14,100 subsidy from the federal government. Even households that earn up to $94,800 per year (400% of the federal poverty line for a family of four) will qualify for at least some subsidies. These households receive less – about $3,000 – to defray the costs of health insurance.

These subsidies accomplish two separate goals. First, they make the mandate to purchase insurance much less onerous for middle-class households. Second, they promote equity by means-testing the level of support and making high-quality insurance plans affordable for all. The law calculates the subsidy levels based on the prices of the silver-rated plans, so even middle-income people can afford generous insurance. Projections suggest that nearly 24 million new people will be covered on the exchanges by the year 2020 (Elmendorf 2011).

One key feature of the new exchanges is that insurance companies offering plans are prevented from charging people higher premiums because they have pre-existing chronic diseases or other predictors of high health expenditures (though smokers may be charged a higher premium). The law also limits the extent to which age can be taken into account in setting premiums. These regulations are a form of *community rating*, in which high- and low-risk customers pay a pooled premium, rather than paying a premium commensurate with their own expected health expenditures. These regulations, together with the insurance mandate, guarantee that younger and healthier people on the exchanges will subsidize the care of older, less-healthy people enrolled in the same plan. This is similar to the cross-subsidization that occurs in Bismarck model nations, where community rating is also required.

As we have seen in Chapter 9, pooling between high-risk and low-risk enrollees is not an equilibrium in a free insurance market. The problem is that people who know that they have a low risk of high medical expenditures will not voluntarily subsidize the care of people who are likely to be more expensive. To address this problem and avoid an adverse selection death spiral on the exchanges, PPACA contains a mandate that every American be covered by either public insurance or a qualified private insurance plan. The aim of this provision is to discourage low-risk people from remaining uninsured, and to prevent people from exploiting the system by only signing up for insurance after being diagnosed with cancer or another major, expensive illness.

Those who disregard the mandate and do not acquire insurance must pay a financial penalty ranging up to 2.5% of income. This penalty is not particularly large compared with the annual premium of a health insurance policy, but those who opt out of the exchanges also forfeit any subsidy for which they would be eligible.

Reduced Medicare spending

Extending health insurance to 35 million people is not cheap. While estimates vary, most predict that once the law is fully implemented in 2014, the cost to the federal government of expanding Medicaid and subsidizing coverage on the exchanges will range between $150 and $200 billion per year. PPACA finances these expenditures by cutting Medicare spending by about $50 billion per year, and levying a variety of new taxes on tanning salons, medical device manufacturers, and real-estate sales (to name but a few).

These large cuts to Medicare spending constitute the third major provision of PPACA. The law specifies the amount that Medicare is to be cut, but does not specify where exactly those cuts should be made. The law empowers a board called the Independent Payment Advisory Board (IPAB), which must recommend and implement cost-containment strategies in the Medicare program by 2014. The board has an unusual amount of freedom.

While in the past Medicare has been statutorily enjoined from considering costs in its decisions about which new technologies to cover, IPAB faces no such restrictions.

It is unclear at this point how IPAB will make its decisions about the best way to reduce Medicare spending without compromising on the quality of care for the elderly. Though IPAB is prohibited from "rationing" care, it may rely in part on cost-effectiveness studies to make its decisions. If so, this would represent a major change for Medicare. Whether such sharp cuts to Medicare and (perhaps) the introduction of cost-effectiveness decision criteria will be politically sustainable once they are implemented in 2014 remains to be seen.

18.7   Conclusion

The American model, with its signature mix of public and private insurance and care can be contrasted with the more egalitarian models popular in Europe and Asia. It is a testament to the political divide between the American and the other models that politicians in America accuse their opponents of advocating European-style health care, while politicians in Europe tarnish opposing health care policies as being too similar to America's. With the introduction of PPACA, the American model is undergoing substantial changes, but it is keeping its distance from both the Beveridge and Bismarck models.

Even if PPACA proves popular and politically sustainable, the American model is not economically sustainable. Further changes are certain to come because the American health care system, and Medicare in particular, is facing an ominous fiscal future. Over the coming decades, expenditures on Medicare are forecasted to rise; under the assumption that costs per enrollee continue to rise at the historical rate of 4.7% each year after inflation, Medicare's annual budget will near $4 trillion in 2040 (Medicare Board of Trustees 2012). This figure is greater than the size of the entire US federal budget in 2011. Even the most optimistic prognosticators agree that Medicare, which accounts for nearly a quarter of health care spending in the US, is on an unsustainable course. The driving forces are the rapid aging of the population and the continual stream of expensive new medical technologies.

This problem is not unique to America. In fact, populations are graying much faster in Europe and Japan; these nations will have to reckon with rising health care costs and make painful compromises even sooner than the US. In the final policy chapter, we explore the phenomenon of population aging and preview some of the tactics governments will use to address it.

18.8   Exercises

Comprehension questions

Indicate whether each statement is true or false, and justify your answer. Be sure to cite any evidence and state any additional assumptions you may need.

1 Nearly half of expenditures on health care in the US are government financed.
2 The take-up rate of health insurance among people with good jobs (that is full-time jobs that have lasted longer than a year) has declined in recent years, and this is an important reason for the increase in uninsurance rates over those same years.

3 In employer-sponsored health insurance in the US, employers pay the largest share of the costs of health insurance.

4 Medicare Part D, which was implemented in 2006, is the federal insurance program for the elderly in the US that provides for prescription drug coverage.

5 In the US Medicare program, by statute, the government is not permitted to take cost-effectiveness criteria into account when deciding whether to cover new medical technologies.

6 The primary source of funding for the Medicare program is from premiums assessed on the elderly population, which is the primary population enrolled in the program.

7 The imposition of federally mandated maternity benefits had no effect on the mean wages of female workers.

8 A primary cause of increasing uninsurance in the US over the past decade is that more employers are deciding to stop providing health insurance coverage entirely.

9 Barriers to care erected by managed care organizations, such as requiring patients to visit gatekeeper physicians prior to seeking specialist care, can increase consumer welfare.

10 Scholars who study managed care organizations tend to pick managed care plans over more traditional health insurance plans.

11 Medicaid creates a work disincentive effect even for people currently not working at all.

12 Suppose that a state grants Medicaid benefits to a worker only if his income is between $5,000 and $10,000 a year. This will not result in a work disincentive because those who are not working at all cannot receive any benefits.

13 The primary sources of funding for Medicaid are payroll taxes (paid by workers), and premiums, deductibles, and copayments (paid by patients).

14 In 2010, there were nearly 40 million people in the US who went without health insurance for the entire year.

15 In the 2010 American health reform law, one primary mechanism for financing the expansion of health insurance to the uninsured involves reducing planned Medicare expenditures.

16 After the American health reform plan is fully implemented in 2014, there will be no more uninsured people in the US.

Analytical problems

17 **Medicaid work disincentive effects**. Consider Figure 18.7, which depicts the labor market disincentive effects of Medicaid. In the figure:
- L is the number of hours worked per year.
- $\bar{I}$ is the income threshold for Medicaid eligibility. If a worker earns less than $\bar{I}$, he is eligible for C free units of health care, which cost p per unit on the open market.
- The solid line indicates the total compensation (wage plus Medicaid benefits) that a worker earns as a function of L, hours worked.
- The slope of the solid line reflects the hourly wage.
- a   The interval from L_1 to L_2 is called the Medicaid notch or, less colorfully, the Medicaid work disincentive region. Explain why an individual does not elect to work between L_1 and L_2 hours.

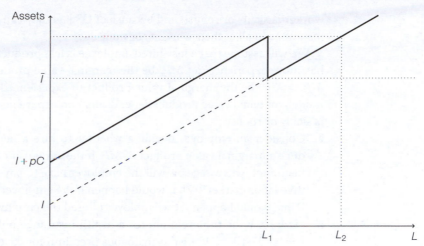

Figure 18.7. *The Medicaid notch.*

b In this model, the value of Medicaid to the worker is set to the price of health care times the quantity of health care transferred (pC). Is pC more than, less than, or equal to the value of Medicaid for most workers? [*Hint:* Would you prefer to have C units of health care given to you, or would you prefer $\$pC$ worth of cash?]

c If the true value of Medicaid were used in the figure instead of the equivalent monetary value, would this shrink or expand the work disincentive region between L_1 and L_2?

d In this model, workers earn the same total assets whether they work L_1 or L_2 hours. Is the worker better off at L_1 or L_2 hours of work?

e If disutility from work were included in the model, would this shrink, expand, or keep the same the size of the region where workers have no incentive to work?

f In your own version of Figure 18.7, draw three sets of plausible utility curves that take assets as a positive input and hours worked as a negative input. Draw one set so that the worker elects to work less than L_1 hours, one set so that the worker elects to work exactly L_1 hours, and one set so that the worker elects to work more than L_2 hours.

g Explain why the utility curves cannot be drawn so as to induce the worker to work between L_1 and L_2 hours.

h Yelowitz (1995) studies a Medicaid reform measure that reduced the Medicaid work disincentive. One of the reforms he studied raised the Medicaid eligibility threshold income level by 33%. Draw a new version of the figure with a new labor–income curve that reflects this change. Explain how this change might induce someone currently working L_1 hours per year to work more, and be sure to draw indifference curves to support your answer.

18 **Job-specific human capital.** In this problem, based on a simplified version of the model in Bhattacharya and Sood (2006), we will explore how linking employment and health insurance provision can (partially) solve the adverse selection problem if the labor market is competitive. Suppose that there are two types of workers – sickly workers with probability p_s of falling ill over the course of the next year, and robust workers with probability $p_r < p_s$ of falling ill. Employers cannot observe whether a

worker is sickly or robust, and because of US law they can only decide to offer health insurance to all of their workers, or none at all.

We will assume that a just-hired employee is less productive than an employee who has more experience; let MP_n be the marginal value product of new employees, and $MP_e > MP_n$ be the marginal value product of experienced employees. In this simple model, marginal value product depends only on experience, not on whether a worker is sickly or robust.

a   Consider an employer deciding whether to hire a new employee who will produce a marginal value product of MP. If the employer offers income and no health insurance, what wage, w, will the employer have to pay the employee in a competitive labor market? What would happen if the employer offered the employee less? What would happen if the employer offered the employee more?

b   Now let V_r be the premium for a health insurance policy covering a robust person, and let $V_s > V_r$ be the analogous premium for covering a sickly person. What wage would an employer pay a robust worker in a competitive labor market if the employer could observe the worker's health state? What wage would an employer pay a sickly worker?

c   In this model, employers cannot tell the difference between robust and sickly workers. That means that they cannot set wages on the basis of worker type. Let θ be the fraction of workers that are sickly at a particular employer. What wage will employers pay workers?

d   Let D be the difference in marginal product between an experienced worker and a new worker ($MP_e - MP_n$). Suppose that robust, experienced workers would prefer not to pool with sickly workers at their firm, and so they seek out a new job with an employer who does not offer health insurance. What will be the wage of the robust worker at the new job during the first year there? Keep in mind, these workers will no longer be experienced because they will be adapting to a new firm. Under what conditions will it make financial sense for the robust worker to change jobs? Your answer should be an inequality that includes D, θ, V_r, and V_s.

e D is a measure of job-specific human capital; as workers learn the job, they become more productive so $D > 0$. However, not every job or industry has the same value for D. In some lines of work D is low, while in others D is high, simply because of the nature of the work. Given the results you have seen in this problem, in which types of industries – high-D or low-D – would you expect there to be a larger fraction of employers offering pooled health insurance to workers?

Essay questions

19 In the US, where most private health insurance coverage is provided by employers, changing employers nearly always means changing health insurance providers. Review the definition of job lock from Section 18.1.

a   Why might the health insurer at a new job balk at providing insurance to a job-switching employee, or charge a high price?

b   Explain why the health insurer at the old job would not also drop coverage or charge a higher price in any given year. [*Hint:* Discuss the observability of any changes to the employee by insurers and legal restrictions.]

   c Describe the nature of the welfare loss arising from this sort of "job lock." Be sure to consider the following question in your answer: Under what conditions can it be economically efficient for employees to quit their jobs?

   d Consider a worker who earns substantially more than he would earn at the next available highest-paying job. Such a situation can arise even in a competitive labor market if, for example, the worker has developed a high level of firm-specific human capital, so that it would be very costly to the firm to replace him. Suppose we call this phenomenon "wage lock." Does your discussion of the welfare loss from Exercise 19(c) apply to wage lock? Does wage lock reflect inefficiencies in the labor market?

Students can find answers to the comprehension questions and lecturers can access an Instructor Manual with guideline answers to the analytical problems and essay questions at **www.palgrave.com/economics/bht**.

19 POPULATION AGING AND THE FUTURE OF HEALTH POLICY

In 1950, a child born in the US could expect to live 68 years – which was an incredibly long time by historical standards and much longer than the life expectancy of a child born at the beginning of the century. Life expectancy continued to climb throughout the 20th century and into the early years of the 21st. By 2009, life expectancy at birth in the US had risen to 79 years, a stunning 11-year increase in six decades.

The story is similar throughout the developed world. In the UK, life expectancy at birth rose from 69 years to 80 years over the same period. In France, it rose from 66 to 81 years; in Japan, life expectancy leapt from 59 to 83 years! Similar rapid growth has occurred in most developing countries as well, although life expectancies still lag behind those in the developed world (Wilmoth and Shkolnikov 2012).

Over this same time period, fertility rates have been falling throughout the world. At one time it was common for nuclear families in Europe and the US to include four or more siblings, but this is no longer the case. In order for a population to exactly maintain its size from generation to generation, each woman must give birth to about 2.1 children over her lifetime to replace both her and the father in the population (Smallwood and Chamberlain 2005). This special fertility rate is often called the population *replacement fertility rate*. In the last few decades, the total fertility rate in the developed world has fallen below that level.

Together, these trends imply that the population of the developed world (and much of the developing world) is *aging*. The term "aging" in demography does not refer to the aging process of individuals but instead the changing age profile of an entire society. When a population's median age rises, or when its share of elderly persons grows, it is said to be aging or sometimes, more colorfully, "graying."

This worldwide decline in fertility, combined with the worldwide increase in life expectancy, is upsetting the familiar demographic of more children than adults and more adults than elderly that has existed unchanged for millennia. In other words, because fewer children are being born and adults are living longer, the age demographics of all societies are shifting. In just the 100-year span from 1950 to 2050, the average age of the world population is expected to jump about 10 years, from 25 to 35, and the ratio of infants (under age 5) to elderly (over age 65) is expected to flip from 5:2 to 2:5 (Rosenberg and Bloom 2006; Haub 2011).

Figure 19.1 shows the United Nations' official estimates of the age structure of Europe projected forward to 2100. In this sort of diagram, called a population pyramid, the vertical axis represents age, while the horizontal axis represents population size for each age. In 1950 Europe, the modal age groups for the population were 15 years old and under. By 2010, the bulk of the European population was between 20 and 50 years old. In 2050, the most common age groups are forecasted to be 60 years and older. These

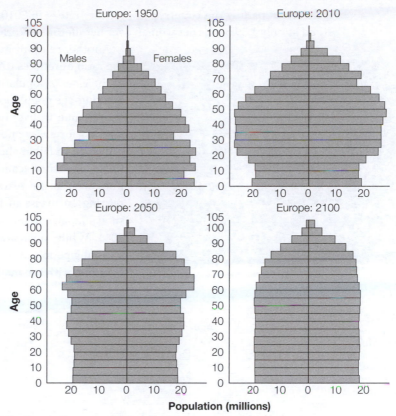

Figure 19.1. *Population aging in Europe.*

Source: United Nations (2011). Reprinted with permission.

massive changes have the potential to disrupt irrevocably the financing of public health systems, and it remains to be seen how well future societies – and their health systems – will weather them.

19.1   Why is the world aging?

Population aging is the result of two major demographic forces working in concert: increasing life expectancies and declining fertility rates. Each trend has its own causes and its own history, but they are both working day by day to turn the youth-dominated world of 1950 into a much older and sicker world in 2050.

Japan is one of the starkest examples of a population rapidly going gray. Indeed, the proportion of elderly in the Japanese population will increase at a far faster rate than in any other industrialized nation. Projections indicate that 27.3% of the Japanese population will be over 65 by 2025, one of the highest rates in the developed world (National Institute of Population and Social Security Research 2002). One benchmark of population aging is the number of years it takes for a country to age from the point when 7% of its population is over 65 years to the point when 14% of its population is over 65. In France, for example, this took 115 years, from 1865 to 1980. But in Japan, that transition happened in just 26 years, from 1970 to 1996 (US National Institute on Aging 2007). The rapid aging of Japan is driven in part by the country's low fertility rate – in 2010, the nationwide fertility rate stood at only 1.39 births per woman over her lifetime (World Bank 2012).

Japan is at the epicenter of the worldwide demographic crisis, with one of the world's highest life expectancies and one of its lowest fertility rates. Credit: © Mihai-Bogdan Lazar – Fotolia.com.

Another relevant measure of population aging is the ratio of retirees to workers. Currently, the ratio of the elderly population (65 years and over) to the working-age population (15–64) in Japan is approximately one to five. In other words, there are five workers for every one retiree. By 2025, this ratio is projected to fall to about one to two. This dramatic shift will occur because Japan's baby boom generation, born in the years after World War II, will be retiring en masse in the next decade. Figure 19.2 shows Japan's population pyramid in 1935 and in 2011. While Japan was once a country dominated by young people, it now has an inverted population pyramid, with the majority of the population above age 40.

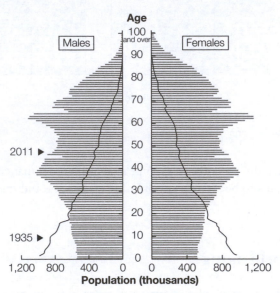

Figure 19.2. *Population aging in Japan.*

Source: Figure 2.1 from *Statistical Handbook of Japan 2012* by Statistics Bureau, Japan. Reproduced with permission.

The aging of Japan is a direct result of the two major demographic trends we have already discussed: increasing life expectancy and decreasing fertility rates. In this section, we discuss the causes of those trends and examine their influence over population aging.

Increasing life expectancy

As recently as the early 19th century, life expectancies were much lower than they are today. For instance, in 1833, French life expectancy at birth was 38 years, while in Sweden it was 42.5. By the early 20th century, life expectancies had risen throughout the developed world. In 1933, the US and the UK had identical life expectancies – 61 years – while Swedish life expectancy had risen to 65 years and French life expectancy to 58 years. Low life expectancies were driven in part by sky-high mortality rates. A child born in the US in

1933 had a 5% chance of dying before the age of one. Today though, child mortality is at historically low levels and life expectancies are historically high (Wilmoth and Shkolnikov 2012). Why has life expectancy been increasing steadily for centuries?

Part of the story is the gigantic strides made in both medical understanding and medical technology in the past few centuries. Riley (2001) compares the leading causes of death in 18th-century London with the leading causes of death in Britain in 1992. The disparity is stark: leading killers in London during the 1700s included tuberculosis, scarlet fever, and infected teeth. In modern times, by contrast, heart disease and lung cancer top the list. Key innovations like vaccines, clean drinking water, and indoor plumbing did much to lower child mortality rates. They also helped eliminate common scourges like smallpox, polio, scarlet fever, malaria, and cholera.

These innovations did much to improve life expectancy in the 19th century, and life expectancy has continued to climb throughout the 20th century. Health economists tend to attribute the ongoing rise in longevity since 1950 to further improvements in medical technology (like antibiotics and improved care of children and mothers during childbirth), as well as lifestyle changes, such as reduction in smoking (Eggleston and Fuchs 2012). Other researchers highlight the importance of improved nutrition in explaining mortality declines, especially in the 19th century. Fogel (1986) estimates that as much as 40% of the mortality decline between 1790 and 1850 in England and the US can be attributed to improved nutrition and the declining frequency of famines.

Another major contributor to increasing life expectancy is the fact that the modern world is simply a more hospitable place to live than the world of two hundred years ago, especially in developed countries. Jobs are safer, wars are rarer, crime rates are lower, food supplies are cleaner, and the physical environment is less squalid. As a result, more and more people are living uninterrupted to a ripe old age. This in turn means that elderly populations – which used to consist only of the few hardy individuals lucky enough to survive the harrowing years of childhood and middle age – are ballooning in size (Eggleston and Fuchs 2012).

Declining fertility rates

The second major trend driving population aging – declining fertility – is perhaps less obvious than increased life expectancy but ultimately just as important. The decline in fertility in the past two hundred years is stark. Women born in England in the 1830s had about five children on average, while German and American women born in the 1860s had about four each. Even with relatively high infant mortality rates, these figures made for robust population growth from generation to generation (Guinnane 2011). Today, birth rates have fallen so far that many countries across Europe are poised for population decline, while birth rates in the US are barely above the replacement rate. Table 19.1 shows fertility rates in 1980 and 2011 for selected countries.

What explains the precipitous decline in birth rates in the industrialized world over the past two centuries? Demographers and economists have presented several theories, none of which have garnered a complete consensus. It seems likely that social factors like the increased availability of effective contraception or increased women's labor force participation have at least played a role in reduced birth rates. Becker (1981) argues that changes in the cost of bearing and raising children decreased the demand for new births over time.

Table 19.1. *Total fertility rate per 1,000 women (selected countries).*

Country	Year 1980	Year 2011
Australia	1.9	1.9
Austria	1.6	1.4
Belgium	1.7	1.8
Brazil	4.1	1.8
Canada	1.7	1.7
Chile	2.7	1.9
China	2.6	1.6
France	1.9	2.0
Germany	1.4	1.4
Greece	2.2	1.4
India	4.7	2.6
Italy	1.6	1.4
Japan	1.8	1.4
Mexico	4.7	2.3
Netherlands	1.6	1.8
Norway	1.7	2.0
Russian Federation	1.9	1.5
Spain	2.2	1.4
Sweden	1.7	2.0
Switzerland	1.6	1.5
Turkey	4.5	2.1
UK	1.9	1.9
US	1.8	2.1

Source: Data from the World Bank (2012).

One of the more intriguing theories is known as the "old-age income security hypothesis." This theory argues that, in centuries past, having children was an effective form of savings by parents. Consider the plight of a young married couple working on a farm. They need to figure out how to get by in case of illness or injury. In this world, kids are a great investment – they can act as caretakers in the event of a disability or as breadwinners once the couple reaches old age. According to this theory, fertility has declined because industrialization allowed children to easily escape their parents' economic influence, and because social insurance programs have come to replace children as providers of income security in old age (Sundstrom and David 1988; Longman 2004). However, this theory is disputed, because there is evidence that children did not serve this function in all societies and because the insurance children provided may not justify the high cost of their upbringing in purely financial terms (Guinnane and Streb 2011; Willis 1979).

Certain industries are especially vulnerable to sharp demographic changes.

Credit: Allen Cox.

Whatever the ultimate causes of demographic change, population aging over the last few decades remains an undisputed fact in many countries. The crucial, unanswered question is whether aging countries like Japan can react quickly enough to accommodate these changes. An older society requires a different health care infrastructure from that of a younger society, including more nursing homes and more physicians familiar with geriatrics and the diseases of the elderly. An older society also needs to reconsider how it finances health care for the elderly as the ratio of elderly beneficiaries to young workers continues to grow. In the rest of this chapter, we explore the immense challenges facing national health care systems and discuss policies to address the destabilizing effects of aging.

19.2   Health care system sustainability

All of the health systems we discussed in the previous few chapters, ranging from Medicare in the US to the National Health Service in the UK to Roken in Japan, were designed long before these destabilizing demographic trends became apparent. They were dreamt up in a historical context where every generation was bigger than the last, and where a massive and continual influx of young people entered the workforce each year to help pay for the older generation's expenses. In some sense, these systems resemble pyramid schemes: the debts of the current generation are borne by the larger generation that follows, whose even greater debts are in turn borne by the even larger generation after that.

This is the sort of health system financing that can succeed in a 1950-style world with high birthrates and ever-expanding populations. But as we have already established, the world of 2050 will be a totally different place. These health systems are predicated on a bedrock assumption of population growth, which seemed eminently reasonable up until the last few decades. In a world of stagnant populations or even population decline, though, these health systems are no longer solvent. The twin forces of rising life expectancies and declining birthrates will ultimately bankrupt these programs unless they are reformed. Case studies of the budgetary predicaments of two health programs – US Medicare and the Japanese long-term care insurance program – will make these predictions clear.

US Medicare

Historically, the revenues collected through the Medicare payroll tax have exceeded the amount spent by the US federal government on Medicare. Over these years, Medicare took in more money than it spent. Each year, the excess tax collections were placed in an account called the Medicare Trust Fund. In 2007, however, Medicare Part A expenditures exceeded payroll tax collections for the first time, and the trust fund has been on the decline since (see Figure 19.3). Over the coming decades, expenditures on Medicare are forecasted to rise, and financing Medicare will pose an increasing and significant challenge (Medicare Board of Trustees 2012).

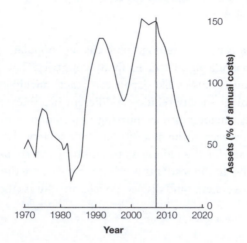

Figure 19.3. *The dwindling Medicare Trust Fund. As of 2013, the Trust Fund is projected to go bankrupt in 2024.*

Source: Medicare Board of Trustees (2012).

There are two main factors driving rising expenditures. First, the US population is expected to age significantly in the coming decades, meaning more Medicare-eligible citizens with more expensive health problems (He et al. 2005). Second, the continual introduction of new medical technologies is increasing Medicare expenditures to unprecedented levels (Shekelle et al. 2005).

In 2010, there were about 40 million people living in the US aged 65 years and older. But the enormous "baby boom" generation, born in the years after World War II, has just begun retiring. By 2030, there will be more than 70 million elderly people swelling Medicare rolls (Figure 19.4). Furthermore, the number of people who are very old – over age 85 – will increase from about 5.7 million in 2010 to a conservative estimate of 9 million in 2030. Since expected medical expenditures increase sharply with age, population aging will place larger and larger burdens on Medicare.

By contrast, the taxes collected to pay for Medicare are projected to rise much more slowly, because the growth of the working-age population will not keep pace with the growth of the elderly population. While there are about 3.5 workers per elderly person in the US today, by 2020 there will be about 2.8, and by 2030 only 2.2. The Medicare trustees forecast that tax income to fund Medicare Part A in 2021 will be about $411 billion, while Medicare Part A expenditures will be about $431 billion – a deficit of about $20 billion for that year. By 2040, the annual budget shortfall for Part A, along with the shortfalls for

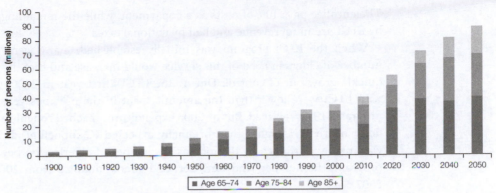

Figure 19.4. *Number of elderly in the US, 1900–2050. Figures from 2020 forward are projections.*
Source: Data from US Census Bureau.

Parts B, C, and D, will run into the trillions of dollars and comprise 3.5% of GDP (Medicare Board of Trustees 2012).

Under current law, when the trust fund is exhausted in 2024, the federal government is not authorized to continue payments for Medicare Part A. However, given political considerations, it seems exceedingly unlikely that Medicare would actually be shut down altogether when that happens. It remains to be seen whether Medicare will remain in its current form or transform into something partially or totally unrecognizable.

Japanese long-term care insurance

The Japanese long-term care insurance program faces a sustainability problem similar to that of US Medicare. The long-term care insurance (LTCI) program was established in 2000 to accommodate the growing population of elderly people who are bedridden or suffering from dementia. Due to a decrease in average family size and an increase in the ranks of working women, traditional sources of home and family care for the elderly are disappearing. This problem is exacerbated by the rapid aging of Japan's population, one quarter of which is projected to be over age 65 by 2050 (Campbell et al. 2009).

Two categories of people are eligible to receive LTCI. The first includes those over the age of 65 who have lived in Japan for at least one year. These enrollees pay a monthly premium that is either a direct payment or a deduction from their pension. The second category includes those between the ages of 40 and 64 with any of 15 types of aging-associated disabilities such as an inability to perform *activities of daily living* (ADLs) including bathing or dressing without aid. The premium paid for both categories is dependent on income, and averages ¥2,087 ($25) per month for first-year enrollees (Murashima et al. 2003).

People who need long-term care apply to the municipal government, and a staff member investigates the level of care needed. The applicant fills out a standardized survey covering 85 items designed to assess the applicant's state of mind and body as well as his care needs. LTCI covers home care (visiting nurse and bathing services), respite care (day care services), and institutional care at a nursing home (Matsuda and Yamamoto 2001).

The enrollee pays 10% of costs as a copayment, while the remaining 90% is covered half by LTCI premium revenue and half by national taxes.

When the LTCI program was initially established, many were concerned that the number of elders in need of this service would increase and that the LTCI budget would quickly grow out of control. During the LTCI's first year in 2000, the costs associated with LTCI were lower than the amount spent in the previous year for the health care programs LTCI replaced. But by 2005 expenditures reached roughly ¥4.3 trillion ($52 billion), nearly 25% higher than originally expected (Campbell et al. 2010). The increase was mainly attributed to the increasing number of elderly who became eligible for the program; the number who were certified almost doubled from 2000 to 2005 (Ikegami 2007).

In response to these growing expenses, the Japanese government reformed the LTCI program in 2005. The policy changes, designed to cut costs, limited the number of institutional beds and increased copayment rates for nursing home room and board (Tsutsui and Muramatsu 2007). In 2006 another amendment was added to further decrease costs. It included new preventive measures – including engaging insured elderly in light physical activity every day – in hopes of decreasing the number of elderly needing assistance (Okamoto 2006). These services were mainly directed at relatively healthy elderly individuals who nevertheless might be at risk of needing extensive care in the future.

The reform enacted in 2005 and 2006 slowed the government expenditure growth rate but did not stop the increase altogether. In 2008, LTCI costs were ¥4.8 trillion ($57 billion) and have been increasing annually ever since (Campbell et al. 2009).

19.3   Forecasting the future of health expenditures

The US Medicare program and Japan's LTCI program are not the only government health care systems facing tough budgetary decisions. In the next few decades, governments all over the world will need to make difficult decisions about how to reform their health care programs. As we have seen, the aging of the population places considerable pressure on traditional financing models which rely in part on the young and healthy to subsidize care for the elderly.

Before governments can even start considering tough decisions about reforming health care programs, they need accurate estimates of future health expenditures to understand the extent of the budgetary shortfall. To make these projections, analysts must consider both trends in aging and trends in overall health. If the future population is healthier at any given age than the current population – if 60 becomes the new 50, for instance – then perhaps the burden of financing health care will be less than would be anticipated given the age distribution alone. In addition, future changes in medical technology will undoubtedly affect future health care expenditures, just as they have affected past health care expenditures.

Future medical technology

Predicting the development of future medical technology is a difficult and perhaps impossible task. In theory, future new medical technology could either raise or lower future health expenditures. One might think that future medical technological developments will

POPULATION AGING AND THE FUTURE OF HEALTH POLICY   **411**

have the same effect of increasing health care expenditures that new technologies over the past few decades have had (see Chapter 13). However, it is also possible that future medical technologies might actually enable doctors to provide better care at a lower cost and reduce overall expenditures (Pardes et al. 1999).

In 1999, a group of researchers at the RAND Corporation were tasked with developing a new forecast of spending for the US Medicare system over the next thirty years. The researchers needed to account for the effects of future medical technology, so they convened a group of distinguished scientists and doctors – leaders in the fields of cardiovascular medicine, neurobiology, and cancer, among other areas. These experts were asked to put forward their expectations about what new technologies were most likely to emerge in their fields, as well as the probability of those innovations actually arising (Goldman et al. 2004).

Table 19.2 lists a selection of the new technologies predicted by this expert panel, alongside estimates of the likelihood of the technologies emerging by 2010 and by 2020. In addition to the median likelihood reported by the panel, Table 19.2 reports the range of probabilities estimated by the RAND panel. While it will be impossible until 2020 to thoroughly evaluate how well these experts did at predicting the future, the table does permit a few preliminary conclusions.

First, the scientific expert panels, such as the one convened by RAND, can be good at identifying new technologies, even if they cannot always foresee the uses to which those

Table 19.2. *New technology predictions by RAND panel.*

Technology	Predicted likelihood by 2010[†]	Predicted likelihood by 2020[†]
Cardiology		
Improved cardiovascular disease prevention	20% (10%–100%)	40% (15%–100%)
MRI angiography as a replacement for coronary catheterization	50% (25%–75%)	100% (100%–100%)
Permanent implantation of left ventricular assist devices	10% (5%–40%)	50% (15%–80%)
Xenotransplants of heart	2% (1%–3%)	2% (1%–3%)
Aging and cancer		
Telemorase inhibitors to treat solid tumors	55% (50%–60%)	100%(100%–100%)
Cancer vaccines as an oncologic treatment	5% (0%–10%)	15% (10%–20%)
Anti-angiogensis to treat solid tumors	85% (70%–100%)	85% (70%–100%)
Drugs to sensitize insulin-receptors and prevent diabetes	50% (50%–50%)	65% (65%–65%)
Compounds that extend lifespan	7% (0%–15%)	25% (0%–50%)
Neurological disease		
Drugs to prevent Alzheimer's disease	25% (10%–60%)	40% (20%–60%)
Drugs to slow the progression of Alzheimer's disease	25% (10%–50%)	40% (10%–70%)
Neurotransplantation to treat Parkinson's disease	10% (10%–15%)	25% (15%–50%)
Stem cell treatment of acute stroke	2% (2%–5%)	20% (5%–20%)

[†]Consensus prediction of experts and range of probability predictions.

Source: Data from Goldman et al. (2004).

technologies will be put. For instance, the panel predicted that MRI angiography, where an MRI machine is used to visualize blocked arteries, would come to replace coronary catheterization as a diagnostic tool in coronary heart disease. In fact, coronary catheterization remains a widely used technology to diagnose heart disease. But MRI angiography is also widely used in 2012 – to diagnose the cause of strokes and to detect certain types of cancer alongside many other uses.

Second, some of the technologies that the panel felt most certain about have proven not to be as successful as they imagined, while others have developed faster than expected. For instance, in the late 1990s, spurred in part by some tantalizing findings by scientists, the panel (along with many others in oncology) had high hopes that a new technology called anti-angiogensis could be used to halt the growth of solid tumors (Folkman 1995). Most cancer cells need blood supply to grow, and they send chemical signals to surrounding tissue, requesting that new blood vessels be built nearby to deliver more blood to the tumor. Anti-angiogensis attempts to interfere with the cancer's chemical signals, preventing the formation of blood vessels to the tumor and ultimately killing the tumor. While there was much optimism in the late 1990s about this technology, the strategy has not resulted in therapeutic advances, at least not to the extent expected then. In other cases, though, the panel was too pessimistic. For instance, in the years since 1999, there have been many advances in stem cell technology that the panel did not anticipate.

This evidence from Goldman et al. (2004) suggests that predicting the future of medical technologies stymies even medical experts. As a result, most forecasts in practice resort to the assumption that future medical technologies will have approximately the same increasing effect on health expenditures that recent technological innovations have had. In the next section, we consider an additional challenge to forecasting future expenditures – predicting the health of the future elderly.

Compression of morbidity

We know that life expectancy has been increasing steadily throughout the developed world over the past decades. While this should naturally be seen as good news, extra life years are not necessarily an unmixed blessing. What if those extra years of life are spent in a partially disabled state? Many elderly people spend the last years of life unable to perform basic activities of daily living (ADLs) such as walking around the house, bathing, or dressing themselves. While living longer is undoubtedly a good thing, living longer in a healthy state is an even better thing. Living longer in a healthy state, however, requires that disabilities are postponed until later in life or eliminated altogether. The phenomenon of disease and disability occurring later and later in life is known as the **compression of morbidity**. Without a compression of morbidity, lengthier lifetimes do not necessarily imply a significant improvement in quality of life (Fries 1980).

Definition	19.1

Compression of morbidity: the phenomenon of disability and illness being delayed or "compressed" into the end of life.

In the 1970s, many American researchers worried that even as mortality rates among the elderly were falling, disability rates among the elderly population were increasing

(Crimmins et al. 1989; Waidmann et al. 1995). Several researchers argued that increases in longevity amounted only to extensions of the time spent in disability by the elderly, not an increase in the actual healthy lifespan, just as surveys found declining numbers of elderly people able to perform basic activities. There were predictions that increases in longevity would inevitably be accompanied by increases in the incidence of disability (Gruenberg 1977). This research found little to no evidence of compression of morbidity in the American population.

These worries abated in the 1980s as disability rates among the elderly in the US began to drop, and indeed continued to drop over the next several decades (Manton et al. 1997, 2006, 2008). A consensus has emerged that the health of the elderly has actually been improving since the early 1980s (Crimmins et al. 1997; Schoeni 2001). This evidence suggests that 60 might actually be the new 50 after all, and that morbidity was indeed becoming more compressed into later years of life.

The main reason why disability rates among the elderly have improved in recent decades is related to improved care for those with chronic diseases like arthritis, heart disease, and hypertension. Elderly people who have already developed a chronic illness are substantially less likely to become disabled today than they would have been decades ago (Aranovich et al. 2009). This is largely because improvements in supportive technology – such as better walking aids – have enabled physically disabled people to avoid becoming disabled in practice.

Despite these documented improvements in elderly health, there is now reason to believe the trend is reversing yet again. During the 1990s and early 2000s, at the same time as disability rates among the older population were declining in the US, disability rates among the *non-elderly* population were increasing (Lakdawalla et al. 2004). This increase in disability was largely due to sharp increases in the prevalence of obesity and the disabling consequences of that obesity (Bhattacharya et al. 2008). Given these recent trends, it is possible that the current generation of Americans might be less healthy in old age than their parents were (Olshansky and Passaro 2005; Flegal et al. 2005).

In the past few decades, many disabled people have been able to enjoy vastly increased mobility thanks to technologies like motorized scooters. Such technologies help compress morbidity into the last few years of life.
Credit: PhotoDisc/Getty Images.

Modeling future health and health expenditures

In the face of these forecasting challenges, analysts have adopted a variety of approaches, each with its own strengths and weaknesses. One popular approach is to assume that health expenditures will continue to grow at roughly the same rate as they have in past years, perhaps after accounting for the state of the broader economy. This simple approach is commonly taken by government accounting agencies tasked with estimating how much should be set aside in next year's budget for health care expenditures.

This smooth-growth approach is ideally suited to forecast next year's health care obligations since health care expenditures are unlikely to fluctuate wildly from year to year. However, such an approach is inappropriate for longer-run forecasts since they fail to account for long-term changes in the age or health structure of the population. They are also inappropriate for answering "what if" questions that are important for healthy policy, such as: What would happen if the government were to adopt policies promoting preventative care or larger families, or what if expensive new treatments are introduced to treat widespread conditions like diabetes or cancer?

One alternative approach is to construct a model that forecasts how the prevalence of a specific disease, such as HIV or hypertension, is likely to evolve and use it to estimate how much care for patients of those conditions will cost in the future. In Chapter 21, we discuss one example of this approach – the susceptible–infected–recovered (SIR) model – applied to infectious diseases. These models are mathematically sophisticated and take into consideration the course of the disease being modeled, as well as the consequences in terms of specific health care services demanded. Even if such models cannot be used to forecast *whether* new medical technologies will be developed to treat the disease, they can be useful for understanding *how* a hypothetical new technology might affect patients and overall costs.

The drawback of single-disease models is that they ignore the problem of **competing risks**. No matter how effective a new medical technology is, we will all die at some point in the future from one condition or another. Suppose, for instance, that a magical inexpensive new medical treatment is developed that could cure all cases of cancer with no side effects. The first and most obvious consequence of this magical treatment is that cancer mortality will drop to zero. Less obvious, however, is that the rate of mortality from all other causes will eventually increase. The magical cancer remedy cures cancer patients, but by doing so, keeps them alive long enough to die of heart attacks instead. In a certain sense, cancer and other diseases compete with each other to be the cause of mortality. As long as death is inevitable, reducing cancer mortality necessarily increases the summed mortality risk of all the other non-cancer causes.

Definition	19.2

Competing risks problem: the inevitable rise in mortality from other causes that results from a reduction in mortality from any one particular cause.

Health care expenditures might even rise overall as a consequence of the new magical cancer treatment, even if that treatment itself is basically costless. This might occur if the costs of caring for heart attack and other conditions are more expensive than caring for cancer (Bhattacharya et al. 2005). This example demonstrates an important general point – a rise in health care expenditures is not necessarily a bad thing. In this case, eliminating the suffering from cancer for free would certainly be a good thing, even if it resulted in markedly higher health care expenditures.

To address the competing risks problem, researchers must model all possible causes of death at the same time. One example of such an approach is the RAND Future Elderly Model, developed by health economist Dana Goldman and his colleagues. The basis of the model is a microsimulation, in which the population of the country is simulated over a number of years (Goldman et al. 2004).

Figure 19.5 provides an overview of how the model works. The model starts in 2013 with a representative cohort of virtual elderly people. Each "person" living in the model is assigned a randomly chosen health and disability history that matches the probabilities found in the population at large. The characterization of health history is detailed, and includes information about heart disease, hypertension, diabetes, and many other medical conditions. Each year, people generate health care costs that are consistent with their own health history.

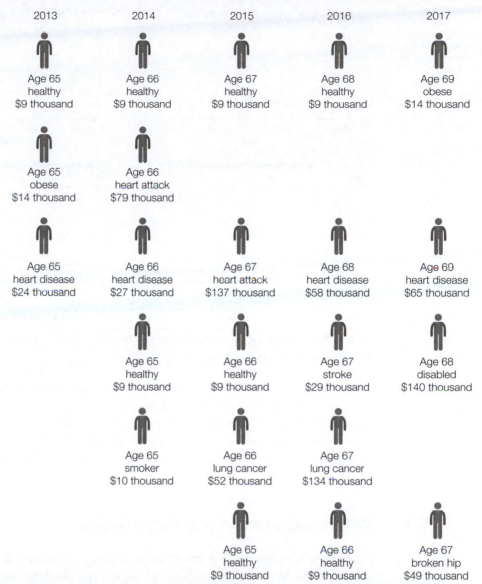

Figure 19.5. *A simplified depiction of the RAND Future Elderly Model using fabricated data. Simulated persons within the model transition between health states based on true-to-life probabilities.*

As the model begins running, the cohort of elderly people ages each year. Some fraction of the simulated people die, with a probability based again on their health status and risk factors in the previous year. Health also changes from year to year, based on past health status and risk factors. Someone who has a history of smoking is more likely to develop emphysema in 2014 than someone who does not. Each year, the sample of elderly people is replenished with a newly entering cohort of 65-year-olds whose health status also reflects national averages.

One use of models like the RAND Future Elderly Model (FEM) is to conduct thought experiments about the effect of possible technological changes in medicine. For instance, suppose that a drug had been developed in the year 2000 that extends lifespan by 10%, but

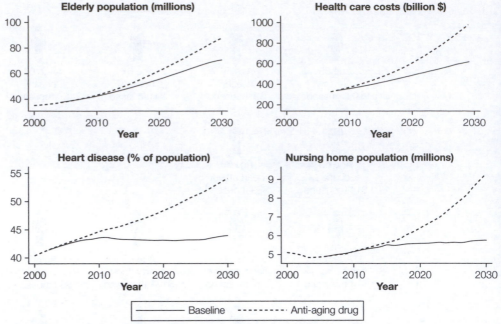

Figure 19.6. *The effect of an anti-aging drug in the Future Elderly Model.*

Source: Data from Goldman et al. (2004).

has no effect on the probability of developing chronic diseases and disability at any given age. Researchers at RAND used the FEM to show this drug would by 2013 have resulted in a much larger elderly population, dramatically increased nursing home costs, substantially higher heart disease rates, and higher health care costs overall (see Figure 19.6). This thought experiment illustrates starkly how important the competing risks problem can be.

19.4   Policy responses to population aging

Confronted with forecasts of unsustainable costs, governments around the world have sought policies that might abate the rise in health expenditures. One often proposed policy is raising the retirement age. Doing so lengthens the amount of time workers contribute to national health care funds, while shortening the amount of time the elderly spend on the government's payroll. Another policy proposal for changing the retirement age is actually redefining it as a predicted time until death rather than a specific age (Shoven 2010).

We focus here on three other policies aimed at coping with aging populations: rethinking preventative care; managing end-of-life care; and promoting higher birthrates.

Chronic disease prevention

One approach to reducing the health cost burden of an aging population is to improve the health of the population as it ages by preventing chronic diseases, such as diabetes, hypertension, and coronary artery disease. This approach is attractive because it potentially carries a double benefit – both reducing the burden of chronic diseases and reducing long-term health care expenditures. This would lower health expenditures despite the competing risks problem because chronic diseases are far more expensive to treat over the course of a lifetime than other conditions.

Chronic disease prevention programs can take many forms. One popular type of program involves lifestyle modification efforts, such as encouraging people to exercise or to eat in healthier ways. While such programs are popular, there is only limited evidence that they can succeed in preventing chronic disease. Even the most successful of these programs seem to have difficulty making good habits last after the intervention ends (Tuah et al. 2011).

Programs focusing on preventing the *progression* of an existing chronic disease exhibit somewhat better results. For instance, intensive management of blood sugar levels in diabetic patients has been shown to prevent diabetes-induced declines in kidney function, though not end-stage renal disease (Coca et al. 2012).

Broadly speaking, there are at least two major difficulties in designing chronic disease prevention programs that reduce total health care expenditures. First, there is the problem of properly targeting the intervention to a population of people who are most likely to benefit from it. The basic outline of the targeting problem is easiest to understand in the context of a program designed to prevent obesity in a young and healthy population. As we will see in Chapter 22, a substantial percentage of young people is likely to become obese over their lifetime. However, not every young obese person stays obese, and similarly not everyone who is thin in youth becomes obese later in life. A population-based intervention aimed at preventing obesity will necessarily be wasting some resources on participants never at risk of becoming obese.

The competing risks problem is even trickier. Even if a prevention program is successful, health costs may rise because the population survives only to spend health care resources on another, perhaps more expensive-to-treat, condition. One way around this problem is to design programs that simultaneously prevent many chronic diseases. This is one reason why healthy diet and exercise programs are so popular – living a healthy lifestyle puts off or prevents many chronic diseases at once. For instance, Goldman et al. (2006), using the FEM, find that a successful population obesity prevention program could be cost-effective in the long run since reducing obesity reduces the risk of many chronic diseases.

Reinventing end-of-life care

Another big opportunity for savings as populations continue to age is reforming **end-of-life (EOL) care**. Unsurprisingly, a substantial share of health care spending goes toward care near the end of patients' lives. For example, in the early 1990s, about 30% of US Medicare resources went to care for the 5–6% of beneficiaries who died each year (Emanuel 1994). In many cases, this disproportionate spending is clinically justifiable, as in the case of emergency surgery for patients with badly clogged arteries, or chemotherapy that may have been able to arrest the spread of a cancer. But some end-of-life health care is wasteful or even prolongs the pain of a dying patient (Gawande 2002). Eliminating these procedures could save money while improving or at least not detracting from clinical care.

Definition	19.3

End-of-life (EOL) care: medical care administered in the last months, weeks, or days of a patient's life.

Patient deaths are hard to predict, so there is no surefire way to tell which procedures and medicines will save a life and which are administered too late to make a difference. But the enormous sums of money involved, and the sense that much EOL care is wasteful and does nothing to extend life or improve patient comfort, have made EOL care a natural target for policymakers looking to cut costs (Emanuel 1994).

Two major strategies for reducing EOL care have emerged. One is the promotion and institutionalization of hospice care and palliative care. Palliative care is described by proponents as an approach that de-emphasizes long-shot medical treatments to combat advancing diseases and instead emphasizes comfort during a patient's final days. Palliative care often involves moving a dying patient to a hospice or his own home, ceasing most medical treatments, and employing specialized nurses trained in caring for the dying. Palliative care has existed for centuries, but only recently have governments sought to promote it in an attempt to reduce costs and improve the experience of dying patients.

One prominent example is the introduction of the Liverpool care pathway (LCP) in the British National Health System, which provides guidelines for caregivers tending to dying patients. The system is designed to ease the transition to palliative care for patients who want it but may not be aware of their options. A 2004 study showed that 64% of Britons would prefer to die at home in the case of a terminal illness, but that only 22% of patients with terminal cancer actually did. Marie Curie Cancer Care, a palliative-care advocacy group, estimates that increasing funds to support cancer patients who want to die at home would actually save about £2,700 per patient by reducing the burden on hospitals (Burke 2004).

Another tactic for reducing unnecessary care at the end of life is proactively making provisions for patients to indicate their own preferences about EOL care. Usually, this is accomplished with an *advance directive* (sometimes called a "living will"), a binding legal document that indicates a patient's wishes regarding EOL care. An advance directive enables a patient to indicate that she does not wish to be resuscitated if her heart stops, or that she does not want to be kept on life support if she sustains major brain damage and enters a vegetative state. An advance directive can also be used to appoint another person (often a spouse or a grown child) to make end-of-life health care decisions if the patient cannot communicate her own wishes.

If these preferences are not documented and a dying patient is unable to communicate, health care providers in some countries are legally obligated to try their best to resuscitate patients and extend their life as long as possible, even if the procedures involved are quite expensive and, in some cases, even if the patient's family protests.

Do palliative care approaches and advance directives actually reduce costs? Numerous studies in this field conducted in the early 1990s found that shifting to hospice care did lead to significant savings, but that savings from advance directives were not as big as optimistic policymakers had hoped (Emanuel 1996).

A recent study presents more hopeful evidence. Zhang et al. (2009) study a group of about 600 American patients with advanced cancer, and track total health care spending in each one's last seven days of life. They find that the 31% of patients who originally reported having had a "discussion about EOL wishes" with their doctors incurred less expenses and enjoyed greater comfort in their last week of life than patients with similar characteristics who had not discussed EOL options with their doctors. The savings were substantial – data suggests that just having a single EOL discussion can save over a thousand dollars in medical bills.

Governments have taken steps to ensure that advanced directives and verbal EOL wishes are respected. Nevertheless, many dying patients do not receive hospice care and do not have advance directives that authorize termination of life support. And yet survey after survey finds that people do not want aggressive medical treatment at the end of life and would prefer to die at home as opposed to a hospital. A 1990 survey found that 57% of patients at Massachusetts General Hospital expressed a desire to document their end-of-life care preferences for doctors, but only 7% had actually created an advance directive (Emanuel and Barry 1991). This disconnect may result from lack of information about options like advance directives and hospice care and also perhaps from a negative stigma attached to such options.

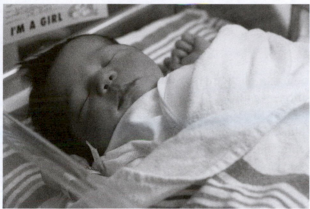

Savior of national health insurance programs? A future taxpayer relaxing in a crib.   Credit: Corbis.

Recent reforms have centered around making sure patients are aware of their ability to direct their own EOL care. But these efforts have met with controversy, like almost any proposal that touches on life-and-death decisions. For example, a proposal in the US to provide Medicare funding for patients to have voluntary EOL consultations with doctors every five years attracted much criticism. In one particularly memorable and effective denunciation, a politician invoked the term "death panels" and speculated that her son with Down syndrome might be deemed unworthy of receiving health care under the new system (Nyhan 2010).

Natalism

Policies to reduce the costs of health care for the elderly are defensible, but may require tough choices about whose benefits to cut and what care to withhold. Some nations have taken a more direct – if longer-term – approach to combating population aging by actively seeking to reverse declining fertility rates. If successful, these efforts may obviate the need to fundamentally restructure social insurance programs. Policies that are designed to encourage childbirth are called **natalist**.

Definition	19.4
Natalism: the practice of encouraging childbirth through government policies.	

Most of these policies use various levers to ease the financial burden of a newborn child. Family policy in Sweden during the 1970s and 1980s included immediate direct and in-kind transfers to the parents of newborns. When compared with similar neighboring countries (and with Swedish mothers in previous generations who did not have benefits), Swedish women during this period had more kids and waited a relatively shorter amount of time before having additional children (Björklund 2006). Sweden also has notably generous paid maternity and paternity leave, including an "equality bonus" for new parents who split time off evenly between father and mother (Mansdotter et al. 2007; Hegedus 2010).

A wave of policies adopted in the early 2000s in countries ranging from Germany to Singapore to Australia provide similar incentives for childbearing. One Russian region, in an effort to reverse the area's population decline, has declared September 12 the "Day of Conception," giving working couples the day off to procreate. The regional government has also offered cash prizes to mothers giving birth the following June 12 (Weaver 2007).

But the undisputed champion of family size promotion is France, which has aggressively pursued family policies since the early 20th century (Chen 2011). In France, having more children can be downright lucrative, as it reduces a family's tax liability and entitles parents to subsidized child care and early education programs (Castles 2003). In 2008, France enjoyed a fertility rate of 1.98, low by global standards but third-highest in Europe (Prioux and Mandelbaum 2007).

19.5   Conclusion

The aging of the world's population is a phenomenon that will challenge health policy in nearly every developed country over the coming decades. The financing model of health and social systems throughout the West relies on large-scale monetary transfers from younger populations to older, retired ones. As populations age, the viability of these financing models is likely to come under substantial stress. Reform, when it comes, will take one of three different forms. First, taxes on younger and older populations will increase. Second, benefits provided by public health systems will become less generous, and there will be great pressure to increase cost-sharing for medical care as a way to raise funds. To some extent, both of these sorts of reforms are already being implemented. In the US, for instance, the 2010 health care reform bill both substantially cut funding for Medicare and increased taxes on working-age populations to fund it.

Third, there will be increasing pressure for private provision of at least some of the services that are currently publicly provided. In Germany, for instance, health expenditures by the government as a percentage of total expenditures declined from about 80% in the mid-1990s to 75% in the mid-2000s (World Bank 2012). Because there is often considerable political resistance against such changes in many countries, at this point it remains far from clear the extent to which governments will adopt these sorts of reforms, or if they come, what form they will take. Nevertheless, as economist Herb Stein once quipped, "if something cannot go on forever, it will stop." Since people value goods, services, and activities other than health care, there is a limit to how much governments can and will finance rising health expenditures caused by aging populations. How governments manage health care policy in the face of population aging will be one of the key domestic policy challenges of the 21st century.

19.6   Exercises

Comprehension questions

Indicate whether each statement is true or false, and justify your answer. Be sure to state any additional assumptions you may need.

1 Population growth in the developed world is contributing to population aging.
2 Japan's population is not aging along with the rest of the developed world.

3 In a world of population decline, many national health systems are no longer solvent because they were predicated on the assumption of population growth.

4 In recent years, each year's Medicare tax receipts have been sufficient to cover that year's services.

5 In the 1970s, researchers were worried that, while Americans were living longer than previous generations, they were actually less healthy during old age than before. This phenomenon is known as the "compression of morbidity."

6 Reducing mortality from one disease necessarily increases the sum of the total mortality risk from all other causes of death.

7 If a costless drug were created that effectively cured a prevalent and deadly disease, health care expenditures would decrease.

8 Disproportionate spending on end-of-life care is never clinically justifiable.

9 Advance directives allow patients to indicate their own preferences about EOL care, but they cannot be acted upon if a dying patient is too sick to communicate with doctors.

10 Aggressive natalist policies have successfully reversed birth rate declines in most European countries.

Analytical questions

11 **Saving a national health insurance plan**. It is the year 2020 and you have just been elected President of Pcoria, a small island nation. Congratulations! Your country has a health care system like the one in the US, except much smaller. The government has a program called Medisure designed to provide insurance for the old and the very old for free. Unlike the American Medicare system, the recipients of Medisure do not face any cost-sharing; that is, recipients pay nothing. To finance the system, each young person pays $1,000 in taxes into the Medisure trust fund. According to your political opponents, the trust fund, with a current balance of $1 million, will reportedly go bankrupt any day now. You are up for re-election soon and have the unenviable task of saving Medisure. Table 19.3 contains demographic information about your island.

Table 19.3. *Pcoria demographic facts.*

Age	Population	Avg. annual medical exp.
Young	100	$0
Old	90	$1,000
Very old	50	$4,000

Your island also has some unique features:

• There is full employment for every member of the young generation, no matter how high taxes get; all of them are able to pay the full $1,000 tax for Medisure.

• There is no inflation and your trust fund does not earn interest.

• Each year, 100 new young people are born.

• Each year, all of the young who survive become old, all of the old who survive become very old, and all of the very old die. A percentage of the young and old die rather than transition to the next state (see Table 19.4).

Table **19.4.** *Mortality rates.*

Age	Death rate
Young	10%
Old	44.44%
Very old	100%

In answering the following questions, it may be helpful to use spreadsheet software.

a   Are your political opponents right in claiming that Medisure's trust fund will go bankrupt? If so, in what year? Assume for these exercises that the trust fund has $1 million as of January 1, 2020.

b   As if things were not already bad enough, your scientists have come up with a breakthrough medical technology that will decrease death rates without affecting per-person medical costs for the elderly. The new death rates are shown in Table 19.5. Will the Medisure trust fund ever go bankrupt now? If so, when?

Table **19.5.** *New mortality rates.*

Age	Death rate
Young	5%
Old	36.84%
Very old	100%

c   Appalled by the answer to the previous questions, you set your scientists to work again. They concoct another "breakthrough" technology that raises each citizen's annual medical expenditures by 50% without having any effect on death rates. Now you have lower death rates *and* higher medical expenditures. Will the Medisure trust fund ever go bankrupt now? If so, when?

d   Suppose that all the scientists are deported and the blueprints of their technological discoveries are lost in an accidental fire. Now the original schedules of death rates and yearly medical expenditures per person hold. You decide that the right way to save Medisure is to raise the retirement age from old to very old. Now the old work and are taxed $1,000 per person, just like the young, while consuming $0 of Medisure health care (hopefully they have other sources of insurance). Will the Medisure trust fund ever go bankrupt now? If so, when? Assume that you are starting over in 2020.

e   Polling reveals people abhor your decision to raise the retirement age and they force you to lower it again. As a firm leader, you consider raising taxes to $2,000 per year on each of the young. While this is bound to be unpopular in the short run, if you save Medisure, it might establish your legacy. Will the Medisure trust fund ever go bankrupt now? If so, when? Assume that you are starting over in 2020.

f   Well, increasing taxes proved even more unpopular than you could have imagined, and you were forced to lower them again to $1,000 per year on each of the young. Ever resourceful, you hit upon another strategy – invest the trust fund in the stock market. You are confident that with the right investments, you can earn 10% per year on the trust fund and save Medisure. Will the Medisure trust fund ever go bankrupt now? If so, when? Assume that you are starting over in 2020.

g   Alas, the stock market venture didn't work out quite as well as you might have liked. You are truly desperate now, so you do the unthinkable. You allow 200 extra young workers to immigrate to your island and force them to pay the Medisure tax (thus making 300 young workers in total). To mitigate the political and fiscal impact, you force them to leave your island before they become old and start using health care. Will the Medisure trust fund ever go bankrupt now? If so, when? Assume that you are starting over in 2020.

h   Your re-election is going to be very close. Your political advisers do not think you can afford to let so many outsiders into the country every year due to xenophobic sentiments. Assuming again that you start in 2020, what is the minimum number of immigrants you need each year to keep Medisure solvent through the next election at the end of 2027?

12 **A simple future elderly model.** In this exercise, you will create a very simple version of the FEM designed at RAND. Our model will follow a cohort of 65-year-olds as they age, and each period of the model will represent one year. In the first version of our model, the elderly will have three states: h (healthy), s (sick with cancer), and r (deceased). In a given period, each elderly person assumes a certain state for the entire period. Between periods, the elderly transition with the following likelihoods:

(1) Healthy to deceased: $P(r_{t+1}|h_t) = \delta$

(2) Healthy to sick: $P(s_{t+1}|h_t) = \rho(1 - \delta)$

(3) Sick to deceased: $P(r_{t+1}|s_t) = \delta + \gamma(1 - \delta)$

where, for instance, condition 1 implies that a person has a δ chance of becoming deceased in period $t + 1$, given that she is healthy in period t.

a   In this model, cancer patients never get cured; that is, they never return to state h once they enter state s. Express this idea in terms of a conditional probability statement like the ones listed above.

b   Create a diagram with circles representing each possible state and arrows between them with transition probabilities. Note that the sum of probability emanating from each state must equal one. [*Hint:* Some or all of the states may have self-directed arrows.]

c   In each period, the elderly incur certain health care costs. Assume $c_h = \$100$ (that is, assume the healthy incur $100 each period). Also assume $c_s = \$500$ and $c_r = \$0$. How much will a cohort of 1,000 healthy 65-year-olds cost during the zeroth period of the model (when they are all still healthy)? How much would you expect they will cost altogether during the first period of the model (on average)? Express your answers in terms of $c_h, c_s, c_r, \delta, \rho$, and γ.

d   Imagine that you follow a cohort of simulated healthy 65-year-olds until they are all deceased (in the next exercise you will no longer have to imagine this – you will model it). Now suppose that γ has decreased because treatment for people with cancer has improved. What effect do you expect this will have on overall combined costs if you ran a new model with a new cohort of simulated healthy 65-year-olds compared with the cohort before this new technology? Explain.

e   Now suppose that ρ decreases, perhaps due to the dissemination of better cancer screening techniques. Explain why you cannot predict the effect of this change on total costs without more information. Explain how this change may lower total costs and how it may raise total costs. Argue that it may be a good development even if it raises total costs.

    f Let's make the model a little more complicated. We introduce a fourth state d (disabled). Assume that healthy people will have strokes with probability $\eta(1 - \delta)$ and become disabled; that is $P(d_{t+1}|h_t) = \eta(1 - \delta)$. Disabled elderly must receive expensive nursing-home care, so $c_d = \$2,000$. Assume for simplicity that people do not get strokes and cancer in the same year, that people with cancer do not have strokes, and that people who are disabled do not get cancer (these are not biologically accurate assumptions). Assume also that $P(r_{t+1}|d_t) = \delta$. Draw an updated circle diagram with these new assumptions.

13 **A simple future elderly model II.** Review the previous exercise before embarking on this one.

    a Use Excel, Matlab, or similar software to build a version of our model. Your model should be able to

- Track a cohort of 100 people throughout several periods.
- Assign and track states to each simulated elderly person in each period.
- Track total costs over each period.
- Randomly generate a new set of states for each subsequent period based on the transition probabilities. *Important:* make sure to design your model so that you can easily change these transition probabilities for each run of the model.

One convenient implementation might involve a spreadsheet or matrix where each column represents a year and each row represents a "person."

    b Assume the following values: $\delta = \rho = \gamma = \eta = 0.1$. Show that the probability of a healthy person remaining healthy in the next period is 0.72.

    c Using these assumed values, run the model five times, starting each time with a cohort of 100 healthy (state h) 65-year-olds in period 0. Run the model until period 35 each time (when the lucky surviving elderly reach age 100). Report your total costs in each of the five runs.

    d Run the model a sixth time but set $\delta(\text{age}) = \frac{\text{age} - 65}{35}$. Why is this a more realistic assumption? How does this affect costs over 35 years?

    e Run the model a seventh time with the new δ function and $\rho = 0.03$ (people are now less likely to get cancer). Does this increase costs over 35 years or decrease costs over 35 years?

    f Run the model one last time with the new δ function, the new ρ, and assume that nursing-home care is getting more efficient: $c_d = \$1,000$. How big of an effect does this have on decreasing overall costs?

    g Explain how cancer and stroke interact in this model.

Essay questions

14 While it may seem intuitively obvious that health expenditures will increase as a population ages – older people after all are less healthy on average than younger people – in fact, several prominent health economists have argued that it is not aging per se, but rather some of the correlates of an aging population that cause health expenditures to rise as a population ages. For instance, Getzen (1992) argues that, at least in part, rising health expenditures with an aging population are due to the higher incomes and resources of the older population; health care is a normal good, so higher incomes lead to higher expenditures. In a similar manner, Zweifel et al. (1999) argue that the real problem with an aging population, at least as far as health care costs are concerned, is that there will be more people who are within a couple of years of dying. Since health care expenditures rise sharply close to the end of life, it is this, rather than population aging by itself, that leads to higher health care expenditures.

- Suppose that population aging in a given country is due entirely to an increase in life expectancy at age 65, rather than any other cause, and suppose further that Zweifel et al. (1999) are right and the rise in the set of people who are close to death causes higher health expenditures. Given these assumptions, would you expect per capita health care expenditures to rise or fall in the near future? What about total health expenditures?

- Suppose that Getzen's finding is accurate, and the reason why population aging is correlated with higher health expenditures is because older populations tend to be richer than younger ones. If that is so, do rising health care expenditures mean higher or lower social welfare? Under these conditions, should policymakers be concerned about higher health care expenditures due to population aging?

Students can find answers to the comprehension questions and lecturers can access an Instructor Manual with guideline answers to the analytical problems and essay questions at **www.palgrave.com/economics/bht**.

VI PUBLIC HEALTH ECONOMICS

20 The economics of health
    externalities   428

21 Economic epidemiology   449

22 Obesity   472

20 THE ECONOMICS OF HEALTH EXTERNALITIES

VI PUBLIC HEALTH ECONOMICS

Up to this point, this book has focused mainly on the economic conundrums caused by health uncertainty. Health events are inherently unpredictable, and the demand for health care is highly uncertain as a result. This creates a market for health insurance, which in turn gives rise to the problems of adverse selection and moral hazard. We have studied how the existence of insurance complicates the relationships between patients, doctors, hospitals, governments, and insurance companies. We found that insurance markets are prone to failure in the face of asymmetric information, and that governments around the world have tried to rectify these failures (with varying degrees of success).

But health has another interesting economic property: it is highly contagious. Unlike other factors that affect your economic wellbeing – for instance, your height, your appearance, or your years of schooling – your health is greatly determined by the health of those around you. If your friends got their flu shots this fall, it is less likely that you will come down with the flu this winter, even if you neglected to get a flu shot yourself. Likewise, if your roommate falls ill with an infectious disease like meningitis or pneumonia, your health could soon take a turn for the worse. Health is therefore a source of many economic *externalities*, both positive and negative.

Externalities are a classic justification for government involvement in markets. In the absence of externalities and asymmetric information, basic economic theory suggests that markets will reach an efficient outcome. In this setting, taxes, subsidies, and price controls are useless at best and harmful at worst. But when externalities do exist, these very same government responses may help the market reach a socially desirable state.

This logic extends to disease as well: the government subsidizes treatments that prevent contagious diseases (like the flu) but not most non-contagious ones (like chronic back pain). This is not because the flu is worth avoiding and back pain is not – it is because people will take sufficient steps to combat back pain on their own, while the same cannot be said of the flu.

For health that is contagious, it does not make sense to consider it solely as a personal status or goal. An entire community or society may be affected by one person's health, so in that sense any group of people has a shared health status. If the people around you or the society you live in is not very healthy, in some sense you are not very healthy either. This notion of *public health* makes clear the need to analyze health externalities.

Public health efforts, like flu vaccination campaigns or quarantines to combat deadly diseases like Ebola virus, can be thought of as a way for the government to combat externalities. The economic way of thinking about public health is presented in the remainder of this chapter.

20.1   Externalities in health

In a typical transaction, a buyer and seller make a voluntary agreement that benefits both. Such transactions are called *Pareto improving* because every party involved is made better off (or, at the very least, not worse off).

But sometimes the effects of a transaction are not contained to just the buyer and seller. An **externality** occurs whenever a market transaction between a buyer and seller has an effect on some third party. These externalities can be positive (as in the case of a well-tended garden on a neighbor's front lawn), or negative (as in the case of pollution spewing from a factory smokestack).

Definition | **20.1**

Externality: any positive or negative effect that a market transaction imposes on a third party (that is, someone other than the buyer or the seller).

There are lots of externalities in the world of health: secondhand smoke, the risk of catching infectious disease from your neighbors, the motivational benefits of living among active people, and the taxes paid to the government to care for sick people. All externalities, positive and negative, can be analyzed using a simple graphical framework. Below, we introduce two standard examples of health externalities – one positive and one negative – and analyze their effects on social welfare.

Before we introduce the formal analysis of externalities, we introduce a key concept in welfare economics: the distinction between **private welfare** and **social welfare**. Private welfare is a measure of the utility of one member of society, while social welfare is a measure of the utility of all members of society. In the presence of externalities, these two quantities will tend to diverge: what is good for one person's private welfare may not be good for the overall social welfare.

Definition | **20.2**

Private welfare: the utility level of one individual within a society. Actions that would increase or decrease this quantity are said to have **private benefits** or **private costs**.

Social welfare: the summed utility levels of all individuals within a society. Actions that would increase or decrease this quantity are said to have **social benefits** or **social costs**.

Herd immunity

Every time an individual is vaccinated against an infectious disease, she protects herself from the disease, but also protects everyone else around her. This is because she can no longer get infected and pass the disease to anyone else. The probability of a random interaction leading to disease transmission is lower as a result of each vaccination. Thus, even unvaccinated people benefit when their neighbors, friends, co-workers, and family become immune through vaccination. This positive externality is called **herd immunity**.

> **Definition | 20.3**
>
> **Herd immunity:** the secondhand immunity that accrues to nonvaccinated people when other people are vaccinated.

Herd immunity is a classic positive externality: the social gain from each vaccination is greater than the private gain from that vaccination. When deciding whether to get vaccinated, people balance the private gains from vaccination – immunity from the disease – against the private costs. These costs may include the price of the vaccine, the possibility of side effects, the time it takes to travel to the doctor's office, and the pain of getting a shot. But a person considering vaccination ignores the social benefits of herd immunity. Because social benefits are greater than private benefits, a private market produces fewer vaccinations than is socially optimal.

To understand what we mean by socially optimal, we adopt the graphical interpretation of externalities due to Bowen (1943) and popularized by Nobel laureate Paul Samuelson. Consider Figure 20.1, the basic diagram of supply and demand for a good (in this case a flu vaccine). As always, the demand curve D indicates how many flu vaccinations are purchased at any given price. S is the supply curve in a perfectly competitive market where marginal cost is constant. The market equilibrates at the intersection of S and D at a vaccination rate of Q^* and at a price P^*.

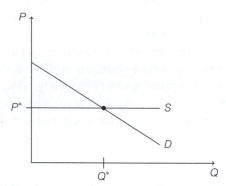

Figure 20.1. *The market for flu vaccinations.*

The demand curve D in Figure 20.1 is called a *private demand curve* because it reflects innumerable private decisions of people in the market about whether they want to be vaccinated at various price levels. These decisions reflect only private costs and benefits and not social costs and benefits. Herd immunity benefits, for instance, are ignored.

Imagine now that the decision to vaccinate is not private but instead public. A social planner who cares about maximizing social welfare decides whether each person gets vaccinated, regardless of that person's desires. The social planner compares the social benefit and social cost of each vaccination. We can draw a new *social demand curve* from the point of view of the social planner. In this case, it is higher than the private demand curve due to the positive externality from herd immunity (Figure 20.2).

The point α in Figure 20.2 represents the private market equilibrium, which does not account for herd immunity. The point β represents the hypothetical market equilibrium that results when the social planner decides who gets vaccinated.

From a social welfare standpoint, β is a better market equilibrium than α. That is, social welfare is highest when a social planner decides who gets vaccinated, as opposed to the

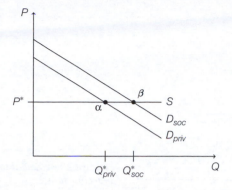

Figure 20.2. *The market for flu vaccinations with private and social demand curves.*

individuals themselves. To see why, suppose that an unvaccinated man named Jay would get only $5 of private benefit out of a flu shot, and that it costs $10 at the local clinic. But the herd immunity benefits of the shot would be worth an additional $15 to Jay's friends and co-workers.

Society derives $20 of benefit from the shot, and it only costs $10, so it is a bargain for the public and the social planner would buy it. But left to his own devices, Jay would not purchase the shot because the private benefits are small. When private individuals do not take herd immunity into account in their vaccination decisions, the rest of society loses out on cheaply available herd immunity that is worth more than it costs.

In an ideal world, Jay would be induced to purchase the socially valuable flu shot even though it is not privately worth it. At α, there are $Q_{soc} - Q_{priv}$ people like Jay. These people do not get vaccinated on their own, because their private benefit is lower than private cost, but it would be socially beneficial if they were to vaccinate.

In general, demand curves reflect the benefit of consuming a good, and supply curves reflect the cost of producing it. So in Figure 20.2, the vertical distance between D_{soc} and S indicates how much more society gains from vaccination benefit than it loses in vaccination costs. This difference is termed **social surplus**. It reflects the gains from trade and measures the wealth that is created by the market's existence. Any social surplus that is lost when individuals make privately motivated decisions – such as the $10 in net benefit that was lost when Jay did not vaccinate – is termed **social loss**. Many introductory textbooks use the term *deadweight loss* instead.

Definition | **20.4**

Social surplus: the difference between the social benefit and the social cost of production in a market.

Social loss: the forgone social surplus due to a market inefficiency such as an externality.

Figure 20.3 helps to quantify the social loss from the herd immunity externality. Region A, shaded dark gray, represents the social surplus that accrues when vaccinations are purchased. Region B, shaded light gray, represents social loss. This is the forgone surplus that is never realized because the market is at α instead of β. The larger that region B is, the more costly it is for the market to ignore the positive herd immunity externality and remain at the inefficient private equilibrium.

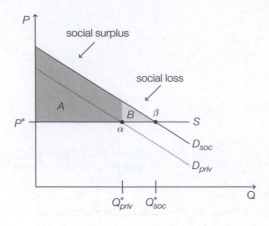

Figure 20.3. *Social loss in the market for flu vaccinations.*

The size of the social loss – that is, the area of B – depends on the elasticity of the demand curve with respect to price. If the demand curve is vertical, representing perfectly inelastic demand, the private demand curve and social demand curve coincide. Exercise 13 of this chapter and Chapter 22 explore this relationship in much more detail.

In this section we have studied the positive externality from herd immunity. The graphic framework we present can be used to analyze any positive externality. In the next section, we study a classic negative externality in health. Social loss from negative externalities can be modeled in an exactly analogous way.

Antibiotic resistance

Humans and animals are not the only creatures who must contend with bacterial infections – fungi must do so as well. In fact, it was a chemical innovation evolved by fungi that formed the basis of the first synthetic antibiotic, penicillin.

Many fungi combat bacteria by secreting molecules containing a β-lactam ring. A β-lactam ring is a chemical structure with four atoms in a square, three carbon and one nitrogen. These β-lactam rings have the happy ability to kill bacteria by preventing them from building and repairing their cell walls. This interferes with the bacteria's capacity to reproduce and grow. Penicillin and other early antibiotics rely on β-lactam rings to combat bacterial infections.

Unfortunately, some bacteria have genes that code for the creation of an enzyme called β-lactamase. This enzyme lyses β-lactam in half and disables its antibiotic properties.

The chemical structure of penicillin. The square at the center of the molecule is the β-lactam responsible for inhibiting the growth and repair of bacterial cell walls.

If only a small fraction of a bacterial population is equipped with β-lactamase, then penicillin can kill off most of the bacteria, and a human immune system can easily dispose of the rest. But if a large share of the bacteria can produce β-lactamase, then penicillin will be rendered ineffective.

Since the introduction of penicillin decades ago, β-lactam-resistant bacteria have become much more common. Bacterial species previously susceptible to pencillin must now be treated with novel antibiotics that use different techniques. This is no coincidence; it turns out that the widespread use of penicillin itself is to blame for the increase in β-lactam resistance.

Imagine a patient who is sick with pneumonia and takes a course of penicillin. After a few days, the β-lactam-sensitive bacteria in his lungs are all dead, but the few surviving bacteria are all penicillin resistant. The gene for β-lactamase is passed on to the next generation of bacteria, further diminishing the effectiveness of penicillin. This phenomenon is called *antibiotic resistance*. The only recourse is for scientists and drugmakers to find new chemical innovations that will be effective even on β-lactamase-producing bacteria. If no new strategy is found, many bacterial infections will become untreatable, just as they were in the days before penicillin.

Hence, the use of antibiotic drugs imposes a negative externality. Every dose of antibiotics breeds more resistant bacteria, which harms everyone in the world who might one day get infected and need effective antibiotics.

Despite this negative externality, the use of some antibiotic drugs may still be socially efficient. For example, the benefits of taking antibiotics for a person with a life-threatening case of necrotizing fasciitis caused by flesh-eating bacteria far outweigh the social costs of slightly increased antibiotic resistance. But in other cases, the social costs of antibiotic use can outweigh private benefits. For example, antibiotics are often inappropriately prescribed to insistent patients with colds or other viral infections. In this case, the health benefits of antibiotic use are zero, but the social costs remain high.

In the Samuelson model, negative externalities like antibiotic resistance can also be depicted with divergent social and private curves (Figure 20.4). This time, the social supply curve is higher than the private supply curve because each dose of antibiotics is more costly to society than simply its marginal cost of production. Patients make antibiotic purchase decisions based on the private price P^*_{priv}, but society as a whole pays the greater price P^*_{soc} whenever an antibiotic prescription is filled. The difference between the two price levels $P^*_{soc} - P^*_{priv}$ is equal to the additional cost of antibiotic resistance.

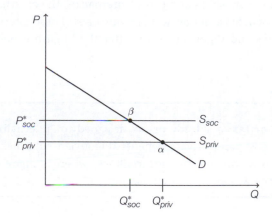

Figure 20.4. *The market for antibiotics.*

Figure 20.5 shows the social loss that arises when patients overconsume antibiotics relative to the socially optimal level. Private consumers would want to consume at point α but notice that for the drugs purchased between Q^*_{soc} and Q^*_{priv}, the social cost of producing them, P^*, exceeds their marginal benefit. Thus, drugs consumed in this region create a net loss for society.

Region A again depicts the social consumer surplus that results from efficient antibiotic use. The surplus is from the use of antibiotics that are worth the cost even when antibiotic resistance is considered. Region B depicts the social loss – this is the negative consumer

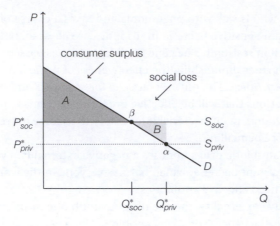

Figure 20.5. *Social loss in the market for antibiotics.*

surplus that arises when consumers purchase antibiotics that produce less benefit to society than they cost. From a social perspective, it would be better if these antibiotics were not taken because they cost P^*_{soc} but produce less benefit than that. Nevertheless, they are purchased anyway, because private consumers do not account for the effects of antibiotic resistance and face the lower price P^*_{priv}.

20.2   Pigouvian subsidies and taxes

If externalities cause social harm, how might government policy restore the social optimum and get us from point α to point β? One strategy governments often use is subsidizing behaviors that cause positive externalities and tax behaviors that cause negative externalities. These subsidies and taxes "internalize" the externality so that people treat social costs and benefits as if they were private ones. These interventions are known as **Pigouvian subsidies** and **Pigouvian taxes** after the English economist Arthur Cecil Pigou (1877–959).

Definition   20.5

Pigouvian subsidy or tax: a subsidy or tax designed to "internalize" an externality by altering private costs and private benefits. Pigouvian subsidies encourage more consumption of goods with positive externalities, whereas Pigouvian taxes reduce consumption of goods with negative externalities.

Herd immunity

As we have previously seen, immunity from disease confers a positive externality. Each person's immunity conveys both safety upon himself and also reduces the risk to his companions or his "herd." If each person considers only the private benefits, then vaccinations will be undervalued and the quantity of vaccinations purchased will be below the optimal amount.

The Pigouvian strategy for reducing the social loss from positive externalities is to provide a subsidy to consumers that raises the private benefits of vaccination to match the social benefit. Figure 20.6 shows the supply of flu vaccines S, the private demand curve D_{priv}, and the social demand curve D_{soc}. Without any intervention, the quantity demanded is Q^*_{priv} and the market price is p_s.

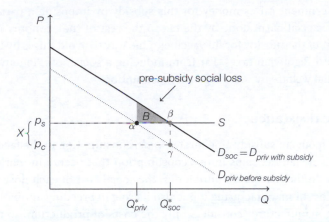

Figure 20.6. *A Pigouvian subsidy in the market for flu vaccinations.*

A social planner seeking to maximize overall welfare notices that marginal social benefit exceeds social marginal cost of each vaccination up to point β. So consuming any amount less than Q^*_{soc} must be socially inefficient. How low would vaccine prices need to fall so that consumers would choose to vaccinate all the way to Q^*_{soc}?

For the Q^*_{soc} unit of vaccination, the consumer only gains p_c in private benefit (point γ), so he is only willing to pay p_c for it. At p_c, consumers demands the socially optimal amount of vaccinations. But since it costs vaccine suppliers p_s to produce that Q^*_{soc} unit, suppliers will not accept anything less than p_s (point β).

Thus, to obtain the socially optimal level of vaccinations, a third party such as the government or a nonprofit organization must provide the difference between the consumer's maximum willing-to-pay price p_c and the supplier's minimum willing-to-sell price p_s. This difference $X = p_s - p_c$ is the optimal Pigouvian subsidy for this market.

In a perfectly competitive market, consumers all pay the same price for the vaccine. So if Q^*_{soc} vaccines are sold, every consumer pays p_c out of pocket. Similarly, the supplier receives p_s per vaccine. Thus, the total subsidy equals the per-transaction subsidy $X = p_s - p_c$ multiplied by the number of vaccines purchased Q^*_{soc}:

$$\text{Total subsidy} = Q^*_{soc} \times X = Q^*_{soc}(p_s - p_c)$$

This amount indicated by the area of the dashed rectangle in Figure 20.6 seems expensive since the total subsidy is greater than the original social loss (region B). Does this mean that the subsidy is not worth enacting? The answer is no.

Before the subsidy, the social loss in Region B represented lost social surplus – due to the herd-immunity externality, people ignored the social surplus available in region B. A Pigouvian subsidy fixes the problem, but it costs the government money as well. This government cost should not be counted as an additional social loss, though, because the subsidy flows directly to consumers. This transfer of funds affects the allocation of welfare in society but not the total welfare. Thus, unlike the social loss from the externality in region B, the subsidy region does not represent forgone social surplus. Even though the subsidy is larger than the social loss, the subsidy is still welfare-enhancing.

This does not mean that subsidies are totally costless. The government must raise money for the subsidy through tax revenue, and most kinds of government taxes, like income taxes, are welfare-reducing because they distort behavior away from the social optimum (Gwartney 1983).

If the government raises money for this subsidy by imposing a particularly distortive tax, then the social harm done by the tax to the rest of the economy may outweigh the social benefit of the subsidy for flu vaccines. One way to avoid this is by funding Pigouvian subsidies with Pigouvian taxes. Far from inducing a social loss, Pigouvian taxes actually increase social welfare by reducing overconsumption.

Antibiotic resistance

Whereas a Pigouvian subsidy ameliorates *under*consumption in the face of positive externalities, a Pigouvian tax reins in *over*consumption that occurs in markets with negative externalities. In the market for antibiotics, the social cost of each dose includes not only the private cost of manufacturing it but also its role in breeding antibiotic resistance. The private drug manufacturer considers only the costs of production, so the private supply curve understates the social cost. More drugs than are socially optimal are purchased, and a social loss results. A per-dose tax on the supplier can align the private and social supply curves.

In Figure 20.7, the optimal Pigouvian tax τ raises the private supply curve from S_{priv} to S_{soc}. Each unit of the drug costs τ more to produce. Because the tax in this case is placed on the supplier, the demand curve D does not change.

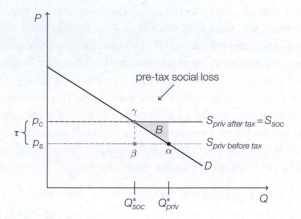

Figure 20.7. *A Pigouvian tax τ in the market for antibiotics.*

As a result of the tax, the consumer pays p_c per antibiotic dose. Of that payment, the government receives τ, leaving the supplier with $p_s = p_c - \tau$. The intersection of the demand curve and the supply curve with the tax now lies at point γ and the socially optimal quantity of antibiotics Q^*_{soc} is produced.

Because only Q^*_{soc} doses of drugs are consumed, lower than the pre-tax quantity Q^*_{priv}, the social loss in triangle B is also avoided. The total tax revenue collected by the government, illustrated by the dashed rectangle, is tax amount τ multiplied by the number of drugs actually sold:

$$\text{Tax Revenue} = Q^*_{soc} \times \tau = Q^*_{soc}(p_c - p_s)$$

Unlike Pigouvian subsidies, whose net welfare effect depends on how they are funded, Pigouvian taxes unambiguously improve social welfare. In fact, Pigouvian taxes generate two welfare-enhancing consequences. First, they curb the overconsumption of goods with negative externalities. Then the collected tax revenue can be put toward other public goods in order to reduce distortionary taxes. This pair of benefits from Pigouvian taxes is known as the *double dividend*.

20.3   The Coase theorem

The Pigouvian strategy for mending inefficient markets with externalities is to apply subsidies and taxes that "internalize" social costs and benefits. In the resulting market, private costs and benefits are aligned with social costs and benefits, so consumers make socially optimal choices.

But the Pigouvian strategy can be difficult to carry out when the size of the externality is unknown or hard to measure – how large a subsidy or tax should be enacted? If a Pigouvian tax or subsidy is too large, it may induce more social loss than it recoups and leave markets more inefficient than before. Ideally, when the effect of an externality is difficult to measure, there would be a way that the market itself could be induced to address its own externalities without Pigouvian remedies.

On first glance, this task may seem impossible – externalities by definition are *external* to the markets or transactions that cause them. But in 1960, Ronald Coase (1910–) showed that, under certain conditions, markets achieve the socially optimal outcomes, even in the face of externalities and in the absence of Pigouvian interventions (Coase 1960). In this section, we introduce the logic of this famous result, now known as the **Coase theorem**, using a parable of Willy Wonka and Dr Wormwood. We then ask whether the theorem applies in the case of the two externalities we have discussed: herd immunity and antibiotic resistance.

A Coasian parable

Suppose in the mythical land of Pcoria, there is a family medical practice run by Doctor Matilda Wormwood, where she meets with patients and treats their conditions. Next door to her practice is a small factory owned by candy magnate Willy Wonka, whose oft-criticized labor practices include the employment of cacophonous Oompa-Loompas to manufacture candy.

All is well until Dr Wormwood builds a new consultation room with a wall abutting the candy factory. Unfortunately, whenever she uses the room to examine her patients, she can barely hear herself think over the din of the Oompa-Loompas' joyous singing. Eventually she decides to take Willy Wonka to court, charging that his noisy employees are depriving her of the peace and quiet she needs to do her work.

The judge who takes the case must decide between two conflicting views of *property rights*. Dr Wormwood argues that everyone has a right to peace and quiet on her own property, and that the Oompa-Loompas should be prohibited from singing loudly enough to disrupt her work. Mr Wonka argues that everyone has a right to do whatever he wishes on his own property, regardless of the noise he makes, and that Dr Wormwood should find a different place to meet with patients.

Whichever rule prevails, an externality will be created. If Dr Wormwood wins the right to peace and quiet, then the mere presence of her practice imposes an externality on nearby property owners, who are legally required to keep quiet during her business hours. If Mr Wonka wins the right to make as much noise as possible, his Oompa-Loompas will impose an externality on Dr Wormwood, who can no longer use her consultation room. The Coase theorem makes a surprising assertion: no matter how the property rights are assigned, the outcome will be the same and that outcome will be socially optimal (as long as certain conditions hold).

Suppose that Willy Wonka will lose \$1,000 each year if he has to close his factory, but that Dr Wormwood will lose \$2,000 each year if she has to shut down her practice. Assuming these outcomes are mutually exclusive, we should hope that the doctor's office stays open in order to maximize social welfare.

First imagine that the judge decides in favor of Dr Wormwood, and declares that she has a right to peace and quiet on her own property. The next day, Willy Wonka shutters his factory and Dr Wormwood resumes treating her patients. Under this assignment of property rights, Willy Wonka is prevented from making candy due to Dr Wormwood's right to tranquility. But from a social point of view, it is worthwhile to shut down Willy Wonka's factory if it allows the doctor's more profitable business to continue. The parties achieve the socially optimal outcome, even if Willy Wonka is not happy about it.

Now imagine that the judge instead decides in favor of Willy Wonka, and declares that he can make as much noise as he wants, even to the point of annoying Dr Wormwood. It seems at first that the socially optimal outcome is not achieved in this case, because Dr Wormwood will have to move elsewhere or stop serving her patients. Shuttering Dr Wormwood's practice costs her \$2,000 a year, whereas the ruling only saves Willy Wonka \$1,000 a year.

But consider what happens if Dr Wormwood offers to strike a bargain with Willy Wonka. She agrees to pay \$1,500 a year to Willy Wonka if he agrees to keep his Oompa-Loompas quiet. This trade is *Pareto-improving*, because both parties are made better off. Willy Wonka makes more money than he would if his factory were operating, and Dr Wormwood can continue her work in peace even though the judge ruled against her property rights. Though Dr Wormwood now only makes \$500 a year, it is still better than shutting down her practice. Again, the parties achieve the socially optimal outcome, because the doctor's office is still operating and producing \$2,000 in profit each year, even though this time Dr Wormwood had to give up some money to get it.

A statement of the Coase theorem

The above parable illustrates the basic principle of the Coase theorem: private negotiations between individuals when there is an externality present can undo the social harm of the externality. No matter how property rights are assigned in any situation, the parties can bargain with each other until the socially optimal configuration is reached.

The Coase theorem

Resources will be used efficiently to maximize social welfare, even in the face of externalities, provided:

- property rights are well defined, and
- transaction costs or bargaining costs are sufficiently low.

The Coase theorem comes with two important prerequisites: in order for the social optimum to be guaranteed, we need well-defined property rights and low transaction costs.

These limitations are easily understood in terms of our example. Before Dr Wormwood's lawsuit was settled, property rights in her case were ill-defined; it was not clear whether Willy Wonka was allowed to pollute her office with noise, or whether she could insist on a quiet environment. This property right assignment is a crucial starting point for any negotiation between Dr Wormwood and Willy Wonka; without property rights, the two disputants are at an impasse.

Even once property rights are assigned, Dr Wormwood and Willy Wonka need to be able to negotiate effectively or the social optimum still may not be achieved. Suppose that Dr Wormwood hates her long-time neighbor and cannot abide the notion of being in the same room with Willy Wonka and his horrid Oompa-Loompas, let alone spending hours negotiating a settlement. Even if they do not come to fisticuffs on first sight, there may be other barriers to negotiation, like language differences or travel costs.

Herd immunity and antibiotic resistance

High transaction costs are often the biggest hurdle to achieving a Coasian bargain. The costs facing multiple parties trying to negotiate can take several forms – distrust, poor enforceability, legal fees, language interpreter services, finding a place to meet – and may be sufficient to deter the parties from making a Pareto-improving deal. We return to our two examples of health externalities and analyze each in light of the Coase theorem.

How would Coasian bargaining play out in the case of the flu vaccine? Consider Jay, who is not willing to vaccinate on his own, but whose vaccination would generate $100 of benefit to his neighbors and co-workers in the form of herd immunity. If those neighbors and co-workers pooled together, they could pay Jay $50, which would be enough to bribe him to get a flu shot. He would benefit because he is being paid, and the others would benefit because they collectively gain $100 worth of herd immunity for only $50.

But this arrangement relies on several assumptions: Jay's neighbors and co-workers must realize that these herd immunity benefits exist, must understand their monetary value, and must trust him to actually get a vaccine after they pay him the $50. Ultimately, transaction costs like incomplete information and enforcement problems might derail this agreement and leave everyone worse off.

Consider next the dilemma of the world population in the case of antibiotic resistance. Suppose a patient, by taking antibiotics, imposes a total externality of $100 on the rest of the world. She would be willing to forgo her medicine for a payment of only $30. By taking the antibiotics, the patient generates a net social loss of $70. It would be socially optimal for everyone else in the world to pool resources and send the patient a check for $30 in return for her halting the antibiotics.

In practice, the transaction costs of such an arrangement would be immense. Assuming the externality is borne equally by the world's seven billion other people, each would save only a millionth of a cent with this transfer. The transaction costs of negotiating and implementing a Coasian bargain in this case would far outweigh the gains to each party in the negotiation.

So while the Coase theorem provides a tidy solution to the problem of externalities, high transaction costs may preclude a Coasian bargain in practice. This means the justification

A seven-billion-person negotiation would be challenging to arrange. Finding a venue to meet would of course be a major obstacle. Other costs would include translator expenses and an extremely powerful megaphone.
Credit: © satori – Fotolia.com.

for Pigouvian taxes and subsidies discussed in Section 20.1 is intact, at least in the cases where transaction costs are too high.

These cases of high transaction costs also illustrate the importance of the initial property rights assignment. In an ideal world with no transaction costs, the Coase theorem says that this initial assignment of property rights is immaterial, because it is the subsequent bargaining stage that ensures optimal outcomes. Recall that in the case of Willy Wonka and Dr Wormwood, the doctor's office remained open and the factory shut down under both property rights allocations. But if transaction costs are high, outcomes are no longer independent of property rights assignment. In these situations, governments should consider which property rights systems are most conducive to bargaining and negotiation.

Antibiotic resistance provides a good case study of how different property rights designations can alter transaction costs. For instance, suppose that the government sets a property right such that someone with a bacterial infection must seek permission to use antibiotics from everyone in the world. In this case, even a single recalcitrant individual could veto the use of the antibiotic. Even if a patient secured the agreement of every person on Earth except one, that last person has a strong incentive to exploit the property regime and overcharge for her assent. This is known as the *hold-up problem*, and arises in other settings such as when developers want to buy several adjacent lots to build a larger building or a highway. Under this property right assignment, no one would ever gain the right to take an antibiotic, even if it were socially optimal to do so.

On the other hand, if the patient has a property right to take the antibiotic, there is no similar hold-up problem, but, as we have seen, there is an impossible coordination problem. The countless people who would potentially be harmed from antibiotic resistance, including many who are not yet born, have no way of coordinating to pay the patient to forgo the antibiotic.

In most countries, a patient has a property right to take antibiotics as long as she secures a prescription from a doctor. Ideally, the doctor serves as a proxy for the interests of the rest of the population and only agrees to the prescription if the benefit to the patient outweighs the social harm from antibiotic resistance. Even if doctors do not always serve as perfect proxies, this property rights assignment avoids both the hold-up and coordination problems of alternate property rights assignments.

20.4   The economics of organ transplantation

To illustrate the complexities of welfare analysis, we develop a case study of organ transplantation markets. Certain diseases like hepatitis and ischemic heart disease attack specific organs of the body, and sometimes when the disease becomes too severe, the besieged organs can lose their functionality. In such cases, the only available treatment may be replacing the sickly organ with a healthy one from another person through a procedure known as an organ transplant.

For example, patients with end-stage renal disease must be given at least one healthy kidney in order to survive without expensive and onerous kidney dialysis treatment. Others suffering chronic liver disease may need a new liver or suffer lethal blood toxicity. And patients with severe coronary artery disease or other heart complications may face an immediate death sentence unless they are given a heart transplant. In each case, the medical procedure is incredibly complex but may extend the patient's life for several years. Organ transplants can replace diseased hearts, lungs, kidneys, livers, and even corneas.

While some organs like a kidney or part of the pancreas can be obtained from a living body, the removal of other organs – the liver, a lung, the heart, or parts of the intestine – would kill the person donating the organ. Donations of these vital organs necessarily come from dead patients. But almost all human organs are viable only very briefly after death and only under specific circumstances. If they are not harvested almost immediately, the organ tissues decay from lack of oxygenated blood and the organs quickly become unusable.

Moreover, organs seem inherently unlike other secondhand goods like used books or clothes – they are less possessions than they are parts of a person. So donating a heart or a liver is not the same as giving away college textbooks or childhood toys. Perhaps it is unsurprising that the organs available for transplant are exceedingly scarce. In January and February of 2012, there were a total of 4,494 organ transplants conducted in the US, whereas there were 114,339 patients on organ waiting lists (United Network for Organ Sharing 2012). The existence of a waitlist imposes a large cost on dying patients and suggests that the market is not doing a good job of supplying organs.

Another oddity of the market for organs is that even the richest people in the world cannot get an organ when they need one. For example, after former Apple CEO Steve Jobs was diagnosed with pancreatic cancer, his doctors told him that he needed a new liver. Despite his vast wealth, it took him many months to secure one. Jobs traveled to many regions in the US to register on the organ waiting list of each region. These lists are managed by the nonprofit United Network for Organ Sharing (UNOS) and allocate organs as they become available based on clinical need, immunological compatibility, and queue position, so Jobs could not pay to expedite this process. Jobs eventually received his replacement liver at a hospital in Memphis, Tennessee, more than 2,000 miles away from his home in California.

Is the apparent dysfunction of the market for organs creating a social loss, or is the waiting list a socially efficient outcome? We study this question using the tools of welfare economics.

Repugnant transactions and negative externalities

Consider a patient on a hospital bed. He has just suffered severe brain trauma as a result of a motorcycle accident. Doctors can attempt to sustain his life, but the prognosis is grim. The patient is comatose but has stated in a living will that he does want to be dependent on artificial life support. Most of his vital organs like his heart, kidneys, and liver may still be usable, but the patient did not specify whether his organs should be harvested for donation.

The patient's family members consider donating the organs. But before they can, the more venal relatives hatch a plan to sell the organs. While keeping the crash victim on life support, they schedule an auction for the organs and widely publicize the event. The next day, the hospital ward is crowded with representatives of people on organ waiting lists throughout the country. The potential bidders submit the accident victim to various stress tests, poking and prodding his organs, and they conclude that organs are in good shape. Envoys of the poor and middle class submit offers, but those are immediately trounced by bids from wealthy tycoons. At the end of the day, the richest bidders have purchased new organs; the relatives toast their new wealth at a local restaurant; and the motorcycle victim is taken off life support and his body is sent to doctors for organ-harvesting.

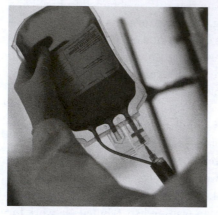

A pint of blood awaiting transfusion. Selling blood or other organs is almost uniformly illegal worldwide. Credit: *PhotoDisc/Getty Images.*

Most people would agree that there is something upsetting about this transaction. Some argue that any act that treats the human body like a commodity is immoral and so organ sales are degrading for the society that permits them. For example, Pope John Paul II said in 2000 that "any procedure which tends to commercialize human organs ... must be considered morally unacceptable, because to use the body as an 'object' is to violate the dignity of the human person" (Roth 2007).

In addition, the allocation of the organs may violate notions of equity. Should a wealthy 78-year-old in stable condition be able to buy a heart because he has more money than the poor 34-year-old dying in an intensive care unit? Both the collection and distribution of organs may cause people to feel that the unfettered sale of organs is repugnant.

This repugnance is a sort of negative externality. People not party to the organ sale suffer knowing that somewhere this kind of organ auction is happening. Many transactions may cause a repugnance negative externality as well. For example, transactions like indentured servitude, prostitution, and serving *foie gras* have all stirred protests that the existence of these practices harms human dignity. Another memorable example of a repugnance externality is the market for dwarf tossing, a pastime in which a larger person pays a smaller person for the pleasure of hurling him as far as possible (Roth 2007).

Hence, repugnance is similar to pollution from nearby factories or increased antibiotic resistance from drug use. As with other negative externalities, the repugnance may cause a social loss. Fortunately, there are multiple ways in which a society can address the repugnance externality in the market for organs.

The Coasian approach: transferable organ property rights

As long as the Coase theorem holds, markets can work out any externality – even an externality like organ sale repugnance – on their own. How would this market for human organs look? First suppose that the conditions of the Coase theorem are satisfied: property rights are well defined and transaction costs of bargaining are low. In this context, property rights to a person's organs could rest with the person herself or with her next of kin after she is dead; as long as the right to an organ is unambiguous and transferable, the market reaches a social optimum.

Suppose the government grants people a transferable property right to their own organs. In this world, people would be free to buy and sell organs, even though some other people may be repulsed by this practice. Consenting adults from developing countries might sell spare kidneys to patients with end-stage renal disease in developed nations. Young motorcyclists might sell the rights to their hearts and livers to organ brokers who would harvest them whenever their clients suffered fatal crashes. The welfare gains of this regime are clear: organ sellers can convert extra or unneeded organs into cash, while those desperate for a transplant no longer face deadly shortages.

However, these transactions would also generate repugnance. But if bargaining costs are low, there is a ready solution: those who are repulsed can pay people not to transact in organs. Organizations opposed to organ selling could give payouts to those who refuse to participate in organ sales. If the repugnance is great enough, and those who feel repulsed are willing to pay to stop the sales, it is possible that no organ transactions would occur at all! In this case, a market for organs with no transactions would be socially efficient.

There is another possible property rights assignment: every person has the right to negate another person's organ sale. This is equivalent to assigning everyone the property rights to everyone else's organs. Those who wished to sell their organs would only be able to sell if they obtained permission from everyone else on Earth. But transaction costs under this assignment would be prohibitively high, due to the hold-up problem highlighted in Section 20.3.

The assumption that organ property rights can be well defined may not be right either. The central difficulty is that most organs can only be harvested after the death of their original owner. In the US, the deceased has nominal rights to his organs after death – if he designated himself an organ donor, in theory his wishes must be respected. In practice, his grieving family may be in shock, distracted by the pain of their loss, and may not want the body disturbed or may be opposed to organ donation. The delicacy of these tragic situations means that doctors often do not feel comfortable harvesting organs from people who have died, even if the deceased was an ardent believer in organ donation during life. In the 1993 National Mortality Follow-Back Survey, 16% of families indicated that they ignored the wishes of their deceased kin with respect to organ donation (Bhattacharya 2004).

By contrast, in some countries such as Spain, the decision to harvest a patient's organs lies with the government, unless that person has explicitly declared that her organs can not be donated. Even grieving families cannot stand in the way of a donation. Predictably, Spain has a much higher organ donation rate than the US, and consequently, the waiting lists for organ donations are shorter there.

Ultimately, the Coase theorem fails to apply in either the US or Spain, because property rights are still not well defined. Neither the next of kin in the US nor the government in Spain can sell the property rights to the organs, so both parties only have a *limited* property right over the organs. They can decide to donate or not to donate but no one has the right to sell the organs.

Because property rights are difficult to define and enforce in the case of organs, and because bargaining costs seem prohibitively high regardless of property rights assignment, a Coasian approach may not succeed in achieving a socially optimal level of organ transactions. We turn next to the Pigouvian approach, where bargaining costs are immaterial.

The Pigouvian approach: an infinite tax

The Pigouvian strategy for internalizing negative externalities is to tax an unwelcome activity so that private individuals face prices that reflect the full social cost of their actions. In this case, the government might apply a tax to organ sales that reflects the amount of moral damage that each repugnant transaction does to fellow citizens. If repugnance is relatively low, this tax might be small and deter very few transactions. But if the repugnance generated by each transaction is great, the optimal Pigouvian tax might be high, enough to discourage most organ sales. And if the repugnance is truly extreme, the optimal Pigouvian tax will rise so high that no one will want to sell any organs at all. A tax this high would be economically identical to a ban on all organ sales.

In real-world organ markets, this is the preferred policy adopted by nearly every government on Earth: an outright ban on any organ sales (organ *donations* are still allowed and encouraged, of course). The only exception as of 2008 was Iran, which permits the sale of kidneys from live donors (Hippen 2008). The ban can be construed as a Pigouvian strategy, but only if every single organ sale generates more welfare loss from repugnance than welfare gain to the buyer and seller. But if there is even one potential organ sale that would increase social welfare, even accounting for repugnance, this infinite "tax" would not be optimal.

The ban on monetary organ transactions accounts for most of the idiosyncrasies of this market, especially the long waiting times for organs. One way governments have tried to shorten waiting lists is through subsidies that provide financial incentive for people to become organ donors. For example, in 2013 Australia initiated a limited pilot program offering six weeks' paid leave at minimum wage for kidney donors (Yosufzai 2013). The financial reward is limited to currently employed citizens, perhaps out of fear that offering payment in exchange for kidneys would create coercive pressure on the unemployed or indigent.

But such a subsidy may actually backfire. In a study of blood donation, Titmus (1970) hypothesized that financially compensating blood donors could actually lower the supply of donations. Providing an economic incentive might undercut altruistic motives and discourage donations. In a field experiment with 89 subjects, Mellström and Johannesson (2008) found that the introduction of a financial reward of 50 Swedish kronor (about $7) for blood donors reduced the donation rate of women from 52% to 30%.

None of the Coasian or Pigouvian policies we have discussed seem to solve the problems of organ transplantation markets. Repugnance and unenforceable property rights combine to undermine potential solutions, leaving behind long waitlists, unharvested organs, and dying patients. This area could benefit from creative thinking about market design (Roth et al. 2005).

One increasingly popular strategy uses non-financial incentives to reduce waiting lists. Israel and Singapore have designed waiting list policies that promote registered donors and demote non-donors (Tabbarok 2010). As a result, individuals anticipating a risk of future organ failure are motivated to register as organ donors themselves. If this system increases donor rolls, it will successfully reduce waiting lists while avoiding the repugnance of a financial transaction.

20.5   Conclusion

While previously we concentrated on market failures arising from information asymmetries and monopolistic competition, this chapter introduced market failures that arise from externalities. When externalities create social loss, a government action such as a Pigouvian tax or a Coasian property right assignment can improve social welfare.

But it is not clear that all externalities justify government response. Is every externality valid? Or are there externalities so extraneous or frivolous that they should be discounted in the social welfare function? Most would agree that children who contract asthma because of neighborhood smog have a valid grievance against local polluters. But at the same time, few would agree that the protests of a bigot who claims harm whenever a family of a different race moves in next door should be included in the social welfare function. These questions are not just philosophical exercises, though – as we saw in the case of organs, the decision to treat organ sale repugnance as a valid externality (rightly or wrongly) has a profound impact on the shape of that market.

In the next two chapters, we examine the welfare economics of two public health topics: infectious disease and obesity. We analyze government interventions such as vaccination programs, quarantine operations, and eradication campaigns using the tools we have introduced in this chapter.

20.6   Exercises

Comprehension questions

Indicate whether each statement is true or false, and justify your answer. Be sure to cite evidence from the chapter and state any additional assumptions you may need.

1 The Coase theorem implies that there are no externalities.
2 Suppose Fred imposes negative externalities on Wilma when he engages in some otherwise productive activity (like yelling "Yabba Dabba Doo!" to encourage himself, for instance). Suppose further that Fred and Wilma know each other well, communicate effectively and trust each other, and generally have low costs from transacting with each other. In this setting, having the government impose a Pigouvian tax on Fred each time he yells "Yabba Dabba Doo!" is the only way to generate socially optimal levels of yelling.
3 In the presence of externalities, private and social welfare diverge.
4 Herd immunity is a negative health externality.
5 Every antibiotic taken causes a net social loss by contributing to antibiotic resistance.
6 Pigouvian taxes always improve social welfare.
7 The Coase theorem says that well-defined property rights and low transaction costs are needed in order for the social optimum to be guaranteed through bargaining.
8 Viable organs, while scarce, are readily accessible to extremely wealthy patients for a high price.
9 A Coasian approach may not succeed in achieving a socially optimal level of organ transactions.
10 Most countries effectively impose an infinite tax on organ sales.
11 Subsidies that provide financial incentive for people to become organ donors may lead to a decrease in donations.

Analytical problems

12 **Demand elasticity and social loss.** Consider two vaccines for different viruses X and Ω. Assume that the marginal cost of producing both drugs is constant and that the fixed cost is small. In other words, assume that the supply curve for both drugs is flat.

a   Suppose that demand for vaccine χ is price elastic, whereas demand for vaccine Ω is relatively inelastic. Plot the private demand curve for both drugs on separate axes.

b   For the sake of example, assume that both viruses have the same externality. Plot the social demand curve for both drugs and label the social loss in each case.

c   Explain intuitively why, all else equal, social loss is greater in the case of elastic demand than it is in the case of inelastic demand.

13 **Secondhand smoke I**. Assume that the daily demand for packs of cigarettes in the tobacco-addicted nation of Pcoria is

$$Q = 100 - P$$

Further assume that the marginal cost of producing a pack of cigarettes is \$6, and that the market for cigarettes is perfectly competitive. Assume that each pack of cigarettes smoked does \$6 worth of health damage to the smoker in the form of increased cancer risk and a total of \$5 worth of health damage to the smoker's neighbors via secondhand smoke. Finally, assume that all Pcorian cigarette consumers are aware of these costs.

a   Assume that a Pcorian smoker named Jay states that he is willing to buy a pack of cigarettes for \$8, but not a penny more. In this market, where the price is \$6 per pack, what are the private benefits and private costs incurred whenever he buys a pack of cigarettes? Is it privately efficient for him to buy a pack of cigarettes at this price?

b   What about the public benefits and public costs? Is it socially efficient for him to buy a pack of cigarettes at this price?

c   Suppose that, due to the introduction of a hyper-effective tobacco fertilizer, the cost of producing a pack of cigarettes plummets to \$1. Now is it socially efficient for Jay to purchase a pack of cigarettes?

14 **Secondhand smoke II**. Review the assumptions from the previous problem, and assume that it still costs \$6 to produce a pack of cigarettes.

a   Draw the private supply curve and the private demand curve in this market. What is the privately efficient quantity of packs purchased per day?

b   Draw the public supply curve in this market. Explain why it differs from the private supply curve, and how this represents the externality from secondhand smoke. Highlight the area(s) of your diagram that represents social loss, and interpret this loss in terms of cigarette smoking.

c   What is the socially efficient quantity of packs purchased per day?

d   Suppose that, due to the introduction of a hyper-effective tobacco fertilizer, the cost of producing a pack of cigarettes plummets to \$1. How does this affect the level of smoking and the level of social loss? Explain.

e   Suppose the government decides to pursue a Pigouvian solution to eliminate social loss. What sort of tax or subsidy would they implement, and what is the resulting quantity of cigarette packs purchased?

f   The opposition party in the Pcorian parliament loudly opposes the proposed tax plan as government meddling. The opposition leader invokes the Coase theorem and says that the socially efficient level of smoking will occur even in the absence of government intervention. How are property rights assigned in this instance? Why might the Coase theorem not apply in this setting?

g Assume that the Coase theorem actually does apply in this setting. The Pcorian parliament passes a new law giving anyone the right to forbid his neighbor from smoking. Who benefits, and who is harmed, by this new law? How will this affect the level of smoking?

15 Consider a patient (let's call her A) with end-stage renal disease, who has been on the waiting list for a kidney for several years. She has no family members with kidneys that are immunological matches, so she is waiting for a kidney from an organ donor. Getting a new kidney would considerably improve A's life, so she is willing to pay a considerable sum – x – to get a replacement kidney.

Consider another patient (let's call him B) who has just died in a motorcycle accident and who has a kidney that is an immunological match for A. When B was alive, he was an altruistic sort of person – in case of his death, he had wanted his organs to go to someone like A (though A and B never knew each other). He expressed his wishes by putting an official sticker, which cost him $0, on his driver's license saying he was an organ donor. He was *so* altruistic, though, that he would have been willing to pay y for this sticker, where $y < x$.

Consider, finally, B's family who (all else equal) would rather bury B with all his organs intact than without them. As a group, they derive z of utility from burying B with all of his organs intact, even after taking into account B's preferences (where $y < z < x$). Assume that the law is ambiguous but that in practice B's family gets to decide what happens to B's body.

These are the only interested parties in this story.

a Describe the socially optimal outcome. That is, what ought to happen with the kidney? Is this a feasible outcome given the laws that regulate organ donation in the US?

b Suppose the laws were changed so that B's family no longer decides what happens to B's body. Instead, all organs are harvested from deceased people by default. (This is analogous to assigning the property rights to B's organs to A and is reflective of current organ donation laws in Spain.) Would the socially optimal outcome happen? Explain your answer (briefly).

c Suppose instead that the law is changed so that again B's family has the right to determine what happens to his body, but B's family can negotiate with A (including, perhaps, a monetary settlement) about B's organs. Would the socially optimal outcome happen? Explain your answer (briefly).

d Who has the property rights to B's organs under current law? (You may expand beyond A, B, and B's family in your answer, if necessary.)

e Based on your answers to the previous exercises, does the Coase theorem apply in this setting?

Essay questions

16 Below is the abstract of a recent NBER working paper entitled "Organ allocation policy and the decision to donate" by Judd Kessler and Alvin Roth (NBER Working Paper No. 17324, 2011):

Organ donations from deceased donors provide the majority of transplanted organs in the United States, and one deceased donor can save numerous lives by providing multiple organs. Nevertheless, most Americans are not registered organ donors despite the relative ease of becoming one. We study in the laboratory an experimental game modeled on the decision to register as an organ donor, and investigate how changes in the management of organ waiting lists might impact donations. We find that an organ allocation policy giving priority on waiting lists to those who previously registered as donors has a significant positive impact on registration.

a The choice whether to register as an organ donor is a decision based on comparing costs and benefits. Suppose that registered organ donors receive priority on organ waiting lists. What are the costs of registering? What are the benefits, How do the benefits of registering vary depending on the potential registrant's health, his age, his blood type, and the organ he is most likely to need? What other factors might affect the potential benefit of registering as an organ donor?

b The health of the organ donor can significantly impact the value of the donated organ. Diabetic donors, for instance, produce lower-quality organs than non-diabetic donors. What effect would the Kessler–Roth scheme have on the average quality of donated organs? How would this affect the potential benefits of registering as an organ donor?

c Suppose the Kessler–Roth scheme is implemented and effective in increasing the number of organs harvested for transplantation. How does the scheme affect the welfare of patients awaiting organ transplants who are *not* registered organ donors? [*Hint:* There are two competing effects.]

Students can find answers to the comprehension questions and lecturers can access an Instructor Manual with guideline answers to the analytical problems and essay questions at **www.palgrave.com/economics/bht**.

21 ECONOMIC EPIDEMIOLOGY

Epidemiology is the study of the patterns of disease spread. Although it is mostly a technical field concerned with the properties of different microbes, epidemiology involves some economics as well. The major contribution from economics to epidemiology is the recognition that people change their behavior in response to the possibility of illness.

There is a wealth of empirical evidence from real-world disease epidemics like HIV and measles showing this to be the case. For instance, people use condoms to protect themselves from HIV, and parents vaccinate their children to prevent measles. People have evacuated entire cities in order to escape the plague.

Understanding how people react to the spread of disease has consequences for accurately measuring the costs of disease, forecasting how diseases are likely to spread, and designing policies that effectively limit the suffering from a disease. If the tendency of people to protect themselves is ignored, then the policies adopted to combat diseases will be less effective than anticipated: vaccine campaigns may underperform, diseases with high true costs may not receive appropriate research attention, and disease eradication efforts may prove surprisingly difficult.

21.1   The demand for self-protection

Self-protective activities, like avoiding sick friends and keeping up to date with immunizations, are commonplace. In many situations, involving both infectious and non-infectious diseases, people are willing to give up desirable things and undertake costly measures to avoid illness. Understanding when and why people engage in self-protection is crucial for designing optimal public health policies to control disease. The key principle is that people have more demand for self-protection when exposure to a disease is more costly.

Disease as a tax

One productive way to think about disease is as a tax. Being sick results in a loss of productive time and is costly in and of itself, even if it does not result in financial loss. Unlike a regular tax, which everyone pays with certainty, disease only directly affects those who happen to become ill. But like a regular tax, people will undertake costly activities to avoid having to "pay" the tax by becoming ill.

Consider J. Wellington Wimpy, a connoisseur of fine cheeseburgers. The problem he faces is that his cheeseburger habit increases the chance that he suffers a heart attack. Eating cheeseburgers and suffering a heart attack for Wimpy is analogous to earning income and paying income taxes. The more cheeseburgers Wimpy eats, the more the "tax" he pays in the form of the heightened risk of a heart attack; the more income Wimpy earns, the higher income tax he pays. And just as each extra dollar earned increases his tax bill, each incremental cheeseburger results in higher expected heart attack costs over Wimpy's lifespan.

This idea of disease as a tax applies to more than just eating cheeseburgers and heart attacks. Exposure to almost any disease can be viewed as a type of good being taxed. The "good" may be as concrete as eating cheeseburgers or a less tangible good like neglecting flu vaccinations, vacationing in malarial regions, or avoiding the use of condoms. The more of this good one consumes, the higher the likelihood of disease and the higher the disease tax.

Excess burden of disease

In the face of the disease tax, consumers may change how they behave to avoid paying taxes. Wimpy, for example, might substitute spinach for cheeseburgers to reduce his risk of a heart attack, thereby lowering his disease tax "bill." But doing so is not costless: he forgoes the pleasure of eating those additional cheeseburgers. Hence, the existence of heart attacks harms not only heart attack victims but also people who change their behavior to avoid them. Analogously, Wimpy could work less, which reduces his income tax bill, but then he also earns less as a result. Any shift from desired activities to less desirable ones in an attempt to avoid disease is the **excess burden** of that disease.

Typically, public health accounts of disease cost do not include the excess burden, which is often hard to measure but can be just as large or larger than direct costs. Philipson (2000) cites the example of polio. As a result of a universal vaccination campaign, there are few if any cases of polio in the US, so the **epidemiological cost** of polio is nearly zero. However, polio still imposes an excess burden, because each year millions of American newborns receive the polio vaccine. The cost of administering the vaccine constitutes an excess burden, even though polio has been effectively eradicated in the US.

Definition	21.1

Epidemiological cost: the direct cost associated with a disease. It consists of the financial and non-financial consequences to the person with the disease, such as lost wages and physical suffering.

Excess burden: the cost associated with the activities people undertake in order to avoid a disease.

Total economic cost: the sum of the epidemiological cost and the excess burden of a disease.

The epidemiological costs and the excess burden of a disease depend on its severity and contagiousness. Consider the difference between the common cold and the Ebola virus. While it may be annoying to catch the cold, the epidemiological cost of each infection is typically low. So even though the common cold is widespread, its epidemiological costs over an entire population are low. Ebola, by contrast, is a deadly and infectious condition, killing the vast majority of infected people within days. However, worldwide cases number in the dozens annually. Thus, the epidemiological costs of the common cold and Ebola may both be low but for very different reasons.

In the case of the common cold, most people take some precautions but few go to extremes. For instance, most do not wear surgical masks or wash their hands eight times a day during the cold season, even though this would reduce the risk of catching a cold. Hence, the excess burden of the common cold is low, because the risk of catching cold does not motivate people to change their behavior very much.

By contrast, in the regions of Africa where Ebola outbreaks periodically occur, people take extensive measures to prevent exposure. During a 2005 outbreak in the Congo, the World Health Organization and the local government quarantined an entire village where cases of Ebola had surfaced. No one was allowed in or out, and uncontaminated food had to be delivered from outside. This costly operation, undertaken to prevent the further spread of the virus, is an example of the high excess burden of Ebola. The grave consequences of catching Ebola motivate dramatic changes in behavior to avoid infection.

Figure 21.1 shows an example of how epidemiological costs and excess burden may vary with disease severity Θ. The horizontal axis represents a spectrum of diseases of increasing severity. As disease severity increases, the motivation for self-protection also increases, so excess burden is monotonically increasing in Θ. If the self-protection is effective, then the frequency of cases will eventually fall with Θ, perhaps to the point where epidemiological costs actually decline for the most severe diseases.

The bubonic plague forced Isaac Newton to evacuate Cambridge University for his hometown of Woolsthorpe in 1664. There, with few people to distract him, he formulated his theory of gravity. In his case, self-protection both slowed the spread of plague and led to a brilliant scientific insight. Credit: Superstock.

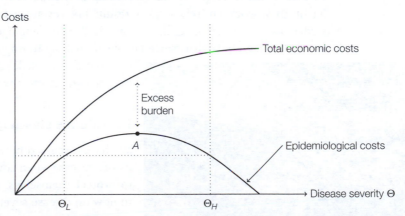

Figure 21.1. *Epidemiological and economic cost of diseases with varying severity.*

Source: Philipson (2000). Copyright (2000), with permission from Elsevier.

Consider a low-cost disease L (like the cold) with severity Θ_L, and a high-cost disease H (like Ebola) with severity $\Theta_H > \Theta_L$. Suppose further that disease L is ten times more common than disease H, but the epidemiological cost of being infected with L is also ten times less costly. Under these assumptions, diseases H and L share the same direct costs. But because disease L does not induce much self-protection, its excess burden is small.

Not coincidentally, Figure 21.1 looks similar to a typical graphical analysis of tax revenue and tax burden as income tax rates increase. The epidemiological cost corresponds to revenue from a tax, and total economic costs correspond to the total costs of the tax, including the tax's excess burden. At low levels of taxation, an income tax

Table 21.1. *Comparison of income tax and various disease "taxes".*

	Income tax	Generic disease "tax"	Example: heart attack tax	Example: influenza tax
What is the good being taxed?	Income	Exposure to the disease	Anything increasing heart attack risk (e.g. cheeseburgers)	Unvaccinated contact with flu carriers
What is the form of payment?	Money paid to government	Increased expected cost of disease	Increased expected heart attack costs	Increased expected flu costs
What are the methods of avoidance?	Work less	Self-protection	Eat fewer cheeseburgers	Get flu shot
What is the excess burden?	Less productive economy	Forgone utility from self-protection	Not getting to eat cheeseburgers	Paying for vaccine, getting a shot

raises little revenue and imposes little excess burden. Correspondingly, a less severe disease imposes low levels of epidemiological cost and excess burden. As the tax rate increases, the revenue generated also increases, *until* point *A* on the graph, when the disincentive to work as a result of the high tax rate causes overall revenue to fall. At the highest tax rates, people do everything they can to avoid paying taxes at all, including quitting work entirely – as a result, tax revenues fall to zero, while the excess burden from the tax skyrockets. This is directly analogous to the case of a severe disease like the Ebola virus since people are willing to impose great costs on themselves to avoid getting sick. Table 21.1 makes the analogy between an income tax and a disease tax explicit.

Prevalence elasticity

We have discussed how people respond to the severity of a disease when considering what actions to take to protect themselves. Though we have focused up to now on disease severity, it is also true that people sometimes respond to how widespread a disease is, especially in the case of infectious diseases. If everyone you come into contact with is a potential carrier of a disease, you might take more precautions than if only one in a million people carry that disease.

At the height of the 2009 H1N1 flu epidemic, attendance at soccer games in Mexico City's Azteca Stadium dwindled to essentially zero.
Credit: © johny007pan – Fotolia.com.

One striking example of self-protection in the face of infectious disease came during the worldwide H1N1 flu epidemic of 2009. When the flu first emerged in Mexico City, the normally bustling metropolis shut down for five days. Parents kept their children out of schools, tourists avoided the Plaza de la Constitución, fans stayed away from crucial football games, and infected patients were quarantined. Only when public reports finally emerged that the flu had been contained through quarantine efforts did people in Mexico City resume their daily lives. It seems clear that residents of Mexico City were assessing their risk of catching the disease when deciding how much to protect themselves.

Public health officials and epidemiologists usually emphasize the pathway illustrated by the success of the Mexico City quarantine and shutdown:

more protection ⟶ **less** disease

Economists in the emerging field of economic epidemiology emphasize a different pathway (Figure 21.2). Economic epidemiology accounts for the possibility that the demand for self-protection from a disease is sensitive to the **prevalence** of that disease – the proportion or percentage of a population suffering from it at a given point in time. This creates the feedback loop in the illustration.

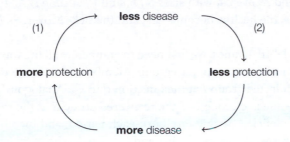

(1)   **less** disease   (2)

more protection   **less** protection

more disease

Figure 21.2. *The reciprocal relationship between self-protection and disease prevalence: (1) self-protection limits the extent of the disease; (2) lower prevalence rates motivate less self-protection. Ultimately, this reciprocal relationship creates a feedback effect that mitigates the effects of self-protection on disease prevalence.*

Definition | **21.2**

Prevalence: the proportion or percentage of a population suffering from a given disease at a given point in time.

Under this view, if a terrible disease suddenly becomes more widespread in a population, demand for protection increases in response. It also implies that any effective campaign for self-protection against a disease, like a vaccine drive, will be ultimately self-limiting. If any such campaign is successful, it reduces prevalence and the population responds by reducing self-protection. This feedback pathway only occurs if people respond to prevalence. This sensitivity to prevalence is called the **prevalence elasticity of demand**.

Definition | **21.3**

Prevalence elasticity of demand for self-protection: a measure of how demand for self-protection from a disease responds to changes in the prevalence of that disease. Often referred to simply as **prevalence elasticity**.

Many epidemiological models and studies do not consider the way demand for self-protection may react to disease prevalence, and implicitly assume a prevalence elasticity of 0. In Section 21.4, we discuss evidence in the literature that prevalence elasticity is nonzero.

21.2   The SIR model of infectious disease

In this section, we introduce a basic epidemiological model of infectious disease, known as the **SIR model** (Anderson and May 1985). This model traces how an infectious disease evolves over time. Such models help us to understand when a population is at its most vulnerable, when an epidemic is at its most virulent, and when its effects are likely to wane. They also help measure the effect of vaccinations and public health interventions such as vaccine subsidies. The SIR model provides a convenient framework for thinking about the reciprocal relationship between prevalence and self-protection.

In the SIR model, the members of a population are classified into three groups: *susceptible*, *infected*, and *recovered*, with sizes S_t, I_t, and R_t at time t. As time passes, babies are born, people die, the healthy become sick, and the sick recover. S_t, I_t, and R_t fluctuate accordingly.

To study the model's dynamics, we first need to enumerate all the ways that members of the population can move from group to group. Members of the susceptible population S fall ill and join the infected group I at the infection rate λ_{SI}. Analogously, the sick recover and move from the infected group I to the recovered group R at the recovery rate λ_{IR}. In this version of the model, Λ_b babies are born each period, and members from all three groups die at their respective rates λ_{d_S}, λ_{d_I}, and λ_{d_R}. Lastly, the vaccination rate v reflects movement from the susceptible group S to the recovered group R. Figure 21.3 displays each of these pathways and their corresponding rates.

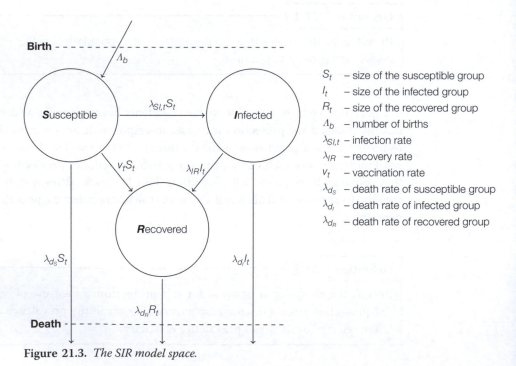

S_t – size of the susceptible group
I_t – size of the infected group
R_t – size of the recovered group
Λ_b – number of births
$\lambda_{SI,t}$ – infection rate
λ_{IR} – recovery rate
v_t – vaccination rate
λ_{d_S} – death rate of susceptible group
λ_{d_I} – death rate of infected group
λ_{d_R} – death rate of recovered group

Figure 21.3. *The SIR model space.*

Figure 21.3 depicts a version of the model where the infected never return to the susceptible pool, since there is no pathway from either the infected or the recovered pool back to the susceptible group. This assumption makes sense when modeling for diseases which confer immunity, such as chicken pox, diphtheria, or pertussis (whooping cough). The SIR model can also be extended to account for broader categories of diseases.

Vaccination rate

Like the demand for nearly all common goods, the demand for vaccinations depends on the price of vaccinations; this has been established through empirical studies like the RAND HIE (see Chapter 2). If the prevalence elasticity of demand for the vaccine is nonzero, then the vaccination rate also depends on the prevalence of the disease (see Section 21.1). Thus, the vaccination rate v is modeled as a function of both vaccination price p and disease prevalence I_t:

$$v_t = v(p, I_t) \tag{21.1}$$

If the effect of prevalence on the vaccination rate is large, then the demand for vaccination is very prevalence elastic, regardless of how price sensitive it is. In fact, the effects of prevalence and price on the vaccination rate move in different directions. Demand increases with prevalence, but decreases with price. Our main goal in studying the SIR model is to determine how a change in vaccine price changes the total number of infected people, while accounting for the effect of prevalence elasticity.

Infection rate

With infectious diseases, the more infected people there are, the more likely it is that a random susceptible person in the population will come in contact with someone with the disease. If no one has the flu, then the probability of contracting the flu is zero. And if everyone but one person has the flu, then the chance that last person will develop the infection is very high.

The infection rate also depends on some properties of the disease. For instance, Hansen's disease, commonly known as leprosy, does not spread readily from person to person even with casual contact. By contrast, the common cold requires just a nearby sneeze or handshake to spread. The SIR model accounts for this by including a disease-specific infectivity constant β, which captures both how often people interact in a community and how contagious the disease is. A highly contagious disease transmitted by proximity such as the common cold virus is likely to have a high infectivity constant, while Hansen's disease has a lower β. The infection rate $\lambda_{SI,t}$ is the product of this infectivity constant β and the number of people infected I_t:

$$\lambda_{SI,t} = \beta I_t \tag{21.2}$$

Transition equations

Next, we specify the transition equations for each population in the SIR model. These transition equations tell us how the size of each population changes over time, and are found by accounting for all entry and exit pathways. To find the change in the size of the susceptible population S at time t, dS/dt, we add up all incoming flows (just the birth rate in this case), and subtract all outgoing flows (infection, vaccination, and death):

$$\frac{dS}{dt} = \overbrace{\Lambda_b}^{\text{birth}} - \overbrace{\lambda_{SI,t} S_t}^{\text{infection}} - \overbrace{v \cdot S_t}^{\text{vaccination}} - \overbrace{\lambda_{d_S} S_t}^{\text{death}} \tag{21.3}$$

$$= \Lambda_b - \beta I_t \cdot S_t - v_t \cdot S_t - \lambda_{d_S} S_t$$

We proceed analogously to find the other transition equations. For the infected group:

$$\frac{dI}{dt} = \overbrace{\lambda_{SI,t} S_t}^{\text{infection}} - \overbrace{\lambda_{IR} I_t}^{\text{recovery}} - \overbrace{\lambda_{d_I} I_t}^{\text{death}}$$

$$= \beta I_t \cdot S_t - \lambda_{IR} I_t - \lambda_{d_I} I_t$$

(21.4)

And for the recovered group:

$$\frac{dR}{dt} = \overbrace{v_t \cdot S_t}^{\text{vaccination}} + \overbrace{\lambda_{IR} I_t}^{\text{recovery}} - \overbrace{\lambda_{d_R} R_t}^{\text{death}}$$

(21.5)

Steady-state populations

For our purposes, we are concerned mostly with the size of the susceptible, infected, and recovered in the *steady state*, where population sizes of all three groups have stabilized. This is interesting from a policy point of view, because changes in policy, such as subsidies for vaccinations, often aim to limit the steady-state population of infected people. Let S^*, I^*, and R^* mark the steady-state sizes. They do not change over time by definition; hence, the derivatives of each with respect to time are zero:

$$\frac{dS^*}{dt} = \frac{dI^*}{dt} = \frac{dR^*}{dt} = 0$$

(21.6)

In the steady state, people still move between the susceptible, infected, and recovered pools, but the net number of people in the three pools does not fluctuate.

Given our specification of the SIR model, we can readily solve for the number of susceptible people in the steady state S^*. This is necessary to find the number of infected people in the steady state I^*, which for policy reasons is the true quantity of interest. The easiest way to derive S^* is analyzing the infected population in the steady state in equation (21.4):

$$\frac{dI^*}{dt} = \beta I^* \cdot S^* - \lambda_{IR} I^* - \lambda_{d_I} I^* = 0$$

(21.7)

Notice that all three terms of $\frac{dI^*}{dt}$ share I^* as a factor. As long as $I^* \neq 0$, we can cancel it out of the equation:

$$0 = I^* \left[\beta S^* - \lambda_{IR} - \lambda_{d_I} \right]$$

$$0 = \beta S^* - \lambda_{IR} - \lambda_{d_I}$$

Finally, we solve for S^*:

$$S^* = \frac{\lambda_{IR} + \lambda_{d_I}}{\beta}$$

(21.8)

Equation (21.8) says that the size of the susceptible population in the steady state S^* is inversely related to the infectivity of the disease β, and directly related to the rate at which people exit the infected population, $\lambda_{IR} + \lambda_{d_I}$. This matches our intuition: if infectivity is high, then the susceptible people are likely to fall ill quickly, but if the infected do not stay infected long, their chances of infecting others is smaller.

Strikingly, S^* does not depend on the price of vaccination, but this does not mean that vaccination prices have no impact on the course of infectious disease outbreaks. We shall see that price affects the number of people in infected population in the steady state.

Price and infectious disease

Recall that the vaccination rate v_t is a function of both the price of the vaccine p and the disease prevalence I_t:

$$v_t = v(p, I_t) \tag{21.9}$$

Our main objective is to see how a change in vaccine price affects the size of the infected population, because this is the main policy-relevant question. Subsidizing vaccination is a popular policy lever, and the SIR model predicts whether and when it will be effective in controlling infectious disease. While it was easy to solve for S^*, finding I^* is analytically difficult. It is much easier to derive an expression for the effect of price on the size of the steady-state infected population:

$$\frac{dI^*}{dp} = -\frac{\frac{dv}{dp}}{\beta + \frac{dv}{dI^*}} \tag{21.10}$$

The magnitude of this derivative reveals how effective a vaccine subsidy can be. Exercise 15 leads interested readers through the derivation of equation (21.10).

Equation (21.10) depends on the infectivity of a disease β, which we have already discussed, along with two other quantities, $\frac{dv}{dI^*}$ and $\frac{dv}{dp}$. The first, $\frac{dv}{dI^*}$, captures the impact of prevalence on the vaccination rate and is related to prevalence elasticity. As more people are infected, the demand for self-protection increases, so $\frac{dv}{dI^*}$ is positive. The second term, $\frac{dv}{dp}$, captures the effect of vaccine price on the vaccination rate. Since the price elasticity of vaccine demand is negative, $\frac{dv}{dp}$ is also negative.

Because the infectivity parameter β is always positive, $\frac{dv}{dI^*}$ is positive, and $\frac{dv}{dp}$ is negative, $\frac{dI^*}{dp}$ must also be positive. This means that vaccine subsidies can be effective at reducing the number of people infected in the steady state:

$$\frac{dI^*}{dp} = -\frac{\frac{dv}{dp}}{\beta + \frac{dv}{dI^*}} > 0$$

Equation (21.10) allows us to evaluate *how* effective a vaccine subsidy can be. A vaccine subsidy is more likely to be effective if:

- ... **vaccine demand is more price elastic.** If the price effect on vaccine demand is high, then the vaccine subsidy is likely to increase vaccine demand substantially. In that case, $\frac{dv}{dp}$ will be large in magnitude and increase $\frac{dI^*}{dp}$. Conversely, if vaccine demand is very price inelastic so people barely take price into account, a vaccine subsidy would not significantly affect behavior.
- ... **infectivity is low.** A low β increases $\frac{dI^*}{dp}$. If infectivity is low, then few people are infected and many more are susceptible. As a result, the market for the vaccine is larger, so the subsidy has the potential to reach more people. Conversely, if infectivity were high, there are fewer people left susceptible, so the market for the vaccine is smaller and the subsidy less effective.
- ... **prevalence elasticity is low.** A low $\frac{dv}{dI}$ increases $\frac{dI^*}{dp}$. A price subsidy for the vaccine reduces the prevalence of the disease in the steady state. If the prevalence elasticity for the vaccine is low, then this reduction in disease prevalence does not trigger a substantial feedback effect that reduces the demand for the vaccine, thereby limiting the effectiveness of the vaccine subsidy. Conversely, if the

prevalence elasticity is high, the reduction in prevalence due to the vaccine subsidy triggers a larger feedback effect that reduces the vaccine demand.

Figure 21.4 revisits Figure 21.2 to see why the existence of a negative feedback effect caused by the demand for self-protection mitigates the effect of a vaccine price subsidy on disease prevalence. A price subsidy increases demand for the vaccine, but its very success in limiting prevalence subsequently decreases demand for self-protection. The subsidy still reduces the prevalence of the disease in steady state, but not by as much as if there were no feedback effect.

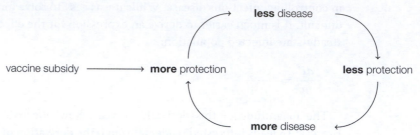

Figure 21.4. *An altered version of Figure 21.2 that reflects the effect of a vaccine subsidy.*

21.3   Disease control

One goal of infectious disease control has been disease eradication – the elimination of any possibility of new infections. This requires not only reducing disease prevalence to zero but also eliminating any non-human reservoirs of the disease. Eradication not only eliminates the mortality and human suffering directly caused by a disease, but also the fear of contracting it. In other words, eradication eliminates both the epidemiological cost and the excess burden of a disease, as there is no longer any need for self-protection.

Despite these benefits, disease eradication is rare. With the exception of the successful campaign to end smallpox, there are no other examples of a worldwide disease eradication. One reason that eradication is difficult is that it is difficult to control the spread of disease in non-human reservoirs. In diseases that are solely human-borne though, the fact that self-protection responds to disease prevalence is the main reason why disease elimination is so difficult. In the course of an eradication campaign, initially successful efforts reduce prevalence to a low level. Moving from that level to zero is difficult, because demand for self-protection may vanish when prevalence is low enough. As long as the disease is not fully eradicated, it may spread from the small number of people who still have it to a broader population because the susceptible population no longer takes precautions against the disease.

Disease resilience

In disease eradication, close may not be close enough. Eliminating all but a few cases of a disease may not be sufficient to eradicate it completely. The remaining few cases of a disease may be capable of infecting many others and starting a new epidemic on their own. It is possible that prevalence can rebound from even low levels.

How can we tell if and when a disease might rebound? Recall the transition equation for the infected population I_t in the SIR model:

$$\frac{dI}{dt} = \beta I_t \cdot S_t - \lambda_{IR} I_t - \lambda_{d_I} I_t$$

A disease is increasing in prevalence when the infected population is increasing in size over time, or $\frac{dI}{dt} > 0$:

$$0 < \beta I_t \cdot S_t - \lambda_{IR} I_t - \lambda_{d_I} I_t$$

$$0 < I_t [\beta \cdot S_t - \lambda_{IR} - \lambda_{d_I}]$$

$$0 < \beta \cdot S_t - \lambda_{IR} - \lambda_{d_I}$$

Rearranging terms, we obtain the condition for increasing prevalence:

$$\lambda_{IR} + \lambda_{d_I} < \beta \cdot S_t \tag{21.11}$$

Thus, disease prevalence is increasing if and only if the infection rate βS_t is greater than the sum of the recovery rate λ_{IR} and the death rate λ_{d_I} (equation (21.11)). The inequality means that prevalence rises when infection spreads faster than the infected people die or recover. Equivalently, prevalence rises when the average infected person infects more than one susceptible person before dying or recovering.

This does not mean that vaccination must be absolutely universal for there to be any hope of eradication. Recall the discussion of *herd immunity* from the previous chapter. Herd immunity, which occurs when vaccinated individuals protect their neighbors and friends from contagious disease, makes disease eradication easier. If a large fraction of a population is vaccinated, then fewer susceptible people remain. As a result, each new infection causes on average fewer than one new infection.

This same story is reflected in equation (21.11). When S_t is small because a large fraction of the population is vaccinated, then the condition is unlikely to hold. With so few susceptible people, the sum of the recovery and death rates exceed the infection rate, and disease prevalence declines over time. The practical implication is that 100% vaccination rates are not necessarily required for eradication. Herd immunity extends the reach of a vaccine, reducing the resilience of a disease.

Vaccine demand and disease eradication

In disease control, there are two competing forces determining disease prevalence: herd immunity and the responsiveness of vaccine demand to prevalence rates. Herd immunity extends the reach of each vaccination, thereby limiting disease spread and lowering prevalence. But because vaccination reduces the prevalence of the disease, it lowers the incentives for others to vaccinate, putting upward pressure on prevalence – recall the feedback loop depicted in Figure 21.2.

At the outset of an eradication campaign, when prevalence levels are high, the herd immunity effect dominates the negative feedback effect of prevalence responsiveness. As the campaign progresses, prevalence declines and the private benefit of vaccinating declines along with it. The negative feedback effect begins to dominate the herd immunity effect. As a result of prevalence-responsive demand, efforts to eradicate disease become progressively more difficult the closer they get to success. Prevalence may even drop so low that demand for self-protection vanishes entirely, possibly allowing the disease to rebound if it is resilient (Figure 21.5).

A competitive vaccine market can never produce a vaccine price low enough to eradicate a disease as long as: (1) the demand for self-protection vanishes at low levels of

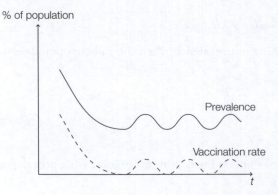

% of population

Prevalence

Vaccination rate

t

Figure 21.5. *For this hypothetical disease, as prevalence falls, the benefits of vaccination fall as well, so the vaccination rate declines. Below a certain prevalence, the vaccination rate may vanish if the price of vaccination is positive. This drop in self-protection leaves a larger susceptible population, which gives an opportunity for disease prevalence to rise again.*

prevalence; (2) at this low level of prevalence, the disease is resilient and increases in prevalence. Under these two conditions, it is only possible to eradicate a disease if there is a subsidy that reduces the vaccine price to zero, or there is a mandatory vaccine program.

The history of measles in Ireland during the 1980s illustrates how vanishing demand and disease resilience combine to thwart eradication efforts. When the measles vaccine was first introduced into Ireland in 1985, the number of measles cases among Irish children dropped from nearly 100,000 in 1985 to only 135 in 1991 (Butler et al. 2002). But the disease lingered as vaccination demand declined. The Irish health authorities fell short of their goal of 95% vaccine coverage. Had they achieved that level of coverage, authorities estimated that herd immunity would have effectively eradicated the disease. As self-protection waned, measles prevalence rebounded: over 4,000 new cases were reported in 1993. Even though Ireland's measles eradication campaign was close to success in 1991, it was evidently not close enough. A reservoir of unvaccinated, susceptible children remained that was large enough to permit measles to reemerge.

If the sick man takes a taxi instead, other bus riders will be spared his germs. Sickness taxes may add insult to illness, but they would help slow the spread of disease.

Credit: Allen Cox.

The welfare economics of eradication

As we have seen, contagious diseases impose harm not only on the infected but also on the susceptible population, both by increasing the probability of disease and necessitating self-protection. Additionally, because the social benefits from vaccination are greater than the private benefits, a private market will not achieve socially optimal levels of vaccination. In economic terms, each case of a contagious disease imposes a negative externality on susceptible people who are exposed, and each vaccination confers a positive externality through herd immunity.

The gap between social and private harm (in the case of contagious disease) and social and private benefit (in the case of vaccinations) results in too much disease and too few vaccinations compared to the social optimum. As discussed in Chapter 20, there are two sets of policies that might cause people to internalize these externalities: Pigouvian and Coasian.

The Pigouvian solution might entail taxes on disease and subsidies for vaccination. The Pigouvian tax would discourage disease spread by taxing activities that could cause transmission of the disease. For instance, parents would be taxed for sending their kids to school sick, and travelers would be taxed for flying on an airplane while contagious. Not only would this tax be difficult to administer and enforce, but it also acts as a form of reverse insurance: the sickest have to pay more.

Much more feasible are Pigouvian subsidies that promote self-protection by paying people to vaccinate. For instance, governments often provide basic vaccinations free of charge to all residents. But sometimes subsidies – even ones that cover the full financial cost of a vaccine – are not enough. The demand for vaccines is determined not only by financial cost but also non-financial considerations like concern about side effects, needle-phobia, or low prevalence. As a result, the Pigouvian subsidy may need to exceed the marginal cost of producing the vaccine to induce widespread vaccination.

In the early 2000s, the Nicaraguan government established a conditional cash transfer program, which paid poor families an average of $272 a year if they completed several essential health tasks, including vaccinating their children against tuberculosis, measles, polio, and diphtheria among others (Barham and Maluccio 2009). The transfer represented nearly 17% of annual household expenditures among people in the program. In addition, the government also provided these vaccines free of charge for all participants. Together, the cash transfer and vaccine campaign served as a Pigouvian subsidy that reduced the effective price of vaccinations below zero. This effort succeeded in raising the vaccination rate above 95% for many of these diseases.

An alternative to Pigouvian taxes and subsidies is the Coasian solution featuring a nego-tiated arrangement or altered property rights. As in the case of the Pigouvian policies, the success of these proposed solutions is measured by the extent to which they internalize the social costs and benefits of infection and vaccination.

Suppose that people have a legal right to remain unvaccinated. A possible Coasian solu-tion might entail a negotiation between an unvaccinated person and all the people who might benefit through herd immunity if he vaccinates. Ideally, the susceptible population would pay the unvaccinated individual to vaccinate. But such a negotiation is infeasible, because of the prohibitive transaction costs involved in identifying all the people who might benefit and actually conducting a successful negotiation.

Instead, many governments have adopted an alternative Coasian solution in which property rights are reassigned: people do *not* have the right to stay unvaccinated. In the US for instance, every state requires that children be vaccinated before enrolling in school. Such vaccination mandates are common throughout the world; the successful smallpox eradication effort relied heavily on this strategy.

Was the smallpox eradication campaign worth it?

Despite the social benefits of eradication, whether an eradication campaign is socially desirable depends on both its costs and its benefits. A truly comprehensive vaccina-tion campaign may be so costly that accepting a low prevalence indefinitely may be preferable.

Consider the epidemiological costs and excess burden of smallpox in 1967 before its eradication (Table 21.2). The disease was eliminated in industrialized nations, so epi-demiological costs were zero. But because the disease existed elsewhere, the need for self-protection persisted even in industrialized countries and excess burden was posi-tive. Meanwhile, smallpox was still endemic in developing countries, so they faced both epidemiological costs and excess burden. The excess burden faced by developing coun-tries is lower than that faced by industrialized nations for two reasons. First, the vaccine penetration rate was much lower in the developing world. Second, the price of vaccine

Table 21.2. *Annual costs of smallpox and the smallpox eradication campaign (millions of 1967 dollars).*

	Epidemiological costs	Excess burden	Campaign costs
Industrialized countries	$0	$150	$7.5
Developing countries	$1,020	$50	$15.4

Source: Fenner et al. (1988). Adapted, with permission, from *Smallpox and its Eradication*, Table 31.1 and Table 31.2, http://whqlibdoc.who.int/smallpox/9241561106_chp31.pdf (date accessed 05.02.13).

administered was higher in the industrialized countries, in part due to the higher liability costs associated with vaccine side effects.

The actual campaign for smallpox eradication lasted 13 years between 1967 and 1979 and cost a total of $298 million. But eradication continues to save $1.2 billion annually in epidemiological costs and excess burden. To assess whether this campaign was worthwhile from the perspective of public health officials in 1967, we compare the discounted value of this cost against the discounted stream of future benefits from smallpox eradication from 1980 onward. This is analogous to the calculation done in Chapter 5 to find the net present value of attending medical school.

Equation (21.12) presents the calculations for the present value of costs and benefits for the smallpox eradication campaign using figures from Table 21.2. In these equations, r represents the interest rate, which is also the rate at which future costs and benefits are discounted. The benefit equation includes the benefits accruing all future generations:

$$PV[\text{Cost}] = \sum_{t=0}^{12} \frac{7.5 + 15.4}{(1+r)^t}$$

$$PV[\text{Benefit}] = \sum_{t=13}^{\infty} \frac{1,020 + 50 + 150}{(1+r)^t} \tag{21.12}$$

The *net present value* is the difference between benefits and costs:

$$NPV = PV[\text{Benefit}] - PV[\text{Cost}] \tag{21.13}$$

In the case of smallpox eradication, the net present value was $18.8 billion at a 4% interest rate. The internal rate of return was 36%, which means the eradication campaign is worthwhile for any interest rate below 36%. These calculations are made from the point of view of worldwide social welfare. Table 21.3 shows similar calculations from the perspective of industrialized nations and developing countries. The last column shows calculations for worldwide societal welfare without accounting for excess burden. From

Table 21.3. *Net present value, internal rate of return, and break-even campaign length.*

	Worldwide	Industrial	Developing	Worldwide (without excess burden)
Net present value (billions)[†][*]	$18.8	$2.3	$16.5	$15.7
Internal rate of return[†]	36%	26%	39%	34%
Break-even length (years)[*]	102	77	109	97

[†] Assuming a campaign length of 13 years.
[*] Assuming interest rate $r = 0.04$.

all these points of view, smallpox eradication was a worthwhile endeavor. By contrast, eradication provides no benefit to the industrialized nations if excess burden is ignored.

21.4   Applications of economic epidemiology

The distinctive contribution that economists have made to epidemiology has been the documentation of the feedback pathway leading from disease prevalence to the demand for self-protection. In this section we present evidence from three disease epidemics in the US: the HIV epidemic, the measles epidemic of 1989–91, and the seasonal influenza epidemic. In each case, self-protection takes a different form, but evidence from all three epidemics suggests that prevalence elasticity is positive. In fact, these empirical examples make clear that demand for self-protection responds not only to prevalence but also to other measures of its perceived threat, such as mortality rate.

Falling HIV incidence in 1980s San Francisco

Suppose that, contrary to the version of the SIR model we studied in Section 21.2, susceptible populations do *not* take the prevalence of a disease into account when deciding whether and how to protect themselves. Under this assumption, the **infection hazard rate** of a rapidly spreading disease increases as the prevalence increases. As the disease becomes more widespread, there are more chances for members of the susceptible population to come into contact with an infected person.

Definition	21.4

Infection hazard rate: the rate at which *susceptible* members of the population become infected with a given disease. This is related to the **incidence** of the infection, which is the rate at which members of the entire population become infected with a given disease.

Now suppose instead that the prevalence elasticity of demand for self-protection is positive. As a disease becomes more widespread, uninfected people seek more self-protection. Given this, it is possible that disease *incidence* will hold steady or even decline as *prevalence* rises. This prediction is in sharp contrast to the corresponding prediction when prevalence elasticity is zero. Just as vaccination campaigns can be self-limiting because people stop seeking self-protection when prevalence falls, epidemics can be self-limiting because people seek more self-protection as prevalence rises. Data from an epidemic showing rising prevalence and *declining* incidence at the same time would be suggestive evidence that prevalence elasticity of demand is positive.

Geoffard and Philipson (1996) find just such a pattern when studying the incidence and prevalence of HIV in San Francisco from 1983 to 1992. This was a period when HIV became extraordinarily widespread in certain San Francisco populations, like gay men and intravenous drug users. In 1982, when AIDS was first emerging into the public consciousness, the city of San Francisco was home to about an eighth of all AIDS cases in the US. The disease spread rapidly, mostly through unprotected sex and infected needles.

Figure 21.6 plots estimated HIV prevalence and incidence among young, unmarried males in certain high-risk San Francisco neighborhoods between 1983 and 1992, using data from 15 waves of the San Francisco Men's Health Survey (Geoffard and Philipson 1996). The incidence of HIV is falling sharply in this period: by 1992, new cases are arising in study participants at less than a tenth the rate that they were in 1983. According to this evidence, prevalence and incidence are inversely correlated. As more and more San Franciscans became infected, HIV spread more slowly than when the infection was in its earliest stages. Despite a higher prevalence rate, and hence more opportunities for the spread of HIV through unprotected sex, infected needles, and tainted blood transfusions, incidence actually declined.

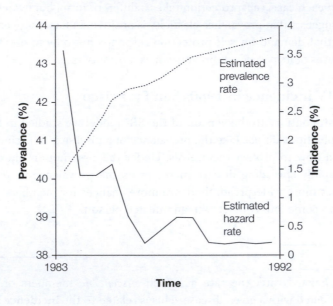

Figure 21.6. *Estimated prevalence and hazard rate of HIV in high-risk San Francisco neighborhoods, 1983–1992.*

Source: P. Geoffard and T. Philipson (1996). Figure 1a from: Rational epidemics and their public control, International Economic Review, p. 608. Copyright (1996) John Wiley and Sons Ltd. Reproduced with permission of Blackwell Publishing Ltd.

Positive prevalence elasticity is not the only possible explanation for the inverse correlation between prevalence and incidence. Other factors that could have led to reduced incidence – like awareness of the mode of transmission of HIV and information about self-protection strategies – were also changing during this time period. Nevertheless, Figure 21.6 provides indirect evidence of a positive prevalence elasticity.

The measles epidemic of 1989–91

A more direct approach for measuring prevalence elasticity involves comparing regions with different prevalence levels at the same time. One example is a study of vaccination behavior during the measles epidemic of 1989–91 (Philipson 1996). Measles is a highly contagious infectious disease that is relatively rare in the developed world due to near-universal vaccination. It is a potentially deadly disease that killed three out of every thousand people infected in the US between 1987–2000 (Perry and Halsey 2004).

From 1989 to 1991, the US suffered a measles epidemic that was attributed to delayed vaccination in children (CDC 1991; Gindler et al. 1992). As a result, measles prevalence spiked: there were nearly nine times as many cases of measles in the US in 1990 as in 1988 (Philipson 1996). The epidemic did not strike all states equally, though. Some states, especially those with large Hispanic populations, like Texas, had particularly elevated levels of measles during the epidemic, while other states, like North Dakota, did not suffer unusually high measles prevalence.

Philipson (1996) investigates whether parents in high-prevalence states responded by having their infants vaccinated at a younger age. The recommended age for the vaccine is 12–15 months of age, but many babies born in non-epidemic years were still unvaccinated at 15 months and even 24 months. If parents in high-prevalence states like Texas brought their children in for vaccinations sooner or more reliably than parents in low-prevalence states like North Dakota, then we would conclude that the demand for vaccinations is prevalence elastic.

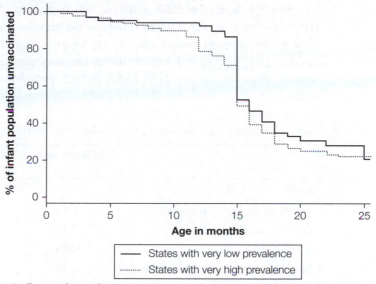

Figure 21.7. *Differential measles vaccination rates by statewide prevalence for babies born in 1989.*

Source: T. Philipson (1996). © 1996 by the Board of Regents of the University of Wisconsin System. Figure 3a reproduced by the permission of the University of Wisconsin Press.

Evidence from national health survey data shows this was indeed the case: infants born in 1989 in high-prevalence states tended to receive the measles vaccine earlier than infants born the same year in low-prevalence states (Figure 21.7). Infants from high-prevalence states were about four times as likely to be vaccinated by the time they reached their first birthday, and still about three times as likely to be vaccinated before age 15 months.

One objection to this evidence is that it derives from an observational study of measles vaccinations rather than a controlled experiment. Perhaps there are difficult-to-observe characteristics about parents in states like Texas that lead to both more measles and earlier vaccinations, and there is no *causal* relationship between the two. However, vaccination rates and timing in high- and low-prevalence states did not differ significantly in 1986, before the measles epidemic (Philipson 1996). This suggests that the differential response during the measles epidemic shown in Figure 21.7 was due to a positive prevalence elasticity of demand.

Condom use in states with high AIDS prevalence

Ahituv et al. (1996) use a similar strategy to measure the prevalence elasticity of demand for condoms during the early days of the AIDS epidemic. Using US national survey data from 1984–90, they calculate rates of condom use for different at-risk groups of single men, such as those living in urban areas and those who were sexually active. They compare rates of condom use for single men in states with high AIDS prevalence and low AIDS prevalence, just as Philipson (1996) compares vaccination rates in states with varying levels of measles prevalence.

Just as we expect parents in high-prevalence measles states to rush their infants in for early vaccinations, we expect at-risk single men in high-prevalence AIDS states to wear condoms more consistently. Table 21.4 shows that the evidence largely fits this hypothesis. In 1984, when the AIDS epidemic was beginning, condom use was not related to HIV prevalence in the different states – perhaps because prevalence was still low in most states or many people did not yet know of the connection between HIV transmission and unprotected sex. By 1990, condom use rates for single men and single men in urban areas were starkly higher in high-prevalence states than in low-prevalence states.

Table 21.4. *Rates of condom use by state and quartile of HIV prevalence.*

	All single men	Single men in urban areas	Sexually active single men
1984			
First quartile (lowest prevalence)	10.6%[†]	10.3%	14.5%
Second quartile	7.4%	4.8%	8.5%
Third quartile	10.4%	8.2%	12.1%
Fourth quartile (highest prevalence)	9.2%	10.6%	12.2%
1990			
First quartile (lowest prevalence)	21.3%	22.2%	25.3%
Second quartile	24.4%	24.5%	26.8%
Third quartile	30.9%	33.4%	29.3%
Fourth quartile (highest prevalence)	30.5%[**]	32.5%[**]	34.1%

[**] Statistically significant discrepancy between the first and fourth quartiles at the 5% level.
[†] Condom use is defined as the percentage of respondents who, when asked the following survey question: "During the last month, have you or your (partner/spouse) used any form of birth control?", said they had used a condom.
Source: Data from Ahituv et al. (1996).

Flu vaccinations

Evidence on positive prevalence elasticity is not confined to HIV and measles. These two diseases tend to strike younger populations, but there is evidence of positive prevalence elasticities in other populations such as the elderly. Mullahy (1999) studies the determinants of flu vaccine demand in the US and finds that more people sought vaccination in states reporting more weeks of widespread influenza during the flu season.

Li et al. (2004) focus instead on disease severity. Rather than studying the effect of influenza prevalence on flu vaccination rates, they study the effect of influenza mortality.

They hypothesize that flu vaccination demand in the current year responds positively to local, state-level influenza mortality from the previous year: if the flu is particularly deadly in a given state one year, wary seniors in that state might be more likely to seek the flu vaccine in the next year. Using US survey data from 1992–97 in conjunction with official flu mortality statistics, Li et al. find that vaccination rates are indeed responsive to lagged mortality rates. They estimate the mortality elasticity of flu vaccine demand to be 0.15.

21.5   Conclusion

As we have seen, economic epidemiology is not merely a theoretical matter. The fact that people alter their demand for self-protection in response to disease prevalence and disease mortality carries consequences for policy. For instance, the US and other nations have spent billions of dollars in Africa for the treatment of patients with HIV but less on the prevention of HIV. This disease treatment has extended the lives of over a million HIV-positive Africans (Bendavid and Bhattacharya 2009). But over the same period, the prevalence of HIV has increased, in part because HIV-positive people are now surviving longer. The optimal mix of spending on prevention and treatment depends on the prevalence elasticity of the populations in these countries. In this and many other disease control efforts, a knowledge of economic epidemiology is vital.

21.6   Exercises

Comprehension questions

Indicate whether each statement is true or false, and justify your answer. Be sure to cite evidence from the chapter and state any additional assumptions you may need.

1 The ratio of a disease's prevalence to its incidence is constant.
2 The expense of opening a secret offshore bank account is an example of the excess burden of US income taxes.
3 A disease that has been eradicated necessarily imposes no welfare loss in the present. (Be sure to include at least one example disease to illustrate your explanation.)
4 A disease that is very uncommon necessarily imposes very little welfare loss.
5 If a disease is shown to have a surprisingly high prevalence elasticity of demand for self-protection, policymakers should conclude that an eradication campaign is going to be more difficult than expected.
6 Public health models that do not take economic epidemiological principles into account often make the mistaken assumption that the prevalence elasticity of demand is essentially infinite.
7 In the SIR model of infectious disease, a high value of β for a disease indicates that people are very fearful of catching it and protect themselves more.
8 The 1989–91 measles epidemic induced parents in states with a high measles prevalence rate to inoculate their children at earlier ages.
9 The version of the SIR model discussed in Section 21.2 is flawed because it does not account for the possibility of prevalence elasticity.

10 For a given disease (with all else equal), if a vaccine has a higher prevalence elasticity of demand, a vaccine subsidy will be a *more* effective tool to control the equilibrium number of people infected with the disease.

11 In the steady-state SIR model, the number of susceptible people is not affected by changes in vaccine price.

12 Most economists believe that the smallpox eradication campaign was not cost-effective because it required so many upfront costs and smallpox was already eliminated in much of the developed world.

13 The phenomenon of herd immunity makes disease eradication difficult because it ensures that diseases will survive until vaccination rates reach 100%.

Analytical problems

14 The SIR-style diagram in Figure 21.8 demonstrates the dynamics of a new disease called fictitia that is sweeping the nation. Fictitia is different from the disease we diagrammed in Section 21.2 in a number of ways:

- There is no vaccine for fictitia and no way to recover from it, so there is no recovered population.
- Fictitia renders patients sterile, so the birth rate is proportional to the size of the susceptible population, not the whole population.
- Fortunately, there are some costly self-protective activities h that people can take to avoid contracting fictitia. Their rate of use depends on both the cost of the activities p and the prevalence of the disease I_t. Specifically, the rate of use $h(p, I_t) = C - \alpha p + \gamma I_t$ for constant C.

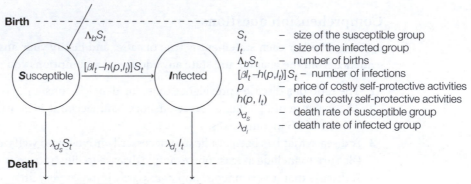

Figure 21.8. *The SIR model space for fictitia.*

a Given these assumptions about the fictitia epidemic, write down the two laws of motion for S_t and I_t in terms of S_t, I_t, C, p, α, β, γ, and the λs.

b What conditions must be true if the populations of infected and uninfected people are in steady state (that is, they do not change over time)?

c Assume $\gamma = 0$. Interpret this assumption.

d Now assume $\gamma > \beta$. Interpret this assumption.

e Assuming $\gamma > \beta$, solve for I^* as a function of C, p, α, β, γ, and the λs. [*Hint*: As a first step, you should add your two equations from part (b) to derive a relationship between I^* and S^*.]

f How does a change in the price of p affect the steady-state level of I^*?

15 In this exercise, you will derive how a change in the price of vaccines changes the steady-state infected population, I^*, in an SIR model – discussed in Section 21.2 – in which the demand for vaccine is affected by the size of the infected population.

  a Recall the formula in the SIR reflecting the size of the susceptible populaton in steady state (please see Section 21.2 for the description of the notation):

$$\frac{dS^*}{dt} = \lambda_b - \beta I^* \cdot S^* - v_t \cdot S^* - \lambda_{d_S} S^* = 0 \tag{21.14}$$

  Take the derivative of equation (21.14) with respect to p. [*Hint:* Remember that v_t is a function of both the price of vaccines and the number of infected people, p and I^*. Remember too that I will change with p, so the derivative of v_t with respect to p requires the use of the chain rule. By contrast, the birth rate λ_b, the infectivity rate β, and the death rate of the susceptible group λ_{D_S} are all constants.]

  b Recall the equation for the steady state-population of the susceptible group S^* in equation (21.8). Does it depend on the price of vaccines p?

  c Using this fact about $\frac{dS^*}{dp}$ that you derived in the last question, simplify the expression you derived in the first part of this question.

  d Now solve for $\frac{dI^*}{dp}$. When the prevalence elasticity of demand for the vaccine $\frac{dv}{dI^*}$ is high, is the the steady-state size of the infected population I^* more or less affected by changes in the vaccine price, p, compared to when $\frac{dv}{dI^*}$ is low?

16 **Eradication of a disease with a vaccine subsidy.** A terrible disease called fictitia is ravaging the woebegone nation of Pcoria. Fortunately, government scientists have just discovered the formula for an effective vaccine. Given current raw material prices, it costs $10 to produce each dose of vaccine.

Assume that Pcoria has 100 citizens, and that the demand for vaccine in the first time period is

$$Q = 100 - \frac{P}{\gamma}$$

where P is vaccine price and γ is disease prevalence.

  a Assume a competitive vaccine manufacturing market and a disease prevalence of 20% ($\gamma = 0.2$). How many citizens demand the vaccine this period?

  b After this initial round of vaccinations, demand for the vaccine plummets because many citizens have been vaccinated and do not need another vaccine. Among the unvaccinated population, demand is now

$$Q = 50 - \frac{P}{\gamma}$$

  The fictitia outbreak has slowed down considerably but the prevalence is still rising. Now assume $\gamma = 0.25$. How many unvaccinated citizens will demand vaccine this period?

  c The demand for vaccine in the third period $Q = 40 - P/\gamma$. Because of the success of the vaccination campaign, disease prevalence is now 10%. How many unvaccinated citizens demand vaccine this period?

  d What does the price need to be for everyone to vaccinate?

    e The Pcorian parliament appropriates funds for a vaccine subsidy in an attempt to wipe out fictitia once and for all. If they subsidize manufacturers by the full production cost of the vaccine, what price will consumers face? Will everyone decide to vaccinate?

17 Suppose that some members of a population are infected with a sexually transmitted virus that causes disease X, and some are infected with another sexually transmitted virus that causes disease Y. Some members of the population may be infected with both viruses. While diseases X and Y are similar in that they are both sexually transmitted diseases, the disease X is much more harmful to its carriers than the disease Y is to its carriers. Condom use is highly effective in preventing the transmission of either disease. Suppose scientists discover a cure for the sexually transmitted disease X. This cure (a vaccination) will eliminate the virus causing the disease X from its carrier before its carrier can suffer any harm from the virus. Everybody is immediately given this vaccination against the disease X.

    a What do you expect to happen to the prevalence of the virus causing the disease X in the population? Draw a graph with time on the horizontal axis and prevalence of the virus causing disease X on the vertical axis.

    b What do you expect to happen to the rate of condom use in the population over time? Add a curve for the rate of condom use to your graph.

    c What do you expect to happen to the prevalence of the virus causing the disease Y in the population? Add a curve for the prevalence of disease Y to your graph.

(Question courtesy of Professor Mikko Packalen, University of Waterloo)

Essay questions

18 The SARS virus is a particularly virulent form of the flu virus that spread through Taiwan and many parts of China in the mid-2000s. In a recent National Bureau of Economic Research working paper entitled "Learning during a crisis: the SARS epidemic in Taiwan" by Daniel Bennett, Chun-Fang Chiang, and Anup Malani (2011), the authors observe that:

> When SARS struck Taiwan in the spring of 2003, many people feared that the disease would spread through the healthcare system. As a result, outpatient medical visits fell by over 30% in the course of a few weeks.

    a Is staying home from seeing the doctor a rational response to an epidemic like SARS?

    b Leaving aside the probability of catching an infectious disease like SARS while going to the doctor, there is a distribution over the marginal benefit that patients gain from an outpatient visit. Some of the most sickly patients benefit a lot, while those with mild conditions probably receive only minor help from seeing a doctor. Which sorts of patients were more likely to stay at home in the face of the SARS epidemic? What is the effect on the excess burden of SARS?

    c Suppose there are some patients who are not susceptible to SARS but whose health is harmed because they skipped a visit to the doctor. Should the harm to these patients' health be counted as part of the excess burden of SARS? Now consider the patient who avoids iatrogenic harm – harm caused by inappropriate medical treatment – because she stayed home instead of going to the doctor.

Should this effect be included in the excess burden calculation? What is the effect on the excess burden of SARS?

19 Consider an infectious disease such as the flu which is spread primarily through virus particles in aerosolized respiratory droplets of already infected people.

   a In the midst of an infectious disease epidemic of this sort, is it privately rational for people to limit their exposure to other people, perhaps by staying home from work or not going to school?

   b An infected person who goes out into public areas and does not take precautions to contain their respiratory emissions clearly poses a negative externality on those around them. Does an uninfected person going out into public areas also pose a negative externality?

   c For a particularly severe disease outbreak of this sort, one possible government response is to exaggerate to the public both the harm that might arise from contracting the disease and the likelihood of contracting the disease. In what ways might such a strategy reduce the harm to the public from the disease epidemic? In what ways might such a strategy increase the harm to the public? [*Hint:* It is extremely unlikely that any particular infectious disease epidemic will be the *last* epidemic a society will face.]

Students can find answers to the comprehension questions and lecturers can access an Instructor Manual with guideline answers to the analytical problems and essay questions at **www.palgrave.com/economics/bht**.

22 OBESITY

In 1989, the typical Cuban consumed an ample 2,899 calories per day. The collapse of Soviet Union led to a dramatic decline in subsidies to Cuba, which in turn led to a collapse of the Cuban economy. By 2000, the typical Cuban consumed only 1,863 calories each day – a daily decline of 1,036 calories, which is a few calories short of a Quarter Pounder and a large order of fries at McDonald's (plus ketchup). As Cubans lost access to working cars, they were increasingly forced to walk everywhere, and the proportion of the Cuban adult population that reported themselves physically active rose from 30% to 67%.

Over this same period, the Cuban annual age-adjusted mortality rate dropped by 18%, diabetes-related mortality dropped by 51%, and heart disease-related mortality fell by 35%. Even if one discounts these statistics for the usual bias in data reporting by opaque regimes, these are astonishing numbers. Calorie restriction, as long as it does not go so far as starvation, is evidently very good for your health.

For a more precise estimate of the effect of starvation, we look to a classic study in nutritional physiology, conducted during World War II by Ancel Keys and his colleagues at the University of Minnesota. For six months, 36 young conscientious objectors volunteered for a strict nutrition regimen in lieu of military service. They were put on a controlled diet that reduced calorie intake by 45% and were required to walk for 22 miles per week. The volunteers ate all their meals together in the laboratory, lived together in the same dormitory, and checked up on each other to prevent cheating (Keys 1950). Thirty-four of the men completed the six months; 19 were still alive – into their 80s – in 2005.

During the period of the experiment, the personalities of the participants changed dramatically. They became obsessed with food. One collected over 100 cookbooks during the experiment. They became irritable and depressed. One recalls "noticing what's wrong with everybody else, even your best friend. Their idiosyncrasies became great big deals . . . little things that wouldn't bother me before or after would really make me upset." Though by some measures the men were more healthy by the end of the experiment, registering lower blood pressure, lower resting heart rate, and lower cholesterol levels, all of them were elated when the experiment finally ended and they could go back to eating as they chose.

These and other findings over the last several decades have confirmed the link between overeating, obesity, and adverse health outcomes. Today's typical American diet, which too often counts donuts and french fries as staples, is not what doctors and nutritionists would like it to be. The result is inexorable: bulging waistlines, chronic disease, missed work days, high health care costs, and premature death.

In recent years, the increasing prevalence of obesity in the US has been heralded as a public health crisis of first order. This in turn has led to proposals of substantive legislative action aimed at reducing body weight, including regulating the fast food industry, mandating smaller portion sizes, and imposing taxes on certain foods. Below, we explore the origins of the obesity epidemic, assess whether or not it is a *public* health crisis in the economic sense, and discuss government interventions to limit it.

22.1   The widespread rise in obesity

The rise in obesity prevalence is a fundamentally economic phenomenon. In particular, it is the technological and social changes that lower the price of calories and raise the opportunity costs of exercise. To make this case, we first need to establish how pervasive the rise in body weight and obesity has been.

Measuring obesity

Is a man who weighs 180 pounds (82 kilograms) obese? It depends whether that person is five feet tall (1.5 meters), or seven (2.1 meters). Clearly, some accounting must be made for height in defining obesity. The standard way to do this is calculate the **body mass index** or BMI.

Definition	22.1

Body Mass Index: $\text{BMI} = \dfrac{\text{Weight in kilograms}}{(\text{Height in meters})^2} = 4.9 \times \dfrac{\text{Weight in pounds}}{(\text{Height in feet})^2}$

By the relatively simplistic BMI measure, all of the participants in the annual World's Strongest Man competition (events include the "Bus Pull" and the "Giant Tire Carry") would be classified as morbidly obese. Credit: © michaeljung – Fotolia.com.

Somewhat arbitrarily, a person is considered clinically obese if his or her BMI is 30 or greater. A person with a BMI between 25 and 30 is not obese by this definition but is considered overweight. A person with a BMI under 18 is considered underweight. The seven-foot-tall man weighing 180 pounds clocks in at a BMI of 17.9, so he is not even overweight (he may in fact be unhealthily light). But a five-foot-tall man with the same weight has a BMI of 35; he is obese.

BMI is widely used in large-scale studies of obesity because both height and weight are relatively easy to measure. The major problem with BMI is that it does not distinguish between fat and muscle weight – by this standard, contestants competing for the World's Strongest Man title are morbidly obese despite their low body fat. Furthermore, for countries with smaller average body-frame sizes, such as China, obesity designations based on a BMI of 30 may understate the extent of excess weight, when compared to countries with larger average body frame sizes, such as Tonga (Swinburn et al. 2011).

Other methods of measuring body fat specifically range from the relatively low-tech subscapular skin fold (which involves a finger pinch and a ruler) to the dual energy X-ray absorptiometry (DEXA) machine. While these may be better measures of obesity, they are more expensive to collect and rarely used in large studies.

Evidence on rising body weight

Figure 22.1 shows that the proportion of adult Americans who are obese has more than doubled between 1977 and 2006. This figure also shows that the rise in obesity prevalence has been (roughly) the same for all Americans, regardless of education. It is still true that adults who have not graduated from high school are more likely to be obese than are college graduates, but both groups have grown more obese during this 30-year period.

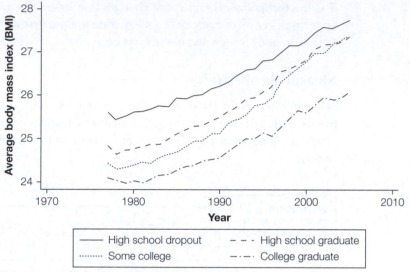

Figure 22.1. *Average body mass index (BMI) by education level in the US.*

Source: Authors' calculations using data from the National Health Interview Survey.

Although there is a widespread perception that the rise in body weight is a modern phenomenon that began only in the last few decades, body weight in the US has been rising in fits and starts for at least the past 150 years. Figure 22.2 shows a graph constructed by economic historians Dora Costa and Richard Steckel. They track the body weight of adult men of different ages in the US using hard-to-find data sources, including Army records dating back to the Civil War. This graph shows, for instance, that the average BMI of a 6-foot-tall 19-year-old in 1864 was just under 22. This had increased to 23 in 1961 and stood at 23.5 by 1991. The rise in body weight among older populations of men was even sharper. In 1900 the average 6-foot-tall 57-year-old man in the US had a BMI just under 23; in 1961 this number rose to over 25 and reached nearly 27 in 1991.

The increase in average body weight has not been confined to the last few decades, nor has it been confined to the US. Figure 22.3 plots World Health Organization data on average body weight obesity levels for 17 OECD (Organisation for Economic Co-operation and Development) countries at various points in time between 1976 and 2002. Every country in this sample has seen its average body weight go up in the past few decades. One curious fact is that the heaviest countries on Earth are all in the Anglosphere. We will see shortly that the reason for this has nothing to do with the English language.

At this point in the argument, there is a lot to explain. Obesity and body weight have been rising over a long period of time and in every developed country on Earth. At the same time, the age-old pattern of the well-fed and wealthy lord exploiting the thin and undernourished peasants has reversed. Today, it is the rich and well-educated who are

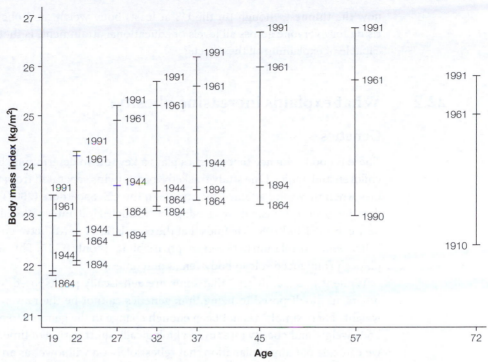

Figure 22.2. *Estimated average body mass index of American males in various age cohorts, 1863–991.*

Source: Figure 2.4 from D. Costa and R. H. Steckel (1997). Long-term trends in health, welfare, and economic growth in the United States. In Steckel, R. H. and Floud, R., editors, *Health and Welfare during Industrialization*, January, pp. 47–90. University of Chicago Press, Chicago, IL.

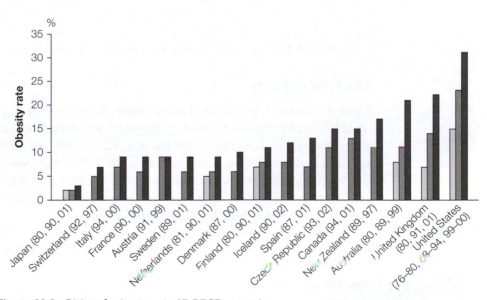

Figure 22.3. *Rising obesity rates in 17 OECD countries.*

Source: Data from OECD Health Data 2003. © OECD (2003) URL: http://www.oecd.org/health/healthpoliciesanddata/oecdhealthdata2003showhealthexpendituresatanall-timehigh.htm.

now the thinnest, though (in the US at least) body weight and obesity rates have been rising for everyone across all levels of educational attainment. Is there any simple theory capable of explaining all these facts?

22.2   What explains increasing obesity?

Genetics

There is good evidence that genetics plays a key role in determining body weight for both children and adults. One study tracked Korean twins separated from their biological families when they were adopted by parents in the US. Sacerdote (2007) collected adult BMI data for over a thousand twins adopted through Holt International Children's Services between 1964 and 1985. He finds that the correlation in BMI between biological siblings is 0.269, while correlation between adoptive siblings is only 0.115. This suggests that genetics plays a pronounced role in bodyweight outcomes.

While it is certainly true that some are genetically predisposed to being heavy, while others are predisposed to being thin, genetics cannot be the reason for the *rise* in body weight. There simply has not been enough change in the genome to explain the change in body weight and obesity rates over a biologically short period of time. For similar reasons, we can rule out any explanation that relies solely on willpower as an explanation. Even if one accepts the idea that people have enough self-mastery to control their own body at will there still remains the question of why willpower has declined so much since World War II and why it has exhibited the strange pattern that we have seen to date. Genetics may help explain why some people are likely to be more overweight than others, but we can reject genetics by itself as an explanation for skyrocketing obesity rates.

Genetics may actually play a small role in the rise in obesity prevalence due to assortative mating. Because overweight people tend to marry each other, and thin people tend to marry each other, the obesity gene pool may become more skewed over time (Katzmarzyk et al. 2002). But this effect is likely far too small to explain the rising obesity rates.

The food industry

Another popular theory for explaining obesity levels accuses fast food restaurants and agricultural corporations of pushing unhealthy, fattening foods, and large serving sizes on an unwary populace. This theory has been advanced by journalists like Eric Schlosser, author of *Fast Food Nation*, and documentarians like Morgan Spurlock, director of *Super Size Me*. Their argument is a variation on the theme that unchecked capitalism is literally unhealthy. In their telling, food habits are driven by the decisions of large corporations that are unconcerned about the health of the populace.

We have already seen evidence that the Cuban calorie crisis may have extended longevity, so it may also be true that restricting food choices can improve health. In addition, there is evidence that living close to fast food restaurants increases body weight, especially among children. But this argument does not account for the fact that economic freedom worldwide is positively correlated with health outcomes. It seems that economic freedom provides people with the opportunity to live a healthy life, even if some choose to do life-shortening things (like eating french fries) that they find enjoyable. Recall the argument presented in Chapter 3 that certain life-shortening decisions may be optimal, because they increase lifetime utility.

The Grossman model assumes people make decisions to perfectly optimize a known and unchanging lifetime utility function. This assumption implies a certain willpower and resistance to impulses. But those who argue that the food industry contributes to the obesity crisis contend that these assumptions are not valid. If the teller at McDonald's offers a customer a super-sized french fry serving, he says yes whether or not the surplus fries are a good decision. We discuss how economists model these potential deviations from the assumptions of the Grossman model in Chapters 23 and 24 on behavioral economics.

However, the incentives the fast food industry has to serve unhealthy food are still insufficient to explain the basic facts of rising obesity. Although the popularity of fast food restaurants may have contributed to rising obesity since World War II, body weight has been increasing since at least the mid-19th century (see Figure 22.2).

Food price trends

The only theory that explains all the data we have discussed so far puts prices in the central role. There are at least three key facts to explain: (1) the rise in average population body weight over the past 150 years; (2) the widespread increase in population body weight in every developed country on Earth; and (3) the parallel increase in average body weight for rich and poor alike. Together, changes in three sets of relative prices – the price of food, the price of physical activity, and the price of housework – explain all of these key facts.

Since the end of World War II, the price of food relative to other goods has been declining more or less monotonically. This price decline has been driven by remarkable improvements in the technology of agriculture. Work that used to require a team of men with mules and shovels can now be accomplished more efficiently by one person with a tractor. Advances in the science of agriculture now permit more food to be grown from the same cropland with less fallow time required. These technological advances have made food production substantially cheaper and driven down its price. Any given calorie type costs less today than it did in 1945.

Figure 22.4 shows the average price of food each year between 1950 and 2000. The law of demand says that (with rare exceptions) a decline in the price of a good will be met with an increase in the quantity consumed of that good. And Americans have responded to these price changes just as expected. Herbert Hoover's 1928 presidential campaign slogan of "a chicken in every pot" was an ambitious promise to a nation in which meat was still a luxury not often consumed. Today it might be seen as a promise (or perhaps a threat) to make Americans consume less red meat. Figure 22.4 also shows that during a few years in the mid-1970s, food prices increased dramatically due to sharply rising oil prices. Consistent with the hypothesis that food prices play a central role, the growth in average American body weight briefly halted during that period.

The decline in the price of food has put a nutritionally rich and varied diet within the reach of nearly every American, rich and poor alike, and has come close to ending frank starvation in the US. It has also permitted people, rich and poor alike, the luxury of eating inexpensively to the point of getting fat. In fact, data show that average daily calories purchased and consumed by Americans have risen since 1975 (Lakdawalla and Philipson 2009). While some have pointed to rising portion sizes at meals as a cause of rising body

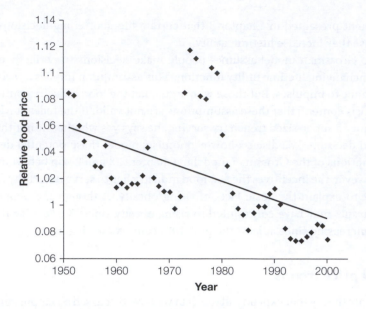

Figure 22.4. *Food prices have fallen steadily since World War II, with the exception of a large uptick during the 1970s energy crisis.*

Source: Lakdawalla and Philipson (2009). Copyright (2009), Figure 2 reproduced with permission of Elsevier.

weight, in fact those rising portions are themselves a consequence of falling food prices. McDonald's could not offer to supersize their fries for 39 cents, for example, if potatoes were not so cheap.

Of course, the decline in food prices has not been confined to just the US, but has occurred in every country that has not disconnected itself from the global economy. It is no surprise, then, to see that average body weight has risen in every developed country on Earth.

A hard-working combine harvester pictured alongside an idle human. Mechanized farming equipment is partially to blame for the obesity epidemic. Credit: © iofoto – Fotolia.com.

This simple story of declining food prices can also explain, to a large degree, why average body weight is higher in some countries than others. One striking fact that is evident from the data on body weight in the developed world is that English-speaking countries – Canada, New Zealand, Australia, the UK, and the US – have heavier populations than the rest of the world. This does not mean that people in the Anglosphere have less willpower to diet than people elsewhere. Rather, this pattern is a consequence of the fact that food is cheaper in these countries because the agricultural trade barriers between them are lower.

Of course, cultural differences matter as well: perhaps the cuisine that Japanese or French consumers favor does promote a thinner lifestyle. But even accounting for these cultural differences, the clear negative relationship between bodyweight and price supports the notion that food prices play a key role.

Declining physical labor and changing lifestyles

Food prices are not the only prices that have changed over the last 150 years. Another key price change is a consequence of the industrial and information revolutions that have occurred during that same time span. The labor economy in the developed world, which once upon a time consisted largely of agricultural jobs, has become dominated by service

and manufacturing jobs. Broadly speaking, jobs in the these industries require less physical activity at work than jobs in agriculture. In addition, within industries, technological
advances have made the typical job less physically strenuous and more sedentary – less
time operating a forklift and more time writing emails.

In short, because technology has expedited so many tasks, the opportunity costs
of manual work – such as hand-delivering a note rather than emailing – have risen
sharply. Workers now need to take time *off* to get exercise. As a consequence,
the typical worker today is less physically active overall than were prior generations of workers. This fact contributes to the rise in body weight in many ways,
especially since leisure-time physical activity has not increased by nearly enough to
compensate.

Other aspects of life have also changed in recent decades, including the widespread
adoption of air conditioning and the automobile. Air conditioning, while a fantastic innovation for people living in warm and humid climes, may contribute to obesity by keeping
temperatures overly steady. Bodies expend energy to cope with hot and cold temperatures, so air conditioning and central heating may be contributing to fat staying on bodies
rather than being burned off.

The automobile, meanwhile, is credited with dramatically reducing average daily walking exercise in developed countries (Keith et al. 2006). The findings of Bassett et al. (2011)
support the idea that increased automobile utilization is contributing to the growing
prevalence of global obesity. They find that countries in Europe, North America, and Australia with the highest rates of automobile use also have the highest obesity rates, while
the countries where the workforce has the most physically active commute modes (such
as walking and biking) have the lowest obesity rates.

It would be interesting to see whether a counterfactual society that never adopted these
lifestyle innovations would have also grown fatter during the last hundred years. Luckily
for researchers, such groups do exist – for example, there are Amish populations in North
America who have disavowed electricity, cars, and other modern technologies for religious reasons. A study of an Amish farming community in Ontario, Canada, found that
both males and females spent much of their time engaged in hard physical labor and that
the average participant walked three times as many steps per day as the average Canadian. One woman logged over 40,000 steps in one day when she woke up before dawn
to help her husband with chores before setting out to work in the hayfield (Bassett et al.
2004).

Unsurprisingly, obesity rates in the Amish village were much lower than in Canada as a
whole; only 4% of the participants qualified as obese, compared to 15% nationwide. There
may be other significant differences between the Amish population and the national Canadian population that explain some or all of this difference, but this is suggestive evidence
that technology and labor have played a role as well.

Labor force participation

Another important social change in the Western world that has contributed to rising body
weight is the increase in labor force participation by women and the simultaneous decline
in the average time spent preparing meals at home. The former is a well-known phenomenon, while the latter is confirmed by national surveys of time use in the US (Cutler
et al. 2003).

This transformation has been aided by technological changes, such as the invention and dissemination of dishwashers and microwaves that make housework much less onerous and hence decrease the relative price of labor force participation. And the increase in labor force participation has also contributed to the rising share of food dollars spent on restaurant food, which is often more calorically dense and fattening than food prepared at home.

Obesity as a side effect of good things

So what is the bottom line? Rising obesity prevalence is the undesirable outcome of a bunch of desirable things: the increased affordability of food, technological changes that make back-breaking labor less necessary and life more convenient, and increased opportunities for women in the workplace. But this abundance and freedom do not come without a cost. This analysis means that, whatever action is taken to address rising obesity prevalence, it will be difficult and costly since it will involve curtailing these evidently desirable things. We could eat substantially fewer calories and live longer – like the Cubans – but doing so would impinge on our ability to enjoy other desirable things, like a good hamburger. We could spend more time preparing food at home, but only at the opportunity cost of pursuing more challenging and exciting careers and enjoying meals at restaurants.

22.3   The costs of obesity

Even if obesity is the side effect of otherwise desirable trends, there are unquestionably substantial costs associated with obesity. These come in the form of myriad medical, financial, and personal costs, including:

- higher health care costs;
- reduced life expectancy;
- increased risk of chronic diseases such as heart disease, diabetes, and hypertension;
- reduced physical mobility and function;
- lower wages;
- social stigma.

If obesity causes bad health, it follows that obesity also leads to higher health expenditures. Studies demonstrate that, in many different insurance coverage settings, obese people spend more on average on health care than thin people (Sturm 2002; Finkelstein et al. 2005). For instance, Sturm (2002) finds annual medical expenditures in the US are 36% higher for obese people than thinner people. The difference in expenditure grows with age and is greater for women than for men (Bhattacharya et al. 2009). Wenig (2012), studying obesity in Germany, finds that disparities in expenditures exist even for overweight and obese children. A separate Canadian study failed to find a significant difference in spending between normal-weight and obese adolescents (Janssen et al. 2009).

These obesity-related costs have a considerable economic impact on many countries, with costs ranging between 0.09% and 0.61% of national GDP in Western Europe and between 0.2% and 0.6% of GDP in Canada and New Zealand (Müller-Riemenschneider et al. 2008). Obesity-related expenses in the US are even higher.

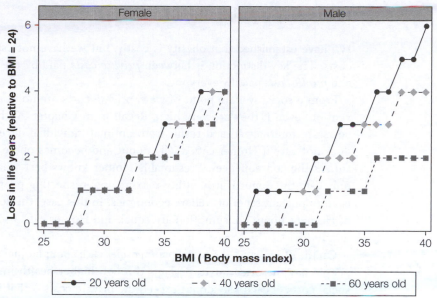

Figure 22.5. *Years of life lost due to obesity.*

Source: Data from Fontaine et al. (2003).

Yet the most dramatic cost of obesity arises from its life-shortening effect. Fontaine et al. (2003) use data from national surveys in the US to plot how life expectancy correlates with increased BMI in different age groups (see Figure 22.5). A 40-year-old white male with a BMI of 35 has a life expectancy three years shorter than a 40-year-old white male with a BMI of 24. The life expectancy drop due to obesity is larger at younger ages, partially because the young have more years left to lose, and because obesity can have a minor beneficial effect in older populations by protecting against frailty.

In examining the life-shortening effect of obesity, Banegas et al. (2003) find that in the European Union, at least 175,000 deaths per year are attributable to obesity. They conclude that at least one in thirteen deaths per year in the EU are caused by excess weight, and that among these deaths 70% were from cardiovascular disease and 20% from cancer.

Clearly, the costs of obesity come in both monetary (e.g. high health care costs) and non-monetary forms (e.g. lower life expectancy). To quantify the total costs of obesity, we need to give a monetary value to the non-monetary costs; we need a measure of the value of a lost year of life. Recall from Chapter 14 that measuring the value of a statistical life-year is a difficult and controversial task. To make the rest of this discussion concrete, we use a moderate value of $200,000 per life-year. Hence, the loss of life from obesity for a 40-year-old white man with a BMI of 35 compared to a 40-year-old white man with a BMI of 24 costs $600,000.

Given the effect of obesity on mortality, differences in annual health expenditures must be interpreted with care. For example, if the obese spend more per year on health care, but live shorter lives, it is possible that obese individuals spend less on health care over their entire lives. However, this is in fact *not* the case. Yang and Hall (2007) show that obesity increases the expected net present value of future health care expenditures for a 65-year-old by over $20,000, even after accounting for the lower life expectancy.

22.4   Is obesity a public health crisis?

We have established that obesity is costly, but we have not established who pays these costs. The key distinction is between *private costs* paid by the obese people themselves and *public costs* paid by everyone.

From a social welfare point of view, private costs are not a mandate for public intervention, even if they are very high. Recall from Chapter 20 that, by definition, private costs are internalized and result from optimal individual decisions. The social planner does not care if Homer eats a jelly donut and becomes obese, as long as Homer alone suffers the consequences. Presumably Homer knows best what makes him happy and only eats the donut if it is utility-maximizing; respecting people's revealed preferences is an important tenet of welfare economics. In this case, the social cost and private cost of Homer's donut consumption are equal, and Homer eats a socially optimal number of donuts.

On the other hand, the social planner *does* care about Homer's jelly donut habit if other people pay the price for it, perhaps through higher health insurance premiums. If the social costs of each jelly donut exceed the private costs – that is, if each donut creates a negative externality – we can no longer trust Homer to choose a socially optimal number of donuts to eat.

An important caveat to this argument is that it assumes that people make decisions that maximize their own utility; one school of thought holds that obesity is the result of mistakes in utility maximization. If this is so, it is no longer true that we can automatically ignore private costs in a social welfare analysis. Later in this chapter and in Chapter 24, we explore this caveat in more detail.

Not everyone analyzes health crises such as obesity this way. For instance, most public health experts argue that a public health crisis arises by definition whenever any undesirable health state becomes sufficiently widespread in the population. From this viewpoint, since obesity poses a significant health problem for millions, public interventions that help people avoid fast food restaurants would yield enormous benefits, even if people enjoy an occasional burger.

The use of the term "public" in the public health argument is not about whether the costs are publicly or privately borne. Rather, "public" refers to the scale of the problem. But for an economist, the distinction between public and private costs, rather than prevalence, determines whether obesity is a *public* health crisis rather than a significant but private problem.

Under this welfare economics rubric, an outbreak of tuberculosis is a public health emergency, but a rise in the prevalence of back pain is not. In the case of tuberculosis, drastic public action like quarantines may be justified. In the case of back pain, an intervention like a subsidy for ibuprofen would not be economically efficient. If the ibuprofen were worth buying, then the patient with back pain would buy it without a subsidy. No government action is justified because, unlike a tubercular patient in a crowded room, a person with back pain inflicts no costs on others. So whether the obesity epidemic is a *public* health crisis under our rubric depends on whether one person's obesity causes a loss in social welfare (also known as a social loss or a deadweight loss).

We consider two potential mechanisms through which obesity imposes externalities: pooled health insurance and contagion through social networks. The rest of this section describes how health insurance might make one person's obesity another person's problem. We discuss the possibility of obesity spreading through social networks in Section 22.5.

Pooled health insurance

Imagine that Homer, Carl, and Lenny are in a pooled health insurance plan. This would occur if the three live in a Beveridge country, like the UK, that joins all citizens in one massive insurance pool, or if they live in a Bismarck country, like Germany, that requires all citizens to join a pooled insurance plan. It could also happen in the US if all the three worked for the same company and subscribed to the same insurance plan, or if all three were enrolled in Medicare or Medicaid.

Because the insurance is pooled, Homer pays the same amount to qualify for health insurance coverage as Carl and Lenny (either through taxes, premiums, or some combination thereof). This is despite the fact that Homer is dangerously obese and likely to generate substantial medical costs in the coming year, whereas Carl and Lenny eat organic greens every day and have not needed or sought medical care in decades.

Pooled health insurance is like splitting a dinner bill with everyone in the same insurance pool. If the pool size is large, Homer pays almost no part of the increased medical bills that are a consequence of his obesity. Suppose that each additional jelly donut Homer eats raises the total medical bill for the entire pool by $1. Because Homer is one of thousands or even millions of members in the insurance pool, his own health insurance premium only rises by a fraction of a cent. By pooling together in the same insurance plan, Carl, Lenny and everyone else in the pool subsidizes Homer's costly jelly donut habit.

In this way, pooled insurance creates an artificial externality where none existed naturally. Simply by entering into a pooled insurance contract, Homer, Carl, and Lenny start affecting each other economically in ways they did not before. But this externality is just as real as any other externality and poses the same danger to social welfare.

While the cross-subsidization induced by pooled insurance seems like a problem – certainly, Carl and Lenny would agree – from a social planner's point of view, it is not certain that social welfare actually declines as a result. If Homer gains a dollar from the insurance cross-subsidization while Carl, Lenny, and the rest of the employees lose exactly a dollar in total, then health insurance induces a transfer but does not create any social loss.

So far, we have no evidence of an obesity-induced public health crisis, even with pooled insurance. But pooled insurance in combination with moral hazard *would* imply a public health crisis.

Moral hazard and health insurance

The incentives created by pooling apply not just to Homer, but to everyone else in the pool as well. For Carl, Lenny, and Homer alike, pooled health insurance reduces the price of unhealthy eating and of avoiding the morning jog. Suppose Carl responds to pooling by joining Homer for jelly donuts, and Lenny starts skipping his yoga exercises. Both realize that any higher medical bills as a result of their obesity will be paid by everyone in their insurance pool. This is a classic case of moral hazard: distortions in price induce changes in behavior that lead to a loss in social welfare (see Chapter 11).

If this assumption holds, pool members eat too poorly, exercise too little, and weigh too much relative to the social optimum. The presence of moral hazard in pooled health insurance implies a true public health crisis.

There is one critically important hitch to this reasoning that bears on whether the obesity epidemic is a public health crisis. Up to now, we have been discussing body weight choices as if they are firmly under our own control. For example, we assumed that Homer, Carl, and Lenny alter their exercise and diet habits on the margin in response to changes in the price of obesity induced by pooled insurance. As anyone who has tried a diet and failed can attest, this is not exactly right. There are many influences on diet and exercise choices that most people can do little about. Though we are evolutionarily programmed to like sugar, fat, and salt, some of us seem constitutionally more resistant to the lure of chocolate cake than others.

Let us suppose for the sake of argument that Homer overeats, not because of pooled insurance, but rather because he simply cannot resist the lure of jelly donuts. He acts the same way whether he is in a health insurance pool or not. That is, his elasticity of demand for donuts with respect to pooled insurance is zero. Under these assumptions, pooled insurance does not change Homer's behavior. If so, Homer's gluttony causes no social loss because there is no moral hazard.

To be sure, pooling still induces a transfer from Carl and Lenny to Homer since his expected medical bills are higher. Homer will be, say, a thousand dollars richer because of his participation in the pool, and the other pool members will be in aggregate a thousand dollars poorer. However, because pool membership does not affect Homer's behavior, there are no additional jelly donuts eaten or any morning jogs forgone because of pooling. Pooling induces a transfer, but it is a (socially) lossless transfer, because Homer's gain exactly offsets the other pool members' loss. Thus, without moral hazard, there is no social loss through pooled insurance due to obesity. Carl and Lenny may not like being in the same pool as Homer, but that does not mean that the obesity epidemic is a public health crisis.

The basic analysis of social loss induced by moral hazard should be familiar from Chapter 11 (see Figure 22.6). Recall that if there is no price distortion or no price sensitivity in the demand for obesity, there can be no moral hazard from health insurance. Therefore,

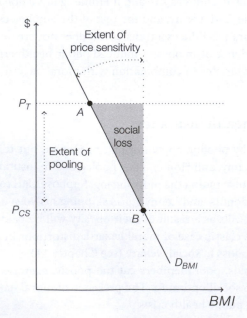

Figure 22.6. *The basic analysis of social loss caused by moral hazard as applied to pooled health insurance. Point A represents the socially efficient equilibrium where people optimize their body weight to balance the benefits of eating fattening foods with the resulting costs of health care. Point B represents the privately efficient equilibrium where people take advantage of the fact that other people in their insurance pool pay most of the costs of their health care. If the demand for obesity is completely price-inelastic, social loss is zero.*

the extent to which the obesity epidemic creates social loss through health insurance depends on one question: To what extent does insurance pooling induce changes in body weight decisions? Put more bluntly, does health insurance make you fat?

Does health insurance make you fat?

For evidence on this question, we can look to evidence from the RAND Health Insurance Experiment (HIE), covered in detail in Chapter 2. The RAND experiment is ideally suited to yield a clean estimate of the effect of generous insurance coverage on the incentive to gain weight. Recall that participants were randomly assigned to plans of varying generosity. Some participants were assigned to the "free plan" and received free medical care. Other participants were assigned to less generous plans that required a copay for health expenditures.

If pooled insurance causes people to eat more donuts and exercise less, then people in the free plan would do exactly that, while people in less generous plans would be more careful about their weight. Over time, the people in the free plan would gain more weight than people in less generous plans.

In fact, there was no such difference observed in the RAND HIE. At the end of the experiment, the people in the free plan had gained about as much weight (on average) as the people in the less generous plans. Figure 22.7 shows that for people on the free plan, 12% entered the experiment obese and 14% were obese by the end. This two percentage point increase in obesity prevalence is similar to and statistically indistinguishable from the increase in the other cost-sharing groups (Bhattacharya et al. 2011).

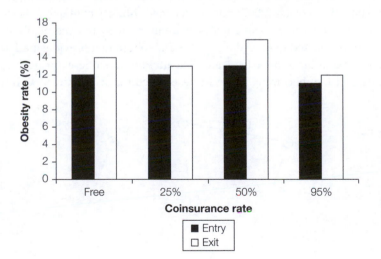

Figure 22.7. *Obesity rates increased the same in the cost-sharing and free plans in the RAND HIE.*

Source: Bhattacharya and Sood 2011.

According to the RAND HIE, more generous health insurance does not make people fat. There is a related question about whether moving from no insurance to some insurance makes enrollees fat. The answer to those two questions may not be the same. As we discussed in Chapter 2, the extent of moral hazard induced by moving from uninsurance to insurance may be different from the moral hazard induced by making insurance more generous. Examination of non-experimental evidence on this point has reached conflicting conclusions (Kelly and Markowitz 2010; Bhattacharya and Sood 2011).

22.5   Obesity contagion in social networks

So far, we have focused on the possibility that one person's obesity could harm another person through the mechanism of pooled health insurance. This is not a traditional public-health externality that arises from contagious disease, but instead an artificial externality that is a byproduct of pooled insurance.

But in recent years, scholarly interest has focused on the connection between social networks and obesity, and the possibility that a person, simply by being obese, can cause his friends and family to become overweight. Under this theory, obesity is a contagious disease that spreads not through physical proximity but instead through links in a social network. If this is the case, increasing obesity actually creates more obesity among the non-obese. We have established that obesity is privately harmful, so evidence that obesity can "spread" from person to person would be reason to call the obesity epidemic a public health crisis after all.

Researchers have used data from a massive study of the residents of a Massachusetts town to test whether social networks actually do spread obesity. The Framingham Heart Study was initiated in 1948 and originally included over 5,000 subjects from the town of Framingham, Massachusetts (Christakis and Fowler 2007). The offspring of these research subjects have also been included in the study, which remains ongoing. Researchers track data on subject health, but most critically they also track the social relationships between subjects. The dataset includes information on which subjects are spouses, siblings, neighbors, and data on which subjects consider which other subjects to be their friends (see Figure 22.8).

After analyzing network data on over 12,000 subjects spanning from 1971 to 2003, Christakis and Fowler (2007) find evidence for obesity contagion. They find that subjects (called *egos* in social network analysis) are more likely to become obese if the people that they are connected to (called *alters*) became obese in a previous period. If an ego identified an alter as his or her friend, and that alter became obese during the study period, then the ego's risk of becoming obese was estimated to increase by 57%. If that alter mutually

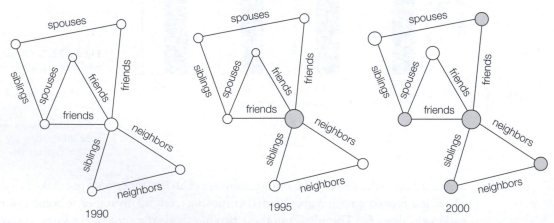

Figure 22.8. *A vastly simplified version of Christakis and Fowler's depiction of the Framingham data set. Each circle represents a subject, and the size of each circle is proportional to the subject's body mass index. The links between the subjects represent ties of friendship, marriage, or kinship. Over time, more people become overweight as obesity "spreads" through the social network. Obese subjects are highlighted in gray.*

Source: Developed from Figure 1 in Christakis and Fowler (2007).

identified the ego as a friend, the ego's risk of becoming obese was estimated to increase by 171%. Effects were smaller but still statistically significant for alters that were spouses or siblings of the egos; the only alters that did not seem to spread obesity to egos were next-door neighbors.

There are some interesting asymmetries in the data when friendship is not mutual. First, suppose an ego perceives the alter as a friend but the alter does not reciprocate (ego-perceived friend). In this case, if the alter becomes obese, the ego is statistically significantly more likely to become obese. On the other hand, suppose the alter perceives the ego as a friend but not *vice versa* (alter-perceived friend). Then the alter becoming obese has no significant effect on the ego's obesity risk. In other words, those we admire have a bigger effect on our body weight than the people who admire us. The data also show that obesity risk increases most dramatically when one person becomes more obese in a *mutually*-perceived friendship.

Some of these effect sizes are striking, but the appearance of obesity contagion may be an illusion. Perhaps if a pair of siblings or friends become obese in quick succession, it is a sign of changing dietary habits or economic conditions, not of one person's obesity causing another's. A second possibility is that people choose friends on the basis of common interests that are fattening. As with most observational studies, questions of causality are not definitively answered.

A natural experiment would be helpful in establishing whether the obesity contagion observed in the Framingham Heart Study is causal. Carrell et al. (2011) use the random assignment of cadets to dormitories at the US Air Force Academy as a natural experiment to measure fitness peer effects. The random dorm assignment allows researchers to measure peer effects without having to worry about selection bias and confounding variables.

The Air Force Academy is also a particularly good venue for study because it measures student fitness when cadets first enter the academy (before they have lived with their dorm mates). Students are retested in subsequent years, after they have spent time with their randomly assigned dorm mates. This test requires cadets to perform pull-ups, sit-ups, a 1.5-mile run, and various other athletic activities.

Carrell et al. (2011) find that the entry fitness scores of a cadet's peers have a significant influence on that cadet's subsequent fitness score. If a cadet is assigned to a dorm with particularly poorly conditioned dorm mates, his performance on future fitness tests tends to suffer accordingly. The least-fit peers have the most deleterious effect on cadet fitness, and the least-fit cadets are most affected by poorly conditioned peers.

This study is of limited applicability off the grounds of the Air Force Academy campus, where people are not assigned randomly to friend groups and are not forced to spend almost all waking hours with them. It also focuses on fitness scores among a relatively fit population with obesity prevalence at or near zero. Nevertheless, it provides evidence from a natural experiment that associating socially with less-fit peers can degrade one's own fitness.

Airman completing a fitness test. "If I can't do this next push-up, it's my roommate's fault." Credit: © mennis2185 – Fotolia.com.

While this evidence is interesting, it does not imply that an obese person causes his or her friends to become obese in the real world, where friendships and associations are not randomly assigned. While it is possible that obesity is contagious, there remains the possibility that the peer effects of obesity seen in the observational data such as the Christakis and Fowler (2007) study are actually evidence of people befriending people who share common interests. If so, the resulting impact on weight is a consequence of the common interest, rather than the effect of one peer on the other.

22.6   Other justifications for public health intervention

So far, we have argued that the only way obesity could be a "public" health crisis – in other words, the only way that government intervention against obesity would be justified – is if obesity causes social loss through externalities. This is the welfarist point of view, because welfare economics assumes that any choices that individuals make that do not affect others (about their health or anything else) must be optimal and should be respected by the government. In this section, we relax that assumption and consider whether there are occasions when governments should discourage or even forbid people from doing things they want to do.

Inadequate nutritional information

The notion that people choose an optimal weight for themselves based on food prices and their budget constraints relies on the assumption that people understand how their food choices impact their health. But there is evidence that consumers are woefully unaware of the nutritional content of much of the food they eat, especially food they do not prepare themselves. This lack of knowledge has been proposed as a justification for nutrition facts labels and, more recently, calorie posting requirements at restaurants (Blaylock et al. 1999).

Burton et al. (2006) found evidence that restaurant diners routinely underestimate the calorie content of the dishes they order. Survey respondents were given short descriptions of various dishes drawn from actual restaurant menus, and asked to estimate the number of calories in each dish. For low-calorie dishes, the respondents' estimates tended to be fairly accurate. The mean estimate was 358 calories for a 370-calorie turkey sandwich and 479 for a 640-calorie chicken breast.

On the other hand, respondents severely underestimated calorie counts for the high-calorie dish fettuccine alfredo (respondents guessed 704 when the true calorie measure was 1,500). Consider this particularly stark example: the average survey taker estimated that a serving of cheese fries with ranch dressing contains 869 calories, whereas laboratory tests revealed that the dish contained over 3,000 calories. Respondents proved equally inept at estimating fat content and sodium content.

Other studies corroborate the inability of consumers to accurately gauge the nutrition content of restaurant offerings. If consumers are not equipped to estimate the nutrition content of the meals they order – and perhaps unaware that they are not equipped – then government interventions may help consumers. Rather than preventing consumers from eating what they want, better nutrition information may help consumers better optimize their food decisions.

Nutrition facts labeling mandates are a popular government response to this problem. A typical nutrition facts label contains information about how much fat, sugar, cholesterol, and sodium is in each serving of food. But requiring nutritional labels is not costless – food providers must expend resources to measure the nutrition content of their offerings and to disseminate that information on their packaging. But they can help alert consumers make informed choices and avert some of the large private costs of obesity.

A similar tactic is requiring restaurants (especially fast food restaurants) to post calorie information on their menus. New York City and Washington state, for instance, both require calorie counts to be posted on menus in chain restaurants, while California requires fast food restaurants to provide calorie information on their menus.

The effectiveness of such measures has been questioned, because many consumers do not respond to this information. A study of New York City fast food restaurants before and after the calorie posting regulations went into effect found that lunchtime calorie purchases did not significantly decline, and that most survey respondents claimed not to use the information at all. But among the 15% of survey respondents who said they used the calorie information, lunchtime calorie purchases fell more than 10% from 863 to 765 on average (Dumanovsky et al. 2011). Even this small change suggests that consumers sometimes use nutrition information to alter their food consumption decisions. Calorie posting requirements may also induce restaurants to compete to offer healthier meals if customers lose interest in their more calorie-heavy offerings.

Nutrition disclosure requirements are not particularly overbearing because they do not restrict consumer choices. Even if a menu item is advertised as containing 14,000 calories, customers may still purchase it. But other policies – like taxes on sugary sodas or New York City's ban on trans fats in restaurants – are more heavy-handed; they may be impeding consumers from making privately optimal eating decisions.

Lastly, even with readily available nutrition statistics, there remains another information problem for food consumers. Consumers may have trouble translating their food choices into health outcomes. How many extra dollars of health care will be required over the course of your life if you eat a double cheeseburger with 12 grams of saturated fat? How much more likely will a heart attack be forty years from now if you choose to eat a 400-calorie donut instead of a 60-calorie apple as a snack this afternoon? These types of questions are next to impossible to answer. Interventions to improve the ability of customers to make this type of judgment are not obvious.

Childhood obesity

As we have seen, obesity rates have been rising across the board – for rich and poor, educated and uneducated, in Europe and America. It is also true that obesity is rising among children (Ebbeling et al. 2002). Over the past several decades, the prevalence of childhood obesity has increased in most industrialized countries, as well as several low-income countries (Han et al. 2010). For example, the prevalence of childhood obesity has at least doubled between the 1970s and 1990s in Brazil, Chile, Finland, France, Germany, Greece, the UK, Australia, and Japan. However, some recent reports suggest that rising childhood obesity rates in some countries such as Australia, France, Sweden, and Switzerland may now be slowly leveling off (Swinburn et al. 2011).

Welfare economics starts from the basic premise that people know what is best for them, and that people's actions reveal their true preferences. But this assumption is less likely to hold when it comes to children, who may be uninformed about health risks, ill-equipped to think about how health decisions now will affect their long-term health, and especially vulnerable to advertising for unhealthy foods. This question of whether children are capable of pursuing their self-interest is especially important in light of the findings that obesity during childhood is associated not only with obesity during adulthood but also with elevated rates of heart disease later in life and ultimately with a shorter life span (Must and Strauss 1999).

If a seven-year-old is unwittingly consigning himself to a lifetime of poor health by drinking sugary sodas and feasting on donuts and ice-cream every day after school, childhood obesity may warrant a government response even in the absence of externalities. Parents bear responsibility for the health and well-being of their children, but governments can play a role in supporting parents in this responsibility, especially during school hours when students are away from their parents' direct supervision.

One obvious way to limit childhood obesity is by making it harder for schoolchildren to access fatty and sugary foods. Common measures include removing sugary sodas and juices from cafeteria vending machines and imposing fast-food-free zones around elementary schools. Other proposals include banning or limiting advertisements aimed at impressionable youth and prohibiting toy giveaways with fast food meals.

While these interventions are quite restrictive, research indicates that they could be effective (Neumark-Sztainer et al. 2005). Currie et al. (2010) find that children living in close proximity to a fast food restaurant are more likely to be obese, while Chou et al. (2008) estimate that eliminating television advertising for fast food chains would reduce obesity among children aged 3—11 by 18%. But there are other studies that dispute these results and find evidence that school interventions do not lead to reduced body weight (Van Hook and Altman 2011; Datar and Nicosia 2012). Perhaps children circumvent restrictions on fatty foods at school by increasing their intake off campus.

Impatience and addiction

Another critique of the welfare economics argument attacks the core assumption that in the presence of perfect information, adults always make rational decisions. What if people gorge on cookies at midnight but regret it the next morning? What if people become addicted to french fries and cannot stop even if they do not want to gain weight? These kinds of scenarios are the focus of an emerging field called *behavioral economics*.

A ban on unhealthy midnight snacks, and a police directive to enter people's homes at midnight and enforce the ban, would certainly reduce obesity. It may even be supported (during daylight hours at least) by the very people whose midnight snacks would be outlawed. Similar tactics could be used to combat tobacco and alcohol addictions as well.

But this kind of muscular government intervention raises profound questions about liberty and the fundamental assumptions of welfare economics. We consider all these questions in much more detail in Chapters 23 and 24.

22.7   Conclusion

The rapid rise of obesity and associated chronic diseases worldwide has inspired policy responses in many countries. New York City voted to ban trans fat in restaurants in 2006; Japan started charging higher health insurance premiums for citizens with waistlines wider than a certain threshold in 2008; and Denmark instituted a tax on all products with saturated fat in 2011.

Recall the result from the RAND HIE which shows that more generous insurance coverage does not seem to change body weight outcomes (Section 22.4). One implication is that laws such as these induce a transfer from the obese to the thin, since obese people are the ones who tend to eat more fat. If there is no moral hazard, then these laws neither increase nor decrease total social welfare. However, since obese people tend to be poorer than thinner people, the transfers may represent a regressive change in income (Powell and Chaloupka 2009).

Taxing other fast foods may also have the unintended effect of tightening access to key nutrients for those who need those cheap sources of food. For example, beef is a primary source of iron for many poor children, and inadequate iron intake can cause anemia, which in turn can have devastating consequences on students' ability to concentrate (among other negative effects). Taxing burgers may reduce obesity but, by raising the price of beef, also increases the threat of childhood anemia (Lakdawalla et al. 2005).

Nutrition is complicated and entwined with income distributions and the economics of insurance markets. A single intervention can have many unintended ramifications. Reducing obesity rates is a worthy goal, but policymakers cannot overlook the economic fundamentals of the problem when they design their interventions.

22.8   Exercises

Comprehension questions

Indicate whether each statement is true or false, and justify your answer. Be sure to cite evidence from the chapter and state any additional assumptions you may need.

1 In the US, the rise in body weight started about 30 years ago.
2 While obesity generally results in higher per-year medical costs, obese individuals do not typically have higher average *lifetime* medical costs than non-obese individuals because they do not live as long.
3 Increasing female labor force participation rates (alongside declining time spent on preparing meals at home) have been implicated as one cause of rising obesity rates.
4 At firms that do not provide health insurance, the wages of obese workers are lower than the wages of non-obese workers with similar levels of productivity.
5 Over the past 15 years, obesity rates have increased sharply for high-school dropouts and for people with only high-school degrees. Rates for college graduates, however, have remained flat.
6 Developed countries with high food price tariffs tend to have lower prevalence rates of obesity.
7 Suppose that there is no wage penalty for obesity at the Springfield Nuclear Power Plant (SNPP). Suppose further that Mr Burns (the boss) offers his employees generous pooled health insurance coverage. Finally, suppose that obese workers at the SNPP are likely to spend more on health care than their thinner colleagues. Without further assumptions, one can conclude that Homer Simpson's gluttony and sloth necessarily causes a large welfare loss.
8 People tend to underestimate the calories counts of food not prepared for them at home.
9 Body mass index (BMI) is a reliable measure of obesity.

10 The only way to combat childhood obesity is through strict government intervention.

11 Genetics plays a role in determining body weight for children and adults.

12 New York has seen a majority of people change their behaviors because of the recent requirement that restaurants list the calorie counts for all their menu items.

13 Many countries in the world have experienced increases in the number of obese individuals in their population, but only the US has seen increases in childhood obesity.

14 Having generous insurance makes you fat because you do not pay the full health costs of eating poorly and not exercising.

15 Having an obese friend increases the likelihood of obesity.

Analytical problems

16 Suppose Homer and Smithers are in the same health insurance pool and they pay the same premium for their health insurance. Suppose further, that the SNPP discriminates against employees on the basis of body weight so that a negative wage penalty is associated with obesity. Finally, suppose Homer eschews exercise and loves jelly donuts much more than Smithers does. As a result, Homer also has much higher expected medical expenditures.

Does Homer impose a negative externality on Smithers? Explain why or why not, and describe carefully any assumptions you need to answer this question.

17 Suppose that in the midst of a financial crisis, Mr Burns is forced to sell the SNPP to wealthy chocolate tycoons. The first thing the tycoons do is reverse Mr. Burns' discriminatory policy against the obese. They eliminate the wage penalty associated with obesity but leave intact the pooled health insurance program, so Homer and Smithers still pay the same premium.

a   Now do Homer's jelly-eating, slothlike habits impose a negative externality on Smithers? Explain the nature of the negative externality. Is there any loss in net social welfare from this externality? Explain why or why not, and describe carefully any assumptions you need to answer this question.

b   How might an adverse selection death spiral arise at the new SNPP?

Essay questions

18 **Obesity contagion and social loss**. In this question, we discuss the research on obesity contagion by Christakis and Fowler (2007) introduced in Section 22.5. They find that people who identify obese people as friends are also more likely to be obese.

a   Does the finding by Christakis and Fowler establish a causal link between a friend's obesity and one's own obesity? If not, propose a different reason for the correlation identified by Christakis and Fowler.

For the rest of this problem, suppose that the effect is causal. In other words, obesity is contagious and being friends with someone who is obese is likely to make you make you obese, even if you are thin initially.

b   Do obese people impose a negative externality on their friends? What is the externality?

c   Suppose the government actively pursues Pigouvian remedies to reduce the social loss from externalities. It taxes smoking to combat the externality from secondhand smoke. It taxes factories to reduce the environmental harm from pollution. If the government also wants to use a Pigouvian tax to alleviate the problem of obesity contagion, what should it tax? Will this tax work? What factors go into deciding the size of the tax?

d   Suppose that people know that obesity contagion exists and can calculate the effect that obese friends impose on them. Would someone ever voluntarily befriend an obese person? What does this mean about the maximum harm an obese person can impose on his friends due to the obesity externality? [*Hint:* It may be helpful to think in terms of the costs and benefits of befriending this person.]

e   Obesity contagion can also travel through familial relations. Unlike in the case of friendships, family kinships – especially between parents and children – are much less likely to be voluntary. How does your answer to the previous question change for family members instead of friends?

f   Recall the concept of excess burden from Chapter 21. For both the cases of friends and family members, what is the excess burden imposed by obesity contagion?

g   Now consider the negative externality caused by a polluting factory. For the sake of this problem, assume that the pollution is concentrated and does not affect anyone or anything outside the factory's immediate radius. Living next to the factory is voluntary, and people are not legally proscribed from moving. For a family living next to the factory, what is the upper bound on the harm caused by the pollution? What might the excess burden be?

Students can find answers to the comprehension questions and lecturers can access an Instructor Manual with guideline answers to the analytical problems and essay questions at **www.palgrave.com/economics/bht**.

VII BEHAVIORAL HEALTH ECONOMICS

23 Prospect theory 496

24 Time inconsistency and
health 525

(23) PROSPECT THEORY

The local theater company is putting on a production of *Rigoletto*, Verdi's famous tragic opera, and opening night is in a few weeks. A lover of opera, you are extremely excited to go and would pay up to $200 for two tickets for yourself and a date – even for seats in the rear balcony. When you find out seats are available for only $75 each, you jump at the opportunity and buy two tickets for a night out on the town.

Eventually opening night arrives, and you step out of a limousine donning your new top hat and carrying the pocket watch you inherited from your grandfather. You have been looking forward to this moment ever since you purchased your ticket weeks ago. But as you step up to the door, you feel for the tickets in your breast pocket and discover they are not there. With a growing sense of dread, you now remember that you left your tickets on the dresser while you were adjusting your cuff links.

Your limousine has already driven off into the night, and even if you hailed a cab you would not be able to go pick up your tickets and get back to the theater without missing most of the show. A kindly usher informs you that tonight's performance is actually not sold out – there are two tickets left in the rear balcony, also for $75 each. But you have already spent $150 for the two tickets that are sitting at home, and suddenly all these expenses are adding up. If you pay for a third and fourth ticket to the show, you will have spent $300 to see a performance that is only worth $200 to you. Your date mumbles something about this being a lot of money to spend on one night out. Dejected, you doff your top hat and head home to watch *Simpsons* reruns instead.

Just as you step away from the ticket window, a fellow opera-lover wanders by with his wife. Just like you, he values two tickets to the opera at $200, but he did not know *Rigoletto* was playing until he sees it on the theater's marquee. Delighted, he steps up to the window and buys the last two tickets that you decided were too expensive.

This story is an illustration of the sunk cost fallacy. Even though you and your fellow opera-lover have the exact same valuation of a night at the opera and face the exact same price for tickets, you made different decisions about whether the last two tickets were worth buying. For some reason, you added the sunk cost of the forgotten tickets to the cost of the new tickets when you were balancing the costs and benefits of an additional purchase. Your fellow opera-lover never bought any tickets, had no sunk cost to think about when he was trying to decide what to do, and maximized his utility.

Some would say that your decision was a "mistake" – a deviation from the rational behavior that economists assume. A rational utility-maximizer would have ignored the sunk cost, purchased the two tickets, and received $200 − $150 = $50 worth of utility. This story and others like it suggest that people may not always act as rationally as standard economic models predict.

Recall from the beginning of this book our discussion of the Grossman model in Chapter 3. The individual in the Grossman model is assumed to correctly make the choices between labor and leisure, and between health and consumption, that maximize his lifetime utility. If individuals behave as rationally as the Grossman model assumes, then the choices they make must be individually optimal. However, the struggles of our opera-lover to optimize over his relatively simple ticket decision call into question the ability of people to maximize something as complicated and multifaceted as their lifetime health.

A relatively young branch of economics known as behavioral economics arose in the 1970s to identify deviations from rationality and help economic theory to cope with these deviations. As we will see, the findings have major implications throughout health economics. In this chapter, we formalize the economic notion of rationality and introduce prospect theory, an alternate model of decision-making proposed by two psychologists Daniel Kahneman and Amos Tversky. In the next and final chapter, we discuss time-inconsistency, a distinct but similar aspect of behavioral economics.

23.1   Modeling decisions under uncertainty

A core goal of economics is describing how people make decisions under uncertainty. Uncertainty is pervasive and it is not entirely obvious what it means to maximize utility when uncertainty exists. When uncertainty exists, decision-makers have to envision all of the possible outcomes, and how their actions might change the likelihood of those outcomes before deciding optimally. These complications are not present when outcomes are certain.

Throughout this chapter, we discuss how people value different *lotteries*, which offer sets of payouts with corresponding probabilities. An example lottery is a game in which the player wins $100 if a coin lands on heads and loses $100 if it ends up tails. This simple lottery has only two outcomes, but lotteries can also include countless possibilities. For example, the purchase of a used car in Akerlof's model for lemons is a lottery between cars of different qualities. A worker's income next year is a kind of lottery as well. He might receive a promotion, he might fall sick, he might buy a winning lotto ticket, or the economy might suffer a recession. Every possible final level of income has its own small likelihood of happening.

Consider the simpler lottery of an individual who will receive I_S if she gets sick and I_H if she does not. This is the same lottery we studied repeatedly in Chapter 7. If she gets sick, then her resulting utility is $U(I_S)$; if she stays healthy it is $U(I_H)$. But at $t = 0$, how should the individual value the *chance* of either I_S or I_H?

Our goal in this chapter is to define a *valuation function* V to describe how people value lotteries with uncertain outcomes such as I_S and I_H. For a lottery L with different outcomes $x_1, x_2, \cdots, x_n$ and corresponding probabilities $p_1, p_2, \cdots, p_n$:

Valuation function: $V(L) = V(x_1, p_1; x_2, p_2; \cdots ; x_n, p_n)$ (23.1)

We have actually seen a valuation function before. Starting in Chapter 7, we implicitly assumed that this function V equals the statistical definition of expected utility over potential outcomes. If p is the probability of sickness, then

$$V(L) = E\left[U(L)\right] = pU(I_S) + (1-p)U(I_H)$$

In this chapter, we explain why economists often make the assumption that the valuation function equals expected utility; cover some empirical evidence that it fails to describe preferences in many circumstances; and introduce prospect theory, which offers a different valuation function.

Modeling rationality

Economists assume that people are "rational," so the valuation function V must reflect this assumption. But what does rationality under uncertainty actually mean? Intuitively, most people would agree that rational decisions made by a single person should be internally consistent. This implies that the valuation function should have three basic mathematical properties to rule out preferences that contradict themselves:

- **Completeness**: When deciding between any two lotteries, a rational individual can always make a judgment about which lottery is preferable, or if he is indifferent between them. The decision depends on the lotteries' potential outcomes, probabilities, and the person's risk appetite. Intuitively, completeness means that a rational actor can always decide which of two alternatives he prefers (or decide that he is perfectly indifferent).
- **Transitivity**: Now consider three possible lotteries A, B, and C. Someone has already decided that she prefers A to B and also that she prefers B to C. This information implies that the individual must also prefer A to C. Transitivity means that people's preferences can never be circular.
- **Independence**: Finally, a preference for one lottery over another should be unaffected by a change common to both lotteries. For example, suppose an individual prefers lottery A to lottery B. If both lotteries were mixed with a third lottery that offered a payout of $0 with certainty, the new lottery A' would still be better than the new lottery B'. In other words, independence means that preferences are unaffected by common alterations.

Definition 23.1

Completeness: for any two lotteries A and B,

- $V(A) > V(B)$, or
- $V(A) < V(B)$, or
- $V(A) = V(B)$.

Transitivity: for any three lotteries A, B, and C,

$$V(A) > V(B) \text{ and } V(B) > V(C) \Longrightarrow V(A) > V(C).$$

Independence: for any three lotteries A, B, and C, and $0 < p < 1$,

$$V(A) > V(B) \Longrightarrow pV(A) + (1-p)V(C) > pV(B) + (1-p)V(C).$$

Expected utility theory

What valuation function V satisfies the "rational" properties of completeness, transitivity, and independence? Is it possible that none exists at all? Two mathematicians, John von Neumann and Oskar Morgenstern, proved that only one functional form for V satisfies all three properties (Morgenstern and von Neumann 1947).[1] It is no coincidence that this one functional form is the same as the statistical expected utility function we have assumed all along to model how people value uncertain prospects.

Valuation function under expected utility theory

For a lottery A with outcomes $x_1, x_2, \cdots, x_n$ and corresponding probabilities $p_1, p_2, \cdots, p_n$:

$$V(A) = V(x_1, p_1; x_2, p_2; \cdots; x_n, p_n)$$

$$= p_1 U(x_1) + p_2 U(x_2) + \cdots + p_n U(x_n) \tag{23.2}$$

$$= E[U(A)]$$

This valuation function is also known as the **von Neumann–Morgenstern utility function**.

The valuation equation in equation (23.2) is the statistical definition of *expected utility* of all the outcomes from lottery A. The theory that people make decisions under uncertainty based on this particular valuation function is known as **expected utility theory**. If expected utility theory is an accurate model of decision-making, then the choices people make maximize the von Neumann–Morgenstern utility function in equation (23.2). The utility function U is not necessarily linear, so risk aversion is accounted for in expected utility theory. In fact, we were taking expected utility theory as given when we studied risk aversion and demand for insurance in Chapters 7, 8, and 9.

Because only von Neumann–Morgenstern utility functions guarantee that preferences are complete, transitive, and independent, it is tempting to equate expected utility maximization with rationality. If the choices people make are not always consistent with expected utility maximization, then there are two possibilities. Either (a) people are not rational in their decision-making under uncertainty, or (b) the completeness, transitivity, and independence properties are not a good definition of rationality.

Studies show that people are averse to closing off options. In a study with a video game that featured disappearing doors, Shin and Ariely (2004) found that people spent inordinate time and energy keeping doors from disappearing even when what lied behind the doors was of little value.
Credit © DTImages Fotolia.com.

Bounded rationality

While expected utility theory has been useful for modeling decisions in a variety of circumstances – such as Akerlof's model of lemons and the Grossman model of the demand for health – two psychologists, Daniel Kahneman and Amos Tversky, have found evidence that rationality is bounded. Under *bounded rationality*, people are hindered by cognitive limitations and as a result they do not always make decisions consistent with completeness, transitivity, and independence.

---

1   Their proof requires other technical assumptions that we omit here. For much more on this topic, see Morgenstern and von Neumann (1947).

Kahneman and Tverky's evidence of discrepancies between the predictions of expected utility theory and the actual decisions people make challenges the proposed valuation function in equation (23.2). Their integration of psychological insights into the study of economics earned Daniel Kahneman the 2002 Nobel Prize in Economics and is the foundation for the study of behavioral economics. Tversky would have undoubtedly won the Nobel Prize alongside his colleague had he not passed away before 2002.

Kahneman and Tversky (1979) studied responses from Israeli university students to a variety of survey questions about decisions under uncertainty. These questions, which offered the respondents different lotteries to win Israeli money, were hypothetical – no actual money changed hands as part of these experiments. It may be dangerous to extrapolate too broadly from surveys in the laboratory to real-world behavior in the field, but surveys are still useful indications of how people might behave. Lab experiments allow researchers to specify exact payouts and probabilities, and control for confounding influences like no real-world study could. Studies of this sort have been replicated many times across a number of different populations and produced consistent results, which lends further credibility to their findings.

The discrepancies we discuss next are the motivation for Kahneman and Tversky's theory of choices under uncertainty called **prospect theory**. Their theory is an alternative to expected utility theory and accounts for bounded rationality by relaxing the assumptions of complete, transitive, and independent preferences.

Several topics covered already have showcased the pervasiveness of uncertainty when it comes to making decisions about one's health. People buy insurance to hedge against the uncertainty of a bad medical diagnosis. The decision to vaccinate depends on the uncertain risk of contagion. Patients considering medical treatments note both the chance of success along with the risk of side effects. If people have serious difficulty maximizing their utility in settings with uncertainty, their health is certain to suffer.

We first share some of the evidence that people make choices that contradict the predictions of expected utility theory, and then briefly introduce prospect theory. Lastly, we discuss the implications of bounded rationality for health economics.

23.2   Misjudging probabilities

Any discussion about decisions under uncertainty must include a discussion of probabilities. Probabilities are a measure of the degree of uncertainty, but in the real world, they can be difficult to estimate. What is the likelihood of an earthquake next year? The chances of catching a cold next week? Or the risk of a global epidemic? Even for the seismologist or the health researcher, estimating the likelihood of these various events is a formidable task. How is the common man supposed to calculate these probabilities as he decides how much insurance to buy?

Unsurprisingly, research has found that people's estimates of the probabilities of rare events are highly susceptible to error (Slovic 1987). For example, people consistently overestimate their probability of being personally affected by risks that are unusual but receive disproportionate news coverage, like tornadoes and floods. Similarly, the frequencies of rare but graphic risks – such as botulism infections or wolf attacks – tend to be over-estimated compared to common but gradual dangers like cancer or heart disease

(Lichtenstein et al. 1978). In general, the salience of an event recorded in one's mind seems to strongly bias one's estimation of the likelihood of that event.

We might conclude that any observed evidence of "irrational" decision-making under uncertainty may just be the consequence of mis-estimated probabilities. However, Kahneman and Tversky show that even when true probabilities are known and explicit, people's stated preferences still seem to violate the properties of rationality. Since respondents are told the actual probabilities in their experiments, any evidence of deviation from rationality they find cannot be the result of mis-estimation.

Overvaluing certainty

Consider the following problem posed to survey takers. Options A and B are two lotteries with different payouts and probabilities.

Problem 1 *Choose either*		
Option A: $2,500 with probability 33%	**Option B:** $2,400 with probability 100%	
$2,400 with probability 66%		
0 with probability 1%		
Chosen by 18%	82%	

Kahneman and Tversky (1979) report that, of the 72 subjects in their study, 82% chose Option B, while only 18% selected the riskier Option A. By itself, this is hardly unexpected. The respondents are exhibiting risk aversion: the certainty of Option B makes it more appealing, even though its expected payout is lower than the expected payout of Option A. For the majority of survey takers, Option A is valued lower than Option B:

$$V(\mathbf{A}) < V(\mathbf{B}) \tag{23.3}$$

If expected utility theory is an accurate description of preferences, the valuation of any lottery equals its expected utility. This fact in conjunction with equation (23.3) means that the expected utility of Option A must exceed that of Option B:

$$V(\mathbf{A}) < V(\mathbf{B})$$

$$\mathrm{E}[U(A)] < \mathrm{E}[U(B)]$$

$$0.33U(2,500) + 0.66U(2,400) + 0.01U(0) < U(2,400) \tag{23.4}$$

$$0.33U(2,500) < 0.34U(2,400)$$

Note that throughout this chapter, we assume that the utility function U is normalized as $U(0) = 0$. Since utility is a relative concept – superior outcomes offer more utility than inferior ones regardless of the absolute level of utility the outcomes provide – we can make this assumption without loss of generality.

The same survey takers were also given the following Problem 2. Notice that the only difference between Problem 1 and Problem 2 is that a 66% chance of winning $2,400 is replaced with a 66% chance of winning $0 in both lotteries.

Problem 2	*Choose either*			
Option C: $2,500 with probability	33%	**Option D:** $2,400 with probability	34%
$0 with probability	67%	$0 with probability	66%
Chosen by	83%		17%

When presented with the two lotteries in Problem 2, 83% of the survey respondents selected Option *C* and only 17% Option *D*. The majority decision in Problem 2 reveals that most people value Option *C* more than Option *D*. By expected utility theory:

$$V(\mathbf{C}) > V(\mathbf{D})$$

$$E[U(C)] > E[U(D)]$$

$$0.33U(2,500) + 0.67U(0) > 0.34U(2,400)$$

$$0.33U(2,500) > 0.34U(2,400)$$

(23.5)

But the conclusion found in equation (23.5) is the precise opposite of the conclusion found in equation (23.4). If expected utility is accurate, the survey responses to Problem 1 imply that most people value a 34% chance of winning $2,400 more than a 33% chance of winning $2,500. However, the choices in Problem 2 refute that implication: people apparently value the 33% chance of winning $2,500 more!

This is our first indication that von Neumann–Morgenstern utility functions may not accurately describe how people value lotteries with uncertain outcomes. This pattern of contradictory responses is known as the Allais paradox after economist Maurice Allais, who originally noticed it during experiments in the 1950s (Allais 1953).

Kahneman and Tversky attribute this discrepancy to the **certainty effect**. Expected-utility maximizers value certainty if they are risk-averse, but these survey results suggest an even stronger preference for certainty than expected utility theory predicts. In Problem 1, respondents seem to be attracted to the certainty of Option *B* even *beyond* what their risk-aversion levels would imply. Once that certainty vanishes in Problem 2, the second lottery loses its special appeal and fewer respondents select it.

Definition	23.2

Certainty effect: the tendency to value lotteries with certain outcomes ($p = 1$) over uncertain lotteries, even more than would be predicted based on risk aversion in expected utility theory.

Table 23.1 introduces Problems 3 and 4, which offer further evidence of the certainty effect. Notice that Problem 4 offers the same options as Problem 3 but reduces the probability of positive gains by 75% in each lottery. Crucially, this reduction eliminates the certainty of Option *B*.

Table 23.1. *Survey questions and responses illustrating the certainty effect.*

Problem 3		Problem 4	
Option A	Option B	Option C	Option D
$4,000 with $p = 0.8$		$4,000 with $p = 0.2$	$3,000 with $p = 0.25$
$0 with $p = 0.2$	*or* $3,000 with $p = 1$	$0 with $p = 0.8$	*or* $0 with $p = 0.75$
80% prefer Option B		65% prefer Option C	

Source: Kahneman and Tversky (1979). With permission of the Econometric Society.

As in the previous pair of problems, the most popular choices in Problems 3 and 4 reveal a contradiction. If the lotteries are valued using expected utility theory:

Problem 3

$$V(A) < V(B)$$

$$E[U(A)] < E[U(B)]$$

$$0.8U(4,000) + 0.2U(0) < U(3,000)$$

$$\frac{4}{5} < \frac{U(3,000)}{U(4,000)}$$

Problem 4

$$V(C) > V(D)$$

$$E[U(C)] > E[U(D)]$$

$$0.2U(4,000) + 0.8U(0) > 0.25U(3,000) + 0.75U(0)$$

$$\frac{4}{5} > \frac{U(3,000)}{U(4,000)}$$

Expected utility theory thus implies that if someone prefers Option B to Option A in Problem 3, she should also prefer Option D to Option C in Problem 4. Unless we believe that people are liable to make decisions inconsistent with their desires, this evidence suggests that the expected utility theory fails to model decision-making in this context. In other words, people seem to be using a valuation function other than the von Neumann–Morgenstern utility function in equation (23.2).

Overvaluing small probabilities

In the experiments conducted by Kahneman and Tversky, the probabilities of different outcomes are specified explicitly, and respondents are assumed to read and understand those probabilities. There is no concern that survey takers will be uncertain about the exact likelihood of each possible payout under each lottery. But even when people know the probabilities of each payout for a fact, there is evidence that they *misjudge* the importance of those probabilities.

Consider the next problem given in the Kahneman and Tversky surveys. It is akin to a choice about buying a five-dollar lottery ticket. You can keep the five dollars (Option B) or gamble it for a small chance of winning $5,000 (Option A).

Problem 5	Choose either		
Option A:	$5,000 with probability 0.1% $0 with probability 99.9%	Option B: $5 with probability 100%	
Chosen by	72%		28%

According to expected utility theory, the majority decision in Problem 5 reveals

$$V(\mathbf{A}) > V(\mathbf{B})$$

$$E[U(A)] > E[U(B)]$$

$$0.001U(5,000) + 0.999U(0) > U(5) \tag{23.6}$$

$$0.001 > \frac{U(5)}{U(5,000)}$$

But as we have discussed in Chapter 7, people tend to be risk-averse and their utility functions $U(I)$ show diminishing returns in income. The first dollar offers more utility than the second dollar and much more than the five-thousandth dollar. In other words, $U(5) - U(0) > U(5,000) - U(4,995)$, and the first five dollars offer a disproportional amount of utility compared to the last five dollars. Just like winning $2 is not fully twice as satisfying as winning $1, winning $5,000 is not a thousand times as satisfying as winning $5. This means that $U(5)/U(5,000) > 0.001$. Hence, there is a contradiction between the majority response to Problem 5 and the implications of risk aversion:

$$0.001 > \frac{U(5)}{U(5,000)} \quad \text{and} \quad \frac{U(5)}{U(5,000)} > 0.001 \tag{23.7}$$

This discrepancy between expected utility theory and empirical evidence suggests that even though survey respondents are explicitly told the probability of winning the lottery – 0.001 in this case – they still misjudge how likely that event is. Whereas expected utility theory says that a 0.001 chance of winning $5,000 has a small impact on expected utility, people seem to overweight that small impact. People select the risky Option A more often than expected utility theory would predict.

The evidence from this problem and others suggest that even when exact probabilities are known, the weights people attach to uncertain events may be different from their actual probabilities. People seem to systematically overweight very low probabilities and underweight medium and large probabilities (see Figure 23.1).

This phenomenon observed in survey results seems to occur in non-experimental settings as well. For example, HIV+ patients show a tendency to overweight their mortality risk immediately after their initial diagnoses when the chances of dying are low. But they underweight mortality risk later on, when their likelihood of dying has increased (Bhattacharya et al. 2009).

In another example, Schoenbaum (1997) shows that light smokers tend to overestimate their mortality risk, but heavy smokers with greater health risks underestimate theirs. Both cases are consistent with the pattern of systematic risk misperception shown in Figure 23.1.

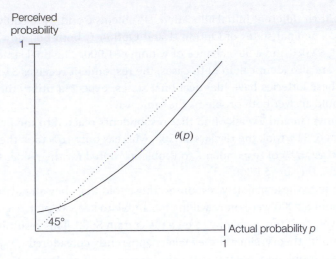

Figure 23.1. *Perceived probabilities and actual probabilities according to Kahneman and Tversky (1979).*

23.3   Framing

In expected utility theory, final outcomes are all that matter. A final prize of $50 should provide you a specific amount of utility, regardless of whether you are given it directly or you were first given a hundred dollars and then forced to return half. In the von Neumann–Morgenstern framework, these two situations are equivalent – either way you walk away with $50 more than you had before the interaction. Intuitively, however, these two scenarios do not feel the same. In the first, we are elated to receive a free gift, but in the second, we feel like something has been stolen from us.

Kahneman and Tversky show that how a final state is reached matters at least as much as the outcome in the final state itself. The *framing* of a problem can affect the perception of how valuable each choice is. Consider the following pair of problems, which were given to different groups of survey takers:

Problem 6	You have just received $1,000. Choose either	
Option A:		**Option B:**
$1,000 more with probability 50%		$500 more with probability 100%
$0 more with probability 50%		
Chosen by 16%		84%

Problem 7	You have just received $2,000. Choose either	
Option C:		**Option D:**
$1,000 less with probability 50%		$500 less with probability 100%
$0 less with probability 50%		
Chosen by 69%		31%

Despite their different initial allocations, Problems 6 and 7 are equivalent in their final outcomes. The final states of Option *A* and Option *C* both boil down to a 50% chance of winning $2,000 and a 50% chance of winning $1,000. The final states of Option *B* and Option *D* are also identical; in both cases, the respondent receives $1,500 with certainty. Because these lotteries have identical final states, expected utility theory would predict people would answer both problems the same way.

Yet Kahneman and Tversky find that respondents reacted to the problems differently. In Problem 6, 84% took the riskless $1,500, whereas only 16% took the gamble in Option *A*. By contrast, 69% of respondents to Problem 7 opted for the riskier Option *C* and only 31% selected the sure $1,500.

According to these majority responses, those told that they already received the maximum amount $2,000 were more willing to gamble to keep all of it. Meanwhile, those who only received $1,000 were happy to take the certain $500. This result is inconsistent with expected utility theory, since survey takers apparently considered not just final states but also how the problems were framed. This discrepancy is analogous to the decisions in the story at beginning of this chapter, where you and your fellow opera-lover valued the last two opera tickets differently because of the different ways the two of you arrived at the decision to purchase them.

Framing can affect the demand for public health insurance plans. The next two problems were given to different groups of Americans in 2009 amid the debate over health care reform in the US.

Problem 8   *Choose either*

Option A: A health insurance plan with no lifetime limit on benefits

Option B: A plan that limits the total lifetime benefits to $1 million but saves you $1,000 a year.

Chosen by   79.5%   20.5%

Problem 9   *Choose either*

Option A: A plan with no limit on lifetime benfits but costs $1,000 more per year.

Option B: A health insurance plan that limits the total lifetime benefit to $1 million.

Chosen by   44.2%   55.8%

Both problems ask how people evaluate the tradeoff between $1,000 a year and unlimited lifetime benefits from their health insurance. Problem 8 frames the $1,000 as a potential savings from accepting a limit, whereas Problem 9 frames it as an additional cost to having unlimited insurance benefits. That subtle distinction encouraged more than twice as many people to select a lifetime limit on benefits (Option B) in Problem 9 (Eckles and Schaffner 2010).

The fact that people change their opinions as a result of framing creates an opportunity for savvy politicians to advance their policy agendas. The framing of health care legislation can matter greatly in how popular it is. If people perceive the legislation as posing additional costs on them, the bill may induce some animus. By framing proposals differently, politicians may be able to garner more support than they otherwise would.

23.4   Loss aversion

Up until now, we have classified people as risk-averse, risk-neutral, or risk-seeking (see Chapter 7). But that may be too simplistic. In fact, some evidence from experimental questionnaires suggest that the same person may exhibit both risk-averse *and* risk-seeking preferences.

Consider two lotteries. The first option gives $3,000 with certainty. The second one offers a 80% chance of winning $4,000 but no money with $p = 20\%$.

Problem 10 *Choose either*	
Option A: $3,000 with probability 100%	**Option B:** $4,000 with probability 80%
	$0 with probability 20%
Chosen by 80%	20%

Risk-averse people prefer the certainty of the sure outcome over the riskiness of the gamble. Choosing between these two lotteries is analogous to choosing whether to buy insurance. In the Kahneman and Tversky experiments, 80% of respondents went for the certain outcome.

Now consider this next problem, a mirror image of the previous problem:

Problem 11 *Choose either*	
Option C: −$3,000 with probability 100%	**Option D:** −$4,000 with probability 80%
	$0 with probability 20%
Chosen by 8%	92%

Risk-averse respondents should prefer the certain loss of Option C, rather than risk the 80% chance of losing even more with Option D. Not only is the certainty appealing, but the expected income loss due the riskless Option C is actually smaller than the expected loss from the riskier Option D. Yet, contrary to this prediction, 92% of respondents opted for the gamble in Option D over the riskless alternative in Option C.

The majority choice in Problem 10 implies that the survey respondents are risk-averse: the certain outcome is more appealing even though it offers a smaller expected gain. The majority choice in Problem 11 implies the exact opposite: the survey respondents are risk-seeking. The certain option is apparently less attractive, even though it offers a *higher* expected value.

The results show that some respondents were both risk-averse and risk-seeking. Specifically, respondents were *risk-averse* when presented with the chance to win money, but *risk-seeking* when given the chance to avoid losses. This tendency is known as **loss aversion**.

Definition   23.3

Loss aversion: a tendency for people to be risk-averse with respect to gains and risk-seeking with respect to losses, and to value the same quantity of income more when it is framed as a loss than as a gain.

Loss aversion can also be viewed graphically. Figure 23.2 shows utility–income functions whose shape would be consistent with the majority preferences in Problems 10 and 11. For the positive prospects offered in Problem 10, the utility from the certain \$3,000 is greater than the expected utility from the gamble. In other words, $U(3,000) > 0.8U(4,000) + 0.2U(0)$. The utility curve in Figure 23.2(a) is *concave*, which reflects risk aversion.

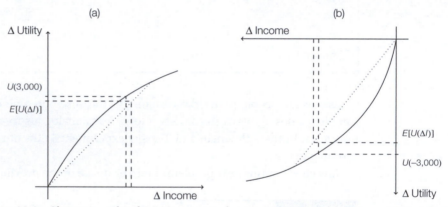

Figure 23.2. *Change in utility from increases or decreases in income. (a) Concave utility-income curve that shows risk-aversion for prospective gains. (b) Convex utility-income curve that shows risk-seeking for prospective losses.*

By contrast, the majority choice in Problem 11 implies that the utility from a certain loss of \$3,000 is lower than the expected utility loss from a gamble with a 80% chance of losing \$4,000. That is, $U(-3,000) < 0.8U(-4,000) + 0.2U(0)$. Reflecting this risk-seeking behavior, the utility curve in Figure 23.2(b) for prospective losses is *convex*.

The curves in both domains also reflect diminishing returns. That is, the perceived difference between a gain of \$100 and a gain of \$200 is much greater than the perceived difference between \$1,100 and \$1,200. Similarly, the loss of \$200 compared to the loss of \$100 feels much worse than the difference between losing \$1,200 over \$1,100.

Figure 23.3 combines the earlier two graphs and shows the effect on utility by both positive and negative changes in income. Its concavity in the positive domain reflects risk-aversion, and its convexity over the negative domain reflects risk-seeking.

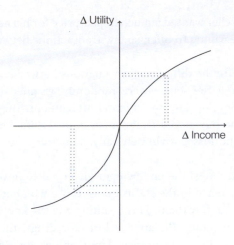

Figure 23.3. *Effect of losses and gains in income on utility.*

The endowment effect

The *S*-shaped utility curve in Figure 23.3 is steeper for losses than for gains. This is another byproduct of loss aversion: people value losses more than equally sized gains. That is, the declining utility from losing a dollar seems to be greater than the increase in utility from gaining a dollar. Researchers have labeled this the **endowment effect**.

Definition	23.4

Endowment effect: the tendency of people to attach greater value to a loss of a given amount than to an equivalent gain.

According to research done by Kahneman et al. (1990), a mug's value lies very much in the eye of its beholder. Credit ImageSource.

A set of famous experiments done by Richard Thaler at Cornell University and Simon Fraser University illustrates the endowment effect. In a simulated market, experiment participants were randomly assigned the role of either a seller or a buyer – half of the participants were assigned to each role. The sellers were all given identical mugs, while the buyers received nothing. Sellers then selected the lowest price at which they would be willing to sell and buyers reported the highest price they would be willing to buy. Presumably the mugs would all end up in the hands of the participants that valued them the most at the outset of the study. Because the roles were randomly assigned, the prediction of expected utility theory was that half the mugs should be traded.

Yet the experiment results showed that the median prices commanded by sellers in each trial were over double the amount that the median buyer was willing to pay. As a result, only 10% of the mugs were actually bought and sold, far less than the approximately 50% predicted by expected utility theory. The same experimental design was repeated with boxes of ballpoint pens with their original price tags still attached, resulting in the same effect. The median seller wanted a much higher price for his newly given commodity than median buyers were willing to offer, so few transactions between buyers and sellers occurred.

The researchers attribute the difference in valuations between seller and buyer to the endowment effect. Though the sellers were randomly assigned to receive their mugs and had no chance to develop any sentimental attachment, they nevertheless valued the objects more than the buyers did (Kahneman et al. 1990). This is further evidence that people treat gains and losses asymmetrically, something not accounted for within expected utility theory.

In the experiment with mugs, the endowment effect led to fewer trades being made, which also caused a persistence in the status quo – those who had mugs kept them and those not given mugs did not buy them. This resulting effect – known as *status quo bias* – appears in many places including the approval of new drugs, the outcome of political elections, and the offering of health insurance plans (Tetlock and Boettger 1994; Kay et al. 2009).

Johnson et al. (1993), for instance, find status quo bias in the health insurance choices of nearly 10,000 Harvard employees during the 1980s. In 1980, the university offered its employees a choice between four different plans; three additional plans were added between 1982 and 1985. A large number of employees did switch when the new plans were introduced, but the researchers find that newly hired employees were ten times more likely to select one of the new plans than comparable employees who were already subscribed to one before 1982. In other words, employees who had selected their plan before 1980 were significantly more likely to be on one of the older plans than new employees were. Since switching costs were negligible, the differential rates of enrollment are evidence of status quo bias.

The importance of reference points

A person who is risk-averse when his assets are positive but risk-seeking when his assets are negative might very well still be "rational." The expected utility theory makes no explicit assumption that people have a consistent risk appetite. But it does assume that a person's utility function does not change shape depending on their circumstances. Consequently, *reference points* are necessary to discuss utility, and when reference points differ, utility evaluations of the same outcomes may also differ (Tversky and Kahneman 1991).

It is easiest to see the importance of reference points in the context of an example. Winter et al. (2003) surveyed elderly people in Philadelphia retirement homes about how long they would want to live if they were physically disabled or cognitively impaired. Frailer individuals reported being more willing to live in poor health circumstances than the healthier elderly did.

This finding is consistent with the predictions of loss aversion and particularly the diminishing returns of health changes. Though the healthy and the frail were evaluating the same hypothetical health conditions, the healthy perceived those conditions as only slightly better than death and therefore expressed less desire to live in those conditions. Conversely, the frail viewed the hypothetical conditions as much better than death.

Figure 23.4 presents a model of loss aversion which can explain the survey results. Person *A*, who is in good health, thinks that the hypothetical level of low health *P* offered

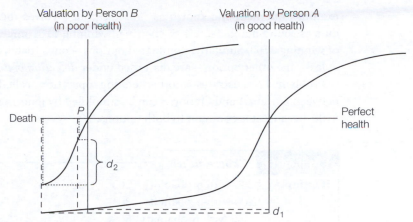

Figure 23.4. *Different evaluations of utility due to different reference points.*

Source: Winter and Parker (2007). Copyright (2007), Figure 2 reprinted with permission from Elsevier.

in the survey gives only d_1 more utility than death. Person B, who starts with a reference point of poorer health, views health level P as d_2 units of utility better than death. Since $d_2 > d_1$, sick people perceive the same medical condition as being a better state than healthy people do.

The importance of reference points in calculating utility under loss aversion has implications for cost-effectiveness analysis. Healthy people with a high reference point may see a treatment as providing very little utility, while someone sick, with a lower reference point, may greatly value that same treatment. Thus, analyzing the benefits of a treatment may depend greatly on which reference point is used (Treadwell and Lenert 1999).

23.5   A formal introduction to prospect theory

Kahneman and Tversky (1979) developed a theory to describe choices under uncertainty that resolves the inconsistencies described above. Their theory, known as *prospect theory*, combines elements of psychology and economics, and relaxes the assumptions that rational preferences are always complete, transitive, and independent. Once those restrictions are relaxed, they can create a more flexible theory capable of explaining the patterns of decision-making we have seen in this chapter.

According to prospect theory, people are boundedly rational; they simplify the problems they face and rely on rules of thumb to evaluate uncertain outcomes. Prospect theory models decision-making under uncertainty in two stages. The first stage, called the *editing stage*, shows how people perceive and organize uncertain options to simplify the decision process. The second stage, or the *evaluation stage*, is where these edited options are assessed against each other and the highest-value prospect is selected. Together, this model accounts for the complexity of uncertainty, the asymmetry of gains and losses, and proclivities to either underweight or overweight particular probabilities.

The editing stage

Prospect theory suggests that, when confronted with a choice of lotteries, people have rules of thumb known as *heuristics* that reduce the complexity of their choice. For example, one heuristic known as *simplification* involves recasting probabilities or pay-outs as round numbers. A 49% chance of winning $101 might be recast as a 50% chance of winning $100. Similarly, dominated options – ones that are unambiguously inferior to at least one other option – are discarded under *detection of dominance*.

Problem 12 illustrates another editing operation called *cancellation*. The choice between Option *A* and Option *B* can be simplified by ignoring the 30% chance of winning $100, because it is common to both options.

Problem 12	*Choose either*		
Option A:	$200 with probability 20%	**Option B:**	$150 with probability 30%
	~~$100 with probability 30%~~		~~$100 with probability 30%~~
	−$50 with probability 50%		−$50 with probability 40%

In addition to canceling common possibilities, people may also *combine* probabilities when a lottery has multiple events with similar payouts. For example, an option that offers a 25% chance of winning $197 and a 15% chance of winning $202 would be combined into a 40% chance of winning $200.

Prospect theory also predicts that people try to separate risky and riskless components. A bet with a 75% chance of winning $150 and 25% chance of winning $200 can be recast as a certain gain of $150 and a 25% chance to win an additional $50. This editing operation is called *segregation*.

Lastly, loss aversion means that individuals consider losses and gains asymmetrically. The selection of a reference point occurs during the editing stage, and outcomes are then *coded* as either potential gains or losses. A final income of $100,000 is coded as a loss for a millionaire but a gain for a pauper.

Table 23.2 summarizes the operations done during the editing stage. While these editing operations may appear straightforward, they make sense of some of the seemingly contradictory findings in Kahneman and Tversky (1979). Recall Problems 6 and 7, which illustrated the effect of framing (they are reproduced in Table 23.3). Although the final states of the two problems were identical, the survey–takers responded to the problems differently. Because the initial allocations are shared across both options of the individual problems, the respondents ignored them through cancellation and focused on the subsequent payoffs. Consequently, the outcomes in Problem 6 were coded as gains and the outcomes in Problem 7 as losses. The discrepancy in responses can be explained by editing.

Thus, the editing stage is the culprit behind some of the observed inconsistencies with expected utility theory. Even the seemingly minor operation of simplification can produce violations of the transitivity of preferences when different options offer similar enough probabilities and payoffs (Tversky 1969). Moreover, when multiple editing operations over a set of outcomes are possible, the order of operations may vary depending on the person and depending on how the problem is framed. Different sequences of operations may generate preferences that are not complete, transitive, or independent. The editing stage reduces the complexity of the decision-making process, but because it substitutes a more tractable problem for the original one, it may fundamentally alter the problem and lead to a different choice.

Table 23.2. *Summary of operations conducted during the editing stage, developed from Kahneman and Tversky (1979).*

Operation	Description	
Simplification	Probabilities and outcomes are rounded.	A 49% chance of winning $101 might be recast as a 50% chance of winning $100.
Detection of dominance	Clearly inferior options are eliminated.	If Option A and Option B share the same probabilities but Option B offers strictly higher payouts for each event, then Option A will be eliminated.
Cancellation	Common events in different options are canceled.	If both Option A and Option B offer a 30% chance of winning $100, then the effect of that outcome is ignored when comparing the two options.
Combination	Common outcomes in the same option are combined.	If an option offers 25% chance of winning $200 and a 15% chance of winning $200, then those will be combined into a 40% chance of winning $200.
Segregation	Risky and riskless components of an option are separated.	An option offering a 75% chance of winning $150 and a 25% chance of winning $200 will be recast as a riskless gain of $150 and a 25% of winning $50.
Coding	Potential outcomes are perceived as gains or losses depending on what reference point is chosen.	A final income of $100,000 is coded as a loss for the rich but a gain for the poor.

Table 23.3. *An example of cancellation and coding during the editing stage.*

Problem 6		Problem 7	
You have just received $1,000. Choose either		You have just received $2,000. Choose either	
Option A	Option B	Option C	Option D
$1,000 more, $p = 0.50$ $0 more, $p = 0.50$ *or* $500 more, $p = 1$		$1,000 less, $p = 0.50$ $0 more, $p = 0.50$ *or* $500 less, $p = 1$	
84% prefer Option B		69% prefer Option C	

Source: Kahneman and Tversky (1979). With permission of the Econometric Society.

The evaluation stage

At the end of the editing stage, the original set of outcomes has been reduced to a simpler formulation. For example, an original set of outcomes $x_1, x_2, \cdots, x_n$ and corresponding probabilities $p_1, p_2, \cdots, p_n$ may be simplified to a smaller set of outcomes $y_1, y_2, \cdots, y_m$ and probabilities $q_1, q_2, \cdots, q_m$, where $m < n$ due to combinations or cancellations. During the evaluation stage, this smaller set of outcomes is evaluated and compared against other options.

Like expected utility theory, the valuation function under prospect theory is a weighted sum of the values of each possible outcome (equation (23.8)).

Valuation function under prospect theory

For a lottery A with a set of edited probabilities q_i and payoffs y_i, $i = 1 \ldots m$, the valuation function is

$$V(A) = V(q_1, y_1; q_2, y_2; \cdots ; q_m, y_m)$$
$$= \theta(q_1)v(y_1) + \theta(q_2)v(y_2) + \cdots + \theta(q_m)v(y_m)$$

(23.8)

where $\theta(q_i)$ is the *weighting function* and $v(y_i)$ is the *value function*.

Prospect theory's valuation function is exactly analogous to the valuation function under expected utility theory in equation (23.2). $\theta(q_i)$ is the analog of probability p_i, and $v(y_i)$ is the analog of $u(x_i)$ and represents the utility from the edited payoff y_i. But as we discuss next, there are crucial differences between the analogous concepts that underscore the differences between expected utility theory and prospect theory.

Evaluation: the value function

The fundamental difference between prospect theory's value function $v(\cdot)$ and the traditional utility function $u(\cdot)$ is that the utility function evaluates absolute income (or other final states), while the value function is calculated relative to a reference point. Prospect theory's value function evaluates *changes* in income, health, or number of mugs, rather than the absolute level of these states.

This means that the value function can account for the effect of reference points that code different outcomes as either gains or losses. While a utility function would always assign a fixed level of utility to a net income of $10,000, a value function treats that final state differently depending on whether it represents an upgrade from $9,000 or a demotion from $11,000.

Therefore, value functions are able to model loss aversion, the tendency for people to be more affected by losses than gains. This means the absolute value of $v(-x)$ is greater than $v(x)$. Value functions can also reflect that people tend to be risk-averse over prospective gains and risk-seeking over prospective losses.

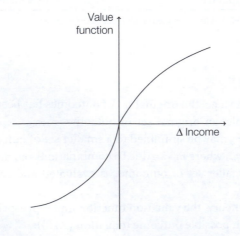

Figure 23.5. *A hypothetical value function for changes in income.*

Figure 23.5 shows one possible value function. It is a reproduction of Figure 23.3 from our discussion on loss aversion. This hypothetical value function is:

- steeper over losses than over gains – people weight losses more heavily than gains;
- concave in the positive domain – people tend to be risk-averse over prospective gains;
- convex in the negative domain – people tend to be risk-seeking over potential losses.

Evaluation: the weighting function

In expected utility theory, the utility of each outcome $u(x)$ is weighted by its probability p. In prospect theory, the value of each edited outcome $v(y)$ is weighted by its decision weight $\theta(q)$. Like probabilities, these decision weights affect how much each outcome is considered. When an outcome is impossible and its probability is zero, then that outcome should not influence the decision at all, so the decision weight of impossible events is also zero, $\theta(0) = 0$. Similarly, the decision weight of a certain event is normalized to one, $\theta(1) = 1$.

Despite this agreement at the extremes, decision weights usually diverge with their associated probabilities and are not beholden to the same rules. For example, the sum of all decision weights do not always add up to one. In fact, they often sum to less than one; that is, $\theta(p) + \theta(1 - p) < 1$. This property, known as *subcertainty*, is related to the certainty effect (Tversky and Fox 1995).

Recall Problems 1 and 2 from our discussion of the certainty effect. Their outcomes and probabilities are reproduced in Table 23.4.

Table 23.4. *Problem 1 and Problem 2 illustrating the certainty effect.*

Problem 1		Problem 2	
Option A	Option B	Option C	Option D
$2,500 with $p = 0.33$		$2,500 with $p = 0.33$	$2,400 with $p = 0.34$
$2,400 with $p = 0.66$ *or* $2,400 with $p = 1$		$0 with $p = 0.67$ *or*	$0 with $p = 0.66$
$0 with $p = 0.01$			
82% prefer Option B		83% prefer Option C	

Source: Kahneman and Tversky (1979). With permission of the Econometric Society.

Most people preferred Option B to Option A and also Option C to Option D. We analyze these revealed preferences with prospect theory's valuation function from equation (23.8). Recall that $v(0) = 0$ and $\theta(1) = 1$.

Problem 1

$$V(\mathbf{B}) > V(\mathbf{A})$$

$$\theta(1)v(2,400) > \theta(0.33)v(2,500) + \theta(0.66)v(2,400) + \theta(0.01)v(0)$$

$$\theta(1)v(2,400) - \theta(0.66)v(2,400) > \theta(0.33)v(2,500)$$

$$[1 - \theta(0.66)]\,v(2,400) > \theta(0.33)v(2,500)$$

Problem 2

$$V(\mathbf{C}) > V(\mathbf{D})$$

$$\theta(0.33)v(2{,}500) + \theta(0.67)v(0) > \theta(0.34)v(2{,}400) + \theta(0.66)v(0)$$

$$\theta(0.33)v(2{,}500) > \theta(0.34)v(2{,}400)$$

Combining the derived inequalities from Problem 1 and Problem 2, we find that:

$$\theta(0.34)v(2{,}400) < \theta(0.33)v(2{,}500) < \left[1 - \theta(0.66)\right]v(2{,}400)$$

Then we focus on the first and third terms in the resulting inequality:

$$\theta(0.34)v(2{,}400) < \left[1 - \theta(0.66)\right]v(2{,}400)$$

$$\theta(0.34) < 1 - \theta(0.66) \tag{23.9}$$

$$\theta(0.34) + \theta(0.66) < 1$$

The last line in equation (23.9) shows that at least a portion of respondents in Problem 1 and Problem 2 exhibit subcertainty. Subcertainty also explains the certainty effect: a guaranteed outcome is weighted more than the summed weights of complimentary outcomes, $\theta(1) > \theta(p) + \theta(1 - p)$. This is a generalization of equation (23.9) and the fact that $\theta(1) = 1$. Hence, subcertainty implies that certain events are valued more than merely probable ones, even more than risk-aversion alone would suggest.

Figure 23.6 shows a hypothetical weighting function under prospect theory. Subcertainty is illustrated by the fact that $\theta(p)$ lies below the 45° line for most probabilities. Hence, $\theta(p) < p$, and if $p_1 + p_2 + p_3 = 1$, then $\theta(p_1) + \theta(p_2) + \theta(p_3) < 1$ for most sets of probabilities.

The hypothetical weighting function $\theta(p)$ is misbehaved at the endpoints. Once an event is guaranteed, its decision weight is 1, but where even the smallest iota of doubt exists, people attach a much lower decision weight. This causes the weighting function to jump at $p = 1$. This is again a manifestation of the certainty effect.

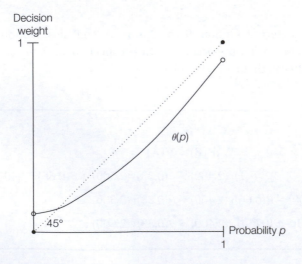

Figure 23.6. *A hypothetical weighting function.*

Kahneman and Tversky's studies also showed that people misperceive very low probabilities, which is why $\theta(p)$ is also misbehaved near $p = 0$. When an event is impossible, it is ignored: $\theta(0) = 0$. But if a sliver of possibility remains, people overweight it compared to its actual probability: $\theta(p) > p$ for very low p. Recall Problem 5.

Problem 5	*Choose either*	
Option A: $5,000 with probability 0.1%	**Option B:** $5 with probability 100%	
$0 with probability 99.9%		
Chosen by 72%	28%	

Using prospect theory's valuation function, the majority decision in Problem 5 reveals

$$V(\mathbf{A}) > V(\mathbf{B})$$

$$\theta(0.001)\upsilon(5,000) + \theta(0.999)\upsilon(0) > \theta(1)\upsilon(5)$$

$$\theta(0.001)\upsilon(5,000) > \upsilon(5) \tag{23.10}$$

$$\theta(0.001) > \frac{\upsilon(5)}{\upsilon(5,000)}$$

Like risk-averse utility functions $U(I)$, the value function $v(x)$ is concave over income. So the first five dollars is worth more than each subsequent five dollars. In other words, the winnings have diminishing marginal returns. This also means that $v(5)/v(5,000) > 0.001$:

$$\theta(0.001) > 0.001 \tag{23.11}$$

Equation (23.11) corroborates the overweighting of very low probabilities shown in Figure 23.6. In this experiment, the probability of winning the lottery is given, so equation (23.11) is *not* evidence of overestimating the probability of winning the lottery. The comparatively higher decision weight arises from overweighting and not overestimation.

Even a survey taker who understands probability theory perfectly and knows the true probabilities still might overweight small probabilities according to prospect theory. In circumstances where the true probability of a rare event is not known, overestimation and overweighting might both occur to inflate the impact of one very unlikely prospect on a person's decision.

23.6   Implications for health economics

The pervasiveness of uncertainty in health makes the findings of Kahneman and Tversky particularly relevant for health economics. Prospect theory prompts us to revisit to some of our conclusions from earlier in this book.

Demand for health insurance

Marquis and Holmer (1996), using data from the RAND HIE, find that prospect theory is better than expected utility theory at describing people's demand for health insurance. At the end of the RAND HIE, participants answered hypothetical questions about their demand for insurance plans now that their experiment-sponsored plans were ending. According to expected utility theory, families with similar incomes and risk of illness would demand similar levels of insurance, regardless of what type of coverage they had during the experiment. However, Marquis and Holmer find that families who were assigned to have less insurance coverage during the experiment were willing to pay much less than families with broader insurance coverage for a new insurance plan after the experiment. The authors argue that this is evidence of consumers treating gains and losses asymmetrically. Those people who were *losing* insurance coverage when the RAND HIE came to an end were much more willing to spend money to maintain it.

This finding also shows evidence of status quo bias. Consumers seem to disproportionately prefer their previous position, even in cases like the RAND HIE, where the previous position was randomly assigned. This has implications for the theory of adverse selection, because it suggests that consumers will not always switch to new plans even if they offer better value in expected utility terms. In fact, Hanoch and Rice (2006) go further to argue that bounded rationality means that having more health insurance choices available can actually harm welfare. They argue that a greater variety of health care options for US Medicare enrollees, far from enabling the elderly to choose more personalized plans, may contribute confusion and cause suboptimal decision-making.

Lotteries can help motivate boundedly rational dieters to lose weight, according to research by Volpp et al. (2008). Credit: © Vladislav Gajic – Fotolia.com.

Interventions and nudges

Prospect theory also suggests that small interventions or "nudges" can have outsize effects. For example, the status quo effect implies that merely adjusting a consumer's initial insurance coverage can have lasting impacts. An insurer that by default enrolls all of its members for annual preventative care visits may have a healthier membership than an insurer that gives patients the option to sign up for visits on their own. Middle-school cafeterias could place leafy green vegetables at the beginning of their lunch lines to encourage tweeners to eat healthier diets. Thaler and Sunstein (2008) write about many other "nudges" that may improve health by framing healthy choices as default options.

Such initiatives can also manipulate dieters' aversion to loss. Volpp et al. (2008) propose a health intervention inspired by prospect theory. In their program, each day, dieters are entered into a lottery that has an expected payout of $3 as well as a 1% chance of paying $100. Only participants who reach their weight loss goal for that day receive money from the lottery. Participants who do not reach their goal do not get paid, but still find out how much money they would have won.

The money that would have been won is purposefully framed as a loss, so individuals who do not reach their goals feel galvanized to avoid "losing" out on lottery winnings in the future. Also, unlike more traditional financial incentive programs, this program used uncertain lotteries as motivation for participants. If these dieting candidates overweight small probabilities, then they value the unlikely chance at a very large payout more than they value smaller, certain awards.

Health technology assessment

Recall from Chapter 14 that patients, doctors, insurers, and policymakers frequently want to quantify the benefit of a given medical treatment. Is a procedure that extends life by eight years but leaves patients deaf better than a traditional treatment that extends life by only five years? How about a medicine that alleviates insomnia but leads to narcolepsy in a fraction of cases?

We discussed the use of cost-effectiveness analysis (CEA) to try to answer these questions. Integral to CEA is the estimation of a quality weight q, which indicates the standard of living of a year. A year in ideal health would have a quality weight $q = 1$, whereas a bedridden year clinging to life might have a quality weight much closer to 0. Two commonly used strategies for estimating quality weights of different health states are the standard gamble and the time-tradeoff question.

- **Standard gamble (SG).** The SG approach offers respondents two options: a health state H with certainty, or a gamble between perfect health and death. The gamble allows respondents to achieve perfect health with probability p or death with probability $(1 - p)$. Researchers offer respondents different versions of this gamble with different values for p.
- **Time trade off (TTO).** Like the SG approach, the TTO method asks respondents to choose between two options: either living for t years with a health state H before dying, or living for a shorter amount of time τ in full health and then dying.

When the implications of prospect theory are considered, there are clear weaknesses to both the SG and the TTO method. The SG approach may be biased because people misperceive probabilities. The evidence discussed in this chapter suggests that responses to gambles may be highly responsive to the question framing. If so, slight alterations within the SG approach can yield different quality weight estimates for the same condition.

Secondly, people's loss aversion can affect the reliability of both SG and TTO. Suppose that researchers want to estimate the quality weight associated with a health state H. Then loss aversion means that respondents with health better than H would report a lower-quality weight than respondents with health worse than H. Which estimate is more valid?

In general, SG estimates of quality weights tend to be higher than TTO estimates (Salomon and Murray 2004). Bleichrodt (2002) argues that this difference can be explained by deviations from expected utility theory. If people have the weighting function shown in Figure 23.6 that overweights small probabilities but underweights moderate ones, then SG estimates are likely to be overestimates. On the other hand, loss aversion may bias TTO estimates either upward or downward.

23.7   Conclusion

Standard economic theory is built around the idea of a rational economic agent. The field of behavioral economics has served to broaden what it means to be rational. The data from the work of Kahneman and Tversky is not evidence of irrationality, nor is it evidence of the rationality predicted by traditional expected utility theory. Prospect theory maintains the fundamental assumption that people always act to pursue their best interest. It merely allows that actual rationality can be a bit quirkier than the "strict" rationality of expected utility theory.

Yet these quirks do raise a question about the role of paternalism. If someone is overvaluing certainty or overweighting small probabilities, is it justifiable for a third party (such as the government) to intervene and correct the weighting? Perhaps a paternalistic intervention could be philosophically justifiable and even economically valuable in some circumstances. But, in practice, distinguishing between someone deviating from rationality and someone with unusual but rational preferences may be difficult or impossible to do.

Suppose someone is willing to pay extreme amounts of money to eliminate all risk about food poisoning from her life. She hires taste testers to sample her food for toxins and hires chemists to analyze her tap water hourly. Most people would say she is spending too much money chasing certainty about her food supply. But then again, she could just be extremely fearful of food poisoning. Is this an instance of someone overvaluing certainty or someone "rationally" pursuing her true preferences? And would a law banning taste testers leave the woman better off (by saving her money), or worse off (by preventing her from reducing uncertainty)?

In the next chapter, we consider time inconsistency, patience, and addiction, and find more examples of people behaving in ways that, from a traditional economic point of view, seem irrational. In that context, we will return to the question of what it means for a set of preferences to be valid or invalid.

23.8   Exercises

Comprehension questions

Indicate whether each statement is true or false, and justify your answer. Be sure to cite evidence from the chapter and state any additional assumptions you may need.

1 Individuals who always make decisions consistent with completeness, transitivity, and independence are exhibiting bounded rationality.
2 Loss aversion is the economics of jealousy: people value what they do not have more than what they do have.
3 During prospect theory's editing stage, the operation of segregation always occurs before the operation of simplification.
4 Expected utility theory offers one possible valuation function that satisfies the properties of completeness, transitivity, and independence of preferences under uncertainty.
5 The certainty effect and subcertainty are opposite phenomena.
6 A typical value function is concave due to risk aversion.
7 Whether a prospect is coded as a gain or as a loss can depend on how that prospect is framed.
8 The endowment effect leads to a stronger status quo bias, because trades are more likely to occur.
9 All perceived probabilities are weighted lower than actual probabilities.
10 Risk-averse individuals have a concave value function for prospective gains and a convex value function for prospective losses.

Analytical questions

11 Consider the following macabre example conceived originally by Richard Zeckhauser. You are forced to play a "game" of Russian roulette, but before the game is played, you are allowed to pay to remove one bullet from the six-chamber gun. You have an initial wealth of $60 and each dollar gives you exactly 1 unit of utility if you are alive but no utility if you die (for the sake of this exercise, assume you have no heirs). In other words, your utility function is

$$U(W) = \begin{cases} W & \text{if alive} \\ 0 & \text{if dead} \end{cases}$$

a   Suppose the gun initially carries four bullets. You have the opportunity to reduce the number of bullets from four to three (and therefore, the probability of dying from 4/6 to 3/6) but it costs $30 to do so. What is your expected utility if you pay the $30? What is your expected utility if you elect not to pay?

b   According to expected utility theory, if it costs $30 to reduce the number of bullets from four to three, would you prefer to pay or take your chances with four bullets?

c   Still according to expected utility theory, what is the maximum you would be willing to pay to reduce the number of bullets from four to three? What is the maximum you would be willing to pay to reduce the number of bullets from one to zero (and thereby reduce the probability of dying from 1/6 to 0)?

d   Zeckhauser finds that most people report more willingness to pay to reduce the probability of dying from 1/6 to 0 than to reduce it from 4/6 to 3/6 (Kahneman and Tversky 1979). Interpret this finding in light of what you have learned about prospect theory.

12 Suppose a new and terrifying disease called bhtitis has been created in a mad scientist's laboratory. In a recently released study, medical researchers determined that the average Pcorian adult has a 0.1% chance of catching bhtitis in the coming year. Suppose all Pcorians have the utility function

$$U = \sqrt{I}$$

where $I = \$100$ if the Pcorian is well and $I = \$0$ if the Pcorian catches bhtitis.

a   An old man hears a brief news item about the research study on the radio, and learns he has a 0.1% chance of catching bhtitis this year. What is his expected utility without insurance?

b   The old man is offered an insurance contract that has a premium of $1 but pays out $100 if the man comes down with bhtitis this year. Will he take the contract, according to expected utility theory?

c   The old man's neighbor also hears about the study, but in a slightly different context. He watches a documentary about the creation of bhtitis and its ghastly symptoms. It features interviews with disfigured victims and talks about the specter of new synthetic diseases. At the end of the documentary, the scientists' finding is mentioned. The neighbor is then offered the same contract and accepts it. Explain this discrepancy with expected utility theory using the principles of prospect theory.

d A third man hears the same news report the first man heard, but due to static on the airwaves he mishears the probability as 1%. Will he buy the same insurance contract if he is an expected-utility maximizer? What about if he shares the tendency to overweight small probabilities?

13 Consider Figure 23.7, which depicts a scenario in the Rothschild–Stiglitz model of adverse selection.

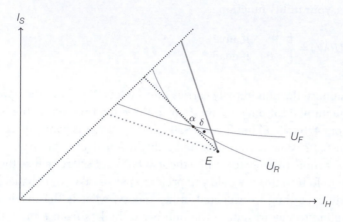

Figure 23.7. *Potential pooling equilibrium α is threatened by contract δ.*

a Explain why α is not a valid pooling equilibrium.

b Explain why your answer to the previous question depends on an assumption that expected utility theory holds.

c Suppose the Pcorian government is trying to maintain α as a pooling equilibrium to ensure universal insurance for its long-suffering populace. The government health minister is familiar with the work of Kahneman and Tversky and wants to take advantage of the fact that Pcorians are loss averse and susceptible to framing. When a private insurance company begins offering contract δ, how should the government frame the tradeoff between α and δ to try to keep robust customers at α?

Essay questions

14 Every year in early January, millions of people resolve to exercise more than they had in the previous year. Inevitably, a substantial portion of people making such a resolution fail to carry through with it in the subsequent weeks and months. One Internet business, stickK.com, aims to help people keep their resolutions by applying behavioral economic precepts.

Customers tell stickK.com their resolution – for example, exercising at least three times a week – and a duration they pledge to adhere to their resolution. They also entrust stickK.com with a money deposit. If the customers meet their resolution, that money is returned. However, if they renege, then a portion goes instead to an *anti*-charity of the customers' choosing. The *anti*-charity is typically an organization that advocates positions opposed by the stickK.com enrollee.

a Identify some of the behavorial economics precepts used in stickK.com.

b Suppose researchers at stickK.com have decided that three months is typically the optimal length for customers – long enough so that fulfilling the resolution becomes a habit and yet not overly long so that customers become exasperated. In unpublished research, Jeremy Goldhaber-Fiebert and Alan Garber show that if stickK.com sets the default contract duration to three months, enrollees tend to gravitate toward three months as their actual contract length.

Is this finding that people pick the suggested contract consistent with prospect theory? Explain why expected utility theory is unable to explain the potential impact of nudges.

c Hence, in practice, the default contract duration, which is set by the people running stickK.com site, can be deliberately used to manipulate the actual choices stickK.com customers make. Is the use of a nudge to alter behavior paternalistic? Does your answer change given that participation in stickK.com is entirely voluntary? Why or why not? [*Hint:* It may be helpful to consider what good or service customers of stickK.com are actually demanding.]

15 At Duke University, tickets for the men's basketball team are highly coveted. The student fans known as the "Cameron Crazies" often camp outside the basketball arena for days leading up to the season's start in hopes of earning the right to buy tickets. Almost every year, the Duke basketball team is invited to play in the NCAA Basketball Tournament, the winner of which is crowned the champion of US college basketball. Tickets for this event are even harder to get. Students who want tickets sign up for a "lottery" and only some are randomly chosen to win the chance of purchasing tickets to the tournament. After the lottery one year, Carmon and Ariely (2000) asked those who won the right to buy a ticket the lowest possible price at which they would be willing to sell their ticket. For those who did not win, the researchers asked the highest possible price they would be willing to pay for a ticket. These results are reproduced in Table 23.5.

Table 23.5. *Selling and buying price for Duke lottery winners and sellers.*

	Median ($)
Selling price (of lottery winners)	1,500
Buying price (of lottery losers)	150

Source: Carmon and Ariely (2000), Focusing on the forgone: how value can appear so different to buyers and sellers, *Journal of Consumer Research*, 27:3, 360-370. With permission from the University of Chicago Press.

a Given the results in Table 23.5, are any of the lottery winners likely to sell their tickets to lottery losers?

b Suppose that the Duke students are answering honestly about their selling and buying prices. Should winning or losing the lottery have any effect on their answers? Why might winning the lottery have such a dramatic effect on the value that students place on the game tickets?

   c   Which aspect of prospect theory is most important in providing an explanation
          for these results?

Students can find answers to the comprehension questions and lecturers can access
an Instructor Manual with guideline answers to the analytical problems and essay
questions at **www.palgrave.com/economics/bht**.

24 TIME INCONSISTENCY AND HEALTH

When he was working as a young graduate student at Stanford in the 1990s, one of the authors would routinely work late at his office and then head home right around midnight. Each night as he walked to his car, he faced a dilemma: which route to take home? His shortest option was El Camino Real, the main arterial route through Palo Alto. With barely any traffic on the roads at that hour, Jay could be home in fifteen minutes if he took that road. Alternatively, he could take Alma Street, a quiet, tree-lined street that would add five or ten minutes to his trip home (Figure 24.1).

The only reason Jay would ever consider taking Alma Street was the presence of a McDonald's on El Camino open late at night. Jay knew that taking El Camino home would tempt him to stop for a snack, and his record on resisting that particular temptation was not great. The appeal of taking Alma was that he would face no such temptation (or, if he did, he would be too far from McDonald's to act upon it).

We can think of Jay's conundrum as a battle between two of Jay's selves. His midnight self, sitting in the parking lot and deciding which route to take home, strongly prefers that Jay not stop for a cheeseburger before heading home and getting to bed. But his 12:15 self always craves a cheeseburger, a side of fries, and a huge Diet Coke, so *that* self strongly prefers that Jay take El Camino so that he can visit McDonald's and not end up stranded on Alma. Behavioral economists would say that Jay exhibited *time-inconsistent preferences* because his various selves had different ideas about the best way for Jay to maximize his utility.

Like prospect theory, the notion of time inconsistency is a major challenge to classical welfare economics, which assumes that all people have consistent, complete, and transitive preferences. If each person actually consists of a multitude of selves with

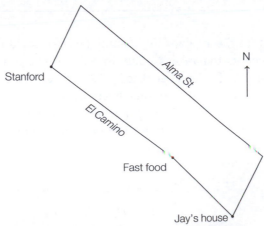

Figure 24.1. *A schematic map of Jay's commute home in Palo Alto, CA.*

vastly different preferences, it is no longer clear how to use revealed preference to infer what policies are optimal. In fact, the possibility that preferences may not be consistent challenges the notion of optimality in economics. Whose utility should be maximized, midnight Jay or 12:15 Jay?

Time inconsistency also raises a whole new set of questions about taxation, commitment devices, and paternalism. Jay's midnight self benefits if he decides to drive down Alma, but his 12:15 self suffers. What is Jay's optimal route? Is that question even well-defined? Is there a different intervention that could benefit all of Jay's selves? And how does this change our thinking about policy responses to uninsurance, addiction, and obesity? This final chapter explores these questions.

24.1   The beta-delta discounting model

Individuals derive utility not only from present joys but also from the anticipation of future happiness. People do not maximize simply their instantaneous utility levels, but instead some function of present and future utility. This is why we pay now for tickets to concerts months in advance, or get flu vaccinations that will not pay off until flu season. To account for this fact, economists model overall utility as a weighted sum of instantaneous utility levels from the present period and all future periods:

$$U_{\text{overall}} = aU_{\text{today}} + bU_{\text{tomorrow}} + cU_{\text{the next day}} + \cdots \tag{24.1}$$

The coefficients a, b, and c are weights that represent the fact that individuals do not necessarily value utility in all periods equally. If they did, we would never observe students procrastinating on homework or workers not saving enough money for retirement. Millennia of human experience confirm that people value utility now more than utility later. In equation (24.1), this translates into $a > b > c$. The vector of weights $\{a, b, c, \dots\}$ is called a **discounting function**.

Definition	**24.1**

Discounting function: a vector of weights that indicates how much an individual values utility in present and future periods.

In theory, one's discounting function could take any shape. Maybe an individual discounts tomorrow's utility by 80% relative to today's, utility the next day by 35%, and utility the day after that by 99%. In general, economists who study time inconsistency assume that discounting functions are monotonically decreasing and reasonably approximated with just two parameters. Equation (24.2) shows a utility function that exhibits *beta-delta discounting*. The original formulation of beta-delta discounting was developed by Phelps and Pollak (1968), and was popularized by economist David Laibson in the 1990s:

$$\begin{aligned} U_{\text{overall}} &= \delta^0 U_{\text{today}} + \beta\delta^1 U_{\text{tomorrow}} + \beta\delta^2 U_{\text{the next day}} + \cdots \\ &= U_{\text{today}} + \beta[\delta U_{\text{tomorrow}} + \delta^2 U_{\text{the next day}} + \cdots] \end{aligned} \tag{24.2}$$

> **Definition** | **24.2**
>
> **Beta-delta discounting** With beta-delta discounting, a discounting function can be specified by two parameters, β and δ, where $0 \leq \beta \leq 1$ and $0 < \delta \leq 1$. Overall utility sums instantaneous utility from period 0 on and is given by
>
> $$U_{overall} = U_0 + \beta[\delta U_1 + \delta^2 U_2 + \cdots]$$
>
> where
>
> - β is the *present bias* parameter that discounts utility in all non-current periods, and
> - δ is the *discount factor* parameter that discounts utility incrementally more in each subsequent period.

The first parameter, delta (δ), should be familiar from our discussions of discounting in the Grossman model, calculations of internal rates of return, and elsewhere. In our model, δ represents the *discount factor* that specifies how much a future period is worth relative to the period before it (δ is assumed to range from 0 to 1 only). The δ term is raised to an incrementally higher power each period, which represents the compound nature of discounting and ensures that the relationship between utility valuation in any two adjacent periods is the same. A δ of 0.95, for example, implies that an amount of utility on a certain day is worth 5% less than the same amount of utility on the previous day. Utility two days from now is worth only $0.95^2 = 90.25\%$ as much as today's utility.

The second parameter, beta (β), adds a twist to the basic discounting scheme we have seen in the Grossman model and elsewhere. As we will see, β captures present bias and creates the sort of time-inconsistent preferences that bedeviled Jay on his commute home. Like δ, β is assumed to range between 0 and 1. The β term is absent from the first term in equation (24.2) but present in all other terms. This means that utility from any future period – any period besides the present – receives an extra devaluation. Alternatively, we could say that utility in the present is especially highly valued, even more highly than it would be based on the discount rate δ alone. This is what is meant by present bias. The closer β is to zero, the more future utility is discounted and the greater the bias toward the present.

24.2   Time-consistent preferences

The traditional way of modeling time preference requires a substantive assumption about the way that people trade off the future and the present. This approach assumes that people are **time-consistent** in their preferences. Imagine a person making a life plan today and then revisiting that plan tomorrow. Time consistency means that tomorrow's self agrees with today's self about the plan. More broadly, this assumption means that all the different selves within a person agree on an overall utility function, and that if a person decides on an optimal long-term plan during one period, future selves agree that the plan is optimal and have no reason to change it (unless new information is uncovered).

> **Definition | 24.3**
>
> **Time-consistent preferences:** preferences shared across all selves, so that future selves will not alter a plan that a previous self found optimal.
>
> Within the beta-delta model, preferences are time-consistent if and only if $\beta = 1$. If $\beta = 1$, the resulting utility function is said to exhibit **exponential discounting** because utility from period t is worth δ^t as much as utility in the current period.

Within the beta-delta discounting model, the only way to achieve time-consistent preferences is to set $\beta = 1$ (we will see a mathematical justification of this statement in Section 24.3). In other words, an assumption of time consistency is equivalent to an assumption that no present bias effect exists. The resulting discounting function is said to be *exponential*:

$$U_{\text{overall}} = U_0 + \delta^1 U_1 + \delta^2 U_2 + \cdots \tag{24.3}$$

The utility function from equation (24.3) should be familiar from our earlier study of discount rates and intertemporal utility. The Grossman model, for instance, assumes that individuals have just these type of preferences, and make decisions about how to spend their time and resources consistent with this utility function. Grossman's agents value the future – not as much as the present, of course – and make decisions or investments that may be painful now, as long as they pay off sufficiently later to justify themselves. A discounting function with higher δ weighs future utility more highly, so higher deltas correspond to more patience and more forward-looking behavior.

The crucial feature of time-consistent preferences is that the relationship between two specific periods is fixed and predictable. Suppose an individual in the Grossman model decides on Monday that he will exercise on Tuesday and eat cookies on Wednesday. He makes this decision based on the tradeoffs inherent in exercising and eating cookies, and he determines that it will be optimal to follow this specific plan. When Tuesday rolls around, he still views the tradeoffs between Tuesday and Wednesday in the exact same way because his preferences are time-consistent. As a result, he agrees with his past self that it is optimal to exercise today (Tuesday) and eat cookies tomorrow. He does not suddenly change his mind and decide to put off exercise and gorge on cookies today. As we will see, this time preference consistency disappears when β falls below 1 and present bias emerges.

Time consistency might seem an unrealistic ideal if it means that plans must never change. What if the gym is unexpectedly crowded on Tuesday and our individual is forced to eat cookies that day instead? Does that mean the individual is no longer time-consistent? We can imagine individuals make not merely simple plans but contingency plans that include instructions under any imaginable circumstance. As long as past and present self agree on the best course in a given circumstance, an individual's preferences are time-consistent.

Nor is time consistency imperiled by the frequent phenomenon of preferences naturally changing over time. Consider a formerly avid tennis player who is aging and is no longer agile enough to play a good game. In his old age he may prefer bocce ball to tennis, but that does not mean his preferences are time-inconsistent, at least not in the sense we mean in this chapter. In this example, both the younger and older selves agree that utility is maximized if the younger self plays tennis and the older self plays bocce ball. With truly time-inconsistent preferences, two selves would disagree about what a specific self should do.

Rational addiction

An optimal puff? According to a study that compared survey responses to mortality data, heavy smokers overestimate their own likelihood of surviving to age 75, while light smokers tend to be slightly too pessimistic about their chances of surviving to that age (Schoenbaum 1997). Credit: PhotoDisc/Getty Images.

So far, our discussion of time-consistent preferences has not considered the potential complication of addictive goods. Addictive goods, by their very nature, change the utility functions of addicts. Each cigarette an individual smokes today increases her demand for cigarettes tomorrow. This could undermine even the optimal plans of time-consistent individuals. Suppose a smoker allows herself one last puff Monday before implementing her plan to quit Tuesday. When Tuesday rolls around this time, her addiction has worsened due to Monday's puff; will her Tuesday self still be on board with the plan to quit?

According to Becker and Murphy (1988), as long as we assume that addicts are fully aware of the addictive nature of their favorite goods, addiction does not create time inconsistency. A fully rational, time-consistent nicotine addict picks the level of smoking in each period to maximize her overall utility. She knows that smoking a cigarette now creates dependency leading to more cigarettes smoked tomorrow and the possibility of serious future health problems. She balances those costs against the upfront utility she enjoys from a cigarette now. If a rational addict pledges to quit tomorrow, then tomorrow she will quit; the plan to quit would not have been made if it had not been optimal from the perspective of all selves, present and future.

Some researchers have used a subtle econometric test to determine if consumption patterns over time fit the Becker–Murphy rational addiction model. Bentzen et al. (1999) find that the consumption of alcohol in Scandinavian countries is in line with time-consistent preferences. Interestingly, there was stronger evidence for rational addiction in countries where strong alcoholic beverages account for higher proportions of total alcohol consumption. Luo et al. (2003) also reject the hypothesis of time-inconsistent consumption with regard to cigarette consumption in Japan.

It is true that the assumptions underlying rational addiction are quite strong: addicts must have time-consistent preferences, and they must be able to anticipate perfectly the costs and benefits of each cigarette they smoke. Whether these assumptions are valid are unresolved empirical issues – for example, Schoenbaum (1997) and Sloan et al. (2003) come to different conclusions about how good smokers are at foreseeing the health consequences of their habit. Nevertheless, Becker and Murphy show that addiction is not inherently irrational.

24.3   Time-inconsistent preferences: myopia and hot brains

Time-consistent preferences are easy to model mathematically, congruent with long-standing economic theory, and philosophically simple. Time-consistent preferences mean the individual is readily modeled as an integrated person with a single utility function whose plans for the future do not gyrate endlessly as different selves take over and exert their idiosyncratic wills.

But a body of evidence from psychological, biological, and economic experiments suggests that in many domains humans and other animals do not exhibit time-consistent preferences (Ainslie 2010). Instead, this evidence suggests that humans use something approximating **hyperbolic discounting**, which features steep discounting of utility in the near future and flatter discounting of utility in the far future. Someone with hyperbolically discounted preferences is **time-inconsistent**: as different selves take over, they will deviate from plans that previous selves deemed optimal.

Definition | **24.4**

Time-inconsistent preferences: preferences such that future selves will sometimes alter a plan that a previous self found optimal. These preferences are also called **myopic**.

Within the beta-delta model, a utility function is time-inconsistent if and only if $\beta < 1$. The resulting utility function is said to exhibit **hyperbolic discounting**.

The beta-delta discounting model provides a tractable way to model these preferences through the present bias parameter β. Because present bias features so prominently in this theory, these preferences are also called **myopic preferences**, after the medical term for nearsightedness. Equation (24.4) displays a hypothetical individual's utility functions and demonstrates how hyperbolic discounting and present bias lead to time-inconsistency:

$$U_{\text{overall}} \text{ in January} = U_{\text{Jan}} + \beta\delta U_{\text{Feb}} + \beta\delta^2 U_{\text{Mar}} + \cdots$$

$$U_{\text{overall}} \text{ in February} = U_{\text{Feb}} + \beta\delta U_{\text{Mar}} + \beta\delta^2 U_{\text{Apr}} + \cdots \qquad (24.4)$$

$$U_{\text{overall}} \text{ in March} = U_{\text{Mar}} + \beta\delta U_{\text{Apr}} + \beta\delta^2 U_{\text{May}} + \cdots$$

It is crucial to recognize that "U_{overall} in January" and "U_{Jan}" are *not* the same thing. The former represents a person's overall utility function that she tries to maximize during January. The latter represents the total utility derived from January, which is only one of many inputs into U_{overall}.

This individual's time-inconsistent preferences can be seen most clearly by comparing how she feels about U_{Feb} and U_{Mar} in January, and how she feels about the same two quantities in February. In January, she discounts February utility by a factor of $\beta\delta$ and discounts March utility by $\beta\delta^2$. In other words, her January self anticipates that her February self will value March utility only $(1 - \delta)$ less than February's utility. If a certain action (like quitting her job and partying all February) will give her some utility in February but cause much suffering in March, her January self will plan not to engage in such bacchanalia.

But what happens to her thinking when the calendar turns to February? Now, she does not discount February utility at all but discounts March utility by a factor of $\beta\delta$. In January, she thought the relative discounting between February and March would be δ, but when February arrives it is actually a steeper discount: $\beta\delta$. If β is significantly less than 1, she has undergone a major change of heart. In January, she thought February's utility was only slightly more valuable than March's, but now she thinks February's is much more valuable. This could change her thinking about whether an unemployed alcoholic binge in February is worth the future pain, because the March costs are now heavily discounted compared to the February benefits. Despite her January plan and despite the reckoning she will face in March, she quits her job in February and celebrates all month.

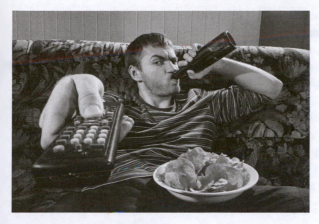

Think of this same discrepancy in terms of Jay's commute home. Jay's midnight self values utility at 12:15am and utility at 12:30am about equally. He knows a cheeseburger will feel good at 12:15 but he will regret it mightily at 12:30. Weighing similarly both the costs and benefits, the midnight Jay does not think a cheeseburger is worth consuming. But as he drives past McDonald's at 12:15, suddenly he values utility from the present much more than his utility at 12:30 – the present bias kicks in. His tradeoff changes and so does his decision: from his 12:15 self's perspective, ordering a cheeseburger is optimal.

This is the essence of time-inconsistent preferences: the different selves within a person do not see eye to eye about the relative valuation of utility in different periods. This is why myopic preferences can lead to behavior that appears pathological or self-destructive. Consider a hyperbolic discounter addicted to smoking. To him, it always seems to make sense to start the grueling process of quitting cigarettes in the *next* period. But when that next period arrives, present bias interferes and suddenly the period after seems like the best time to quit instead.

The notion that a single person does not really have a single utility function has troubling implications for welfare economics and its revealed-preference approach. Welfare economics presupposes that any voluntary action must improve an individual's utility, and that we can draw inferences about an individual's preferences from her actions. A hyperbolic discounter upends this logic, not necessarily because she takes actions that harm her utility, but because her

A tale of two δ's? A short-sighted couch potato pictured alongside forward-looking gym-goers. Credit: © Nomad_Soul – Fotolia.com; Photostock.

utility function is no longer a well-defined or coherent entity; instead, each of her selves has its own utility function. In Section 24.5, we explore the ways that economists have refined their analysis of welfare to accommodate time-inconsistent preferences.

Evidence for time-inconsistent preferences

One way that researchers determine whether discount functions are hyperbolic is by asking survey participants to compare different offers of money. They ask participants to rank payments at different time points, like $1 now versus $2 tomorrow. From the survey responses, researchers can impute discount rates across various time horizons.

This technique was pioneered by Thaler (1981), who found that discount rates varied wildly in both the short term and the long term. Students at the University of Oregon were offered a hypothetical $15 prize on the spot, and were then asked how much would have to be offered so that the participant would agree to delay the prize for a month, a year, or for ten years. The median respondent was indifferent between the original prize immediately and $20 in one month, $50 in one year, or $100 in ten years.

Let us assume the median participant in this study is a beta-delta discounter with exponential preferences. Indifference between $15 now and $20 in a month implies a massive discount rate of 98% per year ($\delta = 0.024$). An exponential discounter who truly was this impatient would also be indifferent between $15 now and approximately $1.47 quadrillion in ten years. And yet the survey participants claimed they were willing to defer the prize ten years for the relatively modest sum of $100. This response implies a more conventional discount rate of 15% per year ($\delta = 0.85$). The wide discrepancy between discount rates for near-future payments and far-future payments suggests that the preferences of the students in this study cannot be described with exponential discounting.

Frederick et al. (2002) analyze over a dozen such studies and calculate the annual discount rate δ implied by the results of each study. They find that the discount rates of participants tend to increase as the time horizon increases (see Figure 24.2). That is, people seem more patient when considering far-future decisions than when considering tradeoffs between the present and the immediate future. This pattern is consistent with the results from Thaler (1981), and seems to contradict the idea of exponential discounting, which would imply that annual discount rates should not increase with the time horizon.

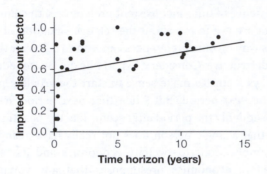

Figure 24.2. *Imputed annual discount rates (δ) from several time-discounting studies.*

Source: Frederick et al. (2002). With permission of the American Economic Association.

Another indication of non-exponential discounting is that people provide inconsistent answers when considering whether to delay a payment. People may prefer $10 today to $11 tomorrow, but simultaneously prefer $11 in 31 days to $10 in 30 days. An individual with an exponential discounting function should answer both questions the same way – at issue is whether it is worth a day's wait to get an extra dollar – but an individual with time-inconsistent preferences (and specifically with a bias for present utility) might be expected to answer the two questions differently. Studies of humans indicate that most respondents do in fact have inconsistent answers to this pair of questions (Green et al. 1994).

These and other studies indicate that exponential discounting is a bad approximation of the way that actual people think about, and act upon, time preference in many domains. Some economists such as Gruber and Kőszegi (2004) state unequivocally: "there is no evidence, psychological or other, that supports time consistent preferences over these time-inconsistent ones in any domain."

One critique of this argument is that people may have non-exponential discounting functions that are nonetheless time-consistent. We have shown that exponential discounting is the only way to achieve time consistency within the beta-delta model, but in theory a discounting function could take any shape, even one that does not fit into the beta-delta framework. As long as selves in future time periods do not overrule the plans of present selves, any discounting function can be time-consistent. Thus, all of the data from the studies above could be explained by non-exponential yet time-consistent preferences. Furthermore, there are many domains of decision-making that have not been studied in the same way, and people making those types of decisions may be time-consistent and even exponential discounters.

Given all the evidence cited in this section, the simplest explanation is that people are time-inconsistent in their decision-making in many domains, and in particular display a bias toward present utility. This does not necessarily mean that individuals have precisely hyperbolic discount rates either, but it does mean that the beta-delta model of discounting with a present bias factor is better than exponential discounting at modeling people's intertemporal preferences.

The hot brain/cold brain model

Bernheim and Rangel (2004) propose an alternate model of time-inconsistent preferences that does not rely on hyperbolic discounting but instead explicitly adopts the view that multiple selves – colloquially, a "hot brain" and a "cold brain" – operate within a single person at the same time. In their model, the cold brain understands the individual's true utility function and always acts rationally to maximize it. The hot brain only appears momentarily in rare circumstances, injecting its own perverse goals and perhaps interfering with the cold brain's plans. Even if the hot brain is only briefly in control, it can have a detrimental impact on the individual's happiness.

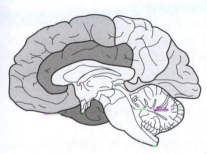

To justify their model, Bernheim and Rangel cite neurological research that suggests addictive goods can effectively hijack a part of the brain called the mesolimbic dopamine system (MDS). Research shows that after repeated exposure to a pleasurable addictive good, the MDS will fire wildly in anticipation of immediate consumption whenever the brain is presented with a cue associated with that good. For laboratory rats, this cue might be a buzzer that always sounds before food is released into a cage. For an addicted smoker, that cue might be another person's burning cigarette.

The rivalry between the hot brain and cold brain in Bernheim and Rangel (2004) is based on the neural relationship between the limbic system and the frontal cortex in the human brain. Neuroeconomics is a nascent field seeking to understand the biology of the utility-maximization process.

Although the MDS's role in decision-making is not understood completely, research suggests that these cues can cause the MDS to fire intensely and overwhelm neuronal signals from the frontal cortex, the area of the brain responsible for impulse control and long-view thinking. With the frontal cortex effectively shut out of the decision-making process, an individual's hot brain takes over and makes short-sighted decisions. Once activity in the MDS subsides and the "hot-brain" moment passes, the cold brain regains control and reinstates the individual's true utility function. But in the short time that the hot brain was in control, the individual may have taken actions leading to irreparable damage. The resulting damage is of little concern to the hot brain, which is mostly (or exclusively) interested in present utility but reduces the utility of the individual in the cold-brain state.

This model seems like an appropriate way to model Jay's commute dilemma as well. If the smell of fries cooking at McDonald's is a cue for Jay's hot brain, that explains why he will stop for a cheeseburger even though his cold brain knew it was a bad idea when he was deciding how to go home. In this case, Jay in his cold-brain state is willing to take costly measures (like a longer commute home) in order to avoid triggering the cue. Bernheim and Rangel highlight cue avoidance as a major goal of the cold brain as it tries to prevent its temperamental counterpart from ever activating.

Although the hot-brain/cold-brain model eschews formal discounting functions, heuristically it can be expressed in terms of beta-delta discounting. Consider equation (24.5), which shows possible utility functions for a cold brain and a hot brain. The cold brain has time-consistent preferences ($\beta = 1$), while the hot brain displays a present bias, $0 \leq \beta < 1$:

$$U_{cold} = \delta^0 U_{today} + \delta^1 U_{tomorrow} + \cdots$$
$$U_{hot} = \delta^0 U_{today} + \beta[\delta^1 U_{tomorrow} + \cdots]$$

(24.5)

If we assume a very small $\beta \approx 0$, then these two equations describe the plight of an individual with cold and hot brains. Usually, the individual makes consistent decisions that take into account future costs. But when his hot brain activates, future utility is discounted heavily by the new β factor, and the individual makes disastrous decisions with almost no regard to how they will affect him in the future. This type of model can explain behaviors like addictive binges that generate a rush of present utility but impose massive future costs. If we make the additional assumption that U_{cold} is the "true" utility function that we should maximize, then even strong-armed interventions to arrest the hot brain's destructive rampages might be justifiable.

24.4   Demand for commitment mechanisms

The traditional, revealed-preference perspective assumes that any constraints placed on a person harms that person's welfare (or in the very best case, leaves it unchanged). All voluntary actions are undertaken to increase utility, so any restriction that denies a voluntary action necessarily also limits utility. Put another way, there is no way to constrain an optimal actor to make him act more optimally than before. The standard theory of demand therefore implies that the demand for *commitment mechanisms* – constraints that people put on themselves – must be zero.

But a heap of empirical evidence from gym members, business students, credit-card users, and many others suggest otherwise (DellaVigna 2009). Some examples of commitment mechanisms that people actually demand include:

- restricted savings accounts that prohibit withdrawals until the holiday shopping season;
- alarm clocks that shred $100 bills each time the snooze button is pressed;
- Antabuse, a drug that creates a violent reaction when alcohol is consumed, akin to an instantaneous hangover;
- GymPact, an iPhone application that pays customers for going to the gym and charges them when they do not; and
- commitment contract websites like stickK.com that donate customer money to abhorrent political causes when an enrollee fails to fulfill a resolution.

In each of these cases, individuals pay money (or at least put money at risk) to constrain their future selves. Some of these examples are difficult to understand from a revealed-preference standpoint – why would you want to constrain future selves if you always act optimally?

Usually, the best way to understand commitment devices is as part of the battle between different selves within the same person. In each case, one self pays money to place a constraint on a second, future self that, in the first self's view, will behave irresponsibly when that future moment arrives. Often the first self takes these drastic measures for the sake of a *third* self from the more-distant future who also benefits if the second self is forced to behave responsibly.

Authoritarian commitment mechanisms

All the commitment mechanisms we cited above involve a tradeoff between the happiness of multiple selves. In each case, a present self elects to impose a constraint on a future self, making the present self better off while making a future self worse off.

The fundamental problem in this case is that the present self does not agree with the future self about what that future self should want to do. By its very nature, a commitment mechanism purchased by the present self will prevent the future self from doing what it wants. We call such a commitment device **authoritarian** because it limits the freedom of future selves, who have no say in the matter of whether the commitment is made.

Definition	24.5

Authoritarian commitment mechanism: a constraint demanded by a present self which benefits that present self but harms a future self.

One classic illustration of an authoritarian commitment mechanism comes from Homer's celebrated epic poem *The Odyssey*. The title character is a war hero returning home from battle with his loyal crew. His route home passed by the home of the Sirens, a mysterious race of beautiful, winged women whose melodious song lures any sailor who hears it to his death on the rocky coastline below their lair. Smart sailors who ventured near the Sirens always plugged their ears so they would not be drawn in.

Curious about their powerful song that no man could live to tell about, Odysseus struck a bargain with his crew. Odysseus had his men tie him to the mast of their ship and promise that they would refuse to untie him no matter how much he pleaded with them to do so. He was then free to unplug his ears and listen to the Sirens' voices without fear of drowning.

Sure enough, as the ship sailed within range of the Sirens, Odysseus entered something resembling a hot-brain state and began struggling against his restraints, begging his crew to disregard his earlier instructions and let him go to the Sirens. They loyally refused, enforcing the will of Odysseus's cold-brain self to the detriment of his hot brain. From a welfare economics point of view, this story begs the question: did this plan benefit Odysseus? We explore this question in more depth in Section 24.5.

Sophisticates and naifs

The willingness to pay for self-commitment only arises if a person is aware of his own time-inconsistent behavior. A person with time-inconsistent preferences might realize that his future selves will be present biased just like his current self; if so, he is a **sophisticated** hyperbolic discounter. By contrast, he might instead assume incorrectly that his future self will be time-consistent. Such a person is a **naive** hyperbolic discounter.

For instance, if midnight Jay does not realize that his 12:15 self will crave a cheeseburger, he naively heads home on El Camino. He thinks he will be able to resist but as soon as McDonald's appears his resolve will falter. If he could have anticipated his own time-inconsistent behavior, he might have chosen a commitment mechanism (like taking Alma Street) instead.

Definition	24.6

Sophisticated hyperbolic discounting: a discounting strategy that takes into account the present bias of future selves. People who are aware of their own time inconsistency are called **sophisticates**.

Naive hyperbolic discounting: a discounting strategy that fails to take into account the present bias of future selves, and instead assumes time-consistent preferences in the future. People unaware of their own time inconsistency are called **naifs**.

A naif will not demand any self-commitment device despite his time-inconsistent preferences; why would he pay money to constrain his future self when he believes his future self will agree completely with his current preferences? An exponential discounter does not demand self-commitment devices because she does not need them – she keeps to her plans even without additional constraints. Naifs, who understand that they have a present bias now but think it will disappear later, similarly have no demand for self-commitment because they mistakenly believe they do not need it. A sophisticate, on the other hand, is willing to pay money for devices that prevent his future selves from taking actions that his present self does not like.

Saving for retirement

One consequential example of time-inconsistent behavior is the failure of a significant fraction of workers to save adequately for retirement (Mitchell and Moore 1998; Scholz et al. 2006). A hyperbolic discounter with a bias for present utility tends not to save much of his weekly paycheck, because utility during the far-future retirement period is heavily discounted. At the end of his working life, his retirement account will be more meager than he would like because impatient past selves opted to spend rather than save.

Sophisticates will seek commitment mechanisms to keep their future selves from undersaving or, worse, making withdrawals from retirement accounts. Laibson (1997) likens such a commitment mechanism to the goose who lays golden eggs from one of Aesop's classic children's fables. In that story, an outwardly normal goose periodically lays eggs made of solid gold. Its owners, impatient with the goose's dilatory production schedule, kill and gut the goose in an attempt to get to all the gold at once. Sadly, the owners discover that no gold was to be found inside – killing the goose was a grievous mistake.

Laibson suggests that most illiquid investments, like real estate, equity in a personal business, or even a regular retirement account are like the unusual goose from Aesop's fable. These investments are valuable commodities, but their value cannot be realized quickly by an impatient future self looking to spend money. Their illiquid nature provides a commitment mechanism because it prevents future selves from raiding the retirement savings.

The rise of easy consumer credit in the US in the 1980s and 1990s may have undermined golden-egg commitment mechanisms like real estate. The widespread availability of personal credit cards and the increasing popularity of home-equity loans means that consumers have more credit and liquidity than they did before. Sophisticated hyperbolic discounters who deliberately store money in illiquid assets may be thwarted when their future selves use the easy access to credit to run up huge debts that effectively cancel out any retirement savings.

The implications for health economics are clear. If people cannot manage to save diligently for retirement, how can they succeed in saving up their health optimally in the Grossman model? The impulse that leads people to raid their retirement accounts is the same one that spurs them to stuff their bodies with potato chips or douse their livers with alcohol. The evidence on inadequate retirement savings suggests that people are probably less healthy than they planned to be when they retire as well. In this way, time-inconsistent behavior undermines many of the conclusions we drew from models throughout this book, and raises the prospect of all sorts of policy interventions that would never make sense otherwise.

Table 24.1 provides example situations involving an individual making decisions over time, and discusses how the actor might behave under different discounting scenarios.

Table 24.1. *Actions and commitment mechanisms under different discounting scenarios.*

	Jay's commute	Smoking addiction	Junk food (Grossman model)
Exponential discounting	Jay always takes El Camino because it is the faster route home. He never stops for a cheeseburger because he has already decided it is not healthy to eat late at night so he has no reason to avoid McDonald's.	The smoker determines his smoking level by optimally trading off current utility and future costs. He is aware that more smoking now will lead to greater tastes for smoking later, and he adjusts his intake to account for the addictive nature of cigarettes.	The individual chooses the optimal amount of junk food to eat in each period based on his lifetime utility function. He optimally trades off future H in order to enjoy Z from the junk food in the present period.
Naive hyperbolic discounting	Jay takes El Camino, thinking he will remember to consider the full future health costs and not want a cheeseburger when he gets to McDonald's. When he drives past McDonald's and smells the fries, he discounts future health costs heavily and decides to order a burger.	A smoker smokes heavily in the current period, planning to quit next period. He ends up saying the same thing when the next period arrives while smoking more than ever.	The individual consumes excessive junk food in each period, thinking that he will cut back next period. He ends up eating more junk food (and dying earlier) than his younger self ever expected.
Sophisticated hyperbolic discounting with authoritarian commitment mechanism	Jay takes Alma to avoid McDonald's. The longer trip home is worth it to his midnight self, but his cheeseburger-craving 12:15 self is harmed.	The smoker hires a coach to rip cigarettes out of his hand whenever he lights them. His current self benefits because he will eventually quit smoking, but some later selves want to smoke and do not like being prevented from doing so.	The individual hires a trainer who will weigh him and fine him for any weight he gains. His current self benefits because this will be an effective way to discourage junk food consumption, but his future selves have to choose between delicious donuts and avoiding fines.

24.5   Behavioral welfare economics

This final section explores an ongoing debate among economists: how best to judge whether an intervention benefits or harms a person with time-inconsistent preferences. Because a single action might benefit some selves within a person while harming others, some of the assumptions of traditional welfare economics no longer apply.

For example, suppose two of Jay's well-intentioned friends, Peter and Tim, take it upon themselves to follow Jay home at midnight to restrain his 12:15 self from going to McDonald's. Under a traditional welfare economics reading, Jay is harmed by this intervention because he is prevented from doing something he wants to do. From a behavioral economics perspective, though, the midnight Jay and 12:30 Jay are both happy with his friends' benevolence, while the 12:15 Jay is quite upset. In this case, the intervention has an ambiguous welfare effect.

Various behavioral welfare perspectives

The debate in behavioral welfare economics centers on whose preferences a society should recognize. Should governments design policies that benefit present selves or future selves? Should they be careful to make sure no selves, present or future, are harmed? Is the cold-brain self the "real" self, or does the hot-brain self have valid preferences too? Below, we list several prominent schools of thought that present different approaches to these questions.

- **Revealed preference**. Gul and Pesendorfer (2001) argue for maintaining the revealed preference framework, even in light of what appears to be time-inconsistent behavior. According to their argument, there is no way to tell what someone's self-interest is besides an analysis of what they actually choose to do. So there is never sufficient evidence to conclude that what seems like suboptimal time-inconsistent behavior is actually suboptimal. Who are we to judge whether someone is making a "mistake," perhaps during a hot-brain period, if that person is the ultimate authority of their own preferences?

- **Long-run preferences**. O'Donoghue and Rabin (1999) argue for an approach balancing the preferences of different selves. Consider a beta-delta discounter trying to optimize behavior over three periods: t, $t + 1$, and $t + 2$. O'Donoghue and Rabin posit a fictional self who exists prior to period t and surveys the situation carefully. This prior self makes an optimal plan using a time-consistent discounting scheme. In this formulation, present bias is considered suboptimal because the fictional self, operating in the calm of the "pre"-period, feels no time-inconsistent effects. Unfortunately, when the actual selves take over, present bias emerges and the individual might deviate from the optimal plan in the absence of commitment mechanisms or government intervention.

Both the revealed-preference perspective and the long-run perspective argue there is a single, underlying utility function that should be maximized. But unlike the revealed-preference approach, the long-run approach holds that individuals frequently fail to maximize correctly due to present bias. The next two approaches suppose that each person is a bundle of multiple selves with different utility functions.

- **Dictatorship of the present**. Laibson (1997) and Gruber and Koszegi (2001) allow for multiple selves within each person that have different preferences. These economists adopt a normative system that values the preferences of current selves over the preferences of future selves. In the words of Cropper and Laibson (1998), "the goal of the government at time t is to maximize the well-being of self t." From this perspective, authoritarian commitment mechanisms are beneficial even though they harm some future selves.

- **Hot-brain invalidity**. In the hot-brain/cold-brain model, Bernheim and Rangel (2004) do not treat each period's self as a different person with different preferences. Instead, they assume that the cold brain – which has control over the individual most of the time – has a time-consistent utility function, and behaves like the exponential discounter discussed in Section 24.2. The problem arises when the hot brain takes over, because that brain does have different preferences – invalid ones, in the view of Bernheim and Rangel. They make the normative argument that the cold brain's preferences should be privileged above the hot brain's preferences.

None of these perspectives has yet established itself as the standard for behavioral welfare economics, and each perspective is vulnerable to critique. Bernheim and Rangel (2007), for instance, question the revealed-preference approach by citing the tragic example of the pedestrians visiting the UK from America who look the wrong way before crossing the street and get hit by a lorry. They argue that looking left instead of right when stepping into a crosswalk cannot possibly be a reflection of anyone's "true preferences," but instead simply a mistake. This is a strong justification for the claim that mistakes exist, and some choices that people voluntarily make are clearly suboptimal.

The other perspectives have also been criticized because they treat some selves preferentially and discount the utility of other selves. The Bernheim and Rangel argument that hot-brain preferences are invalid allows them to conclude that government interventions to restrain the hot brain are useful, but Bhattacharya and Lakdawalla (2004) ask why the utility of the hot-brain is not worth valuing. Anyone with fond memories of an indiscretion during a hot-brain episode knows that these episodes, while potentially unhealthy, can generate substantial happiness.

Table 24.2 summarizes the various perspectives discussed in this section, along with arguments for and against each approach.

Interventions to reduce smoking: a role for paternalism?

Suppose we believe that people in a society are smoking too much due to time-inconsistent preferences. How would each of these different perspectives advise the government to act, if at all?

Some would argue a **paternalistic** approach to public health is warranted. Paternalism refers to any outside constraint imposed by a parent, a friend, the government, or another third party designed to improve someone's wellbeing at the cost of restricting their personal freedom. A mother who forces her son to finish his homework before watching TV is limiting his freedom for the sake of his long-term happiness. Likewise, a government which taxes cigarettes harms smokers but does so in the hopes of helping them quit a deadly habit.

Definition	24.7

Paternalism: any involuntary constraint imposed by a parent, a friend, the government, or another third party designed to improve someone's wellbeing at the cost of restricting their personal freedom.

Table 24.2. *Which utility function should we maximize in the case of time-inconsistent preferences?*

Perspective	Argument	Counterargument
Revealed preference	All voluntary decisions are consistent with the maximization of a single, consistent utility function. Any indication that preferences are time-inconsistent is an illusion that simply indicates a more complex underlying utility function (Gul and Pesendorfer 2001).	This perspective assumes that people never make "mistakes" that do not maximize their own utility. But mistakes like neglecting to look the right direction before crossing the street do occur (Bernheim and Rangel 2007).
Maximize long-run utility	A hypothetical self that exists before any of the other selves evaluates utility as a time-consistent, exponential discounter. This hypothetical self's utility should be maximized (O'Donoghue and Rabin 1999).	This perspective gives preferential treatment to some selves over others.
Dictatorship of the present	Society at time t should maximize social well-being at time t (that is, the utility function of time-t selves), so authoritarian commitment mechanisms or taxes on future selves may be desirable (Cropper and Laibson 1998; Gruber and Koszegi 2001).	This perspective also privileges some selves over others.
Hot-brain invalidity	Decisions made in the hot-brain state are mistakes that result from a faulty decision process, not a time-inconsistent utility function. Each person has one consistent utility function that should be optimized by eliminating hot-brain episodes (Bernheim and Rangel 2004).	This perspective treats the hot-brain self as an irrational actor with invalid preferences, but why ignore its preferences totally?

Conventional welfare economics assumes no role for paternalism on the part of the government or any other outside actors, because everyone always seeks to maximize her own utility and does not need any help doing so. Becker and Murphy (1988), in their exposition of the theory of rational addiction, argue that the optimal cigarette tax is zero. There is no valid role for paternalism in their model because rational addicts are time-consistent. They always act in their own best interests, and always pick the optimal number of cigarettes to smoke each period. Any positive tax would decrease cigarette consumption below the optimal level.

The revealed-preference school of thought agrees with this analysis. People always act in their own best interests (even if they seem to be doing something suboptimal) and need no one to prevent them from smoking too much. In this context, the only positive government intervention is a voluntary one, like a support group to help recovering nicotine addicts.

The long-run preference approach comes to a very different conclusion. If we assume that smokers are beta-delta discounters with present bias, then they are indeed smoking too much from the perspective of their long-run preferences (which exclude present bias effects). In this case, a tax on each pack of cigarettes is appropriate, even if the smokers do not want one. When the tax goes into effect, their present selves may claim that it harms them by reducing their utility. But according to the long-run preference perspective, this tax is good for them. This is a classic paternalistic intervention – it is involuntary but designed to benefit the affected parties.

Under the normative standard of the dictatorship of the present, optimal cigarette taxes are positive as well. If the present self is sophisticated about present bias, these taxes simply serve as a form of commitment device provided by the government for free. Even if the present self is naive and does not want taxes, the taxes should still be imposed – new taxes reduce future smoking and make current smokers who want to cut back happier. Using this paternalistic standard, Gruber and Koszegi (2001) estimate that the optimal cigarette tax in the US is at least one dollar per pack higher than current rates. But recall that their designation of optimality relies on their choice of whose utility function to maximize.

If individuals are time-inconsistent, paternalistic policies can prevent regretful retirements.

Credit: Allen Cox.

The present-biased behavior of the future selves imposes a negative externality on the present self, because future selves smoke more than the present self thinks they should. These intrapersonal externalities – or "internalities" as Gruber and Koszegi (2001) call them – justify a tax on cigarettes consumed in the future just as in the standard case of interpersonal externalities.

The hot-brain invalidity school of thought suggests a different approach for governments trying to limit smoking. Cigarette taxes might not be optimal if they fall mostly on the rational cold-brain smokers who are already smoking the right amount. Instead, interventions should focus on reducing the cues that trigger hot-brain episodes – for example, restrictions on public smoking and cigarette advertisements. Even paternalistic interventions like the temporary arrest of individuals in the hot-brain state may also be justified.

Pareto self-improving commitment mechanisms

Bhattacharya and Lakdawalla (2004) propose a more cautious approach to government intervention in the case of time-inconsistent preferences. They argue that we should eschew paternalistic commitment mechanisms and instead promote a different kind of mechanism designed to benefit some selves without harming any others.

Commitment mechanisms do not have to follow the authoritarian model. In some cases, it is possible to create a more complex commitment mechanism that benefits both present and future selves, and does not force any selves to do anything they do not want to do. Just like a Pareto improvement that benefits some members of society without harming any, this type of commitment mechanism benefits some selves without doing harm to any other selves. These commitment devices are therefore called **Pareto self-improving**.

Definition	24.8

Pareto self-improving commitment mechanism: a commitment mechanism that benefits some selves without doing harm to any other selves.

542   BEHAVIORAL HEALTH ECONOMICS

If all the selves from a person's present and future could somehow congregate and negotiate about whether to take an action, none of them would object to a Pareto self-improving commitment mechanism. Such mechanisms would never be paternalistic because they are always voluntary.

Bhattacharya and Lakdawalla (2004) propose a smoker's bond as an example of a Pareto self-improving commitment device. The bond would resemble a bank account offered by the government where a smoker trying to cut back on cigarettes could deposit money in period t. Then, in period $t + 1$, the new self is offered a choice. He can choose to accept a tax on each pack of cigarettes, in which case he receives the money from the bond; or he can choose to continue smoking without any taxes, in which case he loses access to the bond and the government keeps the money. Under certain assumptions and if the tax is set appropriately, the time-t self can always convince his $t + 1$ self to accept the tax and take the bond money.

The $t + 1$ self smokes less because of the higher marginal cost of cigarettes, but he cannot claim the tax harms him because he accepted it voluntarily. In essence, the smoker's bond is a bribe from a previous self to a subsequent self to behave responsibly.

The same concept can be applied to help Jay with his commute home. Rather than Peter and Tim barring Jay's 12:15 self from visiting McDonald's, they conspire with Jay's midnight self to bribe him instead. Jay's cold-brain self purchases a new video game and gives it to Peter and Tim with instructions only to give it back if Jay successfully avoids McDonald's. Now when Jay's 12:15 self drives past McDonald's, he has strong incentive to stay away and will drive past voluntarily, excited to play the new video game he has earned.

Both Jay's midnight self and his 12:15 self benefit from this arrangement, because the midnight self has convinced Jay to skip McDonald's and the 12:15 self did so voluntarily in return for a video game. This Pareto self-improving commitment device has the added benefit of obviating the need for a detour down Alma. Jay can go the fast way down El Camino confident that his future selves will adhere to his original plan.

There are some limitations to the applicability of Pareto self-improving commitment mechanisms, however. Many authoritarian commitment mechanisms, like Odysseus tying himself to the mast of his ship, harm one self but greatly benefit many other selves. The Pareto criterion for commitment interventions is limiting because it precludes these authoritarian mechanisms, even if they look very beneficial from the perspective of a present self (O'Donoghue and Rabin 1999).

Additionally, Pareto self-improving commitment mechanisms can only work when the future self who is being bribed to behave is responsive to the bribe. Suppose a nicotine addict has a hot brain that will demand cigarettes *no matter what* – not even if it is offered a massive payment to not smoke. No Pareto self-improving commitment device would be able to restrain the hot brain in this situation, though some authoritarian commitment devices might still work.

24.6   Conclusion

The notion of people acting against their own best interests is not new. The ancient Greeks had a term $\alpha\kappa\rho\alpha\sigma\iota\alpha$ (*akrasia*) which signified the lack of control over one's self. The move to incorporate time inconsistency into the neoclassical tradition of economics is more recent. The introduction of time inconsistency, in many ways, poses a fundamental challenge to neoclassical notions of welfare, both individual and social. A time-inconsistent individual makes optimal plans one day and then violates them the next. In this telling, each person is a bundle of quarreling selves rather than a single integrated individual. So what it means for a "person" to prefer one outcome to another is a matter of serious philosophical dispute.

The resolution of this dispute, however, is not merely of philosophical interest. If it is widely accepted that the preferences of the hot brain are invalid and not worthy of policy consideration, then a host of government interventions aimed at curbing hot-brain excesses are justified. On the other hand, if the only legitimate data to judge individual welfare are the preferences people reveal with their actions, then optimal government policy is much more limited in scope.

Time inconsistency can explain many puzzles in health, such as why people buy gym memberships but fail to visit the gym, why people postpone plans to quit smoking (even when they know that smoking kills), why people have so much trouble keeping to a healthy diet, and many other phenomena that are difficult to explain with standard neoclassical economics. The theory of time inconsistency also implies tools that both governments and markets can use to improve the ability of time-inconsistent individuals to keep to their cold brains' plans.

At the same time, the notion of time inconsistency in health policy brings with it philosophical difficulties about the meaning of individual welfare. Ultimately, whether people in a democratic society accept paternalistic policies designed to correct their own decision-making foibles depends on how much trust the people place in their governments to act benevolently on their behalf, and on how much knowledge governments have about such foibles.

24.7   Exercises

Comprehension questions

Indicate whether each statement is true or false, and justify your answer. Be sure to cite evidence from the chapter and state any additional assumptions you may need.

1 There is a massive body of evidence that humans prefer a fixed amount of utility now to that same amount of utility later.
2 If a person discounts utility from future periods, her preferences are time-inconsistent because she does not value utility in all periods equally.
3 Suppose an individual prefers to drink beer during college but enjoys wine more during middle age. This is a classic example of time-inconsistent preferences.
4 Evidence indicates that exponential discounting functions are very rare in humans.
5 According to the hot-brain/cold-brain model, individuals usually have time-consistent preferences but sometimes lapse momentarily into a time-inconsistent frames of mind.
6 Contrary to the predictions of welfare economics, people are willing to pay to have constraints place on themselves.
7 If people demand a self-commitment device, it must be Pareto self-improving; otherwise it would not be demanded by utility-maximizing economic agents.

8 Suppose that a long-time nicotine addict who is trying to quite smoking decides he wants a cigarette, but his friends successfully restrain him. The friends' intervention has an ambiguous effect on the addict's welfare.

9 Economists agree that any intervention at time t which improves the utility of people at time t is necessarily a good intervention.

Analytical problems

10 **Time inconsistency and chocolate**. The latest craze sweeping Pcoria is a new kind of exotic chocolate imported from the faraway alpine nation of Chplandia. Chplandian chocolate is delicious and cheap: each bar produces $2 worth of utility and only costs $1. But unfortunately, it is not very healthy: if a Pcorian eats x bars on any given day, she suffers negative health effects *the next day* that amount to $-\$^1/_4x^2$. But she does not suffer any ill effects on the day she eats the chocolate.

   a Assume Pcorians are beta-delta discounters with $\beta = 1$ and $\delta = 1$, and that each day is a period. Interpret these assumptions about β and δ. Are Pcorians patient? Are they time-consistent?

   b What is the optimal number of Chplandian chocolate bars x^* for each Pcorian to eat each day under these assumptions? [*Hint*: Balance the marginal benefit and marginal cost.]

   c Now assume $\delta = ^2/_3$ instead. How does this affect optimal chocolate intake x^*? Explain intuitively why x^* changes the way it does when δ falls.

   d Bob, a chocolate-loving Pcorian, is doing his grocery shopping for the week and deciding how much Chplandian chocolate to buy. How many bars of chocolate does Bob think he wants to eat tomorrow?

   e When tomorrow actually arrives, will Bob change his mind about how many bars he wants to eat? Explain whether Bob is time-consistent or time-inconsistent in his preferences.

   f Now assume $\delta = ^2/_3$ and $\beta = 0.5$. Explain what β represents and what sort of effect this new β will have on the Pcorians.

   g What is the number of Chplandian chocolate bars $\hat{x}$ that each Pcorian eats each day under these new assumptions, assuming each Pcorian works to maximize the present self's utility function?

   h Assume Bob is a naive hyperbolic discounter. How many chocolate bars does Bob think he will want tomorrow? How many will he actually want?

11 **Time inconsistency and chocolate II**. Pcorians are eating more Chplandian chocolate than ever, and politicians in the Pcorian parliament are starting to propose interventions to reduce chocolate consumption. Assume again that Pcorian citizens are beta-delta discounters with $\beta = 0.5$ and $\delta = ^2/_3$. Review Exercise 10 for information about the costs and benefits of Chplandian chocolate.

   a First take the approach of the dictatorship of the present, and assume that Pcorians are sophisticated hyperbolic discounters. How many bars of chocolate "should" each Pcorian citizen eat today, and how many bars of chocolate "should" each Pcorian citizen eat tomorrow?

   b According to this view, what is the optimal tariff to place on Chplandian chocolate bars starting tomorrow so that citizens will eat the right amount?

c   The Pcorian parliament passes your suggested optimal tariff for a trial period of one day. How much will tomorrow's Pcorians be harmed by this one-day tariff? Compare costs and benefits from the perspective of tomorrow's consumer with the tax to the costs and benefits without the tax.

d   According to the revealed-preference school of thought, what is wrong with this tariff strategy?

e   Is the tariff a Pareto self-improving intervention? Explain why or why not.

f   Suppose the tariff were not a one-day trial, but instead were permanent. Without doing any explicit calculations, explain briefly how that would change your answer to Exericise 11(c).

12 It is October 31 (Halloween night), and thanks to a great pirate costume, you have pulled in a record haul during trick-or-treating – 1001 pieces of candy! Before bed, you have to decide how you will allocate your candy over the next three nights. Your parents have already declared that any un-eaten candy will be thrown away after November 2.

On any given night, your utility from candy is $u(x) = \ln(x)$, where x is the number of pieces consumed that night. In the following exercises, U_0 and x_0 will represent your utility and candy consumption respectively on October 31. The subscripts 1 and 2 denote analogous quantities for November 1 and 2 respectively.

a   Suppose you are a beta-delta discounter. Write down your overall utility from the perspective of your October 31 self as a function of β, δ, x_0, x_1, and x_2. Also write down your overall utility from the perspective of your November 1 self as a function of β, δ, x_1 and x_2.

b   From the perspective of your October 31 self, what is the marginal utility of an additional piece of candy on October 31? That is, find $\partial U_0 / \partial x_0$. Also find $\partial U_0 / \partial x_1$ and $\partial U_1 / \partial x_2$, the marginal utilities from candy consumption on November 1 and on November 2.

c   Assume that you are have time-consistent preferences and a discount rate $\delta = 0.5$. How do you allocate your 1001 pieces of candy between the three nights? [*Hint:* In order to maximize your overall utility, choose a candy allocation that equates your three derivatives from the previous exercise.]

d   Show that you will not elect to reallocate your candy come November 1. That is, show that your original allocation from the night before also maximizes the new utility function on November 1.

e   Let's assume you are still time-consistent but slightly more impatient than we thought; your discount rate is $\delta = 1/3$. Now how do you allocate your 1001 pieces of candy on October 31?

f   Now assume you are actually a hyperbolic discounter, with $\beta = 0.5$ and $\delta = 0.5$. If you are naive, how will you allocate candy on October 31?

g   If on October 31, you follow through on your plan from the previous part, how will you deviate from your plan on November 1?

h   According to the original utility function of the October 31 self, how much utility did the deviation on November 1 cost you? According to your November 1 utility function, how much extra utility did the deviation create compared to the October 31 plan?

i   What tradeoff do your October 31 and November 1 selves disagree about? Be as specific as possible.

13 Review the setup of Exercise 12. Assume you have time-inconsistent preferences ($\beta = 0.5$, $\delta = 0.5$) but are also a sophisticate.

   a Propose two realistic commitment mechanisms in this situation. One should be a authoritarian measure that harms the November 1 self, and one should be a Pareto self-improving measure that weakly benefits all three selves.

   b Suppose for whatever reason that these commitment mechanisms are not available. Now, how much candy do you allot yourself on October 31 for consumption on October 31 in order to maximize your overall utility? Is this more or less candy than you would allot yourself if you were a naive beta-discounter? Explain the difference in these strategies in intuitive terms.

14 **Procrastination and instant gratification at the movies** (exercise adapted from O'Donoghue and Rabin (1999)). Suppose the local movie theater is offering four different movies on the next four Saturdays. And according to your taste in movies, each Saturday's movie will be better than the previous week's movie. You can go to three of the movies, but you must reserve one Saturday to see the doctor. Over the next four weeks, you will choose a Saturday to skip the theater and have your checkup. Your health insurance runs out at the end of the month, so if you haven't seen the doctor yet by the last Saturday, you will be compelled to go then, even if the movie in the theater that afternoon is *really* good.

Table 24.3. *Will you see your doctor today?*

	First Sat	Second Sat	Third Sat	Fourth Sat
Cost of skipping movie	3	5	8	13
Exponential	?	?	?	yes
Naive hyperbolic	?	?	no	yes
Sophisticated hyperbolic	?	?	no	yes

Table 24.3 lists the benefits and costs of choosing each particular Saturday, along with several partially filled rows. A "yes" indicates that you would choose to go to the doctor on that Saturday *given that you have not already done so*, and a "no" indicates you would not. To make your decision each Saturday, you compare your utility from seeing the doctor now to your predicted utility from procrastinating. In order to calculate this predicted utility, you must predict when you will eventually decide to have your checkup if you do not do it now. Assume you are a beta-delta discounter with $\delta = 0.95$.

   a In each blank in the first row, indicate whether you would choose that Saturday to go to the doctor if you had not yet gone and were a time-consistent exponential discounter ($\beta = 1$).

   b In each blank in the second row, indicate whether you would choose that Saturday go to the doctor if you had not yet gone and were a naive time-inconsistent hyperbolic discounter ($\beta = 0.5$).

   c In each blank in the third row, indicate whether you would choose that Saturday to go to the doctor if you had not yet gone and were a sophisticated time-inconsistent hyperbolic discounter ($\beta = 0.5$). [*Hint*: It may help to work backward.]

   d On which day will each type of discounter go to the doctor? Who has a better outcome, the sophisticate or the naif?

Table 24.4. *Will you go to the movies today?*

	First Sat	Second Sat	Third Sat	Fourth Sat
Benefit of seeing movie	3	5	8	13
Exponential	?	no	?	yes
Naive hyperbolic	?	?	?	yes
Sophisticated hyperbolic	?	yes	?	yes

Now assume a different scenario: you need to make three trips to the doctor's over the next four weeks to get a series of vaccinations. So this month, you can only visit the cinema on one Saturday. Table 24.4 lists the benefits and costs of choosing each particular Saturday to attend the movie, along with several blank rows.

e In each blank in the first row, indicate whether you would choose that Saturday to watch the movie if you had not seen one yet and were a time-consistent exponential discounter ($\beta = 1$).

f In each blank in the second row, indicate whether you would choose that Saturday to watch the movie if you had not seen one yet and were a naive time-inconsistent hyperbolic discounter ($\beta = 0.5$).

g In each blank in the third row, indicate whether you would choose that Saturday to watch the movie if you had not seen one yet and were a sophisticated time-inconsistent hyperbolic discounter ($\beta = 0.5$).

h On which day will each type of discounter see the movie? Who has a better outcome, the sophisticate or the naif?

i Explain why the sophisticated discounter has a better outcome when fighting the urge to procrastinate than when trying to delay gratification. Interpret this outcome in terms of the present self "distrusting" the future self in the case of sophisticated hyperbolic discounting.

Essay questions

15 Below is the key empirical finding from a recent NBER working paper titled "Do consumers exploit precommitment opportunities? Evidence from natural experiments involving liquor consumption" by Douglas Bernheim, Jonathan Meer, and Neva Novarro:

> We examine a collection of natural experiments in which states expanded allowable Sunday sales hours for liquor. Our results indicate that consumers increase their liquor consumption in response to extended Sunday on-premise sales hours, but not in response to extended off-premise sales hours.

Sales of alcohol at liquor stores are known as *off-premise sales*, since the alcohol is typically not consumed at the point of sale. In contrast, sales of alcohol at bars and restaurants are known as *on-premise sales.*

a The authors report that:

> One of the most frequently mentioned strategies for exercising self-control is to limit the availability of a problematic good by not maintaining an easily accessed supply.

Consider a sophisticated time-inconsistent consumer who is conflicted about his consumption of alcohol. He wants to stop drinking, but in the presence of chilled beer, he cannot help himself from over-indulging. Give an example of the precommitment strategy described by Bernheim, Meer, and Novarro.

b   Laws restricting liquor sales on Sunday are known as "blue laws." Suppose a community with a blue law decides to relax it and permit liquor stores to be open on Sunday (bars and restaurants are still not allowed to serve alcohol). Consider a time-*consistent* consumer of alcohol. Will the relaxation of off-premise blue laws affect his overall consumption of alcohol? Why or why not?

c   Now consider a time-*inconsistent* consumer of alcohol, currently implementing the precommitment device you described in part (a). Will the relaxation of off-premise blue laws affect his overall consumption of alcohol? Why or why not?

d   Bernheim, Meer, and Novarro find that liquor consumption did not increase as a result of the loosening of off-premise blue laws. What does their result suggest about the time-consistency or time-inconsistency of alcohol consumers?

Students can find answers to the comprehension questions and lecturers can access an Instructor Manual with guideline answers to the analytical problems and essay questions at **www.palgrave.com/economics/bht**.

BIBLIOGRAPHY

Abel-Smith, B. (1992). The Beveridge report: its origins and outcomes. *International Social Security Review*, 45(1–2): 5–16.

Acemoglu, D. and Linn, J. (2004). Market size in innovation: theory and evidence from the pharmaceutical industry. *Quarterly Journal of Economics*, 119(3): 1049–90.

Ahituv, A., Hotz, V. J., and Philipson, T. (1996). The responsiveness of the demand for condoms to the local prevalence of AIDS. *Journal of Human Resources*, 31(4): 869.

Ahmad, N. Z., Byrnes, G., and Naqvi, S. A. (2008). A meta-analysis of ambulatory versus inpatient laparoscopic cholecystectomy. *Surgical Endoscopy*, 22(9): 1928–34.

Ainslie, G. (2010). *Picoeconomics: The Strategic Interaction of Successive Motivational States Within the Person*. Cambridge University Press, Cambridge, 2nd edition.

Akerlof, G. A. (1970). The market for "lemons": quality uncertainty and the market mechanism. *Quarterly Journal of Economics*, 84(3): 488–500.

Allais, M. (1953). Le comportement de l'homme rationnel devant le risque: critique des postulats et axiomes. *Econometrica*, 21(4): 503–46.

Almond, D. (2006). Is the 1918 influenza pandemic over? Long-term effects of in utero influenza exposure in the post-1940 US population. *Journal of Political Economy*, 114(4): 672–712.

Almond, D., Edlund, L., and Palme, M. (2009). Chernobyl's subclinical legacy: prenatal exposure to radioactive fallout and school outcomes in Sweden. *Quarterly Journal of Economics*, 124(4): 1729–72.

Almond, D. and Mazumder, B. (2007). The effects of maternal fasting during Ramadan on birth and adult outcomes. *American Economic Journal: Applied Economics*, 3(4): 56–85.

Amelung, V., Glied, S., and Topan, A. (2003). Health care and the labor market: learning from the German experience. *Journal of Health Politics, Policy and Law*, 28(4): 693–714.

American Hospital Association (2010). *AHA Hospital Statistics*. American Hospital Association, 2011 edition.

Anderson, G. F. (2007). From "soak the rich" to "soak the poor": recent trends in hospital pricing. *Health Affairs*, 26(3): 780–9.

Anderson, G. M., Halcoussis, D., Johnston, L., and Lowenberg, A. (2000). Regulatory barriers to entry in the healthcare industry: the case of alternative medicine. *The Quarterly Review of Economics and Finance*, 40: 485–502.

Anderson, R. and May, R. (1985). Vaccination and herd immunity to infectious diseases. *Nature*, 318(6044): 323–9.

Anell, A. (2004). Priority setting for pharmaceuticals. The use of health economic evidence by reimbursement and clinical guidance committees. *European Journal of Health Economics*, 5(1): 28–35.

Anis, A. H., Guh, D., and Wang, Xh. (2001). A dog's breakfast: prescription drug coverage varies widely across Canada. *Medical Care*, 39(4): 315–26.

Antonovsky, A. (1967). Social class, life expectancy and overall mortality. *The Milbank Memorial Fund Quarterly*, 45(2): 31–73.

Aranovich, G., Bhattacharya, J., Garber, A. M., and MaCurdy, T. E. (2009). "Coping with chronic disease? Chronic disease and disability in elderly American population 1982–1999". NBER Working Paper No. 14811.

Arora, V., Johnson, J., Lovinger, D., Humphrey, H. J., and Meltzer, D. O. (2005). Communication failures in patient sign-out and suggestions for improvement: a critical incident analysis. *Quality and Safety in Health Care*, 14(6): 401–7.

Arrow, K. (1951). *Social Choice and Individual Values*. John Wiley & Sons, New York, 1st edition.

Arrow, K. (1963). Uncertainty and the welfare economics of medical care. *American Economic Review*, 53(5): 941–73.

Asplin, B. R., Rhodes, K. V., Levy, H., Lurie, N., Crain, A. L., Carlin, B. P., and Kellermann, A. L. (2005). Insurance status and access to urgent ambulatory care follow-up appointments. *JAMA*, 294(10): 1248–54.

Association of American Medical Colleges (2011). US medical school applicants and students 1982–1983 to 2010–2011. https://www.aamc.org/download/153708/data/.

Atella, V., Bhattacharya, J., and Carbonari, L. (2012). Pharmaceutical price controls and minimum efficacy regulation: evidence from the United States and Italy. *Health Services Research*, 47(1): 293–308.

Autor, D., Duggan, M., and Gruber, J. (2012). Moral hazard and claims deterrence in private disability insurance. NBER Working Paper No.18172.

Bach, P. B. (2010). A map to bad policy – hospital efficiency measures in the Dartmouth Atlas. *New England Journal of Medicine*, 362: 569–74.

Bach, P. B., Schrag, D., and Begg, C. B. (2004). A study design that should be laid to rest. *Journal of American Medical Association (JAMA)*, 292(22): 2765–70.

Baicker, K. et al. (2013). The Oregon experiment: effects of Medicaid on clinical outcomes. *New England Medical Journal*, 368: 1713–22. http://www.nejm.org/doi/full/10.1056/NEJMsa1212321.

Bakaeen, F. G., Huh, J., Lemaire, S. A., Coselli, J. S., Sansgiry, S., Atluri, P. V., and Chu, D. (2009). The July effect: impact of the beginning of the academic cycle on cardiac surgical outcomes in a cohort of 70,616 patients. *Annals of Thoracic Surgery*, 88(1): 70–5.

Baker, L. C. (2001). Managed care and technology adoption in health care: evidence from magnetic resonance imaging. *Journal of Health Economics*, 20(3): 395–421.

Baker, L. C. (2002). Managed Care. Technical Report, Health Research and Policy, Stanford, CA.

Baker, L. C. (2010). Acquisition of MRI equipment by doctors drives up imaging use and spending. *Health Affairs*, 29(12): 2252–9.

Baker, T. (1996). On the genealogy of moral hazard. *Texas Law Review*, 75(2): 237–92.

Ball, R. M. (1995). Perspectives on Medicare: what Medicare's architects had in mind. *Health Affairs*, 14(4): 62–72.

Banegas, J., Lopez-Garcia, E., Gutierrez-Fisac, J., Guallar-Castillon, P., and Rodriguez-Artalejo, F. (2003). A simple estimate of mortality attributable to excess weight in the European Union. *European Journal of Clinical Nutrition*, 57(2): 201–8.

Banta, D., Kristensen, F. B. R., and Jonsson, E. (2009). A history of health technology assessment at the European level. *International Journal of Technology Assessment in Health*, 25 (Suppl. 1): 68–73.

Barham, T. and Maluccio, J. A. (2009). Eradicating diseases: the effect of conditional cash transfers on vaccination coverage in rural Nicaragua. *Journal of Health Economics*, 28(3): 611–21.

Barnum, H., Kutzin, J., and Saxenian, H. (1995). Incentives and provider payment methods. *International Journal of Health Planning and Management*, 10(1): 23–45.

Barr, D. A., Fenton, L., and Blane, D. (2008). The claim for patient choice and equity. *Journal of Medical Ethics*, 34(4): 271–4.

Barreca, A. I. (2010). The long-term economic impact of in utero and postnatal exposure to malaria. *Journal of Human Resources*, 45(4): 865–92.

Barros, P. P. and Olivella, P. (2005). Waiting lists and patient selection. *Journal of Economics and Management Strategy*, 14(3): 623–46.

Bartel, A., Phibbs, C., Beaulieu, N., and Stone, P. (2011). Human capital and organizational performance: evidence from the health care sector. NBER Working Paper No. 17474.

Barua, B., Rovere, M., and Skinner, B. (2010). Waiting Your Turn: Wait Times for Health Care in Canada. Technical Report, December, Fraser Institute.

Bassett, D. R., Pucher, J., Buehler, R., and Thompson, D. (2011). Active transportation and obesity in Europe, North America, and Australia. *Institute of Transportation Engineers. ITE Journal*, 81(8): 24–8.

Bassett, D. R., Schneider, P. L., and Huntington, G. E. (2004). Physical activity in an Old Order Amish community. *Medicine and Science in Sports and Exercise*, 36(1): 79–85.

Becker, G. S. (1981). *A Treatise on the Family*. Cambridge University Press, Cambridge.

Becker, G. S. (1993). *Human Capital: A Theoretical and Empirical Analysis, with Special Reference to Education*. University of Chicago Press, Chicago, IL.

Becker, G. S. and Murphy, K. (1988). A theory of rational addiction. *Journal of Political Economy*, 96(4): 675–700.

Bekar, C. (2000). Income sharing amongst medieval peasants: usury prohibitions and the non-market provision of insurance. International Institute of Economics and Trade, Conference Proceedings.

Bendavid, E. and Bhattacharya, J. (2009). The President's Emergency Plan for AIDS Relief in Africa: an evaluation of outcomes. *Annals of Internal Medicine*, 150: 688–95.

Bennett, D., Chiang, C. F., and Malani, A. (2011). Learning during a crisis: the SARS epidemic in Taiwan. NBER Working Paper No. 16955.

Bentzen, J., Eriksson, T., and Smith, V. (1999). Rational addiction and alcohol consumption: evidence from the Nordic countries. *Journal of Consumer Policy*, 22(3): 257–79.

Berenson, R. A., Bodenheimer, T., and Pham, H. H. (2006). Specialty-service lines: salvos in the new medical arms race. *Health Affairs*, 25(5): 337–43.

Berndt, E. R. (2005). To inform or persuade? Direct-to-consumer advertising of prescription drugs. *New England Journal of Medicine*, 352(4): 325–8.

Berndt, E. R., Bir, A., Busch, S. H., Frank, R. G., and Normand, S.-L. T. (2002). The medical treatment of depression, 1991–1996: productive inefficiency, expected outcome variations, and price indexes. *Journal of Health Economics*, 21(3): 373–96.

Bernheim, B. D. and Rangel, A. (2004). Addiction and cue-triggered decision processes. *American Economic Review*, 94(5): 1558–90.

Bernheim, B. D. and Rangel, A. (2007). Behavioral public economics: welfare and policy analysis with. In Diamond, P. A. and Vartiainen, H., editors, *Behavioral Economics and its Applications*. Princeton University Press, Princeton, NJ.

Bernheim, D., Meer, J., and Novarro, N. (2012). Do consumers exploit precommitment opportunities. NBER Working Paper No. 17762.

Besley, T., Hall, J., and Preston, I. (1998). Private and public health insurance in the UK. *European Economic Review*, 42(3–5): 491–7.

Bhatt, D. L., Fox, K. A. A., Hacke, W., Berger, P. B., Black, H. R., Boden, W. E., Cacoub, P., Cohen, E. A., Creager, M. A., Easton, J. D., Flather, M. D., Haffner, S. M., Hamm, C. W., Hankey, G. J., Johnston, S. C., Mak, K.-H., Mas, J.-L., Montalescot, G., Pearson, T. A., Steg, P. G., Steinhubl, S. R., Weber, M. A., Brennan, D. M., Fabry-Ribaudo, L., Booth, J., and Topol, E. J. (2006). Clopidogrel and aspirin versus aspirin alone for the prevention of atherothrombotic events. *New England Journal of Medicine*, 354(16): 1706–17.

Bhattacharya, J. (2004). The failure of property rights assignment in organ transplant markets. Unpublished manuscript.

Bhattacharya, J. (2005). Specialty selection and lifetime returns to specialization within medicine. *Journal of Human Resources*, 40(1): 115–43.

Bhattacharya, J. and Bundorf, M. K. (2009). The incidence of the healthcare costs of obesity. *Journal of Health Economics*, 28(3): 649–58.

Bhattacharya, J., Choudhry, K., and Lakdawalla, D. (2008). Chronic disease and severe disability among working-age populations. *Medical Care*, 46(1): 92–100.

Bhattacharya, J., Goldman, D., and Sood, N. (2003). The link between public and private insurance and HIV-related mortality. *Journal of Health Economics*, 22(6): 1105–22.

Bhattacharya, J., Goldman, D., and Sood, N. (2004). Price regulation in secondary insurance markets. *Journal of Risk and Insurance*, 71(4): 643–75.

Bhattacharya, J., Goldman, D., and Sood, N. (2009). Market evidence of misperceived mortality risk. *Journal of Economic Behavior and Organization*, 72(1): 451–62.

Bhattacharya, J. and Lakdawalla, D. (2004). Time-inconsistency and welfare. NBER Working Paper No. 10345.

Bhattacharya, J. and Lakdawalla, D. (2006). Does Medicare benefit the poor? *Journal of Public Economics*, 90(1–2): 277–92.

Bhattacharya, J. and Packalen, M. (2012). Opportunities and benefits as determinants of the direction of technological change. *Journal of Health Economics* 30(4): 603–615.

Bhattacharya, J. and Sood, N. (2006). Health insurance and the obesity externality. In Cawley, J. and Bolin, K., editors, *Advances in Health Economics and Health Services Research*. JAI Press, Greenwich, CT.

Bhattacharya, J. and Sood, N. (2011). Who pays for obesity? *Journal of Economic Perspectives*, 25(1): 139–58.

Bhattacharya, J. and Vogt, W. (2003). A simple model of pharmaceutical price dynamics. *Journal of Law and Economics*, 46(2): 599–626.

Bhattacharya, J. and Vogt, W. B. (2006). Employment and adverse selection in health insurance. NBER Working Paper No. 12430.

Bhattacharya, J., Bundorf, K., Pace N. and Sood, N. (2011). Does Heath Insurance make you fat? In Grossman, M. and Mocan, M. H., editors, *Economic Aspects of Obesity*. University of Chicago Press, Chicago, IL.

Bhattacharya, J., Garber, A. M., Miller, M. and Pedroth, D. (2012). The value of progress against cancer in the elderly. In *Investigations in the Economics of Aging*, ed, D. A. Wise. University of Chicago Press, Chicago, IL, 202–233.

Bhattacharya, J., Shang, B., Su, C. K., and Goldman, D. P. (2005). Technological advances in cancer and future spending by the elderly. *Health Affairs (Project Hope)*, 24(Suppl. 2): W5R53–66.

Bindman, A. B., Grumbach, K., Osmond, D., Komaromy, M., Vranizan, K., Lurie, N., Billings, J., and Stewart, A. (1995). Preventable hospitalizations and access to health care. *JAMA*, 274(4): 305–11.

Birkmeyer, J. D., Siewers, A. E., Finlayson, E. V., Stukel, T. A., Lucas, F. L., Batista, I., Welch, H. G., and Wennberg, D. (2002). Hospital volume and surgical mortality in the United States. *New England Journal of Medicine*, 346(15): 1128–1137.

Björklund, A. (2006). Does family policy affect fertility? *Journal of Population Economics*, 19(1): 3–24.

Black, S., Devereux, P., and Salvanes, K. (2007). From the cradle to the labor market? The effect of birth weight on adult outcomes. *Quarterly Journal of Economics*, 122(1): 409–39.

Blaylock, J., Smallwood, D., Kassel, K., Variyam, J., and Aldrich, L. (1999). Economics, food choices, and nutrition. *Food Policy*, 24(2–3): 269–86.

Bleichrodt, H. (2002). A new explanation for the difference between time trade-off utilities and standard gamble utilities. *Health Economics*, 11(5): 447–56.

Bleichrodt, H. and Johannesson, M. (1997). Standard gamble, time trade-off and rating scale: experimental results on the ranking properties of QALYs. *Journal of Health Economics*, 16(2): 155–75.

Blendon, R. J. and Benson, J. M. (2001). Americans' views on health policy: a fifty-year historical perspective. *Health Affairs*, 20(2): 33–46.

Blendon, R. J., Schoen, C., DesRoches, C. M., Osborn, R., Scoles, K. L., and Zapert, K. (2002). Inequities in health care: a five-country survey. *Health Affairs*, 21(3): 182–91.

Blomqvist, A. (2001). Does the economics of moral hazard need to be revisited? A comment on the paper by John Nyman. *Journal of Health Economics*, 20(2): 283–8.

Bloom, N., Propper, C., Seiler, S., and Van Reenen, J. (2010). The impact of competition on management quality: evidence from public hospitals. Centre for Economic Performance Discussion Paper No. 983.

Blume-Kohout, M. E. and Sood, N. (2008). The impact of Medicare Part D on pharmaceutical R&D. NBER Working Paper No. 13857.

Blumenthal, D. (2008). The lessons of success–revisiting the Medicare Story. *New England Journal of Medicine*, 359(22): 2384–9.

Bodenheimer, T. (1997). The Oregon health plan – lessons for the nation. *New England Journal of Medicine*, 337(9): 651–5.

Bodenheimer, T. and Grumbach, K. (2009). *Understanding Health Policy: A Clinical Approach*. McGraw-Hill, New York, 5th edition.

Bolgiani, I., Crivelli, L., and Domenighetti, G. (2006). The role of health insurance in regulating the Swiss health care system. *Revue francĬaise des affaires sociales*, 6(6): 227–49.

Boseley, S. (2000). Postcode lottery hits heart patient: care lottery is a matter of life and death. *The Guardian*. 12 October. http://www.guardian.co.uk/society/2000/oct/12/futureofthenhs.NHS.

Bowen, H. R. (1943). The interpretation of voting in the allocation of economic resources. *Quarterly Journal of Economics*, 58(1): 27–48.

Brady, T., Robinson, B., Davis, T., Phillips, S., and Amy Gruber (2001). Medicare hospital prospective payment system: how DRG rates are calculated and updated. Technical Report, August, Office of Inspector General, Office of Evaluation and Inspections, San Francisco, CA.

Brekke, K. R. and Sorgard, L. (2007). Public versus private health care in a national health service. *Health Economics*, 601(1): 579–601.

Brickley, J. and Van Horn, R. (2002). Managerial incentives in nonprofit organizations: evidence from hospitals. *Journal of Law and Economics*, 45: 227.

Brown, J. R., Duggan, M., Kuziemko, I., and Woolston, W. (2011). How does risk selection respond to risk adjustment? Evidence from the Medicare Advantage Program. NBER Working Paper No. 16977.

Brown, J. R. and Finkelstein, A. (2007). Why is the market for long-term care insurance so small? *Journal of Public Economics*, 91(10): 1967–91.

Brown, J. R. and Finkelstein, A. (2009). The private market for long-term care insurance in the United States: a review of the evidence. *Journal of Risk and Insurance*, 76(1): 5–29.

Brunello, G., Michaud, P.-C., and Sanz-de Galdeano, A. (2009). The rise of obesity in Europe: an economic perspective. *Economic Policy*, 24(59): 551–96.

Buchmueller, T. C. (1998). Does a fixed-dollar premium contribution lower spending? *Health Affairs*, 17(6): 228–35.

Burgio, G. (1981). The Thalidomide disaster briefly revisited. *European Journal of Pediatrics*, 136: 229–30.

Burke, K. (2004). Palliative care at home to get further funds if it saves money. *BMJ*, 328(March): 544.

Burstein, P. L. and Cromwell, J. (1985). Relative incomes and rates of return for US physicians. *Journal of Health Economics*, 4(1): 63–78.

Burton, S., Creyer, E. H., Kees, J., and Huggins, K. (2006). Attacking the obesity epidemic: the potential health benefits of providing nutrition information in restaurants. *American Journal of Public Health*, 96(9): 1669–75.

Busse, R. (2004). Disease management programs in Germany's statutory health insurance system. *Health Affairs*, 23(3): 56–67.

Busse, R. and Riesberg, A. (2004). Health care systems in transition: Germany. Technical Report, WHO Regional Office for Europe, Copenhagen.

Butler, K., Cafferkey, M., Cronin, M., Doyle, R., Jennings, P., and O'Flanagan, D. (2002). Guidelines for control of measles in Ireland. Technical Report, October, Irish National Disease Surveillance Center, Dublin, Ireland.

Cameron, A., Ewen, M., Ross-Degnan, D., Ball, D., and Laing, R. (2009). Medicine prices, availability, and affordability in 36 developing and middle-income countries: a secondary analysis. *Lancet*, 373(9659): 240–9.

Campbell, J. C., Ikegami, N., and Gibson, M. J. (2010). Lessons from public long-term care insurance in Germany and Japan. *Health Affairs (Project Hope)*, 29(1): 87–95.

Campbell, J. C., Ikegami, N., and Kwon, S. (2009). Policy learning and cross-national diffusion in social long-term care insurance: Germany, Japan, and the Republic of Korea. *International Social Security Review*, 62(4): 63–80.

Card, D., Dobkin, C., and Maestas, N. (2009). Does Medicare save lives? *Quarterly Journal of Economics*, 124(2): 597–636.

Cardon, J. H. and Hendel, I. (2001). Asymmetric information in health insurance: evidence from the National Medical Expenditure Survey. *RAND Journal of Economics*, 32(3): 408–27.

Carlsen, F. and Kaarboe, O. M. (2010a). Norwegian priority guidelines: estimating the distributional implications across age, gender and SES. *Health Policy*, 95(2–3): 264–70.

Carlsen, F. and Kaarboe, O. M. (2010b). Waiting times and socioeconomic status: evidence from Norway. Health Economics. http://onlinelibrary.wiley.com/doi/10.1002/hec.2904/references.

Carmon, Z. and Ariely, D. (2000). Focusing on the forgone: how value can appear so different to buyers and sellers. *Journal of Consumer Research*, 27(3): 360–70.

Carrell, S. E., Hoekstra, M., and West, J. E. (2011). Is poor fitness contagious? Evidence from randomly assigned friends. *Journal of Public Economics*, 95(7–8): 657–63.

Case, A., Lubotsky, D., and Paxson, C. (2002). Economic status and health in childhood: the origins of the gradient. *American Economic Review*, 92(5): 1308–34.

Castles, F. G. (2003). The world turned upside down: below replacement fertility, changing preferences and family-friendly public policy in 21 OECD countries. *Journal of European Social Policy*, 13(3): 209–27.

Caves, R. E., Whinston, M. D., and Hurwitz, M. A. (1991). Patent expiration, entry, and competition in the US pharmaceutical industry. *Brookings Papers on Economic Activity: Microeconomics*, 1991(1): 1–66.

Cawley, J. (2004). The impact of obesity on wages. *Journal of Human Resources*, 39 (September 2000): 451–74.

Cawley, J. and Philipson, T. (1999). An empirical examination of information barriers to trade in insurance. *American Economic Review*, 89(4): 827–46.

CBC (2012). Wait times for patients 'worsening'. http://www.cbc.ca/news/health/story/2012/06/19/wait-times.html.

CDC (1991). Current trends measles – United States, 1987. Technical Report 22, Centers for Disease Control and Prevention.

Chandra, A. and Staiger, D. (2010). Identifying provider prejudice in healthcare. NBER Working Paper No. 16382.

Chen, D. L. (2011). Can countries reverse fertility decline? Evidence from France's marriage and baby bonuses, 1929–1981. *International Tax and Public Finance*, 18(3): 253–72.

Chen, Y. and Zhou, L.-A. (2007). The long-term health and economic consequences of the 1959–1961 famine in China. *Journal of Health Economics*, 26(4): 659–81.

Cheng, A. K. (1999). Cost-utility of the cochlear implant in adults. *Archives of Otolaryngology – Head and Neck Surgery*, 125, 1214–8.

Cheng, A. K., Rubin, H. R., Powe, N. R., Mellon, N. K., Francis, H. W., and Niparko, J. K. (2000). Cost-utility analysis of the cochlear implant in children. *JAMA*, 284(7): 850–6.

Chenot, J.-F. (2009). Undergraduate medical education in Germany. *German Medical Science*, 7: 1–11.

Chevreul, K., Durand-Zaleski, I., Bahrami, S., Hernandez-Quevedo, C., and Mladovsky, P. (2010). France: health system review. *Health Systems in Transition*, 12(6). http://www.euro.who.int/__data/assets/pdf_file/0008/135809/E94856.pdf.

Chiappori, P. and Salanie, B. (2000). Testing for asymmetric information in insurance markets. *Journal of Political Economy*, 108(1): 56–78.

Chou, S., Rashad, I., and Grossman, M. (2008). Fast-food restaurant advertising on television and its influence on childhood obesity. *Journal of Law and Economics*, 51(4): 599–618.

Christakis, N. A. and Fowler, J. H. (2007). The spread of obesity in a large social network over 32 years. *New England Journal of Medicine*, 357(4): 370–9.

Coase, R. (1960). The problem of social cost. *Economic Analysis of the Law*, 3: 1–13.

Coca, S., Ismail-Beigi, F., Haq, N., Krumholz, H., and Parikh, C. R. (2012). Role of intensive glucose control in development of renal end points in type 2 diabetes mellitus. *Archives of Internal Medicine*, 172(10): 761–9.

Cochrane, J. H. (1995). Time-consistent health insurance. *Journal of Political Economy*, 103(3): 445–73.

Cockburn, I. M. and Henderson, R. M. (2000). Publicly funded science and the productivity of the pharmaceutical industry. *Innovation Policy and the Economy*, 1: 1–34.

Cohen, A. (2005). Asymmetric information and learning: evidence from the automobile insurance market. *Review of Economics and Statistics*, 87(2): 197–207.

Cohen, A. and Siegelman, P. (2010). Testing for adverse selection in insurance markets. *Journal of Risk and Insurance*, 77(1): 39–84.

Cohen, R. A., Ward, B. W., and Schiller, J. S. (2011). Health insurance coverage: early release of estimates from the National Health Interview Survey, 2010. Technical Report, Centers for Disease Control and Prevention, Atlanta, GA.

Colombo, F. and Tapay, N. (2004). Private health insurance in OECD countries. OECD Health Working Papers No. 15.

Companje, K.-P., Veraghtert, K., and Widdershoven, B. (2009). *Two Centuries of Solidarity: German, Belgian and Dutch Social Health Insurance, 1770–2008*. Amsterdam University Press, Amsterdam.

Coneus, K. and Spiess, C. K. (2012). The intergenerational transmission of health in early childhood – evidence from the German Socio-Economic Panel study. *Economics and Human Biology*, 10(1): 89–97.

Connor, R. A., Feldman, R. D., Dowd, B. E., and Radcliff, T. A. (1997). Which types of hospital mergers save consumers money? *Health Affairs*, 16(6): 62–74.

Cooper, Z., Gibbons, S., Jones, S., and McGuire, A. (2011). Does hospital competition save lives? Evidence from the

English NHS Patient Choice Reforms. *Economic Journal*, 121(554): 228–260.

Cooper, Z. N., McGuire, A., Jones, S., and Grand, J. L. (2009). Equity, waiting times, and NHS reforms: retrospective study. *BMJ*, 339(7722): 673–5.

Coronado, J. L., Fullerton, D., and Glass, T. (2011). The progressivity of social security. *BE Journal of Economic Analysis and Policy*, 11(1). http://works.bepress.com/don_fullerton/11/.

Costa, D. and Steckel, R. H. (1997). Long-term trends in health, welfare, and economic growth in the United States. In Steckel, R. H. and Floud, R., editors, *Health and Welfare during Industrialization*. University of Chicago Press, Chicago, IL.

Coughlin, T. A., Long, S. K., and Shen, Y.-C. (2005). Assessing access to care under Medicaid: evidence for the nation and thirteen states. *Health Affairs (Project Hope)*, 24(4): 1073–83.

Coulson, N., Terza, J., and Neslusan, C. (1995). Estimating the moral-hazard effect of supplemental medical insurance in the demand for prescription drugs by the elderly. *American Economic Review*, 85(2): 122–6.

Coulter, A., le Maistre, N., and Henderson, L. (2005). Patients' experience of choosing where to undergo surgical treatment. Technical Report, July, Picker Institute, Oxford.

Courbage, C. and Coulon, A. (2004). Prevention and private health insurance in the UK. *Geneva Papers on Risk and Insurance*, 29(4): 719–27.

Crawford, G. S. and Shum, M. (2005). Uncertainty and learning in pharmaceutical demand. *Econometrica*, 73(4): 1137–73.

Cretin, S., Williams, A., and Sine, J. (2006). China rural health insurance experiment. Technical Report, RAND, Santa Monica, CA.

Crimmins, E. M., Saito, Y., and Ingegneri, D. (1989). Changes in life expectancy and disability-free life expectancy in the United States. *Population and Development Review*, 15(2): 235–67.

Crimmins, E. M., Saito, Y., and Reynolds, S. L. (1997). Further evidence on recent trends in the prevalence and incidence of disability among older Americans from two sources: the LSOA and the NHIS. *Journals of Gerontology. Series B, Psychological Sciences and Social Sciences*, 52(2): S59–71.

Cropper, M. and Laibson, D. (1998). The implications of hyperbolic discounting for project evaluation. Policy Research Working Paper 1943.

Cullis, J. G. and Jones, P. R. (1986). Rationing by waiting lists: an implication. *American Economic Review*, 76(1): 250–6.

Culyer, A. J. and Cullis, J. G. (1976). Some economics of hospital waiting lists in the NHS. *Journal of Social Policy*, 5 (July): 239–64.

Currie, J., DellaVigna, S., Moretti, E., and Pathania, V. (2010). The effect of fast food restaurants on obesity and weight gain. *American Economic Journal: Economic Policy*, 2 (August): 32–63.

Currie, J. and Gruber, J. (1996). Saving babies: the efficacy and cost of recent changes in the Medicaid eligibility of pregnant women. *Journal of Political Economy*, 104(6): 1263.

Currie, J. and Stabile, M. (2003). Socioeconomic status and child health: why is the relationship stronger for older children? *American Economic Review*, 93(5): 1813–23.

Currie, J. and Walker, R. (2011). Traffic congestion and infant health: evidence from E-ZPass. *American Economic Journal: Applied Economics*, 3(1): 65–90.

Cutler, D. (2010). Analysis and commentary. How health care reform must bend the cost curve. *Health Affairs*, 29(6): 1131–5.

Cutler, D. M. (1995). The incidence of adverse medical outcomes under prospective payments. *Econometrica*, 63(1): 29–50.

Cutler, D. M., McClellan, M. B., Newhouse, J., and Remler, D. (1998). Are medical prices declining? Evidence from heart attack treatments. *Quarterly Journal of Economics*, 113(4): 991–1024.

Cutler, D. M., Glaeser, E. L., and Shapiro, J. M. (2003). Why have Americans become more obese? *Journal of Economic Perspectives*, 17(3): 93–118.

Cutler, D. M. and Lleras-Muney, A. (2010). Understanding differences in health behaviors by education. *Journal of Health Economics*, 29(1): 1–28.

Cutler, D. M., Lleras-Muney, A., and Vogl, T. (2011). Socioeconomic status and health: dimensions and mechanisms. In Glied, S. and Smith, P. S., editors, *The Oxford Handbook of Health Economics*. Oxford University Press, Oxford.

Cutler, D. M. and Reber, S. J. (1998). Paying for health insurance: the trade-off between competition and adverse selection. *Quarterly Journal of Economics*, 113(2): 433–66.

Cutler, D. M. and Zeckhauser, R. J. (1998). Adverse selection in health insurance. In Garber, A. M., editor, *Frontiers in Health Policy Research*, volume 1. MIT Press, Cambridge, MA.

Danzon, P. M. and Towse, A. (2003). Differential pricing for pharmaceuticals: reconciling access, R&D and patents. *International Journal of Health Care Finance and Economics*, 3(3): 183–205.

Danzon, P. M., Wang, Y. R., and Wang, L. (2005). The impact of price regulation on the launch delay of new drugs – evidence from twenty-five major markets in the 1990s. *Health Economics*, 14(3): 269–92.

Dartmouth Atlas Project (2008). Tracking the care of patients with severe chronic illness. Technical Report, The Dartmouth Institute for Health Policy and

Clinical Practice Center for Health Policy Research, Dartmouth.

Datar, A. and Nicosia, N. (2012). Junk food in schools and childhood obesity. *Journal of Policy Analysis and Management*, 31(2): 312–37.

David, G. (2008). The convergence between for-profit and nonprofit hospitals in the United States. *International Journal of Health Care Finance and Economics*, 9(4): 403–28.

David, G., Lindrooth, R., Helmchen, L. A., and Burns, L. R. (2011). Do hospitals cross subsidize? NBER Working Paper No. 17300.

Dawson, W. H. (1912). *Social Insurance in Germany: 1883–1911*. T. Fisher Unwin, London, England.

De Meza, D. and Webb, D. (2001). Advantageous selection in insurance markets. *RAND Journal of Economics*, 32(2): 249–62.

De Vries, E., Prins, H., Crolla, R., Den Outer, A., Van Andel, G., Van Helden, S., Schlack, W., Van Putten, M., Gouma, D., Dijkgraaf, M., and Others (2010). Effect of a comprehensive surgical safety system on patient outcomes. *New England Journal of Medicine*, 363(20): 1928–37.

Deaton, A. S. (2003). Health, inequality and economic development. *Journal of Economic Literature*, 41(1): 113–58.

DeLeire, T. (2000). The wage and employment effects of the Americans with Disabilities Act. *Journal of Human Resources*, 35(4): 693–715.

DellaVigna, S. (2009). Psychology and economics: evidence from the field. *Journal of Economic Literature*, 47(2): 315–72.

Department of Health (2011). Hospital waiting times and list statistics.

Detsky, A. S. and Naylor, C. D. (2003). Canada's health care system reform delayed. *New England Journal of Medicine*, 349(8): 804–10.

Devers, K. J., Brewster, L. R., and Casalino, L. P. (2003). Changes in hospital competitive strategy: a new medical arms race? *Health Services Research*, 38(1 Pt 2): 447–69.

Devlin, R. A., Sarma, S., and Zhang, Q. (2011). The role of supplemental coverage in a universal health insurance system: some Canadian evidence. *Health Policy*, 100(1): 81–90.

Dimakou, S., Parkin, D., Devlin, N., and Appleby, J. (2008). Identifying the impact of government targets on waiting times in the NHS. *Health Care Management Science*, 12(1): 1–10.

DiMasi, J. A., Hansen, R. W., and Grabowski, H. G. (2003). The price of innovation: new estimates of drug development costs. *Journal of Health Economics*, 22(2): 151–85.

Dionne, G., Gouriéroux, C., and Vanasse, C. (2001). Testing for evidence of adverse selection in the automobile insurance market: a comment. *Journal of Political Economy*, 109(2): 444–53.

DiSesa, V. J., O'Brien, S. M., Welke, K. F., Beland, S. M., Haan, C. K., Vaughan-Sarrazin, M. S., and Peterson, E. D. (2006). Contemporary impact of state certificate-of-need regulations for cardiac surgery: an analysis using the Society of Thoracic Surgeons' National Cardiac Surgery Database. *Circulation*, 114(20): 2122–9.

Dixon, A., Robertson, R., Appleby, J., Burge, P., Devlin, N., and Magee, H. (2010). *Patient Choice: How Patients Choose and How Providers Respond*. The Kings Fund, London, England.

Dolan, P. (1996). The effect of experience of illness on health state valuations. *Journal of Clinical Epidemiology*, 49(5): 551–64.

Dolan, P. (2000). The measurement of health-related quality of life for use in resource allocation decisions in health care. In Culyer, A. J. and Newhouse, J. P., editors, *Handbook of Health Economics*, volume 1. Elsevier Science, Amsterdam, 1st edition.

Donaldson, L. J., Maratos, J. I., and Richardson, R. A. (1984). Review of an orthopaedic in-patient waiting list. *Health Trends*, 16(1): 14–15.

Donelan, K., Blendon, R. J., Schoen, C., Davis, K., and Binns, K. (1999). The cost of health system change: public discontent in five nations. *Health Affairs*, 18(3): 206–16.

Donnelly, L. (2009). Death rates victory after Stafford scandal. *The Telegraph*. 2 May. http://www.telegraph.co.uk/health/healthnews/5264078/Death-rates-victory-after-Stafford-scandal.html.

Dorsey, E. R., Jarjoura, D., and Rutecki, G. W. (2003). Influence of controllable lifestyle on recent trends in specialty choice by US medical students. *JAMA*, 290(9): 1173–8.

Dow, W. and Fulton, B. (2010). Reinsurance for high health costs: benefits, limitations, and alternatives. *Forum for Health Economics and Policy*, 13(2): 1–23.

Doyle, J. J. (2005). Health insurance, treatment and outcomes: using auto accidents as health shocks. *Review of Economics and Statistics*, 87(2): 256–70.

Doyle, J. J., Ewer, S. M., and Wagner, T. H. (2010). Returns to physician human capital: evidence from patients randomized to physician teams. *Journal of Health Economics*, 29(6): 866–82.

Dranove, D. and Satterthwaite, M. A. (1992). Monopolistic competition when price and quality are imperfectly observable. *RAND Journal of Economics*, 23(4): 518–34.

Dranove, D. and Satterthwaite, M. A. (2000). The industrial organization of health care markets. In Culyer, A. J. and Newhouse, J. P., editors, *Handbook of Health Economics*, volume 1. Elsevier Science, Amsterdam, 1st edition.

Duggan, M. G. (2000). Hospital ownership and public medical spending. *Quarterly Journal of Economics*, 115(4): 1343–73.

Dumanovsky, T., Huang, C. Y., Nonas, C. A., Matte, T. D., Bassett, M. T., and Silver, L. D. (2011). Changes in energy content of lunchtime purchases from fast food restaurants after introduction of calorie labelling: cross sectional customer surveys. *BMJ*, 343: d4464. http://www.bmj.com/cgi/doi/10.1136/.

Duncan, G. J. and Holmlund, B. (1983). Was Adam Smith right after all? Another test of the theory of compensating wage differentials. *Journal of Labor Economics*, 1(4): 366–79.

Eastridge, B. J., Hamilton, E. C., O'Keefe, G. E., Rege, R. V., Valentine, R. J., Jones, D. J., Tesfay, S., and Thal, E. R. (2003). Effect of sleep deprivation on the performance of simulated laparoscopic surgical skill. *American Journal of Surgery*, 186(2): 169–74.

Ebbeling, C. B., Pawlak, D. B., and Ludwig, D. S. (2002). Childhood obesity: public-health crisis , common sense cure. *Lancet*, 360(9331): 473–82.

Eckles, D. and Schaffner, B. (2010). Loss aversion and the framing of the health care reform debate. *Forum*, 8(1). http://works.bepress.com/brian_schaffner/1/.

Educational Commission for Foreign Medical Graduates (2012). 2012 information booklet: ECFMG certification. Technical Report, Educational Commission for Foreign Medical Graduates, Philadelphia, PA.

Eggleston, K. and Fuchs, V. R. (2012). The new demographic transition: most gains in life expectancy now realized late in life, 26(3): 137–56.

Eggleston, K. and Hsieh, C.-R. (2004). Health care payment incentives: a comparative analysis of reforms in Taiwan, Korea and China. *Applied Health Economics and Health Policy* 31. http://www.ncbi.nlm.nih.gov/pubmed/15702940.

Eisenberg, J. M. (1985). Physician utilization: the state of research about physicians' practice patterns. *Medical Care*, 23(5): 461–83.

Eldridge, D., Ko, C., Onur, I., and Velamuri, M. (2010). The impact of private hospital insurance on utilization of hospital care in Australia: evidence from the National Health Survey. School of Economics, La Trobe University Working Papers No. 2011.01. http://ideas.repec.org/p/ltr/wpaper/2011.01.html.

Elmendorf, D. (2011). Statement of CBO's analysis of the major health care legislation enacted in March 2010. Technical Report, Congressional Budget Office.

Emanuel, E. J. (1994). The economics of dying: the illusion of cost savings at the end of life. *New England Journal of Medicine*, 330(8): 540–4.

Emanuel, E. J. (1996). Cost savings at the end of life. What do the data show? *JAMA*, 275(24): 1907–14.

Emanuel, L. and Barry, M. (1991). Advance directives for medical care – a case for greater use. *New England Journal of Medicine*, 324(13): 889–95.

Enthoven, A. (1993). The history and principles of managed competition. *Health Affairs*, 12(1): 24–48.

Epstein, D. and Mason, A. (2006). Costs and prices for inpatient care in England: mirror twins or distant cousins? *Health Care Management Science*, 9(3): 233–42.

Escarce, J. J., Jain, A. K., and Rogowski, J. (2006). Hospital competition, managed care, and mortality after hospitalization for medical conditions: evidence from three states. *Medical Care Research and Review*, 63(6 Suppl): 112S–140S.

Evans, R. G. (1974). Supplier-induced demand: some empirical evidence and implications. In Perlman, M., editor, *The Economics of Health and Medical Care*. Macmillan, London.

Fang, H., Keane, M., and Silverman, D. (2008). Sources of advantageous selection: evidence from the Medigap insurance market. *Journal of Political Economy*, 116(2). NBER Working Paper No. 12289, 303–50.

Farber, H. S. and Levy, H. (2000). Recent trends in employer-sponsored health insurance coverage: are bad jobs getting worse? *Journal of Health Economics*, 19(1): 93–119.

Farrar, S., Yi, D., Sutton, M., Chalkley, M., Sussex, J., and Scott, A. (2009). Has payment by results affected the way that English hospitals provide care? Difference-in-differences analysis. *BMJ*, 339(b3047). http://www.ncbi.nlm.nih.gov/pmc/articles/PMC2733950/.

Farrell, P. and Fuchs, V. R. (1982). Schooling and health: the cigarette connection. *Journal of Health Economics*, 1(3): 217–30.

Felder, S. (2008). To wait or to pay for medical treatment? Restraining ex-post moral hazard in health insurance. *Journal of Health Economics*, 27(6): 1418–22.

Fenner, F., Henderson, D. A., Arita, I., and Ladnyi, I. D. (1988). *Smallpox and its Eradication*. World Health Organization, Geneva.

Fihn, S. D. and Wicher, J. B. (1988). Withdrawing routine outpatient medical services: effects on access and health. *Journal of General Internal Medicine*, 3: 356–62.

Finkelstein, A. (2004). Static and dynamic effects of health policy: evidence from the vaccine industry. *Quarterly Journal of Economics*, 119(2): 527.

Finkelstein, A. and McGarry, K. (2006). Dimensions of private information: evidence from the multiple care insurance market. *American Economic Review*, 96(4): 938–58.

Finkelstein, A., Taubman, S., Wright, B., Bernstein, M., Gruber, J., Newhouse, J., Allen, H., and Baicker, K. and Oregon Health Study Group (2011). The Oregon health insurance experiment: evidence from the first year. *Quarterly Journal of Economics*, 127(3): 1057–1106.

Finkelstein, E. A., Ruhm, C. J., and Kosa, K. M. (2005). Economic causes and consequences of obesity. *Annual Review of Public Health*, 26: 239–57.

Fisher, E. S., Wennberg, D. E., Stukel, T. A., Gottlieb, D. J., Lucas, F., and Pinder, E. L. (2003a). The implications of regional variations in Medicare spending. Part 1: the content, quality, and accessibility of care. *Annals of Internal Medicine*, 138(4): 273–311.

Fisher, E. S., Wennberg, D., Stukel, T. A., Gottlieb, D. J., Lucas, F., and Pinder, E. L. (2003b). The implications of regional variations in Medicare spending. Part 2: Health outcomes and satisfaction with care. *Annals of Internal Medicine*, 138(4): 288–98.

Flegal, K., Graubard, B., Williamson, D., and Mitchell, H. (2005). Excess deaths associated with underweight, overweight, and obesity. *JAMA*, 293(15): 1861–7.

Flood, C. M. and Archibald, T. (2001). The illegality of private health care in Canada. *Canadian Medical Association Journal*, 164(6): 825–30.

Flood, C. M. and Thomas, B. (2010). Blurring of the public/private divide : the Canadian chapter. *European Journal of Health Law*, 17(3): 257–78.

Fogel, R. (1986). Nutrition and the decline in mortality since 1700: some additional preliminary findings. In Engerman, S. L. and Gallman, R. E., editors, *Long-Term Factors in American Economic Growth*. University of Chicago Press, Cambridge, MA.

Folkman, J. (1995). Clinical applications of research on angiogenesis. *New England Journal of Medicine*, 333(26): 1757–63.

Fontaine, K. R., Redden, D. T., Wang, C., Westfall, A. O., and Allison, D. B. (2003). Years of life lost due to obesity. *JAMA*, 289(2): 187–93.

Forrest, C. B. (2003). Primary care gatekeeping and referrals: effective filter or failed experiment? *BMJ*, 326(692.1): 692–95.

Fotaki, M. (2007). Patient choice in healthcare in England and Sweden: from quasi-market and back to market? A comparative analysis of failure in unlearning. *Public Administration*, 85(4): 1059–75.

Frakt, A. B. (2011). How much do hospitals cost shift? A review of the evidence. *Milbank Memorial Fund Quarterly*, 89(1): 90–130.

Francis, R. Q. (2010). Independent inquiry into care provided by Mid Staffordshire NHS Foundation Trust January 2005–March 2009. Technical Report, January 2005, The Stationary Office, London.

Frederick, S., Loewenstein, G., and O'Donoghue, T. (2002). Time discounting and time preference: a critical review. *Journal of Economic Literature*, 40(2): 351–401.

Friedman, M. and Kuznets, S. (1945). *Income from Independent Professional Practice*. National Bureau of Economic Research, New York.

Fries, J. (1980). Aging, natural death, and the compression of morbidity. *New England Journal of Medicine*, 303(3): 130–5.

Fuchs, V. R. (1996). Economics, values, and health care reform. *American Economic Review*, 86(1): 1–24.

Fuchs, V. R. (1975). *Who Shall Live? Health, Economics, and Social Choice*. Basic Books, New York.

Fuchs, V. R. (1982). Time preference and health: an exploratory study. In Fuchs, V. R., editor, *Economic Aspects of Health*. University of Chicago Press, Chicago, IL.

Gallini, N. T. (2002). The economics of patents: lessons from recent US patent reform. *Journal of Economic Perspectives*, 16(2): 131–54.

Gambardella, A. (1995). *Science and Innovation: The US Pharmaceutical Industry during the 1980s*. Cambridge University Press, Cambridge, MA, 1st edition.

Garber, A. M. (2011). Competition, integration and incentives: the quest for efficiency in the English NHS. Technical Report 2, Nuffield Trust, London.

Garber, A. M. and Phelps, C. E. (1997). Economic foundations of cost-effectiveness analysis. *Journal of Health Economics*, 16(1): 1–31.

Garber, A. M. and Skinner, J. (2008). Is American health care uniquely inefficient? *Journal of Economic Perspectives*, 22(4): 27–50.

Garber, S., Ridgely, M. S., Bradley, M., and Chin, K. W. (2002). Payment under public and private insurance and access to cochlear implants. *Archives of Otolaryngology – Head and Neck Surgery*, 128(10): 1145–52.

Garcia, T. C., Bernstein, A. B., and Bush, M. A. (2010). Emergency department visitors and visits: who used the emergency room in 2007? Technical Report 38, National Center for Health Statistics.

Garrett, D. (1995). The effects of differential mortality rates on the progressivity of social security. *Economic Inquiry*, 33: 457–75.

Gawande, A. (2002). *Complications: A Surgeon's Notes on an Imperfect Science*. Metropolitan Books, New York.

Gawande, A. (2009). The cost conundrum. *New Yorker*, 1 June 2009.

Gaynor, M., Laudicella, M., and Propper, C. (2011). Can governments do it better? Merger mania and hospital outcomes in the English NHS. NBER Working Paper No. 17608.

Gaynor, M., Moreno-serra, R., and Propper, C. (2010). Death by market power: reform, competition and patient outcomes in the National Health Service. NBER Working Paper No. 16164.

Gaynor, M. and Town, R. J. (2013). Competition in health care markets. In McGuire, T., Pauly, M. V., and Barros, P. P., editors, *Handbook of Health Economics*. Elsevier Science, Amsterdam, 2nd edition.

Gaynor, M. and Vogt, W. B. (2000). Antitrust and competition in health care markets. In Culyer, A. J. and Newhouse, J. P., editors, *Handbook of Health Economics*, volume 1. Elsevier Science, Amsterdam, 1st edition.

Geo (2011). Medicaid and state budgets: looking at the facts. Georgetown University Health Policy Institute. http://ccf.georgetown.edu/index/cms-filesystem-action?file=ccf%20publications/about%20medicaid/medicaid%20and%20state%20budgets.pdf.

Geoffard, P. and Philipson, T. (1996). Rational epidemics and their public control. *International Economic Review*, 37(3): 603–24.

Geoffard, P.-Y., Gardiol, L., and Grandchamp, C. (2006). Separating selection and incentive effects: an econometric study of Swiss health insurance claims data. In Chiappori, P. and Gollier, C., editors, *Competitive Failures in Insurance Markets*. MIT Press, Cambridge, MA.

Georgetown University Health Policy Institute (2011). Medicaid and state budgets: looking at the facts. Technical report, March, Georgetown University Health Policy Institute, Washington DC. http://ccf.georgetown.edu/ccf-resources/medicaid-and-state-budgets-looking-at-the-facts/.

Gerdtham, U. (1991). Price and quantity in international comparisons of health care expenditure. *Applied Economics*, 23(9): 1519–28.

Getzen, T. E. (1992). Population aging and the growth of health expenditures. *Journal of Gerontology*, 47(3): S98–104.

Gieringer, D. (1985). The safety and efficacy of new drug approval. *Cato Journal*, 5(1): 177–201.

Gindler, J. S., Atkinson, W. L., and Markowitz, L. E. (1992). Update – the United States measles epidemic, 1989–1990. *Epidemiologic Reviews*, 14: 270–6.

Ginsburg, P. B. (2010). Wide variation in hospital and physician payment rates evidence of provider market power. Center for Studying Health System Change. https://www.blueshieldca.com/sites/make-care-affordable/documents/variation-hospital-physician-payment.pdf.

Glenngard, A. H., Hjalte, F., Svensson, M., Anell, A., and Bankauskaite, V. (2005). Health systems in transition: Sweden. Technical Report, World Health Organization Regional Office for Europe.

Glotzer, D. E., Freedberg, K. A., and Bauchner, H. (1995). Management of childhood lead poisoning: clinical impact and cost-effectiveness. *Medical Decision Making*, 15(1): 13–23.

Gold, M. R., Siegal, J., Russell, L., and Weinstein, M. (1996). *Cost-Effectiveness in Health and Medicine*. Oxford University Press, Oxford.

Gold, M. R., Sofaer, S., and Siegelberg, T. (2007). Medicare and cost-effectiveness analysis: time to ask the taxpayers. *Health Affairs*, 26(5): 1399–406.

Goldman, D. P., Cutler, D., Shang, B., and Joyce, G. F. (2006). The value of elderly disease prevention. *Forum for Health Economics and Policy*, 9(2). http://www.degruyter.com/view/j/fhep.2006.biomedical_research.1/fhep.2006.biomedicalresearch.1.1004/fhep.2006.biomedicalresearch.1.1004.xml.

Goldman, D. P., Shekelle, P., Bhattacharya, J., Hurd, M., Joyce, G., Lakdawalla, D., Matsui, D., Newberry, S., Panis, C., and Shang, B. (2004). Health status and medical treatment of the future elderly: final report. Technical report, RAND Technical Report TR-169-CMS, Santa Monica, CA.

Goldman, D. P., Bhattacharya, J., McCaffrey, D. F., Duan, N., Leibowitz, A. A., Joyce, G. F., and Morton, S. C. (2001). Effect of insurance on mortality in an HIV-positive population in care. *Journal of the American Statistical Association*, 96(455): 883–94.

Goldman, D. P., Lakdawalla, D. N., Malkin, J. D., Romley, J., and Philipson, T. (2011). The benefits from giving makers of conventional 'small molecule' drugs longer exclusivity over clinical trial data. *Health Affairs*, 30(1): 84–90.

Goldman, D. P. and Smith, J. P. (2002). Can patient self-management help explain the SES health gradient? *Proceedings of the National Academy of Sciences*, 99(16): 10929–34.

Gottfried, J. and Sloan, F. (2002). The quality of managed care: evidence from the medical literature. *Law and Contemporary Problems*, 65(4): 103–37.

Gottlieb, D. J., Zhou, W., Song, Y., Andrews, K. G., Skinner, J. S., and Sutherland, J. M. (2010). Prices don't drive regional Medicare spending variations. *Health Affairs*, 29(3): 537–43.

Gowrisankaran, G. and Town, R. J. (2003). Competition, payers, and hospital quality. *Health Services Research*, 38(6): 1403–22.

Graber, C. (2007). Snake oil salesmen were on to something. *Scientific American* (November). http://www.scientificamerican.com/article.cfm?id=snake-oil-salesmen-knew-something.

Grabowski, H. (2002). Patents, innovation and access to new pharmaceuticals. *Journal of International Economic Law*, 5(4): 849–60.

Grabowski, H. and Vernon, J. (1990). A new look at the returns and risks to pharmaceutical R&D. *Management Science*, 36(7): 804–21.

Grabowski, H. and Vernon, J. M. (1992). Brand loyalty, entry, and price competition in pharamaceuticals after the 1984 Drug Act. *Journal of Law and Economics*, 35(2): 331–50.

Gravelle, H. and Siciliani, L. (2008a). Is waiting-time prioritisation welfare improving? *Health Economics*, 17(2): 167–84.

Gravelle, H. and Siciliani, L. (2008b). Optimal quality, waits and charges in health insurance. *Journal of Health Economics*, 27(3): 663–74.

Green, D. G. and Irvine, B. (2001). *Health Care in France and Germany: Lessons for the UK*. Civitas: Institute for the Study of Civil Society, London.

Green, L., Fristoe, N., and Myerson, J. (1994). Temporal discounting and preference reversals in choice between delayed outcomes. *Psychonomic Bulletin and Review*, 1(3): 383–9.

Grignon, M. and Perronnin, M. (2008). Does free complementary health insurance help the poor to access health care? Evidence from France. *Health Economics*, 219 (June 2007): 203–19.

Grol, R. (1992). Implementing guidelines in general practice care. *Quality in Health Care*, 1(3): 184–91.

Grootendorst, P. (2002). Beneficiary cost sharing under Canadian provincial prescription drug benefit programs: history and assessment. *Canadian Journal of Clinical Pharmacology*, 9(2): 79–99.

Grossman, M. (1972). On the concept of health capital and the demand for health. *Journal of Political Economy*, 80(2): 223–55.

Gruber, J. (1994). The incidence of mandated maternity benefits. *American Economic Review*, 84(3): 622–41.

Gruber, J. and Koszegi, B. (2001). Is addiction "rational"? Theory and evidence. *Quarterly Journal of Economics*, 116(4): 1261–303.

Gruber, J. and KoİNszegi, B. (2004). Tax incidence when individuals are time-inconsistent: the case of cigarette excise taxes. *Journal of Public Economics*, 88(9–10): 1959–87.

Gruenberg, E. M. (1977). The failures of success. *Milbank Memorial Fund Quarterly. Health and Society*, 55(1): 3–24.

Guinnane, T. W. (2011). The historical fertility transition: a guide for economists. *Journal of Economic Literature*, 49(3): 589–614.

Guinnane, T. W. and Streb, J. (2011). Moral hazard in a mutual health insurance system: German Knappschaften, 1867–1914. *Journal of Economic History*, 71(1): 70–104.

Gul, F. and Pesendorfer, W. (2001). Temptation and self-control. *Econometrica*, 69(6): 1403–35.

Gupta, A. K., Poulter, N. R., Dobson, J., Eldridge, S., Cappuccio, F. P., Caulfield, M., Collier, D., Cruickshank, J. K., Sever, P. S., and Feder, G. (2010). Ethnic differences in blood pressure response to first and second-line antihypertensive therapies in patients randomized in the ASCOT Trial. *American Journal of Hypertension*, 23(9): 1023–30.

Gwartney, J. (1983). Labor supply and tax rates: a correction of the record. *American Economic Review*, 73(3): 446–51.

Gwartney, J., Stroup, R., Sobel, R., and Macpherson, D. (2008). *Economics: Private and Public Choice*. South-Western College, Mason, OH, 12th edition.

Hackmann, M., Kolstad, J., and Kowalski, A. (2012). Health reform, health insurance, and selection: estimating selection into health insurance using the Massachusetts health reform. NBER Working Paper No. 17748.

Hadley, J. and Holahan, J. (2003). How much medical care do the uninsured use, and who pays for it? *Health Affairs*: 66–81.

Hall, J. (2010). Health-care reform in Australia: advancing or side-stepping? *Health Economics*, 19(11): 1259–63.

Hall, J., Lourenco, R. D. A., and Viney, R. (1999). Carrots and sticks – the fall and fall of private health insurance in Australia. *Health Economics*, 8(8): 653–60.

Hall, R. E. (2005). Employment efficiency and sticky wages: evidence from flows in the labor market. *Review of Economics and Statistics*, 87(3): 397–407.

Hall, R. E. and Jones, C. I. (2004). The value of life and the rise in health spending. *Quarterly Journal of Economics*, 122(1): 39–72.

Halm, E., Lee, C., and Chassin, M. (2002). Is volume related to outcome in health care? A systematic review and methodologic critique of the literature. *Annals of Internal Medicine*, 137(6): 511.

Ham, C. (1996). Contestability: a middle path for health care. *BMJ*, 312(7023): 70.

Hamilton, B. H. and Bramley-Harker, R. E. (1999). The impact of the NHS reforms on queues and the surgical outcomes in England: evidence from hip fracture patients. *Economic Journal*, 109(1996): 437–62.

Hamilton, B. H., Ho, V., and Goldman, D. P. (2000). Queuing for surgery: is the US or Canada worse off? *Review of Economics and Statistics*, 82(2): 297–308.

Hammitt, J. K. and Haninger, K. (2010). Valuing fatal risks to children and adults: effects of disease, latency, and risk aversion. *Journal of Risk and Uncertainty*, 40(1): 57–83.

Han, J. C., Lawlor, D. A., and Kimm, S. Y. S. (2010). Childhood obesity. *Lancet*, 375(9727): 1737–48.

Handel, B. (2011). Adverse selection and switching costs in health insurance markets: when nudging hurts. NBER Working Paper No. 17459.

Hanning, M. (1996). Maximum waiting-time guarantee – an attempt to reduce waiting lists in Sweden. *Health Policy*, 36(1): 17–35.

Hanoch, Y. and Rice, T. (2006). Can limiting choice increase social welfare? The elderly and health insurance. *Milbank Quarterly*, 84(1): 37–73.

Harris, B. (2004). Public health, nutrition, and the decline of mortality: the McKeown thesis revisited. *Social History of Medicine*, 17(3): 379–407.

Harris, J. (1977). The internal organization of hospitals: some economic implications. *Bell Journal of Economics*, 8(2): 467–82.

Harrison, M. I. and Calltorp, J. (2000). The reorientation of market-oriented reforms in Swedish health-care. *Health Policy*, 50(3): 219–40.

Hassenteufel, P. (2007). Towards neo-Bismarckian health care states? Comparing health insurance reforms in Bismarckian welfare systems. *Social Policy Administration*, 41(6): 574–96.

Haub, C. (2011). World population aging: clocks illustrate growth in population under age 5 and over age 65. Technical Report, Population Reference Bureau.

Hayek, F. (1945). The use of knowledge in society. *American Economic Review*, 35(4): 519–30.

He, D. (2009). The life insurance market: asymmetric information revisited. *Journal of Public Economics*, 93(9–10): 1090–7.

He, W., Sengupta, M., Velkoff, V. A., and DeBarros, K. A. (2005). 65+ in the United States: 2005. Technical Report, December, US Census Bureau.

Healthcare Commission (2009). Investigation into Mid Staffordshire NHS Foundation Trust. Technical Report, March, Commission for Healthcare Audit and Inspection, London.

Hearnden, A. and Tennent, D. (2008). The cost of shoulder arthroscopy: a comparison with national tariff. *Annals of the Royal College of Surgeons of England*, 90(7): 587–91.

Hegedus, N. (2010). The bliss of an 18-month, paid, Swedish paternity leave. http://www.slate.com/articles/double_x/doublex/2010/08/snack_bags_and_a_regular_paycheck_the_happy_life_of_a_swedish_dad.single.html.

Helland, E. and Showalter, M. H. (2006). The impact of liability on the physician labor market. *Journal of Law and Economics*, 52(4): 635–63.

Hendel, I. and Lizzeri, A. (2003). The role of commitment in dynamic contracts: evidence from life insurance. *Quarterly Journal of Economics*, 118(1): 299–327.

Henderson, R. and Cockburn, I. (1994). Racing to invest? The dynamics of competition in ethical drug discovery. *Journal of Economics and Management Strategy*, 3(3): 481–519.

Hendren, N. (2012). Private information and insurance rejections. NBER Working Paper No. 18282.

Hendricks, R. (1991). Medical practice embattled: Kaiser Permanente, the American Medical Association, and Henry J. Kaiser on the West Coast, 1945–1955. *Pacific Historical Review*, 60(4): 439–73.

Hendricks, R. (1993). *A Model for National Health Care: The History of Kaiser Permanente*. Rutgers University Press, New Brunswick, NJ.

Hennock, E. P. (2007). *The Origin of the Welfare State in England and Germany, 1850–1914: Social Policies Compared*. Cambridge University Press, Cambridge.

Henry Ford Health System (2012). Imaging services. http://www.henryford.com/body.cfm?id=47782 (accessed 24 February 2012).

Herwartz, H. and Strumann, C. (2012). On the effect of prospective payment on local hospital competition in Germany. *Health Care Management Science*, 15(1): 48–62.

Hickson, G. B., Altemeier, W. A., and Perrin, J. M. (1987). Physician reimbursement by salary or fee-for-service: effect on physician practice behavior in a randomized prospective study. *Pediatrics*, 80(3): 344–50.

Hinrichs, K. (1995). The impact of German health insurance reforms on redistribution and the culture of solidarity. *Journal of Health Politics, Policy and Law*, 20(3): 653–87.

Hippen, B. E. (2008). Organ sales and moral travails–lessons from the Living Kidney Vendor Program in Iran. Cato Policy Analysis Series No. 614.

Hisashige, A. (2009). History of healthcare technology assessment in Japan. *International Journal of Technology Assessment in Health Care*, 25 (Suppl 1): 210–18.

Ho, K. (2009). Insurer-provider networks in the medical care market. *American Economic Review*, 99(1): 393–430.

Ho, V. (2004). Certificate of need, volume, and percutaneous transluminal coronary angioplasty outcomes. *American Heart Journal*, 147(3): 442–8.

Hoffman, J. R. (1999). Direct to consumer advertising of prescription drugs. *BMJ*, 15(3): 1–4.

Hollingsworth, T. (1965). *The Demography of the British Peerage*. Population Investigation Committee, London School of Economics, London.

Holtz-Eakin, D. and Smith, C. (2010). Labor markets and health care reform: new results. American Action Forum (2010). http://americanactionforum.org/files/LaborMktsHCRAAF5-27-10.pdf.

Horowitz, A. W. and Lai, E. L. (1996). Patent length and the rate of innovation. *International Economic Review*, 37(4): 785–801.

Horwitz, J. R. (2005). Making profits and providing care: comparing nonprofit, for-profit, and government hospitals. *Health Affairs*, 24(3): 790–801.

Hubbard, T. (2002). How do consumers motivate Experts? Reputational incentives in an auto repair market. *Journal of Law and Economics*, 45 (October): 437–67.

Huckman, R. and Barro, J. (2005). Cohort turnover and productivity: the July phenomenon in teaching hospitals. NBER Working Paper No. 11182.

Hunter, D. J. (2009). The case against choice and competition. *Health Economics, Policy and Law*, 4(4): 489–501.

Hurd, M. D., McFadden, D., and Merrill, A. (2001). Predictors of mortality among the elderly. In Wise, D. A., editor, *Themes in the Economics of Aging*. University of Chicago Press, Chicago, IL.

Ikegami, N. (2007). Rationale, design and sustainability of long-term care insurance in Japan: in retrospect. *Social Policy and Society*, 6(3): 423–34.

Iversen, T. (1993). A theory of hospital waiting lists. *Journal of Health Economics*, 12(1): 55–71.

Iversen, T. (1997). The effect of a private sector on the waiting time in a national health service. *Journal of Health Economics*, 16(4): 381–96.

Iversen, T. and Siciliani, L. (2011). Non-price rationing and waiting times. In Glied, S. and Smith, P. C., editors, *The Oxford Handbook of Health Economics*. Oxford University Press, Oxford, 1st edition.

Jachuck, S. J., Brierley, H., Jachuck, S., and Willcox, P. M. (1982). The effect of hypotensive drugs on the quality of life. *Journal of the Royal College of General Practitioners*, 32(235): 103–5.

Jackson, C. K. and Schneider, H. (2011). Do social connections reduce moral hazard? Evidence from the New York city taxi industry. *American Economic Journal: Applied Economics*, 3(3): 244–67.

Jaffe, S. (2009). Health policy brief: Medicare advantage plans. *Health Affairs*, 29 April.

Janssen, I., Lam, M., and Katzmarzyk, P. T. (2009). Influence of overweight and obesity on physician costs in adolescents and adults in Ontario, Canada. *Obesity Reviews*, 10(1): 51–7.

Januleviciute, J., Askildsen, J. E., Holmås, T. H., Kaarbøe, O., and Sutton, M. (2010). The impact of different prioritisation policies on waiting times: a comparative analysis of Norway and Scotland. University of Bergen Working Papers in Economics No. 07/10

Jena, A. B., Seabury, S., Lakdawalla, D., and Chandra, A. (2011). Malpractice risk according to physician specialty. *New England Journal of Medicine*, 365(20): 1939–40.

Jenkins, R. R., Owens, N., and Wiggins, L. B. (2001). Valuing reduced risks to children: the case of bicycle safety helmets. *Contemporary Economic Policy*, 19(4): 397–408.

Johannesson, M., Johansson, P. O., and Söderqvist, T. (1998). Time spent on waiting lists for medical care: an insurance approach. *Journal of Health Economics*, 17(5): 627–44.

Johnson, E. J., Hershey, J., Meszaros, J., and Kunreuther, H. (1993). Framing, probability distortions, and insurance decisions. *Journal of Risk and Uncertainty*, 7(1): 35–51.

Jonsson, E., Banta, H. D., and Schersten, T. (2001). Health technology assessment and screening in Sweden. *International Journal of Technology Assessment in Health*, 17(3): 380–8.

Joyce, B. T. and Lau, D. T. (2009). Medicare Part D prescription drug benefit: an update. *Buehler Center on Aging, Health and Society*, 22(2): 1,14–15.

Kahneman, D., Knetsch, J. L., and Thaler, R. H. (1990). Experimental tests of the endowment effect and the Coase theorem. *Journal of Political Economy*, 98(6): 1325–48.

Kahneman, D. and Tversky, A. (1979). Prospect theory: an analysis of decision under risk. *Econometrica*, 47(2): 263–91.

Kai (2012). Medicaid Benefits: Online Database. http://medicaidbenefits.kff.org/.

Kaiser Family Foundation (2012). Medicaid benefits: online database. http://kff.org/data-collection/medicaid-benefits/.

Kanavos, P. (2003). Overview of pharmaceutical pricing and reimbursement regulation in Europe. *Japanese Pharmacology and Therapeutics*, 31(10): 819–38.

Kaplan, R. M. (1994). Value judgment in the Oregon Medicaid experiment. *Medical Care*, 32(10): 975–88.

Katzmarzyk, P. T., Hebebrand, J., and Bouchard, C. (2002). Spousal resemblance in the Canadian population: implications for the obesity epidemic. *International Journal of Obesity*, 26(2): 241–6.

Kay, A. C., Gaucher, D., Peach, J. M., Laurin, K., Friesen, J., Zanna, M. P., and Spencer, S. J. (2009). Inequality, discrimination, and the power of the status quo: direct evidence for a motivation to see the way things are as the way they should be. *Journal of Personality and Social Psychology*, 97(3): 421–34.

Keeler, E., Buchanan, J. L., Rolph, J. E., Hanley, J. M., and Reboussin, D. M. (1988). *The Demand for Episodes of Medical Treatment in the Health Insurance Experiment*. RAND Corporation, Santa Monica, CA.

Keith, S. W., Redden, D. T., Katzmarzyk, P. T., Boggiano, M. M., Hanlon, E. C., Benca, R. M., Ruden, D., Pietrobelli, A., Barger, J. L., Fontaine, K. R., Wang, C., Aronne, L. J., Wright, S. M., Baskin, M., Dhurandhar, N. V., Lijoi, M. C., Grilo, C. M., DeLuca, M., Westfall, A. O., and Allison, D. B. (2006). Putative contributors to the secular increase in obesity: exploring the roads less traveled. *International Journal of Obesity*, 30(11): 1585–94.

Kelly, I. R. and Markowitz, S. (2010). Incentives in obesity and health Insurance. *Inquiry*, 46(4): 418–32.

Kessel, R. A. (1958). Price discrimination in medicine. *Journal of Law and Economics*, 1 (Oct.): 20–53.

Kessler, D. and McClellan, M. (1996). Do doctors practice defensive medicine? *Quarterly Journal of Economics*, 111(2): 353–90.

Kessler, D. and McClellan, M. (2000). Is hospital competition socially wasteful? *Quarterly Journal of Economics*, 115(2): 577–615.

Kessler, J. and Roth, A. (2011). Organ allocation policy and the decision to donate. NBER Working Paper No. 17324.

Ketel, N. (2011). The effect of occupational licensing on earnings of physicians: evidence from a natural randomized experiment. PhD, University of Tinbergen. http://www.tinbergen.nl/mphil-theses/.

Keys, A. (1950). *The Biology of Human Starvation*. University of Minnesota Press, Minneapolis, MN.

Kim, M. H. (2008). *A Comparison of Health Technology Adoption in Four Countries*. PhD thesis.

Kim, B. and Ruhm, C. (2009). Inheritances, health, and death. NBER Working Paper No. 15364.

Klarman, H. E., Francis, J. O. S., and Rosenthal, G. D. (1968). Cost effectiveness analysis applied to the treatment of chronic renal disease. *Medical Care*, 6(1): 48–54.

Klein, R. (1998). Puzzling out priorities: why we must acknowledge that rationing is a political process. *BMJ*, 317 (October): 959–60.

Klein, R. (2009). Safeguarding NHS standards. *BMJ*, 338(b1958): 1224.

Klein, R. (2010). *The New Politics of the NHS*. Radcliffe Publishing, Abingdon, England.

Kleiner, M. and Kudrle, R. (2002). Does regulation affect economic outcomes? The case of dentistry. *Journal of Law and Economics*, 43(2): 547–82. http://www.jstor.org/stable/10.1086/467465.

Kmietowicz, Z. (2001). Reform of NICE needed to boost its credibility. *BMJ*, 323 (December): 1324.

Koch, P., Schilling, J., Läubli, M., Mitscherlich, F., Melchart, D., and Bellucci, S. (2009). Health technology assessment in Switzerland. *International Journal of Technology Assessment in Health Care*, 25 (Suppl 1): 174–7.

Kowalski, A. E. (2009). Censored quantile instrumental variable estimates of the price elasticity of expenditure on medical care. NBER Working Paper 15085.

Krishnamoorthy, K., Harichandrakumar, K. T., Krishna Kumari, A., and Das, L. K. (2009). Burden of chikungunya in India: estimates of disability adjusted life years (DALY) lost in 2006 epidemic. *Journal of Vector Borne Diseases*, 46(1): 26–35.

Krízová, E. and Simek, J. (2002). Rationing of expensive medical care in a transition country – nihil novum? *Journal of Medical Ethics*, 28(5): 308–12.

Kronick, R. (2009). Medicare and HMOs – the search for accountability. *New England Journal of Medicine*, 360(20): 2048–50.

Kugler, A. D. and Sauer, R. M. (2005). Doctors without borders? Re-licensing requirements and negative selection in the market for physicians. *Journal of Labor Economics*, 23(3).

Lacher, M. (1985). Hodgkin's disease: historical perspective, current status, and future directions. *CA: A Cancer Journal for Clinicians*, 35(2): 88–94.

Lagnado, L. (2004). Medical markup: california hospitals open books, showing huge price differences. *Wall Street Journal*. http://online.wsj.com/article/0,,SB109571706550822844,00.html.

Laibson, D. (1997). Golden eggs and hyperbolic discounting. *Quarterly Journal of Economics*, 112(2): 443.

Lakdawalla, D. and Philipson, T. (1998). Nonprofit production and competition. NBER Working Paper No. 6377.

Lakdawalla, D. and Philipson, T. (2009). The growth of obesity and technological change. *Economics Human Biology*, 7(3): 283–93.

Lakdawalla, D., Philipson, T., and Bhattacharya, J. (2005). Welfare-enhancing technological change and the growth of obesity. *American Economic Review*, 95(2): 253–7.

Lakdawalla, D. N., Bhattacharya, J., and Goldman, D. P. (2004). Are the young becoming more disabled? *Health Affairs*, 23(1): 168–76.

Landrigan, C. P., Barger, L. K., Cade, B. E., Ayas, N. T., and Czeisler, C. A. (2006). Interns' compliance with accreditation council for graduate medical education work-hour limits. *JAMA*, 296(9): 1063–70.

Landrigan, C. P., Rothschild, J. M., Cronin, J. W., Kaushal, R., Burdick, E., Katz, J. T., Lilly, C. M., Stone, P. H., Lockley, S. W., Bates, D. W., and Czeisler, C. A. (2004). Effect of reducing interns' work hours on serious medical errors in intensive care units. *New England Journal of Medicine*, 351(18): 1838–48.

Lanjouw, J. O. (1998). The introduction of pharmaceutical product patents in Indian: "Heartless exploitation of the poor and suffering"? NBER Working Paper No. 6366.

Laudicella, M., Siciliani, L., and Cookson, R. (2012). Waiting times and socioeconomic status: evidence from England. *Social Science and Medicine (1982)*, 74(9): 1331–41.

Lee, R. H. (2008). Future costs in cost effectiveness analysis. *Journal of Health Economics*, 27(4): 809–18.

Lee, T. M. (2004). An EMTALA primer: the impact of changes in the emergency medicine landscape on

EMTALA compliance and enforcement. *Annals of Health Law*, 13(145): 145–78.

Leffler, K. (1978). Physician licensure: competition and monopoly in American medicine. *Journal of Law and Economics*, 21(1): 165–86.

Lehmann, H. and Zweifel, P. (2004). Innovation and risk selection in deregulated social health insurance. *Journal of Health Economics*, 23(5): 997–1012.

Leigh, J. P., Tancredi, D., Jerant, A., and Kravitz, R. (2010). Physician wages across specialties: informing the physician reimbursement debate. *Archives of Internal Medicine*, 170(19): 1728–34.

Lenert, L. A., Cher, D. J., Goldstein, M. K., Bergen, M. R., and Garber, A. (1998). The effect of search procedures on utility elicitations. *Medical Decision Making*, 18(1): 76–83.

Levy, H. and DeLeire, T. (2009). What do people buy when they don't buy health insurance and what does that say about why they are uninsured? *Inquiry*, 45(4): 365–79.

Levy, H. and Meltzer, D. (2004). What do we really know about whether health insurance affects health? In McLaughlin, C., editor, *Health Policy and the Uninsured*. Urban Inst Pr, 1st edition.

Li, Y.-C., Norton, E. C., and Dow, W. H. (2004). Influenza and pneumococcal vaccination demand responses to changes in infectious disease mortality. *Health Services Research*, 39(4 Pt 1): 905–25.

Lichtenberg, F. R. (2005). The impact of new drug launches on longevity: evidence from longitudinal, disease-level data from 52 countries, 1982–2001. *International Journal of Health Care Finance and Economics*, 5(1): 47–73.

Lichtenberg, F. R. and Waldfogel, J. (2003). Does misery love company? Evidence from pharmaceutical markets before and after the Orphan Drug Act. *Mich. Telecomm. & Tech. L. Rev.* 15 (2008): 335–50.

Lichtenstein, S., Slovic, P., Fischhoff, B., Layman, M., and Combs, B. (1978). Judged frequency of lethal events. *Journal of Experimental Psychology: Human Learning and Memory*, 4(6): 551–78.

Lilford, R. and Pronovost, P. (2010). Using hospital mortality rates to judge hospital performance: a bad idea that just won't go away. *BMJ*, 340(c2016): 955–7.

Lindahl, M. (2005). Estimating the effect of income on health and mortality using lottery prizes as an exogenous source of income. *Journal of Human Resources*, 40(1): 144.

Lindsay, C. M. and Feigenbaum, B. (1984). Rationing by waiting lists. *American Economic Review*, 74(3): 404–17.

Lisac, M., Reimers, L., Henke, K.-D., and Schlette, S. (2010). Access and choice – competition under the roof of solidarity in German health care: an analysis of health policy reforms since 2004. *Health Economics, Policy, and Law*, 5(Pt 1): 31–52.

Liu, V., Bhattacharya, J., Weill, D., and Hlatky, M. A. (2011). Persistent racial disparities in survival after heart transplantation. *Circulation*, 123(15): 1642–9.

Lleras-Muney, A. (2005). The relationship between education and adult mortality in the United States. *Review of Economic Studies*, 72(1): 189–221.

Longman, P. (2004). *The Empty Cradle: How Falling Birthrates Threaten World Prosperity and What to Do About It*. Basic Books, New York.

Low, S. A. and McPheters, L. R. (1983). Wage differentials and risk of death: an empirical analysis. *Economic Inquiry*, 21(2): 271–80.

Luft, H. S., Hunt, S., and Maerki, S. (1987). The volume-outcome relationship: practice-makes-perfect or selective-referral patterns? *Health Services Research*, 22(2): 157.

Luft, H. S., Garnick, D. W., Mark, D. H., Peltzman, D. J., Phibbs, C. S., Lichtenberg, E., and McPhee, S. J. (1990). Does quality influence choice of hospital? *JAMA*, 263(21): 2899–906.

Lungen, M. and Lapsley, I. (2003). The reform of hospital financing in Germany: an international solution? *Journal of Health Organisation and Management*, 17(5): 360–72.

Luo, F., Abdel-Ghany, M., and Ogawa, I. (2003). Cigarette smoking in Japan: examination of myopic and rational models of addictive behavior. *Journal of Family and Economic Issues*, 24(3): 305–17.

Lyke, B. (2008). The tax exclusion for employer-provided health insurance: policy issues regarding the repeal debate. Technical Report, Congressional Research Service, Washington DC.

McCarthy, D. and Mitchell, O. (2010). International adverse selection in life insurance and annuities. *International Studies in Population*, 10(2): 119–35.

McClellan, M., McNeil, B. J., and Newhouse, J. P. (1994). Does more intensive treatment of acute myocardial infarction in the elderly reduce mortality? *JAMA*, 272(11): 859–66.

McClellan, M. and Skinner, J. (2006). The incidence of Medicare. *Journal of Public Economics*, 90(1–2): 257–76.

McGrath, P., Wennberg, D., and Dickens, J. (2000). Relation between operator and hospital volume and outcomes following percutaneous coronary interventions in the era of the coronary stent. *JAMA*, 284(24).

McGuire, T. (2000). Physician agency. In Culyer, A. J. and Newhouse, J. P., editors, *Handbook of Health Economics*, volume 1. Elsevier Science, Amsterdam, 1st edition.

Macinko, J., de Oliveira, V. B., Turci, M. A., Guanais, F. C., Bonolo, P. F., and Lima-Costa, M. F. (2011). The influence of primary care and hospital supply on ambulatory care-sensitive hospitalizations among adults in Brazil, 1999–2007. *American Journal of Public Health*, 101(10): 1963–70.

McLeod, H. and Grobler, P. (2010). Risk equalisation and voluntary health insurance: the South Africa experience. *Health Policy*, 98(1): 27–38.

McMahon, M., Morgan, S., and Mitton, C. (2006). The Common Drug Review: a NICE start for Canada? *Health Policy*, 77(3): 138–70.

Madrian, B. C. (1994). Employment-based health insurance and job mobility: is there evidence of job-lock? *Quarterly Journal of Economics*, 109(1): 27–54.

Malani, A. and David, G. (2008). Does nonprofit status signal quality? *Journal of Legal Studies*, 37(2): 551–76.

Manning, W. G. and Marquis, M. S. (2001). Health insurance: tradeoffs revisited. *Journal of Health Economics*, 20(2): 289–93.

Manning, W. G., Newhouse, J., Duan, N., Keeler, E., and Leibowitz, A. (1987). Health insurance and the demand for medical care: evidence from a randomized experiment. *American Economic Review*, 77(3): 251–77.

Mannion, R., Marini, G., and Street, A. (2008). Implementing payment by results in the English NHS: changing incentives and the role of information. *Journal of Health Organisation and Management*, 22(1): 79–88.

Mansdotter, A., Lindholm, L., and Winkvist, A. (2007). Paternity leave in Sweden: costs, savings and health gains. *Health Policy*, 82(1): 102–15.

Mansfield, E. (1986). Patents and innovation: an empirical study. *Management*, 32(2): 173–81.

Manton, K. G., Corder, L., and Stallard, E. (1997). Chronic disability trends in elderly United States populations: 1982–1994. *Proceedings of the National Academy of Sciences of the United States of America*, 94(6): 2593–8.

Manton, K. G., Gu, X., and Lamb, V. L. (2006). Change in chronic disability from 1982 to 2004/2005 as measured by long-term changes in function and health in the US elderly population. *Proceedings of the National Academy of Sciences of the United States of America*, 103(48): 18374–9.

Manton, K. G., Gu, X., and Lowrimore, G. R. (2008). Cohort changes in active life expectancy in the US elderly population: experience from the 1982–2004 National Long-Term Care Survey. *Journals of Gerontology. Series B, Psychological Sciences and Social Sciences*, 63(5): S269–81.

Marchand, M. and Schroyen, F. (2005). Can a mixed health care system be desirable on equity grounds? *Scandinavian Journal of Economics*, 107(1): 1–23.

Marmor, T. R. (2000). *The Politics of Medicare*. Transaction Publishers. New York: Aldine De Gruyter.

Marmot, M. G., Rose, G., Shipley, M., and Hamilton, P. (1978). Employment grade and coronary heart disease in British civil servants. *Journal of Epidemiology and Community Health*, 32: 244–9.

Marmot, M. G., Smith, G., Stansfield, S., Patel, C., North, F., Head, J., White, I., Brunner, E., and Feeney, A. (1991). Health inequalities among British civil servants: the Whitehall II study. *Lancet*, 337: 1387–93.

Marquis, M. S. and Holmer, M. R. (1996). Alternative models of choice under uncertainty and demand for health insurance. *Review of Economics and Statistics*, 78(3): 421–7.

Marquis, M. S. and Phelps, C. E. (1987). Price elasticity and adverse selection in the demand for supplementary health insurance. *Economic Inquiry*, XXV (April): 299–313.

Marquis, M. S., Rogowski, J. A., and Escarce, J. J. (2004). The managed care backlash: did consumers vote with their feet? *Inquiry*, 41(4): 376–90.

Martin, A. B., Lassman, D., Washington, B., Catlin, A., and National Health Expenditure Accounts Team (2012). Growth in US health spending remained slow in 2010; health share of gross domestic product unchanged from 2009. *Health Affairs*, 31(1): 208–19.

Martin, S. and Smith, P. C. (1999). Rationing by waiting lists: an empirical investigation. *Journal of Public Economics*, 71(1): 141–64.

Maskus, K. E. (2001). Parallel imports in pharamceuticals: implications for competition and prices in developing countries. Technical Report, April, World Intellectual Property Organization.

Matsuda, S. and Yamamoto, M. (2001). Long-term care insurance and integrated care for the aged in Japan. *International Journal of Integrated Care*, 1 (September): e28.

Maxwell, A. J., Crocker, M., Jones, T. L., Bhagawati, D., Papadopoulos, M. C., and Bell, B. A. (2010). Implementation of the European Working Time Directive in neurosurgery reduces continuity of care and training opportunities. *Acta Neurochirurgica*, 152(7): 1207–10.

Mechanic, D. (2004). The rise and fall of managed care. *Journal of Health and Social Behavior*, 45 Suppl (2004): 76–86.

Medicare Board of Trustees (2012). 2012 Annual Report of the Boards of Trustees of the Federal Hospital Insurance and Federal Supplementary Medical Insurance Trust Funds. Technical Report.

Mello, M. M., Chandra, A., Gawande, A. A., and Studdert, D. M. (2010). National costs of the medical liability system. *Health Affairs*, 29(9): 1569–77.

Mellström, C. and Johannesson, M. (2008). Crowding out in blood donations: was Titmuss right? *Journal of the European Economic Association*, 6(4): 845–863.

Melnick, G. A. and Fonkych, K. (2008). Hospital pricing and the uninsured: do the uninsured pay higher prices? *Health Affairs*, 27(2): w116–22.

Meltzer, D. (1997). Accounting for future costs in medical cost-effectiveness analysis. *Journal of Health Economics*, 16(1): 33–64.

Meltzer, D. O. (2009). Social science insights into improving workforce effectiveness: examples from the developing field of hospital medicine. *Journal of Public Health Management and Practice*, 15(6 Suppl): S18–23.

Meyer, B. D. and Wherry, L. R. (2012). Saving teens: using a policy discontinuity to estimate the effects of Medicaid eligibility. NBER Working Paper No. 18309.

Michaud, P.-C., Goldman, D., Lakdawalla, D. N., Gailey, A., and Zheng, Y. (2009). International differences in longevity and health and their economic consequences. NBER Working Paper No. 15235.

Mischel, W., Ebbesen, E. B., and Zeiss, A. R. (1972). Cognitive and attentional mechanisms in delay of gratification. *Journal of Personality and Social Psychology*, 21(2): 204–18.

Mitchell, J. M. (2008). Do financial incentives linked to ownership of specialty hospitals affect physicians' practice patterns? *Medical Care*, 46(7): 732–7.

Mitchell, O. S. and Moore, J. F. (1998). Can Americans afford to retire? New evidence on retirement saving adequacy. *Journal of Risk and Insurance*, 65(3): 371–400.

Mitchell, V. S., Philipose, N. M., and Sanford, J. P. (1993). *The Children's Vaccine Initiative: Achieving the Vision*. National Academy Press, Washington DC.

Monheit, A. C., Cantor, J. C., Koller, M., and Fox, K. S. (2004). Community rating and sustainable individual health insurance markets in New Jersey. *Health Affairs*, 23(4): 167–75.

Monstad, K., Engesæter, L. B., and Espehaug, B. (2006). Patients' preferences for choice of hospital. Health Economics Bergen Working Paper No. 05/06.

Morgan, S. G., Grootendorst, P., Lexchin, J., Cunningham, C., and Greyson, D. (2011). The cost of drug development: a systematic review. *Health Policy*, 100(1): 4–17.

Morgan, S. G., McMahon, M., Mitton, C., Roughead, E., Kirk, R., Kanavos, P., and Menon, D. (2006). Centralized drug review processes in Australia, Canada, New Zealand, and the United Kingdom. *Health Affairs*, 25(2): 337–47.

Morgenstern, O. and von Neumann, J. (1947). *The Theory of Games and Economic Behavior*. Princeton University Press, Princeton, NJ, 2nd edition.

Morrison, G. (2005). Mortgaging our future – the cost of medical education. *New England Journal of Medicine*, 352(2): 117–19.

Mossialos, E., Mrazek, M., and Walley, T. (2004). *Regulating Pharmaceuticals in Europe: Striving for Efficiency, Equity, and Quality*. McGraw-Hill International, Berkshire, England.

Mukherjee, S. (2010). *The Emperor of All Maladies: A Biography of Cancer*. Scribner, New York.

Mullahy, J. (1999). It'll only hurt a second? Microeconomic determinants of who gets flu shots. *Health Economics*, 8(1): 9–24.

Müller-Riemenschneider, F., Reinhold, T., Berghöfer, A., and Willich, S. N. (2008). Health-economic burden of obesity in Europe. *European Journal of Epidemiology*, 23(8): 499–509.

Murashima, S., Yokoyama, A., Nagata, S., and Asahara, K. (2003). The implementation of long-term care insurance in Japan: focused on the trend of home care. *Home Health Care Management and Practice*, 15(5): 407–15.

Murphy, K. M. and Topel, R. H. (2006). The value of health and longevity. *Journal of Political Economy*, 114(5): 871–901.

Must, A. and Strauss, R. S. (1999). Risks and consequences of childhood and adolescent obesity. *International Journal of Obesity*, 23 Suppl 2: S2–11.

Nasser, M. and Sawicki, P. (2009). Institute for quality and efficiency in health care: Germany. Technical Report, Commonwealth Fund.

National Cancer Institute (2012). SEER Stat Fact Sheet: Hodgkin Lymphoma.

National Health Service (2012). NHS Constitution. Technical Report, March.

National Institute of Population and Social Security Research (2002). Population projections for Japan: 2001–2050. Technical Report.

Neuman, P., Maibach, E., Dusenbury, K., Kitchman, M., and Zupp, P. (1998). Marketing HMOs to Medicare beneficiaries. *Health Affairs*, 17(4): 132–9.

Neumann, P. J. (2005). *Using Cost-Effectiveness Analysis to Improve Health Care: Opportunities and Barriers*. Oxford University Press, Oxford.

Neumann, P. J., Rosen, A. B., and Weinstein, M. C. (2005). Medicare and cost-effectiveness analysis. *New England Journal of Medicine*, 353(14): 1516–22.

Neumark-Sztainer, D., French, S. A., Hannan, P. J., Story, M., and Fulkerson, J. A. (2005). School lunch and snacking patterns among high school students: associations with school food environment and policies. *International Journal of Behavioral Nutrition and Physical Activity*, 2(1): 14.

Newdick, C. (2007). Evaluating new health technology in the English National Health Service. In Jost, T. S., editor, *Health Care Coverage Determinations: An International Comparative Study*. McGraw-Hill International, New York.

Newhouse, J. P. (1970). Toward a theory of nonprofit institutions. *American Economic Review*, 60(1): 64–74.

Newhouse, J. P. (1992). Medical care costs: how much welfare loss? *Journal of Economic Perspectives*, 6(3): 3–21.

Newhouse, J. P. (1993). *Free for All? Evidence from the RAND Health Insurance Experiment*. Harvard University Press, Cambridge, MA.

Newhouse, J. P. (1996). Health plans and reimbursing health in production providers: efficiency in production versus selection. *Journal of Economic Literature*, 34(3): 1236–63.

NICE (2007). Incorporating health economics in guidelines and assessing resource impact. Technical Report, April.

Nicholson, S. (2002). Barriers to entering medical specialities. NBER Working Paper No. 9649.

Nuscheler, R. and Knaus, T. (2005). Risk selection in the German public health insurance system. *Health Economics*, 14(12): 1253–71.

Nyhan, B. (2010). Why the "death panel" myth wouldn't die: misinformation in the health care reform debate. *Forum*, 8(1). http://www.dartmouth.edu/~nyhan/health-care-misinformation.pdf.

Nyman, J. A. (1999). The economics of moral hazard revisited. *Journal of Health Economics*, 18(6): 811–24.

Nyman, J. A. (2004). Is "moral hazard" inefficient? The policy implications of a new theory. *Health Affairs*, 23(5): 194–9.

Oberlander, J. (2006). Health reform interrupted: the unraveling of the Oregon Health Plan. *Health Affairs*, 26(1): w96–105.

O'Donoghue, T. and Rabin, M. (1999). Doing it now or later. *American Economic Review*, 151(3712): 867–8.

OECD (2012). Data from OECD Health Data 2012 – Frequently Requested Data. © OECD (2012) URL: http://www.oecd.org/health/healthpoliciesanddata/oecdhealthdata2012.htm.

Okamoto, E. (2006). No care for all!? Japan's quest for healthy aging through preventive long term care. In *American Public Health Association Scientific Session*, San Francisco, CA. https://apha.confex.com/apha/134am/techprogram/paper_133089.htm.

Okma, K., Cheng, T., and Chinitz, D. (2010). Six countries, six health reform models? Health care reform in Chile, Israel, Singapore, Switzerland, Taiwan and The Netherlands. *Journal of Comparative Policy Analysis*, 1 (May): 1–42.

Oliver, A. (2003). Health technology assessment in Japan: a case study of one aspect of health technology assessment. *Health Policy*, 63(2): 197–204.

Oliver, A. (2005). The English National Health Service: 1979–2005. *Health Economics*, 14 (Suppl 1): S75–99.

Olshansky, S. and Passaro, D. (2005). A potential decline in life expectancy in the United States in the 21st century. *New England Journal of Medicine*, 352(11): 1138–45.

Or, Z., Cases, C., Lisac, M., Vrangbaek, K., Winblad, U., and Bevan, G. (2010). Are health problems systemic? Politics of access and choice under Beveridge and Bismarck systems. *Health Economics, Policy and Law*, 5(3): 269–93.

Oreopoulos, P., Stabile, M., and Walld, R. (2008). Short-, medium-, and long-term consequences of poor infant health. *Journal of Human Resources*, 43(1): 88–135.

Ortmann, K.-M. (2011). Optimal deductibles for outpatient services. *European Journal of Health Economics: HEPAC*, 12(1): 39–47.

Paolucci, F., Butler, J. R., and van de Ven, W. P. (2008). Subsidising private health insurance in Australia: why, how, and how to proceed? Australian Centre for Economic Research on Health Working Paper No. 2.

Pardes, H., Manton, K., Lander, E., Tolley, H., Ullian, A., and Palmer, H. (1999). Effects of medical research on health care and the economy. *Science*, 283(5398): 36–7.

Pauly, M. (1990). The rational nonpurchase of long-term-care insurance. *Journal of Political Economy*, 98(1): 153–68.

Pauly, M. V. (1974). Overinsurance and public provision of insurance: the roles of moral hazard and adverse selection. *Quarterly Journal of Economics*, 88(1): 44–62.

Pauly, M. V., Kunreuther, H., and Hirth, R. (1995). Guaranteed renewability in insurance. *Journal of Risk and Uncertainty*, 10: 143–56.

Pauly, M. V., Withers, K. H., Subramanian-Viswanathan, K., Lemaire, J., Hershey, John C., Armstrong, K., and Asch, D. A. (2003). Price elasticity of demand for term life insurance and adverse selection. NBER Working Paper No. 9925.

Peabody, J., Bickel, S. R., and Lawson, J. S. (1996). The Australian health care system: are the incentives down under right side up? *JAMA*, 276(24): 1944–50.

Pearson, S. and Rawlins, M. D. (2005). Quality, innovation, and value for money: NICE and the British National Health Service. *JAMA*, 294(20): 2618–22.

Peltzman, S. (1973). An evaluation of consumer protection legislation: the 1962 Drug Amendments. *Journal of Political Economy*, 81(5): 1049.

Penn, R. G. (1979). The state control of medicine: the first 3000 years. *British Journal of Clinical Pharmacology*, 8: 293–305.

Perry, C. W. and Rosen, H. S. (2004). The self-employed are less likely to have health insurance than wage earners. So what? In Holtz-Eakin, D. and Rosen, H. S., editors, *Entrepreneurship and Public Policy*, volume 3. MIT Press, Cambridge, MA.

Perry, R. T. and Halsey, N. a. (2004). The clinical significance of measles: a review. *Journal of Infectious Diseases*, 189 (Suppl 1): S4–16.

Peterson, M. (2009). A systematic review of outcomes and quality measures in adult patients cared for by hospitalists vs nonhospitalists. *Mayo Clinic Proceedings*, 84(3): 248–54.

Phelps, E. and Pollak, R. (1968). On second-best national saving and game-equilibrium growth. *Review of Economic Studies*, 35(2): 185–99.

Philipson, T. J. (1996). Private vaccination and public health: an empirical examination for US measles. *Journal of Human Resources*, 31(3): 611.

Philipson, T. J. (2000). Economic epidemiology and infectious diseases. In Culyer, A. J. and Newhouse, J. P., editors, *Handbook of Health Economics*, volume 1. Elsevier Science, Amsterdam, 1st edition.

Philipson, T. J. and Jena, A. B. (2006). Who benefits from new medical technologies? Estimates of consumer and producer surpluses for HIV/AIDS drugs. *Forum for Health Economics and Policy*, 9(2): 1–33.

Phillips, D. P. and Barker, G. E. C. (2010). A July spike in fatal medication errors: a possible effect of new medical residents. *Journal of General Internal Medicine*, 25(8): 774–9.

Pidd, H. (2010). Avastin prolongs life but drug is too expensive for NHS patients, says NICE. *The Guardian*. http://www.guardian.co.uk/society/2010/aug/24/avastin-too-expensive-for-patients.

Pohl, J. M., Tanner, C., Pilon, B., and Benkert, R. (2011). Comparison of nurse managed health centers with federally qualified health centers as safety net providers. *Policy, Politics and Nursing Practice*, 12(2): 90–9.

Popescu, I., Vaughan-Sarrazin, M. S., and Rosenthal, G. E. (2006). Certificate of Need Regulations and use of coronary revascularization. *JAMA*, 295(18): 2141–7.

Powell, L. M. and Chaloupka, F. J. (2009). Food prices and obesity: evidence and policy implications for taxes and subsidies. *Milbank Quarterly*, 87(1): 229–57.

Powis, D., Hamilton, J., and McManus, I. (2007). Widening access by changing the criteria for selecting medical students. *Teaching and Teacher Education*, 23(8): 1235–45.

Prasad, M., Iwashyna, T., Christie, J., Kramer, A., Silber, J., Volpp, K., and Kahn, J. (2009). The effect of work-hours regulations on ICU mortality in United States teaching hospitals. *Critical Care Medicine*, 37(9): 2564.

Price, J. and Mays, J. (1985). Biased selection in the Federal Employees Health Benefits Program. *Inquiry*, 22(1): 67–77.

Prioux, F. and Mandelbaum, J. (2007). Recent demographic developments in France: fertility at a more than 30-year high. *Population*, 62(3): 417–56.

Propper, C. (1990). Contingent valuation of time spent on NHS waiting lists. *Economic Journal*, 100(400): 193–9.

Propper, C. (1995a). Agency and incentives in the NHS internal market. *Social Science and Medicine*, 40(12): 1683–90.

Propper, C. (1995b). The disutility of time spent on the United Kingdom's National Health Service waiting lists. *Journal of Human Resources*, 30(4): 677–700.

Propper, C. (2000). The demand for private health care in the UK. *Journal of Health Economics*, 19(6): 855–76.

Propper, C., Burgess, S., and Gossage, D. (2008). Competition and quality: evidence from the NHS internal market 1991–9. *Economic Journal*, 118(525): 138–70.

Propper, C., Eachus, J., Chan, P., Pearson, N., and Smith, G. D. (2005). Access to health care resources in the UK: the case of care for arthritis. *Health Economics*, 14(4): 391–406.

Raftery, J. (2010). Paying for costly pharmaceuticals: regulation of new drugs in Australia, England and New Zealand. *Medical Journal of Australia*, 188(1): 26–8.

Raftery, J., Robinson, R., Mulligan, J.-A., and Forrest, S. (1996). Contracting in the NHS quasi-market. *Health Economics*, 5(4): 353–62.

Read, J. L., Quinn, R. J., Berwick, D. M., Fineberg, H. V., and Weinstein, M. C. (1984). Preferences for health outcomes: comparison of assessment methods. *Medical Decision Making*, 4(3): 315–29.

Regidor, E., Martínez, D., Calle, M. E., Astasio, P., Ortega, P., and Domínguez, V. (2008). Socioeconomic patterns in the use of public and private health services and equity in health care. *BMC Health Services Research*, 8(183). http://www.biomedcentral.com/1472-6963/8/183.

Reid, T. R. (2010). *The Healing of America: A Global Quest for Better, Cheaper, and Fairer Health Care*. Penguin Press, New York.

Reinhardt, U. E. (2006). The pricing of US hospital services: chaos behind a veil of secrecy. *Health Affairs*, 25(1): 57–69.

Remler, D. K., Donelan, K., Blendon, R. J., Lundberg, G. D., Leape, L. L., Calkins, D. R., Binns, K., and Newhouse, J. P. (1997). What do managed care plans do to affect care? Results from a survey of physicians. *Inquiry*, 34(3): 196–204.

Reyes, J. (2006). Do female physicians capture their scarcity value? The case of OB/GYNs. NBER Working Paper No. 12528.

Rice, T. (2001). Should consumer choice be encouraged in health care? In John B. Davis, editor, *The Social Economics of Health Care*. Routledge, New York.

Rich-Edwards, J. W., Kleinman, K., Michels, K. B., Stampfer, M. J., Manson, J. E., Rexrode, K. M., Hibert, E. N., and Willett, W. C. (2005). Longitudinal study of birth weight and adult body mass index in predicting risk of coronary heart disease and stroke in women. *BMJ*, 330(7500): 1115.

Riley, J. C. (2001). *Rising Life Expectancy: A Global History*. Cambridge University Press, Cambridge.

Ringard, A. N. (2012). Equitable access to elective hospital services: the introduction of patient choice in a decentralised healthcare system. *Scandinavian Journal of Public Health*, 40(1): 10–17.

Robinson, J. (2011). Hospitals respond to Medicare payment shortfalls by both shifting costs and cutting them, based on market concentration. *Health Affairs*, 30(7): 1265–71.

Robinson, J. C. (1988). Hospital quality competition and the economics of imperfect information. *The Milbank Memorial Fund Quarterly*, 66(3): 465–81.

Robinson, J. C. (2001). The end of managed care. *JAMA*, 285(20): 2622–8.

Robinson, J. C. and Luft, H. S. (1985). The impact of hospital market structure on patient volume, average length of stay, and the cost of care. *Journal of Health Economics*, 4(4): 333–56.

Robinson, J. C. and Luft, H. S. (1987). Competition and the cost of hospital care, 1972 to 1982. *JAMA*, 257(23): 3241–5.

Rodwin, M. and Okamoto, A. (2000). Physicians' conflicts of interest in Japan and the United States: lessons for the United States. *Journal of Health Politics, Policy and Law*, 25(2): 343–75.

Rodwin, V. G. (2003). The health care system under French national health insurance: lessons for health reform in the United States. *American Journal of Public Health*, 93(1): 31–7.

Romanchuk, K. (2004). The effect of limiting residents' work hours on their surgical training: a Canadian perspective. *Academic Medicine: Journal of the Association of American Medical Colleges*, 79(5): 384–5.

Rose-Ackerman, S. (1996). Altruism, nonprofits, and economic theory. *Journal of Economic Literature*, 34(2): 701–28.

Roseboom, T. J., van der Meulen, J. H., Ravelli, A., Osmond, C., Barker, D. J., and Bleker, O. P. (2001). Effects of prenatal exposure to the Dutch famine on adult disease in later life: an overview. *Molecular and Cellular Endocrinology*, 185: 93–8.

Rosenberg, L. and Bloom, D. (2006). Global demographic trends. *Finance and Development: A Quarterly Magazine of the IMF*, 43(3). http://www.imf.org/external/pubs/ft/fandd/2006/09/picture.htm.

Roth, A. E. (2007). Repugnance as a constraint on markets. *Journal of Economic Perspectives*, 21(3): 37–58.

Roth, A. E., Sönmez, T., and Utku Ünver, M. (2005). Pairwise kidney exchange. *Journal of Economic Theory*, 125(2): 151–88.

Rothschild, M. and Stiglitz, J. (1976). Equilibrium in competitive insurance markets. *Quarterly Journal of Economics*, 90(4): 629–49.

Sacerdote, B. (2007). How large are the effects from changes in family environment? A study of Korean American adoptees. *Quarterly Journal of Economics*, 122(1): 119–57.

Saito, K. (2006). Testing for asymmetric information in the automobile insurance market under rate regulation. *Journal of Risk and Insurance*, 73(2): 335–56.

Salomon, J. A. and Murray, C. J. L. (2004). A multi-method approach to measuring health-state valuations. *Health Economics*, 13(3): 281–90.

Sanders, G. D., Bayoumi, A. M., Sundaram, V., Bilir, S. P., Neukermans, C. P., Rydzak, C. E., Douglass, L. R., Lazzeroni, L. C., Holodniy, M., and Owens, D. K. (2005). Cost-effectiveness of screening for HIV in the era of highly active antiretroviral therapy. *New England Journal of Medicine*, 352(6): 570–85.

Sapelli, C. and Vial, B. (2003). Self-selection and moral hazard in Chilean health insurance. *Journal of Health Economics*, 22(3): 459–76.

Sapolsky, R. M. (1995). *Why Zebras Don't Get Ulcers: A Guide to Stress, Stress-Related Diseases, and Coping*. WH Freeman & Company, New York, 1st edition.

Sapolsky, R. M. and Mott, G. E. (1987). Social subordinance in wild baboons is associated with suppressed high density lipoprotein-cholesterol concentrations: the possible role of chronic social stress. *Endocrinology*, 121(5): 1605–10.

Scherer, F. M. (2000). The pharmaceutical industry. In Culyer, A. J. and Newhouse, J. P., editors, *Handbook of Health Economics*, volume 1. Elsevier Science, Amsterdam, 1st edition.

Scherer, F. M. (2010). Pharmaceutical innovation. In Hall, B. H. and Rosenberg, N., editors, *Handbook of the Economics of Innovation*, volume 1. Elsevier Science, Amsterdam, 1st edition.

Schnier, K. E., Horrace, W. C., and Felthoven, R. G. (2009). The value of statistical life: pursuing the deadliest catch. Center for Policy Research Working Paper No. 117.

Schoenbaum, M. (1997). Do smokers understand the mortality effects of smoking? Evidence from the health and retirement survey. *American Journal of Public Health*, 87(5): 755–9.

Schoeni, R. (2001). Persistent, consistent, widespread, and robust? Another look at recent trends in old-age disability. *Journals of Gerontology. Series B, Psychological Sciences and Social Sciences*, 56(4): 206–18.

Scholz, J. K., Seshadri, A., and Khitatrakun, S. (2006). Are Americans saving optimally for retirement? *Journal of Political Economy*, 114(4): 607–43.

Schreyögg, J., Tiemann, O., and Busse, R. (2006). Cost accounting to determine prices: how well do prices reflect costs in the German DRG-system? *Health Care Management Science*, 9(3): 269–79.

Schwartzman, D. (1976). *Innovation and the Pharmaceutical Industry.* Johns Hopkins University Press, Baltimore, MD.

Scitovsky, A. A. and McCall, N. (1977). Coinsurance and the demand for physician services: four years later. *Social Security Bulletin*, 40(5): 19–27.

Scitovsky, A. A. and Snyder, N. M. (1972). Effect of coinsurance on use of physician. *Social Security Bulletin*, 35(3): 3–19.

Scitovsky, T. (1976). *Joyless Economy: An Inquiry into Human Satisfaction and Consumer Dissatisfaction.* Oxford University Press, New York.

Seeman, T. E., Singer, B. H., Rowe, J. W., Horwitz, R. I., and McEwen, B. S. (1997). Price of adaption–allostatic load and its health consequences. *Archive of Internal Medicine*, 157: 2259–68.

Segouin, C., Jouquan, J., Hodges, B., Bréchat, P.-H., David, S., Maillard, D., Schlemmer, B., and Bertrand, D. (2007). Country report: medical education in France. *Medical Education*, 41(3): 295–301.

Seham (1956). Who pays the doctor? *The New Republic*, 9–10 July.

Sen, A. (1979). Economics, personal utilities and public judgements: or what's wrong with welfare. *Economic Journal*, 89(355): 537–58.

Shekelle, P. G., Ortiz, E., Newberry, S. J., Rich, M. W., Rhodes, S. L., Brook, R. H., and Goldman, D. P. (2005). Identifying potential health care innovations for the future elderly. *Health Affairs*, 24 (Suppl 2): W5R67–76.

Sheldon, T. (2004). News pressure mounts over European working time directive. *BMJ*, 328 (April): 2004.

Sherman, M. and Strauss, S. (1986). Thalidomide: a twenty-five year perspective. *Food Drug Cosmetic Law Journal*, 41: 458–66.

Shetty, K. D. and Bhattacharya, J. (2007). Annals of Internal Medicine article changes in hospital mortality associated with residency work-hour. *Annals of Internal Medicine*, 147(2): 73–80.

Shin, J. and Ariely, D. (2004). Keeping doors open: the effect of unavailability on incentives to keep options viable. *Management Science*, 50(5): 575–86.

Shoda, Y., Mischel, W., and Peake, P. K. (1990). Predicting adolescent cognitive and self-regulatory competencies from preschool delay of gratification: identifying diagnostic conditions. *Developmental Psychology*, 26(6): 978–86.

Shoven, J. B. (2010). New age thinking: alternative ways of measuring age, their relationship to labor force participation, government policies, and GDP. In Wise, D. A., editor, *Research Findings in the Economics of Aging.* University of Chicago Press, Chicago, IL.

Shulman, K., Berlin, J., Harless, W., Kerner, J., Sistrunk, S., Gersh, B., Dube, R., Taleghani, C. K., Burke, J. E., Williams, S., Einsenberg, J. M., and Escarce, J. J. (1999). The effect of race and sex on physicians' recommendations for cardiac catheterization. *Journal of the American Geriatrics Society*, 47(11): 1390.

Siciliani, L. and Hurst, J. (2005). Tackling excessive waiting times for elective surgery: a comparative analysis of policies in 12 OECD countries. *Health Policy*, 72(2): 201–15.

Siciliani, L. and Verzulli, R. (2009). Waiting times and socioeconomic status among elderly Europeans: evidence from SHARE. *Health Economics*, 18(11): 1295–306.

Simonet, D. (2010). Healthcare reforms and cost reduction strategies in Europe: the cases of Germany, UK, Switzerland, Italy and France. *International Journal of Health Care Quality Assurance*, 23(5): 470–88.

Sivey, P. (2012). The effect of waiting time and distance on hospital choice for English cataract patients. *Health Economics*, 21(4): 444–56.

Sloan, F. A., Smith, V. K., and Taylor, D. H. (2003). *The Smoking Puzzle.* Harvard University Press, Cambridge, MA.

Slovic, P. (1987). Perception of risk. *Science*, 236(4799): 280–5.

Smallwood, S. and Chamberlain, J. (2005). Replacement fertility, what has it been and what does it mean? *Population Trends*, 119: 16–27.

Smith, A. (1776). *An Inquiry into the Nature and Causes of the Wealth of Nations.* University of Chicago Press, Chicago, 1976 edition.

Smith, J. P. (1999). Healthy bodies and thick wallets: the dual relation between health and economic status. *Journal of Economic Perspectives*, 13(2): 145–66.

Smithells, R. and Newman, C. (1992). Recognition of Thalidomide defects. *Journal of Medical Genetics*, 29: 716–23.

Solomon, D. H., Hashimoto, H., Daltroy, L., and Liang, M. H. (1998). Techniques to improve physicians' use of diagnostic tests: a new conceptual framework. *JAMA*, 280(23): 2020–7.

Sorenson, C., Drummond, M., and Kanavos, P. (2008a). *Ensuring Value for Money in Health Care: The Role of Health Technology Assessment in the European Union.* World Health Organization, Albany, NY.

Sorenson, C., Drummond, M., Kanavos, P., and McGuire, A. (2008b). National Institute for Health and Clinical Excellence (NICE): how does it work and what are the implications for the US? Technical Report, April, National Pharmacuetical Council.

Spenkuch, J. L. (2012). Moral hazard and selection among the poor: evidence from a randomized experiment. *Journal of Health Economics*, 31(1): 72–85.

Stano, M. (1987a). A clarification of theories and evidence on supplier-induced demand for physicians' services. *Journal of Human Resources*, 22(4): 611–20.

Stano, M. (1987b). A further analysis of the physician inducement controversy. *Journal of Health Economics*, 6(3): 227–38.

Starr, P. (1982). *The Social Transformation of American Medicine*. Basic Books, Inc., New York.

Statistics Bureau, J. (2012). Statistical Handbook of Japan 2012. Technical Report, Statistics Bureau, Ministry of Internal Affairs and Communications, Japan.

Steinbrook, R. (2002). The debate over residents' work hours. *New England Journal of Medicine*, 347(16): 1296–1302.

Street, A. and Maynard, A. (2007). Activity based financing in England: the need for continual refinement of payment by results. *Health Economics, Policy and Law*, 2(4): 419–27.

Studdert, D. M., Bhattacharya, J., Schoenbaum, M., Warren, B., and Escarce, J. J. (2002). Personal choices of health plans by managed care experts. *Medical Care*, 40(5): 375–86.

Studdert, D. M., Mello, M. M., Sage, W. M., Desroches, C. M., and Peugh, J. (2005). Among high-risk specialist physicians in a volatile malpractice environment. *JAMA*, 293(21): 2609–17.

Studdert, D. M., Sage, W. M., Gresenz, C. R., and Hensler, D. R. (1999). Expanded managed care liability: what impact on employer coverage? *Health Affairs*, 18(6): 7–27.

Sturm, R. (2002). The effects of obesity, smoking, and drinking on medical problems and costs. *Health Affairs*, 21(2): 245–53.

Sundstrom, W. and David, P. (1988). Old-age security motives, labor markets, and farm family fertility in antebellum American. *Explorations in Economic History*, 197: 164–97.

Sutherland, J. M. (2011). Hospital payment mechanisms: an overview and options for Canada. Technical Report, Canadian Health Services Research Foundation, Ottawa.

Svenson, O. (1981). Are we all less risky and more skillful than our fellow drivers? *Acta Psychologica*, 47: 143–8.

Svorny, S. V. (1987). Physician licensure: a new approach to examining the role of professional interests. *Economic Inquiry*, 25(3): 497–509.

Swartz, K. (2003). Reinsuring risk to increase access to health insurance. *American Economic Review*, 93(2): 283–7.

Swinburn, B. A., Sacks, G., Hall, K. D., McPherson, K., Finegood, D. T., Moodie, M. L., and Gortmaker, S. L. (2011). The global obesity pandemic: shaped by global drivers and local environments. *Lancet*, 378(9793): 804–14.

Syrett, K. (2010). Mixing private and public treatment in the UK's National Health Service: a challenge to core constitutional principles? *European Journal of Health Law*, 17(3): 235–55.

Tabbarok, A. (2010). The Meat Market. *Wall Street Journal*, January 8. http://online.wsj.com/article/SB10001424052748703481004574646233272990474.html?mod=WSJ_hpp_RIGHTTopCarousel.

Taffinder, N. J., McManus, I. C., Gul, Y., Russell, R. C., and Darzi, A. (1998). Effect of sleep deprivation on surgeons' dexterity on laparoscopy simulator. *Lancet*, 352(9135): 1191.

Temple, S. J. (2010). Time for training: a review of the impact of the European Working Time Directive on the quality of training. Technical Report, May, National Health Services, London.

Tetlock, P. E. and Boettger, R. (1994). Accountability amplifies the status quo effect when change creates victims. *Journal of Behavioral Decision Making*, 7 (April 1993).

Thaler, R. (1981). Some empirical evidence on dynamic inconsistency. *Economics Letters*, 8: 201–7.

Thaler, R. and Sunstein, C. (2008). *Nudge: Improving Decisions About Health, Wealth, and Happiness*. Yale University Press, New Haven, CT.

Thomas, D., Frankenberg, E., Friedman, J., Habicht, J.-P., Jones, N., McKelvey, C., Pelto, G., Sikoki, B., Smith, J., Sumantri, C., and Suriastini, W. (2004). Causal effect of health on labor market outcomes: evidence from a random assignment iron supplementation intervention. On-Line Working Paper Series, California Center for Population Research, UC Los Angeles No 070-06. http://www.escholarship.org/uc/item/0g28k77w.

Thomson, S. and Mossialos, E. (2006). Choice of public or private health insurance: learning from the experience of Germany and the Netherlands. *Journal of European Social Policy*, 16(4): 315–27.

Thomson, S., Osborn, R., Squires, D., and Reed, S. J. (2011). International Profiles of Health Care Systems, 2011. Technical Report, November, The Commonwealth Fund.

Titmus, R. M. (1970). *The Gift Relationship: From Human Blood to Social Policy*. Allen and Unwin, London.

Tompkins, C. P., Altman, S. H., and Eilat, E. (2006). The precarious pricing system for hospital services. *Health Affairs*, 25(1): 45–56.

Toole, A. A. (2011). The impact of public basic research on industrial innovation: evidence from the pharmaceutical industry. *Research Policy*, 41(1): 1–12.

Torrance, G. (1986). Measurement of health state utilities for economic appraisal: a review. *Journal of Health Economics*, 5(1): 1–30.

Treadwell, J. R. and Lenert, L. A. (1999). Health values and prospect theory. *Medical Decision Making*, 19(3): 344–52.

Tsutsui, T. and Muramatsu, N. (2007). Japan's universal long-term care system reform of 2005: containing costs and realizing a vision. *Journal of the American Geriatrics Society*, 55(9): 1458–63.

Tuah, N., Amiel, C., Qureshi, S., Car, J., Kaur, B., and Majeed, A. (2011). Transtheoretical model for dietary and physical exercise modification in weight loss management for overweight and obese adults. *Cochrane Database Systematic Review*, 10(8): CD008066.

Tuohy, C. H., Flood, C. M., and Stabile, M. (2004). How does private finance affect public health care systems? Marshaling the evidence from OECD nations. *Journal of Health Politics, Policy and Law*, 29(3): 359–96.

Turquet, P. (2012). Health insurance system financing reforms in the Netherlands, Germany and France: repercussions for coverage and redistribution? *International Social Security Review*, 65(1): 29–51.

Tversky, A. (1969). Intransitivity of preferences. *Psychological Review*, 76(1): 31–48.

Tversky, A. and Fox, C. R. (1995). Weighing risk and uncertainty. *Psychological Review*, 102(2): 269–83.

Tversky, A. and Kahneman, D. (1991). Loss aversion in riskless choice: a reference-dependence model. *Quarterly Journal of Economics*, 106(4): 1039–61.

United Nations (2011). World population prospects: the 2010 revision. Technical Report, Department of Economic and Social Affairs, United Nations, New York.

United Network for Organ Sharing (2012). http://www.unos.org/.

US Department of Justice, Federal Trade Commission, A. D. (2004). *Improving Health Care: A Dose of Competition*. http://www.ftc.gov/reports/healthcare/040723healthcarerpt.pdf.

US National Institute on Aging (2007). Why population aging matters – a global perspective. Technical Report.

van Ackere, A. and Smith, P. C. (1999). Towards a macro model of National Health Service waiting lists. *System Dynamics Review*, 15(3): 225–52.

van de Ven, W. P. M. M. (2011). Risk adjustment and risk equalization: what needs to be done? *Health Economics, Policy and Law*, 6(1): 147–56.

van de Ven, W. P. M. M. and van Vliet, R. C. J. (1995). Consumer information surplus and adverse selection in competitive health insurance markets: an empirical study. *Journal of Health Economics*, 14(2): 149–69.

van de Ven, W. P. M. M., Beck, K., Buchner, F., Chernichovsky, D., Gardiol, L., Holly, A., Lamers, L. M., Schokkaert, E., Shmueli, A., Spycher, S., Van de Voorde, C., van Vliet, R. C. J. A., Wasem, J., and Zmora, I. (2003). Risk adjustment and risk selection on the sickness fund insurance market in five European countries. *Health Policy*, 65(1): 75–98.

van de Ven, W. P. M. M., Beck, K., Van de Voorde, C., Wasem, J., and Zmora, I. (2007). Risk adjustment and risk selection in Europe: 6 years later. *Health Policy*, 83(2–3): 162–79.

van de Ven, W. P. M. M. and Schut, F. T. (2008). Universal mandatory health insurance in the Netherlands: a model for the United States? *Health Affairs*, 27(3): 771–81.

Van Hook, J. and Altman, C. E. (2011). Competitive food sales in schools and childhood obesity: a longitudinal study. *Sociology of Education*, 85(1): 23–39.

Varkevisser, M. and Schut, F. T. (2009). Hospital merger control: an international comparison. iBMG Working Paper W2009.01.

Vassev, P. and Geraci, W., editors (2010). *AAMC Data Book: Medical Schools and Teaching Hospitals by the Number's*. American Association of Medical Colleges, Washington DC.

Veldhuis, M. (1994). Defensive behavior of Dutch family physicians. Widening the concept. *Family Medicine*, 26(1): 27–9.

Viscusi, W. K. (1979). *Employment Hazards: An Investigation of Market Performance*. Harvard University Press, Cambridge, MA, 1st edition.

Viscusi, W. K. (1993). The value of life and of risks. *Journal of Economic Literature*, 31(4): 1912–46.

Viscusi, W. K. (2003). The value of a statistical life: a critical review of market estimates throughout the world. *Journal of Risk and Uncertainty*, 27(1): 5–76.

Viscusi, W. K. (2010). The heterogeneity of the value of statistical life: introduction and overview. *Journal of Risk and Uncertainty*, 40(1): 1–13.

Vladeck, B. C. (2006). Paying for hospitals' community service. *Health Affairs*, 25(1): 34–43.

Vladeck, B. C. and Rice, T. (2009). Market failure and the failure of discourse: facing up to the power of sellers. *Health Affairs*, 28(5): 1305–15.

Volpp, K. G., John, L. K., Troxel, A. B., Norton, L., Fassbender, J., and Lowenstein, G. (2008). Financial incentive-based approaches for weight loss: a randomized trial. *JAMA*, 300(22): 2631–7.

Volpp, K. G., Rosen, A. K., Rosenbaum, P. R., Romano, P. S., Even-Shoshan, O., Wang, Y., Bellini, L., Behringer, T., and Silber, J. H. (2007). Mortality among hospitalized Medicare beneficiaries in the first 2 years following ACGME resident duty hour reform. *JAMA*, 298(9): 975–83.

Wachter, R. M. and Goldman, L. (1996). The emerging role of "hospitalists" in the American health care system. *New England Journal of Medicine*, 335(7): 514–17.

Wachter, R. M. and Goldman, L. (2002). The hospitalist movement 5 years later. *JAMA*, 287(4): 487.

Wadsworth, M. E. and Kuh, D. J. (1997). Childhood influences on adult health: a review of recent work from the British 1946 national birth cohort study, the MRC National Survey of Health and Development. *Paediatric and Perinatal Epidemiology*, 11(1): 2–20.

Waidmann, T., Bound, J., and Schoenbaum, M. (1995). The illusion of failure: trends in the self-reported health of the US elderly. *Milbank Quarterly*, 73(2): 253–87.

Waldman, M., Nicholson, S., and Adilov, N. (2012). Positive and negative mental health consequences of early childhood television watching. NBER Working Paper No. 17768.

Weaver, M. (2007). Russians given day off work to make babies. *The Guardian*: http://www.guardian.co.uk/world/2007/sep/12/russia.matthewweaver.

Weeks, W. B. and Wallace, A. E. (2002). The more things change: revisiting a comparison of educational costs and incomes of physicians and other professionals. *Academic Medicine*, 77(4): 312–19.

Weinstein, M. C. (2005). Spending health care dollars wisely: can cost-effectiveness analysis help? Herbert Lourie Memorial Lecture on Health Policy. Working Paper No. 30/2005.

Weinstein, M. C. and Manning, W. G. (1997). Theoretical issues in cost-effectiveness analysis. *Journal of Health Economics*, 16(1): 121–8.

Weinstein, M. C., Siegel, J. E., Gold, M. R., Kamlet, M. S., and Russell, L. B. (1996). Recommendations of the panel on cost-effectiveness in health and medicine. *JAMA*, 276(15): 1253–8.

Weisbrod, B. (1975). Toward a theory of the voluntary non-profit sector in a three-sector economy. In Phelps, E. S., editor, *Altruism, Morality, and Economic Theory*. Russell Sage Foundation, New York.

Weisburst, S. and Scherer, F. M. (1995). Economic effects of strengthening pharmaceutical patent protection in Italy. *International Review of Industrial Property and Copyright Law*, 26(6): 1009–24.

Weissman, J. S., Zaslavsky, A. M., Wolf, R. E., and Ayanian, J. Z. (2008). State Medicaid coverage and access to care for low-income adults. *Journal of Health Care for the Poor and Underserved*, 19(1): 307–19.

Wenig, C. M. (2012). The impact of BMI on direct costs in children and adolescents: empirical findings for the German healthcare system based on the KiGGS-study. *European Journal of Health Economics*, 13(1): 39–50.

Wennberg, J. E. (1984). Dealing with medical practice variations: a proposal for action. *Health Affairs*, 3(2): 6–32.

Wennberg, J. E., Bronner, K., Skinner, J. S., Fisher, E. S., and Goodman, D. C. (2009). Inpatient care intensity and patients' ratings of their hospital experiences. *Health Affairs*, 28(1): 103–12.

Wennberg J. E., Fisher, E. S., Stukel, T. A., and Sharp, S. M. (2004). Use of Medicare claims data to monitor provider-specific performance among patients with severe chronic illness. *Health Affairs*. http://content.healthaffairs.org/content/early/2004/10/07/hlthaff.var.5.full.pdf.

Werner, R. M., Asch, D. A., and Polsky, D. (2005). Racial profiling: the unintended consequences of coronary artery bypass graft report cards. *Circulation*, 111(10): 1257–63.

Werth, B. (1995). *The Billion Dollar Molecule: One Company's Quest for the Perfect Drug*. Simon & Schuster, New York.

Westman, A., Rosén, M., Berggren, P., and Björnstig, U. (2008). Parachuting from fixed objects: descriptive study of 106 fatal events in BASE jumping 1981–2006. *British Journal of Sports Medicine*, 42(6): 431–6.

Weyden, M. B. V. D., Armstrong, R. M., and Gregory, A. T. (2005). The 2005 Nobel prize in physiology or medicine. *Medical Journal of Australia*, 183(11): 612–14.

Wildavsky, A. (1979). *Speaking Truth to Power: The Art and Craft of Policy Analysis*. LIttle Brown, Boston, MA.

Wilkinson, R. G. and Pickett, K. E. (2006). Income inequality and population health: a review and explanation of the evidence. *Social Science and Medicine*, 62(7): 1768–84.

Willcox, S. (2001). Promoting private health insurance in Australia. *Health Affairs*, 20(3): 152–61.

Willcox, S., Seddon, M., Dunn, S., Edwards, R. T., Pearse, J., and Tu, J. V. (2007). Measuring and reducing waiting times: a cross-national comparison of strategies. *Health Affairs*, 26(4): 1078–87.

Willis, R. (1979). The old age security hypothesis and population growth. NBER Working Paper No. 372.

Wilmoth, J. and Shkolnikov, V. (2012). Human mortality database. http://www.mortality.org/ (accessed September 2012).

Wilson, R. (1987). Returns to entering the medical profession in the UK. *Journal of Health Economics*, 6(4): 339–63.

Winkelmayer, W. C., Weinstein, M. C., Mittleman, M. A., Glynn, R. J., and Pliskin, J. S. (2002). Health economic evaluations: the special case of end-stage renal disease treatment. *Medical Decision Making*, 22(5): 417–30.

Winter, L., Lawton, M. P., and Ruckdeschel, K. (2003). Preferences for prolonging life: a prospect theory approach. *International Journal of Aging and Human Development*, 56(2): 155–70.

Winter, L. and Parker, B. (2007). Current health and preferences for life-prolonging treatments: an application of prospect theory to end-of-life decision making. *Social Science and Medicine*, 65(8): 1695–707.

Wolfe, J. R. and Goddeeris, J. H. (1991). Adverse selection, moral hazard, and wealth effects in the Medigap insurance market. *Journal of Health Economics*, 10(4): 433–59.

Woodrow, S. I., Segouin, C., Armbruster, J., Hamstra, S. J., and Hodges, B. (2006). Duty hours reforms in the United States, France, and Canada: is it time to refocus our attention on education? *Journal of the Association of American Medical Colleges*, 81(12): 1045–51.

World Bank (2012). Fertility rate, total (births per woman). http://data.worldbank.org/indicator/SP.DYN.TFRT.IN. (accessed September 2012).

Wrigley, E., Davies, R., Oeppen, J., and Schofield, R. (1997). *English Population History from Family Reconstitution, 1580–1837*. Cambridge University Press, Cambridge.

Yang, Z. and Hall, A. G. (2007). The financial burden of overweight and obesity among elderly Americans: the dynamics of weight, longevity, and health care cost. *Health Research and Educational Trust*, 43(3): 849–68.

Yelowitz, A. (1995). The Medicaid notch, labor supply, and welfare participation: evidence from eligibility expansions. *Quarterly Journal of Economics*, 110(4): 909–39.

Yilma, Z., van Kempen, L., and de Hoop, T. (2012). A perverse "net" effect? Health insurance and ex-ante moral hazard in Ghana. *Social science and medicine (1982)*, 75(1): 138–47.

Yin, W. (2008). Market incentives and pharmaceutical innovation. *Journal of Health Economics*, 27(4): 1060–77.

Yip, W. C. (1998). Medicare hospital prospective payment system: how DRG rates are calculated and updated. *Journal of Health Economics*, 17(6): 675–99.

Yoshikawa, A., Shirouzu, N., and Holt, M. (1991). How does Japan do it – doctors and hospitals in a universal health care system. *Stanford Law & Policy Review*, 1. Fall 1991: 111–37.

Yosufzai, R. (2013). Live donors to get financial support. Wall Street Journal, April 7. http://www.theaustralian. com.au/news/breaking-news/living-donors-to-receive-financial-support/story-fn3dxiwe-1226614172117.

Young, J., Sumant, R., Wachter, R., Lee, C., Niehaus, B., and Auerbach, A. (2011). "July effect": impact of the academic year-end changeover on patient outcomes. *Annals of Internal Medicine*, 155(5): 309–15.

Zhang, B., Wright, A. A., Huskamp, H. A., Nilsson, M. E., Maciejewski, M. L., Earle, C. C., Block, S. D., Maciejewski, P. K., and Prigerson, H. G. (2009). Health care costs in the last week of life. *Archives of Internal Medicine*, 169(5): 480–8.

Zwanziger, J. and Melnick, G. A. (1988). The effect of hospital competition and the Medicare PPS program on hospital cost behavior in California. *Journal of Health Economics*, 7(4): 301–20.

Zweifel, P., Felder, S., and Meiers, M. (1999). Health care financing ageing of population and health care expenditure: a red herring? *Health Economics*, 496 (April): 485–96.

FIGURES

1.1   US health care expenditure over time   2

2.1   Elastic and inelastic demand curves   8
2.2   Potential bias of measured demand   10
2.3   Emergency and non-emergency visits by age   16
2.4   Data on outpatient and dental care   19
2.5   Demand elasticities of various goods   21

3.1   Illness-avoidance function   32
3.2   Production possibility frontier   34
3.3   Production possibility frontier   35
3.4   Production possibility frontier   36
3.5   Production possibility frontier   37
3.6   Health and productive time   37
3.7   Time tradeoff between labor, play, and health improvement   38
3.8   Time tradeoff between labor, play, and health improvement   38
3.9   Time tradeoff between labor, play, and health improvement   39
3.10   Marginal efficiency of health capital curve   41
3.11   Marginal efficiency of health capital curve   42
3.12   Marginal efficiency of health capital for college graduates and high-school dropouts   43
3.13   Death in the Grossman model   44
3.14   Combined graphs in the Grossman model shifting with age   46

4.1   Causal relationships between health, socioeconomic status, and other variables   51
4.2   Male survival curves by educational attainment   52
4.3   Mortality rate among British ducal families and commoners   53
4.4   Health inequalities by age   53
4.5   Health inequalities by condition   55

4.6   Health inequalities among Canadian children   55
4.7   Health inequalities by race   56
4.8   High and low marginal efficiency of health capital curves   57
4.9   Different production possibility frontiers for the rich and the poor   63
4.10   Allostatic load in the Grossman model   63
4.11   HDL cholesterol levels in baboons and British civil servants by social status   65
4.12   Productive time and health   67
4.13   Time preference and the Grossman model   69
4.14   Causal relationships between health, socioeconomic status, and other variables   71

5.1   Various residency and fellowship programs in the US   80
5.2   Different lifetime income paths for the surfer and the physician   84
5.3   Different lifetime income paths for the surfer and the physician   85

6.1   Recent trends in US hospitals   101
6.2   Recent trends in US hospitals   102
6.3   Prices for common procedures at California hopsitals   116

7.1   Income and utility diagram   127
7.2   Expected utility from uncertain income   129
7.3   Utility and risk aversion   130
7.4   Comparing different insurance contracts   135
7.5   Comparing different insurance contracts   136
7.6   Comparing different insurance contracts   137

8.1   Distribution of car quality   145
8.2   Adverse selection in the used-car market   147
8.3   Adverse selection in the used-car market   148
8.4   Adverse selection in the health insurance market   151

8.5	Adverse selection in the health insurance market	151
8.6	Adverse selection with a guaranteed minimum	155
9.1	Income utility space and $I_H - I_S$ space	162
9.2	Income utility space and $I_H - I_S$ space	163
9.3	Comparing multiple insurance contracts	164
9.4	Comparing multiple insurance contracts	164
9.5	The full-insurance line	165
9.6	The zero-profit line and actuarially-fair insurance	166
9.7	Profitable and unprofitable contracts	167
9.8	The feasible contract wedge	167
9.9	Potential equilibria	169
9.10	Potential equilibria	169
9.11	Potential equilibria	170
9.12	Indifferent curves of robust and frail types	171
9.13	Ideal contract for robust and frail types	171
9.14	Stable equilibrium for heterogeneous customers and perfect information	172
9.15	Pooling equilibrium	173
9.16	Pooling equilibrium	173
9.17	Separating equilibrium	175
9.18	Separating equilibrium	176
9.19	Separating equilibrium	177
10.1	Separating equilibrium in the Rothschild–Stiglitz model	185
10.2	Adverse selection death spiral at Harvard University	189
10.3	Potential study bias in the life insurance market	191
10.4	Per-unit premium cost of life insurance	192
11.1	Social loss from moral hazard	206
11.2	Effect of price distortion and price sensitivity on the social loss from moral hazard	207
11.3	Social loss from different insurance plans	210
11.4	Deductibles, coinsurance, and out-of-pocket expenses	211
11.5	Deductibles and moral hazard	212
11.6	Relationship between insurance coverage and probability of sickness	218
11.7	Relationship between insurance coverage and probability of sickness	219
11.8	Feasible insurance contracts with and without moral hazard	219
11.9	Feasible insurance contracts with and without moral hazard	220
12.1	FDA approval rates for new drugs	233
12.2	Distribution of US drug returns	234
12.3	Rate of innovation and patent strength	236
12.4	Distribution of drug prices in the US and in Italy	239
12.5	Induced innovation in the US	241
12.6	New chemical entities in the US over time	246
12.7	Type I and Type II error	247
12.8	Receiver–operator characteristc curve	248
13.1	Health care expenditures as a proportion of US GDP, 1960–2008	255
13.2	Annual change in various price indices, 1985–2003	258
13.3	The price of a Hodgkin's cure, 1950 and today	261
13.4	Regional distribution of health care spending in the Dartmouth Atlas	267
13.5	Health and health expenditures in La Crosse, WI, and Miami, FL	268
13.6	Possible health production functions for La Crosse, WI, and Miami, FL	269
13.7	HPFs for La Crosse and Miami according to Dartmouth Atlas researchers	271
13.8	Relationship between health care use and supply of hospital beds in various US regions	272
14.1	Several possible treatment options for bhtitis	284
14.2	Cost-effectiveness frontier (CEF) for bhtitis	285
14.3	Relationship between ICERs and the slope of the CEF	285
14.4	Example visual analog scale	289
14.5	Average quality weight estimations from different estimation methods	290
14.6	Tangency between indifference curves and the CEF in the case of uninsurance	293
14.7	Tangency between indifference curves and the CEF in the case of insurance	294
14.8	Rationing and moral hazard	296
15.1	The health policy trilemma	308
15.2	Universal public insurance in the Rothschild–Stiglitz model	310
15.3	Optimal insurance under moral hazard	313
15.4	Health expenditure and life expectancy by country	322
15.5	Three health economies	323
15.6	Three health economies with two HPFs	324
15.7	Separate optima for population subgroups	325

16.1   Basic queue with no price rationing   333
16.2   Queue with price rationing   334
16.3   Queue with perfect gatekeeping   334

18.1   Obesity wage differential   376
18.2   The workforce at BHT enterprises   377
18.3   Distribution of US private health
       insurance customers by plan type   382
18.4   Average length of stay at US hospitals,
       before and after DRG reform   388
18.5   The Medicaid notch   392
18.6   Uninsurance in the US among adults and
       children in 2011   394

19.1   Population aging in Europe   403
19.2   Population aging in Japan   404
19.3   The dwindling Medicare Trust Fund   408
19.4   Number of elderly in the US, 1900–2050   409
19.5   A simplified depiction of the RAND
       Future Elderly Model   415
19.6   The effect of an anti-aging drug in the
       Future Elderly Model   416

20.1   The market for flu vaccinations   430
20.2   The market for flu vaccinations with
       private and social demand curves   431
20.3   Social loss in the market for flu
       vaccinations   432
20.4   The market for antibiotics   433
20.5   Social loss in the market for antibiotics   434
20.6   A Pigouvian subsidy in the market for flu
       vaccinations   435
20.7   A Pigouvian tax in the market for
       antibiotics   436

21.1   Epidemiological and economic cost of
       diseases with varying severity   451
21.2   The reciprocal relationship between
       self-protection and disease spread   453
21.3   The SIR model space   454
21.4   An altered version of 21.2 with a vaccine
       subsidy   458

21.5   Disease resilience   460
21.6   Estimated prevalence and hazard rate of
       HIV in high-risk San Francisco
       neighborhoods   464
21.7   Diðherential measles vaccination rates by
       statewide prevalence for babies born in
       1989   465

22.1   Average body mass index (BMI) by
       education level in the US   474
22.2   Estimated average body mass index of
       American males in various age cohorts,
       1863–1991   475
22.3   Rising obesity rates in 17 OECD
       countries   475
22.4   Global food price trends since World
       War II   478
22.5   Years of life lost due to obesity   481
22.6   Social loss from moral hazard as applied
       to pooled health insurance   484
22.7   Increase in obesity prevalence in the
       RAND HIE   485
22.8   A vastly simplified version of Christakis
       and Fowler's depiction of the
       Framingham data set   486

23.1   Perceived probabilities and actual
       probabilities   505
23.2   Changes in utility from increases or
       decreases in income   508
23.3   Effect of losses and gains in income on
       utility   509
23.4   Different evaluations of utility due to
       different reference points   511
23.5   A hypothetical value function for
       changes in income   514
23.6   A hypothetical weighting function   516

24.1   A schematic map of Jay's commute home
       in Palo Alto, CA   525
24.2   Imputed annual discount rates from
       several time-discounting studies   532

TABLES

2.1 Evidence for outpatient care: (a) RAND HIE Study. (b) Oregon Medicaid Experiment 13

2.2 Evidence for inpatient care: (a) RAND HIE Study. (b) Oregon Medicaid Experiment 14

2.3 Evidence for emergency care: (a) RAND HIE Study. (b) Oregon Medicaid Experiment 15

2.4 Mean health care expenditures in the CRHIE, in yuan 15

2.5 Percentage with preventative pediatric care in three years, by age and care type 17

2.6 Per-capita mental health expenditures, by plan type 18

2.7 Dental care utilization by income level 18

2.8 Antibiotic use in the RAND HIE 18

2.9 Evidence on mortality rates: (a) RAND HIE Study. (b) Oregon Medicaid Experiment 21

2.10 Health indicators by insurance plan in the RAND HIE 22

2.11 Effect of lottery win on health in the first year of the Oregon Medicaid Experiment 23

2.12 Outpatient utilization in Tokyo and Hokkaido, 1999 24

2.13 Outpatient utilization in Tokyo and Hokkaido, 2000 25

2.14 Percentage with preventative care in the three years from the RAND HIE Study 25

2.15 Various measures of predicted annual use of medical services by income group 26

3.1 Activities in the Grossman model 31

3.2 Meal options in the Grossman model 49

4.1 Median wealth by self-reported health status 54

4.2 Summary of evidence for health disparities in different populations 57

4.3 Adult characteristics according to timing of prenatal exposure to the Dutch famine 61

4.4 Improvement in hemoglobin measurement for diabetics by treatment regime and age 72

4.5 Hazard rate of coronary heart disease, stroke, and total cardiovascular disease, compared with average birth rate cohort 73

4.6 Information from the cancer rate study commissioned by the King of Pcoria 73

4.7 Generalized version of Table 4.6 74

5.1 Estimated IRR for various professional careers versus a typical college-degree-requiring job in the US, 1970–1980 86

5.2 Survey data on average hourly wage and work-hours in various medical specialties in the US, 2004–2005 87

5.3 Career options and salary information for Exercises 11 and 12 97

6.1 Surgical mortality rates for various Medicare procedures, by hospital volume 105

6.2 The costs and benefits of nonprofit status under US law 113

6.3 Summary of theories for the existence of nonprofits 115

6.4 Collection ratio at California hospitals by insurance type, 2005 118

7.1 Premium and generosity of different insurance contracts 135

10.1 Information from the human resources department at ASU 199

10.2 BHT-sponsored insurance contracts 200

11.1 Evidence of *ex ante* moral hazard from the RAND HIE 214

11.2 Preventative care test frequency in the Oregon Medicaid 215

11.3 Evidence from the RAND HIE 216

11.4 Health care utilization in the past six months, Oregon Medicaid Experiment 216

12.1 Sample of drug categories with age range of principal users 241

13.1   Technology adoption by nation per million people   256

13.2   Life expectancy of AMI patients in the US Medicare system and average costs of AMI treatment over time (in constant 1991 dollars)   262

13.3   Chronic conditions tracked in the Dartmouth Atlas   265

14.1   Comparison of strategies for HIV screening   281

14.2   Comparison of two lead poisoning treatments   282

14.3   Various drug therapies for bhtitis   283

14.4   Summary of survey methods for QALY quality weight   291

14.5   VSL estimates used by American regulatory agencies   299

14.6   Potential therapies for back pain   303

15.1   Voter preferences in Pcoria   307

15.2   Pathologies present in health care markets   309

15.3   The benefits and costs of various national health policies   320

17.1   Health care technology utilization in select countries following different health policy models in 2010   368

17.2   Health care spending as a percentage of GDP in select countries following different health policy models in 2010   369

19.1   Total fertility rate per 1,000 women (selected countries)   406

19.2   New technology predictions by RAND panel   411

19.3   Pcoria demographic facts   421

19.4   Mortality rates   422

19.5   New mortality rates   422

21.1   Comparison of income tax and various disease "taxes"   452

21.2   Annual costs of smallpox and the smallpox eradication campaign (millions of 1967 dollars)   462

21.3   Net present value, internal rate of return, and break-even campaign length   462

21.4   Rates of condom use by state and quartile of HIV prevalence   466

23.1   Survey questions and responses illustrating the certainty effect   503

23.2   Summary of operations conducted during the editing stage, developed from Kahneman and Tversky (1979)   513

23.3   An example of cancellation and coding during the editing stage   513

23.4   Problem 1 and Problem 2 illustrating the certainty effect   515

23.5   Selling and buying price for Duke lottery winners and sellers   523

24.1   Actions and commitment mechanisms under different discounting scenarios   537

24.2   Which utility function should we maximize in the case of time-inconsistent preferences?   540

24.3   Will you see your doctor today?   546

24.4   Will you go to the movies today?   547

INDEX

Page numbers in *italics* refer to figures and tables.

access
  to care   65–6
  to drugs   249
  see also gatekeeping
Accreditation Council for Graduate Medical
    Education (ACGME)   82
acetylsalicylic acid   230
actuarial fairness   133
acute myocardial infarction (AMI)
  hospital competition and patient outcomes
      112
  price of survival   262–4
  racial discrimination and treatment
      disparities   94–6
addiction
  Grossman model   44–5
  impatience and   490
  rational   529
advanced directives ("living wills")   418, 419
advantageous selection   196–7
adverse selection
  death spiral   150–2, 187, 188–9
  definition   143
  health insurance   187–90
    Bismarck model   362–3
    evidence against   189–90
    Harvard University study   188–9
    market solution   177–9
    policy options   309–12
    predictions of asymmetric information
        models   185–7
    prevention   195–7
  models *see* Akerlof model;
      Rothschild–Stiglitz model
  other insurance markets   190–5
agricultural science   477
AIDS *see* HIV/AIDS
Air Force Academy study   487–8
Akerlof, G.A.   142
Akerlof model of adverse selection (used car
    market)   142–50
  distribution of quality   144–5

government-set price controls   153–4
information assumptions   144–5
market unravels   148–9, 377
seller and buyer utility functions   144,
    152–3
when do cars sell?   145–6
when will buyers buy?   147–8
which cars will sellers offer?   146–7
why not find a better price?   149–50
allostatic load hypothesis   63–4
altruistic-motive theory   114
American Association of Medical Colleges
    (AAMC)   89
American Medical Association (AMA)
    88–9, 90
American model   322
  defining features   372–3
  PPACA reform (2010)   394–7
  uninsurance   393–4
  see also employer-sponsored insurance;
      managed care; Medicaid; Medicare
antibiotic resistance   432–4, 436–7, 439–40
arc elasticity   20
Arrow, K.   2–3, 114
  impossibility theorem   306–7
asymmetric information
  insurance   185–7
  moral hazard   205
  nonprofit hospitals   114–15
  see also Akerlof model; Rothschild–Stiglitz
      model
Australia   217, 330, 341, 344–5
authoritarian commitment mechanisms   535
automobiles/cars
  see Akerlof model
average cost-effectiveness ratio (ACER)   283
  see cost-effectiveness

"baby boom" generation   408
Barker hypothesis *see* thrifty phenotype
    hypothesis
behavioral economics   490, 497

behavioral welfare economics   538–42
  Pareto self-improving commitment
      mechanisms   541–2
  perspectives   538–9
  smoking interventions: role of paternalism
      539–41
Bernheim, B. and Rangel, A.   533, 539, *540*
beta-delta discount model   526–7, 530
Beveridge model   320–1, 328–9
  competition   342–5
    appeal of   342–3
    unease with private markets   343–5
  competition strategies   345–51
    managerial autonomy   350–1
    move away from global budgets   346–8
    NHS internal market (1991)   345–6
    patient choice   346, 348–50
    reforms (2002–8)   346
  elimination of price rationing   331
  health technology assessment (HTA)
      339–42
    controversy surrounding   341–2
    motivations for   339–40
    rise of centralized   340–1
  national systems   329–30
  vs Bismarck model   367–9
  see also   queuing
Bismarck, Otto von   354
Bismarck model   321–2, 354–5
  defining features   355
  history   354
  insurance markets   359–63
    adverse selection   363–4
    managed competition   359–60
    risk selection and elimination   360–2
  national systems   355–8
  price controls   364–7
    clinical distortions   365–7
    gatekeeping   367–8
    negotiating fee schedules   364–5
  vs Beveridge model   367–9
blood donation   444
body mass index (BMI)   473
body weight, evidence of rise in   474–6
bounded rationality   499–500
British civil servants (Whitehall) studies   64,
    65, 66
British National Cohort Study   60
bulk discount   186, 192–3
bulk markups   186

Canada
  Amish farming community study   479
  global budgets   346–7
  health inequalities *55*,   66

Medicare   330, 344
  physician work-hours   83
  prescription drug insurance   217
  queuing   332, 338
cancer treatment costs   264
  Hodgkin's lymphoma   260, *261*
cars *see* Akerlof model of adverse selection
    (used car market); automobiles/cars
Certificate of Need (CON) laws   319
chargemasters   115–16, 117, 118–19
Chernobyl disaster   61–2
child mortality rates   67, 404–5
childhood deprivation: thrifty phenotype
    hypothesis   59–62, 67
childhood obesity   489–90
China Health Insurance Experiment (CRHIE)
    15–16
cholecystectomy   102
cholesterol (HDL)   56, 64, *65*
clinical distortions   365–7
Coase, R.   437
Coase theorem   437–40, 442–3
cochlear implantation   366–7
Cochrane lifetime contract   179
coinsurance and copayment   209–11, 315
community rating   355, 359–60, 363, 396
comparative statics: Grossman model   42–5
competing risks problem   414
competition
  managed   359–60
  and patient outcomes   111–12
  see also Beveridge model
compression of morbidity   412–13
compulsory insurance   311–12, 395–6
  see also Bismarck model
Consolidated Omnibus Budget Reconciliation
    (COBRA)   379
consumption good   29, 33
contagion   428
  in social networks   486–8
  uncertainty and   2–3
copayment
  coinsurance and   209–11, 315
  rates   11, 12, 14, 15–16, 17, 19–20
cost–benefit analysis (CBA)   292–6
cost-effectiveness analysis (CEA)   279–82, 519
  average cost-effectiveness ratios (ACER)
      283
  controlling moral hazard   314–15
  HIV screening and lead poisoning   280–2
  incremental cost-effectiveness ratio (ICER)
      280, 281–2, 282, 285, 292, 293, 314–15
  Medicare   315, 389
  multiple treatments   282–5

cost-effectiveness frontier (CEF)   284–5, 292,
  293, 294
cost of living (COL) index   263–4
cost measurement   285–7
  and effectiveness measurement   287–91
cost-sharing   209–11, 315
cost-shifting   118–19
"cream skimming"   360, 362
Cuba   472

Dartmouth Atlas Project   265–6
  lack of correlation between spending and
      health   266
  Medicare spending variations   265–6
  theories to explain findings   266–74
    local characteristics   269–71
    supply-sensitive care and moral hazard
        272–4
defensive medicine   92–3, 270
delayed gratification and time-discounting
    68–70
Delphi method   291
demand for health care   8–9
  downward-sloping   12–19
    inpatient and emergency room   13–17
    other   17–19
    outpatient care   12–13, 15–17
    pediatric   17
  experiments   9–12
    randomized health insurance   11–12
    other evidence   15–17
    price and health, relationship between
        21–3
    price sensitivity measurement   19–21
diagnosis-related groups (DRGs)   102, 347,
    387–8
dictatorship of the present   538–9, 540–1
differentiated product oligopoly   107–9
direct income hypothesis   62–3
direct-to-consumer (DTC) advertising   249
disability rates   412–13
disability-adjusted life years (DALYS)   288
discount function   526
drug industry *see* pharmaceutical industry

E-ZPass toll collection system   62
education
  and efficiency of producing health   42–3,
      58–9
  time-discounting theory   69–70
efficient producer hypothesis   42–3, 58–9
elasticity of demand   19–21
emergency care
  demand for   13–17
  "last resort" laws   320

employer-sponsored insurance   312, 373–9
  firm-specific human capital   374, 376–8
  job lock   378–9
  wage pass-through   374–6
end-of-life (EOL) care   417–19
endowment effect   509–10
epidemiological cost   450
epidemiology
  applications   463–7
    condom use in states with high AIDS
        prevalence   466
    falling HIV incidence in 1980s San
        Francisco   463–4
    flu vaccinations   466–7
    measles epidemic (1989-91)   464–5
  demand for self-protection   449–54
    disease as tax   449–50
    excess burden of disease   450–2
    prevalence elasticity   452–3
  disease control   458–63
    disease resilience   458–9
    smallpox eradication campaign   461–3
    vaccine demand and disease eradication
        459–60
    welfare economics of eradication   460–1
  SIR model of infectious disease   414, 454–8
equity/inequalities *see* socioeconomic health
    inequalities
European Medicines Agency (EMA)   245, 249
ex ante moral hazard   205, 208–9, 214–15
ex post moral hazard   205, 208–9, 215–17
excess burden of disease   450–2
expected utility   128–9
  theory   498–9, 500
  vs expected income   129–31
expected value   127–8
externalities   429–34
  antibiotic resistance   432–4, 436–7, 439–40
  Coase theorem   437–40, 442–3
  herd immunity   429–32, 434–6, 439–40
  organ transplantation markets   440–4
  Pigouvian subsidies and taxes   434–7,
      443–4
  vaccination   460–1

fair and unfair insurance 132–3, 136–7
fee-for-service (FFS) system   102, 316
  resource based relative value scale (RBRVS)
      388
  vs managed care   380–2, 383
firm-specific human capital   374, 376–8
flu
  H1N1 epidemic, Mexico   452–3
  vaccinations   466–7

Food and Drug Administration (FDA)   230–1, 240, 244, 245–6, 247, 249, 299
food industry   476–7
food price trends   477–8
Framingham Heart Study   486–7
France
    Bismarck model   358, 365, 367
    health care expenditure   318
    insurance   17, 312
    life expectancy   404
    medical education   79
    natalism   420
    nonprofit hospital sectors   320
    private hospital markets   319
free care   328, 331
Fuchs, V.R.   270
    time preference hypothesis   68–70
full insurance
    and partial insurance   133–5, 136–7
    Rothschild–Stiglitz model   165

gatekeeping
    Bismarck model   367–8
    managed care   213, 381
    and monitoring   212–13
    and queuing   315–16, 334–5, 337
general practitioners (GPs)   334–5, 337, 338
generic drug makers   234–5, 237–8
Germany
    ex post moral hazard   216, 217
    fertility rates   405
    health care expenditure   318
    medical education   80
    nonprofit hospital sectors   320
    private hospital markets   319
    sickness funds   360, 362
    thalidomide   244–5
    see also Bismarck model
Ghana   214
global budgets   346–8
Gore, A. (US Vice-President)   391
government-failure theory of nonprofit hospitals   113–14
government-set price controls   153–4, 320, 365–6
Grossman model
    beta-delta discounting   527
    comparative statics   42–5
        aging and endogenous death   43–5
        education and efficiency of producing health   42–3
    day in the life of   28–33
        market budget constraint   31–2
        production of H and Z 30–1
        sick time and productive time   32–3

single-period utility   29
    time constraints within single period   29–30
    health capital   40–2
    health inequalities   42–3, 57–8, 62–3, 67–9, 308, 325
    obesity and food industry   477
    optimal day   33–9
        labor-leisure-health improvement tradeoff   37–9
        optimal H and Z within a period   35–6
        production possibility frontier for H and Z 34–5
    three roles of health in   33
guaranteed renewable contract   179

hay fever   *54*, 55
health capital   33, 40–2
health care expenditure   1–2
    increasing   257–62
    see also aging population
health externalities *see* externalities
health indicators 22
health inequalities *see* socioeconomic health inequalities
health insurance *see* insurance; *specific types*
health maintenance organization (HMO)   381–2, 383–4
health policy *see* policy
health production frontier (HPF)   322–4, 325
health production function (HPF)   268–9, 271
health resource groups (HRGs)   347–8
Health and Retirement Study   66–7, 192
health technology assessment (HTA) 278–9
    Beveridge model *see under* Beveridge model
    Bismarck model   367
    cost–benefit analysis (CBA)   292–6
    cost measurement   285–7
    effectiveness measurement   287–91
    prospect theory   519
    value of statistical life (VSL)   296–300
    see also cost-effectiveness analysis (CEA)
heart attack *see* acute myocardial infarction (AMI)
Helicobacter pylori   261
herd immunity   429–32, 434–6, 439–40
Herfindahl–Hirschman Index (HHI)   108–9
heuristics 511
high-density lipoprotein (HDL)   55–7, 64, *65*
Hill–Burton Act   100–1
HIV/AIDS
    black market reimportation of drugs   237
    condom use in states with high prevalence   466

falling incidence in 1980s San Francisco
463–4
HAART and Medicaid   391
screening   280–1
and viatical settlements markets   193–4
Hodgkin's lymphoma   260, *261*
hospice care   418, 419
hospital bill   115–17
hospitalists   106–7
hospitals
    differing amenities and spending   269–70
    nonprofit   112–15
        altruistic-motive theory   114
        asymmetric information and failure of
            trust   114
        costs and benefits   113
        as for-profits in disguise   114–15
        government-failure theory   113–14
    and other hospitals, relationship between
        107–12
        competition and patient outcomes
            111–12
        differentiated product oligopoly   107–9
        price competition   109–10
        quality competition   110–11
    and payers, relationship between   115–19
        cost-shifting   118–19
        hospital bill   115–17
        uncompensated care   117
    and physicians, relationship between
        103–7
        hospital experience *vs* physician
            experience   105–6
        internal organization   103–4
        rise of hospitalists   106–7
        volume-outcome relationship and
            learning by doing   104–5, 112
    rise and decline of   100–3
        Hill–Burton Act   100–1
        transition to outpatient care   101–3
hot-brain/cold-brain model   533–4, 539–40
hyperbolic discounting   530, 531
    sophisticated and naive   535–6

impatience and addiction   490
impossibility theorem   306–7
income effect of moral hazard   222–3
income inequality hypothesis   53–5, 64–5
income-utility model   126–7, 129–31, 136,
    162–4
incremental cost-effectiveness ratio (ICER)
    280, 281–2, 282, 285, 292, 293, 314–15
indemnity insurance *see* fee-for-service (FFS)
    system

indifference curves   36
    cost-effectiveness frontier (CEF)   292, *293*,
        294
    insurance coverage   218
    rationing   295–6
    Rothschild–Stiglitz model   163–5, 171–2
Indonesia: iron supplement study   67–8
induced innovation *see under* pharmaceutical
    industry
infection hazard rate   463
infectious diseases
    control   458–63
    epidemiological cost and excess burden
        450–2
    prevalence elasticity   452–3
    susceptibility-infected-recovered (SIR)
        model   414, 454–8
    see also HIV/AIDS; vaccination
information asymmetry *see* asymmetric
    information
inpatient care, demand for   13–17
insurance
    contracts   131–5
        comparison   135–6, *137*
        see also Rothschild–Stiglitz model
    declining marginal utility of income   126–7
    full insurance   133–5
    hospital bills   115–17
    partial insurance   136–7
    and price competition   109–10
    prospect theory 517–18
    social *see* Bismarck model
    uncertainty   127–8, 131
    universal   373
    see also adverse selection; moral hazard; risk;
        specific types
internal rate of return (IRR)   85–6, 87–8
international medical graduates   (IMGs) 89
investment good, health as   40
Israel
    Bismarck model   357
    decisions under uncertainty study   500

Japan
    aging population   403–4
    Bismarck model   354–5, 357–8, 363, 364–5,
        366, 367
    hospitals   102, 104, 319, 320
    long-term care insurance (LTCI)   409–10
job lock   378–9
"July effect"   81

Kaiser Permanente plan   380–1
Kefauver–Harris Amendment   245–6

labor market
  declining physical labor   478–9
  disincentive effects of Medicaid   391–3
  participation by women   479–80
  ratio of retirees to workers   404
labor-leisure-health improvement tradeoff
      37–9, 45–7
Laspeyres price index   259, 260, 262–3
"last resort"   laws 320
learning by doing   104–5, 112
liability insurance   93
Liaison Committee on Medical Education
      (LCME)   89
life expectancy   404–5
  and increased BMI   480–1
life insurance   191–3
lifetime insurance contracts   178, 179
"living wills" (advanced directives)   418, 419
long-run preferences   538, 540
long-term care insurance   194–5, 197
  Japan   409–10
loss aversion   507–11

malaria   67, 214, 243
malpractice and defensive medicine   92–3, 270
managed care   380–4
  backlash against HMOs   383–4
  competition between MCOs   110, 111
  research on effectiveness of   382–3
  rise of   380–2
mandatory insurance see Bismarck model;
      compulsory insurance
marginal efficiency of capital (MEC) curve   40,
      41, 42–3, 45–7, 57–8, 69
marginal utility of income   126–7
market concentration measure   108–9
see also Herfindahl–Hirschman Index   (HHI)
means-tested insurance   312
Medicaid   389–93
  cost control   390–1
  PPACA reform (2010)   395
  structuring and financing   389–90
  uncompensated care   117
  work disincentive effects   391–3
medical arms race hypothesis   110–11
medical care consumer price index (CPI)   258,
      259
medical inflation see increasing expenditures
      under technology
medical training see under physicians
Medicare   16–17, 384–9
  Australia   330
  and Bismarck model   366
  Canada   330, 344
  cost control   387–9

cost-effectiveness analysis (CEA)   315, 389
cost sharing   315
diagnosis-related groups (DRG) payment
      system   102
end-of-life (EOL) care   419
expenditure   396–7, 408–9, 411–12
financing   386
history   372
hospital care   116, 117
PPACA reform (2010)   396–7
progressive or regressive?   386–7
structure   384–6
Medicare Trust Fund   408–9
mental health care   17
Mexico
  H1N1 flu epidemic   452–3
  Seguro Popular en Salud insurance program
      213, 215
monopoly rents   88, 90
moral hazard   203–4
  amount   208
  controlling   209–13, 313–17
    cost-effectiveness analysis (CEA)
        314–15
    cost-sharing   209–11, 315
    deductibles   211–12
    gatekeeping and monitoring   212–13
    gatekeeping and queuing   315–16
    private and public insurance   313–14
    prospective payments and
        diagnosis-related groups   316–17
    queuing   332, 333
  definition and examples   204–6
  evidence in health insurance   213–17
  ex ante   205, 208–9, 214–15
  ex post   205, 208–9, 215–17
  graphical representation   206–9
  obesity   483–5
  price distortion   205, 206–7, 208
  and rationing   295–6
  and risk reduction, tradeoff between
        217–21
    private markets   220–1
    public markets   221
  role of asymmetrical information   208–9
  and supply-sensitive care   272–4
  upside of   221–3
    extra preventative care   222
    income effect   222–3
morbidity, compression of   412–13
mortality rates   21–2
  child   67, 404–5
  competing risks problem   414
  Cuba   472
  historic   52

life insurance markets   191–2
and managerial autonomy   350–1
surgical   105
multi-period utility function: Grossman model
    39–40
multiple treatments: cost-effectiveness analysis
    282–5

naive and sophisticated hyperbolic discounting
    535–6
natalism   419–20
National Health Service (NHS) *see* United
    Kingdom (UK)
National Institute for Clinical Excellence
    (NICE), UK   314, 329, 341–2, 343, 344
natural experiments   60–2
net present value (NPV)   84–5
Netherlands   60, 61
    Bismarck model   357
New Zealand   341
nonprofit hospitals *see under* hospitals
Norway   338, 340–1, 349–50
nurse practitioners   89–90
nutritional information   488–9

obesity   472–3
    contagion in social networks   486–8
    costs of   480–1
    evidence of rise in body weight   474–6
    explanations for   476–80
        declining physical labor and changing
            lifestyles   478–9
        food industry   476–7
        food price trends   477–8
        genetic   476
        labor force participation by women
            479–80
        side effect of good things   480
    measuring   473
    as public health crisis   482–5
        moral hazard and health insurance
            483–5
        pooled health insurance   483
        RAND HIE   485
    public health intervention   488–90
        childhood   489–90
        impatience and addiction   490
        nutritional information   488–9
    rise in   473
"old-age income security hypothesis"   406
oligopoly   363–4
    differentiated product   107–9
    vs public provision   317
optimal day: Grossman model   33–9
optimal treatment selection   292–6

Oregon Medicaid Experiment   11–12, 13,
    14–15, 17, 20, 21–3
    access to care   66
    moral hazard   213, 215, 216–17
    proposal   391
orphan drugs, tropical diseases and   243–4
outpatient care
    demand for   12–13, 15–17
    price sensitivity measurement   19–20
    transition to   101–3

palliative care   418
Pareto-improvement   145–6, 152, 429
    commitment mechanisms   541–2
patents *see under* pharmaceutical industry
paternalism, role of   539–41
patient choice   346, 348–50
Patient Protection and Affordable Care Act
    (PPACA)   373, 394–7
"payment-by-results" system, UK   346, 347,
    348
pediatric care, demand for   17
penicillin   242, 432–3
pharmaceutical industry   230–1
    drug life cycle   231–2
    history   230, 242, 244
    induced innovation   232, 240–4
        academic and public institutions
            242–3
        tropical diseases and orphan drugs
            243–4
    patents   233–9
        consumer surplus and innovation, tradeoff
            between   235–6
        in developing countries   236–8
        price controls   238–9
    price controls   238–9, 366
    R&D costs   232–3, 235, 238, 239, 243,
        245–6
    regulation   244–9
        controlled access to drugs   249
        thalidomide   244–6
        Type I and Type II errors   246–8
    uncertainty   232–3
physicians
    agency   90–3
        defensive medicine   92–3
        physician-induced demand (PID)   91–2,
            273
    barrier to entry   88–90
        American Medical Association (AMA)
            88–9, 90
        implicit tradeoff   90
        present-day   89–90

physicians – *continued*
  and hospitals, relationship between *see under*
      hospitals
  racial discrimination   94–6
    evaluating treatment disparities   94–5
    testing for inefficient   95–6
    types   94
  training   79–83
    medical school   79
    residency and "July effect"   80–1
    work-hours   82–3
  wages   83–6
    returns to specialization   86–8
    vs fee-for-service system   380–1
Pigouvian subsidies and taxes   434–7,
    443–4
policy
  aging population *see under* population
      aging
  Arrow's impossibility theorem   306–7
  countering adverse selection in insurance
      markets   309–12
  moral hazard dilemma   313–17
  national comparison   *321*
    health, wealth, and equity outcomes
        322–3
    health equity   325
    health preferences   324–5
    inherent health levels   323–4
    models   320–2
  regulation of provision   317–20
    government-set price controls   320
    private   319–20
    public   317–19
  trilemma   307–9
  uses of value of statistical life (VSL)
      299–300
pooled insurance
  Kaiser Permanente plan   380–1
  obesity   483
  pooling equilibrium   172–4
  see also employer-sponsored insurance
population aging
  European population pyramid   402–3
  fertility rates   405–7
  health care expenditure   407–10
    Japan: long-term care insurance
        409–10
    US Medicare   408–9
  health care expenditure forecasting
      410–16
    compression of morbidity   412–13
    future medical technology   410–12
    models   413–16
  life expectancy   404–5

policy responses   416–20
  chronic disease prevention   416–17
  end-of-life (EOL) care   417–19
  natalism   419–20
  reasons for worldwide trend   403–7
preferred provider organization (PPO)   381–2
prescription drugs, demand for   18–19
prevalence elasticity   452–3
price competition   109–10
price controls
  government-set   153–4, 320, 365–6
  pharmaceutical industry   238–9, 366
  see also Bismarck model
price discrimination   237
price distortion   205, 206–7, 208
price elasticity   16, 17–18
  measurement   19–21
  moral hazard   205, 206–7, 208
price and health, relationship between   21–3
price leakages   237
price rationing, elimination of   331
prioritization strategy   338
private demand curve   430
private health care provision   373
  regulation   319–20, 355
private hospital markets   319–20
probabilities, misjudging   500–5
production possibilities frontier (PPF)   34–5,
    45–7
productive time hypothesis   66–8
property rights *see* Coase theorem
prospect theory   496–7
  decision-making under uncertainty models
      497–500
  expected utility theory   498–9, 500
  framing   505–7
  implications of   518–19
    demand for health insurance   518
    health technology assessment   519
    interventions and nudges   518–19
  introduction to   511–17
    editing stage   511–12
    evaluation: value function   514–15
    evaluation: weighting function   515–17
    evaluation stage   513–14
  loss aversion   507–11
    endowment effect   509–10
    importance of reference points   510–11
  misjudging probabilities   500–5
    overvaluing certainty   501–3
    overvaluing small probabilities   503–4
prospective payments   316–17
public health   428
  see also externalities; obesity

public health care provision   328
  regulation   317–19
public hospitals   113
public institutions and pharmaceutical
    innovation   242–3
public insurance
  moral hazard   221
  and private insurance   309–11, 313–14

quality competition   110–11
quality-adjusted life years (QALYS)   287–9,
    292
  surveys   289–90, 291
queuing   331–8
  and gatekeeping   315–16, 334–5, 337
  optimum length   333–5
  pros and cons   332–3
  reduction strategies   336–8
  socioeconomic status and   336
  welfare loss estimates from   335–6

racial discrimination see under physicians
RAND Corporation: new technology
    predictions   411–12
RAND Future Elderly Model (FEM)   414–16
RAND Health Insurance Experiment (HIE)
    11–12, 13, 14–15, 17, 20, 21–3
  adverse selection   187
  moral hazard   213, 214, 215, 216–17
  obesity   485
randomized experiments
  definition   10
  health insurance   11–12
rare diseases   243
rational addiction   529
rationality
  bounded   499–500
  modeling   498
rationing   293–6
regulation see under pharmaceutical industry;
    policy
retrospective payments   316
revealed preference   538, 540
risk
  accurate prediction of   196
  competing risks problem   414
  and coverage, positive correlation between
    105–6
  heterogeneous types   170–1
  and loss aversion   507–11
  misperceived   195–6
  unobservable   376–7
risk adjustment   362
risk rating   359
risk reduction see under moral hazard

risk selection
  compulsory insurance   312
  and elimination   360–2
Rothschild–Stiglitz model of adverse selection
  completely private insurance vs universal
    public insurance   309–11
  feasible contract wedge   167–8
  full insurance line   165
  [IH-IS] space   162–3
  indifference curves
    in [IH-IS] space   163–5
    for robust and frail   171–2
  information asymmetry   185, 186, 187, 196
    and pooling equilibrium   172–4
  market equilibrium   168–70
  robust and frail
    firm-specific human capital   376–7
    heterogeneous risk types   170–1
    indifference curves for   171–2
    separating equilibrium   174–7
  single-payer system   310
  zero-profit line   165–7

saving for retirement   536–7
screening, HIV/AIDS   280–1
selection bias   60
selective universal health insurance   311
self-protection, demand for   449–54
self-reported health status   53
separating equilibrium   174–7, 363
sickness funds   360, 361–2
single-payer systems   310, 328
smallpox eradication campaign   461–3
Smith, Adam   104
smoking
  interventions: role of paternalism   539–41
  time-discounting theory   69–70
social demand curve   430
social health insurance see Bismarck model
social loss
  herd immunity   431–2
  moral hazard   204, 206–7, 218, 219
social networks, contagion in   486–8
social surplus   431
social welfare   429
socioeconomic health inequalities
  causal relationship   51, 71
  and Grossman model   42–3, 57–8, 62–3,
    67–9, 000, 005
  health production frontier (HPF)   322–3,
    324, 325
  historical   52–3
  hypotheses   58–70
  income levels   53–5
  non-human societies   56

socioeconomic health inequalities – *continued*
    queuing   336
    racial groups   56
    SES health gradient   42
    summary of evidence   56–57
    universal health insurance   55
sophisticated and naive hyperbolic discounting
    535–6
South Africa   363
specialists
    limiting access to   367–8
    wages   86–8
standard gamble (SG)   289–90, 519
Stanford University coinsurance study   216
State Child Health Insurance Program (SCHIP)
    393
statutory health insurance (SHI)   356
subsidies
    cost-shifting   118–19
    mandatory private insurance   395–6
    Pigouvian taxes and   434–7, 443–4
surveys
    demand   9–10
    quality of life   289–90, 291
survival curve   52
susceptibility-infected-recovered (SIR) model
    414, 454–8
Sweden
    Beveridge model   329–30, 340–1, 347, 349
    health care expenditure   318
    life expectancy   404
    natalism   419
Switzerland
    Bismarck model   356–7, 365, 367
    community rating   363
    comparative health economy   322–3, 324,
        325
    risk adjustment schemes   362

targeted and universal screening   280–1
tax(es)
    disease as   449–50
    Medicare   408–9
    Pigouvian subsidies and   434–7, 443–4
technology
    future   410–12
    increasing expenditures   255–62
        cancer and depression   264
        heart attack survival   262–4
        Hodgkin's lymphoma and peptic ulcers
            260–2
        price index measure   258–60
    limiting access to   367–8
    overuse *see* Dartmouth Atlas Project
    see also health technology assessment (HTA)

thalidomide   244–6
thrifty phenotype hypothesis   59–62, 67
time consistent preferences   527–9
    rational addiction   529
time inconsistency   525–6
    beta-delta discount model   526–7, 530
    demand for commitment mechanisms
        534–7
    preferences   529–34
        evidence for   531–3
        hot-brain/cold-brain model   533–4,
            539–40, *533*
        myopia   531
        see also behavioral welfare economics
time preference: Fuchs hypothesis   68–70
time tradeoff (TTO)   289–90, 519
time-discounting theory   69–70
tort reform   93
tropical diseases   243–4

uncertainty
    decision-making under   497–500
    and demand for insurance   127–8, 131
    health and contagion   2–3
    pharmaceutical industry   232–3
uncompensated care   117
uninsurance   116, 117, 393–4
United Kingdom (UK)/National Health Service
    (NHS)
    comparative health economy   322–3, 324,
        325
    fertility rates   405
    Foundation Trusts   350–1
    health expenditure   318
    health resource groups (HRGs)   347–8
    hospitals   112, 113
    internal market   345–6
    Liverpool care pathway (LCP)   418
    Medicines Act   245
    National Health Services Bill   328
    National Institute for Clinical Excellence
        (NICE)   314, 329, 341–2, 343, 344
    patient choice/"NHS Choices"   349, 350,
        351
    physicians   104
      "August killing season"   81
    "postcode lottery"   340, 341
    queuing   332, 338
    see also Beveridge model
universal health insurance   310–11, 328, 355
    health inequalities   55
    partial   373
universal and targeted screening   280–1
unobservable risk   376–7

utility function
    Akerlof model   144, 152–3
    von Neumann–Morgenstern   489–90, 502,
        503, 505
    see also Grossman model

vaccination   460–1
    -preventable diseases   242
    demand and disease eradication   459–60
    flu   466–7
    rate: SIR model   455
    see also herd immunity
value function *see under* prospect theory
value of statistical life (VSL)   296–300
viatical settlements   193–4
visual analogue scale (VAS)   289

von Neumann–Morgenstern utility function
    489–90, 502, 503, 505
vulnerable populations   23

wage pass-through   374–6
wages, physicians *see under* physicians
waiting times *see* queuing
welfare, private and social   429
welfare economics   4
    of eradication   460–1
    see also behavioral welfare economics
Whitehall (British civil servants) studies   64,
        65, 66
women, labor force participation by   479–80
work *see* labor market